Steel and the State

ECONOMIC COMPETITION AMONG NATIONS

Series Editors

*Alan Wm. Wolff, R. Michael Gadbaw,
Thomas R. Howell, and William A. Noellert*

Dewey, Ballantine, Bushby, Palmer & Wood, Washington, D.C.

Paradoxically, in an era of growing economic interdependence, commercial and technological rivalry among nations is intensifying. International competitiveness has moved to the center of the U.S. public policy debate and has become the focus of increasing attention in Europe, Japan, and the developing world. This series examines the public policy issues that affect competition among nations and lead to international economic conflict. Its goals are to contribute to the policy debate by examining underlying sources of economic conflicts, providing policy suggestions for their resolution and fostering the knowledge that can make a more integrated world economy possible.

Titles in This Series

Steel and the State

Government Intervention and Steel's Structural Crisis

Thomas R. Howell, William A. Noellert, Jesse G. Kreier, and Alan Wm. Wolff

Westview Press/Boulder and London

Economic Competition Among Nations Series

Copyright © 1988 by Westview Press, Inc.

Published in 1988 in the United States of America by Westview Press, Inc., 5500 Central Avenue, Boulder, Colorado 80301, and in the United Kingdom by Westview Press, Inc., 13 Brunswick Centre, London WC1N 1AF, England

Library of Congress Cataloging-in-Publication Data
Steel and the state/by Thomas R. Howell . . . [et al.].
    p. cm.—(Economic competition among nations series)
  Bibliography: p.
  Includes index.
  ISBN 0-8133-7676-9
  1. Steel industry and trade—Government policy. I. Howell,
Thomas R., 1949–   . II. Series: Economic competition among
nations.
HD9510.6.S727 1988
338.4'7669142—dc19   88-21030
                                                                                CIP

Printed and bound in the United States of America

The paper used in this publication meets the requirements of the American National Standard for Permanence of Paper for Printed Library Materials Z39.48-1984.

10   9   8   7   6   5   4   3   2   1

CONTENTS

List of Tables

List of Figures

Foreword

The problems of the U.S. steel industry have been a source of public controversy for over twenty years. The industry has grown substantially smaller since the 1960s and hundreds of thousands of steelworkers have lost their jobs. Some steel firms and many steel mills have shut down entirely, profoundly affecting regional economies based on steel and its related industries. An industrial transformation of this magnitude has inevitably given rise to efforts to identify its underlying causes. This book is a contribution to that effort.

The difficulties experienced by the U.S. industry are part of a larger structural crisis which has affected the western world steel industry since 1974. The principal factor underlying the crisis has been the increasing role played by governments in the industry. At the end of World War II, the world steel industry was dominated by private producers. Since the early 1970s, however, virtually all of the substantial growth which has occurred in steel has been undertaken by state-owned firms, and a number of important companies which were formerly privately held have been partially or wholly nationalized (*e.g.*, producers in the U.K., Sweden, Belgium, and France). The wholesale intrusion of the state in this sector has produced a series of major distortions in the world market, including gross overcapacity and a trading environment characterized by cartels, highly restrictive import regimes, subsidies and dumping. The authors of this book show how the increasingly important role played by public authorities in steel served to precipitate and prolong the structural crisis, and to exacerbate its harmful effects.

The national interest requires that the United States have a privately owned, internationally competitive domestic steel industry. In a world competitive environment characterized by extensive government intervention, this requires public policies which fully address such intervention and its effects.

Historically, the U.S. government has acted to offset the effects of foreign government intervention in steel only after substantial injury to the U.S. industry has already occurred. The reactive character of U.S. policy reflects, in part, an inherent reluctance by our government to intervene in the commercial arena, but it also reflects an inadequate base of information available to policymakers concerning industrial policies in other countries.

Because of the growing importance of the phenomenon of government intervention to our industry, and the consequences of this kind of activity to the American national interest, we provided partial support for the research which led to the publication of this book. While the conclusions drawn by the authors are their own and do not necessarily reflect our individual companies' views, we believe that the book is a valuable contribution to the public knowledge of our industry and on the broader phenomenon of state intervention. It is our hope that the book will provide the basis for a more informed public policy discussion of the future of the U.S steel industry.

ARMCO INC.
BETHLEHEM STEEL CORPORATION
INLAND STEEL INDUSTRIES, INC.
LTV STEEL COMPANY, INC.
NATIONAL STEEL CORPORATION
USX CORPORATION

Acknowledgments

The authors would like to acknowledge the contributions of a number of individuals at Dewey, Ballantine, Bushby, Palmer and Wood to the preparation of this study. Audrey S. Winter contributed particularly valuable research and wrote portions of the section on West Germany. Janet H. MacLaughlin provided research and analysis for chapter seven. Karen Magner performed research and translation work with respect to chapter three and assisted in the preparation of the bibliography. Bonnie Ohri provided statistical assistance and was responsible for all of the currency conversions in the study. Susan Forrester provided valuable technical advice in terms of the actual preparation of the manuscript. Lourdes Buenaventura spent many long hours preparing and editing the numerous tables in the study. Sharon von Bergener prepared and edited the final versions of the charts. Bernice Grandsoult typed the initial draft of most of the chapters in the study. The word processing unit at Dewey, Ballantine revised many drafts of the manuscript and we are indebted to Martha Myricks, the supervisor, and Joyce Harris, Reginald Spence, Patricia Brown, Reba Lawson, Nancy Cernick, Dennis Curtin, Julie MacGregor, Wini Parker, Betty Racey, Priscilla Rowe, Karol Smarr, and Debra Williams.

A special note of thanks and recognition is due Susan Byrd for her tireless efforts with respect to the production of the study. She not only edited the manuscript and prepared the bibliography, but also converted the work to typeset format, coordinated the layout and physical production of the text, tables and charts and prepared the initial versions of the charts.

1

Introduction

At the end of 1974, in the wake of the first oil crisis, the world steel industry entered a deep recession. This slump, widely perceived at the time as simply another periodic downturn in an industry known for its cyclicality, proved longer and more severe than any in living memory. Its effects were eventually felt throughout the industrialized and developing world, both in the West and in the centrally-planned economies. Hundreds of steel plants were closed and nearly a million workers laid off in Pennsylvania, Ohio, Wales, Scotland, Lorraine, the Saar, the Ruhr, Luxembourg, Sweden, Austria, and Spain. These dislocations meant economic devastation for entire communities, and, in Europe, led to violent civil unrest. In the United States, the steel industry underwent a series of severe contractions after 1974; over 25 producers went bankrupt, others were forced to merge or retrench drastically, and the work force was cut by two-thirds from over 500 thousand in 1974 to 163 thousand in 1987. The industry suffered a succession of staggering net losses, an estimated $12 billion from 1982 to 1986, raising serious questions about its ability to sustain the level of capital investment needed to be competitive in the 1990s and beyond.

The thesis of this book is that the principal cause of the prolonged structural crisis which affected the western world steel industry after 1974 was pervasive intervention by governments in the market, both before and after 1974, which not only produced enormous distortions, but also has increasingly determined the basic patterns of world steel investment, production and trade.[1] Governments were driven by many motives to intervene in steel, from deliberate pursuit of statist industrial objectives to *ad hoc* actions with no objective more grand than to stave off industrial catastrophe, but the cumulative effect has been the same. In an era characterized by stagnant growth in world steel demand, government actions, occurring more or less simultaneously in many countries, led to excessive and in many cases

---

[1] This book examines the role of state intervention in the carbon steel industry. For the most part it does not address the specialty steel industry, a subject which is worthy of separate treatment.

uneconomic investments in steelmaking plants and prevented the elimination of older facilities. The result was an extraordinary global surplus of steelmaking capacity which, in the years after 1974, led to a generalized regression into mercantilism on a scale seldom seen in the postwar era. Exports were subsidized and dumped, imports were restricted, and national and regional cartels exerted a progressively greater influence on world markets.

In such an environment, actions of governments, rather than market forces, have increasingly dictated short and long-term competitive outcomes in this sector. The resulting shifts in patterns of world steel production and investment have not been efficient, nor do they resemble the outcome that would have occurred under conditions of *laissez faire* competition.

PRELUDE TO CRISIS

The structural recession which developed after 1974 was fundamentally a crisis of overcapacity, a gross imbalance between supply and demand. In the years prior to 1974, far too many steelmaking facilities were built for national markets, or the world market, to support. When world steel demand fell off sharply after 1974, prices plummeted as steel producers desperately sought to maintain their operating rates and to find outlets for their surpluses. Facilities on which construction had begun prior to 1974 continued to come on stream for the remainder of the decade, and altogether new capacity was added, compounding an already serious overcapacity problem. The surplus was to some extent a reflection of faulty investment decisions by private firms, notably in West Germany, which had undertaken major expansion programs in the early 1970s, on the eve of the market collapse. For the most part, however, the surplus was attributable to decisions by government planners, or industrialists working in collaboration with government officials, to undertake "heroic" expansion efforts. These decisions were taken in many countries, reflecting motives ranging from regional development to economic nationalism, but most shared a common characteristic: from a purely economic standpoint, they were irrational.

In Europe, massive public resources were committed to the construction of greenfield steel mills in southern France and southern Italy, far from their natural markets, in order to stimulate local employment and regional industrialization. France's disastrous greenfield mill at Fos-sur-Mer, at the time the largest investment project ever undertaken in that country, was the spearhead of an effort to turn Southern France into a "French California,"[2] and Italy's new mills in the Mezzogiorno were lampooned as industrial

---

[2] Jack Hayward, "The Nemesis of Industrial Patriotism; the French Response to the Steel Crisis," in *The Politics of Steel: Western Europe and the Steel Industry in the Crisis Years 1974-84*, ed. Yves Meny and Vincent Wright (Berlin and New York: Walter de Gruyther, 1987), p. 509.

"cathedrals in the desert."[3]   In Spain, pursuant to an industry-government "Concerted Action Plan," major investments were made in steel facilities in the Valencia region which were intended as a catalyst for the development of that region, but which were so poorly sited that they would become an explosive political issue a decade later.[4]   In Sweden, the state-owned producer NJA undertook a major capacity expansion effort in Norbotten County (an area of high unemployment) which the director of the state holding company called "unrealistic in market and economic terms," in a location where access to the mill would be restricted by harbor ice 4-5 months of the year.[5]   The establishment of such new facilities was generally not accompanied by the closure of older ones; the new capacity, rather than replacing older equipment, "simply added to it."[6]

In Japan, engaged in a frenetic industrialization drive in which steel's role was perceived as pivotal, the government channeled cheap loans to domestic producers and collaborated in a series of cartel arrangements with respect to investment and production.[7]   Such measures drastically reduced the market risks associated with excessive investments, unleashing an extraordinary "capacity expansion race" by the Japanese mills, each of which sought to maintain or expand market share through an aggressive building program. This dynamic, recognized by contemporary Japanese observers as irrational and potentially dangerous,[8] led to the largest growth in steelmaking capacity ever seen in a single country in such a short period; between 1960 and 1975, Japanese capacity grew from 28 to 140 million tons.   The new Japanese facilities were among the most modern and technologically advanced in the world, and were sited at prime seaside locations.   But by the onset of the structural crisis, Japan possessed twice the level of capacity needed to satisfy domestic demand even in peak periods.

THE MARKET COLLAPSE

Under classic *laissez faire* theory, faulty investment decisions are subject to the discipline of the market, and in economic terms the onset of the structural crisis in 1974 should have resulted not only in the curtailment of

---

[3] Alberto Campanna, *Steel in Southern Italy* (Naples: November 7, 1979), p. 24.

[4] Instituto de Promoción Industrial de Valencia, *Repercusiones de la IV Planta Siderúrgica Integral de Sagunto* (Valencia: I.P.I., 1974).

[5] *Skandinaviska Enskilda Banken Quarterly Review* (January 1982).

[6] Patrick Messerlin, "The European Iron and Steel Industry and the World Crisis," in Meny and Wright, *The Politics of Steel*.

[7] Industrial Structure Council, Subcommittee on Industrial Finance Problems of the Central Division Committee, *Kongo No Nozomashii No Arikata Ni Ni Kansuru Hokolu* (1982); *Nihon Keizai* (January 7, 1981); *Oriental Economist* (April 1967).

[8] *Japan Economic Journal* (June 18, 1968; August 31, 1971).

investments but also in the wholesale closure of noncompetitive facilities, retrenchment by producers which had made investment misjudgments, and the elimination of the weakest firms.   In much of the industrialized world, however, that did not occur. The closure of steel mills, and in some cases even the curtailment of expansion plans, was considered unacceptable for a variety of political, social and industrial policy reasons.   Instead, state intervention, which had played a substantial role in precipitating the structural crisis, increased dramatically in the following years.

The European Community

The steel recession struck Europe with full force in 1975. Internal demand fell sharply, and the European Community (EC) mills were rapidly plunged into a crisis of survival by a combination of alarming levels of idle capacity, rising costs, depressed prices, and debt burdens which threatened to break many firms.   To make matters worse, a number of governments and producers, displaying an inexplicable optimism, continued to press forward with intensive expansion plans. By 1981 the Community mills were groaning under an "intolerable" burden of over 50 million tons of surplus raw steelmaking capacity, and a market recovery was nowhere in sight.[9]

Intervention by national governments and the European Commission prevented the collapse of large segments of the Community steel industry after 1975. The largest producers in Belgium, Britain, France, and Italy were virtually bankrupt by the late 1970s and were kept alive only through repeated, massive injections of state aid. The financial failure of the leading steel firms of Belgium, Luxembourg and France led to their progressive takeover by the state, and by the end of the decade over 50 percent of Europe's steel industry was state-owned. All nations in the Community eventually resorted to large-scale subsidization of their steel producers, and between 1980 and 1985, such subsidies exceeded $35 billion.[10]

In addition to national aid programs, the European Commission presided over the formation of a Community-wide system of market controls in conjunction with Eurofer, an association of the major steel producers. The cartel established formal restraints on price and output competition within the Community in the form of production quotas, minimum prices, allocation of market shares by the producers, and import restrictions. The Commission, with a Treaty mandate to combat cartels and monopoly agreements, thus became, in the words of one European analyst, a "switching station for a European steel syndicate."[11]

---

[9] EC Commission, *Comments on the General Objectives Steel 1985*, COM (84) 89 final, February 16, 1984.

[10] EC Commission, *Report from the Commission to the Council on the Application of the Rules on Aids to the Steel Industry*, COM (86) 235 final, August 6, 1986.

[11] *Der Spiegel* (December 6, 1976).

Japan

Japan possessed an enormous capacity surplus at the time the structural recession began. Facing stiff price competition in East Asia from new developing country suppliers, the Japanese mills used their control of the domestic distribution system to insulate their home market from import pressure. The leading producers, working closely with the powerful Ministry of International Trade and Industry (MITI), implemented a succession of joint production cuts to stabilize and raise domestic prices. At the same time the Japanese mills ran their facilities at a high rate, exporting the surpluses at steeply discounted prices.[12] Concurrently, the Japanese government implemented a series of policy measures to enable the industry to adjust to new world competitive circumstances, providing assistance for the acquisition of overseas raw materials, conversion from oil to coal energy, and a variety of forms of steelmaking research and development.

The Developing Countries

In the mid and late 1970s, as the steel recession unfolded, substantial new steelmaking capacity began to become operational in the developing countries. These expansion projects were facilitated by Western world suppliers who sought to offset stagnant steel sales at home by providing state-of-the-art steelmaking equipment and technical assistance to developing nations. The projects, which generally could not attract indigenous private capital, were financed through a combination of developing country government subsidies and loans, concessional export financing by export-import banks in the industrialized countries, international development institutions like the Inter-American Development Bank and the World Bank, and, perhaps most importantly, private banks in the industrialized nations eager to recycle petrodollars. Loans to developing country steel projects, backed by the guarantees of the local government, were so attractive to foreign banks that credit was made available on a virtually unlimited basis.[13] Between 1974 and 1986, gross steelmaking capacity in the developing Western world grew from 54 to 122 million metric tons, but at the same time, countries like Mexico, Brazil and Argentina incurred a huge burden of foreign debt.

As the new steel plants became operational, developing country governments established import restrictions to protect them, with the result that traditional export outlets for mills in the industrialized countries were progressively foreclosed at the very moment that other world markets were contracting. At the same time, developing country suppliers, eager to establish themselves in international markets, launched vigorous export drives. These

---

[12] *Nihon Keizai* (November 23, 1975; February 23, 1976).

[13] *O Globo* (April 19, 1975; February 20, 1978).

efforts intensified during and after 1981, when rising interest rates and a world recession placed extraordinary pressure on developing countries, particularly in Latin America, to achieve a favorable trade balance to service their foreign debt. As a Brazilian Industry Minister put it in 1984, foreign bankers

> *came knocking at my door offering money to buy a steel mill, using political and diplomatic pressure. We bought, and the only way I have to repay the debt is selling steel.*[14]

TRADE WAR

The world steel market had become a commercial jungle by the early 1980s, with many nations seeking to sustain surplus steelmaking capacity by rigorously restricting imports and "cramming" steel into export markets. The chaotic conditions which resulted recall the mercantilism and beggar-thy-neighbor trading practices which characterized the trade wars of the 1930s, described by an American statesman:

> *The attention of governments turned inward. . . . Each for himself and the devil take the hindmost became the general rule. . . . Exports were forced; imports were curtailed. All of the weapons of commercial warfare were brought into play; currencies were depreciated, exports subsidized, tariffs raised, exchanges controlled, quotas imposed, and discrimination practiced through preferential systems and barter deals. Each nation sought to sell much and buy little.*[15]

By the early 1980s, governments were pumping unprecedented volumes of public funds -- billions, and sometimes tens of billions of dollars -- into ailing steel mills to prevent their collapse. Governments made outright grants to failing firms; made purchases of equity capital in firms to which no private investor would commit funds (referred to in the British case as "joke equity");[16] and made low interest loans to uncreditworthy firms, many of which were subsequently written off or converted to equity shares of little or no investment value.[17] Such assistance enabled state-backed producers to continue a high level of operations and maintain employment despite horrific operating losses. By the beginning of the 1980s the state steel enterprises of Brazil, France and Italy ranked among the largest money-losing enterprises

---

[14] Camilio Penna in *Washington Post* (February 21, 1984).

[15] Clair Wilcox, cited in Robert E. Hudec, *The GATT Legal System and World Trade Diplomacy* (New York: Praeger, 1975), p. 5.

[16] *The Economist* (December 20, 1980).

[17] *L'Humanité* (September 21, 1978); *Siderurgia Latinoamericana* (September, 1986).

in the world; state-owned British Steel had achieved the dubious distinction of the greatest lossmaking company in the history of the United Kingdom.[18] In countries such as Spain, Belgium, France, and Italy, the suggestion that steel subsidies might be reduced, and uneconomic mills forced to close, triggered violent social unrest, usually resulting in further injections of public funds to keep ailing producers afloat.[19] Surplus steel produced under such circumstances, so-called "social tons," was disposed of in export markets, usually at prices far below the cost of production.[20] Privately owned firms, which were in many cases better managed and more efficient, were progressively driven to their knees, and in some cases, eliminated from the market.[21]

Domestic subsidies to collapsing firms were by no means the only form of market distortion. Many governments, particularly in developing countries and the Soviet bloc, sought to stimulate steel exports directly through export subsidies and incentives, selective devaluations of the national currency and countertrade transactions. Brazil, South Korea and Argentina offered a variety of special loans to steel companies at low or negative real interest rates in order to finance production of steel products for export.[22] Poland and Venezuela selectively devalued their currency to provide a lower exchange rate for export sales.[23] South Africa established special funds to compensate domestic producers for the lower prices achieved on steel export sales.[24] These measures enabled countries such as Romania and Spain, whose steel industries were completely uncompetitive in international terms, to emerge as substantial exporters.

A third form of government intervention which had profound effects on the international market was the sanctioning (and in some cases the administration) of steel cartels. In the EC, the Commission administered a system of production quotas and minimum prices.[25] In Japan, MITI collaborated with the leading producers to maintain domestic price stability

---

[18] *Sunday Times* (December 27, 1981).

[19] *El País* (February 17, March 6, 1983); *Knack* (March 3, 1982); *Les Echos* (April 2, 1984).

[20] Cockerill, *Annual Report* (1977).

[21] *Wirtschaftswoche* (April 6, 1984); *Metal Bulletin* (January 11, 14, 18, 1983); House of Commons, *Fourth Report from the Industry and Trade Committee*, H.C. 336-II (1980-81), Minutes of Evidence, pp. 124-32.

[22] Consejo Técnico de Inversiones, *Tendencias Económicas 1986*, p. 209; *Siderurgia Latinoamericana* (October 1986), p. 18; *Far Eastern Economic Review* (April 26, 1984); *Resolutions* No. 674 (January 21, 1981), and No. 950 (August 21, 1984).

[23] *Metal Bulletin* (May 24, October 28, 1983); *Rzeczspospolita* (July 1, 1983).

[24] *American Metal Market* (October 18, 1981).

[25] *Official Journal*, L. 291, October 31, 1980.

through joint restraints on production for domestic sales;[26] in South Africa[27] and Spain,[28] joint actions by producers to stabilize domestic prices were sanctioned by government authorities. The stabilization of domestic prices through restraints on quantities available for domestic sales was in each case accompanied by ancillary import restraints.

The steel cartels of the late 1970s and 1980s had a pronounced impact on international competition. Firms participating in cartels tended to operate their facilities at a higher rate than would be warranted by agreed restrictions on production for domestic sale, and to export the surpluses which could not, because of cartel restrictions, be disposed of in the home market. In 1975-1977, a period of stagnant domestic demand, when the Japanese mills were maintaining price stability through a series of joint curtailments on output, they simultaneously launched a massive export drive, increasing their exports by 15 percent at a time when world consumption had decreased by 10 percent. In those three years, the Japanese mills exported almost 100 million metric tons of steel in a depressed world market, sometimes with extremely disruptive effects.[29] In the European Community, efforts to establish a price floor for steel through joint production and delivery restraints were closely linked to the ability of the EC mills to vent their surpluses into the U.S. market; periodic surges of EC steel into the U.S. embroiled the Community in a series of bitter trade disputes with the United States.[30]

A final form of state intervention in steel was the imposition of comprehensive import restrictions. In Japan, despite high domestic price levels and the close proximity of lower cost producers like Korea and Taiwan, imports have been effectively restricted through pressure by the local producers on distributors and customers; penetration rates were held below one percent prior to 1979 and did not exceed 6 percent thereafter.[31] In 1978 the EC established a comprehensive system of import restrictions based on voluntary restraint arrangements with its principal suppliers, which consistently held import penetration levels under 12 percent.[32] South Africa imposed a

[26] *Japan Economic Journal* (October 7, 1975); *Japan Metal Bulletin* (November 27, 1975).

[27] *Metal Bulletin* (June 10, 1979).

[28] Spanish Royal Decree 8978/1981, Article 13(1).

[29] Industrial Bank of Japan, *Quarterly Survey of Japanese Finance and Industry* (October-December 1977).

[30] Sacilor *Annual Report*, 1980, p. 7; *Metal Bulletin* (April 3, 1980; January 19, 1982).

[31] *Japan Economic Journal* (December 6, 1981); *Nikkei Business* (February 22, 1982); *Far Eastern Economic Review* (October 11, 1984); Organization for Economic Cooperation and Development, *The Steel Market for 1986 and Outlook for 1987* (Paris: OECD, 1987).

[32] EC Commission, Communication from the Commission to the Council, *External Commercial Policy in the Steel Sector*, COM (86) 585 final, November 13, 1986.

de facto ban on steel imports for the decade between 1975 and 1985.[33] Developing countries have continued to import steel products which indigenous producers do not make or cannot produce in sufficient quantity, but have generally imposed severe restrictions, often amounting to an outright ban on imports of products which can be made locally.[34]

The net effect of this mix of government policies has been a world trading environment in which most major producing nations seek to dispose of surplus steel in world markets while simultaneously protecting their own domestic markets. The result has been an influx of cheap steel into the comparatively few markets which have remained relatively open to international trade. Such markets have been found in the dwindling number of steel consuming nations of the world that do not possess sufficient steelmaking capacity to meet their needs (such as Middle Eastern nations, China, the Soviet Union, and the city-states of Singapore and Hong Kong); and the United States, which did not implement a system of comprehensive import restraints until 1984, and which did not become effective until 1986.

RESTRUCTURING

Since the beginning of the steel crisis in 1975, in virtually every nation possessing a steel industry there have been efforts to "restructure" the industry to adapt to the crisis, and there have been repeated calls for a general "restructuring" of the world industry. While the term is used to describe, and sometimes to obscure, a multitude of actions, restructuring generally refers to the elimination of older facilities, the modernization and rationalization of remaining facilities, and a balancing of net capacity with market demand, which in the crisis years has usually meant capacity reduction. Restructuring has proceeded unevenly from country to country and its course in each country has been significantly affected by government policies. In general, such policies have tended to facilitate the acquisition of modern plant, but have retarded and complicated the closure of older mills and the reduction of surplus capacity.

Modernization

The principal obstacles to the installation of modern production equipment are financial; the investments required are huge and the risk is large. State-backed firms, however, have generally been able to surmount this hurdle by turning to the government for investment funds. Worldwide, tens of billions of dollars in subsidies have been channeled into investments in modernization. As a result, such firms as British Steel, Sweden's SSAB, France's Usinor and

---

[33] *Metal Bulletin* (December 9, 1983).

[34] *Metal Bulletin* (September 28, 1982); *Nikkei Sangyo* (April 2, 1983); *Korea Herald* (January 16, 1981).

Sacilor, and Belgium's Cockerill and Hainaut-Sambre, all of which were effectively bankrupt and hopelessly in debt by the end of the 1970s, were nevertheless able to undertake intensive investment programs underwritten by the state, and have acquired extensive modern plant and equipment. By contrast, privately owned firms in West Germany, Britain and the United States, which have often been better managed, financially more sound, and more efficient and productive than many of the state-backed firms, have been unable to match the investments of their subsidized rivals, and, in some cases, have seen them pull ahead in terms of the modernity of their facilities.

Capacity Reduction

With respect to the reduction of capacity and the closure of older mills, state involvement has proven more a liability than an asset. In countries like France, Belgium, Britain, Spain and Italy, where the government is deeply involved in the affairs of the industry, decisions to close mills and lay off workers have a political as well as an economic dimension; they are perceived as actions of the state, subject to change, if sufficient agitation is generated, whether through regular political channels or through strikes, riots and other violent actions. It has frequently proven more expedient politically for governments to continue to subsidize uneconomic steel production than to "open a box of lightning bolts"[35] by forcing closures. In other cases, as in Sweden, where class divisions are not as clearly drawn and a long tradition of social welfare exists, the government has achieved closures and work force reductions more smoothly, using generous severance arrangements, worker assistance and regional aid measures.

The steel cartels sanctioned by the EC Commission and the Japanese government have retarded capacity reduction. By restraining competition, the cartels greatly reduce the pressure confronted by each producer to eliminate obsolete or excessive steelmaking plant.[36] Under cartel arrangements, market competition is replaced by a competition between producers to retain or expand their market shares, an exercise in which possession of capacity is almost always an advantage.[37] Under these regimes, producers continually issue joint calls for capacity cuts, but each producer seeks to retain or expand its own capacity and to encourage its rivals to undertake the needed cuts.[38] Elimination of inefficient plant, rather than

---

[35] *El País* (March 6, 1983).

[36] V. Colombo, M. Friderichs and J. Mayoux, "Community Steel Policy: Analysis and Recommendations," in EC Commission, *Communication from the Commission to the Council,* COM (87) 640 final, November 26, 1987 (hereafter, "Wise Men's Report").

[37] *Knack* (June 22, 1983); Ken'ichi Imai, "Tekko," in *Industry and Business in Japan*, ed. Kazuo Sato (White Plains: M.E. Sharpe, 1980).

[38] EC Commission, *General Objectives Steel 1985*, February 16, 1984.

being forced by market pressures, has instead been the subject of protracted and inconclusive negotiations. The continued failure of the EC producers to eliminate surplus capacity led the Commission to end the quota regime on July 1, 1988, although the longer term effects of this measure remain unclear.

Under such circumstances, it is not surprising that restructuring has been taking place unevenly worldwide. The privately owned industries of the U.S. and West Germany have shut down considerable obsolete plant, but in light of their poor operating results over the past decade, have encountered difficulty in raising the volumes of investment capital needed to modernize. Many other European producers, particularly the state-backed firms, have been able to acquire extensive modern plant and equipment, but retirement of older capacity (in Japan as well as Europe) has proceeded much more slowly than is generally perceived to be necessary. Exceptions to the latter problem have been Britain, which undertook drastic facilities and work force reductions under Margaret Thatcher, and Sweden, which has buffered the social shocks associated with work force reductions through a variety of government programs.

In 1987 and 1988, world steel markets have tightened; prices have firmed and spot shortages have developed for some products. It is unclear at this writing whether these developments represent a significant change in the trend of steel consumption since 1974 or merely a strong cyclical upturn, although there is evidence pointing to the latter conclusion.[39] Whether or not the steel market is on the verge of a new era of long-term growth, the interventions which have occurred in the preceding decades will shape competitive outcomes in the coming years.

U.S. STEEL POLICY

The formulation of steel policy in the United States has been shaped by a combination of factors, many of them rather unique. The relationship between the industry and the government has traditionally been adversarial, and no powerful industry ministry has ever sought to promote the industry's international competitiveness. Successive U.S. administrations have embraced a *laissez faire* philosophy towards trade and industrial policy, although imposing import controls from time to time in an inconsistent and relatively ineffective manner. U.S. policymakers have shown an abiding propensity to define trade issues in terms of "fair" versus "unfair" competition, and to commit their resolution to litigation. No U.S. administration, Republican or Democratic, has ever formulated a proactive trade policy in steel. Instead, government policy measures have been implemented on an *ad hoc* basis in response to a succession of crises in the steel sector which threatened to have broader political repercussions if they were not contained.

---

[39] See chapter 2, "An Overview of the World Steel Industry."

In the years immediately following the onset of the structural crisis, the U.S. market experienced a major increase in import penetration, from 12.4 percent in 1973 to 18 percent in 1977 and 1978, principally from Japan and the EC. In 1977, U.S. steel firms filed nearly two dozen antidumping complaints against these producers. The Carter administration, concerned that the litigation would jeopardize U.S. relations with its principal allies, and wishing to craft a response that was less trade disruptive than the imposition of antidumping duties, established the so-called "trigger price mechanism" (TPM), essentially an early warning system for dumping, in return for withdrawal by the industry of the antidumping suits. The TPM appeared to function effectively for about a year, between mid-1978 and mid-1979, but in late 1979, technical flaws in the system caused it to collapse, and the U.S. market experienced a surge of imports from the EC. U.S. steel firms filed another array of antidumping cases against the EC, and the administration, again concerned over possible spillover effects to other issues within the Atlantic alliance, devised a new version of the TPM, which was implemented in late 1980; U.S. firms again withdrew their antidumping cases. This new system functioned well for several months, but in the spring and summer of 1981, it became clearer to EC producers that the new Administration -- more ideologically committed to the notion of "free trade" than the last -- was not responding vigorously to EC sales below trigger prices. At that point, the system simply fell apart; another influx of EC steel followed, and at the end of 1981, U.S. producers filed over 100 antidumping and countervailing duty complaints against EC mills. The investigations conducted by the Commerce Department and the U.S. International Trade Commission resulted in preliminary findings of dumping and subsidization at margins sufficiently high that the application of antidumping and countervailing duties would have effectively excluded some EC mills from the U.S. altogether.

Once again faced with a major confrontation with the EC, the U.S. government negotiated an agreement pursuant to which the Community voluntarily undertook to limit its exports to the U.S. to fixed levels through 1985. This agreement resulted in an abatement of the worst pressure from EC imports; however, even as the agreement was being concluded, a massive new surge of steel from the developing countries was materializing -- import penetration from this source jumped from under 4 percent in 1981 to 7 percent in 1983 and 10 percent in 1984. In 1984, Bethlehem Steel and the United Steelworkers of America brought an action under Section 201 of the Trade Act of 1974 (the escape clause) seeking import relief for most major carbon steel products. At the same time, U.S. Steel filed numerous antidumping and countervailing duty actions against steel imports from developing and "other industrialized" countries, many of which led to affirmative government findings of dumping and subsidization. At the end of 1984, President Reagan denied a recommendation for relief by the U.S. International Trade Commission, but announced his own steel import program, based on bilateral trade agreements or voluntary restraint arrangements with supplier countries, designed to hold the level of import penetration of finished steel in the U.S. market to 18.5 percent and to limit semifinished imports to 1.7 million tons per year.

The Reagan steel program took some time to put into place. Import penetration levels actually increased during the first year of the program. However, by the beginning of 1986 the system was clearly functioning more effectively, and in 1987 import penetration levels had fallen to 21.3 percent.

The twelve years of reactive, often improvised, U.S. trade policies which preceded the effective implementation of the Reagan program in mid-1986 were accompanied by the erosion of a substantial portion of the U.S. steel industry. Each major import influx was accompanied by a wave of layoffs, plant closings, and in some cases, bankruptcies. In contrast to Japan and the EC, where import penetration levels have been consistently held at very low levels (averaging less than 4 percent for Japan and 12 percent for the EC), U.S. import penetration levels progressively increased from 13.4 in 1974 to over 26 percent by 1984. The U.S. industry experienced low or negative profitability for over a decade.

LOOKING FORWARD

American policy toward its steel industry has been erratic and often uninformed. There has been no expression of policy for the longer term. Import restrictions, the primary policy tool, have been sporadic, of uncertain duration, and, until the Reagan program, have been of limited effect. Such uncertainty has created an environment in which investment decisions are put off and ultimately taken in the negative by default. The marked contrast between the shrinkage of the American industry relative to the industries of the rest of the world is due in no small part to the differences in public policies adopted in the United States and abroad.

The apparent rudderlessness of American economic policy as it affects trade is due to the reluctance of American policymakers to reach decisions which intervene in trade or otherwise are believed to impair the operation of the market. The fact that there are exceptions to the application of this principle for worker safety, environmental protection, health care, or other social purposes makes it no less real. Because of the strong belief in a *laissez faire* philosophy as the guiding principle -- that government which governs least governs best -- the realities of international competition for any particular industry are often largely unknown to those in government who are called upon to make complex decisions. These decisions are called for on what seems inadequate notice as political pressures mount or a legal right to redress is invoked.

The following chapters are designed to broaden the base of public knowledge so that policy decisions can be made on a more fully informed basis. The happy assumption that other nations conduct their economies in the same manner that the United States has chosen rapidly gives way to a realization that others define their national interests in terms which differ markedly from our own. If the United States ignores this fact, decisions taken abroad will continue to exercise an undue influence in shaping the U.S. economy. The thesis of this book is that the American policy formulation process can only benefit by being better informed.

2

An Overview of the World Steel Industry

The structural crisis in the world steel industry that began after 1974 has no parallel in this century. The economic fortunes of the world steel industry have generally been more robust; indeed, as shown in figure 2-1, for 30 years after the Second World War global raw steel production grew rapidly at an annual growth rate of 6.16 percent, twice the growth rate experienced from 1900 to 1946, when world steel production increased 2.98 percent per year.[1]

However, this pattern of rapid growth changed abruptly in 1974. If the centrally planned economies are taken out of the world totals, the western economies as a group experienced a decline in production after 1974 of over one percent a year.[2] Production in the western world fell from 494.9 million metric tons in 1974 to 429.5 million metric tons in 1986. Production did increase in the rest-of-world (ROW) category, primarily in the developing nations, but aggregate steel output in the United States, the EC and Japan declined by 122 million metric tons, with half of the entire decline being accounted for by the reduction in production in the United States (table 2-1). The crisis that gripped the world steel industry after 1974 had its origins in a number of interrelated developments in the world economy, most of which

---

[1] Production data are from International Iron and Steel Institute, *Steel Statistical Yearbook 1987* (Brussels: IISI, 1987), table 1.

[2] The western economies exclude the so-called centrally planned economies of the Soviet Union, Eastern Europe and the Asian communist countries. While steel production and consumption have grown rapidly in the centrally planned economies (at a compound annual rate of almost 6 percent since 1950), these countries do not as yet participate to any great extent in the steel markets of the western economies, although they periodically absorb significant exports from the West and are the source of occasional surges of low-priced exports into western markets (see the discussion in chapter 6). The Soviet Union surpassed the United States as the world's largest steel producing country in the 1970s and the share of total world steel production accounted for by the centrally planned economies has increased from 18.8 percent in 1950 to 39.7 percent by 1986.

Table 2-1. World Raw Steel Production by Major Area, 1950-1986
(million metric tons)

	USA	Japan	EC(9)	ROW	Western World	Non-Market Economies	TOTAL
1950	87.8	4.8	48.3	12.1	153.0	35.6	188.5
1951	95.4	6.5	53.5	13.3	168.8	40.6	209.4
1952	84.6	7.0	58.4	15.8	165.7	45.4	211.1
1953	101.2	7.7	57.3	18.0	184.3	50.1	234.3
1954	80.1	7.7	62.6	18.5	168.9	54.0	222.9
1955	106.1	9.4	72.8	21.8	210.2	59.4	269.6
1956	104.5	11.1	77.7	25.4	218.7	63.2	282.0
1957	102.2	12.5	82.0	22.8	219.5	72.3	291.8
1958	77.4	11.8	78.0	23.4	190.6	80.6	271.2
1959	84.7	16.6	84.0	27.4	212.7	93.2	305.9
1960	90.1	22.1	97.9	30.9	241.0	105.1	346.2
1961	88.9	28.3	96.1	34.4	247.7	106.2	353.9
1962	89.2	27.6	94.3	37.3	248.3	109.2	357.5
1963	93.7	31.5	96.5	46.9	268.6	114.4	383.0
1964	115.3	39.8	110.0	46.3	311.4	123.2	434.5
1965	119.3	41.2	113.9	49.6	324.0	132.5	456.4
1966	121.7	47.8	110.2	52.0	331.7	139.3	470.9
1967	115.4	62.1	114.6	54.4	346.6	150.2	496.8
1968	119.3	66.9	125.4	59.4	371.0	157.5	528.4
1969	128.2	82.1	134.7	63.1	408.2	165.2	573.3
1970	119.3	93.4	137.6	68.2	418.5	175.0	593.5
1971	109.2	88.5	128.2	68.7	394.6	185.9	580.5
1972	120.8	96.9	139.2	77.4	434.3	195.8	630.0
1973	136.8	119.3	150.1	85.0	491.3	206.2	697.5
1974	132.2	117.1	155.6	90.0	494.9	215.3	710.2
1975	105.8	102.3	125.3	90.5	423.9	222.0	645.9
1976	116.0	107.4	134.6	94.5	452.6	222.7	675.3
1977	113.7	102.4	126.6	100.5	443.3	232.2	675.4
1978	124.3	102.2	133.3	108.9	468.6	248.2	716.8
1979	123.7	111.8	141.0	120.5	496.9	249.7	746.5
1980	101.4	111.4	128.6	122.3	463.8	252.4	716.1
1981	109.6	101.7	126.3	122.4	460.0	247.6	707.5
1982	67.7	99.5	111.4	119.7	398.4	246.4	644.7
1983	76.7	97.2	109.4	123.6	407.0	256.1	663.1
1984	83.9	105.6	120.2	136.3	446.0	264.0	710.0
1985	80.1	105.2	120.7	144.1	450.2	269.2	719.3
1986	74.0	98.2	110.6	146.6	429.5	282.5	712.0

Source: American Iron and Steel Industry, *Annual Statistical Reports*, various issues.

have been either caused by state intervention or have produced much greater levels of intervention.

The most significant changes have occurred in the relative international location of steel production and consumption. A dramatic shift occurred from the traditional steel producing regions, the United States and the EC, to Japan, other western market economies and the developing nations. Since 1960 the share of the United States and the EC in world production and consumption of steel has fallen by half, while the share of these other nations has doubled.

These changes occurred simultaneously with a slowdown in world steel consumption. In the 1960s world steel consumption grew by over 5 percent per year, but this growth rate fell to 2 percent per year in the 1970s and to 0.5 percent per year in the 1980s. The transition year from high growth to low growth in world steel consumption occurred in 1974, the year of the first world oil crisis.[3] From 1960 to 1974, world consumption increased by 4.95 percent per year, but from 1974 to 1986 the rate of increase was only 0.63 percent per year. However, the only reason for the marginal growth in consumption in the period 1974 to 1986 was increased consumption by the centrally planned economies. The western world economies experienced a decline in raw steel consumption of 0.5 percent per year.[4] Consumption has increased significantly in 1987-1988, but it remains to be seen whether this development represents a fundamentally new longer term trend or simply a cyclical upturn.

Steel trade increased in importance at the same time that consumption was slowing down in the mid-1970s. There was an increase not only in the number of steel exporting countries, but also in the percent of domestic steel production that was exported by many countries.[5] For more developed regions like Europe, steel exports were a means to offset declining domestic consumption. For the newly industrializing countries, exports offered greater scale economies as well as the more traditional benefits of export-led growth

---

[3] The post-1974 world recession and subsequent slow world economic growth and the sharp rise in energy prices all disproportionately affected the steel industry because of the sharp decline, or decline in steel intensity, in such steel intensive heavy capital goods industries as automobiles, shipbuilding, and railways. Meny and Wright, *The Politics of Steel*, pp. 10-11; International Iron and Steel Institute, *Steel Demand Forecasting* (Brussels: IISI, 1983).

[4] Consumption data are from Organization for Economic Cooperation and Development, *World Steel Trade Developments 1960-1983* (Paris: OECD, 1985) and IISI, *Steel Statistical Yearbook 1987*. Part of the decline in crude steel consumption is due to increased efficiency in production, especially the use of continuous casting technology which increases the yield of crude steel to finished steel. Among the western economies, the percentage of continuously cast steel in total steel production increased from 11.8 percent in 1973 to 71.6 percent in 1986. The increase in the use of continuous casting also affects the comparison of crude steel production numbers over time. For example, western world crude steel production in 1986 was 12.5 percent less than the peak reached in 1974. However steel production in ingot equivalents, taking account of the increase in the percent of continuous cast steel, was down only 4.6 percent in 1986 compared to 1974.

[5] *Ibid.*, p. 9.

Figure 2−1: Growth of World Crude Steel Production 1900−1986

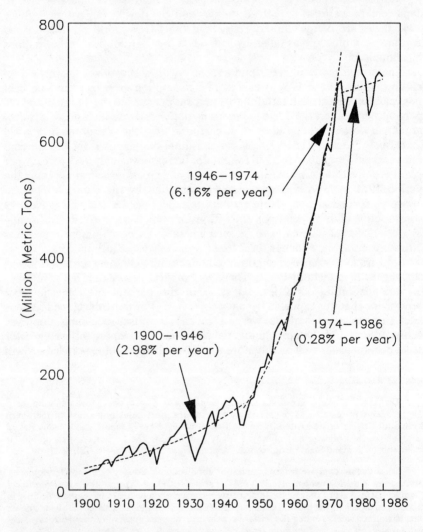

Source: International Iron and Steel Institute, <u>Steel Statistical Yearbook 1987</u> (Brussels: IISI, 1987), Table 1.

Note: Trend lines were computed by regressions of the form ln Production = a + b * Time, where the coefficient b was used to calculate the annual rate of change.

and foreign exchange earnings. In 1950 world steel exports as a percent of world steel production were 10.7 percent. This ratio averaged 26 percent in the 1980s. The importance of steel exports showed a marked increase with the slowdown in world steel consumption after 1974.[6]

Governments in the steel producing countries not only were not passive in the face of these major structural changes in the world steel industry, but were responsible for many of them. Where steel consumption was increasing, developing country governments promoted the installation of indigenous capacity, often by providing extensive subsidies and curtailing imports once production commenced (see chapter 5). In the developed countries, especially in the EC, governments provided incentives for expansion, and subsequently subsidies for operating losses, to meet national industrial, social and regional development objectives (see chapters 3 and 6). Almost every significant producing country, with the exception of the United States, expanded capacity much faster than consumption in the 1970s and early 1980s, increasing the competition in export markets.[7]

The net effect of these developments has been the failure of the world steel market to work efficiently.[8] Investment in productive facilities has far outpaced the growth in consumption and has been largely unrelated to the underlying economic conditions in the industry. Capacity has greatly exceeded demand. Despite upturns in 1979 and 1987-88, capacity utilization rates generally have remained low. In a volume-sensitive industry like steel, where fixed costs are extremely high, chronically low utilization rates have had a devastating effect on profitability.

The political and social forces which gave rise to these global economic distortions are examined in chapters 3 through 7. In order to appreciate the effect which intervention by public authorities has had in this industry, it is worth first reviewing the technology and economics of the steelmaking process, as well as the major global developments in steel production and trade.

---

[6] Export to production data taken from IISI, *Steel Statistical Yearbook*, 1981, 1987.

[7] Because of the large scale of most steel investments, and the length of time between the decision to invest and the time the investment comes on stream, periods of imbalance between supply and demand may occur in various steel markets. However, because of government intervention in world steel markets, this imbalance happened on a global basis for the first time after 1974. On a 1987 dollar basis, steel outlays in the western world were at a peak in the 1971 to 1976 period, averaging $25 to $30 billion per year. This is a major reason why capacity kept expanding through 1982 even though consumption had stagnated after 1974. See Peter F. Marcus and Karlis M. Kirsis, *World Steel Dynamics: Core Report BB* (New York: PaineWebber Inc., January 1988), pp. 1-13.

[8] "It does not work efficiently because of factors such as (1) government investment in steel plants, particularly in developing countries; (2) subsidies to steel plants that increase output and reduce the probability of plant closure; and (3) protectionism in domestic markets for steel products." National Academy of Sciences, *The Competitive Status of the U.S. Steel Industry* (Washington, D.C.: National Academy Press, 1985), pp. 9, 112.

STEEL INDUSTRY TECHNOLOGY AND COMPETITIVE DYNAMICS

Steel is the most important engineering material in industrial societies. Its importance extends from primary manufacturing to construction, and it has always been essential for national security.

The Production of Steel

Almost all molten steel produced in the western nations in 1986 was produced by two means: the hot-metal route involving the blast furnace in combination with the basic oxygen furnace (66 percent) and the cold-metal route using the electric arc furnace (31 percent).[9] The virgin metal intensive basic oxygen furnace (BOF) and the scrap intensive electric arc (EA) furnace are today's conventional steelmaking technologies, replacing the open hearth method which was the conventional steelmaking technology as recently as the mid-1960s.

The process of making steel in an integrated steel plant is made up of six basic operations (figure 2-2): coke production, iron ore agglomeration, ironmaking, steelmaking, casting and finishing.

Coke production is the process for carbonizing coal. The coke is used as an agent in the blast furnace to reduce iron bearing materials (iron ore, pellets, sinter) to molten iron (pig iron). In the blast furnace, the resulting iron is also separated from the large quantity of impurities. Most steel contains much less than 1 percent of carbon. The excess carbon must be removed from the product of the blast furnace in the BOF steelmaking furnace to produce carbon steel.[10]

The BOF steelmaking furnace performs primarily a refining function, removing impurities such as silicon, phosphorous and sulphur through an oxidation process.[11] The EA furnace, unlike the BOF furnace, generally uses almost 100 percent steel scrap. EA technology entails a much smaller capital investment per ton of molten steel produced compared to the BOF or

---

[9] This section relies on the following sources: William J. Vaughan, Clifford S. Russell and Harold C. Cochrane, *Government Policies and the Adoption of Innovations in the Integrated Iron and Steel Industry* (Washington, D.C.: Resources for the Future, 1974); *The Making, Shaping and Treating of Steel*, ed. Harold E. McGannon (Pittsburgh, Pennsylvania: United States Steel, 1971), ninth edition; Congress of the United States, Office of Technology Assessment, *Technology and Steel Industry Competitiveness* (Washington, D.C.: U.S. GPO, June 1980); and National Academy of Sciences, *U.S. Steel Industry*. The percentages of steel production by type of process are from IISI, *Steel Statistical Yearbook 1987*.

[10] Alloy steels are produced by adding various elements such as nickel, manganese, molybdenum, etc. to the molten steel during or after the carbon removal process.

[11] The oxidized impurities leave the molten bath either in the furnace slag or in gases. The metallic charge in the BOF furnace must be at least 70 percent molten iron.

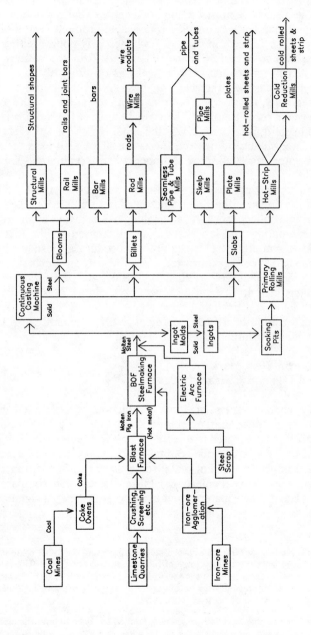

Figure 2-2: Simplified Flow Diagram of Principal Steelmaking Process Steps

Source: Adapted from Harold F. McGannon, ed., The Making, Shaping and Treating of Steel (Pittsburgh, Pennsylvania: Herbick & Held, 1971), p. 2.

integrated process of steelmaking.[12]

After the molten steel attains the desired chemical composition in the steelmaking furnace it must be solidified into a shape that permits further processing so that it can be made into a usable product. The molten steel is poured from the furnace into a ladle whence it is poured either into ingot molds or continuous casting machines. In 1986 in the western producing countries 72 per cent of total crude steel was continuously cast.[13]

Continuous casting, the current best-practice method of producing semifinished steel, involves the pouring of molten steel into the top of open-bottomed water-cooled molds. The cross section of the mold corresponds to the desired semifinished shape. As the molten steel progresses through the mold the outer shell solidifies and forms the shape as it exits the mold. The steel then enters a water-spray chamber where cooling and solidifying are completed.

Continuous casting involves significant savings over the traditional ingot method of making semifinished shapes because it eliminates the sequence of ingot pouring, cooling, reheating and rolling. The savings come from reduced energy consumption and labor hours and increased yield. Increased yield means that less molten steel is required to produce a finished steel product.

Semifinished steel is converted into finished products by mechanical treatment -- hot-rolling, cold-rolling, forging, drawing, extruding, etc. Finished steel products include structural shapes, bars, plates, rails, tubular products, wire, and coated and uncoated sheet steel. Many of these products require some form of additional heat treatment at the steelmill to give them the properties for their intended use.

Competition in Steel Markets:
Supply and Demand Characteristics

Specific characteristics of steel production and demand have direct relevance for product market competition, especially with respect to the volatility of prices compared to quantity changes. Steel production is generally considered to be a large-scale, capital-intensive production process. While integrated production (the hot-metal route using the BOF furnace) is indeed large-scale, it is not particularly capital-intensive when compared to other industries. Energy, raw material and labor costs make up a significant portion

---

[12] The relative cost differences between steelmaking using the BOF route versus the EA route depend largely on the relative price of fuels, scrap and hot metal. The most significant difference between the two processes is the scale of operation and cost of facilities. The EA furnace does not require facilities for making coke (coke oven), iron ore agglomeration (sinter strand) and the production of pig iron (blast furnace).

[13] The traditional, now essentially outmoded, method has been to pour the molten steel into tall, generally rectangular molds where the steel is allowed to cool and solidify into ingots. Most ingots are then removed from the molds and reheated and rolled into shapes known as blooms, billets and slabs. These shapes are referred to as semifinished steel.

of total steelmaking costs. The cold-metal route of steelmaking employing the EA furnace is of significantly smaller scale than an integrated steelworks.

The minimum efficient scale (m.e.s.) for an integrated steelworks ranges from 4 to 8 million tons of raw steel capacity per year, depending on the range of products to be manufactured.[14] The two facilities in a steelworks subject to the greatest scale economies are the blast furnace and the hot strip mill.[15] The m.e.s. has grown continually in the post war period, with the greatest impetus toward bigger facilities provided by Japanese producers in the 1960s and 1970s. The average capacity of large integrated steel plants built since 1950 was 7.6 million metric tons per year (tpy) in Japan compared to 5.0 million metric tpy in Germany, 4.0 million metric tpy in the United Kingdom and 3.9 million metric tpy in the United States (only two plants). The largest steelworks in the western world is the Fukuyama works of Nippon Kokan Kaisha (NKK) in Japan, rated at 16 million metric tpy.[16]

In contrast to the integrated facility, the minimum efficient scale of a plant producing steel via the cold-metal route using the EA furnace (semi-integrated, electric furnace plant or minimill) is many times smaller. Most minimills have an annual capacity of 200,000 to 1 million tpy.[17] Two-thirds of all minimill capacity is in plants of less than 600,000 tons of crude steel per year.[18] Most minimills specialize in standard bar products, small structural shapes and wire rods that can all be made from small diameter billets, the smallest semifinished shape. The integrated plants continue to be the main source of the largest semifinished shape, the slab. Slabs are rolled into sheet

---

[14] Minimum efficient scale (m.e.s.) refers to the rate of output per year at which unit costs reach their minimum. The m.e.s. of a steel plant is determined by the optimal size of each facility (blast furnace, steelmaking furnace, casting operations and finishing mills) and the constraints involved in matching up the facilities with each other to form an optimal flow of materials. On the estimates for m.e.s. see Robert W. Crandall, *The U.S. Steel Industry in Recurrent Crisis* (Washington, D.C.: The Brookings Institution, 1981), pp. 10-12; Walter Adams and Hans Mueller, "The Steel Industry," in *The Structure of American Industry*, ed. Walter Adams (New York: Macmillan Publishing Co., 1982), ch. 3; A. Cockerill, *The Steel Industry: International Comparisons of Industrial Structure and Performance* (Cambridge: Cambridge University Press, 1974); and National Academy of Sciences, *U.S. Steel Industry*, ch. 3.

[15] Crandall, *Recurrent Crisis*, p. 11.

[16] National Academy of Sciences, *U.S. Steel Industry*, table 2-1.

[17] The use of the terms integrated steelworks and minimill (referring to type of establishment) should not be confused with the distinction between an integrated steel firm (where a substantial portion of its crude steel output is produced via the hot-metal route) and a non-integrated steel firm (including minimills but also strip converters, pipe producers, etc.) By the end of the 1970s, a third of the EA furnaces in the United States were operated by integrated steel firms. U.S. General Accounting Office, *New Strategy Required for Aiding Distressed Steel Industry* (Washington, D.C.: GAO, January 8, 1981), EMD-81-29, pp. 1-7.

[18] Robert W. Crandall and Donald F. Barnett, *Up From the Ashes* (Washington, D.C.: Brookings Institution, 1986), p. 9.

products for use in the automotive, capital goods, appliance and consumer goods industries.

The difference in scale, combined with the fact that the minimills do not need to produce hot-metal, means that the capital costs of the two processes differ significantly. Recent estimates of steel plant construction costs in the United States illustrate this large capital cost difference. A 500,000 tpy minimill shipping 450,000 tpy of merchant bar is estimated to cost $284 million, or $631 per ton of shipment capacity. In contrast, a 6 million tpy steel plant, shipping 5 million tpy of typical integrated mill products (hot and cold-rolled sheet, plate, galvanized steel), is estimated to cost $7.33 billion, or $1,465 per ton of shipment capacity.[19]

The differences in scale economies produce differences in geographical concentration of production and have economic, social and political implications.[20] A large integrated steel plant employs thousands of people and can account for most of the economic activity (employment, taxes, income, etc.) in a given community or geographic region. This means that any changes in the plant's economic fortunes have a huge impact on the local economy, one of the major reasons that intervention by national governments has been pervasive. While minimill operations are important, their economic impact, and therefore their social and political impact, is much less than that of integrated works.

The large scale of an integrated plant, with the resultant high fixed costs, means that the capacity utilization of the plant is very important for operating results. The cost savings inherent in large scale operations can only be realized if the plant is run close to its operating potential, normally at least 80 percent of rated capacity; otherwise size becomes a liability.[21] One way to illustrate this phenomenon is to examine the effect of operating rate on productivity for major mills in the United States, Japan and West Germany. In 1987 manhours per ton shipped, calculated at standard operating rates, were 5.59 for Japan, 6.49 for the United States and 6.88 for West Germany. However, when calculated at actual operating rates achieved in 1987, manhours per ton shipped were 6.69 in the United States, 7.54 in Japan and

[19] Marcus and Kirsis, *Core Report BB*, pp. 1-23. The minimill is a direct reduction/electric arc furnace plant while the integrated works is a blast furnace/BOF steelmaking furnace operation.

[20] Kenneth Warren, *World Steel: An Economic Geography* (New York: Crane, Russak and Company, Inc., 1975), ch. 3.

[21] Warren, *World Steel*, p. 72; Donald F. Barnett and Louis Schorsch, *Steel: Upheaval in a Basic Industry* (Cambridge, Massachusetts: Ballinger Publishing Company, 1983), pp. 188-198. Barnett and Schorsch have a very good discussion of the trade-offs between scale and operating rate.

7.73 in West Germany.[22] Thus the U.S. integrated producers, despite having generally smaller plant size than their Japanese competitors, had higher labor productivity because Japanese operating rates in 1987 (approximately 63 percent of gross capacity for the industry) were significantly below the levels for which the plants were designed. The larger the plant size, the greater the penalty is for low operating rates.

The other important implication of the very large size of an integrated steelworks is that additions to capacity take place in very large increments. An integrated works on the order of 8 to 10 million tpy will add raw steel capacity almost equal to the entire annual steel consumption of a newly industrializing country like South Korea. Even for a country like the United States, the largest steel market in the western world, a new integrated plant would represent a capacity addition equal to eight to ten percent of annual consumption.

The relationship between capacity utilization and performance has meant that there are great incentives to operate steel plants at high rates of utilization. Whether this is possible depends on the available market demand and the output and pricing decisions of rival firms.

The demand for steel is derived from the demand for durable goods, such as automobiles and appliances, capital goods and machinery and construction requirements; as a result, carbon steel is price inelastic.[23] The total amount of steel consumed therefore is not sensitive to the average price of steel. Lowering the price of steel will not significantly increase the amount of steel consumed. This means that a steel firm, by lowering its price, can attract sales away from other steel companies, but if all steel firms lower their prices, total steel consumption will show little increase and total revenues from steel sales will decline.

The interaction of demand conditions which are price inelastic combined with the pressures for high operating rates on the supply side can lead to ruinous price competition, especially during periods of economic downturn when all or part of the large fixed costs of the plant and equipment may not be covered by the selling price. Thus, as expressed by one writer, it should

---

[22] Peter F. Marcus and Karlis M. Kirsis, *World Steel Dynamics: Steel Strategist 14* (New York: PaineWebber, Inc., December 1987), p. 42. Operating rate changes can shift the relative position of the low cost producer from year to year. In 1977, for example, when the Japanese rate was 69 percent compared to the U.S. rate of 78 percent, steel production costs were 12 percent higher in the United States than in Japan. The next year, with the Japanese operating rate at 66 percent, and the U.S. rate up to 86 percent, U.S. production costs were 3 percent less than Japanese costs. Congress of the United States, Office of Technology Assessment, *Technology and Steel Industry Competitiveness*, p. 143.

[23] National Academy of Sciences, *U.S. Steel Industry*, pp. 83–85. The demand for high-priced steel products does appear to be sensitive to price. The price elasticity of demand (ϵ_d) measures the percentage change in quantity demanded of a product that results from the percentage change in the price of that product. Saying that the demand for steel is price inelastic means that the ϵ_d is less than 1.0. For example, if the price declines by 10 percent, the quantity demanded will increase by less than 10 percent.

not be surprising that "cooperative agreements to secure orderly competition have a long and colorful history in this industry."[24]

The economic conditions of steel demand and supply have resulted in the protection of most home markets of steel producing countries. Of several exceptions to this norm, the most noteworthy has been the U.S. market, which is the largest in the world and which, despite the implementation of a variety of trade restricting measures since 1968, has been "the most accessible [major] market for steel exports from all countries."[25] A protected home market can insulate a domestic industry from the large cyclical price swings in international steel markets and from dumping. Protection can also provide a sufficient market size and price level to cover fixed production costs, with export prices being required to cover only marginal costs of production. Dumping often occurs as firms try to maintain high operating rates in the face of falling domestic demand by shipping the steel overseas at whatever price is necessary to move it. Generally a protected home market is a necessary condition for dumping to occur.

Under theoretically normal market conditions, low cost producers should displace high cost producers in the world steel market. However, because of the changing economic effects of such factors as operating rates (economic growth) or exchange rates (fiscal and monetary policy), continual swings can occur in the location of low cost producers in the world economy. More importantly, national governments have not been content to let "normal" market forces operate in the world steel industry. As a result, it has not been uncommon for low cost producers to be displaced by higher cost producers with government backing, a phenomenon which is observable within a number of countries as well as across national frontiers.[26]

TRENDS IN PRODUCTION, CONSUMPTION AND TRADE

The United States accounted for 47 percent of total world crude steel production in 1950 and over 57 percent of production among the western economies. By 1986, as shown in table 2-2, the U.S. share of total world steel production had fallen to only 10 percent, and among the western economies to 17 percent. The EC also declined in relative importance from 25.6 percent in 1950 to 15.5 percent in 1986, and among the western economies from 31.6 percent to 25.8 percent, a much less dramatic fall in production than that experienced by the United States. Thus the share of the United States and the EC in crude steel production of the western economies fell from 89 percent in 1950 to 43 percent by 1986, with most of the decline accounted for by the United States.

---

[24] Warren, *World Steel*, p. 90.

[25] Office of Technology Assessment, *Steel Industry Competitiveness*, p. 150. See chapter 7 for a review of U.S. steel import policy measures since the 1960s.

[26] See chapter 3, country sections on West Germany, Italy, and the United Kingdom.

Table 2-2. Geographic Distribution of World Steel Production

	Western World Production (% of Total)		Total World Production (% of Total)	
	1950	1986	1950	1986
United States	57.4	17.2	46.6	10.4
EC	31.6	25.8	25.6	15.5
Japan	3.1	22.9	2.5	13.8
ROW	7.9	34.1	6.4	20.7
CPE	-	-	18.9	39.6
Total	100.0	100.0	100.0	100.0

Source: American Iron and Steel Industry, AISI *Annual Statistical Report*, various issues.
Note: Western world production excludes the so-called centrally planned economies (CPE) of the Soviet Union, Eastern Europe and the Asian communist countries. ROW = rest of world.

The largest production increases came in Japan, which went from 2.5 percent to almost 14 percent of world production over the same period, and the other western economies (primarily the developing nations), which increased their share of world production from 6 percent to 21 percent. Japan's share of steel production among the western economies increased from 3 percent to 23 percent over this period while the respective share of the other western economies went from 8 percent to 34 percent.[27] The major producing countries accounting for the increase in the production share of the "other" group of western economies are Brazil, Korea, India, Spain, South Africa, Mexico and Taiwan.

The changes in the relative shares of world steel production reflect the very large increases in the absolute level of steel production outside of the United States after 1950. In terms of the location of international steel production, the main additions to capacity and production took place in the EC in the 1950s, the EC and Japan in the 1960s, and the EC, Japan and the other western market economies (primarily the developing countries) in the early

---

[27] Data on production shares are from American Iron and Steel Institute, *AISI Annual Statistical Report*, 1959-1986.

1970s. After 1974 the only increases in production took place outside of the
United States, the EC and Japan.

The absolute changes in western world steel production are shown in table
2-3, which shows aggregate changes in production by region for five year
periods beginning in 1955. In the first decade (1955-1964) the major source
of increase in western world steel production was the EC. In the second
decade (1965-1974) the major source of increase in steel production was
Japan. During the last decade (1975-1984) the major source of increase came
from the other western economies, primarily Brazil, Korea, India, Spain, South
Africa, Mexico and Taiwan.

Table 2-3. Changes in Raw Steel Production
(million metric tons)

	United States	Japan	EC(9)	ROW	World
1955-59	25.8	27.7	114.4	43.1	211.1
1960-64	2.3	87.9	100.3	75.0	265.2
1965-69	126.7	150.8	104.0	82.7	464.3
1970-74	14.4	215.1	111.9	110.8	452.2
1975-79	-34.8	10.9	-49.9	125.6	51.7
1980-84	-144.2	-10.7	-64.8	109.4	-110.2

Source: Table 2-1.
Note: The data show the change in raw steel production over the previous 5-year period
compared to the indicated 5-year period. For example, the table indicates that U.S. raw steel
production from 1955 to 1959 was 25.8 million metric tons greater than in the period from 1950
to 1954.

The changes in patterns of world steel production can be partially related
to changes in consumption and trade patterns (table 2-4).[28] Consumption in
the United States, the EC and Japan peaked in 1973 and reached a peak in

---

[28] The data are in the form of ingot equivalents, where apparent steel consumption in ingot
equivalents = steel production in ingot equivalents + net trade in ingot equivalents; where steel
production in ingot equivalents = crude steel production + 0.175 x continuously cast output, and
net trade in ingot equivalents = (imports minus exports of steel mill products) multiplied times
a uniform conversion factor of 1.3. See OECD, *World Steel Trade*, pp. 42-43.

the following year for the other western economies. Consumption has not yet peaked in the developing nations. Consumption in the western world increased from 1960 to 1986 at an annual compound rate of 2.45 percent, but the real increase occurred prior to 1975. From 1960 to 1974, western world

Table 2-4. World Steel Consumption by Major Area, 1960-1986
(million metric tons in ingot equivalents)

	United States	EC(9)	Japan	Developing Countries	Other Western Economies	Centrally Planned Economies	World Total
1960	90.11	81.52	19.46	21.14	27.16	106.02	345.41
1961	89.90	79.20	25.73	23.59	28.54	107.06	354.02
1962	91.36	80.44	22.86	24.29	29.37	110.42	358.74
1963	102.40	84.84	24.62	25.86	31.92	114.57	384.21
1964	118.45	95.61	31.34	29.00	37.85	121.83	434.08
1965	128.12	92.17	28.44	31.30	44.25	131.54	455.93
1966	131.81	92.26	35.40	30.05	43.53	139.58	472.63
1967	126.30	94.66	51.24	32.68	43.16	149.03	497.07
1968	137.90	104.79	50.80	35.87	45.65	157.17	532.18
1969	138.73	119.75	62.73	37.93	50.69	168.18	578.01
1970	127.16	125.99	71.54	42.61	56.63	175.73	599.66
1971	128.02	109.19	60.22	45.91	56.86	186.91	587.11
1972	139.03	121.64	72.71	49.85	58.30	197.07	638.60
1973	151.03	129.26	91.67	59.13	64.17	212.05	707.31
1974	145.60	124.22	80.69	71.80	71.77	219.06	713.14
1975	117.79	102.26	70.41	71.50	65.78	228.34	656.08
1976	131.49	123.06	67.39	74.00	62.94	235.29	694.17
1977	136.06	110.02	66.30	84.04	59.93	239.31	695.66
1978	148.94	108.78	70.61	92.51	58.52	262.49	741.85
1979	144.14	120.42	83.90	97.06	64.52	263.53	773.57
1980	117.98	112.59	85.88	103.73	65.51	262.27	747.96
1981	133.27	102.69	79.28	106.55	64.99	255.01	741.79
1982	88.12	99.50	78.66	102.92	58.82	256.04	684.06
1983	99.23	97.20	75.29	98.94	58.69	274.77	704.12
1984	118.40	104.68	85.80	101.40	63.82	284.50	758.60
1985	113.30	103.79	84.90	108.50	62.01	301.70	774.20
1986	103.60	103.50	81.20	106.90	64.60	310.70	770.50

Source: Organization for Economic Cooperation and Development, *World Steel Trade and Developments 1960-1983* (Paris: OECD, 1985) and Organization for Economic Cooperation and Development, *The Steel Market in 1986 and the Outlook for 1987* (Paris: OECD, 1987).

consumption increased by 4.95 percent per year, but from 1974 to 1986 consumption actually declined by 0.55 percent per year. The only region that experienced an increase in consumption in the 1974 to 1986 period was the

developing countries. The sharpest declines were in the United States and the
EC.[29] Consumption in Japan stagnated.

Table 2-5 compares the rate of growth in consumption with the rate of
increase in production for the main regions of the world. Over the period
1960 to 1986, the rate of increase in production exceeded the rate of increase
in consumption for all regions except the United States. Again, however,
there are two distinct periods that show differing patterns of relative growth.
In the 1960 to 1974 period the growth in production exceeded consumption
by a significant margin in Japan and to a lesser extent in the EC. Production
and consumption in the developing countries and the other western countries
grew at approximately the same rates. In the United States, the growth in
production did not keep pace with the growth in consumption. This situation
changed dramatically after 1974. From 1974 to 1986 consumption declined in
the United States and the EC but production declined even more. In Japan
consumption and production remained at about the same level during the
period. However production growth exceeded consumption increases by a
wide margin in the developing countries and to a lesser extent in the other
western nations.

Table 2-5. Changes in Western World Consumption and Production of Steel
(compound annual rate of change)

	U.S.		EC(9)		Japan		Developing Countries		Other Western Economies	
	Cons.	Prod.	Cons.	Prod.	Cons.	Prod.	Cons.	Prod.	Cons.	Prod.
1960-1986	0.52	-0.40	0.89	0.96	5.43	6.27	6.19	8.79	3.26	4.38
1960-1974	3.25	2.69	2.85	3.27	9.95	12.07	8.49	8.78	6.69	6.70
1974-1986	-2.58	-3.82	-1.39	-1.72	0.05	-0.52	3.11	8.10	-0.81	1.43

Source: Organization for Economic Cooperation and Development, *World Steel Trade
Developments 1960-1983* (Paris: OECD, 1985) and Organization for Economic Cooperation and
Development, *The Steel Market in 1986 and The Outlook for 1987* (Paris: OECD, 1987).
Consumption and production data are based on ingot equivalents.

Obviously these production and consumption patterns have their
counterpart in trade flows; where production exceeds consumption, the

---

[29] The decline in steel consumption in the United States is overstated in recent years because
of the large volume of steel imported in industrial products (automobiles, machinery, appliances,
etc.). The domestic customer base of U.S. steel companies has been eroded with the massive
increase in the trade deficit for manufactured goods in the 1980s. See appendix A for an analysis
of the magnitude of "indirect" steel trade in recent years.

country will be a net exporter and where consumption exceeds production the country will be a net importer.

With few exceptions, the major steel producing countries are all net exporters of steel. Table 2-6 lists the 24 top steel producing countries in the western world, accounting for 95 percent of crude steel production in 1986 and 96 percent of steel exports. Of those 24 countries, only 4 were net importers of steel in the 1980s: the United States, India, Turkey and Yugoslavia. Thus the United States is the only developed country that is a major producer of steel but is not a net exporter of steel. The ratio of U.S. exports to imports of steel products has averaged 0.16 since 1970, with a marked deterioration in that already low ratio in recent years. After the deep recession in 1982 the ratio has averaged only 0.05.

Table 2-6. Major Western World Steel Producing Countries
and Net Export Position

	Crude Steel Production 1986 (1000 metric tons)	% of Total	Cumulative percent	Net Exporter 1980-1986
1. Japan	98,275	22.7	22.7	Y
2. United States	74,032	17.1	39.8	N
3. FRG	37,134	8.6	48.4	Y
4. Italy	22,882	5.3	53.7	Y
5. Brazil	21,233	4.9	58.6	Y
6. France	17,857	4.1	62.7	Y
7. United Kingdom	14,725	3.4	66.1	Y
8. Republic of Korea	14,555	3.4	69.5	Y
9. Canada	14,081	3.3	72.8	Y
10. India	12,197	2.8	75.6	N
11. Spain	11,978	2.8	78.4	Y
12. Belgium	9,722	2.2	80.6	Y
13. South Africa	8,895	2.1	82.7	Y
14. Mexico	7,168	1.7	84.4	Y
15. Australia	6,674	1.5	85.9	Y
16. Turkey	5,928	1.4	87.3	N
17. Taiwan	5,545	1.3	88.6	Y
18. Netherlands	5,283	1.2	89.8	Y
19. Sweden	4,710	1.1	90.9	Y
20. Yugoslavia	4,520	1.0	91.9	N
21. Austria	4,292	1.0	92.9	Y
22. Venezuela	3,402	0.8	93.7	Y
23. Argentina	3,235	0.7	94.4	Y
24. Finland	2,586	0.6	95.0	Y
Total Western World	432,106	100.0	100.0	

Source: International Iron and Steel Institute, *Steel Statistical Yearbook 1987* (Brussels: IISI, 1987).

The fact that the United States is the only major net importer of steel mill products among the western producing nations is a reflection of the trends in production and consumption analyzed above. Over the 1960 to 1974 period, U.S. production did not keep pace with the increase in U.S. consumption, with net imports making up the difference. After 1974, production in the United States declined even more than consumption, again with net imports filling the gap.[30]

For the other major steel producing nations, the period from 1960-1974 was one of significant export growth. Japanese exports increased dramatically from 2.25 million metric tons to 32.22 million metric tons, an increase of over 1,300 percent. EC exports more than doubled, from 15.28 million metric tons to 33.04 million metric tons. Developing country exports, which first began in 1964, grew to 2.9 million metric tons by 1974.[31] After 1974 total exports from both Japan and the EC showed little change, but they remained at the very high levels reached in the 1960-1974 period. EC exports in 1986 were 32.2 million metric tons, down only 2.6 percent from the 1974 level. Japanese exports in 1986 were 37.3 million metric tons, an increase of 15.8 percent over the 1974 level. Dramatic export growth did occur for the steel producing developing countries; exports in 1986 were 24.2 million metric tons, an increase of over 700 percent from 1974.[32]

Export markets became increasingly important after 1974 for the steel producing countries. Figure 2-3 shows that the export-output ratio increased significantly for all major steel-exporting countries, except the United States, between 1970 and 1986. Table 2-7 provides data on the ratio of exports to production for the major steel producing regions from 1960 to 1986. From 1960 to 1974, the ratio for the developed countries averaged 15.4 percent. After 1974 the ratio increased sharply, averaging 25.1 percent from 1974 to 1986. The developing country ratio increased even more, from an average of 10.6 percent from 1964 to 1974 to an average of 21.9 percent from 1974 to 1986.

Not only have export markets grown more important since 1960, but there have been significant longer-term changes in export flows with respect to the countries of origin and destination. Table 2-8 illustrates these changes for the major regions of the world. One major development stands out: the rapid emergence of Japan and the steel producing developing countries as a relative source of world exports. From 1960 to the mid-1970s Japan and the developing countries increased their export share at the expense of the United States and the EC. Since the mid-1970s, the steel producing developing countries have also been increasing their share of world exports, not only at the expense of the U.S. and EC exports but also at the expense of Japanese exports.

---

[30] The trend of steel imports into the U. S. economy is analyzed in more detail in chapter 7.

[31] All export numbers taken from OECD, *World Steel Trade*.

[32] Data on 1986 exports from OECD, *The Steel Market in 1986*. Over 70 percent of steel exports from developing countries are accounted for by what the OECD terms the newly steel-active countries: Korea, Taiwan, Argentina, Brazil, Mexico and Venezuela.

Figure 2–3: Export–Output Ratios for Steel, 1970 and 1986

(exports as a percent of output)

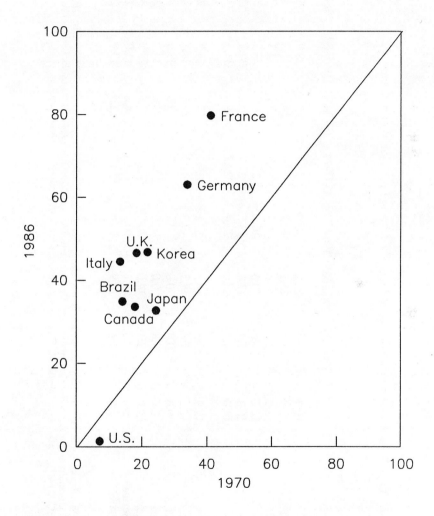

Source: Table 2–7; Organization for Economic Cooperation and Development,
The Steel Market in 1986 and Outlook for 1987 (Paris: OECD, 1987)
International Iron and Steel Institute, Steel Statistical Yearbook 1987
(Brussels: IISI, 1987).

Table 2-7. Total Steel Exports as a Percent of Steel Production by Major World Areas

	1960-62	1963-65	1966-68	1969-71	1972-74	1975-77	1978-80	1981-83	1984-86
EC(9)	19.7	18.7	21.2	19.5	23.7	25.6	28.9	29.8	28.8
Oth. W.Europe	27.0	24.7	25.1	26.1	30.4	34.8	45.2	48.8	60.1
U.S.	3.1	2.9	1.8	4.9	3.8	2.7	3.3	2.7	1.4
Canada	17.2	15.6	13.6	16.1	15.2	16.1	23.5	29.4	28.2
Australia, N.Z	10.3	5.9	13.1	13.6	22.9	39.2	32.3	26.5	24.7
Japan	14.0	24.7	23.0	27.4	29.2	38.6	33.5	33.7	33.4
O.E.C.D.	12.9	13.3	14.3	17.1	19.5	23.3	24.2	26.6	27.3
S. Africa	12.0	7.8	8.3	9.9	13.1	20.1	28.7	25.8	35.1
Oth. Africa	0.0	0.0	0.0	0.0	2.0	9.6	49.0	30.8	33.1
Mid. East	0.0	0.0	0.0	0.0	6.2	12.6	17.0	28.2	21.6
Other Asia	0.0	2.4	14.6	20.0	21.3	23.3	29.3	34.3	30.2
Lat. America	0.0	0.0	9.2	10.8	9.3	4.6	11.0	21.4	31.3
T. Dev. Areas	0.0	1.1	10.9	13.5	13.2	12.6	19.9	27.9	30.3

Source: Organization for Economic Cooperation and Development, *World Steel Trade Developments 1960-1983* (Paris: OECD, 1983), p. 116 and Organization for Economic Cooperation and Development, *The Steel Market in 1986 and the Outlook for 1987* (Paris: OECD, 1987). Ratios were calculated using ingot equivalents for both production and exports.

This overview of trends in production, consumption and trade for the world steel industry has been largely of a statistical nature, to provide a basic understanding of long-term trends. The social and political factors underlying these trends are addressed in later chapters in this book. However, several broad economic, technological and political factors at work are worth summarizing at this point.

Economic, Technological and Political Factors Reshaping the World Steel Industry

The basic economic factor underlying the changing patterns of world steel production and trade is the rapid rate of industrialization that occurred outside of Europe and North America after World War II, first in Japan and later in some of the newly industrializing countries, which resulted in a strong demand for steel mill products. This provided the opportunity for the rapid growth of domestic steel industries, especially as these nations pursued a policy of import substitution. Rapid industrialization, combined with state aid and direction, permitted these nations to build greenfield plants of optimal scale employing the latest advances in steel technology, thereby greatly improving productivity.[33] In some cases, rapid growth also promoted increased profits and cash flow, which increased funds for investment and thereby accelerated further modernization and expansion of facilities.[34]

The opportunity to build large, new plants also allowed firms in expanding regions to take advantage of the discovery of new raw material sources (*e.g*, iron ore from Australia and Brazil) and lower shipping charges by constructing large coastal steelworks. These coastal steelworks, pioneered initially by the Japanese along the region from Kure to Tokyo Bay and imitated by producers in Europe (Belgium, France) and the developing countries (Taiwan, Korea), in some cases acquired a raw material cost advantage over some traditional steel producing locations, at least with respect to certain stages of the production process.[35]

---

[33] The Japanese steel industry, which by the 1970s was considered the best in the world, emerged under the most favorable of circumstances. However, the industry today is beset with problems, many of which stem from the size and scale of earlier investments. As Kenneth Warren has stated, "those fortunate countries which have no great clutter of plants from the past, yet whose demand is sufficient to justify major present extensions, will face the same problems in the next generation when raw material supplies, techniques and a different structure and geography of demand will render still other scales and locations of plant desirable." Warren, *World Steel*, p. 84. See chapter 4 for an analysis of the current state of the Japanese industry.

[34] Barnett and Schorsch, *Steel*, pp. 143-145. In a high growth environment it is also much easier to maintain high operating rates, sharply reducing unit costs.

[35] Klaus Stegemann, *Price Competition and Output Adjustment in the European Steel Market* (Tübingen: Mohr, 1977), p. 161.

Table 2-8. Changes in the Pattern of World Steel Trade, 1960-1986

| | World Exports | | | | |
	1960-62	1970-72	1975-77	1981-83	1984-86
percent from:					
OECD	90.0	84.5	85.0	77.0	72.3
developing countries	1.0	4.5	5.5	15.0	19.5
CPE	9.0	11.0	9.5	8.0	8.2
percent to:					
OECD	49.0	58.0	44.5	41.5	42.6
developing countries	39.0	32.0	38.0	42.5	48.6
CPE	12.0	10.0	16.0	14.0	8.8
Total in million tons	25.6	63.7	87.0	102.7	116.6

| | Exports of OECD Area | | | | |
	1960-62	1970-72	1975-77	1981-83	1984-86
in percent of					
world exports from:					
EC(9)	57.0	34.0	30.0	28.0	24.1
Japan	11.0	32.0	38.0	28.5	26.4
Other Western Europe	9.5	8.5	9.5	14.0	12.5
United States	8.3	6.1	2.7	1.8	0.8
Other OECD	4.2	3.9	4.8	4.7	8.5
Total OECD	90.0	84.5	85.0	77.0	72.3
Total in million tons	23.1	53.9	73.6	78.6	84.4
of which in percent:					
intra-OECD trade	52.0	59.0	44.0	40.5	40.7
to developing countries	37.0	30.0	37.5	42.5	47.4
to CPE	11.0	11.0	18.5	17.0	11.9

| | Imports into OECD Area | | | | |
	1960-62	1970-72	1975-77	1981-83	1984-86
in percent of					
world exports to:					
EC(9)	9.5	13.0	11.0	9.0	5.8
Japan	1.0	0.1	0.2	2.0	2.9
Other Western Europe	21.0	17.0	15.0	12.0	10.1
United States	11.5	23.0	15.5	15.5	18.1
Other OECD	6.0	4.9	2.8	3.0	5.7
Total OECD	49.0	58.0	44.5	41.5	42.6
Total in million tons					
of which in percent:					
intra-OECD trade	94.0	85.5	83.5	75.0	69.0
from develop. countries	0.0	2.5	4.5	14.0	20.3
from CPE	6.0	12.0	12.0	11.0	10.7

Source: Organization for Economic Cooperation and Development, *World Steel Trade Developments 1960-1983* (Paris: OECD, 1985), p. 10 and Organization for Economic Cooperation and Development, *The Steel Market in 1986 and the Outlook for 1987* (Paris: OECD, 1987).
Note: Developing countries refer to non-OECD, non-CPE countries. CPE (centrally planned economies) refers to USSR, Eastern Europe, PRC and North Korea. Steel exports and imports in million metric tons of steel mill products. Intra-EC and intra-CPE trade excluded.

The more mature industrial economies of North America and Europe experienced slower growth in the demand for steel and, after 1974, there was an absolute decline in the amount of steel consumed in these regions. In a slow growth environment the economics of steelmaking, especially in market-oriented economies like the United States, have not favored greenfield investment but rather the piecemeal replacement of obsolescent plants, especially with respect to integrated production.[36] Slow growth also made it more difficult to maintain high operating rates, limited profits and cash flow, making it more difficult to modernize existing facilities.

The fact that the locus of rapidly increasing steel consumption shifted to the newly industrializing regions in the postwar period gave those regions certain advantages with respect to the development of their steel industries versus the established plant and equipment in the traditional steel producing regions, although these were offset by other competitive factors. In the words of development economist Alexander Gerschenkron, these regions enjoyed the advantages of "economic backwardness" in the sense that they could benefit from the already existing technology and know-how of more developed areas combined with lower input costs for labor and raw materials.[37] At the same time, because their new plant and equipment could be acquired with state funds or government-guaranteed foreign loans, a traditional obstacle to industrialization -- the lack of capital -- was not an insurmountable problem. On the other hand, such advantages were offset in most developing countries by high energy costs and costs associated with mismanagement, bureaucratic interference, infrastructural shortcomings, high levels of foreign debt, shortages of skilled personnel, and political and economic instability (see chapter 5).

Differences in the rate of growth in steel consumption were related not only to rates of industrialization but also to a country's stage of industrialization. As an industrial economy matures, it experiences a secular decline in steel demand,[38] so that the demand for steel grows at a slower rate than that of the overall economy. As shown in table 2-5, U.S. steel consumption grew by only 0.52 percent per year over the 1960 to 1986 period

---

[36] There are also disadvantages in a slow growth environment concerning the rate of technological progress. To a significant extent major process innovations and many important product innovations can only be effectively realized with new investment in plant and equipment, often involving whole new facilities. To the extent that slow growth inhibits new investment, this can also inhibit the rate of technological innovation. Bela Gold and Myles G. Boylan, "Capital Budgeting, Industrial Capacity, and Imports," *Quarterly Review of Economics and Business 15* (Autumn 1975): 29.

[37] Alexander Gerschenkron, *Economic Backwardness in Historical Perspective* (Cambridge: Harvard University Press, 1962).

[38] Barnett and Schorsch, *Steel*, pp. 38-43. As an economy matures, the structure of demand for steel changes so that the type of steel produced must also change. The normal pattern, first seen in the United States, is to move from heavier to lighter steel products, especially toward light, flat rolled sheet used in consumer durable goods. Warren, *World Steel*, p. 89. A more detailed discussion is provided in appendix A.

while the growth rate for the EC was only slightly higher at 0.89 percent per year. In contrast, consumption growth was much higher in Japan (5.43 percent), the developing countries (6.19 percent) and the other western economies (3.26 percent).[39] A recent study by the National Academy of Sciences listed four major reasons for the declining intensity of steel usage in industrial nations:

1. the percentage of output by the industrial sector declines relative to the service sector as economies mature;
2. changes in manufacturing equipment and techniques as technology advances (*e.g.*, electronic control processes);
3. improvements in the efficiency of steel usage; and
4. increasing competition from substitute materials.[40]

The sharp differences in demand growth among the steel producing countries provided significantly different opportunities for investment in steelmaking facilities and the attendant adoption of new technologies. The rise of the Japanese industry to world primacy by the 1970s was partially the result of the timing of Japan's steel industry growth. It was in perfect position to take advantage of new steel technologies such as the basic oxygen furnace (BOF) and continuous casting techniques. The development of the Japanese industry in a very fast growth environment also provided the opportunity for Japanese producers to push the scale of production beyond previous experience. This occurred initially with the size of blast furnaces and was later accommodated by increasing the size of BOFs and faster rolling equipment.[41] On the negative side, however, Japanese industrial policies ultimately resulted in a gross overexpansion of steelmaking capacity, with the result that in the 1970s and 1980s the Japanese mills have proven chronically unable to sustain

---

[39] A complicating factor in analyzing trends in consumption is the oil-price shock of 1973-1974. The huge increase in energy prices and the resulting structural changes in the economies of most countries produced what could be called a new level of steel-intensity in all nations. Because of this, the decline in steel consumption after 1974 reflects not just industrial maturity but also a change in patterns of steel usage due to the adjustment to the oil-price shock.

[40] National Academy of Sciences, *U.S. Steel Industry*, pp. 87-88. Perhaps the best illustration of this phenomenon is Japan. Steel consumption in Japan grew extremely rapidly from 1960 to 1974 at an annual compound rate of almost 10 percent. After 1974, the increase in steel consumption almost slowed to a standstill, growing by 0.05 percent per year. While part of this slowdown is related to Japan's adjustment to the oil shock of 1973-1974, the slowdown reflects the industrial maturity of the Japanese economy.

[41] "The consequent emergence of a balanced sequence of individually large capacity operating units, including parallel improvements in materials handling and finishing operations, yielded substantial economies in comparison with smaller scale integrated steel mills." Bela Gold, "Transformation Tendencies in the World Steel Industry and Adaptive Strategies," in *Ailing Steel: The Transoceanic Quarrel*, ed. Walter H. Goldberg (New York: St. Martin's Press, 1986), p. 470.

the high utilization rates necessary to fully realize the scale advantages of the new plants.[42]

In response to the Japanese industry's rapid growth, steel producers in other western nations sought to copy the scale advantages of Japanese plants.[43] This occurred in the major producing states of the EC as well as in the new steel producing states among the developing countries. The risk entailed by such investments was the cost penalty which would be incurred if the new mills were operated at less than rated capacity. In an expanding market environment this risk appeared worth taking, but with the onset of the structural recession in 1974, many producers -- like the Japanese themselves -- found that the operating penalty more than offset the cost advantages associated with increased scale, resulting, in some cases, in disastrous losses.

While technological developments were sharply increasing the optimal scale of plant size, new technologies developed in the 1960s made it possible for a range of steel products to be produced on a relatively small scale. The crucial development was the adaptation of the electric arc furnace to make carbon steel from steel scrap. This innovation, combined with the development of very efficient multi-strand billet casters and improved rolling mills, has resulted in the rapid expansion of semi-integrated producers, the so-called minimills.

The expansion of minimills has occurred worldwide. Since 1973, the share of U.S. steel production accounted for by minimills has increased from 5.2 percent to 18.2 percent in 1986, due in part to the abundant availability and relatively low price of steel scrap.[44] The increasing minimill share of U.S. production stems from their cost advantage in the product markets they serve. The minimills, which average about one-twelfth the capacity of integrated steel plants, can be constructed for less than 50 percent of the investment cost per ton of capacity of integrated plants and may require only half the manhours per ton of finished product.[45] The development of the minimills means that the significant scale advantages of large integrated plants are now limited to specific products and processes instead of across the whole range of steel operations. As a consequence, most U.S. integrated producers now also operate semi-integrated plants or minimills.

While the importance of economic and technological changes in transforming the world steel industry since 1950 should not be overlooked, the

---

[42] See chapter 4.

[43] Cockerill estimated in 1974 that the minimum efficient scale (m.e.s.) of an integrated plant using BOF technology and rolling a wide range of products was approximately 8 million metric tons per year. This compares to an m.e.s. in the mid-1950s of about 2 million tons. It is interesting to note that at the time of Cockerill's study there was no plant in the world meeting the m.e.s. standard and only three countries had plants with capacities in excess of 6 million tons. Cockerill, *The Steel Industry*.

[44] Marcus and Kirsis, *Steel Strategist 14*, p.18. For an analysis of the minimill cost advantage see Crandall and Barnett, *Up From The Ashes*, ch. 2.

[45] Gold, "Transformation Tendencies," p. 471.

role of national governments was critical. State actions have increasingly determined patterns of investment (and disinvestment). The motivation for government involvement in steel industry production and trade is varied, but generally has been directed at economic gains (employment gains and foreign exchange earnings), national security considerations (sufficient domestic supply for steel-using industries) and social policy (promoting regional development or minimizing social adjustment costs).

National attitudes and ideologies with respect to state intervention and international competition are a less tangible factor underlying government intervention (or the lack of it) in steel. Such attitudes, while impossible to assess quantitatively, are important because they are ultimately manifested in government actions, playing an important role in determining whether individual steel industries expand or contract. In 1977, for example, the U.S. Council on Wage and Price Stability (COWPS) advised in a report to the President of the United States that it would be uneconomical for the U.S. steel industry to either modernize or expand. Reflecting a prevailing philosophy which has shaped U.S. policy toward industry and the economy, COWPS argued that "natural" market forces should be allowed to progressively shrink and contract the size of the U.S. steel industry.[46] In many other countries, the philosophy has been diametrically opposed -- the steel industry should expand regardless of technological, raw material and other handicaps, and without regard to short-term market conditions, operating losses, or even the need to earn a return on investment over the long run. A critique of the COWPS report attacked its economic determinism and contrasted it with the policy orientation in Japan two decades earlier.

The essentially hopeless outlook of the COWPS report reflects an overconcentration on the disadvantageous aspects of the U.S. steel industry's position. One cannot help being struck by the dramatic contrast between this approach and that of the Japanese in the 1950's[sic]. Lacking virtually all needed raw materials, without any modern production facilities, and with only the most meager resources of engineers and skilled workmen experienced in contemporary steel technologies, the Japanese considered it quite feasible to undertake a program of development and expansion designed to challenge the world leaders within 15 years. In 1977, on the other hand, the COWPS report examined a steel industry with perhaps the best supply of raw material outside the USSR, with production facilities probably better than those of all countries but Japan, with an unsurpassed aggregation of technological expertise and skilled labor, and with the largest and most affluent market in the world--only to imply that the outlook for the American steel industry was hopeless, for nothing but

---

[46] Council on Wage and Price Stability, *Report to the President on Prices and Costs in the United States Steel Industry* (Washington, D.C.: U.S. Government Printing Office, October 1977). A similar conclusion is reached in a later study by one of the authors of the COWPS report. See Crandall, *The U.S. Steel Industry.*

progressive deterioration can result if neither modernization nor expansion is considered economically feasible.[47]

The changes in the patterns of world production, consumption and trade cannot be explained without analyzing the role of government policies and actions in steel, and the motives and attitudes which underlie those policies. The most important effect of government intervention in the world steel industry has been the expansion of world capacity well in excess of world demand since 1974, and the perpetuation of the capacity surplus through twelve years of stagnant demand and intense trade friction.

THE OVERHANG OF EXCESS CAPACITY SINCE 1974

From the perspective of 1988, when this book is being written, it may seem paradoxical to talk about excess capacity when reports are widespread of a shortage of steel, both in the United States and the world. There is an excess of steel capacity in the world in terms of physical plant and equipment, a situation which has persisted since 1974. However a number of factors -- especially exchange rate movements, production controls in Europe, blast furnace closures for maintenance purposes and improved demand in a number of major markets -- have contributed to tightened availability and rising spot prices in 1988.

Figure 2-4 illustrates the overhang of excess capacity that has developed in western world steel markets since 1974.[48] As the chart in the bottom panel of figure 2-4 illustrates, the average operating rate for the western world steel industry since 1974 has been consistently below 75 percent, the inverse of the pre-1974 period. There is consensus among many analysts of the world steel industry that the principal reason for the development of this capacity overhang beginning in the mid-1970s was government intervention in world steel markets.[49]

Why did the expansion of supply capability get so out of line with demand and why did the situation persist for so long? Prior to 1974 the growth in capacity kept approximate pace with the increase in consumption. After 1974, consumption in the western world stagnated, being 7 percent below the

---

[47] Bela Gold, "Steel Technologies and Costs in the U.S. and Japan," *Iron and Steel Engineer* (April 1978), p. 37.

[48] The capacity figures presented in this section are for gross steelmaking capacity. This refers to engineered or nameplate capacity which is the optimal or theoretic production level that can be attained if a facility operates smoothly, with no production problems. Gross capacity represents an output level that generally cannot be achieved for any sustained period of time. While there are estimates of effective capacity or output levels that are attainable for prolonged periods of time, these estimates can vary over time and by region. Therefore the gross numbers are presented here to use as a basis for time series analysis.

[49] Barnett and Schorsch, *Steel*, pp. 46-47; National Academy of Sciences, *U.S. Steel Industry*, p. 112.

Figure 2−4: Western World Raw Steel Production, Capacity and Capacity Utilization, 1960−1987

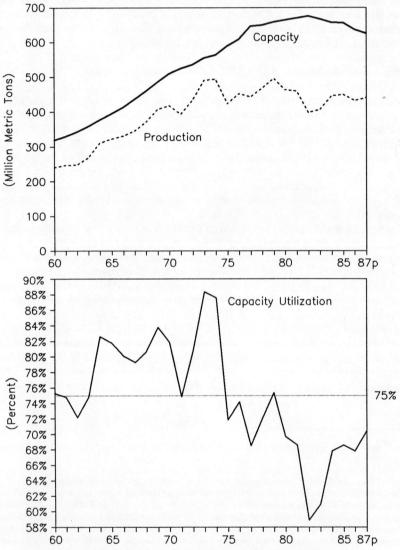

Source: Peter F. Marcus and Karlis M. Kirsis, World Steel Dynamics: Core Report BB (PaineWebber, Inc., January 1988), Exhibit BB−1−5.

tonnage consumed in 1974 by 1986.[50] However capacity kept expanding through 1982 and despite the reductions since then was still 72 million metric tons greater in 1986 than in 1974.

Part, but only part, of the explanation can be attributed to the unexpected stagnation in western world steel demand after 1974, which has proven to be a watershed with respect to steel consumption trends. This can be clearly seen in figure 2-5 which compares five steel production cycles since 1950. In the three cycles prior to 1974 steel production always exceeded the level of production reached in the year before the downturn within two years after the downturn. In each instance production ended the cycle 10 to 20 percent above the previous peak. In contrast, in the two cycles after 1974 steel production never exceeded the previous peak, and generally remained far below it. Based on the experience of the 1960s and early 1970s, most forecasts of world steel consumption were overly optimistic compared to what actually developed.

The other significant factor underlying the capacity surplus was the role played by governments in promoting the establishment of new facilities and the retention of existing ones. While western world consumption growth came to an abrupt halt in 1974, capacity expansion proceeded rapidly, in large part due to government encouragement. By 1982, 55.4 percent of world steelmaking capacity was government-owned.[51] The increasing involvement of the state in world steel was due in part to the growing scale of new integrated steelworks. "As the economical scale of production for steelworks grew to gigantic levels, the capital needed to establish large-scale integrated greenfield plants rose to astronomic sums. Only the most powerful financial groups, or the state, could keep pace with such requirements."[52] As the size of the capital investment increased so did the risk. From start to finish a new integrated works could take from 5 to 7 years and cost $5 billion to $10 billion. Private financial concerns are reluctant to take on such risk, especially in the face of uncertain future steel demand.

As the capacity overhang became difficult to ignore by the early 1980s, with poor operating rates for steel plants around the world, the issue was where capacity reductions would occur. All other factors equal, the high cost and low profit facilities should decline in such a situation while the low cost, high profit facilities should expand or at least maintain their level of

---

[50] See table 2-4.

[51] U.S. Department of Commerce, "Foreign Import Restraints and Unfair Practices in Steel," (Washington, D.C.: U.S. Department of Commerce, September 18, 1984), cited in Kent Jones, *Politics vs. Economics in World Steel Trade* (London: Allen & Unwin, 1986), p. 74. The study shows that outside of the United States and Japan, 75 percent of world raw steel production is produced by state-owned firms. Hogan gives the following percentage breakout for each EC country with respect to steel capacities owned or controlled by the state in 1981: Belgium (57%), Denmark (30%), France (70%), Germany (11%), Ireland (100%), Italy (60%), Luxembourg (0%), Netherlands (36%), United Kingdom (76%). William T. Hogan, *World Steel in the 1980s: A Case of Survival* (Lexington, Massachusetts: Lexington Books, 1983), p. 47.

[52] Goldberg, *Ailing Steel*, pp. 41-42.

Figure 2—5: Comparison of Five
Steel Production Cycles Since 1950
for Western World Producers

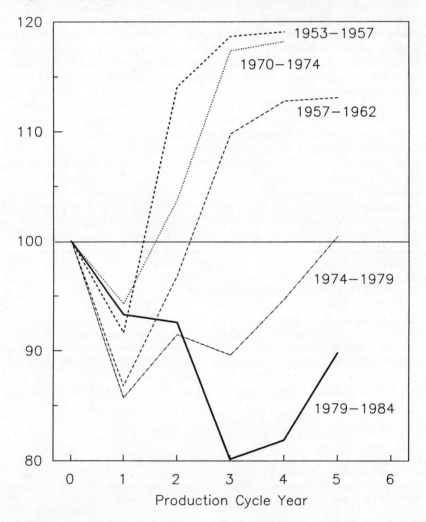

Note: The year preceding the downturn in steel production is equal to 0. The
production index for each cycle is set at 100 for the year preceding the
downturn.

Source: Table 2—1.

operations.[53] Because of government intervention, the adjustment to excess capacity did not follow this theoretic norm. The United States steel industry bore the brunt of much of this initial adjustment because its market was the most open among the producing nations and so became the outlet for much of this excess capacity.[54] The overvalued dollar from 1980 to 1985 made it especially difficult to compete with direct imports and produced a surge in indirect imports.[55] In the European Community, adjustment finally became necessary as the operating subsidies and distortions created by state aid became too severe for the Member States to ignore.[56] By 1986 even the Japanese industry was beginning to undertake modest capacity cuts, in large part due to the effects of the strengthening yen on price competitiveness in U.S. dollars.[57] In developing nations and some non-market economy countries, capacity expansion is still occurring.

The effects of the capacity overhang have been significant. From 1977 to 1984 a survey of the financial performance of 60 major world steelmakers indicates that they lost $22.3 billion.[58] Steel employment in the EC, Japan and the United States was down by almost 800,000 workers in 1986 compared to 1974 (figure 2-6). Capacity reductions in the United States and the EC have been significant. The capacity reductions have reached the point in the United States where the domestic industry no longer has the capability to supply domestic consumption needs. Thus, while there continues to be a surplus of crude steel capacity in the world steel industry, there exists a shortage of domestic capacity in the United States to supply total domestic consumption needs at times of high demand without some level of imports.

Recent Events in World Steel Markets: Shortages in the Midst of Excess Capacity

In the fall of 1987, the first signs of a "shortage" in world steel markets since 1973-1974 began to emerge. By early 1988 spot prices for steel products were continuing to increase and there were reported difficulties in obtaining particular types of steel, especially semifinished, continuous-cast steel, in world markets. Shortages of slabs were reported in Europe, the United States, South Korea, Taiwan and Indonesia and shortages of billets were reported in

---

[53] Over the long-term, facilities with more modern, up-to-date equipment and technology will tend to be more efficient and have lower costs of production. U.S. International Trade Commission, *U.S. Global Competitiveness: Steel Sheet and Strip Industry* (Washington, D.C.: U.S. International Trade Commission, January 1988), USITC Publication 2050, p. xxiii.

[54] Office of Technology Assessment, *Steel Industry Competitiveness*, p. 150.

[55] See the further discussion in chapter 7 and appendix A.

[56] See chapter 3.

[57] See the discussion in chapter 4.

[58] Marcus and Kirsis, *Steel Strategist 14*, table 28.

Figure 2—6: Total Employees in the U.S., Japan, and EC Iron and Steel Industry: 1974—1986

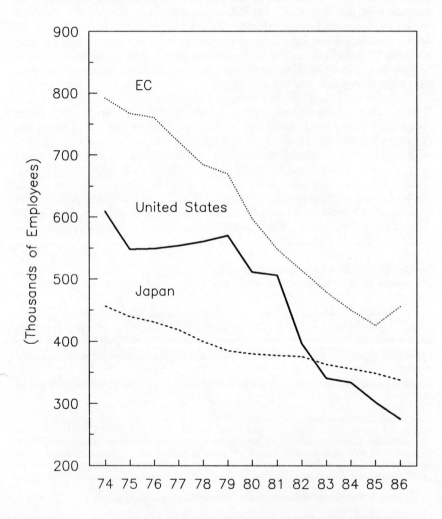

Source: EC — Eurostat, Iron and Steel Yearbook; U.S. — AISI, Annual Statistical Yearbook, various issues; Japan — Japanese Yearbook of Labour Statistics.

Europe and Taiwan.[59] Spot prices for many finished steel products (*e.g.*, hot and cold-rolled coil) were at levels not seen since 1981.[60]

It is possible, but highly unlikely, that the current upturn in steel demand and the spot shortages occurring in the world market reflect a fundamental shift in global demand patterns. However, the current shortage is characterized by one steel analyst as a "price, not a volume, phenomenon," meaning that the shortage is short-term in nature, characterized by a high price for the marginal unit.[61] The more fundamental question is whether an excess of capacity can still be said to exist concurrently with shortages in the world market. How did conditions in the world steel market change from 1986 to 1987 to turn what was generally agreed to be a situation of excess supply to one that, at least for certain products, appears to be characterized by excess demand?

Western world crude steel production in 1987 increased by 3.2 percent over 1986 to 445.9 million metric tons.[62] Since capacity was down by 1.7 percent from the level of 1986, western world capacity utilization increased to 71.2 percent in 1987 from 67.8 percent the previous year.[63] This utilization rate is significantly below the 88 percent operating rate that was reached by the western world steel producers during the last global steel shortage in 1973 and 1974. Based on the annual data alone, there does not appear to be any explanation for why there are shortages in late 1987 and early 1988.[64]

---

[59] *Metal Bulletin* (January 25, 1988), p. 21; International Trade Commission, *Steel Sheet and Strip Industry*, pp. 11-144, 12-31; *Metal Bulletin* (January 18, 1988), p. 27. In the United States, where there are quotas on semifinished steel with the EC and 9 other countries, short supply requests for over 1 million tons of semifinished steel have been filed with the Department of Commerce, mostly for continuously cast slabs, which are not as readily available as slabs rolled from ingots. The short supply requests have been filed, despite the fact that aggregate limits for semifinished steel imports under the quotas were not filled in 1985, 1986 or 1987. United States International Trade Commission, *Monthly Reports on the Status of the Steel Industry* (Washington, D.C.: U.S. International Trade Commission, December 1987).

[60] Marcus and Kirsis, *Steel Strategist 14*, table 4.

[61] Marcus and Kirsis, *Steel Strategist 14*, p. 3.

[62] Preliminary data from the International Iron and Steel Institute.

[63] Preliminary capacity data from Marcus and Kirsis, *Core Report BB*, exhibit BB-1-5.

[64] Capacity utilization in the U.S. steel industry has increased dramatically in late 1987 and early 1988. Through April 23, 1988 capacity utilization has averaged 90.4 percent for the year, compared to 70.8 percent for the same period in 1987.

An analysis of available monthly production data permits a better isolation of production trends.[65] As shown in figure 2-7 western world crude steel production reached a level in October 1987 that was higher than in any month since May 1981.[66] Monthly production has been generally increasing since August 1986. On a quarterly basis crude steel production in the fourth quarter of 1987 was 113.9 million metric tons, the highest level since the fourth quarter of 1983 when production was 114.5 million metric tons. In 1988 production reached 77.5 million metric tons in the first two months of the year, the highest January-February level since 1980. Despite the increasing trend in western world crude steel production in the past 18 months, available western world capacity should be available to support these production levels (figure 2-8).[67]

While there does not as yet appear to be a physical shortage of crude steel capacity in the western world, a number of factors coalesced by late 1987 and early 1988 that caused the tightening of world steel markets.

A major factor is the continued decline of the dollar with respect to most of the major world currencies, especially the Japanese yen and the currencies of the Western European nations. At current exchange rates (and operating rates) Japanese producers' dollar costs are the highest among developed country producers, despite the fact that their equipment and facilities remain the best in the world. The Japanese mills are in a downsizing mode, are reluctant to add more workers and are preparing to "wind back their overall export tonnage during 1988."[68] Among EC producers, only British Steel has dollar costs below U.S. producers, and this is an anomaly reflecting the fact that British Steel's debt and capital costs have largely been absorbed by the government.[69] Thus incentives for EC and Japanese producers to supply world export markets (which are denominated in U.S. dollars) have been sharply

---

[65] Steel consumption in the western world increased 6.1 percent in 1987, according to the International Iron and Steel Institute, from 426 million metric tons in 1986 to 452 million metric tons in 1987. In the United States, the western world's largest market, apparent steel consumption increased for the first time since 1984. Apparent consumption of all steel mill products increased from 90.26 million tons in 1986 to 96.23 million tons in 1987, an increase of 6.6 percent. Domestic shipments were up in 1987 by 9 percent. While apparent consumption increased in 1987 over 1986, the 1987 consumption level was still below the levels of 1984 and 1985. United States International Trade Commission, *Monthly Report on Selected Steel Industry Data* (Washington, D.C.: U.S. International Trade Commission, March 1988).

[66] Monthly production data are from the 29 reporting countries in the IISI survey. These 29 countries accounted for 92 percent of total western world crude steel production in 1986. IISI, *Steel Statistical Yearbook 1987*, table 3.

[67] Based on their estimate of western world effective capacity, Marcus and Kirsis indicate that western world capacity utilization increased throughout 1987, from 81 percent in January to 91 percent in October. This compares to their estimate of effective capacity utilization during the last steel shortage of 100 percent in 1973 and 99 percent in 1974. Marcus and Kirsis, *Steel Strategist 14*, p. 5.

[68] *Metal Bulletin* (December 24, 1987), p. 23; *Wall Street Journal* (April 21, 1988), p. 21.

[69] Marcus and Kirsis, *Steel Strategist 14*, exhibit D.

Figure 2—7: Western World Monthly Crude Steel Production, January 1970 through February 1988

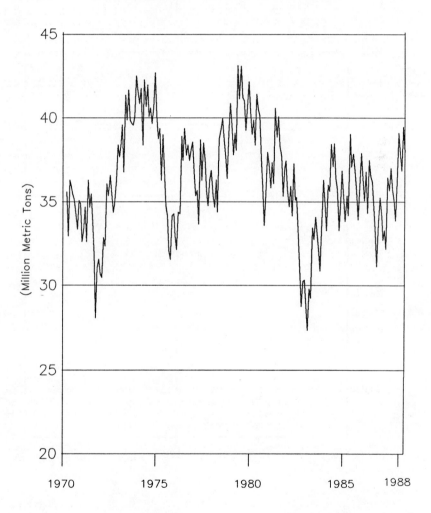

Source: International Iron and Steel Institute. Monthly production data from 29 reporting countries which accounted for 93% of total western world crude steel production in 1986.

Figure 2—8: Western World Monthly Crude Steel Production and Capacity at Annual Rates, January 1970 through February 1988

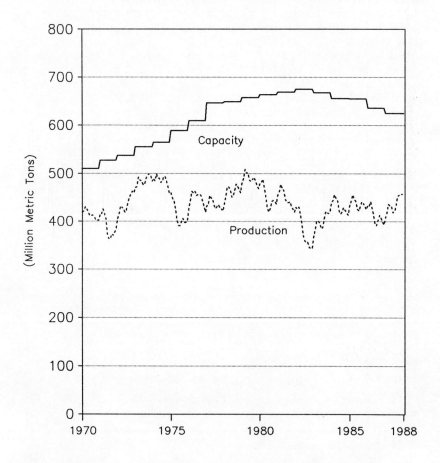

Source: For production data, see figure 2—7; for capacity, see figure 2.4. Production and capacity data presented are 3—month moving averages at annual rates, not seasonally adjusted. Monthly capacity data assumed to be equivalent to 8.3% of annual capacity.

curtailed.[70] For example, the average domestic sales price for steel products in Japan is reported to now be up to 30 percent higher than the average export price.[71]

While Japanese mills appear reluctant to expand output given their loss of competitiveness, EC producers also remained subject to production controls in the first half of 1988 in HR and CR coil and sheet, plate and heavy sections.[72] Production controls in the EC were cited in late 1987 as a source of a world shortage in galvanized sheets; while EC mandatory production quotas on this product were eliminated at the beginning of 1987, its necessary raw material, cold-rolled coil, remained subject to production quotas.[73] Some traders in Europe indicated that were it not for the quotas there would be ample supplies of HR and CR coil and other flat products, compared to the current short supply situation.[74] Others have indicated that the quotas are tight only for British Steel Corporation and that EC mills, together with imports from outside the EC, are meeting current demand. The problem is that supply is not sufficient to meet current demand *and* the desire of buyers to build up their stocks.[75] It is unclear at this writing how the elimination of EC production controls in mid-1988 will affect this situation.

Thus a third factor explaining the current shortage situation is inventory accumulation. Part of the tightness in current steel markets is due to inventory building. When prices were falling or depressed, buyers carried minimal inventory. Now that prices are rising, buyers want to accumulate inventory ahead of price increases.[76] Most analysts expect that when the inventory rebuilding stops (perhaps by as soon as the second half of the year) buyers will quickly reduce orders, depressing prices.[77]

---

[70] "Steel mills in the U.S.A., EC and Japan are determined not to hire any new workers because of the great cost of laying them off. In fact, the Japanese mills seem sure to go through with their 30% employee cutbacks by 1990." Marcus and Kirsis, *Steel Strategist 14*, p. 3. In economic terms, dollar depreciation has increased the dollar costs of steel production in countries whose currencies have appreciated significantly with respect to the dollar. This has caused a shift in the supply curve so that at any given dollar price, steelmakers in these countries are willing to supply less steel than previously.

[71] U.S. International Trade Commission, *Steel Sheet and Strip Industry*, p. 9-16.

[72] The efforts of Japanese producers to adjust to the appreciation of the yen are documented in the "Yen Shock" in chapter 4. The discussion of EC production controls is presented in chapter 3.

[73] *Metal Bulletin* (September 7, 1987).

[74] *Metal Bulletin* (December 24, 1987), p. 21; *Metal Bulletin* (January 25, 1988), p. 19.

[75] *Metal Bulletin* (January 28, 1988), p. 21.

[76] *Metal Bulletin* (January 22, 1988), p. 23.

[77] *Wall Street Journal* (April 21, 1988), p. 12. Some evidence of this has been observed recently at steel service centers in the Southwest United States. *American Metal Market* (April 11, 1988), p. 1.

A fourth significant factor in the current shortage is the temporary closure of a number of facilities around the world for maintenance (primarily blast furnace relines) during the same time that demand began to pick up. Among plants with current or recent temporary closures of some facilities for maintenance are Cosipa and Usiminas (Ipatinga) in Brazil; South Korea's Posco; Nasco in the Philippines; Bethlehem, Armco and USX in the United States; and CSC in Taiwan.[78]

The market for slabs (primarily continuously cast slabs) has tightened significantly in late 1987 and early 1988.[79] Trade in slabs has increased in the past few years, especially in the United States, as uneconomic blast furnaces have been shut down but finishing facilities have remained in operation.[80] Brazil, a major world supplier of slabs, has fewer slabs for export in 1988 as a result of blast furnace relines at Siderbrás group plants.[81]

A sixth factor accounting for tight steel markets is the activity of international producers' cartels. One such group, the International Rebars Exports and Producers Association (Irepas) was established in Madrid in October 1985 to attempt to stabilize international prices for billets and rebars through agreements on price, attempts to balance supply and demand levels, and other market regulation measures. Originally a Spanish initiative, Irepas has progressively expanded to embrace most significant national rebar industries, who have periodically met and agreed on price increases, generally about $10 per ton.[82] On February 6, 1987, *Metal Bulletin* reported that producers of seamless pipes, exasperated by depressed world prices, "seem to have come to the conclusion that joint action on prices is necessary;" a number of meetings had been held "between European, Japanese, and Latin American producers, resulting in the current higher price levels." In mid-1987, reports surfaced that Japanese and European producers had joined in a "conspiracy" to raise the international price for hot and cold-rolled sheets.[83]

---

[78] *Metal Bulletin* (January 18, 1988), p. 27; *Metal Bulletin* (January 18, 1988), p. 23; *Metal Bulletin* (January 25, 1988), p. 22.

[79] *Metal Bulletin* (January 25, 1988), p. 21.

[80] United States International Trade Commission, *Monthly Reports on Status* (December 1987), pp. i-ii.

[81] *Metal Bulletin* (February 8, 1988), p. 19; *Metal Bulletin* (February 29, 1988), p. 23. *American Metal Market* reported that "Brazil's Companhia Siderurgica de Tubarão (CST) steel mill, the country's biggest slab producer, recently said it has only a limited amount of slabs available for short-supply sale to United States firms." *American Metal Market* (March 15, 1988), p. 1.

[82] Irepas meetings have been attended by representatives from Brazil, Japan, Argentina, Venezuela, South Korea, Italy (te Bresciani), and South Africa, although some South African producers did not participate because of domestic allegations that Irepas was "a cartel aimed at enforcing higher prices on the world market." *Metal Bulletin* (November 15, 29, December 6, 20, 24, 1985; January 14, February 7, April 4, 18, July 26, 1986; July 16, September 7, 1987).

[83] *Metal Bulletin* (June 16, 1987).

Other factors that explain the current shortage conditions include increased import demand on world markets from China and the USSR and the fact that many mills in the United States are running flat out. Thus, despite the fact that current exchange rates make U.S. steel producers among the world's low cost producers, the substantial capacity reductions of recent years means that U.S. mills cannot take advantage of current export opportunities and meet domestic demand at the same time.[84]

While it is still too early to make a definitive conclusion about the duration of current shortage conditions, available evidence by the summer of 1988 suggests that the tight market conditions may not persist beyond the end of 1988 and may already be lessening.[85] More importantly, current conditions do not appear to indicate that the overhang of excess capacity in the world steel industry has been fully corrected. Continuing restructuring efforts, especially in the Japanese and EC industries, indicate that this is the conclusion of the world's steelmakers as well.[86]

---

[84] *Metal Bulletin* (December 21, 1987), p. 19.

[85] For example, high carbon plate inventories in the southern United States by the end of May 1988 were reported to be putting downward pressure on prices. *American Metal Market* (June 1, 1988), p. 1. In addition, short supply requests for steel slab imports at the Department of Commerce have suddenly ended. *American Metal Market* (June 30, 1988), p. 1. Finally, industry analyst Peter Marcus recently stated that the U.S. steel industry is now overproducing and that soft-pricing is already evident in cold-rolled and galvanized sheet, oil country tubular goods and wire rod. *American Metal Market* (June 22, 1988), p. 2.

[86] A recently completed study indicates that the elimination of a further 81 million tons of excess capacity remains the fundamental task of the steel industries in the developed world. Bernard Keeling, *World Steel - A New Assessment* (London: The Economist Intelligence Unit, Ltd., February 1988), p. 98.

3

The European Community

The European Community is the western world's largest steelmaking bloc and, after the United States, its largest steel market.[1] In many parts of Europe, steelmaking has a tradition going back centuries, and has been not only one of the principal sources of employment, but also the very cornerstone of many regional economies. The economic crisis which convulsed the European steel sector after 1974 destroyed communities, exacerbated ethnic and national tensions, and threatened a much more serious political crisis if it were not contained. The imminent collapse of large segments of the Community steel industry prompted a succession of escalating market interventions by the governments of the Member States and the European Commission to stave off such a catastrophe. These actions enabled much of the steel industry to survive the crisis, and may ultimately provide the foundation for a more competitive European industry. However, public intervention created major market distortions both within and outside the Community, and was the basic factor underlying the succession of bitter steel disputes which characterized the Community's relations with the United States in the late 1970s and 1980s.

The basic problem confronting the Community steel industry in the years since 1974 has been a massive burden of excess capacity (figure 3-1). As recently as 1981, the European Commission estimated excess capacity in the EC steel industry at 50 million metric tons.[2] Public intervention impeded the reduction of this surplus, preventing competitive pressure from eliminating the less efficient producers and facilities. After 1975 European governments poured subsidies into failing producers in amounts which can only be regarded as incredible, even by the standards of this heavily subsidized industry -- totalling about 35 billion dollars in the years 1980-85 alone. In addition, the European Commission imposed a comprehensive system of market controls

---

[1] In 1986, raw steel production in the EC was 110.6 million metric tons and steel consumption (ingot equivalents) was 103.5 million metric tons. Unless otherwise indicated, all data and references to the European Community refer to the EC (9).

[2] EC Commission, *Comments on the General Objectives Steel 1985*, February 16, 1984.

on the Community steel industry, seeking to stabilize prices through production and delivery quotas, mandatory and "recommended" minimum prices, import protection, and the division and allocation of market shares among firms by Eurofer, an association of European steel producers. While such measures may have succeeded in preventing the wholesale collapse of the Community steel sector, they also diminished the competitive pressure on producers to cut capacity. At the beginning of 1988, after over a decade of restructuring efforts and significant reductions since 1981, the Community still carried a capacity surplus estimated by the Commission at 30 million metric tons.

Intervention by the public authorities in the steel market proved extraordinarily controversial, reflecting the divergent industrial philosophies of the Member States. France and Italy have a long tradition of state intervention in key industrial sectors and view an activist role by the state in the market not only as appropriate but often essential, particularly in periods of crisis. West Germany and the Netherlands favor a liberal, market-oriented approach to industrial policy and strongly oppose overt intrusions by governments into the market. Britain has zigzagged between a heavy state intervention under prior Labour and Conservative governments and an increasingly market-oriented approach under Margaret Thatcher. The Commission has not only been forced to mediate these fundamental differences among the Member States, which have repeatedly led to bitter controversy, but has itself been pulled between its Treaty mandate to preserve a market-oriented environment in steel and the economic and political imperatives of the steel crisis, which have drawn it into a progressively more interventionist role.

Escalating intervention by national and Community authorities inevitably affected external markets; Community restrictions on imports, implemented after 1978, limited access to the western world's second largest market at a time of global oversupply; and outside the Community, subsidized and dumped steel from the European mills caused the eruption of a series of major trade disputes with the United States. Perhaps more fundamentally, while the Community's subsidy measures and market controls have created significant market distortions (and been variously denounced for that reason by economists, journalists, and academic analysts) they have also made possible the emergence of a far more efficient and productive Community steel industry, which will be a major international competitive force in the 1990s and beyond.

THE STEEL CRISIS IN THE COMMUNITY

At the onset of the steel crisis in 1975, the Community steel industry was characterized by a number of serious structural weaknesses. Many European facilities were antiquated and located at inland sites (near traditional sources of coal and ore) where transportation costs were significantly higher than at newer seaside locations. Most European steel industries were overmanned

Figure 3−1: EC Raw Steel Production and Capacity, 1960−1987

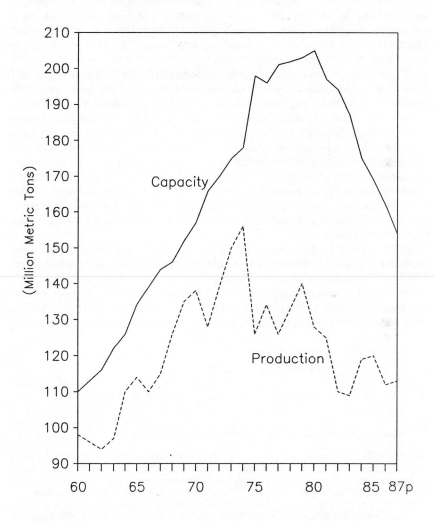

Source: Crude steel capacity from Peter F. Marcus and Karlis M. Kirsis, World Steel Dynamics: Core Report BB (PaineWebber, Inc., January 1988), Exhibit BB−1−5.

and suffered from comparatively high wage costs. Energy and raw material costs were high and were to rise sharply after 1973. Finally, in the late 1960s and early 1970s, the European industry had undertaken a "frenetic and uncoordinated" expansion effort,[3] which substantially increased the Community's capacity without rationalizing the industry's structure. Between 1965 and 1975, 64 million metric tons of new steel capacity were added in the EC countries; the establishment of new facilities, however, was not accompanied by the closure of older, less competitive ones, and, "new investments, far from substituting for existing capital, simply added to it."[4] The cost of these investments (table 3-1) forced many European producers to incur dangerously high burdens of debt.[5]

The European expansion programs undertaken in the decade prior to 1975 were implemented for a variety of reasons, some of them only marginally related to economic considerations. In Italy, the state-owned Finsider group constructed a giant greenfield mill at Taranto, distant from its natural markets in the north, to facilitate regional development and employment in Italy's less developed southern region, the Mezzogiorno. In France, driven by an industrial nationalism shared by "all sectors of political opinion," a succession of state-financed plans to expand the steel industry were pressed forward despite the industry's considerable structural and financial weaknesses.[6] After 1970, an intensive cycle of investment throughout the Community seems to have been driven, to a considerable degree, by little more than rivalry between the Member States.[7]

1974 was the last good year for the Community steel industry. Consumption fell sharply at the beginning of 1975, to 102.3 million tons from 124.2 million tons the prior year, and prices fell 35 to 40 percent from 1974 levels. Steel consumption recovered in 1976 to 123.1 million tons, but fell again to 110.0 million tons in 1977 and 108.8 million tons in 1978.[8] During these years, new plant continued to come on stream, with the result that by

---

[3] Meny and Wright, *The Politics of Steel,* p. 13.

[4] *Ibid.*

[5] *Ibid.*

[6] Hayward, "The Nemesis of Industrial Patriotism," pp. 502-503.

[7] After 1970, the West German industry, largely privately-owned, took the lead in undertaking ambitious investments, prompting a competitive response in Italy, Britain, and France, where steel production was dominated by the government. The state-owned British Steel Corporation launched a massive expansion program in 1972, subsequently criticized as "totally unrealistic and wildly expensive," citing as an important justification the parallel expansion efforts in neighboring European States. J.J. Richardson and G.F. Dudley, "Steel Policy in the U.K.: The Politics of Industrial Decline" in Meny and Wright, *The Politics of Steel,* pp. 330, 339. "The imitative investment behavior of those industries dominated by public capital generated perverse external effects which governments failed to perceive before 1974-75 and were subsequently unable to resolve." Messerlin in Meny and Wright, *Ibid.,* p. 123.

[8] Data from table 2-4.

Table 3-1. EC Steelmakers' Planned Expanded Investments Despite the Onset
of Worldwide Recession in 1974-75

Total Annual Advance Declaration of Investments
Made To The European Commission
(million U.S. dollars)

	1971	1972	1973	1974	1975	1976
Germany	274	478	146	540	512	645
Belgium	25	118	265	309	370	9
France	201	66	91	359	479	326
Italy	132	201	259	964	386	104
Luxembourg	29	2	24	30	11	34
Netherlands	8	-	46	161	-	-
U.K.	NA	NA	NA	431	923	599

Source: *Bulletin of the European Communities*, February 2, 1976, Table 2
Converted to U.S. dollars from ECUs at average annual exchange rate given by International
Monetary Fund.
Conversion: 1971: 1.00; 1972: 1.08; 1973: 1.2; 1974: 1.25; 1975: 1.23; 1976: 1.22

1977, the industry was operating at a 60 percent average utilization rate.[9]
Consumption recovered somewhat in 1979 to 120.4 million tons, then fell again
in the wake of the second oil crisis, to 97.2 million tons by 1983. In 1986, steel
consumption in the EC was still at a very low level, 103.5 million tons, or
virtually the same as it had been eleven years earlier in 1975.

By and large failing to recognize the "structural" nature of the recession,
European governments and producers after 1975 continued to implement the
ambitious expansion plans they had mapped out in the early 1970s.[10] Even
into the early 1980s many of the Community's economic decisionmakers
resisted capacity reduction initiatives and, in some cases, pressed forward new

---

[9] Heusdens and de Horn, "Crisis Policy in the European Steel Industry in the Light of the
ECSC Treaty" in 17 *Common Market Law Review*, February 1980, p. 34.

[10] See *Bull. EC* 5-1975, point 2239 (July-August 1976); *Debates of the European Parliament*,
July 5, 1977, p. 54.

expansion plans with an "overoptimism which in some cases bordered on the extravagant and perverse."[11]

By the late 1970s it was fully evident that the recession in demand which had begun in 1975 did not represent another cyclical downturn but a fundamental change in the pattern of steel demand. Virtually all major producers were suffering unheard-of losses, the industry's debt burden was growing phenomenally, and in some Member States, massive workforce reductions had occurred or were under way. Between 1974 and 1980 the Community steel industry lost nearly 200,000 jobs, and some regions, such as the Saar, Luxembourg, Lorraine, and a number of areas of Britain suffered economic devastation.[12] In Germany, by the early 1980s, losses were estimated to be running at a rate of $550,145 per company per day;[13] in Italy, the "disastrous mess"[14] in the steel industry was characterized by *La Repubblica* as "the major economic disaster in the history of industrialized Italy;"[15] in France, the crisis which enveloped the steel industry was described as "the greatest mess we have seen in France for thirty-five years." [16]

The Crisis Policies of the European Commission

The European Commission has played a more active role in steel than in most other Community industrial sectors, reflecting the fact that its powers over the coal and steel industries under the Treaty of Paris are more substantial than those which it exercises over other industries pursuant to the Treaty of Rome. While the Commission's powers in steel are substantial, they are subject to significant limits. The Commission has no mandate to formulate and implement Community-wide industrial policy in steel, and the Member States have continued to pursue their own policies, which are often not only divergent but inconsistent with basic Community rules.[17] Because the Commission's actions are subject to ratification by a unanimous Council of

---

[11] Meny and Wright, *The Politics of Steel*, p. 14.

[12] Employment declined from 792,191 in 1974 to 597,873 by 1980. A further decline in employment of 140,000 occurred by 1986, bringing employment to 456,300. Eurostat, *Iron and Steel Statistical Yearbook*, various issues.

[13] Meny and Wright, *The Politics of Steel*, p. 6. All conversions to U.S. dollars at the average annual exchange rate given by International Monetary Fund for the respective year.

[14] *Il Borghese* (November 21, 1981).

[15] *La Repubblica*, October 3-4, 1982, cited in Meny and Wright, *The Politics of Steel*, p. 5.

[16] Michel Freyssenet, *La Sidérurgie Française 1945-79. L'Histoire d'un Faillite. Les Solutions qui s'Affrontent* (Paris: Savelli, 1979) cited in Meny and Wright, *The Politics of Steel*, p. 504.

[17] The Founding Treaties of the Community contain no industrial policy mandate, reflecting the differences in economic philosophies which divide the Member States. The principal cleavage is between the *dirigiste* approach favored by the French and Italians and the economic liberalism advocated by the Germans.

Ministers, it is cast in the role of broker between conflicting Member States rather than that of ultimate authority.

The Treaty of Paris, which established the European Coal and Steel Community (ECSC), provides the legal foundation for the Commission's actions regarding steel.[18] The Treaty, based on *laissez faire* principles, provides for the elimination of internal tariff barriers and prohibits (under most circumstances) subsidies and cartels. At the same time, the Treaty empowers the Commission to prescribe and enforce rules of price competition;[19] to enforce the Treaty's prohibitions on anticompetitive agreements[20] and also to exempt certain activities from those prohibitions;[21] to enforce the prohibition on subsidies by national governments or, under some circumstances, to approve such subsidies;[22] to raise funds for disbursement to the industry for a variety of purposes;[23] to collect data from producers and, on the basis of such data to review investments;[24] and to impose market controls, including price controls, in a recession, and, in the event of a "manifest crisis," to impose mandatory production quotas to forestall a collapse of market prices.[25] The authority to regulate foreign trade resided with the individual Member States except to the extent they saw fit to delegate that authority to the Commission.

After 1974, the Community's massive surplus of steelmaking production capacity constantly threatened to produce a price collapse and a frenzied competition for market share among the Community mills. The Commission's

---

[18] The ECSC created a free trade zone for coal and steel and required the Member States to surrender some of their sovereign power to a central European entity, the High Authority. In 1967, the executive of the ECSC was merged with that of the European Economic Community (the EC, formed pursuant to the Treaty of Rome), and the functions of the High Authority are now exercised by the Commission.

[19] Article 60.

[20] Articles 65 and 66.

[21] Articles 65(2) and 66(2) and (3).

[22] Articles 4 and 67.

[23] Article 54. The Commission has always enjoyed a degree of influence over the steel industry because of Article 54 of the Treaty of Paris, which authorizes the Coal and Steel Community to provide industrial investment loans to the industry. ECSC funds are raised through a combination of borrowing on international capital markets and levies on the steel industries of Member States. Because of its quasi-governmental stature, the ECSC can raise debt capital at interest rates significantly below those available to individual firms, and these savings are passed on in their entirety to steel firms, to which the funds are reloaned at cost; in addition, the loans have often been given an additional interest reduction for a specified time period. Between 1952 and 1982, the ECSC extended a total of 5.1 billion EUA in loans to the steel industry ($5.6 billion at $1.1/EUA). ECSC *Financial Report* (1982).

[24] Articles 46, 47 and 48.

[25] Articles 58, 59 and 61.

concern has been that in such an event, rather than permit severe injury to their national industries, the Member States would establish protective measures at their own frontiers, prompting retaliatory moves which could lead to the breakup of the Common Market. Reducing the capacity surplus, however, was a politically explosive issue, since plant closures had a dramatic impact on employment in regions of the Community which were already severely depressed. Most Member States chose instead to subsidize their national producers; this had the effect of preserving jobs and regional economies over the short run, but it also sustained uneconomic producers and facilities and progressively eroded the strength of the unsubsidized firms.

The Commission has attempted to respond to these complex problems in several interrelated ways. It has used the powers available to it to encourage the phasing out of national subsidies. It has presided over a system of market controls designed to hold competition in check through the establishment of production and delivery quotas (until 1988), mandatory minimum prices (until 1986), and import protection. Finally, it has sought to encourage restructuring of the industry -- closure of obsolete mills, layoff of redundant workers, reduction in aggregate capacity, and the modernization of the remaining facilities.

Given its lack of sweeping authority over the industry, the Commission has been required to use a carrot-and-stick approach to pursue these objectives. The carrots included its ability to provide financial assistance for investment and restructuring; social aids for worker retraining and reconversion; and its use of market controls to afford the European mills a degree of protection from adverse market conditions. The sticks included its ability to veto the subsidy proposals of the Member States, its power to disapprove investment plans of individual firms, and the power to impose fines on firms that engaged in overproduction or price discounting in violation of the Commission's directives.

The interrelated issues of national subsidies, overcapacity, and the Commission's market control measures remain a tangle which, at this writing, have defied all efforts at comprehensive resolution. Despite the Commission's growing recognition of the need to move toward "market-oriented" solutions to the steel crisis, it was placed in the anomalous position of using its power to approve additional subsidies and quotas, which themselves were part of the problem, as an inducement to producers to close facilities. In mid-1988, thirteen years after the onset of the steel crisis, the Community still carried a capacity surplus estimated at 30 million metric tons; and while quotas were eliminated on July 1, 1988, the extent to which a competitive regime would follow remained problematic and the issue of subsidies remained a matter of controversy.

The Effort to Control Subsidies. The most divisive aspect of the steel crisis in the Community has been the issue of subsidies to the industry by the governments of the Member States. By any measure the sheer volume of European steel subsidies since 1974 has been stupendous. The West German

Iron and Steel Federation estimated in 1987 that the governments of the Member States had granted $44.8 billion in subsidies to the steel industry between 1975 and 1985, over three fourths of which was paid after 1980.[26] The EC Commission approved over $35.5 billion in subsidies to the steel industry between 1980 and the end of 1985, nearly two thirds of which was "aid for continued operation" -- subsidy injections to keep failing firms afloat (tables 3-2 and 3-3). Moreover, during this period substantial subsidies were granted which were not reported to or approved by the Commission. In 1982 the German Steel Federation charged that in Britain, fully one-half the cost of producing a ton of rolled steel was being paid for by the government.[27] In Luxembourg, in 1981 subsidies to the steel industry accounted for three percent of total national expenditures, and placed a severe strain on the taxpayers of the Grand Duchy.[28] Borrowing by governments to finance the losses of European steelmakers reached such a magnitude that in 1982, it was reportedly crowding other borrowers out of the financial marketplace and driving up interest rates.[29]

One of the most singular aspects of the European steel crisis was the role played by wholly or partially state-owned firms which suffered losses of such magnitude that they could not have long survived without continuing injections of state aid, but which, with such aid, were able to engage in sustained, vigorous price competition, both within the Community and abroad.[30] Within Europe, aggressive price discounting by the ailing nationalized firms brought about a progressive weakening and partial collapse of the private sector.[31] The privately-owned German producers, despite their superior efficiency at the outset of the crisis, progressively lost strength in the face of such competitive

---

[26] Wirtschaftsvereinigung Eisen und Stahlindustrie, *Funfzehn Fragen and Fakten zur Europaischen Stahlpolitik* (December 1987), Anlage V.

[27] Wirtschaftsvereinigung Eisen und Stahlindustrie, *Practical Experience with Governmental Assistance to the Steel Industry of the European Community* (February 1982).

[28] The government was forced to raise the cost of public telephone calls, and to increase taxes on alcohol, cigarettes, and gasoline to offset the cost of the steel subsidies. *Europe*, No. 3588 New Series (April 15, 1983); No. 3691 New Series (September 19-20, 1983).

[29] *Metal Bulletin* (March 23, 1982). A Dutch delegate to the European Parliament, commenting on a new round of Belgian steel subsidies, stated that they placed "An enormously heavy burden on the next generation. . . . [These steel subsidies are] merely being cast into a bottomless pit which is getting bigger day by day." *Debates of the European Parliament*, May 6, 1981, p. 110.

[30] The German Iron and Steel Federation indicated in 1983 that over the past seven years none of the major nationalized enterprises of France, Italy, Belgium and Britain had had losses of less than 20 percent of their turnover. Together these firms lost nearly 20 billion dollars during that period. *Europe*, No. 3625 New Series (June 10, 1983).

[31] *Metal Bulletin* (January 11, 14, 18, 21, 25, March 25, 1983); *Hannoversche Allgemeine* (January 12, 1983).

pressure.[32] A study by the Bremen Economic Research Committee concluded in 1983 that the German industry was losing its technological edge over its competitors "as a direct consequence of the fact that other countries supported their steel industries with state cash."[33] At length, the German government felt compelled to expand its own aid programs to even the balance;[34] in effect, the crisis gave rise to a subsidy competition, "an aid race," between the Member States.[35]

Background. The eruption of a "subsidy steeplechase"[36] in the Community steel market would appear anomalous in light of the Paris Treaty's flat prohibition on government subsidies to the steel industry. However, strict enforcement of this prohibition during the decades following enactment of the Treaty would have precluded the expansion of a number of national industries, and the period prior to the mid-1970s saw a "gradual whittling away of the [Treaty's] clear-cut prohibition of subsidies." During the rapid growth years of European steel, large scale government financial aid facilitated the addition of new steelmaking capacity which, under competitive conditions, would never have been built, and enabled steel firms to "keep alive" obsolete capacity which "under normal conditions would no longer be used."[37] Some of these aid programs eluded the attention of the EC authorities altogether,[38] and while

---

[32] The *Deutsches Allgemeines Sontagsblatt* commented on March 6, 1983 that the German Producers "are somewhat punchdrunk from the blows they have received and are unlikely to weather the subsidies race against the state-owned steelmakers of France, Italy and Belgium." Denmark's steel producer, Det Danske Staalvalsevaerk, complained in 1983 that subsidies to its European competitors were placing it in an "exposed position," and Denmark's government warned that the subsidies of its neighbors jeopardized the existence of the Danish steel industry. *Berlingske Tidende* (November 23, 1987); *Metal Bulletin* (May 10, 1985).

[33] *Metal Bulletin* (May 24, 1983).

[34] *Wirtschaftswoche* (April 6, 1984); *Metal Bulletin* (January 31, February 7, 1984). A curious testament to the competitive power of failing, subsidized firms was a 1987 offer by privately-owned German firms to participate in salvaging the bankrupt German producer Maxhutte to prevent it from becoming another subsidized rival. The Bavarian Land government had stated that it would ensure the survival of Maxhutte "regardless of the cost," and the privately-owned German mills feared that "Maxhutte set up under such conditions would pose a serious threat to the market." *Metal Bulletin* (October 19, 1987).

[35] Ingo Friedrich, EC Committee on Economic and Monetary Affairs, in *Debates of the European Parliament*, May 6, 1981, pp. 101-102.

[36] *Neue Zürcher Zeitung* (January 7, 1982).

[37] Heusdens and de Horn, "Crisis Policy."

[38] The German Iron and Steel Industry Association observed that under this system "those Governments in the EC that wished to wrongfully grant assistance to their steel companies did so within the scope of non-specific, regional or general assistance schemes. Notification was a matter of discretion. The EC Commission consequently lacked any kind of overview of subsidization in the steel industry that rapidly achieved considerable dimensions after 1975, particularly in Belgium, France, Great Britain and Italy. . . . The Commission obviously had no

they did object to particularly flagrant violations of the subsidy prohibition, their efforts at enforcement were less than vigorous, and for the most part ineffectual.[39]

Thus, by the time the European steel market collapsed in 1974, a *de facto* pattern of systematic large-scale government aid to the steel industry had already been established, and the Community's institutional checks on such aid had been compromised. The Commission, belatedly recognizing the threat which the subsidy race posed to the Common Market, was placed in the anomalous position of needing to seek and establish new legal prohibitions on subsidies despite the "perfectly clear" treaty proscription, which had largely become a dead letter during the years of weak enforcement by the Commission.[40]

The Aids Codes. The German producers and the Bonn government continually pressed the Commission to adopt measures to bring the subsidy competition under control.[41] These efforts led the Commission to adopt the First Aids Code in 1980, which established a number of limits on the conditions under which state aid could legally be granted to steel firms. This action proved spectacularly ineffective -- the volume of subsidies actually rose in the years following the promulgation of the First Aids Code,[42] and in exasperation the West German government threatened to impose countervailing duties and quotas at the border on steel shipments from Member States which continued to subsidize their national producers.[43]

---

knowledge at the time of the financial assistance amounting to $2.2 billion each with which the governments of Belgium and Italy had already supported their steel industries." Wirtschaftsvereinigung Eisen and Stahlindustrie, *Practical Experience.*

[39] The High Authority was criticized in 1969 by the Economic Affairs Committee of the European Parliament for its "frankly disappointing" response to massive French aid measures which were "inconsistent with Article 4(c)." European Parliament, *Working Documents*, Doc. 12 (April 24, 1968), p. 11.

[40] Heusdens and de Horn, "Crisis Policy."

[41] In May 1978 the German delegation submitted a draft "subsidy code" to the EC Council of Ministers which would require that all aid measures be made public and satisfy a set of strict criteria. Even weakened versions of the German proposal did not win unanimous support in the Council. The final version adopted -- which became the ECSC's First Subsidy Code -- "obviously undermined the original aim of developing an instrument which could significantly slow down particular subsidization practices." Fritz Franzmeyer, *Industrielle Strukturprobleme und Sektorale Strukturpolitik in der Europaischen Gemeinschaft* (Berlin: Duncker and Humblot, 1979).

[42] In a letter to Chancellor Kohl in 1983, the German producers estimated that the total subsidy per ton had been $42 in the years 1975-80; following enactment of the Subsidies Codes, the figures had climbed to $97 per ton. *Europe*, No. 3625 (New Series), June 10, 1983.

[43] Governments proved uncooperative with the Code and "did not meet their obligation to advise the Commission of proposed assistance or did so only with considerable delays." *Practical Experience*; *Bull. EC*, 2-1980, point 2.1.22; *Metal Bulletin* (April 3 and 7, 1981).

At length, under intense pressure from Germany, a Second Aids Code was adopted in mid-1981. Its salient features were (a) a requirement that operating subsidies cease after December 31, 1984; (b) a prohibition on investment subsidies after December 31, 1985; and (c) a requirement that state aid must be part of a "systematic restructuring program" involving capacity reduction, modernization, and financial restructuring.[44] However, according to the Germans, the Second Code was "disdained" by other national governments, who continued to pump massive "unreported or unapproved assistance funds" into their industries "within five months of the effective date of the Second Subsidy Code."[45]

In 1983 the Commission approved a wide-ranging series of subsidy proposals in France, Britain, Italy and Belgium, and in protest, the Bonn government again threatened to impose countervailing duties at the border on steel from these countries.[46] In retrospect, it was clear that a substantial volume of aid was being granted during this period in breach of the Commission's rules; in 1987, the Commission found that $388.5 million in state aid had been granted illegally by the French government to the state-owned firms Usinor and Sacilor between 1982 and 1985,[47] and that Belgium had illegally paid $185 million to a Belgian producer, Tubemeuse, through 1985.[48]

It was evident soon after the adoption of the Second Aids Code that the complete phaseout of subsidies by 1984-85 would be problematic. France adopted a new steel plan in 1984 which featured an infusion of $1.7 billion from the government to be granted to Usinor and Sacilor through 1987; President Mitterand, noting the Commission's 1985 deadline, merely voiced

---

[44] Under the Second Code, restructuring was required to result in a net reduction in capacity; the Code required that the "amount and intensity" of aid be progressively reduced. *Bull. EC*, No. 6-81, pp. 18-19.

[45] *Practical Experience.* The Germans charged that "The EC Commission has shown itself to be *too weak* up to now either to promote restructuring of the steel industry in the European Community in accordance with the basic principles of the Common Market or to resist the growing pressure of national politics. The demand for transparent policies concerning assistance since the start of the crisis is still not met" (original emphasis). In April 1983 the Commission initiated proceedings against France, Italy, Germany, Belgium, Luxembourg and Britain — *i.e.*, virtually the entire membership — for the grant of subsidies to the steel industry without notification to the Commission. EC Commission, *Fifth Report on the Application of the Rules for Aids to the Steel Industry*, COM (84) 142 final, March 8, 1984.

[46] The German mills, while acknowledging the increasing support which they were receiving from their own government, complained with considerable justification that this aid was dwarfed by that of their rivals. *Europe*, No. 3715 (New Series), October 22, 1983.) In 1984 the German Iron and Steel Federation estimated that during the 1980-85 period, the German industry (excluding Saarstahl) would receive $1.2-$1.4 billion in subsidies. By contrast, Finsider would get $8.4 billion, Usinor-Sacilor $7.2 billion, and British Steel $5.2 billion during the same period. Wirtschaftsvereinigung der Eisen und Stahlindustrie, *EG Stahlpolitik vor Neuer Bewahrunsprobe, Positionspapier der Deutschen Stahlindustrie* (Dusseldorf: 1984).

[47] *Metal Bulletin* (March 31, 1987).

[48] *De Standaard* (February 2, 1987).

the hope that France would be granted an exception.[49] Following a heated dispute in the spring of 1985, the Council of Ministers agreed to extend the cutoff date for operating subsidies to December 31, 1985, and also agreed that governments would be allowed, prior to the cutoff date, to grant aid which reduced steel companies' debt burdens, since such aid did not "directly affect the marketplace."[50] The German industry complained that this action "opened the door for a flood of further subsidies," and left national governments "free to take on the debts of producers which have failed to cut unviable plant and even built up capacity during the steel crisis."[51] The 1985 agreement on subsidies supposedly linked the grant of additional aid to the closing of capacity by the aid recipient, but as the German producers pointed out, the amount of aid allowed bore no fixed relationship to the amount of capacity eliminated.[52] Thus, by the fall of that year, the German producers were complaining that $3.7 billion in aid had been authorized by the Commission in exchange for capacity cuts of only 1.7 million tons per year by the German industry's competitors.[53]

Despite these problems, the Community's prohibition on further operating and investment subsidies to the steel industry became effective on December 31, 1985. During the preceding five year period, the Commission had authorized steel subsidies totaling a staggering $34.1 billion (table 3-2).

Subsidies After 1985. The formal prohibition of subsidies after 1985 by no means heralded the end of the issue in the Community. The prohibition was not absolute; the Commission's new rules permitted state aid to the steel

---

[49] *Metal Bulletin* (April 6, 1985). By late 1984, it was evident that the year-end deadline for phasing out operating subsidies could not be met -- France and Italy formally requested extensions of the deadline, and Finsider, Usinor, Sacilor, Cockerill-Sambre and British Steel all reportedly required continuing operating aid. Ruprecht Vondran of the German Iron and Steel Institute commented in *Handelsblatt* (April 5, 1984), that "one hears with astonishment of subsidy plans in neighboring countries such as France which are designed to be in force for another 4 years yet, calculated from today on. If these indications should solidify into certainty, the German steel industry expects Bonn to draw very serious political conclusions from such a violation of the law."

[50] Virtually all of the Member States took advantage of this decision to extend additional operating aid to their steel firms. EC Commission, *Report,* August 6, 1986.

[51] The German government put a better face on the arrangement, stressing the importance of adhering to the final December 31, 1985 cutoff date for operating and investment aid. *Metal Bulletin* (March 29, May 8, 1985).

[52] The volume of aid allowed relative to the amount of capacity to be eliminated was negotiated by the Commission with each member state on a case-by-case basis. The Commission indicated that it was not possible to reach a decision on the amount of closures required relative to a particular amount of aid "simply on the basis of a mathematical calculation." In October 1985, the European Court of Justice rejected a legal challenge to this policy by the German industry. *Metal Bulletin* (August 30, September 3, October 8, 1985).

[53] *Metal Bulletin* (September 27, 1985).

Table 3-2. Subsidies to the Community Steel Industry Cleared for Payment by the Commission between January 1980 and December 1985 (million U.S. dollars)

	Grants	Loans	Conv. debt to capital	Low interest loans	Loan guarantees	Other	Total
Cockerell-Sambre(BE)	87	1,171	1,686	185	772	-	3,902
Other Belgian	77	32	35	-	164	-	308
Danish Steel	-	39	-	-	-	42	80
Arbed Saarstahl(GE)	834	-	-	1	172	29	1,035
Other German	1,946	-	-	66	753	-	2,766
Sacilor/Usinor	148	8,207	-	-	685	-	9,040
Irish Steel	42	160	-	-	58	-	261
Finsider(IT)	793	6,637	-	2,888	504	-	10,823
Other Italian	2,215	-	-	294	-	-	2,509
Arbed/MMRA(LX)	209	163	-	27	224	-	629
Hoogovens(ND)	88	220	-	-	135	-	443
Other Dutch	8	-	-	-	-	-	8
British Steel	225	5,287	-	-	-	-	5,513
Other U.K.	65	-	-	-	-	-	65
Total	6,740	21,915	1,721	3,461	3,467	70	37,376

Source: *Report from the Commission to the Council on Application of the Rules on Aids to the Steel Industry*, COM (86) 235 final, August 6, 1986. Converted to U.S. dollars at average annual exchange rate given by International Monetary Fund. Conversion: 1980-1985; .989 dollars per ECU.

Table 3-3. Purpose of Subsidies to the Community Steel Industry Cleared for
Payment by the Commission between January 1980 and December 1985
(million U.S. dollars)

Country	Investment	Research & Development	Closures	Aid for Continued Operation	Emergency	Total
Belgium	711	-	117	3,371	12	4,211
Denmark	13	-	-	67	-	80
Germany	1,108	161	612	1,921	-	3,802
France	3,006	-	299	5,055	-	8,360
Ireland	-	-	-	261	681	942
Italy	3,949	-	43	225	9,113	13,332
Luxembourg	435	-	15	174	-	624
Netherlands	231	-	-	220	-	451
U.K.	1,768	48	1,025	2,737	-	5,578

Source: *Report from the Commission to the Council on Application of the Rules on Aids to the Steel Industry*, COM(86) 235 final, August 6, 1986.
Converted to U.S. dollars at average annual exchange rate given by International Monetary Fund Conversion: January 1980 - December 1985: .989 dollars per ECU.

industry for research and development, for environmental protection measures, and to finance the cost of closing facilities. Aid granted to the steel industry pursuant to general regional aid schemes was permitted provided that it did not lead to an increase in capacity.[54] Many forms of state aid to the steel industry continued; a 1985 study performed for Britain's National Economic Development Office calculated the value of various forms of "indirect aid" to the steel industry at between $1.60 and $10.80 per ton of steel in Britain, France, Germany and Italy (table 3-4).[55] Subsidies approved prior to the cutoff date were granted after that date, and France devised a scheme to "effectively circumvent" the aid prohibition through state purchases of

---

[54] *Official Journal*, L. 340 (December 18, 1985).

[55] The study raised fears that British Steel would be disadvantaged because of the relatively low level of Britain's indirect steel subsidies. *Daily Telegraph* (June 9, 1986).

convertible debentures from its nationalized producers.[56]   In 1987, Italy's
Finsider group received a $1.5 billion loan from government banks, triggering

Table 3-4: Summary of Indirect State Aid Schemes to the European Steel
Industry 1985 (million U.S. dollars)

	France	Germany	Italy	U.K.
Labor related schemes	47.7	95.8	61.8	16.1
Transport aid	122.2	221.8	98.3	2.6
Total indirect aid	169.9	217.6	159.9	18.7
Reduction in cost per ton of steel delivered	10.8	10.4	7.8	1.6

Source: Environmental Resources Ltd., *Indirect State Aids in the EEC and Their Impact on the
EEC Steel Industry*, September 1985, prepared for the U.K. National Economic Development
Office.
Converted to U.S. dollars from ECUs at average annual exchange rate given by International
Monetary Fund.
Conversion: 1985: 1.3

vigorous German protests and an investigation by the Commission.[57]   In 1988,
Italy's state holding company, IRI, announced that it would guarantee all of
Finsider's debts; the Commission charged that this could only be done through
the use of public funds and therefore constituted a breach of the aids ban.[58]
The German producers and the Bonn Government charged that France, Italy
and Belgium were continuing to subsidize their steel industries covertly and
illegally, citing the fact that plants in these countries had aggregate losses of
$2.2 billion in 1986 and $6.6 billion between 1984 and 1986, the inference
being that such losses virtually mandated additional government support.[59]

---

[56] *Le Monde* (November 12, 1985); *Le Figaro* (November 11, 1985).

[57] *Corriere Della Sera* (January 24, 1987); *Metal Bulletin* (September 21, October 29, 1987).

[58] *American Metal Market* (June 21, 1988).

[59] *Journal of Commerce* (April 21, 1987). A German industry spokesman stated that although
they had no "hard and fast proof, . . . [they] suspect[ed] that new subsidies are being shelled out
just the same." In the spring of 1987, German Economics Minister Bangemann complained to
the Commission about illegal steel subsidies being granted by the other Member States. *Die Welt*
(April 24, 1987); *Handelsblatt* (April 24, 1987); *Osnabruker Zeitung* (September 19, 1987).

Perhaps more significantly, by mid-1987 the steel producers of a number of Member States were openly requesting that the Commission once again permit subsidies to flow to the steel industry.[60] A Committee of Wise Men appointed by the Commission to study the industry's restructuring problems in late 1987 found that Italy's Finsider group, in particular, needed "special aid to offset its debts, which at present preclude any hope of a revival."[61] The prospect of a renewed subsidy competition, made more dangerous by a prospective lack of transparency, was a principal factor underlying the Community's decision to extend its system of market controls, which restrained intra-Community competition, through 1989. The basic concern was that if these controls were phased out,

> *there [would] be a renewed rash of backdoor and illegal national support schemes for steel of the kind which prompted the Davignon scheme [market controls] in the first place. . . . Whether the Community and indeed the Commission really have the stomach for a return to a mix of open price war and clandestine subsidy war must be a matter of considerable doubt.[62]*

In early 1988, West Germany's Economic Minister, Martin Bangeman, wrote to the Commission complaining that Italy, Belgium and Britain were not complying with the subsidy prohibition. Bangeman charged that public sector enterprises like Finsider were receiving increases in state capital to cover their operating deficits. The Commission rejected Bangeman's charges and raised its own questions about aid provided by the government of Saarland in West Germany to its producer, Saarstahl.[63] These exchanges, coupled with reports from various member states about schemes being contemplated or implemented to circumvent the subsidy prohibition,[64] suggest that the Commission's prohibition has driven state aid measures underground or caused them to be extended in different forms, but has not eliminated them.

---

[60] The *Stuttgarter Zeitung* reported on June 1, 1987 that "It has been no secret for some time that major steel producers in France, Belgium and the Saar would not be able to survive this year and next without subsidies."

[61] *"Wise Men's Report."* The Wise Men reported in 1987 that "Companies in the Community do not receive any support described as aid, but do receive considerable loans to cover operating deficits from banks (more often than not public ones) which do not seem unduly concerned about recovering the debts in question. When the time comes, and if the company cannot pay the interest on these loans, or if it has been decided, late in the day, to close it down, it can be expected that the Community will be asked to give its absolution for past errors."

[62] *Financial Times* (March 17, 1987).

[63] *European Report*, No. 1379 (February 10, 1988).

[64] *La Croix* (May 6, 1987); *Le Monde* (November 12, 1985); *Le Figaro* (November 11, 1985).

The System of Market Controls

The structural recession which began in 1974-75 quickly became a crisis of survival for much of the Community steel industry. With the gap between production capacity and demand widening rapidly, prices fell sharply as individual producers desperately sought to push their steel onto a depressed market, resulting in "ruthless infighting" for market share.[65] Between 1975 and 1980 the Commission was drawn into a succession of market interventions to stave off catastrophe, progressively assuming the role of the administering authority of a Community-wide steel cartel. Although implemented as emergency measures, many of the Commission's crisis measures became institutionalized, and proved politically difficult to phase out.

While the system administered by the Commission grew to be highly complex, and underwent many modifications over time, its essential aspects remained the same throughout. The Commission's crisis measures sought to maintain price stability within the Community, primarily by limiting the quantity of various types of steel available in the internal market. This was done by restricting import volume and production and sales of steel by Community mills through "voluntary" or (after 1980) mandatory quotas on production and delivery of specified steel products. The Commission sought to buttress the quota system through various "flanking measures," such as the enforcement of floor prices for imports and some domestic product lines ("mandatory minimum prices"), and by establishing voluntary minimum prices in other product areas ("guidance prices"). Violators of the mandatory quota and minimum price rules were punished by fines.

The Community's system of market controls has had several significant effects. By restraining intra-Community competition, the system enabled Community producers to "carry" their surplus capacity by preventing a competitive shakeout.[66] The system tended to preserve less efficient producers and mills by alleviating competitive pressures within the Community. The system also had significant effects in external markets, both because it limited access to the Community market and because it fostered low-priced sales by European firms outside of the Community.[67]

Background. European observers do not fail to comment on the irony that the Commission, with a Treaty obligation "to combat cartels and monopoly

---

[65] *Pourquoi Pas* (May 12, 1977); *Handelsblatt* (January 31, 1985).

[66] This was the conclusion of the three "Wise Men" who studied the system on behalf of the Commission in 1987. "Wise Men's Report." The German steel producers have pointed out that the winners of a competitive free-for-all would be the heavily subsidized firms. Thus, while they initially opposed the establishment of a system of market controls by the Commission, by the mid-1980s they were among the strongest proponents of preserving the system, which they felt was necessary to hold their subsidized rivals in check.

[67] See EC Commission, *General Objectives Steel 1990*, COM (85) 450 final, July 31, 1985.

agreements,"[68] after 1975 became the "Brussels European Steel Cartel."[69] In fact, however, the Commission's extension of market controls across the Community steel industry was only the culmination of a long series of developments which had eroded the Paris Treaty's prohibitions on anticompetitive agreements in the decades prior to the crisis. At its inception, the Treaty provided for a more competitive regime in steel than any which then existed within the Member States, placing a considerable burden on the European authorities to give the prohibition real effect.[70] They chose instead to condone collusive activity.[71] Moreover, in the 1960s, the EC authorities began to encourage and officially sanction combinations which had plainly evident anticompetitive purposes and effects.[72] In part this was due to their belief that larger economic units were necessary to take advantage of new production technologies.[73] However, an additional explicitly stated goal was the prevention of excessive price competition among ECSC producers and the maintenance of "market discipline."[74] This concern stemmed from their fear of a "collapse of prices" -- proliferating discounting competition that could injure the industry.[75]

By the time the 1974-75 crisis occurred, most of the Community's integrated steel producers had been consolidated into a few large national

---

[68] *Kolner Stadt-Anzeiger* (September 25, 1976).

[69] *Frankfurter Allgemeine Zeitung* (July 2, 1976); *Der Spiegel* (December 6, 1976).

[70] Prior to World War II virtually all of Europe's steel industries were organized into national cartels. On the eve of the Treaty of Paris, national steel industries were still engaging in a variety of practices designed to limit competition. See generally E. Hexner, *The International Steel Cartel* (Westport, Ct.: Greenwood Press, 1943, 1976), pp. 110-138; L. Lister, *Europe's Coal and Steel Community* (New York: Twentieth Century Fund, 1960), p. 128.

[71] The authorities took a benign view of collusive behavior as long as "enough" competition existed, and in their view, it did. Between 1952 and 1964 there were no reported cases of enforcement of Article 65 of the Treaty of Paris, which prohibits anti-competitive agreements, despite the fact that such activity was widespread. Stegemann, *Price Competition and Output Adjustment*, pp. 198-200; *Business Week*, (September 3, 1966); ECSC, 15th *General Report* (1967); *Le Soir* (September 24, 1976).

[72] One German observer commented that "During the past few years, a change has taken place in regarding the attitude to concentration in the steel industry. In many instances the industry is even being urged by the High Authority to accelerate the formation of large, efficient units. . . ." F. Horders, "Konzentrationstendenzen in der Europaischen Wirtschaft," in *Stahl und Eisen* (March 20, 1969), p. 232.

[73] European Parliament, *Working Documents*, Doc. 12, April 24, 1968, pp. 10, 12-13.

[74] In its 15th *General Report*, the High Authority stated with approval that "steel market discipline can be strengthened when top-level policy decisions come into progressively fewer hands. . . . This process continued in 1966 all over the Community, in the form of the establishment either of selling agencies or communities of various kinds, some of them on a cross-frontier scale."

[75] European Parliament, *Working Documents*, Doc. 12, p. 10.

groups, through nationalization of private firms (Britain), evolution of a dominant state-controlled steel sector (Italy), or by government-induced merger (France).[76]   In West Germany, where the industry was more heterogeneous and largely remained in private hands, the nation's steel producers grouped themselves into four "Walzstahlkontore" (joint sales agencies) in 1967, enabling them to reach agreements on output levels and prices in a manner reminiscent of Germany's pre-war steel cartel, the Stahlwerksverband.[77]   In 1971 the *Kontore* were succeeded by four "Rationalization Groups," which enabled the German mills to divide product markets among themselves, reducing the number of competitors and facilitating price coordination.[78]

By 1975 the largest European producers had also forged a series of transnational links, contributing to price stability in the Community as a whole. The Luxembourg producer Arbed was incorporated into one of the German rationalization groups. Together with the Belgian producer Cockerill, Arbed jointly controlled Sidmar, one of the leading Belgian firms, a relationship which enabled Arbed, Cockerill and Sidmar to regulate price competition in the Benelux region.[79]   The German producer Thyssen developed a relationship with the two consolidated steel groups in France,

---

[76] In Britain "the creation of the British Steel Corporation (BSC) amounted to a cartelization of 14 nationalized private firms," and in France, "duopolistic control (Usinor and Sacilor) was imposed on the industry by the state." Patrick A. Messerlin, "The European Iron and Steel Industry," p. 126.

[77] Stegemann, *Price Competition and Output Adjustment*; *Journal Officiel*, p. 1374/67 (April 2, 1967). Under this system, Germany's 29 steel producers distributed all of their steel through only four joint sales agencies *(Kontore)*, each of which offered only one price for each type of product, thus "substituting stability for earlier chaos and anxiety in the establishment of market prices." H.S. Kohler, "Vertrachliche Formen der Zusammenarbeit in der Produktion und beim Verkauf Stahlerzeugnissin," in *Stahl und Eisen* (April 17, 1969).

[78] The basic goal was that each of the four groups should produce most types of steel products, but that within each group, each member should produce different products. To this end, a number of enterprises deliberately abandoned further investments in some product lines, and the Commission "agreed that specialized agreements could contain possible quantitative financial or equalization measures between the enterprises concerned for certain specified products." EC Commission, *First Report on Competition Policy* (1971), p. 44; Specialisierungs- und Kooperationsvertrag Nord, Section 13 (1976).   B. Roper, *Rationalisierungseffekte der Wahlzstahlkontore und der Rationalisierungsgruppen*, (Berlin: Duncker and Humblot, 1974); H.C. Kohler, *Schriftenreihe der Wirtschaftsvereinigung Eisen und Stahlindistrie Zur Wirtschafts-und Industriepolitik* (Dusseldorf: Wirtschaftsvereinigung Eisen und Stahlindustrie, 1977).

[79] The High Authority approved this arrangement despite the propensity toward "an oligopolistic market" and its recognition that "in fixing the prices of the enterprise controlled, the controlling enterprises will inevitably take into account their own prices for the same or similar products, and very possibly agree all prices." ECSC *General Report*, May 1963, p. 324. When Sidmar commenced operations, the parent companies formed a joint sales agency for flat products. The Commission approved this arrangement even as it recognized that the "liberty to remain competitors between themselves . . . has been abandoned in the new agreements." *Journal Officiel*, No. 49, 1967.

Usinor and Sacilor, through the joint control of the French steel producer of flat products, Solmer.[80] The north German firm Hoesch entered into a series of cooperative arrangements with the only integrated Dutch producer, Hoogovens, which culminated in a merger in 1972.[81]

As a result of the various combinations which occurred in the years prior 1974-75, when the structural crisis developed, virtually all of the ECSC's integrated steel producers had already been consolidated into a few large groups and fairly sophisticated techniques of industrial organization for controlling price competition had already been developed. That fact greatly facilitated the establishment of a Community-wide system of market controls following the onset of the crisis.[82]

The First Crisis Measures. After 1975, as the magnitude of the economic crisis facing the industry became apparent, pressure began to build for direct intervention in the market by the European authorities. Specifically, the Commission was urged to invoke the "manifest crisis" measures of Article 58 and impose production quotas and other stringent measures -- in effect, to form an anti-crisis cartel to restrict price competition through collective restraints on output.[83] The Commission initially rejected this option in favor of "recommended" production cutbacks designed to stabilize prices.[84] In early 1976, the Commission implemented the Simonet Plan,[85] which sought

---

[80] In approving the joint control by three of the ESCS's largest producers of a producer of flat products, the Commission acknowledged that "competition between these groups in relation to investments and flat products will be restricted. . . ." EC Commission, Fourth Report on Competition Policy (1975), p. 70.

[81] *Neue Zürcher Zeitung* (November 20, 1980).

[82] Viscount Etienne Davignon, the principal architect of the Community's anti-crisis measures, later observed that "For us it was nevertheless a matter of great importance that the German steel industry agreed with a joint policy. Through this it became possible to come to a joint approach in the form of anti-crisis measures." *NRC Handelsblad* (February 10, 1978).

[83] Article 58 of the ECSC Treaty provided that the Commission could, in the event of a "manifest crisis" in the steel industry, impose a system of mandatory production quotas, quantitative import restrictions, and/or minimum prices. Before such drastic measures could be implemented, however, the Commission was first required to attempt to resolve the crisis through "indirect means of action" specified in Article 57 of the Treaty -- methods such as "cooperation with government to regularize or influence general consumption" and "intervention in regard to prices."

[84] The Commission published revisions of its periodic forecast of short-term supply and demand trends, the "Forward Programme for Steel," recommending a reduced total of steel production, with a suggested allocation of that total among the member states. The Forward Programme was not binding on the members, but there was an expectation that their production should not greatly deviate from the Commission's "forecasts."

[85] Named for the Commissioner charged with primary responsibility for the steel sector, the plan was formally adopted by the Commission in December 1976, effective in January 1977. The Commission sent notices to 30 groups and 40 companies notifying them of the "voluntary quotas to which they were expected to adhere." *Official Journal*, C.304 (December 23, 1976).

commitments by individual companies to limit production voluntarily. These measures proved ineffective; many ECSC firms did not adhere to the guidelines, exceeding their "voluntary" quotas and engaging in extensive discounting.[86]

The Formation of Eurofer.   Given the failure of the Commission's measures, the steelmakers themselves began to discuss the need for an effective Community-wide cartel, although the French sought a scheme which would be administered by the Commission, while the Germans desired an industry "club" independent of the political authorities.[87] The Germans forced the issue by joining together with Arbed (Luxembourg) and Hoogovens (Netherlands) to form an "international steel union," Denelux, which was designed to "defend its members' interests both within the EC and on a world scale."[88] This "pan-German cartel" so alarmed the Commission and several Member States that they rapidly assented to the formation of a strong Community-wide association of all the major steel producers, Eurofer.[89]

A symbiotic relationship rapidly developed between this new steelmakers' "Club" and the Commission, providing the basis for the first true pan-European steel cartel since the 1930s (table 3-5).[90] The formation of Eurofer created a producers' group through which the Commission could more readily secure industry compliance with its increasingly stringent market control directives.   Eurofer played an important part in shaping and enforcing the Commission's measures to control steel competition on a continental scale. The Commission's Treaty powers effectively legalized collusive price and output agreements arrived at by Eurofer, and its power to regulate imports and to punish firms which engaged in unauthorized discounting enabled it to protect the Community price floor more effectively than the earlier associations of private producers.

---

[86] *Pourquoi Pas* (May 12, 1977).

[87] *Der Spiegel* (December 6, 1976).

[88]   *Metal Bulletin* (February 6, 1976).

[89] *Pourquoi Pas* (August 25, 1976). The French and Belgians feared that Denelux would divide up the German and Benelux markets, impose its own price levels, and exclude outsiders from those markets. The Commission feared that this would lead to a breakup of the common market for steel, and "became less hostile to the formation of Eurofer, which would not involve the same dangers." European Parliament, *Working Documents*, Doc. 198/77, July 4, 1977, p. 9. One of the architects of Denelux, H.C. Kohler, later commented that the real purpose of its formation was to induce the Commission and Germany's neighbors to "reorganize the steel industries Club." *Metal Bulletin* (April 1, 1977), Kohler; *Schriftenriehe der Wirtschaftsvereinigung Eisen und Stahlindustrie zur Wirtschafts Industriepolitik* (1977), p. 8.

[90] A French delegate to the European Parliament complained that the Treaty of Paris "prohibited the reconstitution of the old Konzerns and cartels. How has the Commission, the guardian of the treaties, ensured respect for these objectives? What is Eurofer if not a powerful cartel dominated by the giants of the steel industry like the Krupps and Thyssens?" Remarks of Mr. Ansart in *Debates of the European Parliament*, July 5, 1977, p. 50.

Table 3-5. Market Controls on Steel: The Commission/Eurofer Partnership

Item	Commission	Producers' Association
PRODUCTION	Fixes production ceilings and quotas (voluntary prior to October 1980, mandatory in many categories thereafter)	Agrees on allocation of among members
PRICE	Establishes "guidance" prices Fixes mandatory minimum prices for some products (until 1986)	Agrees on price levels to levels at or above figures fixed by the Commission
DISTRIBUTION	Monitors delivery to ensure compliance	Agrees on delivery quotas consistent with Commission production quotas
ENFORCEMENT	Levies fines against producers violating price minima and (after October 1980) production quotas Monitors prices, output and delivery to enforce compliance	Jawboning of members to adhere to price and output restraint
IMPORTS	Negotiates restrictive bilaterals Enforces import price minima and ban on alignment on imports from nations subject to bilaterals	
ANTITRUST	Exempts producers from Paris Treaty's prohibitions on anticompetitive arrangements	

The Davignon Plan. In early 1977, EC Commissioner Etienne Davignon, who had assumed the steel portfolio from Simonet, advanced a series of more drastic market control proposals which were officially adopted in April, the so-called "Davignon Plan." In addition to continuing the voluntary production restraints introduced under Simonet, for the first time the Commission took direct steps to stop price discounting. "Guidance" (recommended) minimum prices for certain products were published,[91] alignment on imported steel (*e.g.*, matching import prices) was prohibited, and mandatory minimum prices were imposed on rebars, a product where price competition had been particularly intense.[92]

The Davignon Plan was immediately tested on several fronts. A number of northern Italian electric furnace producers, popularly known as the "Bresciani,"[93] ignored the voluntary production quotas on rebars, and following the imposition of mandatory minimum prices, continued to sell them at prices well below the legal floor.[94] The Commission instituted a two-tier price system to allow some limited legal discounting by the Bresciani,[95] but at the same time, levied fines against a number of them for undercutting the minimum legal prices.[96] Davignon sought to persuade the Bresciani to adhere to the Commission's volume and price guidelines, suggesting that they find an outlet for their excess production somewhere outside the Community, which they subsequently did.[97] The Bresciani agreed to enter into quantitative restraint agreements with other ECSC nations, and formed a joint "sales

---

[91] *Bull. EC* 6-1977, point 2.1.15. While adherence to "guidance" prices was voluntary, it became mandatory as soon as producers published list prices conforming to the guidance prices, since they were legally bound to adhere to their published list prices.

[92] *Official Journal*, L. 114 (May 5, 1977).

[93] For a description of these firms see *Metal Bulletin Monthly* (September, 1978).

[94] *Metal Bulletin* (October 25, 1977; April 18, May 12, 16, 1978).

[95] The Commission fixed guidance prices, to which other producers were expected to adhere, at higher levels than the minimum price level, which constituted the legal floor for the Bresciani. This created a "zone" of legal discounting for the Bresciani designed to remove the incentive to engage in illegal discounting. Heusdens and de Horn, "Crisis Policy."

[96] *Official Journal*, C. 133 (June 7, 1978); C. 186 (August 4, 1978); C. 206 (August 30, 1978).

[97] Davignon pointed out that "it was strange that while some traditional steel producers were exporting rebars at a considerable loss, efficient producers were kept out of those markets. He added that it should not be impossible to pass on orders entailing losses to the Bresciani. The Commission may even help the Bresciani to find alternative outlets for their steel. . . ." *Metal Bulletin* (October 14, 1977.) A French delegate commented in the European Parliament in 1979 that the Bresciani, having found third country outlets, were no longer a threat to "Community discipline." *Debates of the European Parliament*, April 25, 1979.

office" in Milan to monitor their shipments to other ECSC countries.[98] By early 1979, price-cutting by the Bresciani had moderated.[99]

The Davignon Plan was also threatened by an influx of low-priced imported steel, which prompted a wave of defensive price-cutting by the European mills. At the end of 1977 the Commission adopted a decision to seek, on an urgent basis, a series of voluntary restraint agreements with the principal exporters to the Community market. Using the threat of unilateral restrictions as a lever, in 1978 the Commission concluded fifteen restraint arrangements with exporting nations, in which these countries accepted an actual or *de facto* quota (based on their "traditional" patterns of trade) and agreed to respect the Community's pricing rules.[100] These new arrangements, according to contemporary industry observers, stabilized the import situation and "permitted a certain increase in steel price levels."[101]

During this period the Commission, although constantly criticized as indecisive, demonstrated that it could play an important role in a system of collective restraints on competition that were not available to the old national steel cartels. Discipline of mavericks is a perennial problem in a cartel, but the Commission had the power to punish companies that exceeded their quotas or undercut the agreed minimum prices, and in the case of the Bresciani, it showed that it could induce a heterogeneous group of recalcitrant firms into a semblance of cooperation with collective restraints on price and output.[102] More significantly, the Commission could effectively restrict

---

[98] The Industrie Siderurgiche Associate (ISI), an association of many Bresciani producers, established this bureau in Milan under Commission supervision in June 1978 to ensure adherence by the Bresciani to quotas. In effect this self-monitoring of deliveries by the industry was comparable to the efforts of Eurofer (which the Bresciani refused to join) to ensure adherence of its members to production quotas. *Metal Bulletin* (June 16, 1978).

[99] This was partially attributable to rising scrap prices, which increased cost pressure on the Bresciani. *Metal Bulletin* (February 6, 1979).

[100] EC Commission, Communication from the Commission to the Council, *Concerning the Negotiation of Arrangements on Community Steel Imports for 1986*, COM (85) 535 final, October 14, 1985.

[101] *Metal Bulletin* (August 1, 1978). The Community's import arrangements are described later in this chapter.

[102] Thyssen Chairman Dieter Spethmann acknowledged this in a May 23, 1983 interview with *Der Spiegel*, when violations of output and price restrictions were discussed: "*Der Spiegel*: You are not only the Thyssen-chief, but also chairman of the Steel Trade Association. This office gave you the possibility, after all, to check such violations. Spethmann: Here you misjudge. The association is okay. But only the Commission can punish violations."

imports, thus bringing under control one of the most serious vulnerabilities of the old private producers' cartels.[103]

Manifest Crisis. The Davignon system was progressively strengthened and extended throughout 1977, and functioned reasonably well in 1978 and 1979, buoyed by the recovery of the European economy.[104] Compliance with the price and output restrictions was not universal, however, and the Commission levied fines against about 20 firms in 1978-79 for infringing price rules.[105] In the summer of 1980, U.S. steel producers commenced antidumping actions against the Community, causing a sharp fall in ECSC exports to the U.S., and steel demand in the auto and construction industries also fell sharply.[106] The sudden development of a major steel surplus triggered a struggle for market share as ECSC producers attempted to maintain sales volume through price discounting.[107] Attempts to encourage further voluntary production cuts failed, the internal unity of Eurofer broke down, and by Fall, it was evident that the original Davignon plan, based on voluntary quotas and "guidance" prices, was coming unraveled.[108]

---

[103] In Germany, for example, the *kontore* could not restrict imports; the most they could achieve was to restrain German mills from matching import prices. The German mills simply allowed "interlopers" to sell their steel at lower prices with the hope that the volume of lost sales would not be too great. Under the principal of "equal sacrifice," the German firms then spread the impact of such lost sales by redistributing orders among the *kontore* members. Such self-restraint required extraordinary industry discipline, and became increasingly difficult after 1975, as the volume of imports increased. Stegeman, *Price Competition and Output Adjustment*; *Der Spiegel* (December 6, 1976); *Handelsblatt* (January 31, 1975).

[104] Davignon's early 1977 measures were supplemented in December 1977 by the extension of mandatory minimum prices to hot-rolled wide strips and merchant bars, by increased Commission compliance monitoring, by extension of the minimum prices to steel stockholders and by a raising of guidance prices. *Official Journal*, L.352/1; L.352/8; L.352/4; L.352/11; (December 28, 1977); L.353/1 (December 31, 1977).

[105] *Metal Bulletin* (October 28, 1980); *Bull. EC* 7/8-1980, point 2.1.22.

[106] Sacilor *Annual Report* (1980); *Metal Bulletin* (July 4, 1980).

[107] Davignon called it a "senseless, self-destroying battle," and said that "European steelmakers should be prepared to learn from Japan, where overproduction has been swiftly quashed by a close consensus of all parties involved. Rather than criticizing the Japanese, Europe should imitate them." *Metal Bulletin* (September 19, 1980).

[108] *Elseviers Weekblad* (October 18, 1980). The problem within Eurofer was "intransigence on the part of a few producers who feel that they are not getting a fair deal under present arrangements." Most notably this included Klöckner, a German producer which had recently constructed a new hot strip mill, which wished to expand production, and which opposed production quotas and price restraints. Klöckner quit Eurofer in mid-1980, and was later widely blamed for having destroyed the arrangement. Similarly, the Italians felt that they would not be required to cut production when their home market was buying significant quantities of imported steel. *Wirtschaftswoche* (June 26, 1981); *La Repubblica* (October 28, 1980); *Metal Bulletin* (September 12, 1980).

At length, in October 1980, the Commission declared a state of "Manifest Crisis" in the Community steel industry and asked the Council of Ministers to approve a system of mandatory production quotas pursuant to Article 58 of the Treaty of Paris.[109] Despite some reservations by the Germans, the Council gave its approval, and the Commission issued an order imposing mandatory quotas on October 31.[110] Mandatory quotas were fixed on four main categories of product, with the remaining steel products subject to voluntary quotas. Each firm was required to report daily to the Commission concerning its production, about 100 inspectors were engaged to supervise compliance, and fines were prescribed for violators.

The new system continued the traditional Commission-Eurofer partnership. The Commission fixed the initial quota levels, but permitted companies to exchange, buy and sell quotas among themselves, after which it ratified this sharing out of the market. While the Commission backed the quotas with official sanctions, as a practical matter it relied heavily on the Eurofer members to police themselves and to bring infractions to the attention of the Commission. The new system worked so well in 1981 and early 1982 that the European mills enjoyed "remarkable success" in implementing "sharply increased prices;" a testament to the effectiveness of the new quota regime was the increasing criticism levied against it by steel consumers.[111] The mandatory quotas were regularly extended after 1980, with even the German producers calling for their extension.[112]

The Restructuring Impasse

After the implementation of "manifest crisis" measures in 1980, the Commission pointed out at intervals that the crisis measures are temporary expedients to be maintained only so long as necessary to permit the industry to restructure, eliminating the capacity surplus that made the crisis measures

---

[109] *Bull. EC*, 10-1980, point 1.1.5.

[110] *Official Journal*, No. L. 291 (October 31, 1980). The Germans were reluctant to veto the crisis measures altogether; a veto "would have created large cracks in the very structure of the Community, and was being advocated by Germany's right wing opposition party, the CDU." German Economics Minister Lambsdorff said that "we have no reason to rejoice over the agreement," but without the agreement "the German industry would have faced serious difficulties as state-owned companies in other European countries would have thrown the market into confusion with dumping prices." *Metal Bulletin* (October 28, November 4, 1980, June 30, 1981).

[111] *Metal Bulletin* (September 29, November 6, 10 and 13, 1981); *Bull. EC* (March 1982).

[112] *The Economist* (June 25, 1983). Controls were tightened further in 1982-83 by reducing production quotas and adopting more stringent production rules. EC Commission, *Forward Programme For Steel For the Third Quarter of 1983*, *Official Journal* No. C 175/3 (July 2, 1983); *Metal Bulletin* (December 7, 1982; February 18, March 18, April 12, 15, 1983).

necessary in the first place.[113]   Restructuring, however, has proven extraordinarily difficult and politically divisive to achieve, and the industry grew increasingly comfortable with the quota regime, which permitted deferral of difficult capacity reduction decisions. The Commission's efforts to force a resolution of the restructuring impasse have increasingly led it to use its power to authorize production quotas (and to approve state aid) to induce producers to undertake capacity cuts.[114]

Although European steel demand peaked in 1974, the Community's steelmaking capacity continued to increase until 1979, reflecting faulty expansion decisions made immediately before and in some cases after the onset of the structural crisis.[115] By the end of 1981 the EC nations had surplus crude steelmaking capacity of over 50 million metric tons, an "intolerable structural imbalance."[116] In a fully competitive regime, with no government interference, most of this surplus would have been eliminated by market forces. However, governments, anxious to avoid the mass layoffs entailed by closure of large facilities, "[poured] cash into supporting a fundamental structural inefficiency."[117]

Between 1980 and 1987, the Community industry eliminated about 32 million metric tons of raw steel capacity leaving a balance of about 140 million metric tons (table 3-6). Employment levels fell from a high of 792,191 in 1974 to 456,300 in 1986.[118] However, significant as these cuts may have been, they were inadequate, and even these reductions were achieved only after extraordinarily bitter wrangling among the Member States. After 1985, the attempt to achieve further closures on the scale seen necessary by the Commission has proven even more divisive, since further cuts would affect

---

[113] EC Commission, *General Objectives Steel 1985*, COM (83) 239 final, April 22, 1983, p. 8.

[114] European Parliament, *Working Documents*, Doc. 1-238/83, May 3, 1983, p. 26.

[115] Eurostat. The Commission attributes this phenomenon to several factors. High prices in 1973-74 encouraged producers to keep in production "or even restart marginal and inefficient plants"; during the same period "extensive investment programmes" were undertaken which led to a net capacity increase of about 15% over 1973; while investments slowed markedly after 1977 and some capacity surpluses that alone more than cancelled out plant closures." EC Commission, *General Objectives Steel 1985*, April 22, 1983, pp. 41-42; ECSC Staff Reports, *Analysis of Certain Aspects of Steel Restructuring Policies*, January 31, 1981, pp. 8-9.

[116] EC Commission, *Comments on the General Objectives Steel 1985*, COM (84) 89 final, February 16, 1984. The Commission complained in 1983 that "since 1974 . . . enormous imbalance between supply and demand have been created in all product categories," and it indicated in early 1983 that despite capacity cuts implemented since 1980, *"The surplus capacity already evident in 1980 will be even greater in 1985,* if the present stagnation in demand continues, if it is not substantially reduced by the policy of restructuring and the application of the aids code." (original emphasis) *Ibid.*, p. 42.

[117] EC Parliament, *Working Documents*, Doc. 1-238/83, p. 28.

[118] Eurostat.

Table 3-6. Community Reduction in Hot-Rolling Capacity - First Phase 1980 - 1986 (thousand metric tons)

Member State	Capacity in 1980	Capacity at the End of 1985	Net Reduction (Increase) 1980-85	1986 Cuts Demanded byCommissionin Return for Approval Of Subsidies in 1985	TotalReductions at the end of Steel Aids Regime
Belgium	16,028	13,098	2,930	256	3,436
Denmark	941	875	66		66
Germany	51,869	45,140	6,729	36	6,729
Greece	4,317	4,710	(393)		(393)
France	26,869	21,469	5,400	745	6,145
Ireland	57	333	(276)		(276)
Italy	36,294	29,984	6,400	800	7,200
Luxembourg	5,215	3,920	1,045		1,045
Netherlands	7,597	5,865	1,732		1,732
U.K.	22,840	18,064	4,776	655	5,431
Total	172,027	143,368	28,623	2,492	31,115

Source: EC Commission, *Report from the Commission to the Council on the Application of the Rules on Aids to the Steel Industry 1984-85*, COM (86) 235 final, August 6, 1986.

larger facilities and a younger segment of the workforce.[119]

The issue of steel closures aggravated basic fissures in the Community polity. Italy viewed its neighbors' calls for cuts in its steel facilities as an attempt to perpetuate its status as a less developed member of the Community and an outlet for the manufactured products of the more industrialized

---

[119] The Community's workforce reductions between 1974 and 1987 were achieved, in significant part, by giving early retirement to older workers and by refraining from hiring new workers. This produced a "bulge" in the middle age groups (25-49) which could not be reduced through early retirement schemes or by a freeze on new hires. *European Report* No. 1314, May 16, 1987; *General Objectives Steel 1990*, July 31, 1985, p. VI/13.

Member States.[120] The Germans showed an abiding distaste for an economic union with states that heavily subsidized major industries, and reacted strongly to proposals that their own industry should contract to accommodate less efficient, and in their view, less well-managed state-backed firms. The British, who had slashed their own steel workforce by two thirds, saw no need to make further sacrifices, and harbored major reservations over the muddled affairs of the Community, of which steel was seen as a classic example. The issue of steel closures threatened the very national cohesion of Belgium. Under such circumstances, while there had long been a consensus that significant additional capacity cuts on a Community-wide basis were a necessary objective, this consensus broke down over the issue of the extent of specific cuts to be undertaken by each nation and producer. Each company and Member State sought to emerge from the crisis with its own capacity relatively intact.

The Community's first round of facility closings, which took place roughly between 1980 and 1985, involved smaller plants (mainly in long products) whose elimination, with some exceptions, did not have a disproportionately severe regional employment impact and did not significantly alter individual firms' relative competitive standing. By 1986, however, the Community's principal remaining surplus was in the larger integrated mills, the largest steel plants in Europe. Closure of one or more of these facilities would not only have a devastating impact on employment in regions which were already depressed, but in some cases, would virtually eliminate the company operating the mill. The problem was perhaps most acute in the area of hot-rolled strip; the Community simply possessed too many hot strip mills, and the issue of which ones should close has, at this writing, proven impossible to resolve, involving a complex web of social, economic and political issues (table 3-7).[121]

---

[120] The Member States frequently pointed out that while they have phased out capacity between 1974 and 1982, the effect of these closures was nullified by Italy, which continued to expand its uneconomic state steel sector. Italy felt that its actions were wholly justified on the basis of Italy's growth in steel demand. ECSC Staff Report, *Analysis of Certain Aspects of Steel Restructuring Policies*. *The Economist* commented on June 25, 1983 that "In 1974-82 Italy actually increased its steel output by about 1%. . . . Italy, whose state-owned steelmaker is a huge lossmaker, cut (ooh, ow) just 4% of its jobs."

[121] In Italy and France, where the issue of steel plant closings occasionally triggered violent civil disturbances, hot strip mills were located in areas of chronically high unemployment, where the impact of large scale job losses could not be mitigated and could have unpredictable social and political effects. Germany possessed six hot strip mills, a number of them poorly sited for historical reasons; one way to resolve the problem was for several German firms to merge, permitting one or more hot strip mills to be shut down. However, all German merger efforts collapsed. In any event, the Germans believed they had been leaders in reducing capacity and that their own hot strip mills were profitable and should not be closed. *VDI Nachrichten* (December 18, 1987); *Financial Times* (September 28, 1987).

Table 3-7. EC Commission 1985 Projections of Community Capacity Surplus in 1990 With Accession of Spain and Portugal (million metric tons)

Product Category	Expected Maximum Production Potential	Required Maximum Production Potential	Surplus (Tons)	Surplus (Percent)
Hot-Rolled Strip	79.1	66.3	12.8	16.2%
Reversing-mill plate	15.0	9.5	5.5	36.7
Heavy sections	15.6	11.6	4.0	25.6
Light sections	39.1	25.9	13.2	33.8
Wire rod	16.7	15.4	1.3	7.8
Cold rolled sheet	50.1	41.0	9.1	18.2

Source: EC Commission, Communication from the Commission to the Council, *General Objectives Steel 1990*, COM (85) 450 final, July 31, 1985.

The Elsinore Commitments. Serious efforts at the Community level to reach a solution to the capacity problem did not really begin until the fall of 1982. A major catalyst was the trade dispute with the United States, which, by limiting Community exports to the U.S., forced additional tonnages onto the Community market, and precipitated a collapse in prices.[122] In the fall of 1982, in the wake of these developments, the Council of Ministers met at Elsinore, Denmark, in an atmosphere of acute crisis, to devise a plan to address the problems of the steel industry. For the short run, to stabilize the market, the Ministers agreed to a package of tighter market control measures,[123] actions which did in fact enable the Community mills to achieve

---

[122] See also chapter 7 and the discussion of exports later in this chapter. Many European firms blamed the heavily subsidized producers for the discounting. *Metal Bulletin* reported on September 10, 1982 that "the most competitive pricing policies appear at the moment to be operated by the state-backed integrated steelmakers." The Bresciani charged Italsider, the state-owned producer, "with slashing its prices to 60 percent of its production cost." Eisa, the association of independent steel producers, charged that state-owned French and Belgium firms were guilty of "grave infringements of price discipline." *Metal Bulletin* (October 5, 22, 1982).

[123] Tighter production quotas were set for the first quarter of 1983, and guidance prices and ECSC pricing rules were modified to limit the scope of legal discounting. The guidance prices were lower than the peak which prices reached in July 1982, but were about 10 percent higher than prevailing market levels. The pricing rules were modified to limit the extent of alignment permitted on another producer's prices. Alignment on the lowest price in the ECSC was no longer permitted; alignment was limited to the level of prices at certain "representative" mills. *Metal Bulletin* (November 30, December 17, 1982).

Table 3-8. EC Commission Order on Capacity Reduction, 1983
(million metric tons)

Member	Maximum Possible Production 1980	Additional Cuts Reduction Commitments Given After Elsinore*	Asked by Commission
Germany	53.1	4.8	1.2
Belgium	16.0	1.7	1.4
France	26.7	4.7	.6
Britain	22.8	4.0	.5
Italy	36.3	2.4	3.5
Luxembourg	5.2	.6	.4
Netherlands	7.3	.3	.7

Source: Commission Decision of June 29, 1983.
* Includes closures realized since 1980.

substantial price increases in early 1983.[124] More fundamentally, the Ministers committed themselves in principal to Community-wide capacity cuts of 30-35 million metric tons per year, agreeing that pursuant to this commitment, each nation would submit its own proposal for capacity reduction to the Commission. However, after Elsinore, when the commitments were submitted and added up, the Commission found that the Members had only pledged cuts of 18.4 million metric tons, despite the fact that credit was given for closures already made since 1980.[125]

At this juncture, in a departure from past practice, the Commission published an order declaring how much additional capacity needed to be cut, and how much each country was expected to reduce (table 3-8).   The Commission fixed a deadline of January 31, 1984, by which time each Member was to submit a restructuring plan, providing both the specifics on capacity cuts and the Member's requests for approval of state aids proposals.   The Commission indicated it would approve the grant of aid only if the

---

[124] "The very restrictive production quotas set by the Commission for the first quarter of 1983 provided the framework for an advance in prices from the very low levels of the second half of 1982." EC Commission, *Forward Programme for Steel for the Third Quarter of 1983*; *Official Journal* C.179/3, July 2, 1983. See also *Metal Bulletin* (March 18, April 12 and 15, 1983).

[125] EC Commission, *General Objectives Steel 1985*, April 22, 1983, p. 11.

restructuring plan satisfied its criteria. The Commission put additional teeth in this decision by adjusting the production quotas of each Member upward or downward to reward or punish them for their comparative progress in capacity reduction.[126]

Unexpectedly, the latter action precipitated a breakdown in the unity of Eurofer, whose members could not reach agreement on the sharing out of the reduced quotas. The quota reductions fell most heavily on the Italians, who were enraged; demonstrations erupted in Genoa, Taranto, and Bagnoli (near Naples), and the Italian government threatened to return to a "free market," e.g., veto an extension of the quotas and run its mills at a higher rate.[127] The Germans, who normally supported the notion that infringements of the price and quota rules should be strictly punished, were compromised by the still-unresolved problem of the German producer Klöckner, which continued to exceed its quota in defiance of the Commission.[128] With Eurofer in disarray, the Commission attempted to continue operating the cartel itself, setting quotas and guidance prices without a reinforcing consensus from the producers, but by the end of 1983, it was clear that such measures were inadequate. Prices fell dramatically.[129] At the end of 1983, with Eurofer still unable to reach agreement, the Council of Ministers approved draconian new market control measures to reestablish a viable price floor.[130] Perhaps

---

[126] *Official Journal*, L. 208/12 (July 31, 1983); *Europe* No. 3699 (New Series) (September 30, 1983).

[127] *Europe* No. 3658 (New Series), July 27, 1983. The Commission asked Italy to cut 3.5 million tons of capacity and proposed to reduce its production quota by nearly 1.5 million tons. This would free some plants to operate rates so uneconomically low that they would close. Genoa, the site of the Cornigliano Works, where large cuts were imminent, was described as a "powder keg," and it was feared the proposed cuts would "bring about a level of social and political tension difficult to control." *L'Espresso* (June 26, 1983).

[128] Klöckner continued to produce steel in excess of its quota on the grounds that the quota forced it to operate its hot strip mill at an uneconomically low rate. The Commission levied a draconian fine on Klöckner, but the Bonn Government would not collect the fine because to do so would bankrupt the firm. A Klöckner bankruptcy would have been one of Germany's largest corporate failures, and would have seriously jeopardized the re-election prospects of Chancellor Helmut Kohl's conservative-liberal coalition. The impasse over Klöckner fundamentally compromised the German position that violators of the quota regime should be strictly punished. *Der Spiegel* (June 20, 1983); *Financial Times* (February 13, 1983); *Wirtschaftswoche* (June 26, 1981).

[129] *Europe* No. 3706 (New Series) (October 10/11. 1983); *Europe*, No. 3729 (New Series) (November 14/15, 1983); *Financial Times* (October 17, 1983; January 5, 1984).

[130] Mandatory minimum prices were established for flat-rolled products and structurals, and an enforcement system was established whereby producers were required to pay a security deposit of a designated amount per ton of flat products sold into a national government account, to be refunded at the end of the following month. If the firm engaged in unauthorized overproduction or price discounting, the Commission would direct the member government to forfeit an appropriate amount from the security deposit. In addition, a system of independent verification of billing and a check on receipts for flat products was established. Commission decisions 3715/83, 1716/83 and 3717/83; Official Journal, L. 373 (December 31, 1983); See EC

fortunately for the Community mills, demand began to increase significantly in 1984, and that fact, coupled with tight production controls, enabled producers to implement substantial price increases in the spring.[131] Eurofer was able to compose its internal differences, and by the end of the year was once again working with the Commission to maintain market stability.[132]

Meanwhile, complete and partial restructuring plans trickled in to the Commission from the Member States, linked to requests for approval of new tranches of state aid.[133] Pursuant to these plans, between 1982 and 1985, Community gross steel capacity was reduced by about 25 million metric tons.[134] The Commission observed at the end of 1985 that the cutbacks agreed to at Elsinore in 1982 were "on track" and that by years' end, 32 million metric tons of capacity would have been eliminated since January 1980. However, it was increasingly evident that these cuts, painful and controversial as they had been to achieve, were altogether inadequate.[135] The Commission concluded at the end of 1985 that another 20 million metric tons in cuts would be necessary.[136]

Restructuring under Narjes.   Karl-Heinz Narjes took over the Commission's steel portfolio from Davignon in 1985. Narjes signaled his intention to phase out the system of market controls established under his predecessor and indicated his willingness to let market forces resolve the overcapacity problem if an agreement on closures could not be reached.[137]

Commission, *Steel: Short Term Measures*, COM (83) 691 final, November 14, 1983.

[131] EC Commission, *Forward Programme for Steel for the Third Quarter of 1984*, SEC (84) 891/2, June 8, 1984; *Official Journal*, L. 148 (June 4, 1984).

[132] *Europe* No. 3859 (New Series) (May 28/29, 1984). Klöckner reached a "complex" settlement of the issue of its fine. Details of the settlement were not made public, but the agreement reportedly involved reduction of Klöckner's fine in return for a commitment to undertake unspecified increments of capacity reduction. *Metal Bulletin* (April 27, 1984.) Klöckner rejoined Eurofer, whose members agreed to contribute increments of their quotas to enable Klöckner's hot strip will to operate at a more economic utilization rate. *Europe* N. 3883 (New Series) July 4, 1984.

[133] *European Report*, No. 1043 (May 19, 1984).

[134] Marcus and Kirsis, *Core Report BB*, Exhibit BB-1-5.

[135] The Commission observed in 1984 that Community utilization rates would be unsatisfactory even after the proposed cuts were undertaken. *Comments on the General Objectives Steel 1985*, February 16, 1984. The *Wall Street Journal* commented on May 7, 1984 that "Even by 1986, when and if all the current plant closure plans are implemented, Europe would still have [capacity for] . . . 50% more finished steel products a year than it needs."

[136] Commission Decision No. 3485/85/ECSC; *Official Journal* L. 340/5 (December 18, 1985); *European Report*, No. 1314 (May 16, 1987); No. 1331 (June 18, 1987).

[137] The market controls were loosened somewhat in 1985; mandatory quotas were removed from rebars and coated sheets, and the mandatory minimum prices were eliminated at the end of 1985. *Official Journal*, L. 351 (December 28, 1985); C. 239 (September 20, 1985).

Eurofer, however, strongly opposed the end of the quota regime, and 1986 and 1987 were consumed with inconclusive maneuvering, with the Commission seeking cuts from the industry and Eurofer pursuing extension of the quota regime by the Commission.

In mid-1986, Narjes indicated that the Commission would not seek a renewal of the anti-crisis measures when they expired at the end of 1987,[138] and that it would eliminate quotas on wire rods, merchant bars, galvanized sheets and light sections at the end of 1986.[139] Eurofer partially forestalled these measures by advancing its own proposal, under which the Commission would temporarily extend the market controls while its own members implemented a voluntary capacity reduction scheme.[140] Although the Council of Ministers agreed to maintain the quotas pending the development of Eurofer's plan, Eurofer proved incapable of reaching a consensus among its members on capacity cuts of the magnitude required.[141] In the wake of this failure, production quotas were eliminated on galvanized sheets, but, notwithstanding the Commission's stated intention in 1986, were retained on HR and CR sheet, plate, heavy sections, wire rods, and merchant bars (table 3-9).[142] The failure of the Eurofer restructuring scheme was not altogether unwelcome because it gave

member states a convenient excuse to defer politically uncomfortable decisions about whether or not to change the quota system that supports prices and helps to keep inefficient steel companies alive.[143]

In July 1987, the Commission unveiled a new capacity reduction proposal. Acknowledging that firms lacked adequate financial incentives for closures, the Commission proposed to impose a levy on steel products which were produced under the quota arrangements (HR coil, sheet, structurals and plate) which would be used to create a fund to pay producers for "the irrevocable and permanent closure" of hot-rolling capacities in several categories. The Commission left open the possibility that the quota system could be extended beyond 1988, but warned that it would terminate the system on August 1, 1988

---

[138] *Metal Bulletin* (June 27, 1986).

[139] *Metal Bulletin* (September 23, 1986).

[140] *Metal Bulletin* (October 23, 1986).

[141] The producers proposed 15.3 million tons of cuts, but the Commission sought cuts totaling 24.2 million tons. The shortfall was greatest in flat-rolled products, which embraced some of the largest mills in Europe. Because of the scale of closures which had already been undertaken, "the struggle to avoid the chopping block this time round [was] fierce." *Financial Times* (March 17, 1987); *European Report*, No. 1300 (March 21, 1987).

[142] *Bull. EC* 5-1987, Point 2.1.30.

[143] *Financial Times* (June 8, 1987).

Table 3-9. European Commission Mandatory Production Quotas for Community Steel Producers, 1984-87 (million metric tons)

Category	Item	1984		1985				1986				1987			
		3	4	1	2	3	4	1	2	3	4	1	2	3	4
Ia	HR coil	5.2	5.7	5.7	5.8	4.1	4.1	3.8	4.1	3.8	3.5	3.5	3.8	3.8	4.1
Ib	CR Sheet	3.6	3.8	3.9	4.0	3.4	3.3	3.3	3.6	2.9	2.9	3.1	3.4	3.2	3.3
Ic	Galvanized Sheet	0.9	1.0	0.9	1.0	0.9	0.9	0.9	0.9	0.8	0.8	-	-	-	-
Id	Other coated Sheet	0.7	0.9	0.9	0.9	0.8	0.8	-	-	-	-	-	-	-	-
II	Quarto Plate	1.3	1.4	1.4	1.4	1.3	1.3	1.3	1.4	1.1	1.3	1.2	1.2	1.1	1.3
III	Heavy Sections (Structurals)	1.1	1.1	1.2	1.2	1.1	1.1	1.1	1.3	1.0	0.9	1.0	1.1	1.1	1.2
IV	Wire rod	2.7	2.8	3.0	2.9	2.6	2.6	2.5	2.2	2.2	2.3	2.3	1.3	2.1	2.3
V	Reinforcing Bar	1.8	1.9	1.9	2.0	1.7	1.9	-	-	-	-	-	-	-	-
VI	Merchant bar	2.2	2.4	2.5	2.4	2.2	2.1	2.1	2.2	2.1	2.1	1.8	1.7	1.7	1.9

Source: EC Commission, Forward Programme For Steel, various issues.

Notes: Some quotas were adjusted subsequent to publication by the Commission. All quotas rounded to nearest hundred thousand tons.

if the commitments to closures proved inadequate.[144]   Narjes' proposal succeeded in achieving a rare consensus within the Community, if only in opposition to it.[145]

The Council of Ministers reviewed the Commission's proposals in September 1987. While agreeing on a need to link the extension of the quota regime to cuts in capacity, they deferred a decision on quota extension until December, asking the Commission to appoint a panel of "Three Wise Men" to advise the Commission and the Council on how to secure commitments from the steel firms on closures, "under the hypothesis of continuing for a limited period a quota system and the creation of appropriate financial incentives."[146]   Pursuant to this "latest exercise in passing the buck",[147] the Three Wise Men conducted their investigation between October 10 and November 15, 1987. As the Commission reported,

It emerged that the industry was not in a position to contemplate satisfactory restructuring arrangements or to give undertakings in this connection. Furthermore, the possible arrangements proved to be to a large extent independent of the continuation of the quota system.[148]

The Wise Men's Report was a scathing indictment of the state of the Community steel industry. The Wise Men noted the distortions which years of subsidies had caused in the Community market, and the general unwillingness of the industry to make commitments to capacity reduction. They condemned in particular the system of production quotas, which "protected" the Community's steel industry:

While they do not actually prevent rationalization from taking place, they go too far in softening the financial and commercial pressures to act quickly in order to adapt to the foreseeable market situation. . . . It is obvious that, having been protected by a quota system for seven years, and having become accustomed to the system being extended,

---

[144] EC Commission, Communication from the Commission to the Council, *Steel Policy*, COM (87) 388 final/2, September 11, 1987.

[145] *European Report* No. 1319 (June 6, 1987). The German producers attacked the proposed linkage of the quota systems to restructuring; the Commission's proposal favored firms that had delayed making the necessary cutbacks; these companies would get the closure aid which other firms would be required to finance. Virtually all other interested parties found fault with the proposal. *Metal Bulletin* (July 27, 30, August 6, September 21, 1987).

[146] *Metal Bulletin* (September 24, 1987).

[147] *Financial Times* (November 25, 1987).

[148] *EC Commission, Communication from the Commission to the Council Amending COM (87) 388 Final/2 of 17 September 1987*, COM (87) 640 final, November 26, 1987.

the companies are not prepared to give adequate undertakings
regarding closures in order to justify extending the system.[149]

The Wise Men concluded that the entire system should be scrapped through
progressive increases and eventual elimination of production quotas.

Pressure from the Member States for retention of the quota system,
however, was too great. At the end of December 1987, the Council of
Ministers agreed on an extension of the quota regime for six months in four
product categories, Ia and b (hot coil and CR sheet), II (heavy plate) and III
(heavy sections).[150] The Member States agreed to transmit to the Commission
firm restructuring commitments for 7.5 million metric tons of hot strip
capacity, and for 75 percent of the overcapacity in categories II and III. The
quotas were to be raised by 2 percent in the second quarter of 1988. The
"reference production threshold" below which small steelmakers are excluded
from the quota system was raised from 36 thousand tons to 200 thousand tons.
In addition, the Commission established safeguards to induce firms which had
received debt annulment through bankruptcy but which continued producing
to undertake restructuring measures.[151]

Table 3-10: EC Surplus Capacity in 1987
(million metric tons)

Product Area	Utilization Rate In 1986	1986 Capacity Surplus (per EC Commission)	Proposed Cuts
HR Coil	71.5%	7.6	3.725
Plate	57.0	4.1	2.700
Beams	60.0	3.0	.870
Light Sections	60.0	6.7	3.030
Wire rod	65.0	2.9	3.885
CR Sheet	63.0	9.2	1.050

Source: *European Report* No. 1298, March 18, 1987

---

[149] *Wise Men's Report*, p. 6.

[150] *Official Journal*, L. 25 (January 29, 1988).

[151] *European Report* No. 1370 (January 9, 1988).

Finally, in mid-1988, the quota regime was ended. The Commission gave the industry a deadline of June 10 to propose additional capacity cuts as a condition for extending the quotas; when this requirement was not satisfied, the Commission announced that it would end the quota regime effective July 1. This time the Council of Ministers backed the Commission, and the mandatory production quota system which had been in force since 1980 terminated on July 1. The buoyant steel market was instrumental to the decision -- Narjes indicated that in light of increased production levels, it was no longer possible to point to a "manifest crisis" in steel justifying the use of quotas pursuant to Article 58. Narjes emphasized, however, that the Commission would "continue to protect the steel industry against unfair competition from third countries."[152]

It was not immediately clear what sort of market regime would follow the elimination of the mandatory quotas. The producers of flat-rolled products were discussing a return to the "voluntary" arrangements of the 1977-80 period, when the Commission set production targets and "guidance" prices to induce market discipline by the producers.[153] However the Commission rejected any return to voluntary controls.[154] Another possibility was that the producers would seek to regulate production and pricing informally themselves without any sanction from the Commission, in effect resurrecting the old producers' "Club" of the pre-1975 era. However, such actions would contravene Article 65 of the ECSC Treaty; while the Commission took a benign view of such activity in the past, it is unclear that it would do so this time. Moreover, the producers' "Club" did not prevent a collapse of price discipline in 1975 and it is unlikely that an informal producers' group would suffice in any sharp market downturn. A third possibility was that the elimination of quotas would be followed by a period of severe price competition, with the weaker producers (and perhaps some of the stronger ones) receiving clandestine subsidies to ensure their survival.

External Relations, 1978-88

Given the Community's sheer size, in terms of steel consumption and production,[155] and the volume of its trade, it was inevitable that the dramatic market interventions undertaken by the Commission and by the governments of the Member States since the onset of the structural crisis would have a pronounced impact on the world steel market. Import restrictions imposed

---

[152] EC Commission, *European Community News* (June 29, 1988).

[153] *Metal Bulletin* (May 2, 1988) The flat-rolled producers were "habitues of voluntary discipline under the Eurofer arrangements, and could be expected to operate a Commission-led voluntary delivery system effectively."

[154] *Financial Times* (June 26, 1988).

[155] The Community accounts for 5.8% of the world's steel imports and 24.1% of its exports (table 2-8).

by the Commission since 1978 have limited access to the western world's second largest steel market, and the Commission's and the Member States' steel policies have forced large quantities of low-priced European steel onto the export market.

Import Restrictions. The Community established a comprehensive system of import restrictions in 1978 which has been maintained through 1988. This system has consistently held import penetration of the Community market to a level of about 10 to 12 percent of consumption during a period when substantial additional capacity was being added abroad and the international market was frequently glutted with cheap steel:

> *A happy island has been created in the EC, in which prices are kept artificially high, while all around bitter competition has been unleashed among the world's producers. . . .*[156]

Given the state of overcapacity and depressed demand which characterized the world steel market after 1975, the Community's implementation of import restrictions in 1978 had a "preemptive effect" on import growth[157] and increased import pressure on more open markets thereafter as Community suppliers sought other export outlets.[158]

Prior to the structural crisis the Commission did not administer a comprehensive system of import protection in steel, although a variety of protective policies were in existence at the beginning of the crisis. A common Community system of import quotas had been in effect since 1963 with respect to the state trading countries, coupled with a ban on alignment on import prices from these countries. This lapsed after 1973, but five individual Member States maintained their own national quantitative restrictions on imports from those countries.[159] Japanese exports to the Community were limited by agreement to 1,150,000 metric tons after 1971.[160] The European national cartels were able to restrict imports to some extent by threatening customers with a cutoff of their main source of supply if they bought imported

---

[156] *L'Espresso* (June 11, 1978).

[157] See also Geoffrey Shepherd, "Japanese Exports and Europe's Problem Industries" in Laukas Tsoukalis and Maureen White, *Japan and Western Europe* (New York; St. Martin's Press 1982), p. 132.

[158] Following the Community's conclusion of a voluntary restraint arrangement with South Africa in 1977, for example, South African producers concluded that "alternative markets had . . . to be found in a hurry," and shortly thereafter, the U.S. market experienced a massive surge of steel imports from South Africa, which shot up from 21 thousand tons in 1976 to 463 thousand in 1978. *The Star* (Johannesburg) (February 14, 1977); *Financial Mail* (July 29, 1977).

[159] EC Commission, *General Objectives Steel 1980 to 1985, Official Journal*, C. 232 (October 4, 1976).

[160] Japan Iron and Steel Federation, *Japan's Iron and Steel Industry 1972*, p. 37.

steel.[161] Antidumping and countervailing duty actions could be brought against dumped or subsidized imports in particular product areas.

This loose aggregation of formal and informal measures and practices, however, proved inadequate to prevent a surge of imported steel into the Community market after the onset of the structural crisis. Penetration rates increased from 6.0 percent in 1974 to 11.3 percent in 1977.[162] The Commission's subsequent efforts to establish controls on internal competition would clearly have failed had this influx not been stemmed; it was self-evident that "crisis measures" which sought to stabilize prices through collective restraints on production volume could be fatally compromised by an unregulated flow of imports. The initial difficulties experienced by the European authorities in stabilizing internal prices in 1976-77 were substantially attributable to the lack of effective control mechanism for imports.[163] Simonet had rejected import restraints.[164] The Davignon Plan established a surveillance system designed to monitor the prices of third country imports, pursuant to which antidumping measures would be triggered in appropriate cases, but these measures soon proved inadequate, and their failure threatened to undermine the Davignon Plan.[165]

The Voluntary Restraint Agreements. In December 1977 the Commission developed a far more comprehensive and stringent system of import control measures. Most importantly, a decision was made to conclude, on an expedited basis, "bilateral arrangements with some twenty countries which will give the Community steel market the respite it needs to reorganize. . . ."[166] In 1978 the European authorities negotiated a series of restrictive bilateral

---

[161] Activities of one such group, the so-called "Tin Plate Club," are noted in Craig R. MacPhee, *Nontariff Barriers to International Trade in Steel* (Ann Arbor: University of Michigan, 1970), p. 243.

[162] Eurostat.

[163] The import influx consisted largely of Japanese steel which the Europeans charged was dumped, reflecting the breakdown of a Community-Japan agreement. *Handelsblatt* reported on October 29/30, 1976 that "The EC steel industry is all the more aggrieved about the new Japanese export offensive as, following an agreement with the Japanese at the onset of the steel crisis at the end of 1974 and early 1975, the Japanese were ceded markets in third countries in the expectation that they would then 'as little as possible' disrupt the EC market. This little-publicized agreement worked reasonably well until sometime in the first half of 1976. Since then, however, in the words of a German steel boss, 'those guys are suddenly back again.'"

[164] *Metal Bulletin* (October 21, 1977).

[165] *Metal Bulletin* (October 21, 1977). This system required licensing of all imported steel. While import licenses were granted virtually automatically, prices were noted in the license – affording a means of monitoring import price levels. The authorities recommended to the Member States a series of information and consultation procedures designed to ensure a quick response to dumping, and accelerated antidumping procedures were established. *Official Journal* L. 114 (May 5, 1977); *Bull. EC* 4-1977, point 2.1.15.

[166] Davignon in *Bull. EC* 1-1978, point 2.2.32.

agreements with most of the principal exporters to the ECSC market.[167] These "contractual" arrangements fixed quantitative limits on the volume of steel to be shipped to the European market by each bilateral partner. The basic principle of the agreements was to allow the signatory to maintain its "traditional" trade (*e.g.*, market share) in the Community, in return for a pledge to respect volume and price restraints.[168] Community producers were prohibited from matching prices of imported steel from nations with which bilateral restraint agreements had been concluded, a measure designed to prevent low-priced imports from triggering a defensive chain reaction of discounting by European producers.[169] An interim protective system of minimum "trigger" prices was implemented pending negotiation of the bilateral agreements; thereafter these measures remained in effect for those nations with which agreements were not concluded.[170]

Almost immediately upon negotiation of the agreements in 1978, the success of the new policy was apparent.[171] Jacques Ferry, President of Eurofer and a critic of prior import policies, stated in August 1978 that the

> *Davignon Plan ... has permitted a certain increase in steel price levels inside the EC and a degree of restraint of exports from third countries. [The system of agreements] seems to be coming into force in a satisfactory manner.*[172]

---

[167] Austria, Finland, Norway, Sweden, Portugal, Spain, Australia, Hungary, Poland, Romania, Czechoslovakia, South Korea, and South Africa. "Special arrangements" were concluded with Japan and Switzerland.

[168] Third countries were offered a series of inducements for entering into the agreements, which include non-application of base price rules, renunciation by the EC of antidumping action, and a "penetration margin" on delivered prices (3 percent for EFTA nations, and 4 and 6 percent for specialty and ordinary steel from other nations, respectively). The trading partner offered the Community "respect for traditional trade flows, taking account of the development of the market." EC Commission, *Summary of Arrangements for Iron and Steel Products* (Brussels, April 5, 1983); EC Commission, Communication from the Commission to the Council, *Concerning the Negotiation of Arrangements on Community Steel Imports for 1986*, COM (85) 535 final, October 14, 1985, pp. 3-4. The "penetration margin" was phased out for EFTA producers in 1986. *Metal Bulletin* (April 22, 1986).

[169] *Bull. EC* 1-1978, point 2.2.35; Commission Decision No. 527 of 1978; *Official Journal*, L. 73/16, 1978 amending *Official Journal*, L. 95, 1982.

[170] Trigger prices were fixed for the Community market reflecting "lowest production costs in third countries in which normal conditions of competition existed." Import prices were required to be stated on import licenses. In appropriate cases involving a disparity between actual prices and trigger prices, antidumping and countervailing duties could be imposed. Heusdens and de Horn, "Crisis Policy," p. 57.

[171] Countries which had concluded agreements were, on the whole, adhering to them, and other nations indicated a willingness to enter into similar agreements. *Metal Bulletin* (September 26, 1978).

[172] *Metal Bulletin* (August 1, 1978).

The system implemented in 1978 has continued in operation, with some modifications, through 1988. The bilateral agreements, which are renegotiated annually, require exporting nations to distribute their exports regionally within the Community according to "traditional patterns of trade."[173] The agreements contain a so-called "triple clause" which states that imports should be spread out over the year, throughout the Community and across the product range.[174] Exporting countries which have not negotiated agreements with the Community are expected to observe minimum import prices fixed by the Commission.[175] The arrangements with the EFTA countries do not contain explicit references to quantities, merely providing that exporters would observe "traditional trade flows" and that the Commission could call for "speedy" consultations in the event that these patterns are not observed.[176] The "special understanding" with Japan involves a commitment by Japan to respect EC price rules and not to overstep its "traditional pattern of trade" [e.g., market share] with the EC.[177]

The Community's system of import restrictions is regarded by the Commission as a success.[178] Individual Member States have sometimes taken a less sanguine view,[179] but in fact, the Community's import volume has been substantially reduced by implementation of this system -- imports originating in countries with which an arrangement had been made reached 9.3 million

---

[173] Communication from the Commission to the Council, *Concerning the Negotiation of Arrangements*, October 14, 1985.

[174] *Ibid.*; *Metal Bulletin* (December 17, 1985).

[175] These are "trigger prices" based on the Commission's calculation of the production costs of the world's most efficient producers.

[176] The Free Trade Agreements between the Community and the EFTA countries prohibited quantitative restrictions on trade. This requirement was circumvented by the use of vague language in the agreements alluding to traditional trade flows, coupled with a clear expression by the Commission of its expectations with respect to these countries. EC Commission, Communication to the Council, *External Commercial Policy* in the Steel Sector, COM (86) 585 final, November 13, 1986, pp. 24-25.

[177] *Metal Bulletin* (March 4, 1986).

[178] EC Commission, *External Commercial Policy*, November 13, 1986.

[179] Several weaknesses in the system became apparent over time. When ECSC demand fell in 1982, import quotas based on a fixed volume of steel allowed importing nations to expand their proportionate share of the Community market. As a result, under pressure from the steelmakers, the Commission negotiated new agreements in 1983 reducing many nations' quotas, usually by 12.5 percent. In addition, low-priced imports from nations not covered by agreements have continued to cause intermittent problems, despite the fact that such imports are subject to floor prices. Finally, import pressure has affected members unevenly, despite the so-called "triple clause" in the bilaterals which requires third countries to spread their imports regionally and stagger them over time. *Europe* No. 3709 (New Series) (October 14, 1983); *Metal Bulletin* (August 6, October 29, November 5, 23, 26, 30, 1982; February 11, September 2, 1983).

tons in 1977, but fell to an average of 6.8 million tons in the 1983-85 period.[180] All parties have agreed that the success of the import controls is essential to the continued functioning of the Community cartel.[181]

Developments Since 1986. The strengthening of various European currencies against the dollar produced an increase in imports in 1986, leading to calls from Eurofer to tighten existing Community import restrictions,[182] and the Commission took steps in 1987 to strengthen them. Demands by Brazil and South Korea for an increase in their quotas were rejected; Brazilian threats of retaliation did not materialize.[183] Venezuela was brought into the agreements system with the negotiation of a restraint arrangement in 1987.[184]

Maintaining the system of import restrictions has entailed a substantial degree of friction with the Community's trading partners. The accession of Spain and Portugal to the Community, for example, caused a series of acrimonious disputes when the restraint agreements were renegotiated in 1986; the Commission proposed to allow exporting countries an increase in their volume to the ECSC based on their export volume to Spain and Portugal in 1983-84, a period which exporters like Japan and Brazil argued was "not representative."[185] The Commission permitted a 3 percent increase in import quotas for the Community as a whole in 1986, but exporters charged that this did not fully reflect actual growth in demand in the Community market.[186] Nevertheless, the Community has held the trump card in its negotiations --

---

[180] EC Commission, *External Commercial Policy*, November 13, 1986, p. 8.

[181] In late 1983 the Commission observed that "Effective application of the internal element of the steel plan presupposed that the external element remains in force. . . . [Council deliberations] recognized the need to maintain the internal element of the anti-crisis measures until the end of 1985; at this point a need also exists, therefore, to maintain for the year 1984 the outward defense (external element) which guarantees the proper operation of the internal element." Commission Communication to the Council "Steel: External Measures, 1984," COM (83) 589 final, (October 10, 1983). See also *European Report* No. 986, October 12, 1983; *Metal Bulletin* (November 26, 1985).

[182] *Metal Bulletin* (June 6, July 1, 1986). Eurofer sought restraint agreements with additional exporting countries, including Algeria, Yugoslavia, Mexico and Argentina.

[183] *Metal Bulletin* (April 10, 1987).

[184] *Ibid.*

[185] *Metal Bulletin* (January 14, 1986).

[186] *Metal Bulletin* (February 4, 1986).

access to its market -- and the exporting nations have generally felt compelled, after a period of protest, to accede to the terms offered by the Commission.[187]

Exports. The Community's steel production capacity exceeded internal consumption by an increasingly wide margin in the years after 1975. The capacity overhang exerted an enormous downward pressure on prices in the Community market and continually threatened to force producers to operate at uneconomically low rates. Exports were a natural outlet for the internal pressures engendered by the Community's capacity surplus, enabling the Community mills to operate at higher utilization rates, facilitating efforts to stabilize internal prices (by removing surplus inventories from the Community), and permitting the Member States to avoid, or at least delay, confrontation of the political and social problems entailed by capacity reduction.

Because of the sheer size of the Community's capacity surplus, however, European export volume during the structural crisis has been massive, and these exports have been made in a depressed international market in which many established and emerging steel exporting nations have also been seeking to expand their export presence. Community steel exports were generally made at prices below those prevailing within the Community and below the average cost of production of Community producers.[188] Community exports to the U.S. precipitated a bitter and protracted series of transatlantic trade disputes.[189] Traditionally, it is not unusual for steel producers to seek export outlets to compensate for a drop in domestic orders, and such exports are often made at prices lower than those prevailing on the domestic market, that is, dumped. Historically, the European mills have been no exception to this

---

[187] The Commission frequently offers an agreement as an alternative to the institution of antidumping agreements against the exporter; this prospect enabled the Community to secure a new restraint arrangement with Venezuela in 1987. *Metal Bulletin* (April 10, 1987.) A Brazilian negotiator commented in 1986, after Brazil accepted terms which it had protested, that "This seemed to be the most the Commission would offer us, so we decided to sign the agreement as this is the surest way of being able to continue to export at good prices without having antidumping suits taken out against us." *Metal Bulletin* (March 4, 1986).

[188] The Commission stated in 1985 that in Community export markets, "steel is sold at marginal prices for a large number of steel undertakings. . . . In fact, *export prices in general only cover marginal costs*, and too high a differentiation between internal and external prices would come to subsidizing sales to third countries by Community consumers." (original emphasis) *General Objectives Steel 1990*, July 31, 1985, p. II.5.

[189] See chapter 7.

pattern.[190]   Similarly, for many years state-subsidized firms (including European mills) have exported steel and gained a pricing advantage as a result of state aid. Recognizing the potential for international conflict inherent in such trading practices, international agreements have defined permissible administrative measures which can be taken to counter dumped or subsidized exports which cause injury to a domestic industry. These are the imposition of antidumping and countervailing duties.[191]

The structural crisis in steel, however, gave rise to trade conflicts which threatened simply to overwhelm these mechanisms. The volume of European subsidies to national producers was enormous; the economic pressure on the Community mills to export was intense, particularly after the establishment of Community-wide production restraints; and the volume of trade involved was massive. The application of trade remedies by the U.S. government against the Community mills under such circumstances might well have resulted in the virtual exclusion of European steel from the U.S. market, which could have had severe economic effects in Europe and, in the view of some observers, created cracks in the Atlantic alliance.

Most analyses of the transatlantic steel dispute have focused on the measures taken by the United States government to restrict European steel access to the U.S. market and the political environment in which those measures were implemented.[192]   But the U.S. measures were a secondary rather than a primary element of the dispute.   U.S. trade policy is fundamentally reactive, and in the transatlantic steel dispute, U.S. policy measures were a response to economic distortions which had occurred in the Community and which were attributable to the industrial policies of the Commission and the individual Member States, that is, national subsidies and the Commission's crisis measures.

---

[190] See Stegemann, *Price Competition and Output Adjustment,* pp. 204-206. Sacilor explained in its 1977 *Annual Report* (Appendix II, p. 5), "The prolongation of such a poor market could not fail to cause a new drop in the prices of steel products on the markets outside the EEC, where each producer tried to provide himself with the full complement of transactions necessary to avoid having to suffer new declines in activity. . . ." Arbed noted in its 1977 *Annual Report* (p. 17) that "Along with other European steelmakers, Arbed had to make up for this sharp contraction [of Community steel demand] by stepping up its exports, which in general are less remunerative."

[191] The General Agreement on Tariffs and Trade (GATT) authorizes contracting parties to impose antidumping and contervailing duties to offset the price effects of dumped and subsidized imports (Articles VI, XVI and XXIII). These rules have been refined in GATT Codes interpreting the GATT provisions on subsidies and dumping. A number of contracting parties to the GATT, including the EC and the U.S., administer systems providing for antidumping and countervailing duties consistent with the GATT rules.

[192] These measures are described in chapter 7. See generally Hues van der Ven and Thomas Grunert, "The Politics of Transatlantic Steel Trade" in Meny and Wright, (1987); Michael Borrus, "The Politics of Competitive Erosion in the U.S. Steel Industry," in *American Industry in International Competition,* ed. John Zysman and Laura Tyson (Ithaca: Cornell University Press, 1983).

Subsidies and Exports. The application by the United States of its countervailing duty law to EC steel exports in 1982 threw into sharp relief the issue of the impact of European steel subsidies on international steel competition. The Community reacted with anger and dismay at the notion that the U.S. might offset EC steel subsidies with *ad valorem* countervailing duties. The basic EC argument was that all EC state aids were granted only to finance restructuring, not to subsidize commercial operations; that a condition of the Commission's approval of subsidies was that they be accompanied by a reduction in steel capacity; and that such aid measures should not be countervailable.[193] The U.S. Department of Commerce took the position that the motives underlying a government's grant of a subsidy were not relevant, provided that the subsidy conferred a benefit on the recipient.[194]

The Commission's own treatment of the state aids issue within the Community raises questions about the positions which it took on the issue in the transatlantic trade dispute. The Commission's 1986 report on state aids indicated that between 1980 and 1985, it had approved a total of $35.6 billion in subsidies by Member State governments to the steel industry, of which $21.8 billion, or well over half, was in fact subsidies for continued operations.[195] Within the Community, the Commission closely monitored the disbursement of such operating subsidies, precisely because it recognized that they were sometimes used "to finance disruptive price cuttings."[196]

While a substantial proportion of the total Community steel subsidies was allotted to "restructuring" or awarded under the rubric of "regional aids," this distinction is not particularly significant from the standpoint of international competition. Government funds applied to restructuring, investment, or indeed against any other expense, ultimately free up company resources for other uses. In extreme cases, Community mills reportedly diverted restructuring aid to subsidize operating losses.[197] Even where this did not occur, various forms of restructuring, regional, transport and labor aid schemes ultimately resulted in cost reductions for European mills; a 1985

---

[193] See *Metal Bulletin Monthly* (January 1986); Van der Ven and Grunert (1987), p. 160; Mary Francis Dominick, "Countervailing State Aids: A Case for International Consensus," in 21 *Common Market Law Review* 355 (June 1984).

[194] *Certain Steel Products from the United Kingdom*, 47 F.R. 39384, September 7, 1982 (final).

[195] EC Commission, *Report*, August 6, 1986.

[196] EC Commission, *Fourth Report on the Application of the Rules for Aids to the Steel Industry*, COM (83) 178 final, April 1983.

[197] *Metal Bulletin* (September 10, 1982). The fact that restructuring aid was linked to capacity reduction commitments is not particularly significant from a competitive standpoint. As the German producers pointed out, there was no formula linking a particular volume of subsidies to a fixed level of capacity reduction, so that as in the case of Italy, a huge volume of subsidies might be approved in return for a relatively small level of closures. More fundamentally, such aid conferred cost savings on the recipient which could be translated into aggressive international pricing, irrespective of whether net capacity was or was not reduced.

study prepared for the British government concluded that such aid conferred benefits to steel producers which could be quantified on a cost-savings-per-ton basis.[198] For this reason the Community Member States have carefully monitored their neighbors' aid programs with deep suspicion.

The impact of subsidies on the Community's export markets has been similar to their effect within the Community itself, where aggressive pricing by the subsidized firms threw the private sector into crisis. Heavily subsidized firms like British Steel, Usinor and Sacilor could export at a loss to the United States more or less indefinitely, and appear to have done so.[199] Without a continued flow of subsidies, this situation would have been quickly self-correcting; the weakest firms would have contracted substantially or collapsed altogether as their losses mounted.[200] With state aid, however, many European mills could be extraordinarily price competitive, and made major inroads in export markets. While the subsidies themselves were often justified as a way of maintaining employment, they gave rise to charges that the Community was "exporting unemployment" as its subsidized exports forced privately-owned mills abroad to retrench.[201]

The Impact of Market Controls. The cartelization of the Community market under the aegis of the Commission appears to have had the effect of stimulating low-priced (and often dumped) exports. That fact should not be particularly surprising; the old national cartels in the Community had fostered dumping in export markets as a convenient way to dispose of surpluses that might otherwise have jeopardized efforts to maintain a stable price floor,[202] and the Community producers tended to regard the world market "as a

---

[198] Environmental Resources Ltd., *Indirect State Aids and Their Impact on the EEC Steel Industry* (London: Environmental Resources, Ltd., September 1985).

[199] PaineWebber estimated in 1984 that the steel producers of France and Great Britain suffered a pretax loss on every ton of steel shipped to the U.S. between 1976 and 1983; the average per ton loss was calculated at $67.38 and $70.24 for France and Britain, respectively. PaineWebber, *World Steel Dynamics* (February 1984).

[200] A staff member of the U.S. International Trade Commission observed in 1980 that European government financial aid enabled "those steel industries to sell steel at less than the cost of production over the long run. . . . Many steel operations in Europe would close today if they had to sell at cost." U.S. International Trade Commission Investigation No. 731-TA-18/24 (1980), hearing transcript at pp. 42-43.

[201] The Belgian producer Cockerill noted in its *Annual Report* for 1977 how it had responded: "The regression of the volume of orders originating from the EEC has brought Cockerill in 1977 to increase its effort of marketing towards more distant countries. On various occasions, the desire to maintain a reasonable level of activity in its plants has compelled Cockerill to accept orders, called in the language of the profession 'social tons,' whose price does not cover the fixed production expenses."

[202] See Roper, *Rationalisierungseffekte*, pp. 20, 109.

marginal outlet mopping up shortfalls in internal demand."[203] As it struggled to establish a Community floor price and to enforce production quotas, the Commission encouraged European mills to find outlets for their excess production outside of the Community. The quota system was designed to permit increases in production quotas to the extent that a firm could demonstrate that the extra production was for export rather than for sale within the Community.[204] As the U.S. Mission to the European Communities expressed the problem in 1977:

> *Voluntary restrictions on domestic deliveries, combined with "reasonable" behavior by importers, may lead to diminished supply, and, therefore, to artificially increased prices in the EC domestic market as compared to the world market. This in turn creates the danger that there will be dumping of steel produced for export or diverted to export markets by the restrictions of domestic deliveries.*[205]

The relationship between the restraint of price competition within the Community and the export patterns of the European mills is illustrated by the interplay between the Community's efforts to stabilize its internal prices and its external trade relations with the United States prior to the establishment of the U.S.-EC voluntary restraint arrangement in 1982. Periods during which the Community managed to maintain an internal price floor through output restraints were characterized by surges of low-priced ECSC exports to the United States.[206] Conversely, when steps were taken in the United States to restrict Community exports to the U.S. the result was the weakening or even collapse of the Community's own internal price floor, a phenomenon which suggests that the Community's internal market control efforts, when successful, enabled the Community to shift surplus production (and the "collapse of prices") into export markets.

The Bresciani offered one of the first examples of this dynamic. In 1977, price-cutting by the Bresciani was threatening to undercut the price floor established in the Davignon Plan. Davignon urged the Bresciani to seek

---

[203] EC Commission, *General Objectives Steel 1985*, p. 27.

[204] The quota system permits an increase in a firm's quota allotment if export orders are secured. Firms must demonstrate evidence of export or their production will be deemed to have been sold within the ECSC. See Commission Decision No. 2177/83 of July 23, 1983, *Official Journal*, L. 208/3, Section 12 and Article II(6). Thus in the spring of 1984 Davignon indicated he would allocate additional quota shares to Italy if that country could demonstrate export orders secured from the Soviet Union. *Europe* No. 3777 (New Series) (January 28, 1984).

[205] Aide Mémoire of the U.S. Mission to the European Communities, January 14, 1977.

[206] While in 1981-82 this was partially attributable to the appreciation of the dollar against European currencies, such surges have also occurred when the dollar was comparatively weak, *e.g.*, in late 1979 and early 1980.

outlets for their products outside the Community, and, internally, to agree to
observe quotas and price minima for shipments to Member States. Davignon
suggested that export orders "entailing losses" might be shifted from other
Community producers to the Bresciani to assist this process,[207] and in 1979 a
French delegate to the European Parliament commented that "the Bresciani
are no longer a threat to the European market because they have found other
outlets in third countries."[208] In early 1980, Bresciani exports to the U.S.
dropped sharply following the filing of trade complaints by U.S. producers, a
fact which was blamed for a surge of low-priced internal Community
shipments by the Bresciani, "who have been absent from this market for quite
a while" and were "moving back into the Southern German and French
markets in force, which is causing prices to tumble swiftly."[209] In effect, when
the Bresciani's export outlet was reduced, the result was immediate disruption
of price discipline in the Community.

Exports to the U.S. In late 1979, during a period when prices were fairly
firm within the EC -- and when the dollar was comparatively weak -- large
quantities of low-priced Community steel were being exported to the United
States, much of it dumped or subsidized.[210] These exports were alleviating a
substantial amount of the pressure placed on the Community internal market
by the ECSC's surplus capacity.[211] In March 1980, however, U.S. Steel filed
antidumping actions against Community producers,[212] and within months the
Community price floor collapsed, a fact which was widely attributed to the

---

[207] *Metal Bulletin* (October 14 and 28, 1977).

[208] *Debates of the European Parliament*, April 25, 1979, p. 107.

[209] *Metal Bulletin* (April 3, June 13, 1980).

[210] At that time the *Financial Times* estimated that if U.S. producers made full use of the
antidumping and countervailing duty laws, "According to European experts, as much as 3 million
tons of EC steel products would be barred from the U.S. . . ." *Financial Times* (December 6,
1979).

[211] Davignon told the European Parliament in mid-1980 that "Here and now, I pledge my
word to Parliament that I will try to do everything -- and of course in the negotiations I will not
adopt a position on any particular formula -- to arrive at arrangements which will preserve our
industry's exporting capacity to the United States, which is one of the indispensable factors in
maintaining and restructuring [the Community steel] industry." *Debates of the European
Parliament*, July 10, 1980, p. 265.

[212] U.S. Steel filed against all major Community producers, and the U.S. International Trade
Commission made a preliminary finding that European sales at less than fair value had injured
the U.S. industry. 45 F.R. 20, 150 (1980).

diversion of steel intended for the American market back into the Community market.[213] Sacilor noted in its 1980 *Annual Report*:

> *The antidumping suit filed by U.S. Steel, by the threat it posed during long months to importers had the effect of partly closing the American market to European exporters. It resulted in a very great excess of supply over demand on the market in the EC, which led small mills and certain large ones into a price war and caused, in June/July, the collapse of the Eurofer agreements.[214]*

However, following the imposition of mandatory quotas and other tighter controls in October 1980, the Community steel industry was able to implement a series of internal price increases.[215] Throughout 1981 and early 1982, despite falling demand, a progression of increasingly tight output restrictions enabled the steelmakers to force internal prices to levels high enough to provoke a widespread outcry from consumers.[216] During this period Belgian Minister of Economic Affairs Mark Eyskens commented on the importance of the U.S. market as an outlet which absorbed seven percent of the total output of the troubled, heavily-subsidized Belgian firm Cockerill-Sambre:

> *If the United States settles into protectionism and closes its borders to European steel, the European production will have to be sold elsewhere, that is to say on the European market. . . . The induced effects scare me.[217]*

During the same period that the cartel was enabling the EC mills to raise internal prices, Community export prices were falling, and beginning in mid-

---

[213] *Metal Bulletin* reported on April 3, 1980 that Belgian firms, among others, were responsible for falling prices in Germany: "One Belgian group is understood to be refusing new U.S. orders until the present uncertainty is cleared up. This has directed larger tonnages toward West Germany. . . . Stocks are building up (causing additional problems for business which already has high interest rates to cope with) and with prices falling there is a rush to sell."

[214] Sacilor, *Annual Report* (1980),p. 7. The fall in demand from some industrial sectors, such as autos, also contributed to the surplus, but Sacilor's perspective is instructive, p.7.

[215] When the Community adopted mandatory quotas, concern was expressed in the OECD that the measures might induce "an artificially high level of exports to the USA or other countries." *Metal Bulletin* (November 4, 1980).

[216] *Metal Bulletin* (February 3, July 17, July 31, September 19, October 2, October 30, November 27, 1981); Part III.E. *infra*.

[217] *Le Soir* (January 15, 1981).

1981, a surge in Community exports to the U.S. developed.[218] By October, the U.S. market was experiencing a major influx of European steel, much of it sold far below trigger price levels; in November 1981, Davignon was reportedly

> *distinctly displeased with the [European] mills at present . . . for having provoked U.S. antidumping action by supposedly reckless export tactics.*[219]

During the same period European export price-cutting was also affecting Canada -- in January 1982 Canadian steelmakers filed suits alleging dumping by West Germany, Luxembourg, and Britain.[220]

In November 1981, U.S. Government fired a "warning salvo" of antidumping actions against France and Belgium; these were followed by an extensive filing of private antidumping and countervailing duty actions against the Community nations in January 1982. The prospect that U.S. trade sanctions might result in a "floor" on EC export prices to the U.S. posed an immediate threat to the Community's own internal price floor. *Metal Bulletin* observed on January 19, 1982 that "the remarkable discipline displayed by most EC mills in the past few months will clearly come under enormous pressure. . . ."[221] In June and August 1982 the U.S. imposed sanctions on a wide range of steel products from the Community designed to offset margins of dumping and subsidization.[222] Franz Schuser of the German Chamber of Commerce and Industry observed in *Wirtschaftsdienst* (August 1981) that

---

[218] *Metal Bulletin* reported that on February 27, 1981 that "Although some mills report more [export] selling activity, one suspects that this is only being achieved through price concessions. Third country export prices are often -- through rebates -- far below published levels, for a buyer with a firm order can almost dictate his terms." Original forecasts had estimated that the Community would ship 3 million tons to the U.S. in 1981. By October, it appeared that the figure would be nearly double that, 5 million tons. The U.S. Commerce Department commenced an investigation of "surges" in imports of certain types of steel from Europe and elsewhere in the second quarter of 1981. *Metal Bulletin* (August 28, September 4, 1981).

[219] *Metal Bulletin* (November 6, 1981). The 1981 European export surge to the U.S. is described in more detail in chapter 7.

[220] *Metal Bulletin* (November 10, 1981; January 15, 1982).

[221] *Metal Bulletin* went on to speculate that the Community producers might respond simply by dumping in other third country markets -- "barred from the USA [they] may attempt to move their steel by dumping it in already depressed third countries."

[222] In June the Commerce Department made a preliminary finding of subsidization against six ECSC nations in the pending countervailing duty actions. In August preliminary determinations of dumping were made against five ECSC nations. U.S. importers of the European products were required to post a bond equivalent to the estimated per ton margin of dumping or subsidization pending a final determination. See 47 F.R. 117, June 17, 1982.

The justification of these proceedings has been indirectly conceded by EC officials who admit that European steel products are in some cases sold at well below domestic price levels in the United States and thus dumped.

U.S. imports from the Community began to fall sharply, from a high of 747,000 tons in June 1982 to 346,000 tons in October.[223] Significantly, when dumping in the U.S. market was thus restrained, the Community's internal price floor once again began to break down -- discounting began in a few product lines in the late summer of 1982, developing into a general price collapse in the fall. The connection with the U.S. trade dispute was evident to many observers. *Metal Bulletin* reported on November 16, 1982 that

The European steel price cartel is again failing to keep the market up, and discounting is once more becoming widespread. . . . Some industry quarters blame the trade dispute with the USA. Curbs on European exports in the past few months have diverted larger tonnages onto the EC market and non-US export markets, creating heightened tensions in the output quotas and concerted pricing arrangements which are supposed to be keeping the Community market afloat.[224]

The fact that the establishment of "floor" prices on Community exports to the U.S. caused the collapse of the Community's own internal price "floor" indicates the extent to which the success of the Community's system of internal market controls depended upon the Community's ability to dispose of a portion of its surplus production in the United States market.[225] Given

---

[223] In October the U.S. and the Community agreed to settle the dispute, with U.S. producers withdrawing their trade complaints in return for a commitment by the Community to limit the volume of its exports to specified percentages of U.S. domestic consumption. By the time the agreement was concluded, prices had already begun to fall within the EC.

[224] Similarly, a West German producer complained in *American Metal Market* in June 1982 that following the imposition of antidumping and countervailing duties by the U.S. Government, "we have to compete against subsidized competitors in Europe and we get all the tonnages back which they can't export to the United States." British Steel Chairman Ian MacGregor commented in 1981 that by commencing countervailing duty actions against the European mills, "The Americans are threatening to stop all European imports because all European steel is subsidized. If this happens, European producers will try to sell more of their steel in our market. This will put pressure on prices, and the higher prices we need to cut our losses could easily collapse." *American Metal Market* (December 30, 1981).

[225] One European account of the dispute noted that the publication of preliminary countervailing duty margins against the EC mills in the summer of 1982 "threatened to undermine the carefully orchestrated and painfully achieved manifest crisis regime, which had just been renewed for another year. Drastic changes in export patterns could interfere with the existing allocation of production quotas, putting the whole crisis regime in jeopardy." Eurofer members developed a "sharing key" among themselves for dividing and allocating the Community share of the U.S. market. This was based on an optimistic assumption of the volumes of EC steel the U.S. was prepared to absorb. The prospect of a harder line by the U.S. threatened to

the interplay between the Community's internal and external markets, it is not coincidental   that the Community's first serious effort to confront the overcapacity problem, the Council of Ministers meeting at Elsinore in late 1982, came at the point at which the conclusion of a VRA with the United States limited the Community mills' ability to use the U.S. as an outlet for surplus production.[226]

STEEL POLICIES OF THE MEMBER STATES

Belgium/Luxembourg

The Belgian steel industry already confronted fundamental problems when the structural recession began in 1975, and in the crucible of the steel crisis, the greater portion of the industry would have quickly collapsed without major government intervention.   But while state aid was forthcoming on a truly massive scale, the fragmentation of economic decision making within Belgium prevented it from being applied in a coherent or systematic fashion.   For the most part badly managed, saddled with obsolete equipment, and racked with labor unrest, the industry staggered from one crisis to the next, sustained only by continuing injections of public money.   The steel crisis severely aggravated communal antagonisms within Belgian society, causing the fall of one Belgian government and at times appearing to threaten the continued existence of the Belgian state.   In 1988, after over a decade of heavy subsidies and economic, political and social turmoil, it remained unclear whether major segments of the Belgian industry could survive without new infusions of state funds.

The formulation and implementation of a Belgian national industrial policy in steel was immensely complicated by the country's division into two linguistic regions, Flanders (Dutch) and Wallonia (French).[227] Wallonia, the birthplace of the industrial revolution in continental Europe, has undergone a long economic decline; Flanders was an underdeveloped agricultural region until relatively recently, when it began to industrialize.   In the postwar era the central government tended to divert resources from the growing region of Flanders to offset the economic difficulties of Wallonia, an arrangement which was reasonably acceptable to the Flemings until economic stagnation began

---

make development of a new sharing key "an extremely complicated, if not impossible process," and contributed to the breakdown of Eurofer's internal unity. Van der Ven and Grunert (1987), p. 161.

[226] The U.S.-EC trade dispute of 1981-82, and subsequent U.S.-EC trade relations in steel are addressed in chapter 7.

[227] The country has been governed at the national level by a succession of multiparty coalitions dominated by the Flemish majority, but important economic powers are exercised by the regional governments of Flanders and Wallonia.

(Million metric tons)

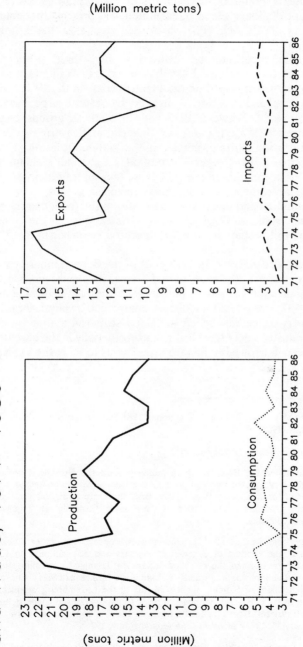

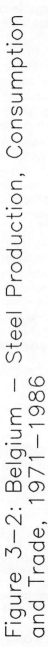

Figure 3-2: Belgium – Steel Production, Consumption and Trade, 1971–1986

Source: International Iron and Steel Institute, _Steel Statistical Yearbook_, 1981, 1987. Production and Consumption refer to crude steel; Exports and Imports refer to semi-finished and finished steel.

to overtake Flanders in the late 1970s.[228] The steel crisis exacerbated these divisions, since it required the taxpayers of Flanders to subsidize the crisis-ridden mills of Wallonia; Flemish resentment was principally countered by the Socialist Party of Wallonia (PS) which used steel as a "battle horse against Flanders."[229]

The Belgian steel industry evolved around three primary poles of production, the Charleroi and Liège basins, both in Wallonia, and Sidmar, a greenfield facility established on the Flemish coast in the 1960s. Historically the Belgian steel industry was controlled by several large Franco-Belgian financial groups.[230]   Between 1955 and 1975, these groups engaged in a complex sequence of acquisitions and financial maneuverings which resulted in the concentration of the ownership of the Walloon mills into relatively few hands, principally the Cockerill group at Liège and Hainaut-Sambre at Charleroi.[231] The main significance of these tangled transactions, which made the industry a "combat zone for rival financial groups,"[232] was that they distracted attention and diverted resources from the fundamental competitive problems confronting Belgian steel.   As a result, the industry was extraordinarily ill prepared when the structural crisis began in 1975.

Structural Weaknesses. In 1975 most of the Belgian industry's equipment was obsolete, and with the exception of Sidmar its plants were located inland, where transportation costs were higher. The various financial consolidations of the 1955-1975 period had not been accompanied by physical rationalization of the industry's facilities, which remained scattered among many separate sites. The industry's debt level had risen substantially in the early 1970s as the steel producers borrowed to finance investments to meet the anticipated steel

---

[228] Anthony Mughan, "The Belgian Election of 1981; the Primacy of the Economic," in 5 *West European Politics* (1982), p. 301.

[229] *La Nouvelle Gazette* (April 13, 1985).

[230] These included the Boel Group (a family group); the Bruxelles-Lambert Group (a consolidated group of Belgian financial houses); the Cobepa Group (a Belgian firm managing the investments of the Banque du Paris et Pays Bas); the Frère-Bourgeois Group; the Launoit Group (a family group); and the Group of the Société Générale de Belgique, Belgium's principal holding company.

[231] In Liège, the various steel producers were consolidated under Cockerill-Ougree-Providence, itself the product of a series of mergers and acquisitions. In Charleroi, the industrialist A. Frère formed the so-called "Charleroi Triangle," controlling the steel firms Hainaut-Sambre, Laminoirs de Ruau, and Thy-Marcinelle-Monceau (TMM). Cockerill originally held a 22 percent share of Sidmar, but it sold this to the Luxembourg producer Arbed, the majority owner, in 1975. Several independent firms (notably Boel and Clabecq, both located in Wallonia near Charleroi) have remained a factor in the Walloon steel industry. *Neue Zürcher Zeitung* (February 26, 1977); *Metal Bulletin Monthly* (July, 1976).

[232] Michael Capron, "The State, the Regions, and Industrial Redevelopment. The Challenge of the Belgian Steel Crisis," in Meny and Wright, *The Politics of Steel*, p. 699.

boom of the late 1970s.[233] Its raw materials, transportation, and particularly its labor costs were comparatively high, and productivity was poor.[234] The industry was dangerously reliant on sales outside of Belgium, which, after 1964, accounted for over 75 percent of Belgian production. An extremely low percentage of the industry's output consisted of sophisticated finished products such as pipes and coated sheets; the Belgian industry was to a considerable degree a supplier of semifinished and commodity products to other nations.[235] The management of the Belgian firms was widely criticized, even by itself.[236]

By 1975 the industry had already become heavily dependent upon public financial support. At the beginning of the structural crisis, pursuant to a variety of regional development aid schemes, the government was providing the industry with capital grants, interest free loans, rebates on interest paid to private financial institutions, loan guarantees, preferential railroad rates, and exemptions from real estate taxes for investments in plant.[237] Between 1955 and 1975, the steel industry accounted for one fifth of all government investments in Belgian industry.[238] This aid was initially provided on an unconditional basis to the privately-owned Belgian firms, but as the industry's competitive problems became more apparent in the mid-1960s, it was accompanied by some extension of the state's influence into industry affairs.[239]

---

[233] Spécial (May 24, 1978).

[234] By the early 1970s Belgian labor costs were doubling every four years. Spécial (May 24, 1978). In October 1976, Julien Charlier, the Director General of Cockerill, indicated that "the company is suffering from a lack of productivity which is very wide ranging at all levels. There are frequent production stoppages." Metal Bulletin (October 26, 1976).

[235] Deutsche Zeitung (June 16, 1978); Capron, "The Challenge of the Belgian Steel Crisis," pp. 698-700.

[236] On February 26, 1977 the Neue Zürcher Zeitung reported that "As the company [Cockerill] frankly confesses its administration is not well developed. Planning, investments and modern management have been neglected."

[237] These benefits were made available pursuant to two regional industrial promotion laws, the Law of July 18, 1959, and the Law of December 30, 1970.

[238] National Secretary of the Belgian Metalworkers' Union in Pourquoi Pas (December 20, 1979).

[239] In 1966, the steel sector's trade unions, alarmed by the mismanagement of the industry and plans to close outdated plants, called for the formation of a tripartite industry-labor-government round table on steel, which led to the formation of the Comité de Concertation de la Politique Sidérurgique (CCPS). This entity devised a general investment program for the national steel industry, and only the investment projects approved by the CCPS were eligible for public assistance. The CCPS intervened on a number of occasions to promote acquisitions by Cockerill which enabled that firm to consolidate its hold on steel production in the Liège region. The influence of the CCPS waned after 1971, however, when the strengthening of the steel market enabled the producers effectively to ignore it. Capron, "The Challenge of the Belgian Steel Crisis," pp. 703-704.

The Collapse. The structural crisis which began in 1975 enveloped the Belgian industry rapidly; production fell by 30 percent in that year and increased only marginally in 1976.[240] The Walloon firms were the most seriously affected. By early 1977 the Charleroi group (dominated by Hainaut-Sambre) was, by its own admission, "nearly bankrupt," while Cockerill, at Liège,

> *frankly admits to having deteriorated to such an extent that private financial backers would have to shrink away from investing in the modernization of the traditional business.*[241]

By 1978 the losses of the Belgian steel firms were so severe that had Belgian commercial law been strictly applied, several firms would have been required to enter bankruptcy proceedings. The industry's debt was reportedly between $2.2 and $2.5 billion with annual interest alone exceeding $222 million.[242] In these desperate circumstances the steel companies appealed to the state for an emergency injection of financial aid, warning that denial would result in massive layoffs.[243]

In March 1977 a "National Steel Conference" was convened, in which government, firms, and the unions jointly attempted to devise a solution to the steel crisis. In return for a commitment not to lay off any workers before the end of 1977, and not to further expand the country's already-excessive production capacity, the Walloon steel producers were granted a low interest government loan of $251 million, a sum which "it proved easy to extort from the Belgian government."[244] An American consulting firm, McKinsey, was asked to analyze the industry's prospects; the resulting report was "unflattering" and recommended substantial capacity cuts, concentration of Belgian production around the country's most efficient mills, $726 million in productivity enhancing investments, and the layoff of 7,000 workers.[245]

---

[240] *Metal Bulletin Monthly* (July 1976).

[241] *Neue Zürcher Zeitung* (February 26, 1977).

[242] *Deutsche Zeitung* (June 16, 1978).

[243] "Belgium's steel bosses have applied . . . pressure to politicians and unions: if they do not receive approximately 10 billion Belgian francs [$279 million] in state guaranteed credits before long, to as great an extent possible interest-free, so goes their threat, then more companies will close down this year and thousands of jobs will be lost . . . in a crisis their enterprise supported its workers, who otherwise would be living off the state." *Neue Zürcher Zeitung* (February 26, 1977).

[244] *Deutsche Zeitung* (June 16, 1978).

[245] McKinsey & Co., *Un Programme de Redressment pour la Sidérurgie Belgo-Luxembourgeoise* (Brussels: McKinsey & Co., 1978).

The Claes Plan. Following a Second National Steel Conference in April 1978, the government presented the so-called Claes Plan, developed by the Belgian Minister of Economic Affairs on the basis of the McKinsey report. The Claes Plan, which was adopted both by the unions and the private sector in the fall of that year,[246] called for specific measures to improve productivity, restructure the industry, and upgrade its technological base.[247] The Plan created the Comité Nationale Planification et de Contrôle (CNPC) for the steel industry, ostensibly a tripartite group to oversee public and private steel investments, but in fact a body which the steel producers were able to manipulate to secure additional injections of government funds.[248] From the government's perspective, such measures were essential since the wholesale collapse of the Walloon steel industry would have had intolerable social and political consequences.[249]

The Claes plan, while calling for government financial assistance to the steel industry pursuant to a restructuring program, required concessions by the unions and management. Government loans to the steel firms were to be progressively converted to equity shares, leading to a "partial nationalization" of the industry; management was also asked to accept the closure of some obsolete facilities. The financial groups which owned the steel firms were to match the government's contributions on a 50-50 basis. Private and public contributions were to be channeled to the industry through a holding company, the Ste. Financière de la Sidérurgie (SFS). Labor was to accede to the elimination of 8,000 jobs in Liège and Charleroi. These arrangements left unclear who would make the basic planning and investment decisions for the industry; steel management and Claes himself indicated that the government's role would be limited.[250] Due to the lack of effective decisionmaking, the modernization and productivity improvements envisioned by the Claes Plan for

---

[246] The accord was ratified by Royal Decree No. 30 of December 15, 1978; *Moniteur Belge* (December 29, 1978); Capron, "The Challenge of the Belgian Steel Crisis," p. 709n.

[247] The foundation for this agreement had been established through parallel arrangements worked out by the major Belgian and Luxembourg producers for the establishment of three rationalization cartels, the so-called Hanzinelle Accords. These called for the division of product markets according to product specializations of individual firms. The three cartels were to consist of Arbed-Sidmar; the Charleroi triangle (dominated by Cockerill) and the "independents," Boel, Clabecq, and Fabrique de Fer.

[248] Capron, "The Challenge of the Belgian Steel Crisis," p. 710.

[249] "[Belgian Economics Minister Willy Claes indicated that] steel was a priority for state action; the several thousand million francs [hundred million dollars] which the state had already spent to keep steelmaking in Belgium afloat were only the first step. Although the industry was bankrupt in commercial terms, economic and political criteria meant that the government could not let steelmaking go under." *Metal Bulletin* (April 19, 1978).

[250] *Spécial* (May 24, 1978); *La Libre Belgique* (November 23, 1977), cited in Capron, "The Challenge of the Belgian Steel Crisis," p. 711.

the most part were not implemented.[251] The government acquisition of equity shares in the steel firms, however, took place over the course of 1979 "at enormous expense to the government," which paid nearly three times the stock exchange value of the shares which it acquired.[252]

The steel situation deteriorated substantially in 1980. The operating losses of the steel enterprises soared; Cockerill's loss of $232 million was a threefold increase over 1979.[253] The financial groups which had committed to match the government's contributions refused to pay, stating "laconically that without state guarantees the money could not be raised."[254] With increasing frequency, the steelmakers demanded short-term cash infusions from the government simply to enable them to stave off imminent insolvency. Such demands, which had "nothing to do with the money needed to finance the plans for reorganizing the sector,"[255] were generally granted.[256] The *Neue Zürcher Zeitung* commented on November 27, 1980 that

---

[251] *Knack* (March 3, 1982); Capron, "The Challenge of the Belgian Steel Crisis," pp. 710-711.

[252] Capron, "The Challenge of the Belgian Steel Crisis," p. 712. The government acquired an interest in Cockerill (28.9 percent), Hainaut-Sambre (30.9 percent) and Thy-Marcinelle (42.3 percent). In return for new shares of stock issued by these companies the government wrote off substantial portions of the firm's outstanding indebtedness to the government -- transforming prior loans into purchases of stock which had no market value to commercial investors. The stock was paid for at prices grossly inflated over the current market price; the government paid $44.36 per share for Cockerill's stock at a time when the market value was under $17 per share. In addition, the obligation of Belgian steel firms to repay interest and principal on outstanding government loans was suspended for a period of five years; in 1980 alone, this measure relieved Belgian steelmakers of roughly $410 million in interest payments. The restructuring plan called for $1.5 billion in new investments, to be financed 50-50 by the industry and the government. *L'Echo de la Bourse*; Cockerill *Annual Report*, 1979; *Metal Bulletin* (January 5, 1979, February 1, 1980).

[253] *Metal Bulletin* (May 1, 1981).

[254] *Neue Zürcher Zeitung* (January 14, 1981). While the government contribution was paid, the holding companies contended "that they only agreed to the setting up of the SFS, not to actually pay their 50 percent contribution." *Metal Bulletin* (September 19, 1980).

[255] *Le Soir* (July 9, 1980).

[256] *Le Soir* (September 10, 1980). *Le Soir* reported on July 9, 1980 that "For leading Walloon steel enterprises, suffering from financial leukemia, the remission will have been a short one -- barely a year, following the last transfusions of public capital. In September, we are told, Cockerill in Liège and Triangle in Charleroi will together ask the state to advance them between 5 and 7 billion [$171 and $240 million] to enable them to survive. Cockerill received a 1.2 billion Bfr. [$41 million] 'survival credit' from the government in the summer of 1980 to "meet immediate liquidity problems." *Metal Bulletin* (August 15, 1980) The following spring the government pumped another $53.9 million into Hainaut-Sambre to enable it to meet its payroll. *Metal Bulletin* (April 16, 1981) Emergency loans backed by government guarantees totaling $273.9 million were reportedly extended to the steel industry in late 1980 and 1981. *Standard* (April 23, 1981).

Since the summer break, the Ministry of Economic Affairs has been forced at almost monthly intervals to grant state guarantees for emergency credit [to steel firms] to bridge the most urgent dates of payment to the utmost. A few days ago, the Leuttich Cockerill Works had no ready answer to persistent rumors of bankruptcy other than pointing to the fact that the Belgian government had obligated itself to plug all the holes.

One Belgian analyst pointed out that since the state had taken share holdings in steel, an "intolerable Indian wrestling match" had developed between state and private shareholders, with the private owners seeking progressively to disengage from the industry, leaving the state to assume its financial burdens and the costs of prior mismanagement. The Minister of Economic Affairs, charging that "the shortcomings of [Cockerill's] financial management reach unbearable proportions," indicated that the government "adamantly refused" to assume the financial burdens of the private shareholders, but the company's fate was "mortgaged by the social imperative of its 45,000 workers."[257] In the end, despite such protestations, the state would pay.

The Formation of Cockerill-Sambre. At the beginning of 1981, the managements of Cockerill and Hainaut-Sambre announced their intention to merge the two firms, and "Cockerill-Sambre was born into sorrow" in June 1981, consolidating most of the Walloon steel industry in the Liège and Charleroi basins under one management.[258] While the merger was undertaken for a variety of political motives, it held out the prospect that duplicative operations could be eliminated.[259] The government took an 81 percent share of the merged company to be managed by a state entity, the Société Nationale de Participations et de Financement de la Sidérurgie (SNS).[260] The government underwrote a massive financial rescue plan, estimated to involve $1.6 billion in direct government aid, in the form of loans (debentures) and subscriptions of new equity to cover prior debt and to provide funds to cover "cash drains" and new investments (table 3-11). The success of the rescue plan depended on the "rather optimistic" assumptions that steel prices would

---

[257] *Le Soir* (September 10, 1980).

[258] *Metal Bulletin* (June 26, 1981).

[259] Cockerill's management was fearful of reports that the Liège producers would integrate with Arbed and Sidmar, leaving Cockerill to bear the brunt of the restructuring of the Walloon industry. Conversely, if most of the Walloon industry were united under one giant producer, it was unlikely that the state would find it politically feasible to reject its pleas for public funds. The president of the principal Walloon political party strongly supported the merger, seeing an opportunity to strengthen his party by becoming the champion of the Walloon industry. Capron, "The Challenge of the Belgian Steel Crisis," p. 716.

[260] *L'Echo de la Bourse* (June 30, 1981).

rise by 40 percent over the next four years and that sales volume would increase by 20 percent; should these conditions not be met, the government would "be confronted with the decision of whether or not new billions should be thrown into the bottomless hole of the Walloon steel industry."[261]

Table 3-11. Belgian Government Financial Assistance for the Rescue of Cockerill-Sambre 1981 (millions U.S. dollars)

	Debentures	Shares	Total
CONSOLIDATION OF DEBT			
1977-78 relay credit	-	403	403
1978 relay credit	51	-	51
1979-80 relay credit	225	-	225
CONTRIBUTION OF NEW FUNDS			
To cover future cash drains	297	297	593
To cover one third of new investments	247	-	247
TRANSFORMATION OF 1984/85 DEBT SERVICE CHARGES	67	-	67
TOTALS	886	699	1,586

Source: *L'Echo De La Bourse* (June 30, 1981)
Converted to U.S. dollars at average annual exchange rate given by International Monetary Fund. Conversion: 1981: 37.1

Flemish criticism of the massive aid program was muted somewhat by large additional grants of aid to Sidmar and several other independent Belgian firms.[262] For reasons of "equal treatment," roughly $431 million in subsidies were to be made available to Sidmar (which had been profitable in 1980), and

---

[261] *Neue Zürcher Zeitung* (June 27, 1981).

[262] *Echo* (May 20, 1981); *Tijd* (August 4, 1981).

to some specialty steel firms in Flanders which had "no use for the full amount."[263]

It was evident almost immediately that with respect to Cockerill-Sambre, even the huge new aid program was little more than a stopgap measure.[264] From the moment of its formation in 1981 Cockerill-Sambre was losing $26.9 million per month, and needed $140.1 million just to survive through the end of the summer; the government patched together a package of short-term financial assistance which was channeled to the ailing firm through the state entity SNS.[265] In early 1982 a Flemish business group estimated that a total of $6.5 billion in government funds would be paid to Cockerill-Sambre between 1981 and 1985, excluding new financial commitments decided after May 1981.[266]

The Steel Crisis in Luxembourg. The restructuring of Belgian steel inevitably involved the Grand Duchy of Luxembourg, because of both natural proximity and the substantial presence of Luxembourg capital in the Belgian industry. Steelmaking dominates the economic life of Luxembourg, which at the beginning of the structural crisis produced more steel per capita than any other nation in the world.[267] The principal Luxembourg producer was the privately-owned Arbed, "disproportionately powerful inside tiny Luxembourg,"[268] whose annual turnover substantially exceeded the national budget of the Grand Duchy.[269] Arbed controlled a group of firms in

---

[263] *Neue Zürcher Zeitung* (June 27, 1981).

[264] A Dutch delegate to the European Parliament commented that "The new [aid] measures are designed to make up for a loss of 25 billion Belgian francs [$673.8 million], while future losses are put at 22 billion Belgian francs [$592.9 million], and that too is going to be met by the Belgian government. The government is also financing 9 billion [$242.5 million] worth of investment, and that is not all. . . . The effect of these debts on the Belgian budget will be felt up to the year 2005, and will place an enormously heavy burden on the next generation. . . . [This aid] is merely being cast into a bottomless pit which is getting bigger day by day." *Debates of the European Parliament*, May 6, 1981, p. 110.

[265] The SNS was able to borrow funds from a number of sources which were transferred to Cockerill-Sambre, and the SNS arranged to absorb the firm's debts through the end of 1981. Capron, "The Challenge of the Belgian Steel Crisis," p. 719.

[266] *Metal Bulletin* (January 26, 1982). By late 1982 Cockerill-Sambre was reportedly diverting government funds earmarked for "restructuring" to meet current expenses (*Metal Bulletin*, September 10, 1982) and warning that it was "inconceivable" that the $262 million government contingency fund for financing cash drains could last until 1985 -- and indeed, this fund was exhausted by mid-1983. *Metal Bulletin* (September 10, 24, 1982; September 9, 1983). Cockerill-Sambre suffered annual operating losses estimated at $323 million and $262 million in 1981 and 1982. *Neue Zürcher Zeitung* (November 23, 1982).

[267] *Metal Bulletin Monthly* (July, 1976).

[268] *Europe* (January-February 1982), p. 38.

[269] *Neue Zürcher Zeitung* (October 21, 1977).

neighboring states, most notably Sidmar in Belgium and a number of subsidiaries in the Saar, which enabled it to influence the investment decisions of its neighbors and to "participate in the subsidy blessings of bigger state treasuries."[270]

Prior to 1979 Arbed did not receive massive, direct government aid, although it was discreetly extended a variety of forms of government assistance on a more modest scale.[271] Arbed championed free competition and continued an intensive investment program following the onset of the structural crisis.[272] These investments proved extraordinarily ill-timed, however; in 1977 Arbed was operating at only 60 percent of capacity, and was simultaneously confronting an "explosion" in production costs, primarily in the form of higher salaries.[273] Arbed suffered a succession of major operating losses, and in 1979 it was forced to turn to the state for a comprehensive bailout.[274] Arbed signed a "tripartite agreement" with government and labor, pursuant to which the firm received major commitments of government financial aid and promised to undertake a new investment program.[275] The Arbed bailout had a substantial impact on the taxpaying citizens of the Grand Duchy; between 1980 and 1984 steel subsidies accounted for an estimated 3 percent of all state expenditures.[276]

By early 1983, Arbed was again in need of state assistance, and the Grand Duchy submitted a new rescue plan to the Commission for approval. Under

---

[270] *Neue Zürcher Zeitung* (November 27, 1980).

[271] The Luxembourg government absorbed a percentage of Arbed's labor costs through payments from the state Unemployment Fund to Arbed's "Anticrisis Division" Arbed *Annual Report*, 1980, p. 27. Arbed's 1975 *Annual Report* described a capital investment program under which expenditures of $57 million were made possible through "coordination between Arbed and the Luxembourg government in the matter of investment, with the aim of maintaining employment in Luxembourg." *Ibid.*

[272] *Neue Zürcher Zeitung* (November 27, 1980).

[273] *Pourquoi Pas* (May 12, 1977).

[274] Arbed had pressed forward with an ambitious investment program despite the world steel crisis and its own operating losses, drawing down its financial reserves. *Pourquoi Pas* (May 12, 1977); *Metal Bulletin* (March 23, 1979).

[275] The European authorities summarized this program as follows: "A program of assistance to the steel industry including subsidies of 25% for capital investment expenditures of $682.5 million during the investment period 1980 to 1984. Added to it are certain tax incentives, loans in the amount of $682,594 at reduced interest, state guarantees for CECA loans, and subsidies in favor of the Anticrisis Division." EC Commission, *Initial Report on Application of Disciplinary Measures in the matter of Assistance to the Steel Industry*, COM(81) 71 final, February 23, 1981.

[276] *Neue Zürcher Zeitung* (November 27, 1980). The money was raised through a combination of government borrowing, increases in the value added tax, increase of excise taxes on cigarettes, gasoline, and alcohol, and an increase in the cost of phone calls from $.06 to $.09. By 1983, the state, with a 22 percent equity share in Arbed, had become the largest shareholder. *Europe* No. 3588 (New Series) (April 15, 1983); No. 3691 (New Series) (September 19-20, 1983).

the plan, which was approved in early 1984, the government provided an injection of $311.5 million to Arbed, acquiring a 24.5 percent share in the company, which was to scale back its investment program substantially and cut hot-rolled capacity from 5.2 million tons in 1980 to 3.9 million tons in 1985. The government also proposed to acquire some of the Sidmar shares held by Arbed. Instrumental to Commission approval was Arbed's entry into a rationalization arrangement with Cockerill-Sambre designed to reduce redundancies and facilitate closure of some facilities. Beween 1980 and 1985, the Commission approved $497.2 million in subsidies for the steel industry of Luxembourg.[277]

The Political Dimension. In Belgium, by the early 1980s the seemingly insatiable demands of the Walloon steel industry for public funds were producing "clear signs of strain" on the Belgian treasury, and had become a major political issue.[278] The Flemish majority was increasingly restive over what was viewed as Flanders' cross-subsidization of Walloon steel, and the Flemish press mounted "a vitriolic campaign against the seemingly unlimited amounts of state cash which the ailing Walloon steel industry will need."[279] Flemish criticism was only partially mitigated by major subsidies to Flemish producers Sidmar and ALZ.[280] For their part the Walloons resented what they felt was favoritism in steel policy decisions toward Flemish producers (notably Sidmar) and emphasized employment concerns in Wallonia,[281] where the steel firms provided the economic backbone of the region:

> *Politicians, employers, and union leaders joined together tempting figures, according to which it would be much cheaper to subsidize a job in the steel industry at approximately 200,000 Bfr. [$6,839] than it would be to support an unemployed person at as much as 500,000 Bfr. [$17,098] annually.*[282]

The principal political lines of conflict were drawn between the Walloon Socialist Party (PS), which demanded immediate government action to ensure the survival of Cockerill-Sambre, and the conservative Flemish Popular Christian Party (CVP), which sought to link any further aid to Walloon steel

---

[277] EC Commission, *Report,* August 6, 1986.

[278] *Metal Bulletin* (February 1, 1980).

[279] *Metal Bulletin* (May 1, 1981).

[280] In 1981 the Belgian government decided to grant Sidmar $78.1 million to cover former losses, $56.6 million for new investments, and $223.7 million drawing rights for future losses or covering long-term debts. ALZ was to get $7.2 million for former losses, $29.6 million for investments and $26.9 million in drawing rights. *Tijd* (August 4, 1981); *Echo* (May 20, 1981).

[281] *Neue Zürcher Zeitung* (November 27, 1980).

[282] *Neue Zürcher Zeitung* (January 14, 1981).

to concessions from the PS on indexation of wages as the first step toward a "Thatcherite" policy of austerity.[283] In September 1981 the impasse between the CVP and the PS over steel policy caused the collapse of the Belgian government, and the election of a new coalition under Wilfred Martens.

While these internal problems were serious, Belgium also confronted mounting external pressure from the EC Commission to bring its steel subsidies under control. Beginning in late 1980 the Commission began to criticize Belgian subsidy programs, to press for employment and capacity cuts at the Walloon mills, and to question some aspects of proposed Belgian restructuring measures.[284] In June 1981 the Belgian government notified the Commission of the restructuring plan which it proposed to implement in conjunction with the Cockerill-Sambre merger.[285] The Commission refused to approve the Cockerill-Sambre restructuring plan, particularly the "erroneous, unrealistic and quite impossible" proposal to maintain 8.5 million metric tpy of steelmaking capacity. The Commission asked the Belgian government first to clarify, if it could, how the plan would enable the firm to achieve profitability by 1985, producing a deadlock between the Belgian government and the Commission.[286] With the restructuring plan thus stalled, the Belgian

---

[283] Capron, "The Challenge of the Belgian Steel Crisis," p. 746. Some Flemish groups supported a "dévolution" or "régionalization" of steel policy; that is, Wallonia should pay for the cost of supporting its own steel industry. The CVP supported continuation of a national steel policy, but alarmed the Walloons by proposing to "study" whether the financial responsibility for supporting regional steel producers should devolve on the regions. Le Soir (June 19, 1981); Le Peuple (March 13/14, 1982).

[284] The Commission expressed concern that the Belgian subsidies would not actually make the industry competitive; that production capacity would be expanded rather than reduced; and that the Belgian aid programs violated the Commission's Subsidy Code. The Commission, citing these concerns, suspended its own aid program for Belgian steel. Neue Zürcher Zeitung (January 14, 1981).

[285] The proposal involved $2 billion in subsidies, including $1.6 billion in operating aid, and called for the phaseout of 3.2 million metric tons of crude steel capacity and 5000 jobs.

[286] La Libre Belgique (January 2, 1982). Relations between Belgium and the Commission were further clouded by the revelation that a number of Belgian subsidy and investment decisions had been made without notification to the Commission. In early 1982, the Commission happened to read in Cockerill-Sambre's house magazine that the company was about to complete work on a new hot strip mill at Carlam, a capacity expansion project which had never been notified to the Commission. The project was surrounded with allegations of financial malpractice, with industry sources alleging that Cockerill-Sambre had siphoned off government operating subsidies and channeled them into financing the Carlam expansion. The Community was already burdened with a huge surplus of hot coil capacity, and the Commission refused to approve the Carlam investment, despite the fact that work was almost complete. Metal Bulletin (February 19, 1982).

government was required to support Cockerill-Sambre with a succession of short-term injections of aid to enable it to continue operations.[287]

In the winter of 1982, the continuing impasse between the Commission and the Belgian government over the restructuring of Cockerill-Sambre prompted unusually violent demonstrations by steelworkers at the EC offices in Brussels, in which hundreds of people were seriously injured. Cockerill-Sambre's Liège and Charleroi mills were closed by strikes; in March, Liège, which would bear the brunt of closures sought by the Commission, was paralyzed by striking steelworkers, and strikers blocked roads in Namur and East Flanders, interrupting communications with Germany and the rest of Belgium. These events raised the prospect of serious civil unrest spreading across Wallonia, jeopardizing the cohesion of the Belgian state.[288]

The Vandestrik Interlude.   In mid-March 1982, after months of drift in steel policy, the Commission approved a tranche of $503.2 million in Belgian government subsidies to Cockerill-Sambre for some aspects of the firm's restructuring program, but reiterated its opposition to the overall restructuring plan.[289] The aid was approved on the condition that outmoded facilities in Liège and Charleroi be shut down and that the funds be employed to modernize remaining facilities.   The Belgian government appointed M. Vandestrik the acting chairman of Cockerill-Sambre; in addition, the government negotiated major new loans for Cockerill-Sambre from private banks, backed by a state guarantee.[290]

In May 1982 Vandestrik announced a comprehensive restructuring program for Cockerill-Sambre.[291] The new plan, which initially appeared to offer hope for the company, began to founder almost immediately. The EC Commission indicated that it was not prepared to grant immediate approval

---

[287] *Neue Zürcher Zeitung* (January 7, 1982). In August 1981 the Commission approved an extension of $140.1 million in government-guaranteed short-term credits to Cockerill-Sambre. In December the Commission approved a further $110.5 million in government guarantees, and the conversion of the July $140.1 million credit into equity capital. Wirtschaftsvereinigung Eisen und Stahlindustrie, *Practical Experience* (1982).

[288] *Knack* (March 3, 1982); *Metal Bulletin* (February 16, 19, March 5, 12, 23, 1982).

[289] *Le Soir* (March 19, 1982); *Metal Bulletin* (March 23, 1982).

[290] The agreement provided for the continuity of existing lines of credit, provided a state guarantee for $196.9 million already loaned to Cockerill-Sambre, and provided for $196.9 million in additional medium term credit. *Cockerill-Sambre Acier No. 5*, 1982: in Capron, "The Challenge of the Belgian Steel Crisis," pp. 723-24.

[291] The principal features of the plan were a 52 percent reduction in steelmaking capacity, to 6.1 million tpy. by 1985, co-production arrangements with other regional producers, and rationalization of remaining production, with Charleroi and Liège each supporting one flat and one non-flat operation. The plan called for the government to convert $328.2 million in frozen debts and $109.4 million in interest rebates to "working capital;" 3,900 jobs would be cut. Steel workers were asked to accept a wage freeze through 1984. *L'Usine Nouvelle* (May 13, 1982); *Metal Bulletin* (June 4, 1982).

for the plan, and that deeper capacity cuts than those envisioned by Vandestrik would be required. Worse, by mid-1982 Cockerill-Sambre confronted yet another cash crisis; by the end of October 1982 the company had "swallowed" 90 percent of the subsidies allotted to cover its operating losses between 1981 and 1985, and was reportedly drawing on funds intended for investment and restructuring to cover immediate operating expenses.[292] Vandestrik resigned in November, and Eurofer President Claude Etchegary, a board member of Cockerill-Sambre, also resigned, chiding Vandestrik and the Belgian government for their failure to draw up strategic plans for the company's future.[293]

Cockerill-Sambre's immediate financial crisis was resolved by releasing the remaining $153 million that had been intended to cover its operating losses through 1985, and the provision of another $129 million in government credits.[294] By this point Cockerill-Sambre had become "the show room of the Walloon disaster,"[295] a "bottomless pit" into which subsidies were poured "without a sign of light at the end of the tunnel."[296] By the end of 1982, even Walloon politicians were beginning to question whether it might not be better to stop "sooner rather than later the senseless subsidizing of the steel sector."[297]

The Gandois Plan. In early 1983 the Belgian government retained a French consultant, Jean Gandois, to develop a new plan for the restructuring of the Belgian steel industry which would, among other things, return Cockerill-Sambre to profitability by the end of 1985. Gandois was instructed to develop a proposal for the "filialization" of Cockerill-Sambre's healthy divisions, turning them into self-managing subsidiaries, in order to prune the remaining unprofitable operations.[298] The "Gandois Plan" was submitted to the Belgian government in May 1983; it proposed the closure of one melting shop each in Liège and Charleroi, a net reduction in capacity of 1.4 million tons and numerous other structural changes designed to cut costs and rationalize operations.[299] The work force would be reduced by 7,900 by 1986.

---

[292] *Neue Zürcher Zeitung* (November 23, 1982); Capron, "The Challenge of the Belgian Steel Crisis," p. 725; *Metal Bulletin* (September 10, 1982).

[293] *Metal Bulletin* (December 24, 1982).

[294] Capron, "The Challenge of the Belgian Steel Crisis," p. 726.

[295] Belgian Minister for New Technologies in *L'Evénément* (March 1984).

[296] *Neue Zürcher Zeitung* (November 23, 1982).

[297] *Metal Bulletin* (December 31, 1982).

[298] Jean Gandois, *Mission Acier; Mon Aventure Belge* (Paris: Duculot, 1986); *Metal Bulletin* (January 7, 1983).

[299] *Metal Bulletin Monthly* (September 1983).

Semifinished products would be transferred between Liège and Charleroi to achieve maximum utilization at each site, and any shortfalls would be met through cooperative arrangements with other regional producers. Financing the plan would be problematic in light of the EC Commission's cutoff date of December 31, 1985 for subsidies, and Gandois proposed two possible solutions -- extension of the deadline, or an immediate injection of $1.5 billion in subsidies into Cockerill-Sambre.[300]

Table 3-12: Financing the Gandois Plan 1984-1987
(million U.S. dollars)

Restructuring Cockerill-Sambre debts [1]	1,065
Funds for Restructuring National [2] Wallonian Sectors (FSNW)	539
Belfin credits for investments [3]	221
SNCI credits [3]	30
State aid for employment adjustments [4]	181
Total	2,036

Source: Mark Singlet, *La Subsidiation de la Siderurgie Belge: Un Bilan Provisoire* (Brussels: Université Libre de Bruxelles, 1986-87).
Converted to U.S. dollars at average annual exchange rate given by International Monetary Fund. Conversion: 1984 - 1987: 49.8

---

[1] National Government
[2] Regional funding by Wallonia for investments and operating aid
[3] Belfin and SNCI are entities through which the state participates in the steel sector.
[4] To be matched by $125,321 in employer contributions.

The Belgian government adopted the Gandois recommendations in July 1983, and Gandois was appointed chief executive officer of Cockerill-Sambre. The plan called for nearly $1.96 billion in new state aid. The huge subsidy burden (table 3-12) called for by the Gandois Plan was allocated among the regions pursuant to an elaborate compromise which averted major new

---

[300] *Metal Bulletin* (May 27, 1983). The total cost of the Gandois restructuring was estimated at $1.9 billion. The Belgian government notified the EC Commission of its intention to grant total aid of $1.6 billion. Capron, "The Challenge of the Belgian Steel Crisis," p. 755.

outbreaks of communal violence.[301] Meanwhile, by the fall of 1983 Cockerill-Sambre had exhausted the $430 million in subsidies provided under the 1980 restructuring plan, and another injection of $23.4 million was forthcoming from the government in late 1983 to enable the company to continue operations.[302]

In 1984, a rationalization arrangement was reached between Belgium and Luxembourg. Arbed's Luxembourg works was to specialize in non-flat rolled products; Sidmar in hot and cold-rolled flat products, Cockerill-Sambre's Liège works in cold-rolled and coated flat products, and its Charleroi mills in hot-rolled flat products. However, the plan involved controversial closures, including, most notably, the Valfil wire rod mill in Wallonia, where workers went on strike. It was also characterized by continuing distrust between Flemish and Walloon elements which made it unclear how successfully rationalization could be carried out; in discussing the proposed arrangement, a Walloon spokesman characterized it as a "marriage of convenience" rather than love between Cockerill-Sambre and Arbed, and remarked that there was

> no reason why Sidmar, which has been invited to the reception, should eat the whole cake, rifle the silverware and steal the tablecloth and napkins to boot.[303]

In order to nullify Walloon criticism that Wallonia was being asked to accept sacrifices that benefited Flanders, the Belgian government acquired a stake in Sidmar which would eventually reach 49 percent.[304] The acquisition involved conversion of state-guaranteed debt to non-voting preferred stock and the purchase of ordinary shares by the state. The Commission indicated that in its view the Belgian government had overvalued the shares acquired in Sidmar, but was "prepared to consider that a higher price could be considered normal for the purchase of a blocking minority." A similar government share purchase was arranged for another Flemish producer, ALZ.[305]

New government aid to the Belgian industry was barred by the EC Commission at the end of 1985. However, despite the energetic restructuring

---

[301] The central government undertook the consolidation of Cockerill-Sambre's $1 billion debt, part of which was converted to capital, but the Wallonia regional government assumed full responsibility for financing the actual restructuring, at a cost of about $528.3 million, through "Funds for Restructuring the National Wallonia Sectors" (FSNW). These funds were raised, in part, through a regionalized tax system in which death taxes were paid to local Walloon authorities instead of the national government, with the proceeds used to subsidize Cockerill-Sambre. A similar arrangement was made with respect to Flanders, which used the funds to subsidize a variety of industries in that region. *Metal Bulletin* (July 29, 1983).

[302] *Metal Bulletin* (September 9, 1983).

[303] Jean Gol in *Le Soir* (December 2, 1983).

[304] *La Cité* (January 1, 1984); *Neue Zürcher Zeitung* (January 14, 1984).

[305] EC Commission, *Report*, August 6, 1986.

plan begun under Gandois and continued by his successor, Cockerill-Sambre continued to incur severe operating losses, which consistently exceeded the forecasts of its executives,[306] and the company's operating costs remained higher than those of its competitors.[307] Management announced "austerity" measures in 1986 designed to cut costs, involving wage reductions and layoffs, but these triggered further labor unrest in Cockerill-Sambre's mills.[308] One Walloon source commented that "M. Gandois' calculations were false. Today his successor is faced with a company that . . . is not integrated and cannot attain success on the date anticipated by Gandois as imposed by the Community."[309] The company's pattern of continuing losses, unless reversed, meant that it would require further injections of public money; Gandois, who returned to Cockerill-Sambre's management on a part-time basis in 1987, commented that

> *It would be unrealistic to think, and hypocritical to say that the new period of restructuring which the European steel industry is facing can be achieved without state aid.*[310]

The Balance. By the end of 1986, after more than a decade of crisis, the Belgian steel industry had contracted substantially, but had by no means disappeared. However, this contraction would have been far more dramatic without state intervention; indeed, much of the Belgian industry, particularly in the Charleroi-Liège basins, might well have shut down. It will probably be impossible ever to calculate the precise amount of government subsidies poured into the industry during this period, although one recent study arrived at the figure of $6.7 billion between 1977 and 1987.[311]

The Belgian experience underscores the competitive paradox which confronts privately-owned steel producers pitted against state-backed firms; state backing ultimately enables even inefficient, chronic loss-making firms like Cockerill-Sambre to survive and continue to invest. Much of the Belgian steel industry, "according to the criteria of business economics, should have closed its gates long ago,"[312] and certainly was in no condition to undertake an ambitious investment program. Backed by the state, however, Belgian steel

---

[306] Cockerill-Sambre lost $101 million in 1985, $89.4 million in 1986, and $34.8 million in the first half of 1987. *Metal Bulletin* (August 10, 1987).

[307] *L'Echo de la Bourse* (October 1, 1987); *Metal Bulletin* (June 6, 1986).

[308] *Metal Bulletin* (January 23, 1987).

[309] *La Wallonie* (May 13, 1986).

[310] *Metal Bulletin* (June 2, 1987).

[311] Marc Singlet, *La Subsidisation de la Sidérurgie Belge: Un Bilan Provisoire* (Brussels: Universite Libre de Bruxelles, 1986-87).

[312] *Neue Zürcher Zeitung* (November 23, 1982).

investments grew from $3.5 billion in 1976 to $3.7 billion in 1986, notwithstanding an unbroken string of massive losses by Cockerill-Sambre, the dominant producer.[313] That firm, effectively bankrupt at the beginning of 1982, was at that moment installing three new continuous casting lines at considerable cost.[314] During the catastrophic decade between 1976 and 1986, the Belgian steel industry's continuous casting ratio grew from 5.7 percent to 72.4 percent. By 1987, although still troubled by labor problems, Cockerill-Sambre was enjoying operating results which were an improvement over prior years.[315] As Belgian Economic Minister Mark Eyskens commented in 1982, subsidies had made such investments possible:

> *With regard to our 27 billion Bfr. [$591 million] [subsidy] plan, the Commission has given us the green light for 21 billion Bfr. [$460 million]. Cockerill was worn out and had no future. This is the reason it was necessary to proceed with an all-around modernization! Cockerill will once again become a beautiful plant.*[316]

France

Through much of the postwar era the French government has held out much higher objectives for the national steel industry than the industry was capable of achieving. In a succession of national steel plans in the 1960s and 1970s, the industry, urged on by the government, built new steel plants (without closing or modernizing old ones), and financed their investments through massive borrowing arranged or facilitated by the state. When the steel crisis struck in 1974, the French industry did not possess the resources to withstand it, and between 1978 and 1981 the industry, in a state of financial collapse, was progressively nationalized and its debts wiped out by the state. By 1981 the industry was grossly overmanned and in need of restructuring, but these moves were delayed by the arrival of a Socialist government committed to maintaining employment. Under the Socialists, an ambitious new government steel plan, launched in 1982, proved abortive, with the state forced to advance enormous sums to cover the industry's losses. These losses, however, like prior ones, were ultimately made good by the state. Between 1974 and 1986, the French steel industry received an estimated $17.2 billion in subsidies.[317] Although the EC Commission barred steel subsidies as of the end of 1985, the French government has periodically argued that the ban

---

[313] Eurostat.

[314] *Industries et Techniques* (April 20, 1982).

[315] *La Cité* (May 26, 1987). In 1986, Cockerill-Sambre managed to realize a positive cash flow for the first time in a number of years. *La Wallonie* (May 26, 1987).

[316] *L'Usine Nouvelle* (May 13, 1982).

[317] *L'Usine Nouvelle* (September 4, 1986).

(Million metric tons)

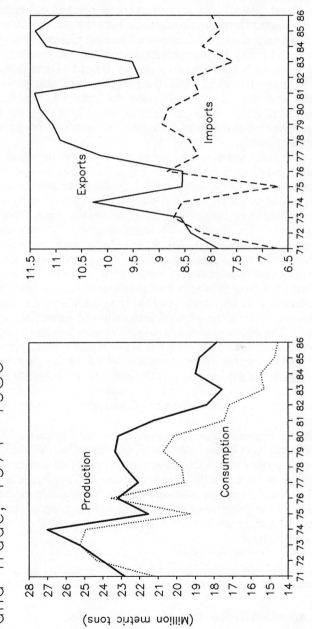

Figure 3-3: France - Steel Production, Consumption and Trade, 1971-1986

Source: International Iron and Steel Institute, Steel Statistical Yearbook, 1981, 1987. Production and Consumption refer to crude steel; Exports and Imports refer to semi-finished and finished steel.

should be terminated, and devised a variety of schemes to circumvent it.

Since the Second World War the French government has played an active role in fostering the development of industry through implementation of a series of national "plans," a loose framework of government guidelines and initiatives developed through consultations between the private sector, the government, labor unions, and a national Planning Commission. While the plans were not binding on the private sector, the government influenced conformity with them through a variety of tax, fiscal and administrative incentives.[318] In the 1960s and 1970s, the French government became actively involved in a series of sectoral plans to enhance the international competitiveness of the French steel industry, which for a time was held up as the principal working example of "concertation" between the private sector, government and labor.

The French steel industry was ill prepared for the demands which the government's ambitious industrial policy goals would place upon it. At the end of World War II the industry consisted of a large number of relatively small firms owned by family financial groups. French steel mills were poorly sited in inland locations, principally in Lorraine and the Nord; French facilities were technologically backward, and their owners generally lacked the financial resources for modernization. Much of the industry used low grade ore from Lorraine, which increased production costs. The government, mindful of the need to rationalize the industry, encouraged a series of mergers and consolidations, but these primarily took the form of financial combinations -- the establishment of an intricate array of holding companies and jointly owned subsidiaries, rather than the physical integration of industrial facilities and production.[319] The fragmentation of the industry gave its trade association, the Chambre Syndicate de la Sidérurgie Francaise (CSSF), a uniquely important role; the CSSF reconciled internal conflicts within the industry, acted as the intermediary between the industry and the government, helped to raise capital to finance industry investments, and reportedly even provided a forum for price fixing and the establishment of production quotas for French steelmakers.[320]

The CSSF's financial arm, the Groupement de l'Industrie Siderurgique (GIS) was instrumental not only in raising much of the capital for the industry's expansion of the 1960s, but as a mechanism for industry-government planning of the direction of the industry's growth. The GIS annually issued a steel industry debenture on the bond market, raising debt capital that was then re-loaned to individual steel firms at market rates, an advantage for the many firms which were weak credit risks; the government absorbed a portion

---

[318] U.S. International Trade Commission, *Foreign Industrial Targeting and its Effects on U.S. Industries: Phase II: The European Community and Member States*, U.S.I.T.C. Pub. No. 1517, April 1984.

[319] *Metal Bulletin Monthly* (June 1976); Hayward (1987), p. 505.

[320] *Business Week* (September 3, 1966).

of the interest on the GIS loans.[321]   Between 1952 and 1964 GIS loans accounted for about 72 percent of the outstanding bonded indebtedness of the French steel industry, or about 44 percent of the industry's long-term debt. The GIS had a 12-member council and a 4-man committee, with representatives from two government ministries and the state Planning Commission, who allocated GIS funds to ensure that the investments to which they were directed were consistent with public policy.[322]

The Steel Convention of 1966. The French industry borrowed heavily in the early 1960s to finance investments in expansion and modernization, and by the mid-1960s it was grossly overextended financially; in addition, it was apparent that it faced major short and long-term competitive liabilities, notably the poor siting of its plants.[323] Accordingly, the industry's leaders, headed by CSSF President Jules Ferry, approached President Pompidou with a formal request for additional public financial assistance, at a point when the French government was formulating its fifth national plan. After protracted industry-government negotiations, a "Convention" was reached between the two sides in July 1966. Under this "contractual" arrangement, the government pledged to provide the industry with extensive financial assistance, to seek to reduce the industry's coal and coke costs, and to explore ways to reduce the industry's transportation costs. In return, the industry agreed to consolidate its companies into two groups, based on Lorraine and the Nord; to undertake investment and rationalization plans to enhance productivity; and to develop a system of worker retraining to assist employees displaced by the anticipated productivity improvements. In the words of one critic, in return for state funds, the steelmakers were asked only to "concentrate, cooperate, and cartelize." The CSSF was "informally delegated a part of public authority to handle the distribution of state funds and moneys raised by the grouped loans, and became the privileged negotiating partner of the state."[324]

The Fos Debacle. In the early 1960s the French government and industry began planning the establishment of two "Japanese style" greenfield mills at

---

[321] John H. MacArthur and Bruce R. Scott, *Industrial Planning in France* (Boston: Harvard University Press, 1967), p. 198.

[322] The GIS was dominated by industry "insiders" who reviewed all major firms' investment plans (pursuant to the review of loan applications), and were thus in a position to exercise influence over investment patterns in the industry." A company could have pressure brought to bear on its investment programs by the threat of an unfavorable action on its [loan] dossier." *Ibid.*, p. 200.

[323] By 1965 annual debt service charges were 8 percent of sales, at a time when working capital and internal cash generation were insufficient to support ongoing operations. Some firms were "virtually bankrupt" and were being kept alive only by state aid. MacArthur and Scott, *Industrial Planning.*

[324] Christian Stoffaes and Pierre Gadonniex, "Steel and the State in France," in 4 *Annals of the Public Economy* 405 (1980).

seaside locations, utilizing modern steelmaking technology, one at Dunkirk and the other at Fos-sur-Mer near Marseilles. The Dunkirk facility was built in 1963; its construction "would not have been possible without the financial support and restructuring assistance of the French government."[325] The Fos-sur-Mer project was delayed until the late 1960s; its eventual location on the Mediterranean coast, far from its natural markets, was dictated by political rather than economic factors. The principal institutional proponent of the Fos location was the Regional and Spatial Development and Planning Agency (DATAR), which saw the greenfield mill as a way to develop the south into a "French California," creating 170,000 direct and indirect jobs, France's "Mediterranean answer to Rotterdam on the North Sea, the southern Europort."[326]

The greenfield mill built at Fos-Sur-Mer was the largest investment project ever undertaken in France. The mill was built by Solmer, a subsidiary of Wendel-Sidelor, one of the principal Lorraine steel groups. Wendel-Sidelor attempted to finance Solmer's $1.8 billion first stage expansion effort through a combination of heavy borrowing and public loans, which covered about one fourth of the total investment.[327] Wendel-Sidelor ran into serious financial problems virtually as soon as construction was begun in 1971, and it became apparent that the project simply could not be financed primarily through private capital. By then, the "government seemed to be trapped by its own propaganda . . . too many commitments had been entered into with firms and local authorities" to cancel the project.[328] In 1972 the government, under pressure from creditors of the Fos project, arranged for Usinor to assume joint control of Solmer with Wendel-Sidelor. Solmer went bankrupt in 1973, but was revived by a succession of new government loans.[329] By 1976, 3.5

---

[325] U.S. International Trade Commission, *U.S. Strip and Sheet Industry* (1988), p. 8-1. The Dunkirk facility was established by Usinor, assisted principally by the Ministry of Industry's Steel Division, which helped select the site and secure public financial assistance. Government aid took the form of loans from the Treasury and the Credit national, a government bank. Hayward, "The Nemesis of Industrial Patriotism," p. 508; Stoffaes and Gadonneix, "Steel and the State in France."

[326] Hayward, *Ibid.*, p. 508.

[327] Stoffaes and Gadonneix, "Steel and the State in France."

[328] Hayward, "The Nemesis of Industrial Patriotism," p. 509.

[329] Following Solmer's insolvency, "In the greatest secrecy, a new finance plan was worked out, in which the Usinor group participated, and public assistance was increased by 800 million francs [$177.7 million]. But this was not sufficient since, in 1975 the Government committed 1.4 billion [$326 million] more to the operation of Fos." (Parliamentary Debates, National Assembly, *Journal Officiel* at 5813 (October 9, 1978). One French Senator commented that the new funds were extended "under terms which were even more extravagant than before. Of course, the interest rate was 6.75 percent, but with unheard-of deferment of the repayment of principal — seventeen years. . . . This was a neat trick indeed." Anciet Le Pors in Parliamentary Debates, Senate *Journal Officiel* at p. 2688 (October 18, 1978).

million tpy of capacity had become operational at Fos, but on this scale the facility was "uneconomic to run."[330]

The Fos-sur-Mer fiasco contributed substantially to the disasters which engulfed French steel after the onset of the structural crisis. In order to finance the project, Wendel-Sidelor had taken on a huge burden of debt, which Usinor assumed when it took joint control of Solmer, and this indebtedness contributed substantially to the collapse of both Usinor and Wendel-Sidelor several years later. Solmer absorbed investment capital that could have been used to modernize and rationalize existing facilities elsewhere in France, whose productivity was extremely poor by world standards. The older mills were neither shut down nor upgraded, and industry executives were subsequently chided for "not following Clausewitz' precept, according to which one must strengthen one's strong points and abandon the weak points."[331] Thus, by 1974, on the eve of the crisis, the French steel industry had accumulated debts of $5 billion, and little had been done to address its fundamental structural problems; the industry's output per worker was 175 tons, compared with 202 tpy in the Community as a whole and 252 tpy in the United States.[332]

The First Crisis Years. The French industry suffered severely from the beginning of the structural steel crisis; 1975 was the "worst year since the War for French Steel."[333] The French industrialists and planners displayed a dogged unwillingness to abandon ambitious expansion goals for the industry, predicated on assumptions of market growth which proved wildly optimistic. France's Seventh Plan forecast two alternative growth rates for domestic steel demand in the years 1974-79, an "optimistic" scenario, based on growth rate of 3 percent, and a "pessimistic" scenario which placed growth at 1.7 percent. In reality, demand declined by 17 percent.[334] The industry failed to meet the objectives laid down for it in 1975, the last year of the Sixth Plan, and almost immediately after the Seventh Plan was launched in 1976, it was recognized that government funding was inadequate. In early 1977, under a new *"Plan Acier,"* another $469 million in low interest government loans were extended

---

[330] *Metal Bulletin* (November 19, 1976).

[331] *Le Figaro* (January 30, 1979).

[332] Stoffaes and Gadonneix, "Steel and the State in France."

[333] *Metal Bulletin* (December 9, 1985). The Usinor and Sacilor groups lost money on steel operations in every year between 1975 and 1978, the year that both firms were partially nationalized. Usinor and Sacilor *Annual Reports; Metal Bulletin* (February 10, 1978).

[334] Commisariat Général au Plan, Ministère de l'Industrie et de la Recherche, *La Documentation Française 1976*, pp. 21, 42, cited in Hayward, "The Nemesis of Industrial Patriotism," p. 520.

to the industry.[335] To a substantial degree, such government subsidies after the onset of the crisis in 1975 were a political *quid pro quo* for employment and investment actions by the French mills desired by the government; in 1975, confronting imminent local elections, the Prime Minister asked the steel firms not to lay off workers and to sustain a high level of investment.[336]

The French steelmakers' principal strategic response to the protracted slump in domestic demand was to mount a vigorous export drive to offset the loss of home sales, although this led to extensive sales of French steel abroad at uneconomic prices.[337] In 1978 Michel Rocard made the following remarks in the French National Assembly:

> *Let's speak plainly. Under pretext of protecting foreign markets, for four years exports have been made at "dumping" prices, and our steel industry has not recovered. Why? Because the owners, like the governments that authorized the practices, gave the crisis a cyclical analysis.*[338]

As the crisis deepened, the steelmakers' financial condition deteriorated dramatically. By 1978 the industry's medium and long-term debt exceeded total annual turnover, and Usinor and Sacilor appeared in the *Fortune* classification of the biggest money-losing enterprises in the world. The steelmakers covered their growing losses by continued heavy borrowing, much

---

[335] The new loans carried an interest rate of 2 percent for the first five years (9.5 percent thereafter) at a time when the commercial prime rate in France exceeded 11 percent. Parliamentary Debates, Senate, *Journal Officiel* at 2706 (October 18, 1978).

[336] Hayward, "The Nemesis of Industrial Patriotism," p. 523.

[337] Two French analysts commented that "To offset the drop in home consumption, producers sought to find the missing outlets abroad by bringing their prices into line with the very modest prices charged for large-scale exports. In this way production of French firms fell off less than elsewhere and the level of capacity was, if anything, rather better. However, this volume of production was maintained on poor financial terms" (Stoffaes and Gadonneix). On December 19, 1979, *Metal Bulletin* reported with respect to French steel that "On the domestic and other EC markets there was a marked decline [in demand] and it was only a "spectacular recovery" on third country markets which enabled orders and deliveries to surmount their 1976 levels. . . . Outside the EC, prices had weakened during the latter part of 1976, and this downward movement continued throughout the year, and for many products prices returned to their very worst levels of 1975."

[338] Parliamentary Debates, National Assembly, *Journal Officiel* at p. 5817 (October 10, 1978). Usinor explained in its 1977 *Annual Report* (Appendix III, p. 13) that "the European steelworkers, and most particularly, the French steelworkers, have been active on the international market, where the prices are nonetheless disastrous, in 1977 to try to make up, at least partly, for the decline in domestic demand and to provide a minimum operation for their installations."

of it financed or guaranteed by the French government.[339] The steelmakers remained reluctant to retire capacity and "the State indeed did not look kindly upon the shutting down of production units and the abolition of jobs."[340] At the same time, the French steelmakers continued to engage in aggressive price-cutting both inside and outside the Community,[341] and pressed for further capacity expansion projects of dubious economic value.[342]

Partial Nationalization (1978). By mid-1978 the steelmakers were virtually bankrupt, and the French government was forced to launch another comprehensive industry "Rescue Plan." Under this plan, the bulk of the enormous outstanding debt held by the governmental and government-backed entities was, in effect, written off, and the government acquired a controlling equity interest in Usinor and Sacilor.[343] The debt held by the French treasury (FDES) was converted into "participating loans" bearing a token annual interest rate of 0.1 percent.[344] Debts held by other government institutions and GIS was converted into similar loans, but rather than forfeiting interest, these entities were compensated by a state-funded "Steel Amortization Fund"

---

[339] Many of the loans were extended by the Fonds de Développement Économique et Social (FDES), a special account in the French Treasury which extended loans on favorable terms (low interest, long-term, lenient security requirements) for "conversion and adoption of commercial structures." Additional loans were provided through the GIS and the Crédit National, a government bank. *Certain Steel Products from France,* 47 F.R. 39332, September 7, 1982 (final).

[340] Stoffaes and Gadonneix, "Steel and the State in France," p. 15.

[341] In June 1978 the European Commission imposed heavy fines on Usinor for selling hot coils in the Community below the ECSC legal minimum, *Metal Bulletin* (July 2, 1978). Sacilor and Usinor were fined by the Commission (Usinor heavily) for price violations in early 1984. *Official Journal,* C. 34 (February 9, 1984).

[342] The steelmakers, for example, sought government funds to double the capacity of the Solmer plant at Fos despite the fact that there was "no certainty that the additional 3.5 tons of steel will be needed, at least by 1980." *Metal Bulletin* (November 19, 1976).

[343] *L'Humanité* (September 21, 1982); *Activités Industrielle Lorraines* (October 1978). Two finance companies were created in which government institutions held majority shares. These companies acquired blocks of equity shares in Usinor and Sacilor, through the so-called "accordion treatment" — the steel firms' capital was reduced, then increased by consolidating loans held by the finance companies. The finance companies also acquired majority interests in holding companies which held additional equity shares in Usinor and Sacilor. "La Situation et L'Avenir de la Sidérurgie," *Journal Officiel* at p. 28 (July 3-4, 1979).

[344] The Finance Committee of the French National Assembly noted that "by setting a symbolic rate of interest, a sum of several hundred million francs [several million dollars] will be abandoned [by the Treasury] each year." Assemblée Nationale, *Rapport* No. 568 (October 5, 1978).

(Caisse d'Amortissement pour l'Acier, or APA).[345] It was recognized at the time that, in effect, these measures meant that the steel industry's massive debts would never be repaid (or would be covered by the government).[346] The rationale was to give the French industry a "second financial wind," relieving them of their financial burdens and reducing their levels of indebtedness to those of their foreign competitors.[347] The following dialogue occurred in the French Senate at the time the Rescue Plan was being reviewed:

> *Anciet LePors: The Government spent in September 1977 -- one year ago -- 1.3 billion francs [$265 million] to achieve this objective of 32 million tons at an interest rate of 2 percent for the first eight years, and 9.5 percent after that. What does any of this mean now? That was a year ago.*
>
> *Gerard Ehlers: They'll never pay.*[348]

Under the Rescue Plan, the industry was to improve its productivity through 21,750 layoffs in 1979 and 1980;[349] while some limited capacity cuts and work force reductions were achieved, such cuts were fought by the unions, which adamantly opposed work force reductions.[350] The steel plan was vigorously denounced by the French Communist Party and its affiliated union, the CGT, which sought to stir xenophobic reactions by associating proposed work force cuts with the "German forces" and a "German-dominated" EC Commission.[351] Steelworkers staged a series of *"coups du poing"* -- raids by

---

[345] The APA served "as a relay between the debtor companies and the creditors to assure them payment of their interest, and the repayment of their credits at the fixed maturities." *Journal Officiel* (July 3-4, 1979), p. 28. The former majority shareholders of Usinor and Sacilor were required by the government to "abandon" loans which they had extended to the two companies. Sacilor *Annual Report* 1979, p. 43; Usinor *Annual Report* 1978, p. 7.

[346] Sacilor noted in its 1979 *Annual Report* (pp.41-42) that in addition to nominal interest payments, no principal would be paid until at least 1984. Sacilor further noted that considering the "conditional character of the repayment of the loans" and "the special modalities of their repayment," the outstanding principal could be considered part of Sacilor's net assets for net worth purposes -- suggesting, in other words, that neither interest nor principal would be repaid.

[347] *L'Humanité* (September 21, 1978).

[348] Parliamentary Debates, Senate, *Journal Officiel* at 2689 (October 18, 1978).

[349] *Le Monde* (January 18, 1979).

[350] In 1979 Jules Ferry, head of the Chambre Syndicale, argued that "the French steel industry should aim at maintaining its share of EC steel capacity at present level." *Metal Bulletin* (February 6, 1979). The industry and government faced substantial pressure from unions to defer or abandon portions of the Rescue Plan which called for work force reductions. *L'Humanité* (September 21, 1978); *Le Figaro* (September 21, 1978); *Metal Bulletin* (April 10, 1979).

[351] *Le Drapeau Rouge* (December 30-31, 1978).

small groups of activists to block roads and railroads and occupy office buildings to protest job cuts.[352] "Bombs, battering rams and protest marches" shook steel towns such as Denain and Longwy. However, the Communists suffered a setback when most other steel unions assented to a "social pact" with management which barred outright dismissals, but achieved work force reductions through early retirement, alternative employment schemes, and large voluntary departure bonuses.[353]

Mitterrand's Plan Acier. The condition of the French industry continued to worsen in the aftermath of the 1978 Rescue Plan. In May 1981 Socialist François Mitterrand was elected President, having pledged to reject industrial decline and to establish ambitious new steel mills in areas worst hit by the crisis. In the fall of that year, Usinor and Sacilor, in a state of total financial collapse, were virtually completely nationalized; $2.6 billion in outstanding government debt was converted to equity, giving the state an 86 percent share of Usinor and a 93 percent share of Sacilor. The Budget Minister, appalled at the "stupendous failure" of the "massive financial gamble to which the steel policy community had collectively committed $7.4 billion of public money," called the collapse of Usinor and Sacilor "the greatest scandal since Panama."[354] Undaunted, the Mitterrand government released an ambitious new "*Plan Acier*" in April 1982, pursuant to which it planned to revitalize the industry through massive new government capital investments and closer coordination of the operations of Usinor and Sacilor.[355]

Mitterrand's *Plan Acier* was based on three scenarios involving varying estimates of French steel consumption in 1986, developed by Professor Pierre Judet of Grenoble University. Judet's pessimistic scenario indicated that France would need 20 million metric tons of production capability by 1986; a "middle" scenario, envisioned a need for 21.8 million metric tons; and an optimistic scenario calling for a production capability of 24 million metric tons. Any steel plan based on either the "pessimistic" or "middle" scenarios would require a complete overhaul of the French steel industry involving major closings and work force reductions, particularly in Lorraine.[356] Although the EC Commission regarded even Judet's pessimistic scenario estimates as too

---

[352] *Le Monde* (January 18, 1979).

[353] *Financial Times* (January 19, 1980).

[354] Hayward, "The Nemesis of Industrial Patriotism," p. 526.

[355] *Metal Bulletin* (January 29, April 23, 1982; April 15, October 1, 1983). A total of $3.8 billion was earmarked for Usinor and Sacilor through 1986. "If the FFr 22 billion [$4.9 billion] of rescue-finance poured into steel at the end of 1978 and the FFr 13 billion [$2.8 billion] of aid for the period 1978-81 is taken into account, the total state contribution to French steel over a period of eight years has been over FFr 60 billion [$12.9 billion]." *Steel Times* (November 11, 1982).

[356] President Mitterrand had visited Lorraine in 1982 and promised that layoffs and closures in the steel industry were out of the question. *Ibid.*

high, pushed by the unions, the socialist government for political and labor reasons chose to take the Judet Report's "high option" for its *Plan Acier* and based the two groups' investment plans for the years 1982-86 on it.[357]

By the time the *Plan Acier* was adopted, based on Judet's "optimistic" scenario, the French government was already adopting austerity measures which made the consumption estimates on which the optimistic scenario was based completely unrealistic. Nevertheless, in June 1982, the cabinet adopted the Plan based on the "incredibly ambitious, not to say foolhardy" objective of 24 million metric tons of steel in 1986.[358] The government committed to provide Usinor and Sacilor $2.7 billion for investments over a period of five years;[359] in addition, it was estimated that the Treasury would be required to spend $761 to $913 million annually to subsidize the losses of the state steel firms, $304 million to cover debt repayments, and $456 million to $608 million to cover the costs associated with work force reductions.[360]

The *Plan Acier* began coming unravelled virtually from its inception. With consumption falling in 1982, it was quickly apparent that the projected capacity of 24 million metric tons by 1986 was "utterly unrealistic;" nevertheless, Usinor and Sacilor proceeded with investments on the basis of the Plan,[361] for "having geared up the industry for an increase in output it proved difficult to engineer a change in direction."[362] Both firms suffered staggering losses in 1982, and worse prospects were seen by 1983.[363] The number of jobs to be eliminated under the Plan, 12,000, was regarded by observers as "much too low;"[364] yet even these proposed work force reductions triggered major civil disturbances across the steelmaking regions of France.[365] Such disturbances were particularly difficult for a left-oriented government to ignore, and decisions on work force reduction were delayed.

In early 1983, Sacilor and Usinor called for a "rethink" of the *Plan Acier*, a "return to square one."[366] With even labor unions criticizing the Plan as

---

[357] *Metal Bulletin Monthly* (September 1983).

[358] Hayward, "The Nemesis of Industrial Patriotism," p. 528.

[359] *Metal Bulletin Monthly* (September 1983).

[360] *Le Monde* (September 30, 1982), cited in Hayward (1987), p. 529.

[361] *Metal Bulletin Monthly* (September 1983).

[362] *Financial Times* (October 13, 1986).

[363] The state firms suffered a combined loss of $1.3 billion in 1982 and $ 1.9 billion in 1981. *Les Echos* (March 5, 1984); *Le Monde* (March 7, 1984); *Steel Times* (June 1983); *L'Usine Nouvelle* (June 2, 1983).

[364] *L'Usine Nouvelle* (December 16, 1982).

[365] In 1982, demonstrators blocked the Tour de France bicycle race at Denain, calling the Premier a "traitor." *Les Echos* (September 27, 1982).

[366] *Metal Bulletin* (April 29, 1983).

"unrealistic and utopian," in late 1983 the French government conceded that a downward revision in the projected 1985 production targets would be needed, and that a link needed to be established between industry profitability and government aid.[367] The government's action reflected a growing concern over the mounting losses of the major public sector enterprises and ultimately, over the entire direction of Mitterrand's economic program.[368] With Usinor and Sacilor calling for massive new injections of state aid, the Mitterrand government took the position that such aid would only be forthcoming if the two firms could devise a new plan for restoring the industry to profitability, a government stand which, if adhered to, would virtually ensure large-scale layoffs.[369]

After months of difficult negotiations between the government, labor and Usinor and Sacilor, the government unveiled a new steel plan in March 1984.[370] The new plan called for a series of plant closings that would eliminate some redundancies between Usinor and Sacilor, but which would entail an unprecedented cut of 20-50,000 jobs. An infusion of 15 billion francs (over \$2 billion) in government subsidies would be granted for new capital investments with the objective of restoring Usinor and Sacilor to profitability by 1987, \$720 million of which would be forthcoming in 1984.[371] The job cuts called for by the new plan touched off a "political and social cyclone" in France.[372] Riots broke out in the steelmaking regions, government offices were ransacked by steelworkers in Lorraine, and polls showed that the Socialist government enjoyed less public support than any party in power since the Fifth Republic.[373]

---

[367] *Financial Times* (October 15, November 24, 1983).

[368] While Usinor and Sacilor had suffered the largest losses, nationalized firms in the chemical, automobile, coal and shipbuilding sectors were also incurring progressively greater losses. *L'Usine Nouvelle* (June 2, 1983). *Le Nouvelle Economiste* commented on March 26, 1984 that "2 steel industry groups, which continue to battle it out among themselves, will be soaking up 5.5 billion francs [\$.6 billion] in appropriations -- an amount, moreover, which isn't even adequate for their needs."

[369] *Le Nouvelle Economiste* (March 26, 1984); *Metal Bulletin* (November 29, December 30, 1983). In early 1984, Usinor and Sacilor asked the government for an infusion of \$1.6 billion to finance their 1984 operations. The government rejected the request; the Ministry of Finance declared that "the government is no longer in a position to finance such sums." *Steel Times* (March 1984).

[370] *L'Usine Nouvelle* (January 26, 1984); *Les Echos* (March 23, 1984).

[371] *Metal Bulletin* (April 3, 1984).

[372] *Les Echos* (April 2, 1984).

[373] *Business Week* (April 23, 1984). One labor leader stated that "The anger of the steelworkers and the blast furnace is rumbling. We share it. Scrapping steelworks in Lorraine and four modern ones in Fos that run well . . . will involve the death of the coal mines, a source of wealth many countries envy us for, and has absolutely nothing to do with any modernization plan. . . . We cannot accept such human, industrial, and financial waste. We are therefore going to pursue and expand union actions among the broadest possible group of workers with the

The proposed $720 million in new subsidies for 1984, while substantial, represented a 15 percent cut from 1983 levels and was only about half the amount sought by Usinor and Sacilor, and virtually ensured that substantial closures and job cuts would be necessary.[374] Over the following months, announcements of new closures, usually attributed to cuts in state subsidies to steel, triggered new violent actions by steelworkers.[375] Notwithstanding the anger of displaced workers, who wished for a higher level of public expenditure, the government withstood considerable internal and external pressure to cut its subsidies to steel. The Ministry of Finance was eager to "reduce the ruinous demands made on public funds by the steel firms,"[376] and France was under mounting pressure from the EC Commission, which had set the deadline of December 31, 1985 as the cutoff date for further subsidies. Nevertheless, in the fall of 1984, Usinor and Sacilor called on the government to write off their accumulated debts of $1.5 billion and $1.4 billion, respectively, and *Le Monde* surmised (in the event, correctly) that it was unlikely that the French state would reject these demands.[377] At the end of 1984, the government announced its intention to grant $3.1 - $3.4 billion in subsidies to the steel industry between 1984 and 1987, notwithstanding the Commission's deadline; about $1.7 billion would be devoted to investments, the remainder to "wiping out existing debts."[378] France joined with Italy in demanding that the 1985 deadline be extended.[379]

The Move Toward Greater Concentration.   As Usinor and Sacilor struggled to achieve financial viability, the consolidation of the French steel industry continued. The state steel firms absorbed a number of the remaining private sector firms which had become insolvent, including the venerable Creusot-Loire, which had cast cannon for Napoleon's *Grande Armee* (acquired by Usinor in 1984), and Forges et Laminoirs de Bretagne (acquired

---

support of the populations concerned to make it impossible to apply the bad decisions that have been adopted." *Les Echos* (April 2, 1984).

[374] *Les Echos* (March 5, 1984); *Le Monde* (March 7, 1984); *The Economist* (March 10, 1984). The impetus for the subsidy reduction came from the Minister of Industry, Laurent Fabius, who wished to channel state funds away from steel toward "sectors with a future," particularly telecommunications. *Le Monde* (March 6, 1984).

[375] In 1985, cuts in state funding were blamed for the announced plan to close a universal beam mill operated by Unimétal, a joint subsidiary of Usinor and Sacilor near Valenciennes. The announcement prompted angry protests by workers, who destroyed a section of the permanent way of the main railway line and dumped steel in the river Escaut to block navigation. *Metal Bulletin* (August 2, 1985).

[376] Hayward, "The Nemesis of Industrial Patriotism," p. 531.

[377] *Le Monde* (October 5, 1984).

[378] *Les Echos* (December 6, 1984); *Le Monde* (December 7, 1984).

[379] *Financial Times* (March 26, 1985).

by Sacilor in 1984).[380] Usinor moved aggressively into downstream steel products, acquiring a number of pipe and tube facilities, controlling interests in the pipe and tube operations of Vallourec, control of Valexy, a maker of small diameter pipes, and control of Profilafroid, a number of cold-formed sections.[381] A joint venture, Unimétal, was formed by Usinor and Sacilor to operate the non-flat rolled steelworks of the Usinor and Sacilor groups, laying the groundwork for a series of facility closures; in early 1986, Sacilor took full control of Unimétal, leaving Usinor primarily a producer of flat-rolled steel and pipe.[382] Both Usinor and Sacilor overhauled their organizations, turning all of their operating divisions into separate subsidiaries, with Usinor and Sacilor remaining purely holding companies.[383] The French government had been seeking to nudge Usinor and Sacilor toward greater cooperation since the early 1980s, and in the fall of 1986, a single individual, François Mer, was appointed by the state as chairman of both Usinor and Sacilor. Finally, in 1987, the two state groups were merged, becoming Usinor-Sacilor, and activities of many of the two groups' operating subsidiaries were consolidated.

The consolidations, while commanding a great deal of media attention, did not immediately restore the state steel sector to financial or operational viability. Constant changes in management and policies, coupled with closures and job cuts, left management and the work force demoralized. Poor management resulted in low yields and productivity.[384] Usinor and Sacilor suffered aggregate losses of $977.5 million in 1985, $1.8 billion in 1986, and an estimated $250 million in 1987.[385] However Usinor-Sacilor reported that it expected to show a profit in the first six months of 1988 and to finish the year in the black, reflecting the company's restructuring efforts as well as increasing demand from the auto, construction and appliance industries.[386]

The improvement in Usinor-Sacilor's position also reflected continuing state financial support. Government steel consultant Jean Gandois concluded in mid-1986 that the state steel sector would need further public financial aid,[387] and to a substantial degree, state aid had been arranged or was forthcoming after the Commission's December 31, 1985 cutoff date. The state

---

[380] *Metal Bulletin* (August 7, 1984).

[381] *Metal Bulletin* (July 10, October 23, December 28, 1984). By 1987, some of these takeovers were "regarded as having been mistakes, imposed on the steel groups by the state for reasons other than strictly industrial or commercial ones." *Metal Bulletin* (January 6, 1987).

[382] *Metal Bulletin* (January 15, 1988).

[383] *Metal Bulletin* (October 8, 1985).

[384] *Financial Times* (October 13, 1986).

[385] *Metal Bulletin* (February 22, 1988); *Financial Times* (May 5, 1987).

[386] *Wall Street Journal* (May 20, 1988).

[387] *La Tribune de l'Economie* (June 25, 1986); *Le Nouvelle Economiste* (July 11, 1986); *L'Usine Nouvelle* (September 4, 1986).

injected new equity of $561.7 million each into Usinor and Sacilor in 1985, and secured EC Commission approval prior to the deadline for a new injection of $674 million to be made in the years 1985, 1986, and 1987.[388] At the end of 1985, Usinor and Sacilor issued an estimated $2.2 billion in convertible bonds, with subscription reserved for the state or the public sector; the French press, commenting on this transaction, indicated that the state hoped to inject $3.4 billion into the steel sector between 1985 and 1987, and that "this form of capital raising effectively circumvents the legislation drawn up by the European Commission to end subsidies to the steel industry."[389] In late 1986, the French government announced it would "regularize" the balance sheets of Usinor and Sacilor by converting $7.3 billion in "shareholders advances" (i.e., state loans) into equity shares.[390]

Italy

The experience of the Italian steel industry demonstrates how social and political pressures can foster fundamentally irrational patterns of investment in an industry dominated by state-owned companies. Finsider, the state-owned entity that produces virtually all of Italy's pig iron and more than half of its steel,[391] has been in a state of continual financial crisis since the mid-1970s; its accumulated losses from 1976 through 1987 totalled more than $11 billion. Yet Finsider, the fifth largest steel maker in the world in 1987,[392] has failed to make the capacity reductions which offer its only real chance for profitability. Italy's massive subsidies to the Finsider group, and its continued emphasis on expansion through the initial phase of the steel crisis, have been the source of bitter conflict with other Member States in the Community. Despite the Commission's ban on state aid, Finsider will collapse without additional government help on a large scale, a dilemma which seriously jeopardizes the future of the Community's aid prohibition.

The Italian steel industry was created largely by the state to meet the needs of a rapidly developing society and to spur economic progress in its most backward regions. By the mid-1970s, these goals had to a great extent been achieved: Italy had become an industrial society, self-sufficient in steel

---

[388] La Tribune de l'Economie (January 7, 1987).

[389] Le Monde (November 12, 1985); Le Figaro (November 11, 1985). The Commission approved this arrangement as long as it was implemented prior to January 1, 1986.

[390] American Metal Market (September 25, 1986). Perhaps the best indicator that a new round of massive subsidies was seen as likely, notwithstanding the Commission's ban, was the lively speculation in Usinor and Sacilor stock by private investors: "Speculating over future subsidization programs, private investors have taken up about 20 percent of Usinor's shares and 9 percent of Sacilor's shares, directed by the nationalized banks and other institutional investors over the past three years at very low prices." Ibid.

[391] IRI Group Yearbook 1987, p. 20.

[392] Metal Bulletin (February 15, 1988).

production, and its less-advanced regions had been substantially integrated into the national economy. However, the state had also created a political constituency determined to resist all efforts to contain the expansion of, much less reduce, steelmaking capacity. With the onset of the steel crisis, when it became apparent that demand growth was slackening and that expansion plans should be curtailed, the government confronted a volatile coalition of southern legislators and voters, industrial unions, leftist political parties and steel industry managers opposed to a more conservative program. Under pressure from these groups, the government continued to expand capacity for nearly a decade in the face of depressed prices and stagnant demand, resulting in an unbroken string of staggering losses.

Large scale government financial aid has enabled the Italian steel industry to resist capacity cuts tenaciously. Despite continual prodding from the European Commission, Finsider did not make any significant cuts in capacity or employment until 1983; in that year, with the EC deadline on state aid approaching, the Italian steel industry began to rationalize. However, even then its actions were inadequate in light of the problems it confronted; Finsider did not close large mills, and it relied on early retirement schemes and other incremental measures to trim its work force. At present, Finsider finds itself in a fundamentally untenable position, suffering huge losses which the state is not legally permitted to make good, but which only the state can pay.

Public Ownership and Public Purpose.   The Italian   government's participation in the industrial and commercial fields is conducted through *"enti,"* or state-owned corporations. IRI, founded by Mussolini in 1933, is the largest ente.[393]   IRI is divided into a number of *"finanziarie"* -- financial companies which in turn control operating companies. Finsider -- Società Finanziaria Siderurgica -- is the 99.82 percent IRI-owned company for the state steel sector. The company, founded in 1937, controls dozens of operating companies in steel and related sectors. Ultimately, Finsider, like all the state-owned corporations, is answerable to the Italian government.[394]

As a state-owned corporation, Finsider has generally been viewed as a tool for the achievement of certain policy goals. First among these, in the early years, was the creation of an efficient volume producer of steel as a base for the industrialization of the Italian economy. Oscar Sinigaglia, Finsider's first President, envisioned the creation of large coastal integrated steel mills, which

---

[393] IRI controls more than seventy-five percent of the state's financial, commercial and industrial holdings and accounted for nearly four percent of Italian value-added in 1985. IRI *Group Yearbook 1987,* p. 15.

[394] Two "Interministerial Committees," CIPI and CIPE, "lay down general guidelines within the framework of Government economic policy" for the operation of state enterprises. The Ministry of State Holdings supervises the implementation of these guidelines, and a Parliamentary commission oversees the management of the state enterprises and the allocation of state funds. *Ibid.,* p. 14.

142

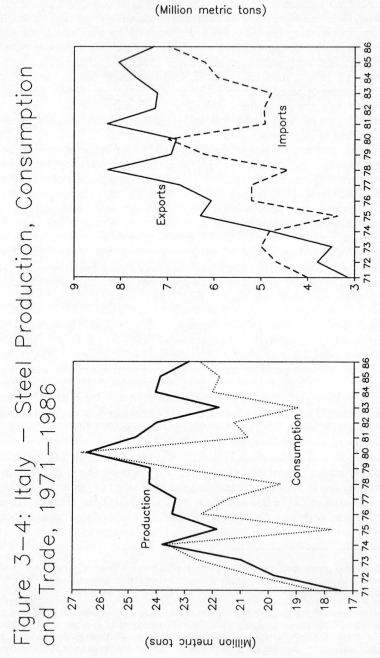

(Million metric tons)

Figure 3-4: Italy — Steel Production, Consumption and Trade, 1971–1986

Source: International Iron and Steel Institute, Steel Statistical Yearbook, 1981, 1987. Production and Consumption refer to crude steel; Exports and Imports refer to semi-finished and finished steel.

would receive iron ore, coal and other raw materials by sea, serving as a springboard to propel Italy's economy into a new phase of development.[395] Although Sinigaglia's plans were interrupted by the Second World War, his ambitious program was resumed after the close of hostilities. By the late 1940s, Finsider was operating several coastal integrated steel mills. In 1956, Finsider decided to build a greenfield mill at Taranto, on the heel of the Italian boot.[396] The huge new mill, which was constructed in phases between 1960 and 1976, accounted for nearly seventy percent of Finsider's total production in 1977.[397]

Northern Italy has always been wealthier than the South, and the boom that swept the North in the fifties and sixties only served to aggravate that division. The great system of state holdings was seen as a tool to narrow the gap by stimulating Southern development. As early as 1957, state-owned corporations were required by law to channel a portion of their investment to the Mezzogiorno.[398] Accordingly, Finsider's ambitious development plans called for the construction or rehabilitation of steel mills in Taranto, Naples, and Gioia Tauro, all of which are located in the South. In theory, the placement of massive industrial facilities in these underdeveloped areas would generate a wave of development throughout the region.[399]

Expansion and Crisis. In the fifties and sixties, it seemed that Finsider could accomplish its goals. The ambitious expansion program undertaken by the state, culminating in the construction of the massive integrated mill at Taranto, boosted steel production from approximately six million tons in 1955 to almost twenty-four million tons in 1974.[400] In 1974, the year in which the steady climb in steel consumption in Italy and the world peaked, the Italian steel industry was operating at a reasonably robust 83 percent of capacity. Italsider, the main Finsider operating subsidiary, turned a small profit after four years of losses. Modern facilities at Taranto and Naples produced steel for Italian industry and employed thousands of workers.

---

[395] A. Wormald, "Growth Promotion: The Creation of a Modern Steel Industry," in *The State As Entrepreneur*, ed. S. Holland (London: Weidenfeld and Nicolson, 1972), pp. 94-97.

[396] *Ibid.*, pp. 97-99.

[397] Masi, "Nuova Italsider-Taranto and the Steel Crisis: Problems, Innovations and Prospects," in Meny and Wright, *The Politics of Steel*, p. 479.

[398] *Laws* 634 (1957) and 717 (1965).

[399] The policy of Southern development is discussed in Campanna, *Steel in Southern Italy*. Campanna, a former President of Finsider, acknowledged that the regional development impact of these mills "did not come up to expectations." *Ibid.*, p. 23. Further, the decision to locate these mills in the South was not without costs. The Italian steel market is centered in the North, and high transportation costs put the southern mills at a competitive disadvantage. *Ibid.*, p. 24.

[400] A. Harris, *U.S. Trade Problems in Steel* (New York: Praeger, 1983), p. 200.

Underlying these encouraging indicators, however, were significant structural weaknesses. The rapid growth of the state-owned steel sector rested on a narrow financial base. Finsider managed to generate only fourteen percent of its total investment requirements out of cash flow;[401] the remainder was borrowed or provided by the government. The state contributed eighteen percent of total fixed investment for the construction of the Taranto mill.[402] Despite this considerable state assistance, Finsider had to borrow substantial sums in the private markets to finance its Taranto mill and other projects. As a result, debt service was equal to almost twenty percent of revenues by 1977.[403] Finsider also faced serious labor problems. Worker unrest was endemic; for *each* worker the steel industry lost 2.8 days annually to labor conflicts in the years 1974-77.[404] Meanwhile, average hourly labor costs soared 1065 percent between 1960 and 1978.[405]

The onset of the steel crisis saw a drastic decline in the demand for steel just as Finsider's Taranto works became fully operational. The Taranto mill, Europe's largest, could achieve significant scale economies if operated at full capacity but would incur devastating cost penalties if forced to operate at a lower rate, which is in fact what occurred. Italian consumption plummeted 25 percent and Italsider, Finsider's largest operating company, plunged into what would prove to be a permanent state of deficit operations. Between 1975 and 1980 alone, Italsider incurred losses totalling more than $2.3 billion and the company has never subsequently broken even (table 3-13).

The initial Italian response to falling domestic demand was to launch a massive export drive. In 1975, exports surged nearly 32 percent, to 38 percent of production, and exports to the United States quadrupled. In that year, the Italian steel industry generated a trade surplus of more than $1.1 billion.[406] Despite the fact that the industry was suffering heavy losses, it continued to export in order to maintain employment. Undaunted by growing trade friction

---

[401] Aldo Sorci, "L'Evoluzione del Settore Siderurgico in Italia," in *L'Industria Siderurgica*, ed. L. Selleri and D. Velo (Milan: Giuffrè Editore, 1986), p. 100.

[402] The government provided $123 million in the form of contributions to the IRI "Endowment Fund." The Cassa per il Mezzogiorno, a government-funded institution dedicated to the development of the South, provided $44.6 million in capital grants and $238 million in subsidized loans. Additional funds were provided by the European Investment Bank. A. Wormald, "Growth Promotion," pp. 100-102.

[403] J. Eisenhammer and M. Rhodes, "The Politics of Public Sector Steel in Italy: From the 'Economic Miracle' to the Crisis of the Eighties," in Meny and Wright, *The Politics of Steel*, p. 442.

[404] *Ibid.*, p. 427. Alberto Campanna, former President of Finsider, categorized the company's losses due to labor unrest as "astronomical." Campanna, *Steel in Southern Italy*, p. 26.

[405] J. Eisenhammer and M. Rhodes, "The Politics of Public Sector Steel in Italy: From the 'Economic Miracle' to the Crisis of the Eighties," in Meny and Wright, *The Politics of Steel*, p. 428.

[406] A. Harris, *U.S. Trade Problems in Steel*, p. 201.

arising out of Italy's aggressive export tactics, the Minister for State Holdings declared in October 1982 that the state steel industry would increase exports 50 percent by 1985.[407]

Table 3-13. Italsider and Nuova Italsider: Summary of Performance, 1975-1986

Company	Year	Sales (Mil $)	Profit (Mil $)	Raw Prod. (Mil NT)	Profit ($/NT)
Italsider	1975	2696	(106)	11.5	(9)
Italsider	1976	2633	(150)	11.9	(13)
Italsider	1977	2697	(453)	11.2	(40)
Italsider	1978	3242	(420)	11.5	(37)
Italsider	1979	4062	(321)	10.7	(30)
Italsider	1980	4119	(804)	11.9	(68)
Italsider	1981	3827	(800)	12.1	(66)
Nuova Ital.	1982	3462	(761)	11.1	(69)
Nuova Ital.	1983	2736	(766)	10.1	(76)
Nuova Ital.	1984*	2697	(460)	14.9	(31)
Nuova Ital.	1985*	3083	(240)	14.8	(16)
Nuova Ital.	1986*	3480	(376)	14.4	(27)

* Production Data for Finsider as reported by IISI.
Source: Italsider, Nuova Italsider *Annual Reports*.
Converted to U.S. dollars at average annual exchange rate given by International Monetary Fund.
Conversion: 1975: 652.8, 1976: 832.3, 1977: 882.4, 1978: 848.7, 1979: 830.9, 1980: 856.4, 1981: 1136.8, 1982: 1352.5, 1983: 1518.8, 1984: 1757.0, 1985: 1909.4, 1986: 1490.8

---

[407] Gianni DeMichelis, in *L'Espresso* (November 28, 1982).

At the same time that the steel industry was generating a large trade surplus, domestic groups were urging the Italian government to protect the home market.[408] Although the EC Commission was supposedly managing the Community's import policies, the Italian government closed a number of customs posts important to steel importers and did not reopen them until the Commission brought the matter before the European Court of Justice.[409] When EC measures to limit imports from third countries failed to satisfy Italy, the government did not hesitate to impose unilateral restrictions.[410]

Table 3-14. Italian Capacity Utilization

	Percent
1974	83
1978	68
1979	65
1980	67
1981	61
1982	58
1983	55
1984	65
1985	66

Source: Eurostat Commission

In spite of the crisis, proposals to curtail Finsider's expansion plans met with fierce resistance. Based on the optimistic market forecasts of the early 1970s, Finsider planned to double the capacity of its Taranto plant and to build a new integrated steel works at Gioia Tauro in impoverished Calabria.[411] Although the Gioia Tauro project ultimately was scaled back, Italian steel-making capacity continued to increase until 1981, making Italy one of the principal sources of the Community's capacity surplus. As capacity increased, utilization rates sank from 83 percent in 1974 to an abysmal 55 percent in 1983 (table 3-14). Incongruously, employment in the Italian steel industry actually

---

[408] *La Repubblica* (October 28, 1980).

[409] *Metal Bulletin* (February 13 and May 15, 1981).

[410] In 1982 Italy imposed restrictions on imported tube and pipe fittings from third countries, despite Commission opposition. *Official Journal*, No. L 86/22 (March 31, 1983).

[411] J. Eisenhammer and M. Rhodes, "The Politics of Public Sector Steel in Italy," pp. 429-430.

rose by 3,900 workers between 1974 and 1980.[412] *Il Borghese* observed on November 22, 1982 that

> *ever since 1968, we read in Italsider's annual reports that the market is growing steadily softer, with supply outpacing demand; that consequently "softened" prices turn out to be lower than predicted; yet as a counter corollary to this, we see in the very same annual reports that there are still more programs for plant expansion and consequent increases in corporate indebtedness. We would cite by way of example the doubling of capacity in the unmanageable Taranto plant and the start of expansion at Gioia Tauro. . . . Now the government is being called upon for more trillions for the public sector steel industry. . . .*

The costs to the government were immense. Between 1977 and 1981, the government, through IRI, pumped nearly $2.2 billion into the Finsider group in the form of "recapitalizations." During the same period, the steel industry received approximately $2.7 billion in capital grants, soft loans, and interest subsidies pursuant to Italy's newly enacted Industrial Reconstruction and Reconversion Act, designed to aid financially distressed sectors, and $81 million in capital grants from the Cassa per il Mezzogiorno (table 3-15).

Restructuring.   Italy's relentless, heavily subsidized expansion during the early years of the steel crisis put it on a collision course with the EC Commission and the other Member States, who by the beginning of the 1980s were struggling with the issue of how to effect major cuts in Community capacity. The Commission's Aids Code effectively rendered some forms of Italian state aid illegal, and required the elimination of most forms of aid by the end of 1985.[413]   The Commission's post-Elsinore decree on capacity reduction in June 1983 fell most heavily on Italy; it called for 3.5 million metric tons in capacity cuts and conditioned further approval of subsidies and production quotas on compliance. This action provoked a violent reaction in Italy, and was the prelude to several years of "arm wrestling" between Italy and the Commission over the issues of closures, quotas, and subsidies.[414]

The Commission's principal leverage was its ability to approve additional tranches of state aid for Finsider, whose situation was becoming increasingly desperate. The company's 1983 losses were almost $1.4 billion, and new capital injections were essential; in January of 1984, the company announced that unless immediate state assistance was forthcoming, it would be unable to

---

[412] *Ibid.*, p. 428.

[413] *Official Journal*, L. 228/14 (August 7, 1981).

[414] As the Italians saw it, the production quotas proposed by the Commission required Italy to produce less steel than it consumed, a situation which one union leader characterized as "unthinkable and unacceptable". *L'Espresso* (June 26, 1983).

Table 3-15. Direct Italian Government Financial Aid To The Steel
Industry,1977-81 (million U.S. dollars)

	Increases in Capitalization	Aid under Law 675 (year end balances)	Grants from the Cassa per il Mezzogiorno
1977	–	74	3
1978	733	1,001	4
1979	354	333	17
1980	689	1,348	57
1981	380	*	NA
Total	2,156	NA	NA

Source: Italsider *Annual Reports*, 1977-80; Minutes of CIPI Meetings.
Converted to U.S. dollars at average annual exchange rate given by International Monetary
Fund.
Conversion: 1977: 882, 1978: 849, 1979: 831, 1980: 856, 1981: 1,137.
* 1981 aid included $219 million in capital grants and $77 million in low interest loans.

meet payroll for the month.[415] Finsider incurred further losses in 1984 and
in 1985 (table 3-16). Using this situation to best advantage, the Commission
unblocked state aid in increments as the Italians appeared to make some
concessions on capacity. All told, the EC approved almost $13.8 billion in aid
to the Italian steel industry between 1980 and 1985.[416]

The most direct source of state funds to meet Finsider's losses came
through recapitalizations. Under this method of financing, the state
contributed money to IRI's "Endowment Fund;" IRI, in turn, made the funds
available to Finsider through the purchase of shares. The Italian government
also requested EC approval for $186 million in regional aid grants to the
industry between 1981 and 1985.[417] Much of the regional aid was made
available through the Cassa del Mezzogiorno, which was empowered to give

---

[415] *Financial Times* (January 4, 1984).

[416] This figure may be an underestimate. German steel makers believed that Italy awarded
additional aid to Finsider, approximately $3.2 billion, without EC consent. Reuters North
European Service, November 13, 1984.

[417] *Official Journal*, L. 227/24 (June 29, 1983).

Table 3-16. Finsider's Losses (million U.S. dollars)

1976	(225)
1977	(568)
1978	(684)
1979	(638)
1980	(1,450)
1981	(1,874)
1982	(1,081)
1983	(1,379)
1984	(908)
1985	(592)
1986	(657)
1987	(1,235*)

Sources: J. Eisenhammer and M. Rhodes, "The Politics of Public Section Steel in Italy: From the 'Economic Miracle' to the Crisis of the Eighties," in *The Politics of Steel: Western Europe and the Steel Industry in the Crisis Years 1974-84*, p. 443; IRI *Annual Reports*, 1984 and 1985; *Il Mondo Economico* (June 29, 1987); *The Financial Times* (January 18, 1988).

Converted to U.S. dollars at average annual exchange rate given by International Monetary Fund.

Conversion: 1976: 832, 1977: 882, 1978: 849, 1979: 831,1980: 856, 1981: 1,137, 1982: 1,353, 1983: 1,519, 1984: 1,757, 1985: 1,909, 1986: 1,490, 1987: 1,296.

* Estimated

outright grants and low-interest loans to eligible industrialization projects. Other incentives for undertaking economic activity in the South included preferential rail rates, tax exemptions and reduced social security payments for certain workers.[418] 54 percent of Finsider's investments and 37 percent of its employees were in the South in 1985;[419] thus, the company was well positioned to take advantage of these programs.

State financing of an early retirement scheme was a less visible form of state aid which served to reduce Finsider's personnel costs. Under this plan, steel workers were allowed to retire at age 50. The program came into effect in 1984 and, by January of the following year, between six and seven thousand workers had taken advantage of it.[420]   Finsider considered the plan "fundamental" to its goal of shedding 26,500 employees between 1984 and 1986.[421]

---

[418] *CCH Common Market Reporter* ¶ 26,618.

[419] IRI *Group Yearbook 1987*, pp. 18, 129.

[420] *Il Mondo Economico* (January 10, 1985).

[421] Sorci, "L'Evoluzione del Settore Siderurgico in Italia," p. 109.

The Private Sector. Italy's private producers are primarily smaller companies that operate scrap-based mills, such as the Bresciani in Northern Italy. While these companies do not have the huge fixed costs of the state-owned integrated mills, and have traditionally been vigorous competitors, their financial situation was worsening by 1980. A sharp rise in the cost of scrap and of the energy inputs necessary to melt it put these small producers under pressure,[422] and by the early 1980s Italy's beleaguered private companies were complaining that they could not compete with subsidized state steel.[423] Finsider's management urged that any Italian capacity reductions taken at the behest of the EC come at the expense of private producers; Parliament therefore passed legislation that paid private producers to cut capacity.[424] *Il Mondo Economico* reported on April 16, 1985 that 54 steel producers had sought 480 billion lire ($251 million) under the program. This sum, it remarked, is "A drop in the sea compared to the quantity of public money poured into Finsider: the [Law] 46 has, however, sufficed to make numerous champagne corks pop in the Brescian valleys and the plains of Friulia, but not to resolve the question of excess capacity." A few years later, after $638.9 million had been spent, *L'Espresso* summed up the program this way: "The proof of how badly Law 193 of 1983 was made is shown by the fact that, after so many awards for dismantling, Italian productive capacity has simply risen, and the Minister has always refused to furnish a detailed breakdown of expenditures."[425]

The Continuing Italian Dilemma. The Italian steel industry should have begun 1986 in reasonably good condition; trillions of lire had been spent to modernize facilities and to reduce costs, and domestic consumption was at its highest level in six years. Finsider forecast in 1985 that in 1986 it would earn a profit for the first time in decades.[426] Instead, the company suffered losses of $657 million in 1986, and was expected to report a massive $1.2 billion loss for 1987.[427] In May of 1986, Finsider was once again forced to seek the

---

[422] *Metal Bulletin* (August 1, 1980; August 17, 1982).

[423] *Metal Bulletin* (August 2, 1982).

[424] *Law* 46, Article 20 and *Law* 193.

[425] *L'Espresso* (October 4, 1987). The government also requested EC approval to subsidize the energy costs of private producers, and to provide them with low-interest loans. When the price of scrap soared, the government provided subsidies of $.03 per kilo on imports. *Il Mondo Economico* (January 10, 1985).

[426] *Il Mondo Economico* (July 1, 1985).

[427] *Financial Times* (January 18, 1988).

assistance of the state.[428] Outraged German steel producers complained that the Italians were violating the Aids Code,[429] and the European Commission agreed to investigate.[430]

In explaining the spectacular failure of the Italian state steel industry to generate a profit, management cited a familiar list of woes: a structural drop in demand in the developed world; competition from aggressive producers such as Korea, Brazil and Mexico; the imposition of market barriers in important export markets. But as *L'Espresso* remarked: "Steel is in crisis in all the world. But elsewhere it makes a profit from time to time."[431] The persistence of the Italian dilemma lies in factors specific to that nation.

Finsider officials have laid the blame for the company's problems on undercapitalization and resultant high finance costs.[432] Clearly, these costs have had an impact on Finsider's profitability. Ultimately, however, Finsider's debt was in great part incurred due to overambitious expansion projects undertaken to achieve political objectives, continuing management problems and a stubborn refusal to reduce its substantial capacity surplus.[433] *Il Mondo Economico* remarked on May 26, 1986 that:

When, on Monday, June 27 [1986], Finsider holds a special session to plug up, with the last injection of public funds authorized by the Community, the hole of 1985, it will be clear to everyone how deceptive was the excuse of financial burdens adopted for so many years to justify the disasters of the old State Holdings: the companies closed in red not because they are strangled by high interest rates, but they pay too much money to the banks because they administer badly the

---

[428] *Il Mondo Economico* (May 12, 1986). In late 1986, Finsider "increased its capital" by the issuance of $1 billion worth of new stock, 99.9 percent of which was purchased by IRI. Finsider *Annual Report 1986*, p. 33. Without this recapitalization, "the survival of the firm would have been impossible." *Ibid.*, p. 18. Nevertheless, Finsider needed more subsidies: "The uncertain market for future years," the *Report* notes, "brings forward once again the problem of an adequate endowment of its own resources, necessary to compensate for the effect of the negative economic results of 1986 and above all to recompose the disequilibrium that would otherwise continue to manifest itself vis-a-vis the most efficient competition." *Ibid.*, p. 20.

[429] *Journal of Commerce* (April 21, 1987); *Metal Bulletin* (September 21, 1987). Under the new Aids Code, the only state aid permitted to EC steel producers was to finance research and development, environmental protection, and closures. *Official Journal*, L. 340 (November 27, 1985).

[430] *Financial Times* (September 17, 1987).

[431] *L'Espresso* (June 28, 1987).

[432] Sorci, "L'Evoluzione del Settore Siderurgico," p. 100.

[433] The banks remained willing to loan Finsider money because they were confident that the government would not allow Finsider to collapse. Similarly, Finsider managers continued to invest in the expectation that the state would eventually "bail them out." Eisenhammer and Rhodes, "The Politics of Public Sector Steel in Italy," p. 443.

*production and sale of their products. Is this the discovery of the egg
of Columbus? Very true, but not rarely it is the simplest things that
are forgotten when one speaks of the grand strategies that should
from 1986 on allow the complete self-financing of a group that up until
now hasn't gone into bankruptcy only because the state shareholder
has always put his hand in his wallet burning trillions of lire to plug
up the leaks in the blast furnaces.*

Italy's state steel sector was condemned to seemingly perpetual losses
because efficiency and profitability were subordinated to political and social
goals.[434] Within the industry itself, according to one observer, there had
developed an ethic of "productivism."[435] Rather than placing the industry on
a sound competitive footing, management focused on raising production, an
orientation which may be acceptable in times of growing domestic demand,
but which is counter-productive in an industry suffering from enormous
overcapacity. Even after the management of IRI, under President Romano
Prodi, recognized the need for adjustment, the political consensus within
Italian society required to take the necessary actions was not present. The
Board of IRI, on which were represented the five parties of the governing
coalition, was paralyzed by political in-fighting.[436] The Directors were
unwilling to approve steps that might threaten their parties' political base.
The industry's restructuring plans, which called for the cancellation of large
projects in the Mezzogiorno, produced angry protests; the plans, it was
alleged, were a Northern capitalist plot to prevent Southern development.[437]
Even the Christian Democracy, Italy's largest party and Prodi's primary
backer, was dependent on the Southern vote and therefore hesitated to take

---

[434] One author declared that "steel-making has an essential function: not so much for the
profits that it can insure for the company or a few beneficiaries, but for the dynamic that it can
imprint on the entire economic process." E. Capecelatro, *L'"Affaire" Accaio, Manipolazione di
una Crisi* (Lerici, 1979), p. 81.

[435] J. Eisenhammer & M. Rhodes, "The Politics of Public Sector Steel in Italy," p. 423.

[436] *Financial Times* (July 7, 1987).

[437] A Socialist Parliamentarian wrote that "Certainly, the [steel] crisis exists, it is vast, but
we are obliged to say to ourselves, to our friends, and above all to the young, that in this moment
it would be wrong, absurd and intolerable that the poorest regions of our country pay the price
of the general crisis. . . ." G. Mancini, *Il Caso Gioia Tauro* (Reggio-Calabria: Casa del Libro
Editrice, 1977), p. 102. The fight to save Gioia Tauro "is a national battle that expresses the will
of non-subjection to the bulldogs of the private Italian economy or the European and Eastern
economies, in which are united the workers of the Mezzogiorno and, in the same class interests,
the workers of the North." *Ibid.*, p. 12. Another author complained that Finsider's steel plan,
which would cut back expansion at Gioia Tauro and Bagnoli, constituted the "punishment" of the
South, excluding it from the "vast world of steel production." He believed that the plan was a
conspiracy to aid the private sector by reducing the state's role in steel. E. Capecelatro, *L'
"Affaire" Accaio.*

actions that could adversely impact the impoverished region. As one Italian observer remarked, Prodi was a "prisoner of the parties."[438]

A powerful labor movement also impeded restructuring. Every announcement of cuts brought workers into the streets.[439] The opposition Communists, whose hard core of support lay in the organized labor movement, supported these efforts.[440] In response to Finsider projections in 1986 that the workforce should be cut by 12,000 employees by 1988, a senior union leader responded: "This news makes me sick; it is at the same time surprising and disconcerting; I hope that Finsider disavows or clarifies this news; otherwise a very delicate phase in its relations with the union will open."[441] In those cases where employment was cut, few workers were actually laid off. Instead, employees were offered early retirement. Affected workers also were provided generous severance benefits, the costs of which were absorbed by the state.[442]

In June 1988 the Italian government unveiled the state steel sector's third rescue plan in the last seven years, which, if implemented, would radically restructure the sector. A new company, Ilva, would retain the more viable companies of the Finsider group, while the biggest loss-makers would be spun off into a separate entity for sale or liquidation. The plan foresees employment cuts of 20,000 workers and the reduction of capacity by 1.3 million metric tons, and projects that Finsider will reach the break-even point in 1990; in the meanwhile, the Italian government is to provide an additional $5 billion in aid.[443] However, the plan has stirred union protests and political opposition.[444] Irate officials of the European Commission threatened to bring legal action if the Italian government did not provide full details of the

---

[438] *L'Espresso* (June 28, 1987; June 26, 1983).

[439] For example, plans to close the Cornigliano works in Genoa resulted in a general strike. *Financial Times* (September 16, 1983). Similarly, plans to close the Bagnoli works in Naples met with fierce opposition from labor. J. Eisenhammer, "Longwy & Bagnoli: A Comparative Study of Trade Union Response to the Steel Crisis in France and Italy," in Meny and Wright, *The Politics of Steel.*

[440] *Ibid.*

[441] Franco Lotito, Secretary General of UIL, quoted in *La Stampa* (April 5, 1986).

[442] One mechanism for easing the blow of unemployment was the Cassa Integrazione Guadagni (CIG). The CIG provided steel workers affected by restructuring with eighty percent of salary up to a total of forty hours per week. Eisenhammer and Rhodes, "The Politics of Public Sector Steel in Italy," p. 429. As of December 31, 1986, 4,925 workers were receiving benefits from the CIG. Finsider *Annual Report 1986*, p. 32.

[443] *Financial Times* (June 15, February 10, 1988); *Metal Bulletin* (February 22, February 15, 1988).

[444] *Financial Times* (June 17, May 6, March 9, 1988); *Metal Bulletin* (April 14, 1988). In response to the announcement that employment at Bagnoli would be pared by 1,200 jobs, steelworkers seized two of Naples' antique public buildings, smashing art and furniture, and injuring the mayor.

restructuring and seek approval before providing any aid to the sector.[445] IRI's 1988 announcement that it would guarantee all of Finsider's debt was denounced by the Commission as illegal.[446] However, the alternative to further government assistance appeared to be the collapse of the state steel sector; the "Three Wise Men," appointed by the EC in 1987 to make recommendations for the future of the European steel industry, commented:

> It should be added that the Community must rapidly consider the case of Finsider. This major Italian public enterprise, which has made considerable investments as part of the development of the Mezzogiorno, must undertake in-depth reorganization in order to ensure its viability and its future. This presupposes not only major industrial decisions but also special aid to offset its debts, which at present preclude any hope of a revival.[447]

Great Britain

The British Steel Corporation (BSC), the state-owned firm which produces about 85 percent of Britain's steel, has for many years been regarded, in the words of one of its chairmen, as "a broken-down outfit that is not very good,"[448] the object of Parliamentary investigations and the butt of public criticism and ridicule for its inefficiency, huge losses, and dependence on government aid for survival. It has come as no small surprise, therefore, that since 1985 BSC has become profitable and achieved major gains in efficiency and productivity.[449] BSC's transformation has been widely viewed as a triumph for Margaret Thatcher's Conservative government, which encouraged the drastic reduction of BSC's work force, began to wean the company from subsidies, and overhauled its production facilities. However, BSC achieved its current state as a result of measures which the Conservatives tend to regard with disapproval; these include the government's forgiveness of huge amounts

---

[445] *American Metal Market* (May 2, 9, 1988); *Financial Times* (May 4, 6, 1988). Karl Narjes, the EC Industry Commissioner, complained that Finsider continued to receive $3.9 million per day in subsidies in violation of the Aids Code. *American Metal Market* (April 27, 1988). Commission officials suspected that the Italian government was effectively guaranteeing credit to Finsider by extending loans through state-owned banks. *Financial Times* (May 4, 1988). The Commission, showing increasing impatience with the situation, threatened to bar sales of Italian steel in the rest of the Community. *American Metal Market* (May 2, 1988). In June, the Commission enlarged the scope of its investigation to encompass loans to Ilva, the new holding company for the state steel sector. *Financial Times* (June 16, 1988).

[446] *American Metal Market* (June 21, 1988).

[447] Communication from the Commission to the Council, COM(87) 640 final, November 26, 1987.

[448] *Financial Times* (July 8, 1987).

[449] Marcus and Kirsis, *Steel Strategist 14.*

of debt and massive subsidies which helped finance BSC's current capital plant and sustained it through years of heavy operating losses. Without these measures it is unlikely that BSC would be profitable today, since it would still be carrying heavy financial costs. In the end, BSC's recovery can hardly be regarded as a triumph of market principles; if anything, it only demonstrates that an industry can be restored even under very adverse circumstances if the government is prepared to commit enough money to the endeavor.

The British steel industry was nationalized after World War II by the Labour government which came to power in 1945. The Conservatives, returning in 1951, restored the industry to private ownership. Ironically, while the Conservatives have been the traditional proponents of *laissez faire*, politically-motivated intervention by a Conservative government led to one of the worst strategic blunders in the industry's postwar history, the 1958 decision to establish a new steelworks at Ravenscraig, in Scotland, which could not be justified in economic terms. The consequences of this decision continue to plague the British steel industry three decades later.[450]

In 1967, Harold Wilson's Labour government once again nationalized the industry, acquiring and merging Britain's fourteen largest private steel companies to form the British Steel Corporation.[451] BSC was given a statutory duty to satisfy the steel requirements of British industry. It was legally answerable to the Department of Industry, and ultimately, to Parliament, but as a practical matter, because of its expertise, British Steel's management enjoyed considerable autonomy, and experienced only "spasmodic bouts of relatively ineffectual intervention by government."[452] In fact, BSC management's independence, its refusals to divulge aspects of its corporate plans to Parliament, and the "grave lack of communication" between BSC and the Department of Industry frequently led to controversy and at times erupted into public furor.[453]

By the time the British steel industry was nationalized in 1967, the industry, like the British manufacturing sector generally, had entered a steep financial,

---

[450] The Ravenscraig mill was designed to provide steel for "downstream" consuming industries in Scotland that did not yet exist and, for the most part, did not materialize. As a result, today it is distant from its markets and a financial drain on BSC. The Conservatives, eager to secure regional support in the General Election of 1959, supported this project and another in Llanwern, in Wales, pressing them on two private firms that doubted the prudence of the investments and lacked the resources to undertake them. The government provided initial financing under the Iron and Steel (Financial Provisions) Act of 1960, but the cost of developing the two sites greatly exceeded original estimates and reduced both firms to a state of near bankruptcy. Richardson and Dudley, "Steel Policy in the U.K.," pp. 312-13.

[451] About 15 percent of Britain's steelmaking remained in private hands.

[452] Richardson and Dudley, "Steel Policy in the U.K.," p. 309.

[453] In a highly publicized episode in the late 1970s, for example, BSC's management was accused by a Parliamentary committee of misleading the government as to its financial condition. House of Commons, *Fifth Report from the Select Committee on Nationalized Industries*, H.C. 238 (1977-78), "Financial Forecasts of the British Steel Corporation."

156

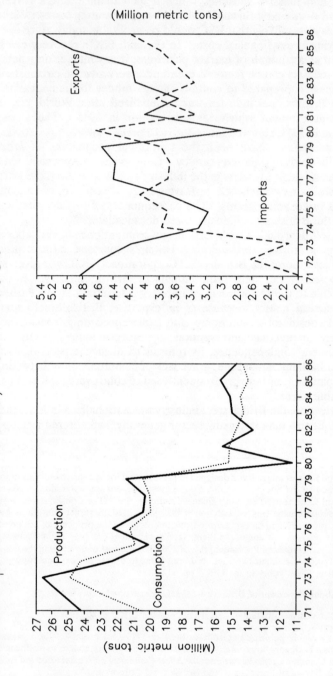

Figure 3-5: United Kingdom – Steel Production, Consumption and Trade, 1971–1986

(Million metric tons)

Source: International Iron and Steel Institute, Steel Statistical Yearbook, 1981, 1987. Production and Consumption refer to crude steel; Exports and Imports refer to semi-finished and finished steel.

technological, and competitive decline. On the eve of nationalization, the industry was fragmented among numerous firms, a number of them on the brink of financial ruin. Most of its equipment was obsolete, underutilized, and of sub-optimum scale, and used high-cost, low quality British coking coal. The industry was seriously overmanned; labor unions resisted technological change and tenaciously defended archaic and restrictive labor practices. Productivity had deteriorated relative to most of Britain's principal foreign competitors. The management of the newly-formed British Steel complained that it had inherited "not only a great deal of obsolescent plant, but also much plant which had lacked sufficient maintenance expenditure and which subsequently proved defective when driven to maximum levels of output."[454]

The inherited facilities were scattered all over the United Kingdom, and each region had a local constituency within the Corporation; in effect, upon nationalization fourteen fractious and geographically diverse manufacturing concerns were replaced by a single company racked by internal differences rooted in regionalism. Reflecting these centrifugal forces, the Corporation's so-called "Heritage Strategy" (1967-73), which emphasized the modernization and expansion of the most efficient assets inherited from the private sector, entailed a program of incremental investments at widely dispersed sites.[455]

The Ten Year Development Strategy. In 1970 the Conservatives returned to power but, in a departure from the past, made no serious moves to denationalize the steel industry. Instead, the management of British Steel developed and launched an extraordinarily ambitious "Ten Year Development Strategy," with the acquiescence, if not the full approval of the Conservative government. The Ten Year Development Strategy formed the basis of British Steel's capital planning through the decade of the 1970s and was to contribute substantially to the disasters which overtook the Corporation.[456] The original strategy formulated by the management of British Steel was extraordinary, calling for an expansion of British steelmaking capacity from 27 million metric tons in 1973 to over 40 million metric tons in 1980. In the cruel perspective of hindsight, the Plan was hopelessly misguided; actual British steel consumption was only 15 million metric tons in 1980, 37 percent of the target set by the BSC in 1972. Even in the early 1970s, when it appeared that demand would continue to increase, the plan caused "alarm and incredulity" within the Department of Industry, which established an oversight body, the Joint Steering Group (JSG) to "review" the plan. The JSG Report, released

[454] House of Commons, *First Report from the Select Committee on Nationalized Industries,* (H.C. 62-11, Minutes of Evidence, April 7, 1976, pp. 24, 26.

[455] The principal features of the "Heritage" investments were the replacement of open hearth furnaces with basic oxygen facilities, and the development of a transportation infrastructure that would enable the Corporation to begin to source foreign ore and coking coal. *First Report of the Select Committee,* H.C. 62-I (1977-78).

[456] *Ibid.,* Para. 123.

in early 1972, recommended that British Steel scale down its target to a capacity level of between 28 and 36 million metric tons by 1980. In the fall of 1972, however, a new Secretary of State for Trade and Industry was appointed, Peter Salker, who was "generally regarded as possessing a more adventurous spirit than his predecessor," and who was more inclined to embrace BSC's aggressive investment strategy. The Department ultimately adopted an investment plan only slightly modified from the original British Steel proposal.[457]

Even the slightly scaled down Ten Year Strategy was "an extremely ambitious plan;" it envisioned expansion of British steelmaking capacity to 38 million metric tons by the early 1980s.[458] Obsolete facilities would be completely replaced with modern ones through intensive investments at five existing coastal sites.[459] A deepwater ore port would be established at Hunterston in Scotland, a limited amount of electric arc capacity would be installed for the bulk production of general steel products. The cost of implementing the Ten Year Strategy was fixed at $5.4 billion, a figure which, in the event, proved wrong by several orders of magnitude.[460] Thus, the Corporation committed itself to an expansion effort of unprecedented scale on the eve of the sharpest and most protracted market contraction since the depression of the 1930s.

Sources of Capital. The course on which BSC was embarking would ultimately swallow an extraordinary volume of public money. In 1984 a Committee of Parliament estimated that the Corporation had received over $15.6 billion in external financing since 1967; such financing consisted of government capital infusions and government guaranteed loans, many of which were ultimately written off.[461] Two analysts observed in 1987 that

Enormous amounts of public money have been pumped into the BSC for the purposes of restructuring, and also as a direct subsidy. Nearly all of this cash has never been seen since, and has been written off by governments with a shrug of resignation to the inevitable.[462]

---

[457] Richardson and Dudley, "Steel Policy in the U.K.," pp. 318-319.

[458] *First Report of the Select Committee,* H.C. 62-I (1977-78), Para. 120 and 122.

[459] Port Talbot, Llanwern, Ravenscraig, Scunthorpe and Lackenby. 12 million metric tons of high cost capacity would be closed.

[460] *First Report of the Select Committee,* H.C. 62-I (1977-78); *Minutes of Evidence,* BSC Memorandum (April 7, 1976), Para. 5.5.

[461] House of Commons, *First Report of the Trade and Industry Committee,* H.C. 344, 208 i-v (1983-84), "The British Steel Corporation's Prospects," para. 8.

[462] Richardson and Dudley, "Steel Policy in the U.K.," p. 309.

Upon its formation in 1967, British Steel assumed a capital debt to the government of $2 billion; this debt was restructured in 1969, with $1.6 billion converted into so-called "public dividend capital" (PDC),[463] which was to become a principal source of the Corporation's capital over the next decade. Ostensibly, PDC was equity capital on which the Corporation was obligated to pay the government a dividend when it was profitable, but BSC was not profitable for a decade after 1975; under such circumstances, PDC took on the quality of "an interest-free, non-repayable advance -- in effect, a grant."[464] PDC was characterized as "really only a dodge to save BSC paying interest on Treasury loans;"[465] "joke equity,"[466] and a device to pass "the payment of that interest on capital to the taxpayer."[467]

British Steel was also authorized to borrow capital funds in amounts up to a ceiling fixed by acts of Parliament. Domestically, the Corporation borrowed from the government administered funds for the nationalized industries (the Consolidated Fund and its successor, the National Loans Fund (NLF)), at relatively low interest rates.[468] In addition, the Corporation borrowed from foreign lenders; since repayment of all foreign loans was guaranteed by the Treasury, the interest rates secured were those obtaining for loans with very low risk.[469]

An integral feature of the Ten Year Strategy was the closure of obsolete mills and reduction of the work force, with the Corporation's plan calling for a maximum of 50,000 job cuts.[470] As they become known, these plans gave rise to grass roots political movements in various parts of Britain to lobby the Corporation and the government to rethink the proposed closures. In early 1974, Labour returned to power, having promised in the election campaign to review all of British Steel's proposed closures, each of which was located in areas with strong Labour constituencies.[471] The new government postponed most of the proposed closures pending a review of the Corporation's plan by

---

[463] United Kingdom, Iron and Steel Act of 1969.

[464] United Kingdom, Chancellor of the Exchequer, *The Nationalized Industries*, (London: HMSO, March 1978), p. 30.

[465] *The Economist* (January 24, 1981).

[466] *The Economist* (December 20, 1980).

[467] House of Commons, *Second Report of the Select Committee on Nationalized Industries*, H.C. 127 (1977-78), "British Steel Corporation," Vol. II, p. 68.

[468] The NLF is a depository of money raised by government borrowing. Loans from the NLF are not generally available; they are limited to nationalized firms. The rate British Steel paid the NLF reflected "the rate at which the Government itself can borrow." British Steel was also authorized to borrow from the NLF's predecessor fund, the Consolidated Fund.

[469] British Steel *Annual Report*, 1980-91, p. 36.

[470] *First Report of the Select Committee*, H.C. 62-I (1977-78), Para. 127.

[471] Richardson and Dudley, "Steel Policy in the U.K.," p. 332.

Lord Beswick, a Labour government official. The Beswick Review, completed in February 1975, represented a compromise between the Corporation's restructuring plans and the sensitivities of the localities, and a number of proposed closures were deferred. The net effect of the Beswick Review was to prolong the life of open hearth plants for a number of years, frustrating the Corporation's plan to convert its steelmaking capability completely to basic oxygen and electric furnace facilities by 1980-81.[472] An ex-Labour MP commented in 1979 that the Beswick Review "took over 12 months, and the result was a report in 1975 extending the life of most of the plants involved until 1979-81. I estimate that this act of political expediency cost the BSC some 350 million pounds [$700 million] between 1975 and March 1980."[473]

The First Crisis Years. The Beswick Review was still underway when the structural crisis began to affect the British industry; in 1975, steel demand fell to its lowest levels since the 1930s. Curiously, BSC found that it was "unable to produce sufficient steel" to satisfy domestic needs, a reflection of labor disputes (three times as many in 1975 as in 1971) and delays in implementing its investment program. BSC suffered from "gross overmanning at all levels;" by its own admission, it suffered from "failings on quality," in some cases because the necessary plant was not available, but in other cases even when it was.[474] As a result of these competitive failures, the Corporation saw its share of the British market eroded by foreign steel, which took an 18 percent share of the U.K. market in 1975-76, compared with 5 percent in 1969.[475]

British Steel's management initially viewed the recession as another cyclical downturn, and its main concern in 1976 was that it would lack the capacity to meet the "rapid upturn in demand" anticipated in 1977.[476] The Corporation, although reporting estimated losses of over a $1.8 million a day, remained eager to press ahead with its investment program.[477] In mid-1976, the Corporation's Chairman, Sir Monty Finniston, indicated to the House of Commons that the eventual cost of that investment program might run as high as $16.2 billion; profitability could only be achieved after 1980, with completion of new facilities at Port Talbot and Redcar. The government raised BSC's borrowing limit from $3.6 to $7.2 billion in 1976, although there

---

[472] *First Report of the Select Committee*, H.C. 62-I (1977-78), Para. 128-29.

[473] *Metal Bulletin* (October 9, 1979).

[474] Memorandum submitted on behalf of the British Steel Corporation, *First Report of the Select Committee*, H.C. 62-II (1977-78) April 7, 1976, Para. 4.5.

[475] *Ibid.*; *Metal Bulletin* (October 9, 1979).

[476] To this end, BSC secured government financial support to stockpile steel during the recession "to meet demand in 1977-78." *First Report of the Select Committee*, H.C. 62-II (1977-78), Minutes of Evidence, p. 34.

[477] *Metal Bulletin* (July 30, 1976). British Steel lost $459 million in the financial year ended April 3, 1976.

was considerable grumbling over the commitment of such huge capital investments to a plan which showed clear signs of going awry.[478]

As the crisis deepened, the full implications of the Ten Year Development Strategy began to become apparent. The Plan had launched capital investments aiming at a target of 38 million metric tons of crude steel, but it was evident by the late 1970s that 15 million metric tons would suffice to cover domestic needs. The new investments had created plants which were highly efficient if run at full capacity, but extraordinarily costly if forced to operate at lower rates, which was in fact the case. While the plan could be scaled back, some investments had already been made, and the curtailment of the plan led to severe imbalances in capacity at individual sites. The investment projects at Port Talbot and Redcar, for example, involved "very expensive" new efforts that resulted in "unbalanced" facilities -- upstream iron and steelmaking capacity was expanded substantially, while downstream strip capacity was not; the "rounding out" of these plants depended on a growth in sales volume which, by the late 1970s, had become "unlikely." The result was that "the unit costs of the works' finished product [were] increased by the cost of the excess upstream capacity."[479]

Abandonment of the Ten-Year Strategy. At the end of 1976, a new BSC Chairman, Sir Charles Villiers, abandoned the Ten Year Development Strategy in favor of a more conservative (but still, under the prevailing circumstances, highly ambitious) objective of 30 million metric tons of capacity by 1982. Nevertheless, British Steel's financial situation continued to worsen dramatically; in the fall of 1977 Villiers testified that any private firm "losing money at the rate we are would now be in receivership or liquidation."[480]

The political support necessary to sustain an ambitious expansion effort was rapidly eroding. In early 1978, the House of Commons' Select Committee on the Nationalized Industries charged that "the Corporation's management is incapable of making a forecast for a few months ahead which stands any chance of achieving even a minimal level of accuracy," strongly implying that Villiers' 30 million metric ton investment plan was based on forecasts designed

---

[478] Conservative M.P. Anthony Nelson exclaimed in the House of Commons that it was "nothing less than fantastic that we should be considering doubling the size of the capital employed by this major British industry, which will consume 8 percent of the prospective public deficit in the next year alone, without an adequate prospectus." *Metal Bulletin* (April 30, July 16, 1976).

[479] *First Report of the Select Committee,* H.C. 62-I (1977-78), Para. 138. At Redcar, a major new blast furnace had been built at a cost of $875 million, and was "awaiting a steelworks whose future [was] conjectural." At the same time, the continuous casting facility at Scunthorpe lacked sufficient ironmaking capacity to be fully utilized, and the rolling mill capacity at Lackenby greatly exceeded that site's iron and steelmaking capability." *Ibid.*

[480] *Second Report from the Select Committee,* H.C. 127 (1977-78) Vol. I, p. ix.

to mislead Parliament.[481] The Corporation was unkindly characterized in the press as an "open industrial drain down which government after government has poured taxpayers' cash."[482]

In the spring of 1978 the government released a new White Paper on British Steel, signaling a fundamental change in policy. Villiers' capacity target of 30 million metric tons by 1982 was abandoned, and no new long-term target was set; the White Paper contained "no capacity targets, no promises for exaggerated, unneeded schemes in Labour strongholds."[483] The Corporation was to invest only to finish projects underway or to improve product quality; priority would be given to replacing worn-out equipment and to small schemes (entailing investment of up to $3.8 million) to ease local bottlenecks.   Plans to add electric arc furnaces and to establish new steelmaking capacity and a plate mill at Redcar were abandoned.[484]

However, because of BSC's deteriorating financial position, even these scaled-down proposals placed demands on the Corporation which could not be satisfied without new government aid measures. British Steel's borrowing limit was raised from $7.6 to $10.5 billion, with the view widely expressed that "a large part of BSC's 4 billion pound [$7.6 billion] debt to the government will eventually be written off."[485] In addition, the Corporation received "handouts described as 'subscriptions of capital' under Section 18(1) of the Iron and Steel Act."[486] This so-called "New Capital" supplanted public dividend capital and NLF loans as the principal source of direct government aid; British Steel received injections of New Capital in 1979, 1980 and 1981 totaling $1.7, $2.1, and $2.5 billion, respectively (table 3-17).[487] By 1979, British Steel was losing $2 million per day, or, in the words of a former

---

[481] "There would seem to be only two explanations for the fact that evidence was given to the sub-committee in May which was liable to cause the committee to be seriously misled as to the corporation's likely prospects. The first is that the corporation turned a blind eye to the real danger that the world market situation would worsen rather than improve and had continued to base its forecasts on the most optimistic assumptions. If in fact the corporation failed to make alternative forecasts, this would suggest, at the very least, a lack of prudence. The only other possibility is that the BSC deliberately avoided revealing the true situation to the sub-committee." *Second Report from the Select Committee*, H.C. 127 (1977-78).

[482] *The Economist* (March 25, 1978).

[483] *Ibid.*

[484] British Steel Corporation, *The Road to Viability*, Cmnd. 5226 (1978).

[485] *The Economist* (March 25, 1978). The American Embassy in London reported that British Steel's debts "will almost certainly have to be written off by a government-arranged capital reconstruction of the corporation's finances." U.S. Embassy, London, No. R. 1820032, December 1978.

[486] *The Economist* (March 25, 1978). The provision of the 1975 Act authorizes the Secretary for Industry to pay British Steel "such sums as he sees fit," with the approval of the Treasury.

[487] British Steel, *Annual Reports*.

Corporation director, a cost to the taxpayer of "38 pounds [$80] a week to keep every BSC employee in a job."[488]

Table 3-17. British Steel Sources of Funds and Operating Deficits, 1974-1980 (millions U.S. dollars)

Sources of Funds	1974-75	1975-76	1976-77	1977-78	1978/79	1979/80
Public Dividend Capital	105	764	882	779	-	-
New Capital	-	-	-	-	1,624	1,919
NLF Loans	(183)	291	289	378	(308)	(443)
Foreign Loans	503	409	385	233	(15)	(74)
Short Term Borrowings	288	(2)	119	12	65	(199)
Operating Profit (Loss) after tax	171	(568)	(171)	(758)	(590)	(1,092)

Source: House of Commons, *Fourth Report from the Industry and Trade Committee*, H.S. 336-I (1980-81); Memorandum Submitted by British Steel Corporation, Minutes of Evidence, pp. 9-10.
Converted to U.S. dollars at average annual exchange rate given by the International Monetary Fund. Conversion: 1974: 2.34; 1975: 2.22; 1976: 1.8; 1977: 1.75: 1978: 1.91; 1979: 2.12.

The Return of the Conservatives. In the spring of 1979 a Conservative government returned to power under Margaret Thatcher. The new Industry Secretary, Sir Keith Joseph, prescribed "shock treatment" for British Steel, cutting its annual borrowing limit from $1,470 to $945 million and declaring that the government would not finance its losses after 1980-81.[489] Sir Keith indicated that in 1981-82 "BSC is unlikely to get any hand-out at all for any purpose." These actions "concentrated the minds of BSC's management," which announced that it would slash its workforce by 52,000 jobs by August

---

[488] *Metal Bulletin* (October 9, 1979).

[489] House of Commons, *Fourth Report from the Industry and Trade Committee*, H.C. 336-I (1980-81), Para. 29.

1980.[490] This provoked a "disastrous" strike by the steel workers which severely affected the Corporation's production and market position.[491]

The Conservative government's ambitious breakeven targets, and its commitment to end "handouts" to the Corporation, were soon abandoned as unrealistic. British Steel's losses for 1979-80 of $1.1 billion were the highest trading loss ever recorded by a U.K. company. By the summer of 1980 its cash position was "clearly desperate," and Villiers informed the Industry Secretary that unless the company's borrowing limit could be raised, British Steel would face liquidation, complaining later that his efforts to reform the company were like "running up a down escalator." In 1980-81, BSC suffered another record loss of $1.5 billion (after having forecast profits of $104 million) and the House of Commons Industry and Trade Committee remarked that

> *The catastrophic shortfall of performance against target was another in a line of successive failures to meet targets set in good faith. . . . We cannot overlook the fact that most forecasts in the past ten years have been wildly inaccurate.*[492]

British Steel was a painful embarrassment for the Conservative government, in light of its ultimatum that the Corporation must achieve breakeven and wean itself from state aid.[493] Ultimately, during 1980 the government wrote off $2.3 billion of the Corporation's debt and raised the ceiling which it had imposed on British Steel's borrowing; government support for BSC totaled $2.3 billion by the end of 1980 above and beyond the forgiven debt.[494]

In June 1980 Villiers was replaced as Chairman of BSC by Ian MacGregor, an American who was accused by the unions of having been brought in as the government's "hatchet man," and who did in fact achieve substantial cuts in the

---

[490] This proposal even left the European Commission aghast, although it had been pressing the Member States for cutbacks. The Commissioner for Social Policy "expressed amazement" that the British government proposed to eliminate 52,000 jobs so quickly. Richardson and Dudley, "Steel Policy in the U.K.," p. 343.

[491] During the strike, U.K. steel weekly production fell to 58.8 thousand tons (seasonally adjusted), compared with 381 thousand tons during the same period in 1979. *Fourth Report*, H.C. 36-I (1980-81), point 10. *The Economist* (January 19, 1980); *Metal Bulletin* (March 18, 25, 1980). The strike was settled with an agreement providing for a 15.5 percent pay increase for steelworkers and an enabling agreement on productivity which the Corporation hoped would permit it to eliminate 12,000 jobs.

[492] *Fourth Report*, H.C. 336-I (1980-81), Para. 16.

[493] *Metal Bulletin* (July 1, 1980).

[494] Richardson and Dudley, "Steel Policy in the U.K.," p. 345.

Table 3-18.   British Steel's Balance Sheet Before and After Financial
Reconstruction, 1981 (millions U.S. dollars)

Assets	Before	Reconstruction	Post Reconstruction
Fixed Assets, Investments, and Long Term Debtors	3,792		3,792
Working Capital	1,622		1,622
Short-Term Borrowings	(649)		(649)
	4,766		4,766
Liabilities			
Capital	9,774	(6,084)*	3,691
Reserves (Deficit)	(7,361)	7,118	(243)
Long-Term Borrowings	2,312	(1,034)**	1,278
Minority Interest	41		41
	4,766		4,766

* Write-off of $6,084 million of "New Capital."
** Write-off of $1,034 million in outstanding debt from the National Loans Fund.
Source: House of Commons, *Fourth Report from the Industry and Trade Committee*, H.C. 336-I (1980-81), Table 4.
Converted to U.S. dollars at average annual exchange rate of $2.0279 per pound given by the International Monetary Fund.

workforce during his term. At the end of 1980 MacGregor advanced a new corporate plan which was characterized as "essentially a short term survival plan" when BSC, "after years of subsidies and declining public confidence," was "on the brink of a precipice."[495] The MacGregor plan called for 20,000 job cuts but no major closures. Britain's principal steel union, the ISTC, opposed MacGregor's plan and sought to mobilize resistance to it. The workforce, however, was increasingly demoralized by the apparent inevitability of further

---

[495] House of Commons, Fourth Report, H.C. 336-II (1980-81), Para. 2; Memorandum Submitted by British Steel Corporation, March 11, 1981, *Minutes of Evidence*, pp. 1-18.

cutbacks and was divided in its desire to resist by attractive severance terms which were offered. MacGregor went over the heads of the union leadership, submitting his plan to the workforce for a vote, with a warning that the Corporation's survival was at stake, and won majority approval.[496]

While these measures held out some hope for the longer term, the Corporation's immediate financial problems needed to be addressed. At the beginning of 1981 the Thatcher government was compelled to secure Parliament's approval for a huge new aid program for British Steel, designed to "bury past blunders" and put the Company on a sound financial footing (table 3-18).[497] The government wrote off $8.4 billion of BSC's debt and public dividend capital. As The Economist commented on the latter, "there never was any dividend; now there is to be no capital."[498] British Steel's borrowing limit was raised to $14.4 billion, although the writeoff of debt and PDC enabled it to be lowered to $8.4 billion. Provision was also made for replacement of $1.5 billion in outstanding loans by New Capital, which would replace interest bearing debt with interest free capital [which would] not fall due to be repaid."[499] A new capital injection of $1.5 billion was provided for 1981-82.[500] During the Parliamentary hearings which addressed the financial restructuring, the following exchange took place between an M.P. and BSC Chairman McGregor:

> Mr. Kenneth Carlisle, M.P.: What is your opinion of a policy in which operating losses are met by subscriptions of non-repayable, unremunerated capital which inevitably means a financial reconstruction in the future?
>
> Mr. MacGregor: It is a phenomenon that does not exist in the real world. I do not know what I should say. It is a sort of fairyland in which somebody gives you presents.[501]

The BSC's financial situation, to a substantial extent a reflection of bad strategic decisions made in prior years, overshadowed the fact that the

---

[496] Meny and Wright, The Politics of Steel, p. 69; Metal Bulletin (December 16, 1980); Richardson and Dudley, "Steel Policy in the U.K.," p. 345.

[497] This "reconstruction," "a euphemism for writing off enormous amounts of outstanding debt," provided for the elimination of all outstanding principal due the National Loans Fund ($1,224 million), and the elimination of $7.2 billion of public capital. Fourth Report, H.C. 336-I (1980-81), Points 3 and 57.

[498] The Economist (January 24, 1981).

[499] Fourth Report, H.C. 336-I (1980-81), Para. 61.

[500] Fourth Report, H.C. 336-I (1980-81), Para. 3; The Economist (January 24, 1981): Metal Bulletin (February 17, 1981), Para. 3.

[501] Fourth Report, H.C. 336-II (1980-81), Minutes of Evidence, May 20, 1981, p. 51.

Corporation was pressing forward with a series of rationalization measures which would have significant impact in the future. In the year ended March 31, 1981, 45,500 jobs were cut, leaving the Corporation with 120,900 employees. BSC reduced its energy consumption substantially and began converting its facilities from oil to coal. Productivity improved, particularly at several sites (Port Talbot, Llanwern). These improvements, while significant, were not immediately reflected in the Corporation's bottom line; the Corporation suffered an enormous loss of $1.3 billion in 1981-82, and another loss of $644 million in 1982-83.[502] In 1982, the government had little choice but to write off another $1.8 billion of BSC debt; it also raised the external financing limit for 1982-83 from $657 to $1,035 million.[503]

A fundamental strategic problem confronting the BSC was the fact that it produced steel at too many major sites -- five -- to achieve maximum efficient scale, given its production volume. The problem was compounded by the fact that one of these sites, Ravenscraig in Scotland, lacked geographically contiguous markets for its products. The management of BSC, recognizing the problem, wished to close operations at one major site, with Ravenscraig the most likely candidate,[504] but closure of one of the major sites was a volatile political issue. Rumors that BSC was contemplating a major closure periodically swept steel producing regions, prompting intensive lobbying efforts to keep the sites open. In 1982 reports that BSC planned to shut Ravenscraig and concentrate HR coil production at Llanwern and Port Talbot touched off a political furor in Scotland; George Younger, the Secretary of State for Scotland, indicated that a Ravenscraig closure might prompt him to resign.[505] Intensive lobbying by a wide range of Scottish interests followed, and the Thatcher government, facing general elections, "stopped Mr. MacGregor from losing votes by shutting down Ravenscraig."[506] The Department of Industry told BSC to prepare its corporate plan for 1982-85 on the basis that

---

[502] BSC *Annual Report*, 1982-83; *Metal Bulletin* (July 10, 1981, January 15, June 11, July 16, 1982).

[503] *Fourth Report from the Industry and Trade Committee*, H.C. 308 (1981-82) p. 2; BSC *Annual Report*, 1982-83.

[504] Chairman Ian MacGregor commented in 1981 that: "The technique in Japan is to produce an enormous amount of tonnage in one site. You have site costs in our case on a very larger number of sites. . . . These are many, many problems facing us because of [our failure to reduce the number of sites]. We have major iron and steel making sites in Scotland, Tee-side, Scunthorpe, two place in Wales -- that is too many for 14 million tonnes." *Fourth Report*, H.C. 308, 61 -- i and ii (1982-82), *Minutes of Evidence*, p. 20.

[505] Richardson and Dudley, "Steel Policy in the U.K."

[506] *The Economist* (July 9, 1983).

steelmaking would continue at all five sites in December 1982.[507] A member of Parliament remarked to BSC's Chairman several years later that

> *There is no secret about the fact that two years ago you wanted to close [Ravenscraig]. Everyone knew that. It was a political decision that stopped it.*[508]

The House of Commons Select Committee on Nationalized Industries charged that this decision would prove "extremely costly and its consequences must delay the development of a thoroughly efficient, cost competitive UK steel industry in a changing world."[509] BSC's Deputy Chairman told Parliament in early 1984 that BSC's "viability is not compatible with the criteria of maintaining five integrated sites . . . we're still losing money."[510]

The Private Sector. The formation of British Steel in 1967 left 100 British steel companies in private hands, ranging in size from very small entities with under 25 employees to companies whose output was only slightly smaller than the size which would have qualified them for nationalization.   The private firms, which accounted for about 15 percent of Britain's steel production, were particularly strong in the production of more profitable "downstream" finished products for the engineering industry, such as cold-rolled strip, forgings, tool steel, pipes and tubes, and bars.[511] The private sector initially weathered the structural crisis better than BSC, in part because of BSC's inefficiency and pricing policies, but at the end of the 1970s it, too, began to experience significant difficulties.[512]

The private sector's problems partially stemmed from stagnant demand, but it was also evident that private producers were adversely affected by a new aggressiveness in BSC's pricing. Until the end of the 1970s BSC had adhered to list prices in an attempt to cover its costs; this had, in the view of its Chairman, cast it in it the role of "patsy" and "tended to create some parts of

---

[507] *First Report*, H.C. 208-i-v (1983-84), "The British Steel Corporation's Prospects," point 8. BSC Chairman MacGregor was of the view that the cost of keeping Ravenscraig open would be $180 million per year. *Financial Times* (March 29, 1983).

[508] House of Commons Trade and Industry Committee, *The British Steel Corporation*, H.C. 444-i (1984-85), Mr. Crowther, M.P., *Minutes of Evidence*, p. 12.

[509] *Metal Bulletin* (March 11, 1983).

[510] *Metal Bulletin* (February 14, 1984). BSC assessed a plan under which part of Ravenscraig would close and the remainder would supply semifinished slabs to a joint venture set up with U.S. Steel. This plan foundered, in part because of opposition to it in the U.S.

[511] These firms formed the British Independent Steel Producers Association (BISPA) to represent their interests in the context of an industry with "mixed" public-private ownership.

[512] *Fourth Report*, H.C. 336-I (1980), Para. 34.

the private sector" by opening up market opportunities for private firms.[513]
However, in late 1980 BSC began a new policy of aggressive pricing, designed
to expand its market share in the U.K.[514] While this policy was directed at
imports, it severely affected private producers in the U.K. as well. BISPA, the
private producers' association, testified before Parliament in 1981 that

> We do not believe that the Corporation is deliberately seeking to
> destroy independent companies by price-cutting.   We do, however,
> point out that even a sincerely expressed intention to "roll back
> imports" and to "regain market share" is, given the indivisible nature
> of the steel market, bound to have the same effect. It could not be
> done without access to public funds, and cannot be done without
> damage to private producers.   Both are occurring at the present
> time.[515]

Perhaps inevitably, the charge was "bandied about" the House of Commons
that BSC was "using public funds to undercut . . . private sector
competitors,"[516] and BSC's Chairman allowed as how, "in the struggle between
us and major foreign competitors," the private U.K. firms may have been
hurt.[517]

The Conservative government was forced to confront the unpleasant fact
that its continued subsidization of BSC had contributed to the financial straits
of the private sector. In 1981 a Junior Minister resigned his post in protest
over the government's steel policy, charging that

> over the last two years huge handouts had been given to BSC in order
> to enable it to reorganize and compete with foreign competition. This
> support . . . had also subsidized competition with U.K. private
> producers which had led to private firms becoming unprofitable,
> closing down, and shedding jobs.[518]

---

[513] *Fourth Report*, H.C. 336-II (1980-81), *Minutes of Evidence*, March 11, 1981, p. 26.

[514] One private firm testified before Commons in 1981 that "there does seem to be a desire
on the part of the British Steel Corporation to put a lot of steel through – to use their cold-
rolling outlets to put a lot of steel on the market at prices which one finds very difficult to
match." *Ibid.*, Mr. Lee, *Minutes of Evidence*, April 8, 1981, p. 130.

[515] Memorandum Submitted by the British Independent Steel Producers Association (S28),
Fourth Report, H.C. 336-II (1980-81), *Minutes of Evidence*, April 8, 1981, p. 125.

[516] Mr. Crowther, M.P., in *Fourth Report*, H.C. 336-II (1980-81), *Minutes of Evidence*, March
11, 1981, p. 21.

[517] *Ibid.*, Mr. MacGregor, p. 25.

[518] *Metal Bulletin* (May 22, 1981).

The government announced shortly thereafter that $44 million would be made available to private firms to promote "rationalization and restructuring," but the private sector did not respond to this program with enthusiasm.[519] The scheme, ended in 1984, was proclaimed a success by the government after the allocation of $45 million to the private sector, but private firms were less enthusiastic, referring to the program as a "sop to compensate for the vast sums of government cash given to BSC."[520]

The private sector figured prominently in the planning of the Thatcher government, however, since it was hoped eventually to privatize the entire British steel industry. The Iron and Steel Act of 1981 repealed BSC's statutory duty to supply the steel needed by British industry; the Corporation was free to pursue such market opportunities as it saw fit. The government reorganized British Steel into autonomous "profit centers," each of which was to operate as a separate business, with the notion that pieces of the Corporation might be spun off,[521] and some of the Corporation's activities were formed into separate companies. So-called "Phoenix" projects were implemented to "hive off" segments of BSC's operations by merging them with those of private sector firms, particularly in areas of competitive overlap. By early 1986, British Steel had established eight joint ventures with the private sector, and large segments of its operations had been spun off into private businesses.[522]

Turnaround. The BSC suffered a series of unforeseen mishaps in the early 1980s which for a time masked substantial improvements underway at the corporation. The problems included bad weather, a severe recession, depressed prices, the trade dispute with the United States, and finally a major strike by the nations' coal miners in 1984, which resulted in blockades of three of BSC's five integrated works and strikes at two of BSC's unloading docks.[523] Partially reflecting these problems, BSC's performance in 1982-83 was

---

[519] The weaknesses of the scheme were cited as the "low level of the grant available" and the fact that they were made on a 25-75 basis, with the private firms expected to foot 75 percent of the cost of rationalization.

[520] *Metal Bulletin* (March 16, 1984). A British M.P. commented in 1981 that "there is a clear impression in the private sector that [public aid to steel] has been hogged by the public sector." Mr. Cockeran, *Fourth Report*, H.C. 308 (1981-82), *Minutes of Evidence*, December 9, 1981, p. 37.

[521] *Fourth Report*, H.C. 336-I (1980-81), Para. 88.

[522] Phoenix One involved the establishment of a joint venture by BSC and a private engineering company; the joint venture, Allied Steel and Wire, acquired some bar and wire rod facilities of the BSC. Phoenix Two merged the specialty steel facilities of BSC and the engineering group GKN to form a joint venture, United Engineering Steels (UES). *Metal Bulletin Monthly* (April 1986).

[523] *Fourth Report*, H.C. 308, 61-i and ii (1981-1982), *Minutes of Evidence*, pp. 40-41; *Financial Times*, July 13, 1984.

"ghastly," with the Corporation losing a record \$1.6 billion,[524] and the miners' strike "dashed all hopes" that BSC might break even in 1984.[525]

Despite these problems, as early as 1982, there were clear signs that BSC was on the mend. The Corporation was making substantial improvements in efficiency and productivity which were manifested in occasional monthly operating profits, the first in many years.[526] By the beginning of 1986, the workforce had been cut to 61,000 from a peak level of 220,000, and this would be reduced to 55,000 with the "hiving off" of segments of BSC to the private sector.[527] Product quality improvements had been achieved through extensive modernization of older plant.[528] These efficiency improvements were substantially reinforced by the weakening of the British pound against other foreign currencies after 1986. BSC's fortunes were further bolstered by strengthening demand in 1986 and 1987, which was accompanied by rising prices. The Corporation reported a modest profit of \$49 million in 1985-86, which increased to \$261 million in 1986-87; by mid-1987, all BSC divisions, with the exception of seamless pipes, were profitable.[529] A company which six years previously had been "on the brink of a precipice," had become a "sunburst" industry.[530]

Even more startling was steel analyst Peter Marcus' conclusion in late 1987 that British Steel was the lowest cost steel producer among the major steel-producing countries, with costs substantially below those of the Japanese mills (although he did not calculate as "costs" various BSC expenses, such as debt, that were simply absorbed by the state). Marcus attributed British Steel's newfound advantage to (a) the weakening of the British pound, (b) strenuous cost reduction efforts, particularly the reduction in the workforce, (c) the ability to purchase raw materials at international spot prices, (d) substantial capital investments in improving efficiency, (e) sharply reduced interest costs, reflecting government write-off of long-term debt and (f) low depreciation

---

[524] *Financial Times* (August 31, 1983).

[525] *Financial Times*, July 13, 1984. The coal strike cost BSC an estimated \$234 million. House of Commons Trade and Industry Committee, *The British Steel Corporation*, H.C. 444-i, Mr. Haslam, *Minutes of Evidence*, p. 1.

[526] Productivity improved from 122 tons per man year in 1974 to 300 tons in 1985, and BSC estimated that its costs were lower than those of their West German and Japanese competitors. House of Commons *First Report from the Trade and Industry Committee*, H.C. 181 (1983-84), "The British Steel Corporation's Prospects."

[527] *Metal Bulletin* (October 15, 1985; March 4, 1986).

[528] Metal Bulletin (June 13, 1986). In 1987 British Steel's Scunthorpe works became the first integrated steel mill in the world to win an independent quality assurance rating, from Lloyd's Rating Quality Assurance. *Metal Bulletin* (June 16, 1987).

[529] *Financial Times* (July 8, 1987); *Metal Bulletin* (July 9, 1987).

[530] *Financial Times* (July 8, 1987).

expenses per ton.[531] Exchange rate movements were particularly favorable to the Corporation, with the dollar weakening against the pound while the Deutschmark strengthened against the pound.[532] BSC moved aggressively to capitalize on its new cost advantage, acquiring foreign steel stockholders and establishing sales operations in Canada, Europe, Hong Kong and Turkey to develop export opportunities.[533]

BSC's financial performance would have been even stronger had not political pressure continued to frustrate Corporation initiatives to undertake major closures. BSC operated three large hot strip mills, and it calculated that it could save $135 million annually if it could close one of these.[534] When it became known that BSC was contemplating such a move, involving a closure at either Llanwern or Ravenscraig, the Secretary for Scotland reiterated his opposition to a major Ravenscraig closure, steelworkers' representatives denounced the initiative in Parliament, and the House of Commons Trade and Industry Committee issued a report stating that "now is not the time to close a hot strip mill."[535] At length, bowing to such pressures, the government gave a guarantee that it would defer any large-scale closures at the five sites for three years, until August 1988.

The Thatcher government had set forth an objective for BSC to "break even before interest in 1984-85 and thereafter to earn a real return on its capital," with the ultimate objective of complete privatization. These objectives were set in the context of a dramatic cut in the level of public money to the nationalized industries generally, which were projected to be virtually independent of government support for capital or revenue expenditure by 1986-87.[536] In the fall of 1986, a spokesman for the Conservative government indicated that the government would proceed with the complete privatization of British Steel if it were returned to power in the next election (in 1987).[537] Following the Conservative victory, and BSC profits in 1986, which were the highest of any integrated producer in Europe, BSC Chairman Sir Bob Scholey stated his intention to see the corporation privatized by 1990 or sooner.[538] In early 1988 Parliament began considering

---

[531] Marcus and Kirsis, *Steel Strategist 14.*

[532] Since raw materials prices are dollar denominated, the weakening of the dollar against the pound reduced BSC's raw materials costs; since European steel prices are primarily affected by the Deutschmark, a strengthening of the mark against the pound enhanced the competitiveness of BSC's steel products on the Continent.

[533] *Metal Bulletin* (July 13, 1987).

[534] *First Report*, H.C. 344, 208-i-v (1983-84), para. 27.

[535] *Ibid.*, para. 33.

[536] *Ibid.*, para. 8.

[537] *Metal Bulletin* (September 9, 1986).

[538] *Financial Times* (July 8, 1987).

legislation to privatize BSC by 1989.[539] The government indicated it was still considering whether to retain a share (possibly as much as 51 percent) in BSC after privatization.[540]

While it may be tempting to regard British Steel's recovery as a triumph of market principles, it is worth noting the contribution made by government policy measures to the change in the firm's fortunes. The Corporation's substantial capital investments in efficiency enhancing equipment were basically financed with public funds either in the form of capital injections or loans subsequently written off. The cost of much of this money to BSC was effectively zero, at a time when a private company with BSC's earnings record would have had difficulty raising money on any terms. Similarly, the sharp fall in BSC's interest expenses reflected the government's decision to forgive much of its outstanding debt. The layoffs and plant closures which did so much to enhance BSC's efficiency were likewise partially financed with public money.[541] Wholesale workforce reductions were carried out in a political environment characterized by a government prepared to support company management in bruising confrontations with labor.

To some observers BSC's revival may be regarded as a successful return to market principles after decades of excessive, wasteful and distorting public market intervention. From another perspective, however, the Corporation's recovery is an example how even a virtually bankrupt and heavily indebted firm can leapfrog all of its rivals within a relatively short time frame given a sufficient volume of government financial support.

West Germany

At the outset of the structural recession, the West German steel industry was the largest and most powerful in Europe, reflecting not only its technological and managerial superiority, but also its ability to "exploit to [its] best advantage a dual principle of free competition and collective discipline to present a hard competitive front."[542] The structural recession shook the German industry, however, pitting it against heavily subsidized foreign rivals, eroding its traditional solidarity, and ultimately forcing it to turn to the state for financial assistance. Between 1975 and 1988 the German industry suffered substantial losses, weakening of its control over the market, and a decline in

---

[539] *Financial Times* (January 4, 1988). These moves were greeted with misgivings in some quarters; however, at the end of 1987 the British Iron and Steel Consumers Council published a paper warning that "there must be some doubt" about the ability of BSC to maintain long term viability and competitiveness if it were denied all access to government financial assistance following privatization. *The Guardian* (December 10, 1987).

[540] *Metal Bulletin* (February 18, 1988).

[541] These factors led the West German steel producers to complain in 1988 that BSC "is still benefitting artificially from the elimination of its debt." *Financial Times* (May 27, 1988).

[542] J. Ferry in *Metal Bulletin* (November 28, 1978).

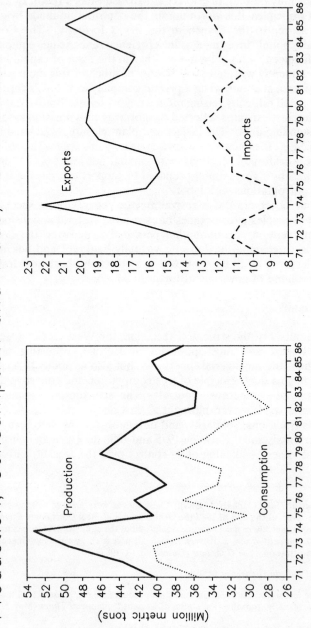

(Million metric tons)

Figure 3–6: Federal Republic of Germany – Steel Production, Consumption and Trade, 1971–1986

Source: International Iron and Steel Institute, Steel Statistical Yearbook, 1981, 1987. Production and Consumption refer to crude steel; Exports and Imports refer to semi-finished and finished steel.

investment relative to its neighbors, all of which were attributed to the steel subsidies in other Member States. The German Economics Minister complained in 1982 that "the entire matter no longer has anything to do with market economy."[543] The relative decline of the German industry and the unraveling of its cooperative structure have implications for the Community as a whole, since the disarray among the German mills has undercut the Commission's efforts to achieve a Community-wide consensus on restructuring.

Background

Germany's initial phase of industrialization in the late nineteenth century has been characterized as "organized capitalism," in which institutions such as banks, industrial groups, and the state jointly determined the direction of industrial development. While German economic policy in the post-1945 period has been implemented under the rubric of the so-called "social market economy," synthesizing the market with the welfare state, many aspects of German prewar industrial organization remain. Large banks and insurance companies own blocks of stock in most major German firms and play an important role in steering investment and other strategic decisions, not only for individual firms but entire industrial sectors. German industrial associations are more powerful and effective than in most other countries. The government's function is to create a political and legal climate to support this system by supplying research and educational facilities and, where necessary, financial backing in the way of tax advantages and subsidies. At the same time, the governments of the German states (Länder) frequently play an activist role in industrial promotion.

While Germany has over two dozen steel producers, almost all German raw steel production is concentrated in the hands of seven steel combines: Thyssen, Klöckner, Krupp, Mannesmann, Hoesch, Saarstahl, and Peine Saltzgitter, the latter being Germany's only state-owned firm. The German industry has historically been one of the most efficient in Europe; at the onset of the structural recession it enjoyed the most advanced facilities and, in the view of some observers, the best management in Europe.[544]

The German mills had a tradition of industrial solidarity dating back to the nineteenth century which remained strong in the twentieth. The prewar German steel cartel, the Stahlwerksverband, was probably the most influential in Europe. While the cartels and konzerns were broken up by the Allies at the end of the war, the steel industry maintained a cooperative structure and an abiding distrust of government meddling in industrial matters. During the severe recession of 1966-67, the German steelmakers formed four regional cartels, the Walzstahlkontore ("rolled steel joint sales agencies"), whose

---

[543] Otto Lambsdorff in *Der Spiegel* (November 8, 1982).

[544] *Rheinischer Merkur/Christ und Welt* (February 12, 1988).

purpose was to create a geographic zone of price stability around their principal markets, the major industrial centers of Germany.[545] Under the *kontore* agreements, all producers retailed their steel through four joint sales agencies (*kontore*) rather than individually. Price competition was avoided through the four agencies' joint adherence to published list prices and collective refusal to align on lower prices quoted in the German market by non-German producers.[546] Orders were shared among the steelmakers in order to discourage firms disadvantaged at any particular point from defending themselves with price cuts.[547] When the *kontore* worked properly, they enabled producers to extract prices from consumers that were as beneficial to the steelmakers as any government subsidy, and which required no surrender of autonomy to political authorities.[548]

In 1971, the Commission refused to reauthorize the *kontore*. However, it did grant the German steelmakers a four-year exemption (continually authorized thereafter) to form "Rationalization Groups" which accomplished the same essential purpose as the *kontore*.[549] Through these groups, product markets were divided to eliminate interfirm competition by reducing the number of producers of each item, thereby facilitating price coordination.[550] The basic goal was that each of the four groups would produce most types of steel products, but that within each group, each member was to concentrate on only a few products, foregoing products that competed with those of other group members.[551]

The First Crisis Years

At the outset of the structural crisis the German producers were, with a few exceptions, "undoubtedly the best equipped and most productive in the

---

[545] Although such practices are inconsistent with the Treaty of Paris, the European authorities were sufficiently concerned by the rash of price cutting which had coincided with the recession of 1967 that they authorized a derogation from the Treaty to permit them. *Official Journal* L 1274/67 (April 2, 1967); Stegemann, *Price Competition and Output Adjustment*, p. 246.

[546] Stegemann, *Price Competition and Output Adjustment*, p. 247.

[547] Thus, during the steel recession of 1976, *Der Spiegel* reported on December 6 that "in accordance with the principle of equal sacrifice" better employed combines were shifting orders to the lesser occupied ones.

[548] One of the architects of the *kontore* credited them with improving producers' profit margins by $2.50 per ton in 1968. H.C. Kohler, "Vertragliche Formen der Zusammenarbeit in der Produktion und beim Verkauf Stahlerzeugnissen," in *Stahl und Eisen* (April 17, 1969).

[549] *Journal Officiel*, L. 161 (July 19, 1971).

[550] Technically, the overt fixing of quotas was prohibited and use of joint sales agencies was restricted. Some joint sales arrangements were allowed. *Bull. EC* 9/10 - 1971, Point 16.

[551] EC Commission, *First Report on Competition Policy* at 44 (1971).

EC."[552] The industry was fragmented, by European standards, but most individual producers enjoyed cost advantages over virtually all foreign competitors, and the potentially adverse effects of fragmentation were partially offset by the regional groupings. Under these circumstances, when the crisis began, the German producers made a logical, but mistaken, strategic decision to wait out the recession, assuming that market pressure would weed out their less efficient foreign rivals in Belgium, France and Italy. The basic misjudgment by the German mills was their underestimation of the extent to which governments would intervene to prevent such a shakeout from occurring, and the lack of institutional constraints within the Community to offset the effects of such intervention. As a result, in steel, "the devil took not the hindmost, but the first," *i.e.*, the Germans.[553] In 1977 a German observer commented that

> *The British Government takes over the giant losses of the nationalized mammoth steel concern, British Steel Corporation. According to the European Coal and Steel Community, this is no subsidy. The agreement expressly prohibits subsidies as an act of unfair competition. But the French and Belgian governments pump billions into their steel industries in order to safeguard jobs in mills, which are three times as old as the oldest German plant. At present, the price situation in the steel markets is influenced more by a competition of subsidies than by performance. The victims of this competition are the German steel mills.*[554]

German Subsidies. Despite its public anti-subsidy stance, the German industry has been the beneficiary of substantial government financial aid, although such assistance was extended more discreetly and did not equal, in terms of sheer volume, the extraordinary subsidies granted by governments in France, Belgium, Italy and Britain. As *Der Spiegel* observed (June 10, 1983), "In all fairness it should be mentioned that subsidies are being paid to the steel industry even in Germany. The difference is that such assistance is much better concealed in Bonn." The federal government bailed out Krupp, one of the largest producers, when it went bankrupt in 1967. Loans at subsidized rates of interest had been granted to German steelmakers,[555] and research and

---

[552] *Rheinischer Merkur/Christ und Welt* (September 30, 1977).

[553] *Ibid.*

[554] *Ibid.*

[555] In March 1980 the German Ministry of Economics and the state of North Rhine-Westphalia jointly extended a loan of $133 million to the ailing Dutch-German combine Estel for the construction of a new steel plant, with interest set at 4 percent and repayment deferred until three years after start-up of the new facilities. The loan was harshly criticized by other West German steelmakers. *World Business Weekly* (April 28, 1980); *Journal of Commerce* (April 10, 1980).

development was subsidized.[556] The government offered a variety of financial benefits for new investment,[557] and German land and local governments maintained their own aid programs for the steel industry.[558] A joint federal-land program, the "Joint Task for the Improvement of the Regional Economic Structure," provided investment subsidies to steelmakers.[559] The one state-owned German firm, Peine-Salzgitter, had its substantial losses partially offset by periodic injections of new government capital.[560]

The German mills also benefited substantially from the federal government's acquisition of the failing German coal industry. Through the 1960s the principal German steel producers owned and operated coal mines; by the late 1960s the cost of coal produced in these mines had become so high that its continued use threatened the cost-competitiveness of German steel. Closure of the mines, however, would have resulted in an unacceptable level of losses charged against the German mills' financial statements, as well as the loss of a captive domestic source of a key raw material. In 1968, an agreement between the producers and the federal government created Ruhrkohle AG, jointly owned by the producers and the government.[561] In 1969, the producers' coal mines were transferred to Ruhrkohle, enabling them

---

[556] "Beschluss der Bundesregierung zur Deutschen Stahlindustrie," *Bulletin* 71/5.623 (August 5, 1981).

[557] The German government offered "investment premiums," among other things, for investments in fixed assets ordered between November 1974 and July 1975. The benefits included cash premiums of 7.5 percent or more of the cost of the investment. Extension of these benefits triggered a rush by German steelmakers to invest in new equipment within the allotted time period to secure the subsidy. See Peine-Salzgitter *Annual Report*, 1974-75, p. 6; *Investment Incentives Guide* (August 20, 1980).

[558] For example, under the Ruhr District Action Program, former pits and other industrial sites in the Ruhr were bought from steel firms at high prices by land and commune governments, and $175 million were paid for the conversion of environment-polluting plants. Josef Esser and Werner Väth, "Overcoming the Steel Crisis in the Federal Republic of Germany," in Meny and Wright, *The Politics of Steel*, p. 645. See also *Kölner Stadt-Anzeiger* (October 17, 1987).

[559] Under this program, designed to create jobs in specific regions in the 1970s, Peine-Salzgitter received investment subsidies at two sites of 20 and 25 percent, respectively; Maxhutte a 25 percent subsidy for a plant at Sulzbach-Rosenberg; and Hoesch, Krupp, Thyssen and Mannesman 5 percent subsidies for investments in the Ruhr. Esser and Väth, "Overcoming the Steel Crisis," p. 645.

[560] Peine-Salzgitter suffered losses of over $381 million between 1974 and 1981. These losses were transferred to its government-owned parent company, where they were partially offset by injections of new government capital into the parent totalling $244 million between 1977 and 1979. Peine-Salzgitter *Annual Reports*. As steelmaker Willi Korf commented in 1981, "then there is Salzgitter — a state-owned enterprise, which, as everyone knows, is safe from any mishap." *Wirtschaftswoche* (June 26, 1981).

[561] *Hüttenvertrag*. A 27 percent share of Ruhrkohle was held by VEBA, a holding company originally formed by the goverment of Prussia, in which the Bonn government now holds a 43.75 percent share.

to avoid closures and the writeoff of large losses.[562] In addition, the federal government agreed to pay the difference between Ruhrkohle's published prices and the lower world market price for coal.[563] In effect, this arrangement has enabled the German mills to maintain a secure domestic source of coal while paying only the world market price rather than the price warranted by Ruhrkohle's actual production costs.

Erosion of Industrial Solidarity. A sensible strategic response to the crisis, in the view of many West German and foreign observers, might have been for the industry to consolidate around the most efficient facilities, close the older plants, and run the remaining mills at a higher rate. Consolidation would not only have reduced unit costs but also enabled the industry to restore a degree of price control over its home market. For an industry with a long tradition of "rationalization groups" and other manifestations of industrial solidarity, such a consolidation appeared by no means impossible. Nonetheless, the German producers consistently proved unable to agree on any coherent plan of industry action. In part, this was due to the stronger firms' desire to wait out the collapse of the weaker ones.[564]

German disunity was exacerbated by the "Klöckner Affair." In 1973, Klöckner had brought on stream a huge new hot strip mill in Bremen, the most modern in Europe, which had cost the firm approximately $374 million. The hot strip mill had been primarily designed to meet the needs of the German shipbuilding industry, which itself was in a deep recession when the structural recession began in 1974. The Commission's production quotas were based on a percentage of 1974 production, which for Klöckner's strip mill had been very low, so that the quotas would force the mill to run at an uneconomically low utilization rate. Klöckner responded by periodically running its mill at a rate which exceeded the quota allocated to it by Eurofer, which in several instances caused price discipline in the Community to collapse. The other German producers, recognizing that the Community cartel was the principal mechanism restraining heavily-subsidized producers in other Member States from a ruinous bout of increased production and heavy discounting,[565] were furious at Klöckner's subversion of the crisis regime.

---

[562] *Grundvertrag* (July 18, 1969). The companies transferring properties to Ruhrkohle received "contribution claims" against it, which were to be redeemed if Ruhrkohle became profitable.

[563] The government pays the subsidy to Ruhrkohle, which furnishes coal to the steel mills at reduced prices.

[564] For example, in the late 1970s the federal and land governments were looking for a buyer to save the Saar steel industry. The German producers in the Ruhr district declined, hoping that a sacrifice of Saar capacity would ultimately benefit them.

[565] *Wirschaftswoche* (June 26, 1981).

The Klöckner affair served to poison the environment in which restructuring was attempted.[566]

By the beginning of the 1980s, it was apparent that heavy subsidization would prevent the market shakeout for which the German producers had been hoping, and the German mills began turning to their own government for aid to offset that of their foreign rivals. The federal authorities were philosophically opposed to sectoral intervention, and approached it only haltingly, as the crisis weakened progressively wider segments of the German industry. As one observer described this process, "there is not so much a conversion (to state interventionism) but rather a phased withdrawal (from market principles)."[567] The first and most dramatic intervention was in the Saar, where the onset of the crisis quickly threw the local steel producers into a struggle for survival.

The Steel Crisis in the Saarland

Notwithstanding German criticism of steel subsidies in other Member States, one segment of the German industry, the steel sector of the Saarland, has been characterized by the same sort of large-scale subsidization of uneconomic production that has occurred in France, Belgium, Britain and other neighboring states. The Saar, like the Charleroi/Liege basins, Luxembourg and Lorraine, was an old inland steelmaking region where steel and coal had dominated the local economy for generations. The region had been administered by France prior to 1957, and consistently lagged behind other regions of Germany in economic development. The Saar steel industry consisted of small plants of sub-optimum scale; they suffered from high inland transport costs, excessive concentration on bulk steel, and a fragmented ownership structure.[568]

The steel crisis hit the Saar industry first and hardest.[569] By 1977, the federal and land governments were faced with the choice of "either total

---

[566] Ruprecht Vondran of the German Iron and Steel Industry Association indicated in referring to the cartel that "we have gotten through the deluge of subsidies pouring in by existing within an air bubble artificially created by policy. . . . Since among our neighboring countries public aid has risen higher and higher, only the measures taken by the authorities have provided breathing room." *Handelsblatt* (April 5, 1985).

[567] *Financial Times* (June 18, 1981). In the view of one German Economics Minister, the industry had brought on its own problems with its "grotesque errors." *Der Spiegel* (June 20, 1983).

[568] Meny and Wright, *The Politics of Steel*, p. 5.

[569] From 1974 to 1977, the unemployment rate in the Saarland rose from 3.9 percent to 7.4 percent, as compared to a 2.7 to 5.3 percent rise for all of Germany. Moreover, the rate of utilization in Saar steel firms fell to 48.8 percent in 1977; whereas it stood at 58 percent for Germany as a whole. Esser and Väth, "Overcoming the Steel Crisis," pp. 648, 650.

collapse, or total government-backed restructuring" of the Saar steel sector.[570] The German industry showed no interest in any commitment to the Saar, and as a result the federal and land governments turned to Arbed, in adjoining Luxembourg. Under a compact agreed by company shareholders and the unions, Arbed received the shares of and the business control over the two Saar plants then in operation, Neunkircher Eisenwerke and Rochling-Burbach, resulting in the formation of a new entity, Arbed Saarstahl. This firm immediately received massive injections of financial aid from the Bonn government and the Saarland government.[571]

Notwithstanding such state support, Arbed would soon come to rue its commitment. The initial aid, while substantial, soon proved inadequate, and after 1981, Bonn was plagued by regular calls for public assistance to ensure Saarstahl's year-to-year survival. By 1983, Saarstahl had "soaked up" more government funds than any other German company in steel or any other West German industry ($862 million), yet there was little hope that the aid granted would be sufficient to resolve its problems.[572]

In 1984, the EC Commission began to express concern as to whether Saarstahl's restructuring measures would restore the Company's profitability by the end of 1985, the target date for the cutoff of subsidies.[573] By the end of 1984, Arbed was making known its interest in disposing of the troubled firm.[574] However, Saarstahl's situation was so dismal that Dillinger, the other Saar producer, whose combination with Saarstahl might have created a more competitive entity, showed little interest in acquiring the firm.[575] Arbed

---

[570] *Ibid.*

[571] The federal government pledged $647 million for new investments, $448 million in bank guarantees and $238 million in immediate cash for social measures. It also agreed to support the long-range plan of establishing one pig iron plant and one coking plant for the entire region. Estimates were that $498 million and $249 million would be necessary for these respective ventures. The Saar government agreed to provide $60 million from its regional development fund for the rescue, and to subsidize 20 percent of the costs of a new blast furnace in Volkingen. Esser and Väth, "Overcoming the Steel Crisis," p. 659; *World Business Weekly* (April 28, 1980), p. 9.

[572] *Metal Bulletin Monthly* (September 1983); Esser and Väth, "Overcoming the Steel Crisis," p. 663; *Financial Times* (Feb. 3, 1984), p. 3; *Metal Bulletin* (February 28, 1984), p. 29.

[573] *Metal Bulletin* (March 2, 1984), p. 23. The Saar government had to give Saarstahl credit of $10.5 million in the form of a bridging loan which was to have been repaid by the end of February 1984. *Metal Bulletin* (Feb. 28, 1984), p. 29.

[574] It was reported that even executive members of the IG Metal trade union were of the opinion that Saarstahl should be allowed to go bankrupt before any further last-minute rescue packages were mounted. *Handelsblatt* (Nov. 2, 1984), p. 15.

[575] The federal and land governments, which retained an option under the original takeover agreement to acquire 76 percent of the company's shares from Arbed AG for a symbolic $.35 amount, also showed no interest in becoming fully responsible for Saarstahl. *Financial Times* (December 29, 1984).

offered to sell its shares in Saarstahl to the federal government, but Bonn refused to make any new commitment to the ailing firm.[576]

1985 was an election year and the pre-election period was marked by a good deal of posturing with regard to the future of Saarstahl, the Saarland's largest employer. Despite indications from Bonn before the election that additional aid might be forthcoming,[577] after the Christian Democrats were defeated the central government stated that it would not provide any further operating subsidies to Saarstahl.[578] The remainder of 1985 was spent in protracted negotiations between the industry, the Commission, the federal and land governments over the amount of funding required to restore Saarstahl's viability.[579] Just before the year's end -- which also marked the end of the Commission's legal authority under the subsidies code to authorize operating aids -- the Commission approved $161 million for the 1986-87 period for Saarstahl.[580]

It was fully apparent that in order to survive, Saarstahl needed to enter into a rationalization arrangement or merge with another steel firm. Three steel companies, Thyssen, Krupp and Klöckner, expressed interest in rescuing Saarstahl.[581] However, the Saar government was skeptical about whether the goals of these firms, which would surely involve capacity cuts, would be compatible with the land's plans for regional employment.[582] Instead, an agreement was worked out with Dillinger whereby in May 1986, the federal and land governments acquired 76 percent of Saarstahl's shares and the remaining 24 percent remained with Arbed. Dillinger took over management of Saarstahl pursuant to a control agreement, but it did not bind itself financially or otherwise to Saarstahl.[583]

---

[576] *Metal Bulletin* (July 9, 1985).

[577] *Financial Times* (January 29, 1985), p. 27.

[578] *Die Welt* (April 4, 1985), p. 4.

[579] Losses in the order of $69.1 million were being forecast for 1986, and the governments were being called upon to write off Saarstahl's $552.9 million in debt. *Metal Bulletin* (March 1, 1985), p. 25; (May 21, 1985), p. 41.

[580] *Metal Bulletin* (July 9, 1985, August 6, 1985).

[581] The real goal of these firms would have been to work out a global German plan for long products, Saarstahl's principal product. *Metal Bulletin* (February 18, 1986), p. 27.

[582] *Metal Bulletin* (March 11, 1986).

[583] The arrangement with Dillinger needed considerable financing from the private banking sector ($161.2 million) and a substantial writeoff of debt by the government. While initially reluctant to write off $324.8 million of Saarstahl's debt, the ruling Christian Democratic government ultimately bowed to pressure from the Social Democrats to pledge the full amount. The government's change of heart was reportedly due to its recent poor showing in elections in Schleswig-Holstein, and fear that it could lose important elections in Lower Saxony, where it was vulnerable on employment issues. *Metal Bulletin* (March 25, 1986), p. 25; *Global Analyst Systems* (March 21, 1986).

When the steel market began to weaken in 1986 Saarstahl was placed under severe strain, and in June 1987, it announced that it would go bankrupt unless more financial assistance was forthcoming.[584] As additional assistance would have contravened the EC prohibition against new subsidies, it was unclear how the company would be able to secure its future without its *argenterie de famille.*[585] In 1987 the land government agreed to take over $235 million of Saarstahl's debt and buy land from the company for $21 million.[586]

The Korf Insolvency. One sidelight of the Saar steel crisis was the 1983 insolvency of an international group of steel firms owned by entrepreneur Willi Korf.[587] Korf had been a pioneer of minimill technology and a fierce competitor in the German market. Korf's need to seek *Vergleich* protection was attributed by observers to a variety of factors inside Germany and abroad,[588] but Korf himself charged that his group's problems stemmed entirely from subsidized competition and the Commission's output quotas.[589] One of his two principal German companies, Badische Stahlwerke, competed with Arbed Saarstahl in southern Germany, and Korf was incensed that "the Arbed Saarstahl plant was being kept alive artificially with the help of government subsidies amounting to billions [while] his own plant . . . a far more efficient operation, would be seriously hurt."[590] Korf's feelings were sufficiently strong on this score that Badische Stahlwerke ultimately brought a legal action against the Bonn government for subsidizing Saarstahl and causing the financial collapse of Badische.[591] Korf's difficulties appeared to reflect a fundamental distortion created by subsidies in the Community and abroad -- inefficient producers were prevailing over more efficient ones. As Korf remarked in 1981,

---

[584] *Die Welt* (June 30, 1987), p. 1; *Die Welt* (November 3, 1986), p. 17; *Handelsblatt* (November 3, 1986), pp. 15, 17.

[585] *La Tribune de l'Economie* (October 7, 1987). In October 1987, Saar Finance Minister Hans Kasper announced that Saarstahl needed a minimum of $83.7 million to get through 1988. *Metal Bulletin* (October 29, 1987), p. 41.

[586] The land government was also interested in purchasing Saarstahl's loss-making steel processing subsidiary, Techno Saarstahl, to ease Saarstahl's financial strain. *Metal Bulletin* (October 29, 1987), p. 41.

[587] Korf's holdings included Badische Stahlwerke in Southern Germany, a majority interest in Hamburger Stahlwerke, and holdings in France and the United States.

[588] Among other problems, the Korf group was reported to be overleveraged and suffering from the losses incurred on its U.S. operations. *Metal Bulletin* (January 14, 18, 1983).

[589] *Metal Bulletin* (January 18, 1983).

[590] *Der Spiegel* (December 27, 1982).

[591] *Metal Bulletin* (July 12, 1985).

The sad thing is that in the other countries obsolete capacities are artificially kept alive while in our country the steelmakers with their modern installations are fighting for survival.[592]

The Restructuring Stalemate

While the Saarstahl crisis was a headache and an embarrassment for the Bonn government, a potentially much more serious problem became evident in 1980 as the steel crisis began to engulf the principal German producers in north Germany and the Ruhr. These firms had weathered the initial years of the structural recession relatively well, but their position had begun to deteriorate seriously by the end of the decade of the 1970s,[593] and in the spring of 1981, several large German producers issued calls for infusions of state aid, including Krupp, Klöckner and Hoesch.[594] That summer the federal government announced its commitment in principle to provide financial help to the steel industry amounting to $800 million. This aid, which was to be spread among the German mills rather than targeted to specific problems, was criticized as a "modified sprinkler system," and the aid total was seen as much too small. One analyst commented that "the innocence is gone, and yet no real sin has been committed."[595]

Bonn noted that the Hoesch and Krupp investment proposals envisaged potentially duplicative facilities, and indicated that state funding would be conditioned on the development of an industry plan to rationalize facilities and eliminate redundant facilities. As a practical matter, this meant a reduction in the number of major producers through merger, and closure of some major plants. This proved impossible to achieve.

The first German restructuring initiative was a 1981 proposal for a joint venture between Krupp and Hoesch (whose union with the Dutch producer Hoogovens was breaking up) to be called "Ruhrstahl."[596] Protracted negotiations through late 1981 and 1982 -- which involved possible participation by Peine-Salzgitter and Klöckner in the combination -- were

---

[592] *Wirtschaftswoche* (June 26, 1981).

[593] *Die Welt* (June 30, 1987).

[594] *Die Welt* (June 19, 1981); *Metal Bulletin* (March 19, May 29, June 5, 26, July 13, 1981).

[595] *Handelsblatt* (August 3, 1981).

[596] The Hoesch-Hoogovens union was weakened by the fact that the Dutch firm was required to cover over $476.1 million in losses for its German partner between 1976 and 1981. Estel, the parent company, was dissolved in 1982. *Der Spiegel* (August 10, 1981); *Metal Bulletin* (September 21, 1982).

inconclusive.[597] The Bonn government balked at aid levels requested by the steelmakers to launch the new combination.[598] Hoesch was irritated by Krupp's plans to enter a specialty steel joint venture with Thyssen,[599] and the Hoesch-Krupp negotiations were characterized by a "narrow-minded and humiliating inability to agree on simple questions."[600] By early 1983, the Hoesch-Krupp talks were "widely assumed to be dead."[601] This episode demonstrated the limitations of the German banks as facilitators of industrial rationalization; the Dresdner Bank had encouraged Krupp, its affiliate, to merge with Hoesch, whose own bank, the Deutsche Bank, had also supported the merger.[602]

In 1982, the Bonn government, exasperated by the steelmakers' inability to develop a viable restructuring plan, appointed a panel of three "moderators" to serve as "marriage brokers" between the large German firms and to develop a restructuring plan for the German industry that would enable it to survive economically.[603] In January 1983 the moderators presented a plan for the restructuring of the German industry over a period of three years. The basic feature of the plan was the creation, through amalgamation, of two large steel groups which would dominate German steel production.[604] While the plan envisioned capacity reductions, "no existing steel location is to be abandoned,"

---

[597] The state-owned producer, Peine-Salzgitter, feared that a Krupp-Hoesch combination would confront it with two "huge competitors, Ruhrstahl and Thyssen, and to top it all, Ruhrstahl would be helped on its feet by none other than Salzgitter's owner -- the government." Klöckner faced a similar dilemma. *Frankfurter Rundschau* (January 16, 1962).

[598] *Metal Bulletin* (August 24, 1981).

[599] Hoesch was caught by surprise by this agreement, as was the land government of North Rhine-Westphalia, which had pledged substantial financial aid to the Krupp-Hoesch combination. land Economic Minister Jochimson indicated that "Ruhrstahl, in the generally anticipated form, is dead." *Stuttgarter Zeitung* (August 28, 1982). Krupp Manager Alfons Goedde intimated in *Der Spiegel* (November 14, 1983) that Thyssen may have initiated the specialty steel arrangement with Krupp as a means of "torpedoing" Ruhrstahl, which might have proven a formidable rival for Thyssen.

[600] *Metal Bulletin* (November 10, 1981).

[601] *Metal Bulletin* (January 24, 1983). The land Minister charged that the reorganization plans were "being sunk through organized though hidden opponents." *Frankfurter Allgemeine Zeitung* (December 17, 1982).

[602] Meny and Wright, *The Politics of Steel*, pp. 83-84.

[603] The three-man panel included a steel executive, a reorganization expert, and an official from the Deutsche Bank. *Rheinischer Merkur/Christ und Welt* (December 10, 1982).

[604] The moderators pursued certain basic objectives: 1) for major products at least two independent suppliers of equal rank should operate in the marketplace; 2) large suppliers should produce a broad range of products; and 3) no producer should achieve predominance. The Plan contemplated 3 hot strip sheet rolling mills in each group -- which would entail a closure of one such mill by each group. *Neue Zürcher Zeitung* (January 28, 1983); *Wirtschaftswoche* (January 28, 1983).

and joint sales agencies similar to the *kontore* would be formed pending the amalgamations.[605] Although the federal government agreed to support the Plan with "financial and external economic assistance," the Plan ran into difficulty almost immediately.[606] The land government of North Rhine-Westphalia rejected the plan, citing a long list of objections.[607] The producers, who were supposed to draw up a plan implementing the moderators' recommendations, would not do so.[608] The "Ruhr Group" was seen as an inherently weaker combination; the *Deutsches Allgemeines Sonntagsblatt* observed on March 6, 1983 that

> *The restructuring of the German steel industry is in danger of developing into a two-class society: Thyssen and Krupp Stahl (of which little will remain) on the one side and several rather lackluster mini-stars and satellites on the other.*

Klöckner, a virtual pariah among the German mills, was shunned as a merger partner by Hoesch and Peine-Salzgitter, who were more interested in exploring a possible union with Arbed -- a firm which the moderators had excluded from the Plan.[609] Hoesch's Chief Executive indicated he would not tolerate reductions in his own firm's operations to accommodate a union with Klöckner, "the most unloved child in the steel industry." Klöckner was teetering on the brink of bankruptcy, and Hoesch in particular was dubious about a merger with "the outsider" (Klöckner) which would entail assumption

---

[605] This was an attempt to restore price discipline among German producers, which had been destroyed by the Klöckner affair -- "Joint sales, it is hoped, will achieve price stabilization in all markets." If necessary, the Plan contemplated measures at the border to protect price stability in the German market from disruption by subsidized steel. *Neue Zürcher Zeitung* (January 28, 1983).

[606] *Metal Bulletin* (February 1, 1983).

[607] The land believed that the commissioning of the Plan had undermined Ruhrstahl. Objections included the fact that the Rhine group was concentrated in one land, whereas the Ruhr Group was dispersed among four, raising the danger of political differences, and the lack of balance between the two groups in terms of technology and location.

[608] The federal government took the view that the moderators' plan was "not sacred," and that it would accept "any better suggestions," but one official commented, "I can't see them finding any better solution." *Metal Bulletin* (March 18, 1983).

[609] "Klöckner had already been ostracized by the other steel companies months ago" (*Der Spiegel*, June 20, 1983); in any event, its heavy debt burden made it a highly unattractive merger partner, and its controversial wide strip mill at Bremen was viewed as "an albatross that should not be allowed to burden any new grouping arising from the moderators' report." *Metal Bulletin* (March 18, 1983); *Deutsches-Allgemeines Sonntagsblatt* (February 20, 1983).

of its financial liabilities.[610] Hoesch and Peine-Salzgitter in turn could not agree on a plan of union between themselves.[611]

At a summit meeting in Bonn held in March 1983, Economics Minister Lambsdorff persuaded the producers to complete plans for cooperation in time for their submission to Brussels by March 31, the deadline for state aid applications. The plan finally submitted called for a merger of Krupp and Thyssen and "close cooperation" between Hoesch and Peine-Salzgitter. Klöckner was left to fend for itself.[612]

Virtually immediately after the submission, however, the hastily-prepared plan began coming unraveled. Krupp and Thyssen -- originally the strongest supporters of the Plan -- began arguing over who would shoulder Krupp's existing liabilities.[613] Thyssen and Krupp wanted Bonn to relieve them of Krupp's debt, but Klöckner argued that if Krupp's debts were written off, Klöckner should receive similar relief.[614] Shortly thereafter, "war broke out" among the German mills over Klöckner's defiance of the Commission's quotas, and North Rhine-Westphalia's Jochimson charged that rather than seeking a real solution, the steel companies were merely trying to "topple each other in the hope of benefitting from their collapse."[615] In October, the Krupp-Thyssen negotiations broke down, leaving the German restructuring effort in a state of "disarray."[616]

In 1984, Krupp and Klöckner quietly began a new series of merger talks.[617] When these talks became known, however, a public controversy erupted over the inevitable job cuts that would most likely accompany the merger. The Lower Saxony land government was particularly displeased with the merger plan, as it would have resulted in the closure of a mill in Osnabruck.[618] With 1985 an election year in the Social Democrat-controlled North Rhine-Westphalia, which would also be potentially affected by the proposed merger, the ruling Christian Democratic government refused to contribute the full

---

[610] *Financial Times* (February 23, 1983).

[611] *Metal Bulletin* (March 22, 1983).

[612] *Metal Bulletin* (March 22, April 6, 1983).

[613] Thyssen indicated it could not take on these liabilities. *Metal Bulletin* (April 15, 1983).

[614] *Metal Bulletin* (September 6, 1983).

[615] *Metal Bulletin* (May 4, June 3, 1983).

[616] *Financial Times* (October 17, 1983. Krupp Manager Alfons Goedde commented that "We had the impression that in certain phases of the negotiations Thyssen was not very interested in the progress of the talks. Thus, I would not like to rule out the possibility of whether perhaps the strategy was to cause the negotiations to fail." *Der Spiegel* (November 14, 1983).

[617] *Frankfurter Allgeine Zeitung* (October 26, 1984), p. 16; *Handelsblatt* (October 26, 1984), pp. 1, 25.

[618] Bonn was focusing already on the elections scheduled for 1986 in DCU-controlled Lower Saxony, which it did not want to risk losing. *Financial Times* (July 11, 1985), p. 22.

$121 million in restructuring subsidies requested for the merger.[619] That fact, combined with Lower Saxony's unyielding opposition, led the firms to abandon the effort.

The failure of the Krupp/Klöckner merger appeared for a time to mark the end of attempts at cooperation within the German industry. However, in early 1988, Krupp, Mannesman and Thyssen unveiled a plan for restructuring of that portion of the Ruhr industry located in Duisburg which stopped short of actual merger. Under this plan, Krupp would close its Rheinhausen steelworks, transferring production of pig iron, raw steel and semis to Mannesmann's Huckingen works, which could then be run at full capacity, operated as a joint venture between Krupp and Mannesmann. Krupp's former rail and structurals production from Rheinhausen would be transferred to Thyssen's Bruckhausen plant.[620] The proposed Rheinhausen closure provoked a dramatic five month long grass roots movement in the city to block the move.[621] However, Krupp adhered to its plan to close the mill, supported by the Bonn government, which pledged about $300 million to foster the region's development, matched by similar funds from the land government of North Rhine-Westphalia.[622]

Even taking the Rheinhausen closure into account, after years of merger discussions, government restructuring packages, and intense media attention, the German industry's rationalization efforts had produced realtively modest results. "The limited amount of concrete restructuring success [was] out of all proportion to the discussion and rhetoric expended on the problem."[623] The slow progress of restructuring was mitigated, to an extent, by better market conditions in 1985 and 1986. However, in 1987, the German mills, hampered by a strong Deutschemark, slid back into a loss position. They charged that their competitors were still being "kept alive" by state aid, and asked for offsetting aid from Bonn. The federal government pledged additional benefits to laid off workers, retraining benefits, incentives for investments in alternative industries, but stopped short of offering aid to producing enterprises.[624]

---

[619] *Frankfurter Allgemeine Zeitung* (April 12, 1985), p. 15; *Handelsblatt* (April 12, 1985), p. 1.

[620] *Metal Bulletin* (February 22, 1988). Thyssen and Mannesman agreed to absorb some of the workers from the Krupp facility.

[621] *Süddeutsche Zeitung* (January 14, 1988); *Rheinischer Merkus/Christ und Welt* (January 29, 1988).

[622] *New York Times* (June 6, 1988).

[623] *Metal Bulletin Monthly* (September 1983).

[624] *Metal Bulletin* (January 20, April 3, 1987). The German producers faced another potential embarrassment when the Bavarian producer Maxhutte fell into financial difficulties in 1987 and filed for bankruptcy. The Bavarian land government stepped in to offer "bridging" loans for the bankrupt firm, and Bavaria indicated its willingness to take a 49 percent stake in a reorganized Maxhütte, prompting a critical inquiry by the Commission over a potential breach in its subsidy prohibition rules. At length, a compromise was worked out in which a reorganized Maxhütte was established, jointly owned by the Bavarian government, five leading steel producers (10% each)

The Netherlands

The Netherlands, while supporting some aid programs for its one integrated producer, Hoogovens, was traditionally an outspoken opponent of the far heavier subsidization of the steel industry in neighboring states.[625] However, in the 1980s the Dutch government, too, has expanded the scope of its financial assistance to the steel industry. The government has offered favorable loans, injections of equity capital, and "special assistance" funds to cover Hoogovens' losses incurred while it was part of a combination with the North German producer Hoesch known as Estel.[626] Between 1980 and 1985, the Commission authorized a total of $430 million in state aid for Hoogovens.[627]

---

and Düsseldorf auditors. *Metal Bulletin* (May 1, June 19, July 13, November 5, 1987; February 1, 1988.)

[625] Pursuant to the Wet Investeringskening (WIR), Dutch enterprises since 1978 have been granted "premiums" by the government for investments in capital plant and for environmental and energy-related investments. The premiums are paid in the form of tax credits; if the premiums exceed tax liability, a direct cash payment is made to the firm by tax authorities (Rijksbelastingdienst). The Dutch government has extended substantial support to Hoogovens for research and development. Hoogovens has also received subsidies for pollution control. *Act of July 18, 1978, Statue Book 368*; Ministry of Economic Affairs, *Bedrijfstakverkenning 1980 Basismettaalindustrie*, pp. 89-117.

[626] The European Authorities summarized this program as follows: "Investment premiums of Fl 200 million [$74.9 million], state-guaranteed loan of Fl 200 million [$74.9 million], loan or holding of Fl 80 million [$29.9 million], low-interest loans of Fl 24 million [$8.9 million], and conversion of a commercial-rate loan of Fl 200 million [$74.9 million] to a participating loan. There would be assistance of Fl 570 million [$213.4 million] (loan or holding) to cover the Estel losses, which have still to be borne by Hoogovens after the reversal of the merger between the two." EC Commission, *Preliminary Study of Steel Aids*, November 1982, p. 74; *Metal Bulletin* (February 12, July 21, October 1, 1982).

[627] EC Commission, *Report*, August 6, 1986.

4

Japan

The spectacular postwar development of the Japanese steel industry is frequently cited as an example of successful industrial policy.[1] Devastated by the War, in the following three decades the Japanese industry emerged as one of the largest, most technologically advanced and efficient steel industries in the world. Today its plants are highly automated and generally employ continuous casting and other state-of-the-art technologies. The principal Japanese mills are of large scale and located at sites where access to deepwater transportation minimizes shipping costs. Japanese scientists and engineers continually develop refinements in the steelmaking processes which are adopted by other steel industries around the world. Japan is the world's leading steel exporter.

However, these achievements have come at a price. The Japanese steel industry has achieved and sustained its present state, in significant part, through a government-sanctioned system which restrains competition in the domestic market. The Japanese steel industry depends heavily on cartel arrangements and stringent restriction of imports to maintain the solvency of its massive plants. Between 1960 and 1975, this system contributed to an extraordinary competition to expand facilities, in which the Japanese industry installed far more production capacity than could possibly be supported by demand from domestic consuming industries, even in peak periods (figure 4-2). The large Japanese mills are only truly "efficient" if they can be operated at a relatively high rate, and the drive to find outlets abroad for their surpluses has caused economic dislocations in other countries and brought Japan into a succession of jarring collisions with its trading partners. At this writing, largely reflecting the cartelization of the domestic market, the Japanese mills have made little progress in reducing their capacity surplus, despite a general recognition dating back to the early 1970s that the industry was far too large for its markets to sustain.

---

[1] See generally Eugene Kaplan, *Japan: The Government-Business Relationship* (Washington: U.S. Department of Commerce, February 1972).

192

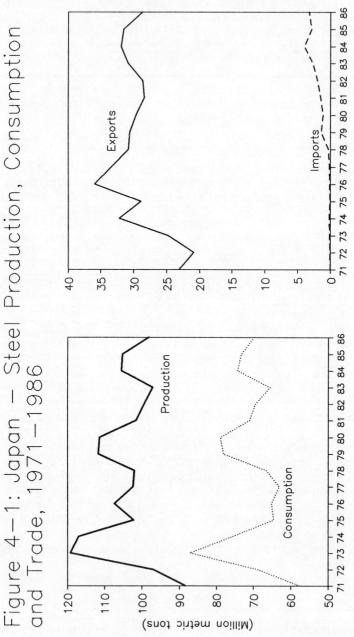

Figure 4-1: Japan – Steel Production, Consumption and Trade, 1971–1986

(Million metric tons)

Source: International Iron and Steel Institute, Steel Statistical Yearbook, 1981, 1987. Production and Consumption refer to crude steel; Exports and Imports refer to semi-finished and finished steel.

The expansion of Japanese steelmaking capacity between 1960 and 1975 defies superlatives. During this period Japanese gross crude steel capacity grew from 28 million metric tons to 140 million metric tons, the largest expansion in such a time frame in the history of the world steel industry. The creation of this massive production base in Japan was one of the most significant developments in world steelmaking of the entire postwar era -- not merely because of its sheer size, but also because of its impact on global steel competition. One recent European analysis suggests that "the meteoric rise of the Japanese industry in the 1960s is perhaps the major cause of the [current] structural imbalance in the world steel industry."[2]

Government policies, particularly those of the Ministry of International Trade and Industry (MITI), played a critical role in this expansion. The government ensured that capital was available, and on favorable terms; it oversaw a system of investment coordination which made it possible for steelmakers to "take turns" constructing greenfield mills of large scale; it encouraged the adoption of advanced steelmaking technologies; and it assisted in the acquisition of overseas raw materials, an important benefit given Japan's paucity of the natural resources required for steelmaking.   MITI also participated in the establishment and refinement of a system of controls on competition which unhinged Japan's growing steel industry from the discipline of the market, resulting in an explosive growth which was "rational," from the perspective of technology and efficiency, but "monstrous"[3] in terms of the size of the industry which Japan really needed or which Japan and other world markets could realistically support. Since 1975, MITI has been forced to cope with a succession of domestic and external steel crises which have at their root the extraordinary expansion which its own prior policies unleashed.

THE INDUSTRY-GOVERNMENT RELATIONSHIP

Japan's postwar political structure has proven highly conducive to government-guided industrial growth. At the end of the War, Japan already possessed a long tradition of government supervision of the economy, as well as the recent experience of a government-directed war effort. In contrast to nations like Britain, where steel policy was caught up in a perennial tug-of-war between successive Conservative and Labour governments, one political party, the Liberal Democratic Party (LDP), with an abiding commitment to industrial growth, has held power throughout the postwar era.[4]   One government body, MITI, has enjoyed wide-ranging influence over the Japanese

---

[2] Meny and Wright, *The Politics of Steel*, p. 11.

[3] The term is from the *Japan Economic Journal* (August 31, 1971).

[4] The business community enjoys substantial influence within the LDP and for over three decades a consensus has prevailed within the party that industrial expansion should be an overriding national goal. The steel industry's leading firms are also among the leading Japanese corporate contributors to the LDP. *Metal Bulletin Monthly* (December 1986).

Figure 4–2: Japanese Crude Steel Capacity and Apparent Consumption, 1960–1986

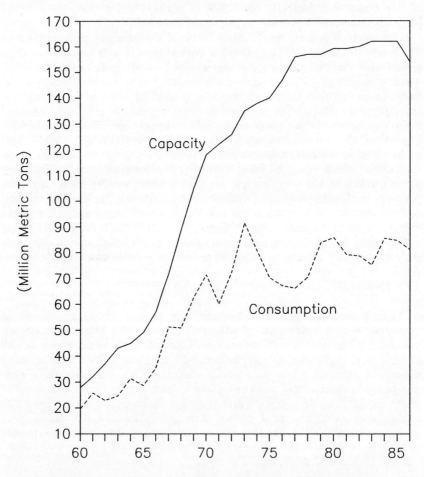

Source: Crude steel capacity from Peter F. Marcus and Karlis M. Karsis, World Steel Dynamics: Core Report BB (PaineWebber, Inc., January 1988), Exhibit BB–1–5; apparent consumption in ingot equivalents from Organization for Economic Cooperation and Development, World Steel Trade Developments 1960–1983 (Paris: OECD, 1985) and OECD, The Steel Market in 1986 and the Outlook for 1987 (Paris: OECD, 1987).

steel industry, which at one time included the power to control imports and the import of technology, to provide financial assistance, to regulate the allocation of raw materials, and to influence industry structure.[5] While MITI no longer wields many of these powers, the events of the "Yen Shock" period (1985-88), when MITI intervened in a variety of ways to help the steelmakers to surmount a crisis precipitated by a rapid shift in exchange rates, demonstrate that its influence in the affairs of the industry remains substantial in the late 1980s.

The Japanese government directly or indirectly controlled the steel industry throughout the entire period from the Meiji Restoration to the end of the Second World War.[6] Although the state-owned steel conglomerate, the Japan Steel Company (Nittetsu), was dissolved at the end of the War, the relationship between the government and the steel industry remained unusually close. The leading executives of the major steel firms were often former MITI officials who made the "descent from heaven" into leadership positions in the steel industry.[7] Steel executives were heavily represented on many industry-government deliberative councils and associations whose views were solicited to develop a consensus on the direction which government policy toward the steel industry should take.[8]

MITI deserves much of the credit for the postwar reconstruction of the steel industry and its subsequent rapid expansion in the 1960s. In 1950 the Japanese Cabinet directed MITI to devise a comprehensive strategy to develop

---

[5] MITI's prewar antecedent was the Ministry of Commerce and Industry (MCI), which played an important role in promoting Japan's strategic and military industries. First in Manchuria and later in Japan, the officials of MCI developed the ability to foster new, advanced-technology industries, and came to appreciate that this could only be done in close collaboration with Japanese industrial groups, the prewar *zaibatsu*. In 1943 portions of the MCI bureaucracy were merged into the Ministry of Munitions, which oversaw Japan's war production and exercised authority over industrial planning, energy, and the supervision of factories. MCI was reconstituted after the War and emerged as MITI in 1949, when it was merged with the Board of Trade and acquired authority over international trade as well as industrial policy. As a result of this institutional history, MITI's cadres acquired extensive experience in promoting new industries, in working closely with large industrial groups, and in wielding broad authority over Japanese industry. See generally Chalmers Johnson, *MITI and the Japanese Miracle* (Stanford: Stanford University Press, 1982).

[6] At the turn of the century, the government established the Yawata Mill, Japan's first large modern steel facility. Most of Japan's private steel firms came into being at the time of the First World War. During the Depression, the Japan Steel Company was formed by merging Yawata with the six largest steel companies, with the government holding a 70 percent share. The government assumed full operational control over the industry in 1941 and retained it until the end of World War II. Kaplan, *Japan*, pp. 138-39.

[7] MITI Vice Minister Tomisaburo Kirai, for example, retired from MITI in 1955 to become the president of Yawata Steel, Japan's largest steel firm. When Nippon Steel was formed in 1970 through the merger of Japan's largest steel firms, Yawata and Fuji, all of its chief executives were former officials of MITI or MCI. Johnson, *MITI and the Japanese Miracle*, p. 283.

[8] The most significant of those is the Industrial Structure Council, composed of academics, government officials and businessmen, which advises MITI on long-range industrial issues.

a competitive steel industry. MITI implemented the First (1951-55) and Second (1955-60) Rationalization Programs, which placed heavy emphasis on capital investment for plant modernization and new plant construction. MITI controlled investment levels by regulating the import of machinery and technology and allocating domestic loans to the industry. Government assistance was provided in the form of government loans, import protection, and tax breaks and infrastructural improvements.[9] The steel industry was allowed greater autonomy over its own development after 1960, but the government continued to provide a variety of forms of assistance to the industry which played a substantial role in the Japanese industry's spectacular ascent.

Capital

One of the most important government policies during the industry's rapid-growth period was the use of its influence over the banking system to ensure a flow of plentiful, low-cost capital to the industry, enabling it to finance its massive expansion, for the most part, with borrowed funds. During the high-growth period of the 1960s, the government held interest rates at artificially low levels, substantially reducing the cost of raising capital through bank loans. This naturally created an excessive demand for loans and made possible a system of credit rationing to industrial sectors whose promotion was desired by the government.[10] Japan's 13 city banks, which were the primary lenders to Japan's industrial corporations, were heavily dependent on the Bank of Japan (BOJ) for funds,[11] and the BOJ's criterion for providing those funds was that the city banks make their own loans in accordance with government

---

[9] For a summary of these programs, see Tsutomu Kawasaki, *Japan's Steel Industry* (Tokyo: Tekko Shimbun Sha, 1985).

[10] MITI's Industrial Structure Council commented in 1982 that "In the face of the artificial low interest rate, at times it was impossible to adjust the demand for and supply of funds through changes in the money rate, so credit allocation was carried out. But as can be seen in the adjustment of debenture flotation and the granting of credit by the Bank of Japan, priority was given to supplying funds to export industries and the key industries." Subcommittee on Industrial Finance Problems of the Central Division Committee, Industrial Structure Council, *Kongo No Nozomashii No Arikata Ni Ni Kansuru Hokolu* (September 29, 1982).

[11] The city banks were chronically in an "overloaned" position -- that is, their loans frequently equaled or exceeded their holdings, forcing them to borrow from the Bank of Japan. Bank of Japan, Economic Research Department, *The Japanese Financial System* (Tokyo: Bank of Japan, 1972), p. 22.

priorities.[12] In the 1960s, the steel industry was one of the government's leading industrial priorities.[13]

The government also provided the industry direct loans and tax benefits. Government loans were channeled through the Fiscal Investment and Loan Program (FILP), an entity in the Ministry of Finance independent of the general account budget which loans government funds to public financial institutions (such as the Japan Development Bank and the Export-Import Bank of Japan), which in turn make loans on favorable terms to Japanese industry.[14] Such loans were significant not only for their own sake but as a signal that MITI favored the recipient, and "the company that received a JDB loan could easily raise whatever else it needed from private resources."[15] In addition, the Long Term Credit Bank of Japan channeled a substantial volume of government funds into the steel industry for equipment acquisition and long-term working capital.[16] While MITI's desire to provide tax benefits for the industry led to recurrent conflicts with the Ministry of Finance, numerous

---

[12] Article 1 of the *Bank of Japan Law* provides that "the purpose of the Bank of Japan shall be to adjust currency, to regulate financing, and to develop the credit system in conformity with policies of the state so as to ensure appropriate application of the state's total economic power." Article 2 of the same law provides that "the Bank of Japan shall be operated exclusively with a view to accomplishing the purposes of the state." Translated in *Japan Echo* (1977), p. 100.

[13] The *Japan Economic Journal* reported on February 2, 1965 that MITI Vice Minister Sahashi had met with Bank of Japan Governor Usami to explain the "government's industrial policy for developing 11 different industries deemed most important for the nation's economic growth [including steel] and wish to have funds extended to them on an effective basis. . . . Sahashi reportedly told Usami that mere scattering of financing funds would deter sound development of industries . . . [structural alloy steel] will require special financial aid of about 4.5 billion yen [$12.4 million] in the January-March period, for which all-out cooperation of bankers is needed. Groupings of minor firms will be promoted on a long-range basis. Capital investments should be focused only on convertors."

[14] The FILP was financed by deposits made in Japan's Postal Savings system. Public financial institutions like the Japan Development Bank were authorized to borrow from this pool of funds to make loans to industrial customers approved by MITI. In 1953-55, JDB loans to the steel industry accounted for 10.6 percent of the industry's investment in new plant. The JDB and Export-Import Bank of Japan continue to make loans to the steel industry in the 1980s. See generally Johnson, *MITI and the Japanese Miracle*, pp. 210-12, and Yukio Noguchi, "The Government-Business Relationship in Japan: The Changing Role of Fiscal Resources," in Kozo Yamamura, ed. *Policy and Trade Issues of the Japanese Economy* (Seattle: University of Washington Press, 1982).

[15] Johnson, *MITI and the Japanese Miracle*, pp. 210-212.

[16] The Long Term Credit Bank (LTCB) along with several similar banks (the Hypothec Bank and the Industrial Bank of Japan) are private banks to which the government extended the privilege of issuing bank debentures, which was severely limited under Japan's commercial code. The *quid pro quo* for this privilege was that the banks "serve as a pipeline through which the government can channel funds into the private sector by purchasing bank debentures." LTCB *Annual Report* (1981)). The LTCB commented in its 1962 *Annual Report* (p. 8) that "the loans of our banks give priority to key industries." The steel industry was the largest single recipient of the LTCB's financial assistance; in 1981, the LTCB had outstanding loans to the steel industry for equipment capital of 348.5 billion yen, or $2.5 billion at 140:1. LTCB, *Annual Report* (1981).

tax measures favorable to the industry were implemented during the high growth period, including generous depreciation allowances and a variety of export-promoting tax measures.[17]

Greenfield Mills

One of the most distinctive features of the Japanese steel industry is the significant number of greenfield steel mills of large scale constructed after 1960 at prime seaside locations where transportation costs are lowest.[18] Construction of such mills required non-enforcement of Japan's Antimonopoly Law to permit the Japanese producers to "take turns" building such facilities, as opposed to incremental expansion efforts at existing sites (table 4-1).[19] The government shouldered much of the burden of establishing the transportation infrastructure to support these projects, subsidizing the construction and improvement of a series of deepwater steel port facilities capable of accommodating giant ore and coal ships.[20] The government took extensive measures to promote another priority industry, shipbuilding, which enabled Japan to build a fleet of giant, efficient coal and ore-carrying ships to serve the steel industry's bulk raw materials needs.[21]

Technology

A striking feature of the Japanese steel industry to many observers is its technological leadership. MITI, which from the 1950s through 1970 controlled

---

[17] Until 1976, under the *Enterprise Rationalization Law*, a 25 percent first year depreciation charge for approved equipment for designated industries (including steel) was allowed. The steel industry was one of the principal industrial beneficiaries of the Reserve for Overseas Market Development (in effect until 1972). Under this system, extra expense incurred in initial foreign market penetration could be spread over a five year period for tax purposes. The purpose of this provision was to increase cash flow to management. E. Hadley, *Japan's Export Competitiveness in Third World Markets* (Washington, D.C.: Georgetown University, 1981), pp. 29-30.

[18] *Oriental Economist* (April 1967), pp. 266-67.

[19] See below, "The Capacity Expansion Race," for a description of this practice and its consequences.

[20] Eleven harbors were overhauled to accommodate 40,000 DWT ore carriers serving the steel industry. The cost of these renovations was subsidized by the national treasury and by local authorities. Kawasaki, *Japan's Steel Industry*, pp. 452-453.

[21] Ship construction was funded by long-term, low interest loans from the Japan Development Bank (JDB). Ship purchases also received JDB loans, and interest rates for purchases of Japanese-made ships were subsidized. The industry received a variety of tax benefits, including special depreciation allowances. Export financing was provided by the Japan Export-Import Bank, and between 1950 and 1969, exports of ships amounted to 59 percent of all credit extended by that bank. Finally, the industry received a "sugar subsidy" -- shipbuilders were licensed to import raw sugar, which because of exchange and import restrictions, could be sold in the domestic market at a lucrative profit. See generally General Accounting Office, *Industrial Policy: Case Studies in the Japanese Experience* (Washington, D.C.: GAO, 1982).

Table 4-1. Japanese Integrated Producers Agreed Construction Starts, Fiscal Year 1969

Producer	Works	Facility
Yawata	Kimitsu	No. 3 Blast Furnace
Yawata	Kimitsu	Wire Rod Mill
Yawata	Kimitsu	Structural Mill
Yawata	Sakai	Structural Mill
Fuji	Oita	No. 1 Blast Furnace
Fuji	Oita	No. 2 Blast Furnace
Fuji	Oita	Hot Strip Mill
Fumi	Nagoya	Structural Mill
Nippon Kokan	Fukuyama	No. 4 Blast Furnace
Nippon Kokan	Fukuyama	Hot Strip Mill
Nippon Kokan	Fukuyama	Cold Strip Mill
Sumitomo	Kashima	No. 1 Blast Furnace
Sumitomo	Kashima	Structural Mill
Kawasaki	Mizushima	No. 3 Blast Furnace
Kawasaki	Mizushima	Structural Mill
Kawasaki	Chiba	Cold Strip Mill
Kobe	Kakogawa	Cold Strip Mill

Sources: *Oriental Economist* (August 1969); *Japan Economic Journal* (November 18, 1969)

the import of technology into Japan, played a major role in the Japanese industry's early adoption of the basic oxygen furnace (BOF), an Austrian invention which permitted a 20-40 percent reduction in unit costs from those of older open hearth furnaces.[22]   Given the rapid expansion of the steel

---

[22] MITI brokered an arrangement whereby one Japanese firm, Nippon Kokan, would licence BOF technology from Austria and disseminate it to the rest of the Japanese steelmakers, who would share the royalty costs. MITI's Iron and Steel Section actively promoted the adoption of the BOF, arguing that it was the solution to the periodic scrap shortages which plagued the Japanese industry.

industry in Japan at this time, Japan was able to lead all other nations in adopting the BOF; by 1961, Japan had 20 BOFs in operation, while the United States, with a much larger industry, had only 14.[23] MITI has remained active in promoting the import of steelmaking technologies and, in the 1970s and 1980s, in funding research and development to develop new steelmaking techniques.[24]

At present, through its Agency for Industrial Science and Technology (AIST), MITI sponsors a number of joint R&D projects involving "a great deal of expense, risks, and long-range period." These projects are typically conducted jointly by representatives of MITI, the leading steel firms, and Japanese universities.[25] MITI also has funded a new generation of joint R&D projects designed to enhance the energy efficiency of Japan's steel production. It makes annual subsidy grants for R&D for "important technologies" to individual firms, grants to Japanese steel firms, and recommends annual Japan Development Bank funding for R&D and pilot projects by individual steel firms for improvement of energy efficiency and conversion from petroleum to alternative energy sources. MITI continually encourages Japanese steelmakers to conduct joint R&D with other firms and to share new technologies with each other.[26]

Raw Materials Acquisition

Japan's domestic iron ore and coal deposits are wholly inadequate to support its steel industry,[27] and the government has traditionally assisted the Japanese mills in acquiring essential overseas raw materials.[28] Following the

---

[23] The story of Japan's adoption of the BOF is told in Leonard H. Lynn, *How Japan Innovates; A Comparison with the U.S. in the Case of Basic Oxygen Steelmaking* (Boulder, Colo: Westview Press, 1982). As discussed in chapter 7, a number of observers believe that the U.S. industry adopted the BOF technology at an optimum rate, given its specific economic conditions.

[24] MITI frequently intervened in the negotiations of licensing agreements to ensure that Japanese firms received the lowest possible royalty rates and most favorable terms, a practice that was sharply criticized by the OECD in 1968.   Organization for Economic Cooperation and Development, *Liberalization of International Capital Movements: Japan* (Paris: OECD, 1968), pp. 57-58.

[25] *Kogyo Gijutsu* (August 1979); *Japan Steel Bulletin* (September 1981); *Tekko Kaiho* (August 1, 1976).

[26] *Tekkokai* (April 1, 1981).

[27] The Japanese mills must import 99 percent of their iron ore and 95 percent of their coking coal. U.S. International Trade Commission, *Steel Sheet and Strip Industry*, p. 9-2.

[28] In 1981 the Director of MITI's Basic Industries Bureau commented with respect to steel industry raw materials acquisition that "huge amounts of funds are necessary for development investments, and infrastructures are also necessary. . . . MITI also will give support as the occasion may require, by consolidating to the conditions necessary to cope with moves to tackle matters foresightedly. It will do all it can as the state. . . . As to financial conditions, too, I think it is necessary to give incentives, if necessary." Atsushi Mano in *Tekko Shimbun* (July 20, 1981).

First Oil Shock in 1973, MITI, the Ministry of Finance and the Overseas Economic Planning Agency established the foreign currency loan system, which enabled Japanese steel firms to secure long-term, low interest loans for overseas raw materials development projects.[29] Low-interest loans were provided by the Export-Import Bank of Japan to develop overseas deposits of coal and ore.[30] Government loans have been made to finance the stockpiling of raw materials at overseas locations, particularly Australia.[31] The Export-Import Bank has also made substantial loans to the steel industry for spot imports of raw materials on an "urgent" basis.[32]

In order to avoid competitive bidding up of the purchase price by individual Japanese firms, the government has permitted the formation of raw materials purchasing consortia by Japanese firms, pursuant to which one Japanese firm is designated to represent the entire industry in purchasing negotiations.[33] In the scrap market, which is subject to particularly volatile price changes, MITI has repeatedly intervened directly in the scrap market to prevent dramatic price fluctuations from disrupting steelmaking operations.[34]

---

[29] The *Japan Metal Bulletin* reported on August 24, 1978 that "Agreement has been reached among the Ministries of Finance, International Trade and Industry and Economic Planning Agency that foreign currency loans for resource development in abroad will be set up by the end of August, that the term of the loans will be from 1 year to 10 years, that the interest rate will be less than 7 percent per annum, that the loans will be issued up to 70 percent of the total amount of funds required and that the amount of dollar loans will be 70 percent of the total amount leaving 30 percent to Japanese yen. The loans will have no ceiling in amount to individual applicants."

[30] Export-Import Bank, *Annual Report 1970-77*. In 1981, the Export-Import bank was reportedly extending $1 billion in loans for the development of coal mines in China pursuant to a project supervised by Mitsui. *Japan Metal Bulletin* (January 27, 1981).

[31] In 1978 the Ministry of Finance loaned $260 million to the Japanese steelmakers at an interest rate of 4.75 percent to finance the stockpiling of iron ore pellets in Australia. *Japan Metal Bulletin* (March 18 and June 13, 1978).

[32] In 1978 and 1981, loans of $213 million and $8.2 million respectively were made to Japanese firms for "urgent" imports of iron ore. Export-Import Bank of Japan, *Annual Reports* FY 1979, FY 1981.

[33] The so-called joint purchasing system accounted for the majority of all raw materials acquired by the Japanese industry. The system enabled Japanese firms to agree in advance among themselves on the maximum prices they would pay for imported materials. *The Japanese Steel Industry 1969*, pp. 59-60; *Japan Metal Bulletin* (September 20, 1970).

[34] The Japanese steel firms established a system of scrap purchasing cartels in 1955 to eliminate "suicidal competition" in the purchase of scrap; these cartels remained in existence for 19 years. During the First Oil Shock, MITI established a "Stabilization Council" for scrap purchases, and a Steel Scrap Import Association was organized to prevent competitive bidding for imported scrap. Government funds were provided to assist in the establishment of scrap stockpiles. MITI has monitored scrap distribution directly, and when scrap prices have risen sharply (after the Second Oil Shock and during the 1987 construction boom), MITI has directed the release of stockpiled scrap and billet to stabilize prices. *Nihon Kogyo* (February 10, September 17, 1975); *Japan Metal Bulletin* (April 2, August 3, October 3, 1974; June 14, 1975; July 5, November 13, November 20, 1979; February 16, 1980); *Far East Iron and Steel Trade*

During a 1987 scrap shortage, MITI pressured integrated steelmakers to release inventories of scrap and billet to stabilize the domestic price of scrap for the electric furnace mills producing construction steel products.

THE SYSTEM OF MARKET CONTROLS

The measures employed by the Japanese government to promote the steel industry through the early 1970s played an important role in the industry's emergence as one of the largest producers of steel in the world. However, the government's steel policies were also responsible for the enormous distortions which occurred during the course of the industry's expansion, and which have not yet been resolved. At their root is a system of market controls, supervised by MITI and tolerated, if not condoned, by Japan's antitrust authorities, which came into being in 1958 and which has not changed in its essential elements since the mid-1960s.[35]

Production restraints, conducted under MITI's supervision, are the central element of the Japanese system.[36] Since 1965 Japanese steel producers have voluntarily submitted their quarterly production plans to MITI, which publishes "guideposts" forecasting steel demand for the coming quarter. The guideposts are voluntary, do not establish mandatory production quotas for individual firms, and are not always adhered to in practice. However, their normative intent and effect is evident,[37] and in some cases, they have been the

---

Reports (December 1957).

[35] "Japan has had, since 1958, a price fixing panel to regulate the domestic market, in which the State (MITI), the combines and the steel traders cooperate in a corporatist manner." Esser and Väth, "Overcoming the Steel Crisis in the FRG," p. 627.

[36] It has proven impossible for Japanese steel firms to regulate price competition through agreements on price levels. The real price which is obtained by each producer in its sales is known to the seller and buyer, but is difficult for third parties to monitor -- even government authorities. In Japan the complexity of the steel distribution system exacerbates this difficulty. The bulk of Japanese steel sales (about 80-90 percent) are conducted through middlemen, usually trading companies (*sogo shosha*). Sales not made through trading companies are usually "large lot" sales made directly to big buyers, such as automobile manufacturers. In addition, small service centers purchase steel from the trading companies and resell it to local users at the so-called "market" price. MITI's Industrial Structure Committee observed in 1973 that "it is a very complicated distribution system, and this is one reason for the unstable market price." *Tekkokai* (August 1973). Joint restraints on production, however, are much easier for competitors and government authorities to monitor.

[37] The Industrial Bank of Japan commented in 1977 that producers' output decisions "are based on MITI's quarterly guideposts." *Quarterly Survey of Japanese Finance and Industry* (October-December, 1977) p. 6; *Nihon Keizai* observed on January 7, 1981 that "The production in the [guidepost] demand-supply prediction for July-September 1980, when the reduced production started, was 27.5 million tons. The actual result during this term was 27.32 million tons. Six leading companies' rate of reduced production during this period was around 5.7 to 6.7 percent. This is too equal of a pace to be a coincidence."

precursors of formal cartels.[38] MITI makes clear the degree of production restraint which is needed to maintain "supply-demand balance;" in publishing the guidepost for the first quarter of 1988, for example,

> MITI consider[ed] it appropriate that crude steel production be slightly held down to 25,500,000 tons to keep supply and demand of ordinary steel products in good shape at the end of March next year.[39]

Not surprisingly, MITI's guideposts occasionally trigger furious protests by producers, who are well aware of the correlation between the guideposts and actual producer behavior.[40] The guideposts provide a framework permitting the producers to maintain collective restraints on production sufficient to prevent an erosion of prices.[41] Thus, typically, table 4-2 depicts the virtually identical joint crude steel production curtailments undertaken by the largest five steel producers in the third quarter of 1985 "in line with the guidepost figure for crude steel production in the coming quarter announced by the Ministry of International Trade and Industry."[42]

Reinforcing the guidepost system, the leading integrated producers have for many years met on a weekly basis in the presence of MITI officials in the "General Meeting of the Market Situation Countermeasures Committee, "popularly called the "Monday Club," to exchange market data and discuss

---

[38] When a formal depression cartel was established in crude steel in 1972, the existing MITI guideposts formed the basis for the cartel's production quotas. *Tekkokai* (March 1973).

[39] *Japan Metal Bulletin* (December 24, 1987).

[40] In 1982, three associations of steel producers "earnestly asked" MITI to "drastically reduce" its production guidepost figures for the third quarter. Their concern reflected the fact that MITI's publication of guideposts is not merely an academic exercise; the producers believed that by reducing its guidepost figures, MITI would firm up domestic prices. The *Japan Metal Bulletin* reported on June 17, 1982 that "MITI was finally asked to reduce its steel production guidepost figures for the July-September quarter by 1 million to 1,500,000 tons from the April-June quarter. Without the drastic cutback of production, there is no hope for the upturn of market tone and the market prices of steel products in the forthcoming July-September quarter, MITI was told by those 3 organizations at the end of the meeting, according to the circles concerned."

[41] Practices such as the steel guideposts are occasionally characterized as mere vestiges of Japan's government-backed industrialization drive of the 1960s which are gradually disappearing. This is inaccurate. In steel, MITI's guidepost system has been actively employed during the "Yen Shock" period of 1986-87 to help sustain market stability in steel. *Japan Metal Bulletin*, (September 27, December 20, 1986; January 24, June 30, December 24, 1987). Moreover, the practice has spread to high technology industries outside the steel sector; MITI guideposts formed the basis for production restraints designed to stabilize prices by Japanese semiconductor producers in 1986-87. See *Mainichi* (March 26, August 9, 1987); *Nihon Keizai* (March 26, 1987).

[42] *Japan Metal Bulletin* (June 22, 1985). At the same time, the steering committee of the Electric Furnace Steelmakers' Association decided in a meeting that "production curtailment of ordinary steel should be continued so that overall output by its members will be cut by some 400,000 tons during the coming quarter." *Ibid.*

Japanese Integrated Steelmakers Joint Production Curtailments
.ced in June 1985 (thousand metric tons)

Firm	Crude Steel Production July-Sept. Quarter	Crude Steel Production April-June Quarter	Volume Decrease	Percent Decrease
Nippon Steel	7,350	7,010	340	4.6
Nippon Kokan	3,100	2,960	140	4.5
Kawasaki Steel	2,820	2,690	130	4.6
Sumitomo Metal	2,820	2,690	130	4.6
Kobe Steel	1,660	1,580	80	4.8
Total	17,750	16,930	840	4.7

Source: *Japan Metal Bulletin* (June 22, 1985).

appropriate production levels and other "market countermeasures."[43] The system of guideposts, information exchange, and regular meetings, ultimately designed to maintain price stability through fine-tuning of production levels, is a *de facto* government-administered cartel. That fact has become more evident during severe downturns in domestic demand, when the publication of "voluntary" guideposts has sometimes proven insufficient to forestall overproduction and a rash of competitive price-cutting -- requiring MITI to show its hand in more overt fashion. On those occasions MITI has exercised "administrative guidance," directing steelmakers to reduce production to

[43] "Many elderly gentlemen come to the Steel Assembly Hall at Kayaba-chu, Nihonbashi, Tokyo, in their black limousines on every Monday. They take the elevator from the underground parking lot to the 7th floor, and walk straight toward Conference Room No. 704. There are signs which says 'General Monday Meeting' at the entrance. The members at the meeting are board members from 8 leading steel companies. They sit around the rectangular table with the Director from MITI at the head seat. . . . All those attending the Monday Meeting explain it as an ordinary place to exchange information between government officials and the private sector. However, people think about it as the 'counselor's office for steel' or the 'core office for a cooperative system between the government and the private sector.'" *Nihon Keizai* (January 7, 1981).

specified levels to stabilize prices,[44] and in extreme cases, has sanctioned the formation of formal cartels to fix production quotas and in some cases, to establish mandatory minimum prices. Under such arrangements, MITI has legal authority to discipline firms which, by engaging in unauthorized overproduction, constitute a threat to price stability.

The position of Japan's antitrust authorities in the face of such activities has been curious. Japan has an Antimonopoly Law, which was enacted during the American Occupation and patterned on U.S. antitrust principles.[45] U.S. antitrust notions, however, have never enjoyed full acceptance in Japan, which has a much stronger tradition of collective and cooperative behavior. Widespread layoffs and bankruptcies of major firms, for example, normal by-products of a competitive market, are regarded with extreme apprehension in Japan.[46] Following its enactment, the Antimonopoly Law was amended to permit the formation of "depression" and "rationalization" cartels,[47] and numerous other laws were subsequently enacted authorizing the formation of various kinds of cartels,[48] in what one analyst characterized as a "systematic

---

[44] Administrative guidance is a uniquely Japanese phenomenon. It usually takes the form of directives issued by MITI to the industry, generally formulated after extensive discussion and negotiation with and among the steel producers. Guidance most frequently reflects an industry-government consensus; its legal significance is unclear, but it definitely serves to induce, if not compel, compliance in most cases. The *Oriental Economist*, paraphrasing a MITI official, defined administrative guidance in September 1974 as "an approach whereby through gentle persuasion with avoidance of such legally enforceable administrative actions as orders or injunctions achievement of a specific administrative purpose is achieved in line with today's free economic systems."

[45] Law No. 54 of 1947, the "Law Concerning the Prohibition of Private Monopolies and the Maintenance of Fair Trade."

[46] If a major firm goes bankrupt, or many smaller firms in a given sector fail, officials from MITI and other industrial ministries are called to account by the Diet. "The officials cannot avoid accountability by pointing out that the firms' managers are the responsible parties." Iyori Hiroshi, "Antitrust and Industrial Policy in Japan: Competition and Cooperation," in *Law and Trade Issues of the Japanese Economy*, ed. Gary R. Saxonhouse and Kozo Yamamura (Seattle: University of Washington, 1986).

[47] Depression (sometimes called recession) cartels may be formed when prices undercut the average cost of production; they enable an industry to agree on output and/or price levels. Antimonopoly Law, Article 24-3. Rationalization cartels enable the industry to agree on "rationalization," *i.e.*, regulation of investment to permit more efficient production, Antimonopoly Law, Article 24-4.

[48] For example, provisions of the Medium and Small Enterprise Organization Law authorizes such enterprises to form cartels for prevention of excessive competition (enacted in 1958), rationalization (1962) and joint economic business (1957). Provisions of the *Export and Import Trading Law* permit the formation of cartels for the regulation of exports and the control of imports. Many steel cartels have been formed pursuant to the provisions of these laws.

undoing of the American-inspired Antimonopoly Act, both in letter and spirit."[49]

The Antimonopoly Law is enforced by the Japan Fair Trade Commission (JFTC), an independent government agency which occupies an insecure position in Japan; periodic efforts have been mounted by the business community to abolish the JFTC's independent status and sharply curtail its authority.[50] Under these circumstances, the JFTC has generally directed its enforcement efforts toward smaller industries, such as taxicabs and retail rice sales, which are not strategic international sectors under MITI's influence. The JFTC's occasional intrusions into strategic sectors have led to confrontations with MITI in which the JFTC has suffered significant setbacks. Since its dramatic, highly publicized failure in 1970 to block the merger of Japan's two largest steel firms to form Nippon Steel,[51] a move sponsored by MITI, the JFTC has limited its activities in steel to occasional questioning of particularly egregious examples of concerted action by the large producers.[52]

The Japanese system of market controls in steel is little understood outside of Japan, but it has had pronounced effects in the world steel market. Most importantly, cartelization removed the considerable risk which characterizes steel investments in a market economy, and played a major role in the extraordinary "capacity expansion race" which ultimately brought on stream steelmaking capacity grossly in excess of Japan's domestic or export needs. Like steel cartels in other countries, the Japanese system facilitated a recurrent pattern of countercyclical exporting, which has had disruptive, and occasionally devastating effects in export markets. The Japanese system absolutely requires import protection in order to function, and Japan's system of protection has effectively restricted foreign access to one of the world's principal steel markets. Finally, not surprisingly in light of its own tradition of industrial organization, the Japanese industry has demonstrated a propensity to enter into international arrangements with groups of foreign

---

[49] Yamamura, "Success That Soured: Administrative Guidance and Cartels in Japan," in *Policy and Trade Issues of the Japanese Economy*, ed. Kozo Yamamura (Seattle and London: University of Washington Press, 1982), p. 81.

[50] A major effort to weaken the Antimonopoly Law was mounted in 1983 by the Federation of Economic Organizations (Keidanren), headed by Yoshihiro Inayama, the former Chairman of Nippon Steel, whose enthusiasm for industrial cooperation had earned him the sobriquet "Mr. Cartel." *Japan Times* (March 9, 1983); *Nihon Keizai* (March 8, 1983).

[51] The *Japan Economic Journal* observed after this episode that "MITI gloated apropos of the Yawata-Fuji merger; 'It has now been confirmed that Japan's antimonopoly policy will not act independently of its industrial policy.'"

[52] For example, in the steel recessions of 1975-76 and 1982, the steelmakers were able to implement price increases despite severely depressed demand through the implementation of joint cuts in production. The JFTC criticized this activity and questioned the steelmakers, but took no stronger action. *Metal Bulletin* (May 21, 1982); *Japan Metal Bulletin* (May 13, June 17, June 24, July 8, July 17, August 10, November 15, l; December 16, 1975).

steel producers who, likewise uninhibited by significant antitrust concerns, have sought to maintain international price stability through collective action.[53]

Import Protection

An effective system of import protection is a *sine qua non* of an effective cartel, and Japan's imports of steel products have always been negligible by the standards of other industrialized nations, usually accounting for only a few percentage points of domestic consumption.[54]   From a purely legal perspective, the Japanese market is one of the most "open" in the world; given Japan's status as the world's largest steel exporter, formal protective measures have been regarded as impolitic both by government and industry. Imports are controlled instead through a low-visibility system which features pressure on distribution channels and customers coupled with informal "understandings" reached with major exporters. Minor disruptions of this system by occasional "disorderly" imports have caused reactions approaching panic in the Japanese industry, but on the whole the system has functioned far more effectively than government-administered systems of protection in most other major industrialized countries.

The periodic alarm expressed by Japanese steelmakers and trading firms over imports which do not exceed a few percentage points of domestic consumption seems "laughable" to "observers from the USA or other markets plagued by low-priced imported steel,"[55] but it highlights the basic vulnerability of the Japanese system. Even a small influx of "disorderly" imports -- products whose volume and price are not regulated by domestic producers and traders -- can disrupt efforts to maintain domestic price stability through agreed restraints on production, which is the foundation of the whole Japanese

---

[53] The latter phenomenon is observable in 1986-88 and is addressed later in this chapter.

[54] Even in the late 1980s, with the yen at record highs, significant import penetration has been largely confined to a few product areas, notably hot-rolled coil and plate.

[55] *Metal Bulletin Monthly* (March 1986).

system.[56]   Following an increase in import volume in 1981, the *Japan Economic Journal* (December 8, 1981) observed that

> *It may sound strange that piddling import of 1,300,000- 1,400,000 tons of foreign steels should be making such a big fuss in the steel industry which annually exports as much as 30 million tons of its own steel to the entire world. What really hurts the industry, however, is that it is rapidly losing its price controlling power in the face of aggressive advances of steel industries of new industrializing countries.*

Prior to the early 1960s, the Japanese market was protected by formal government measures.[57]   In 1960-62 these restrictions were phased out pursuant to a broader series of liberalization measures affecting the Japanese economy.   Nevertheless, Japan's steel imports remained virtually nil thereafter -- until the late 1970s, imports never accounted for even one percent of domestic steel consumption, by far the lowest import penetration ratio of any major steelmaking nation.

The principal barrier to imports was (and remains today) the leading steelmakers' influence over the domestic distribution network, and, to some extent, over customers.[58]   Japan's imports of steel are conducted primarily by *sogo shosha* (trading companies) who also handle the bulk of the domestic sales of Japan's steel producers.   The producers exert pressure on foreign steel suppliers to utilize the *sogo shosha* as intermediaries for their exports

---

[56] This is underscored by the fact that in the heavy plate and HR coil markets -- product lines where the steelmakers' attempts to control imports have been relatively unsuccessful -- price stability has proven correspondingly difficult to maintain.   In 1983 the major Japanese steel producers decided to force up their price of steel plates by jointly cutting back their production -- a device that worked effectively until November, 1983, when a surge of imported plate disrupted the market and forced the domestic producers to expand their output of plate to retain market share.   The *Japan Metal Bulletin* reported on January 12, 1984 that "Throughout last year, the major steelmakers made joint efforts to cut production on steel plate and a few other items, even declining part of their customers' buying proposals, with the result that the local market mostly stayed tight of supply, with prices propped up to reasonable levels.   Some importers, however, cashed in on the situation and made voluminous imports of steel plate, which soared to 149,000 tons in last November, as compared to 51,000 tons last January.   Hence [Nippon Steel's] decision to safeguard its own users against inroads of foreign-made products [by expanding production]."

[57] The Japanese government controlled imports through Law No. 228 of 1949, the Foreign Exchange and Foreign Trade Control Law, which required that any Japanese citizen who acquired foreign exchange through trade turn it over to the government, which had the power to approve or disapprove each purchase with these funds.   This enabled MITI to determine which commodities could be imported into Japan.

[58] Toyota, for example, one of Japan's largest steel consumers, purchased its first imported steel in 1987.   *Japan Metal Bulletin* (November 28, 1987).   Japanese shipbuilders indicated in 1978 that they would reduce the quantity of their purchases of steel from Taiwan "if the Japanese steel producers are strongly opposed to it." *Japan Metal Bulletin* (December 14, 1978).

to Japan.[59] The trading companies are in turn subject to influence from the Japanese steel producers, upon whom they depend for a substantial portion of their business.[60] Traditionally, the *sogo shosha* simply refused to handle foreign steel in the normal course,[61] although when shortages threatened on the domestic market, they could arrange for imports on a spot basis, in close coordination with the domestic steel producers.[62] A Korean journal commented in 1987 that

> *Import of iron and steel into Japan faces a . . . restriction by large steel mills which put strong pressure on distributors demanding use of domestic products only. Any user of imported steel will run the risk of being cut off from supplies from domestic mills. . . . This is the marketing environment that Korean exporters must face in Japan.*[63]

At the end of the 1970s, the startup of modern, competitive steel facilities in Korea and Taiwan, coupled with export-forcing practices by countries like Brazil and Romania, resulted in an increase in import pressure on the Japanese steel market.[64] Beginning in 1979, a trickle of low-priced Korean and Taiwanese steel imports into Japan began to become noticeable, particularly in the Kansai region, which is geographically closest to Korea.[65] This caused consternation among Japanese steelmakers, who, worried about

---

[59] In 1980, Nippon Steel, concerned over the need for more "orderly" imports of low-priced Korean pig iron (priced $17.64 per ton lower than domestically produced pig iron) concluded an agreement with South Korea's Pohang Iron & Steel Co. (POSCO). As part of this agreement, POSCO agreed to utilize three Japanese trading companies for its exports to Japan (Mitsui, Mitsubishi, Nissho Iwai), limiting the quantity to 10,000 tons per quarter, with future quantities to be agreed upon. The trading companies, in conjunction with Nippon Steel, were to designate 6 domestic dealers to handle the final transfer to consumers. *Japan Metal Bulletin* (November 1, 1980).

[60] "As a rule they [the *sogo shosha*] refrain from dealing in imports of steel materials because of pressure from blast furnace steelmakers, particularly Nippon Steel Corp." *Oriental Economist* (February 1983), p. 13. "Foreign [steel] exporters have claimed that their large Japanese competitors have warned the major trading houses that any bending to permit imports will see them taking their trading business elsewhere." *Metal Bulletin Monthly* (December 1986).

[61] "Major trading firms . . . say they are strictly refraining from imports of . . . steel items from the developing countries." *Japan Metal Bulletin* (November 14, 1978).

[62] See *Japan Metal Bulletin* (February 14, 18, 23 and 28, 1967).

[63] *Korea Businessworld* (March 1987).

[64] The Korean and Taiwanese mills could produce competitive grades of steel at a lower cost than their Japanese counterparts, and because of their geographic proximity to Japan, transportation costs did not cancel this advantage. "Pohang Iron Steel Co. [POSCO], the largest South Korean steelmaker, appears to have become more internationally competitive than major Japanese steelmakers, steel industry sources here revealed recently." *Japan Economic Journal* (January 26, 1982).

[65] *Japan Metal Bulletin* (February 19, 1980).

"fatal price pandemonium," were "becoming frantic, saying 'we've got to find some way to stop this.'"[66] One of the steelmakers' primary concerns was the fact that the steel was not entering the market through normal channels -- the established *sogo shosha* -- but was being distributed in clandestine fashion by smaller trading houses, so that prices and volumes could not be monitored.[67] The importers were small trading firms which distributed the steel to secondary wholesalers in the Kansai district (Osaka and Kobe); the driving force behind the underground distribution network was the low price of imported steel.[68] The *Japan Economic Journal* reported on December 6, 1981 that

> *Customs-cleared steel products from such nations as ROK are tightly covered by canvas sheets on Japanese ports during the daytime. When night falls, importers get busy obliterating the imprints of producing countries. With the telltale imprints removed, the steel products are loaded on trucks having no company names and secretly transported to users. Why this clandestine operation? Importers are afraid of the wrath they may very well incur when their action is known to blast furnace steelmakers. They are running the risk of being eliminated from the traders' list of the steelmakers.*[69]

The small traders demonstrated considerable ingenuity in circumventing efforts at surveillance by the Japanese producers; Nippon Steel reportedly organized an effort to monitor the distribution of Korean steel through Tokyo (by tailing the delivery trucks) in order to determine who was buying it. This

---

[66] *Japan Economic Journal* (December 6, 1981); *Japan Metal Bulletin* (June 27, 1981).

[67] The covert nature of the steel import distribution system was widely reported. Kamia Haruki, Executive Director of Nippon Kokan, indicated in 1981 that "we do not know by what routes the imported steel is distributed." *Nikkan Kogyo* (September 7, 1981); *Nikkei Sangyo* (October 27, 1981). Some *sogo shosha* had themselves been dealing in imported steel themselves since 1981, which was "regarded as a betrayal by Japan's integrated steelmakers." *Japan Metal Bulletin* (July 7, September 15, 1981). *Nippon Kogyo* reported on December 9, 1982 that "The increase in imported steel cannot help but destroy the steel distribution system. Thus the steelmakers, using such large *sogo shosha* as Mitsui and Mitsubishi Shoji, are trying to trace the entire distribution channel down to the very roots of the imported steel. But the reality is they cannot be traced, because they are buried underground."

[68] *Nikkei Sangyo* (October 27, 1981). *Nippon Kogyo* reported on December 9, 1982 that "In the case of Korean steel imports, it is clear that the agents are Korean trading companies, such as Samsung. As for the rest, they are "store sold" directly to the user, such as construction companies and pipe welding companies through brokers and steel trading companies, which are numerous in the Kansai area."

[69] *Oriental Economist*, (February 1983); *Japan Economic Journal* (December 6, 1981).

was thwarted by moving the steel into Japan through Osaka at night by barge, making pursuit more difficult.[70]

In addition to seeking to "grasp" the distribution channels, the Japanese steelmakers sought to restrain imports at their source, through "understandings" with foreign producers.[71] In 1979, Japanese producers, disturbed by low-priced imports from Taiwan, approached Taiwan's principal producer, China Steel Corporation, and secured a series of agreements pursuant to which China Steel would limit its exports to an agreed quantity and price, and would use agreed distribution channels.[72] In 1982, after receiving "unofficial" overtures from Nippon Steel and other Japanese producers, Korea's Pohang Iron and Steel Company agreed to restrain its exports to Japan in order to permit the Japanese firms to implement domestic price increases.[73] Similarly, in late 1986, a Korean producer of structurals, Inchon Steel, reportedly agreed with the Japanese steelmakers to limit its wide-flanged beam exports to Japan to 3,500 tons per year which would be sold at the same level as Japanese producers' prices.[74]

In late 1983, a new organization, the Japan Iron and Steel Importers' Association (JISII), was established which subsequently has played an important role in preventing the domestic market from being disrupted by low-priced imports. JISII consisted initially of a number of the small trading companies in the Kansai region which handled most of Japan's imported steel

---

[70] *Nikkei Business* reported on February 22, 1982 of an episode in which "a small freighter secretly entered Osaka Port and unloaded steel materials on the wharf. At the same time, several young men came running out and covered the cargo with sheeting. Several hours later, waiting until just around dusk, the cargo was re-loaded onto a barge. This barge meandered through the rivers of Osaka and eventually disappeared into the darkness. This cargo was actually 20,000 tons of hot coil manufactured by the Pohang Iron Works in the ROK. There are reasons for these strange maneuvers which make one think of smuggling. They were for the purpose of evading the pursuit of influential manufacturers, such as Nippon Steel. These leading manufacturers, who self-claim to be the leaders of the industrial circles concerned, control the amounts and prices of steel materials imported from the ROK, Taiwan and elsewhere, in virtual fact. Especially in "Tokaki" (made up by 13 companies), which is formed by steel material companies affiliated with Nippon Steel, the said manufacturers' wishes are enforced thoroughly. However, some importing firms are importing less expensive steel materials "secretly," partly because of the requests of the users. Until recently, a large part of these imported steel materials was unloaded at Tokyo Port. However, recently, most of the unloading is done in Osaka Port. That is because, in the case of Tokyo, the cargo is followed by trucks (belonging to trucking enterprisers who are under the control of the influential manufacturers) and the users become known. In the case of Osaka, it is possible to evade the pursuit of trucks, if the cargo is placed on a barge and it meanders through the canals."

[71] The Chairman of the German firm, Thyssen, opened a sales affiliate in Japan in 1978 and was asked by the President of Nippon Steel "to refrain from selling steel in Japan." *Japan Economic Journal* (November 14, 1978). Thyssen subsequently filed a formal complaint in Japan, alleging that its export efforts had been thwarted. *Metal Bulletin* (April 8, 1982).

[72] *Japan Metal Bulletin* (June 23, 1979; December 15, 1981).

[73] *Nihon Keizai* (February 11, 1982).

[74] *Metal Bulletin* (October 7, 1986).

but who professed a desire to foster "orderly" marketing of imported steel.[75] The objective of JISII, whose members handled most of Japan's imported steel, was to prevent internecine price competition among trading firms from depressing the value of their inventories. They achieved this by jointly manipulating supply and demand levels like the domestic steelmakers, reaching agreed limits on the volume that would reach the end users; indeed, the JISII's import limits were implemented in conjunction with the domestic producers' production restraints in order to facilitate price increases.[76]

Reductions in the volume of imported steel were an important part of JISII's initial efforts.[77]   In April 1984, soon after its formation, JISII announced that

> *imports of steel plate and sheet from nearby countries such as South Korea and Taiwan will be reasonably reduced. . . . According to the proposed import policy for far-flung countries, only three countries such as Brazil, Rumania and Spain will remain regular suppliers of steel plate and five countries . . . of hot-rolled steel sheet in the near future.*[78]

---

[75] The *Japan Metal Bulletin* reported on December 20, 1983 that "Several importers in the Kansai District . . . met last week and decided to set up a Japan Iron and Steel Importer's Association . . . as of December 22, and called on importers across the country to join it. Of some 3 million tons of ordinary steel products to be imported this year into this country, about 80 percent is being handled by importers located in the Kansai District. So it is no wonder that Wazai, Ryusho and other influential importers in the district should have taken the initiative in setting up an association, with a view to channeling imported steels orderly on the home market on a long-term basis."

[76] The *Japan Metal Bulletin* reported on June 20, 1985 that "At its regular meeting last week, the [JISII] recommended its members to continuously hold down imports of steel sheet and plate in the coming July-September quarter. . . . Major steelmakers have recently decided to cut back on their production in the coming July-September quarter by 200,000-300,000 tons, probably followed by another production cut in the October-December quarter, so that steel inventories for home consumption may be trimmed to 5 million tons by the end of this year. So the Institute has determined that its members would be better off to hold down imports of sheet and plate for another [3] months, so that steel market may regain a firm tone, with prices making reasonable rebounds then. Meanwhile, it will make contact with the relative overseas steelmakers for a cooperative stand."

[77] *Metal Bulletin* (January 20, 1984). The *Japan Metal Bulletin* reported on January 19, 1984 that "In an effort to maintain orderly imports of steel products, the Japan Iron and Steel Importer's Institute, which was set up last December, decided at its members' meeting last week that their planned imports of steel plate and hot-rolled sheet in coil for the January-March quarter should be reasonably reduced, according to an Institute official. As a result, the member firms would arrange to take about 246,000 tons of steel plate in the quarter instead of 416,000 tons earlier planned, cutting their order by 170,000 tons." The import cuts were allocated by country. Romania's shipments were to be cut from 250 thousand tons to 130 thousand; Brazil's from 100 to 88 thousand; Bulgaria's from 34 to 15 thousand. *Ibid.*

[78] *Japan Metal Bulletin* (April 24, 1984).

In June 1984, JISII's Vice Chairman Tanimoto visited Eastern European governments to ask that their steelmakers book their export sales to Japan through the JISII, and that agreement be reached on price, quantity, and delivery channels.[79]

By the summer of 1984 it was apparent that JISII and the steelmakers had succeeded in stemming the import influx. South Korea indicated that it would

> reduce monthly supply of steel plate at 30,000 tons and hot-rolled steel sheet in coil at 50,000 tons as a more stabilized sales program for the Japanese market on a medium perspective.[80]

JISII reported that import volume would continue to fall through the end of 1984 as its members further reduced their purchases from foreign sources.[81] The *Far Eastern Economic Review* reported on October 11, 1984 that

> In the past 18 months or so imports from South Korea have shown signs of leveling off, but this appears not to have been the result of market factors such as the weakness of the yen. Instead it seems that the Japanese steel industry itself may have been instrumental in reducing the inflow of South Korean steel. One way in which the industry seems to have been able to restrain imports is by "exercising pressure" -- an expression used by steelmakers themselves -- on the distribution channels through which South Korean steel reaches Japanese end-users.

The Japanese system, which insulated the domestic market from "disorderly" imports, proved very effective in preventing an import influx as the yen strengthened against the dollar after 1985. As the "dollar tumbled on the money market" in late 1985, while "tempted" by the falling price of foreign steel, major importers "avoid[ed] any speculative purchases for the sake of orderly marketing to regular users or dealers."[82] While rumors circulated

---

[79] "Tanimoto explained how the Institute was organized last December with the objective of promoting steel imports through orderly marketing. He told how a rush of import arrivals in the past few months from countries in Eastern Europe, the Far East and South America caused the local market to lose supply-and-demand balance. . . . The JISII considers it a high time to offer its service for coordinating orderly import activities. While it does not have any intention of becoming a contract party for steel imports, it will try to work out plans for adequate quarterly imports from East European countries, specifically discussing the quantity, price, and supply channels that will be beneficial both to exporters and importers." *Japan Metal Bulletin* (June 24, 1984).

[80] *Japan Metal Bulletin* (July 5, 1984).

[81] *Japan Metal Bulletin* (August 14, 1984).

[82] *Japan Metal Bulletin* (October 5, 1985).

about a possible influx of low-priced imports, this did not occur.[83] The JISII's president, Hiroyuki Hori, announced that its members would

> *take cautious stand to hold imports of steel products at a realistic level, and that the Institute will serve the function of storing surplus supplies to ensure orderly marketing at reasonable prices as far as possible.*[84]

Despite the strong yen, import pressure actually slackened in 1986 and 1987 (a phenomenon partially attributable to temporary production interruptions in Taiwan and Korea) and only an occasional isolated surge (such as a sudden influx of Romanian hot coil in the spring of 1987) jeopardized domestic price stability.[85]

Fear of retaliation by Japanese steel producers still operates as a powerful deterrent for the *sogo shosha* to handle imports. In late 1987 one U.S. steel firm was approached by a Japanese steel consumer and its affiliated trading company seeking to import a high grade steel product from the U.S. firm. The Japanese trading company asked the U.S. firm to ship the steel through a "dummy" company instead of the trader, in order to keep its name out of the transaction and avoid jeopardizing its relationship with Japanese steel producers. The Japanese consuming firm also wanted to keep its name out of the transaction for a similar reason.[86]

The Japanese government's role with respect to the various import-regulating mechanisms employed by Japanese steelmakers and traders is anomalous. On the one hand, the government has refrained from imposing import-restricting measures which are pervasive in other nations; at the same time, the government has tolerated private activities that would be illegal in many other countries (and are arguably illegal in Japan) but which restrict

---

[83] In late 1985, JISII members were "nervous" over reports that four importers were contemplating purchases of 30-40 thousand tons of hot coil from SOMISA of Argentina -- they were concerned that "any excessive imports may disturb orderly marketing efforts pursued by JISII members in past months." Accordingly, the traders gave a "sigh of relief as the four JISII importers have collectively purchased a moderate 15 thousand tons from SOMISA to be distributed into their regular sales channels." *Japan Metal Bulletin* (September 19, 1985).

[84] *Japan Metal Bulletin* (October 17, 1985).

[85] *Japan Metal Bulletin* (May 30, 1987). The *Far Eastern Economic Review* observed on July 2, 1987 that "steel manufacturers in the newly industrialized countries appear to have failed to break into Japan's import market despite the higher yen."

[86] U.S. industry source, 1988.

imports much more effectively than most government-administered programs of protection.[87]

The *de facto* closing off of Japan's domestic steel market to all but a trickle of foreign steel has had two pronounced effects on the world competitive environment. First, emerging steel industries of East Asian nations like Taiwan and Korea are limited in the extent to which they can penetrate Japan's large domestic market, despite their growing cost advantage over the Japanese mills and they must find outlets in other countries.[88] More fundamentally, Japan's system of import protection has made possible the continued functioning of the system which regulates competition among domestic producers, and which has had a variety of pronounced effects both in Japan and in its external markets over the past three decades.

The Capacity Expansion Race

The modern history of the Japanese system of market controls is divisible into two phases. Between 1960 and 1970, the integrated steel industry could be characterized as an unstable cartel, with individual producers competing for market share through aggressive expansion programs. Following the formation of Nippon Steel in 1970, the industry was transformed into a stable cartel, with Nippon Steel assuming the role of unchallenged leader and enforcer of price stability. The dynamics of the Japanese steel cartel in the 1960-75 period would be little more than a historical footnote today but for the fact that during this period virtually all of Japan's present steelmaking plant was brought on stream.[89] The enormous, unprecedented buildup which occurred during this period continues to exert pressure on world markets, and the same dynamics which gave rise to it hamper efforts to reduce it.

Ironically, the origins of Japan's present capacity surplus lie in MITI's desire, at the beginning of the 1960s, to ensure that Japan's steel industry would expand in a rational manner. At that time, domestic steel demand was increasing at a rate of 17 percent per year, ample credit was available, and it was obvious that the industry would expand rapidly, but the form which that

---

[87] The Japan Fair Trade Commission, charged with enforcing Japan's Antimonopoly Law, concluded in 1983 that Japanese trading companies did not refrain from handling foreign steel, despite the fact that specific restrictive actions by the traders were openly reported on a regular basis in the Japanese media. Similarly, MITI appointed an official to "investigate the reasons" for the establishment of JISII, but it has not moved against the group. *Metal Bulletin* (January 20, 1984).

[88] In 1984 U.S. Trade Representative William Brock charged that Japanese import barriers were a factor underlying the increase in U.S. steel imports from Korea. *Kyodo* (October 1, 1984); *Metal Bulletin* (October 5, 1984).

[89] *Nihon Keizai* estimated in 1981 that 11.1 percent of Japan's steelmaking plant had become operational between 1960 and 1965; 22.6 percent between 1965 and 1970; and 52.5 percent between 1970 and 1975, for a total of 76.2 percent. *Metal Bulletin* (November 13, 1981).

growth would take was problematic.[90] The minimum efficient scale of a greenfield steel mill was 6-7 million tons of crude steel capacity, but it was recognized that if all of Japan's steelmakers invested in such mills simultaneously, the result would be grossly excessive capacity. On the other hand, under a market oriented system in which each producer was left to its individual investment decisions, the steelmakers were likely to opt for incremental expansion at existing facilities, a practice which would involve diminished risk for individual firms, but which would not result in a national industry of optimum scale and efficiency.[91] What was needed, it was felt, was a mechanism to regulate investment plans to enable the Japanese producers to "take turns" installing facilities of the desired scale.[92]

Given Japan's lack of antitrust constraints, it is not surprising that an informal investment cartel developed after 1960 to facilitate a "rational" pattern of new mill construction.[93] Under the arrangement, the steel firms met annually within the Japan Iron and Steel Federation to discuss and exchange data concerning their prospective investment plans, and sought to reach a consensus on which facilities would be built, and over which time frame.[94] MITI took part in these meetings, enabling the steelmakers to avoid the operation of the Antimonopoly Law,[95] and published a report, based on the outcome of the negotiations, recommending an orderly investment

---

[90] *Tekkokai* (August 1972).

[91] This is in fact what happened in the United States, where coordination of investment plans among producers is precluded by the antitrust laws. See Cockerill, *The Steel Industry*, pp. 113-115.

[92] Ken'ichi Imai, *Tekko*, translated in Sato, *Industry and Business in Japan*, p. 211.

[93] At the end of the Second Rationalization Program, the producers were given leeway by MITI to plan their own investments. A MITI survey of producers' investment plans revealed, however, that if all were implemented, a large capacity surplus would be created. "Under such circumstances, the self-arrangement meeting of equipment investments was commenced." Kawasaki, *Japan's Steel Industry*, pp. 108-109.

[94] Kaplan, *Japan: The Government-Business Relationship*, pp. 144-45. In 1960, MITI Vice Minister Matsuo had proposed a steel industry law which would establish a formal investment cartel, with an exemption from the Antimonopoly Law. The industry preferred self-coordination legitimized by MITI supervision. Johnson, *MITI and the Japanese Miracle*, p. 269.

[95] The agreements among producers with respect to facilities investments were regarded as "outside the purview of the Antimonopoly Law." *Japan Economic Journal* (August 4, 1970). In 1966 MITI and the JFTC exchanged memoranda on the subject. The JFTC, while careful not to concede that the investment agreements did not violate the law, stated that "exchange of information" among producers concerning investment did not infringe the law. This exchange of notes conferred "quasi-official approval" on the investment cartel. "Memorandum on the Operation of the Antimonopoly Law with Respect to the Promotion of Structural Improvements in the Industries." (November 1966). See also Ken-ichi Imai, "Iron and Steel," in *Industry and Business in Japan* (White Plains: M.E. Sharpe, Inc., 1980).

schedule.[96] If company presidents could not reach an agreement, MITI arbitrated, and in some cases the Industrial Structure Council served a mediating role.[97]

Table 4-3. Japanese Integrated Producers' Agreed Rolling Mill Construction Start-ups, April 1967 - April 1968

Producer	Works	Facility
Yawata	Kimitsu	Cold Strip Mill
Yawata	Kimitsu	Hot Strip Mill
Yawata	Sakai	Large Shape Mill
Fuji	Nagoya	Plate Mill
Nippon Kokan	Fukuyama	Large Shape Mill
Kawasaki	Mizushima	Large Shape Mill
Kawasaki	Mizushima	Hot Strip Mill
Kawasaki	Mizushima	Cold Strip Mill
Sumitomo	Kashima	Hot Strip Mill
Sumitomo	Kashima	Cold Strip Mill

Source: *Japan Economic Journal* (June 27, 1967).

The investment cartel made the construction of huge greenfield seaside mills economically feasible.[98] However, the substitution of this essentially political process for the market as the principal determinant of the rate of

---

[96] The industry theoretically was free to accept or reject MITI's recommendations, and the more aggressive firms, such as Sumitomo, sometimes did, usually because they wished to expand capacity beyond the levels set by MITI. However, a pattern of adherence was more common. *Japan Metal Bulletin* (January 9, 1971).

[97] Kaplan, *Japan: The Government-Business Relationship*, p. 45.

[98] In the United States, by contrast, where the antitrust laws are vigorously enforced, such practices were altogether out of the question.

capacity expansion encouraged excessive investments.[99] Investment cartels, like production cartels, required the establishment of quotas for the member companies, and in the negotiations over investment quotas, a firm's relative capacity itself conveyed the greatest bargaining leverage. Possession of capacity became an end in itself, to a considerable extent divorced from market factors such as forecast demand.[100] A firm's ability to expand depended upon a bargaining process, so firms tended initially to submit plans calling for major expansion, and then to negotiate down from those levels.[101]

Market risk, which serves as a natural brake on excessive investments, was substantially reduced because of the recognition that during periods of recession, joint production restraints would stabilize domestic prices and imports would not be permitted to jeopardize that stability. During the 1960s, the period of most frenetic capacity expansion, recessions in steel demand occurred in 1962, 1964-65, and 1967-68.[102] On each occasion, the leading integrated steel producers met and agreed on production quotas and

---

[99] Bela Gold has suggested that the practice of "rationing the allocation of permission to build" new blast furnaces was an important factor encouraging Japanese management to build increasingly large units, and that the size of the resulting blast furnaces was probably in excess of the minimum efficient scale under European or U.S. conditions. Bela Gold, "Evaluating Scale Economies: The Case of Japanese Blast Furnaces," *The Journal of Industrial Economics* 23 (1974/75): 1-18.

[100] Deadlocks in negotiations could be broken by mutual agreement to allow a larger number of facilities to be constructed or to revise upward projections of demand in order to permit increased facilities expansion. The *Oriental Economist* observed in April 1967 that negotiations on the producers' investment schedules were likely to become stalled. "How, then, will the investment adjustment program be finalized? As one of the conceivable programs for finalization of the problem, the number of blast furnaces to be constructed in the future may be increased from 8-9 units provided for under the basic plan of the Japan Iron and Steel Federation. . . . The demand target by the federation also may be advanced on the ground that it is underestimated." However, the *Oriental Economist* went on to note (p. 269) that if such a settlement were made, based on a mutual agreement to increase forecasts of demand, "it will become easier for steel companies to compromise in future negotiations for investment adjustment. Such a formula of settlement may be criticized as marking the revival of a free-for-all in an equipment race."

[101] In 1961, the Japanese producers submitted investment proposals for a total of 19 new blast furnaces. Imai, *Tekko*, pp. 219-220. The *Oriental Economist* reported in April 1967 that "Plant and equipment schedules of leading steel companies in fiscal 1967 are far larger than their counterparts in fiscal 1966. . . . Opinion is apparently divided on the feasibility of such large plant and equipment investment projects by steel manufacturers. Those in favor urge that such capital investment projects should be positively propelled on the ground that demand for steel products has been increasing at an unexpectedly rapid tempo. Those against such projects hold that over-equipment in the steel industry will become more noteworthy, if large-scale investments are left unmolested, and will cause a loss to the national economy."

[102] *Tekkokai* (August 1972).

appropriate price levels,[103] effectuated through "voluntary" agreements pursuant to MITI's administrative guidance.[104]

Restraint of price competition does not eliminate interfirm rivalry; it simply forces that rivalry to adopt other forms. With price competition held in check, and with the risk of serious losses in a recession buffered by the inevitability of production restraints, the principal concern of the Japanese producers was that their rivals would expand their facilities more rapidly, resulting in their own relative decline in standing within the national industry.[105] With investment decisions not tempered by the fear of recession, the competition between Japanese mills developed into a furious race to expand capacity, with only the most tenuous of connections between the rate of expansion and the actual state of the steel market. The "excessive equipment investments grew . . . monstrous in nature."[106] Contemporary Japanese observers commented on the anomaly of an industry expanding its production capacity while simultaneously implementing joint production restraints because of the surplus in existing capacity relative to the needs of the national market.[107]

The most intense period of new building occurred between 1965 and 1974 when an incredible 93 million metric tons of additional steelmaking capacity

---

[103] The *Japan Economic Journal* reported on January 1, 1965 with respect to one such meeting that "In their desperate attempts to rehabilitate the domestic steel market, Japanese steel manufacturers have imposed on themselves a series of stringent production curtailments through agreements. . . . It was agreed that each firm will set up a proper, generally acceptable price rate and it will not try to undersell others, that all firms will not try to get a larger share in production and capital investments and that wherever mutually agreeable restraints on production, marketing and capital spendings are not possible, a decision through mediation by a third party such as the Ministry of International Trade and Industry will be respected. On the day following the conference, Yawata announced a price tariff of its own. Fuji and other rival firms followed suit on the next day by announcing matching tariffs."

[104] Formal cartels were sometimes established in individual finished steel product lines such as plates. *Asahi Shimbun* (June 19, 1966); *Nihon Koygo* (June 29, 1965.) There was little substantive difference; the "voluntary" production restraint agreements were effective cartels. See comments of Takeo Kitajima, Chairman of the JFTC, in *Oriental Economist* (July 1966, p. 419).

[105] The amount of a firm's production capacity determined the size of its production quota in a cartel, and also served as the benchmark for determining the level of future investments which that firm would be permitted -- in both the short and long run, capacity was equated with market share. In 1968, for example, Yawata announced that it was planning to construct a second blast furnace at its Kimitsu works; a principal motivation was that "boosting the Kimitsu Steel Works capacity to a level of 4,500,000 tons annually would ensure its market share. . . ." *Japan Economic Journal* (February 20, 1968).

[106] *Japan Economic Journal* (August 31, 1971).

[107] The *Japan Economic Journal* observed in an editorial on May 3, 1966 that "the contention supporting free competition in equipment and cutback in output in case supply exceeds demand is not acceptable. Antidepression cartels or production cutback of crude steel on the basis of Government guidelines are, as pointed out earlier, essentially of an "emergency aid" nature. It is both unreasonable and illogical that production facilities be increased on the basis of such extraordinary steps."

Table 4-4. Crude Steel Capacity Expansion in Japan Compared to Western World Capacity Expansion 1965-1974 (million metric tons)

| | Annual Change in Capacity | | |
	Japan	Total Western World	% of Total
1965	4	19	21%
1966	8	18	44%
1967	15	23	65%
1968	17	23	74%
1969	16	27	59%
1970	13	24	54%
1971	4	16	25%
1972	4	11	36%
1973	9	18	50%
1974	3	9	33%
Cumulative	93	188	49%

Source: Peter F. Marcus and Karlis M. Kirsis, *World Steel Dynamics: Core Report BB* (PaineWebber: January 1988), Exhibit BB-1-5.

was put into place. As shown in table 4-4, this was equal to 49 percent of total capacity expansion in all Western countries. The capacity expansion was driven by the ambition of two smaller integrated firms, Sumitomo and Kawasaki, to expand their market share.[108] The market leaders, Yawata and Fuji, initially attempted to show investment restraint in the face of this challenge, but in so doing, their market share was eroded, and in 1967 Yawata launched a massive new expansion effort, stating that "we are determined to recover our former share."[109] The expansion competition was punctuated with periodic "truces," when expansion projects were suspended pursuant to mutual

---

[108] *Japan Economic Journal* (January 25, March 8, 1966).

[109] *Sankei* (September 9, 1967); *Japan Economic Journal* (October 18, 1966).

agreement, but these were circumvented through expansion at existing mill sites and were followed by intense periods of new building. The expansion competition gave rise to furious disputes in the investment cartel; MITI and the Industrial Structure Council mediated these disagreements, which were generally resolved by companies permitting each firm to undertake major new construction efforts, based on mutual acceptance of wholly unrealistic projections of future steel demand.[110] The capacity expansion race culminated in the mid-1970s with the construction of several giant new facilities on tracts of land reclaimed from the sea, just as the world steel market entered the structural recession.[111]

The Emergence of a Stable Cartel, 1970-88

The irrationality and risk inherent in the "reckless" capacity expansion competition of the 1960s did not escape MITI and the Japanese steel industry leaders.[112] Shaken by the 1965 "Sumitomo incident," in which that firm defied MITI's administrative guidance with respect to production curtailment,[113] the presidents of the two largest Japanese firms, Yawata and Fuji, began discussions of a merger of the two firms, a proposal which MITI enthusiastically supported.[114] While the merger was publicly couched in terms of international competitiveness, its basic purpose was to create a firm so large that it could discipline the other firms, bring the competition for market shares under control, and provide the basis for a more stable cartel.[115] The JFTC publicly opposed the merger, and with consumers expressing concern over "monopolistic price increases," it sought an injunction from the Tokyo

---

[110] In 1967, in the midst of a recession in steel demand, the Industrial Structure Council approved the start-up construction of five blast furnaces and ten rolling mills in fiscal 1967. *Japan Economic Journal* (May 20, June 27, 1967). Investments agreed in 1971 targeted a steelmaking capacity of 150 million tons, but in that year total steel production (domestic and export) was only 88.4 million tons. Kawasaki, *Japan's Steel Industry*, p. 148.

[111] A major force behind this effort was Nippon Kokan, the number three producer, which brooded over its loss of market share from 13 percent in the prewar period to 9.2 percent in the postwar era, and sought to redeem its former share through the construction of massive new greenfield facilities. *Zaikai Tembo* (December 1985).

[112] *Japan Economic Journal* (June 18, 1968).

[113] See generally Johnson, *MITI and the Japanese Miracle*, p. 270; *Nihon Kogyo* (November 26, 1965); *Mainichi* (December 2, 1965); *Asahi* (November 28, 1965).

[114] Johnson, *MITI and the Japanese Miracle*, p. 277.

[115] As the *Oriental Economist* later recounted (May 1968, p. 28): "What prompted President Yoshihiro Inayama to jump at the idea of merger between his company and Fuji Iron and Steel, then? One of the possible reasons is his devotion to a cartel as the most effective tool to business prosperity. . . . [Fuji] President Shigeo Nagano is far from adverse to the idea of a Yawata-Fuji merger. His opinion is that, if the Yawata-Fuji merger paves a ground for formation of a cartel, it is quite all right."

High court to block it.[116] MITI rallied support for the merger within the government and business communities, however, and the merger was approved in October 1969.[117]

Table 4-5. Market Shares of the Leading Integrated Producers Following The Yawata-Fuji Merger (percent of total production)

	Nippon Steel	Nippon Kokan	Kawasaki	Sumitomo	Kobe
Pig Iron	44.1%	16.5%	14.5%	13.3%	6.6%
Crude Steel	35.5	13.6	12.2	12.0	5.1
Heavy Rails	86.4	----	----	----	----
Cold-Rolled Sheets	41.6	15.7	12.9	5.8	----
Tinplate	57.7	10.5	6.1	----	----
Wire Rods	38.7	----	2.6	11.3	18.8
Heavy Structurals	51.2	9.6	19.3	1.0	2.2
Plates	35.6	20.0	18.3	11.5	4.3
Sheet Piles	96.3	.9	2.5	----	----
Wide Hoops	49.1	19.1	16.8	9.3	----
Electric Sheets	57.7	10.5	6.1	----	----

Source: *Oriental Economist* (April 1970).

---

[116] *Nihon Keizai* (May 8, 1969).

[117] The Chairman of the JFTC immediately resigned. *Japan Economic Journal* (September 2, November 4, 1969); Kaplan, *Japan: The Government-Business Relationship*, p. 151.

The creation of Nippon Steel established a single producer with a dominant market position in virtually every major steel product category (table 4-5).[118] The notion that a single firm with such a dominant position could serve as a catalyst for transforming the industry "from competitive oligopoly to cooperative oligopoly"[119] was put to the test almost immediately, when a protracted recession developed in mid-1970. Throughout 1971 the producers agreed on and implemented a series of uniform "voluntary" production cuts pursuant to MITI's administrative guidance.[120] This arrangement did not, however, stabilize prices,[121] and in late 1971, the major producers were authorized to form a formal depression cartel for crude steel production.[122] By May of 1972, the market was recovering and steel prices were rising,[123] but the producers managed to secure an extension of the cartel through December of that year, ultimately enabling them to implement a series of sharp price increases.[124]

The success of the crude steel depression cartel in 1972 established a pattern for the Japanese industry for the next two decades. The cartel was recognized

---

[118] The *Oriental Economist* commented in April 1970 that "Domestic steel users particularly are closely watching the moves of the new company. Many of them take the view that the advance of the prices of major steel products since the early part of 1969 has been closely associated with the birth of Nippon Steel Corporation. . . . It will be when the steel market becomes weaker due to the easing of the supply-demand balance that Nippon Steel will be required to play its assigned role. It is generally expected that the steel market will begin to weaken in 1971-72 at the earliest. Whether Nippon Steel Corporation will take the occasion to expand its market share at the sacrifice of market confusion or take the initiative for stabilization of the market on the basis of cooperation should be closely watched."

[119] *Oriental Economist* (August 1971).

[120] The *Japan Economic Journal* reported on August 10, 1971 that "steel industry circles revealed recently that major blast furnace makers were enforcing their current crude steel production cutback along standards agreed among themselves. . . . The recent revelation by the steel industry circles means, however, that the cutback actually is being conducted jointly by the six major blast furnace makers through the intervention of MITI."

[121] *Nihon Keizai* (February 24, 1971); *Nihon Kogyo* (June 16, 1971); *Yomiuri* (June 1, 1971).

[122] This was reinforced thereafter by the formation of depression cartels in bars, structurals, plates and ingots. The cartel was enforced by a system of resident and traveling inspectors who monitored production at each mill and ensured adherence to the cartel restrictions on production. *Nihon Keizai* (November 3, 1971); *Tekkokai* (August, 1972); *Japan Economic Journal* (November 9, 1971); *Japan Metal Bulletin* (January 13, 20, March 4, April 25, 1972).

[123] *Tekkokai* (August 1972).

[124] The *Oriental Economist* observed in November 1973 that "Such accord was unthinkable prior to the formation of Nippon Steel. In early 1972, under the cover of the 'depression cartel,' price increases were negotiated with such big and regular industrial users as the ship-builders, the motor vehicle manufacturers, and the producers of electrical machinery and appliances. Then, although the steel market had already recovered, the 'depression cartel' was not dissolved until the end of 1972, resulting in a rather severe shortage of steel, and sharp upsurge of steel prices."

as a "blessing to the industry."[125] The *Oriental Economist* commented in November 1973 that Nippon Steel's emergence as an industry leader had

> resulted in a change in the steel industry situation from that of competition to harmonious accord. *Whereas previously the big producers had vied with one another for increase of market share in an "oligopoly of small fry," the Yawata-Fuji merger brought about a change to an "oligopoly under Nippon Steel leadership." Also from about this time, the behavior of the top executives of the steel companies became extremely cautious. . . . Their judgment was that if substantial growth of demand appeared unlikely it would be wiser to cooperate than compete, thus to reap the rewards of price increases.*[126]

Those rewards were manifested in 1973-74, when in "anticipation" of shortages of oil and electric power, Nippon Steel announced a 20 percent production cut, and "inevitably" the other Japanese firms followed suit,[127] giving rise to sharp price increases and widespread charges of profiteering by the steelmakers.[128]

The Export Outlet (1962-1977)

The phenomenal expansion of Japan's steelmaking capacity in the 1960s and 1970s was paralleled by the dramatic growth of Japan's steel exports -- by the mid-1970s, Japan was by far the world's largest steel exporter, shipping well over 40 million metric tons abroad (ingot equivalent) in both 1976 and 1977. However, over the years "the behavior of Japanese steel suppliers in world markets [has been] the subject of intense scrutiny."[129] Through 1978 the basic charge of the Japanese industry's critics was that the industry pursued a policy of countercyclical exporting, maintaining high operating rates through periods

---

[125] *Ibid.*

[126] The Industrial Bank of Japan observed in late 1973 that after dissolution of the cartel, "the market moved in a firm sentiment thanks to the willingness of steel companies to maintain the cooperative system fostered during the period of the cartel and thanks to the rapid increase in demand. . . . Surrounded by such a severe environment, the Japanese steel industry is proceeding toward an orderly structure which in a sense, may be regarded as a cartel." *Quarterly Survey of Japanese Finance and Industry* (July-September 1973), p. 3.

[127] *Nihon Keizai* (December 12, 1973).

[128] *Mainichi* observed on January 24, 1974 that as a result of these price hikes, Nippon Steel had generated near-record profits which were being concealed by manipulation of its depreciation rates. It commented that "because of the oil crisis, industry circles have been having a sense of crisis by crying "this is terrible, terrible . . . . Nevertheless, as they raised the prices of products beforehand in anticipation of a rise in the production cost, and there are appearing some big enterprises in the materials industries which are now being forced to make known their abnormal profits." *Nikkan Kogyo* (March 3, 1974).

[129] Ingo Walter, "Protection of Industries in Trouble -- the Case of Iron and Steel," in 2 *The World Economy* 155, 178 (May 1979).

of slack domestic demand, and exporting the surpluses -- if necessary, at deeply discounted (often dumped) prices.[130]

Japanese accounts of the steel industry's trading practices in the 1960s and 1970s support the view that the industry as a whole pursued a countercyclical export strategy through 1977.[131] Given the structural characteristics of the Japanese industry, this pattern should not be particularly surprising. In the 1960s and early 1970s the Japanese firms were operating new mills of optimum scale which had been acquired with borrowed funds. Their fixed costs were very high, and they needed to maintain a high operating ratio in order to break even.[132] This problem became progressively more urgent as the gap widened between the Japanese mills' effective capacity and domestic demand. By the 1970s, with capacity exceeding domestic demand by a ratio of about two to one, there was simply no way all Japanese producers could operate at a rate approaching full capacity even during boom periods by relying on domestic sales. Exports on a large scale were essential in order to sustain a high operating rate and thus the industry's solvency.[133] The need to expand export

---

[130] This view was articulated in American Iron and Steel Institute, *Steel and the World Economy* (Washington: AISI, May 1977) and in U.S. International Trade Commission, *Carbon Steel Plate From Japan*, U.S.I.T.C. Pub. No. 882, April 1978, p. A-9.

[131] Typically, *Nihon Keizai* observed on June 12, 1974 that "After 1961, iron and steel exports increased in the years 1962, 1965, 1968 and 1971, when the country was in a period of recession or retrocession. . . . The manufacturers sought an outlet for surplus production, which was caused by a decline in demand at home, in the expansion of exports. Moreover, overproduction in Japan reached serious proportions in any period of recession, because equipment investments had been increased greatly in time of prosperity. The manufacturers, therefore, tried to expand exports, even by reducing export prices to a level lower than the prices on the home market. As a result, they were suspected of dumping by importer nations." The Iron and Steel Administration of MITI's Heavy Industries Bureau commented in 1969 that "During each of these three recessions [1957-58, 1961-62, and 1964-65] there were decreases in steel demand, and steel exports increased in order to compensate for the drop in domestic demand." Japan Iron and Steel Federation, *Japan's Iron and Steel Industry 1969*, p. 116.

[132] By 1972 the breakeven operating rate was between 80 and 100 percent of capacity. "The industry can do profitable business only under full operation. If it is not in full operation, the business does not pay, at an 80 percent operation level, it cannot make any profits." Director of Nikko Research Center Shishido in *Tekkokai* (August 1972). "An 80 percent operating rate by new Japanese facilities is more difficult than an 80 percent rate by the mixed facilities of other countries." Director of MITI's Heavy Industries Bureau in *Tekkokai* (August 1972).

[133] The Industrial Bank of Japan observed with respect to the domestic steel recession of 1972 that "the steelmakers, anxious to maintain the level of production at their much expanded facilities, turned as in previous times of recession, to intensive export selling." *Quarterly Survey of Japanese Finance and Industry* (April-June 1972), pp. 1-2.

volume was particularly acute in time of domestic recession, when production controls were in effect.[134]

Ideally, when slack domestic demand required an expansion of export volume, it would have been most desirable to make such exports at high prices. However, slumps in domestic demand generally coincided with global recessions, so that the Japanese mills were pushing their exports onto a depressed world market at discounted prices, giving rise to recurrent charges of dumping.[135] All of Japan's steel exports are handled by trading companies (*sogo shosha*), and the steel firms and the trading companies engaged in mutual finger pointing as to who was responsible for the periodic fall of export prices. The root cause of the problem, however, was the existence of a massive steel surplus and pressure to dispose of it overseas. [136]

The 1975-77 Export Drive

With the onset of the structural recession in late 1974, Japanese steel firms, like other world steel producers, began to experience a dramatic slump in demand. Initially the producers responded, as they had in the past, with a series of concerted production cuts to maintain stable domestic prices.[137] The recession continued to worsen through 1975, and by October the Japanese steel industry was suffering the "worst slump in its history." MITI sought to foster production cuts by setting "guideposts" for reduced production and requiring steel producers to submit their production curtailment programs to MITI for review.[138] The production cuts enabled the steel producers to effectuate a series

---

[134] The *Oriental Economist* commented (August/September 1978) that "The rapid increase of exports of steel products has been principally ascribable to the protracted slump of domestic demand. In other words, steelmakers have had to increase export sales to erase dulling domestic demand for mill products so that they might manage to prevent the operation rate from declining heavily. Exports were excluded from the production restrictions, which served to "enforce export indirectly." Kawasaki, *Japan's Steel Industry*, p. 124.

[135] "The tendency of decline of export price, compared with domestic price was a characteristic feature of this term" (the 1965-66 recession). Kawasaki, *The Japanese Steel Industry*, p. 125.

[136] *Japan Metal Bulletin* (November 27, 1971); *Nihon Keizai* (February 27, 1966).

[137] *Nihon Keizai* reported on January 16, 1975 that "Such concerted action of the iron and steel firms for curtailment of production . . . is a product of the cooperation structure which has been established firmly, on the basis of monopoly, in iron and steel industry circles since Nippon Steel was founded five years ago."

[138] *Japan Economic Journal* (October 7, 1975); *Japan Metal Bulletin* (November 27, 1975).

of domestic price increases in the summer and fall of 1975 despite vociferous objections from steel consuming firms[139] and the JFTC.[140]

At the same time that MITI's guideposts were helping the steelmakers raise domestic prices through joint production cuts, however, export prices fell sharply. The *Japan Economic Journal* reported on November 18, 1975 that

> *Export prices of steel products, such as heavy plates, bars and angles, have been rapidly sagging, according to trading sources. Chiefly responsible for the price decline, sources said, are the slowing down of demand in such major markets as Southeast Asian countries and the U.S. ...*

Significantly, despite the fact that foreign demand was depressed, Japanese export volume began to increase, and MITI, concerned about dumping charges, sought to persuade the steel producers to conduct "orderly" exports.[141] However, export prices fell substantially through the latter half of 1975; the average unit price of exported steel products in October was $310, $42 less than the average unit price for the April-September 1975 period.[142] In late September, the industry leaders, Nippon Steel and Nippon Kokan, were

> *earnestly advising their comrade steelmakers to refrain from cheap exports of their steel products as they might provoke a dumping charge abroad. The advice is being made because a move is being discerned in*

---

[139] *Nihon Keizai* reported on November 11, 1975 that "MITI on the 10th revised its outlook (guidepost) on supply and demand of ordinary steel materials. . . . Major iron and steel companies, including Nippon Steel, are making strenuous efforts to reconstruct the market by strengthening reduced production, including suspension of blast furnace operation, aiming at realizing the second raise of prices of steel materials by 3,000 yen/ton [$10.11/ton]. Especially for this reason, MITI's revision of the guidepost by quantitative reduction is considered to mean its supporting the creation of an environment for the price raise." *Nihon Keizai* (June 6, 1975); *Yomiuri* (July 9, 1975).

[140] The JFTC complained that "the price raises carried out by the six major steelmakers in August had the same effect as that of monopolistic enterprises as their price raises were in effect the collusive price raises prohibited by Antimonopoly Law." *Japan Metal Bulletin* (December 16, 1975). The JFTC began questioning the big six steelmakers "on the suspicion that they may have violated the Antimonopoly Law in raising the prices of rolled steel recently, according to informed sources. . . . The Commission suspects that the steelmakers had 'intimidated' the major steel users by telling them that steel delivery to them might be suspended if the customers did not agree to price raises." *Kyodo*, 0:46 GMT (November 5, 1975). However, the JFTC took no action.

[141] *Nihon Keizai* reported on November 23, 1975 that "behind the increases in the amount of exports, there is an aspect where various iron and steel manufacturing companies are making an export drive intentionally in an attempt to break the deadlock in stagnation of domestic demand. So, export prices are still at a low level. MITI intends to guide industry circles toward the establishment of export order on the grounds that if left as is, there is a fear of incurring criticism from foreign countries as to dumping."

[142] *Japan Metal Bulletin* (December 6, 1975).

*the industry circles that some steelmakers are offering their products
for exports at cheaper prices than for domestic customers for whom
they have recently raised the price by an average of 6,800 yen/ton
[$23/ton].*[143]

Notwithstanding such concern, low export pricing continued and the volume
of Japanese exports rose.[144] Export prices fell precipitously through 1975,
bottoming out in the first quarter of 1976 at a level only 68 percent of that of the
first quarter of 1975.[145] During the same time period, Japanese export volume
was rising rapidly, peaking in 1976 in the quarter following the lowest price
quotations.[146] The impact of the surge in low-priced Japanese exports was felt
all over the world; in 1975 Australia imposed quantitative restrictions on the
import of Japanese flat-rolled sheets, and at the end of that year Canadian
producers filed complaints charging the Japanese mills with dumping bars and
structurals.[147] The Japanese and Europeans (who were also seeking to force
exports) engaged in intense price competition in East Asia and South
America.[148]

In the United States, the Japanese export drive touched off the worst trade
dispute the two nations had experienced in this sector to date. In the fall of
1976, the American Iron and Steel Institute brought an action pursuant to
Section 301 of the Trade Act of 1974, charging that a bilateral agreement

---

[143] *Japan Metal Bulletin* (September 20, 1975). *Nihon Keizai* indicated on November 23, 1975
that "what is feared at this point is export prices which are still at a low level. It is believed this
is attributable to the fact that as iron and steel manufacturers not only in our country, but also
in various countries, including Europe, have been gasping due to the stagnation in demand for
a long time, have inevitably turned to low-priced competition. However, in actuality export
prices are extremely low. . . . Because of this MITI has summoned Japanese steel executives]
and requested them to exercise self control over low-priced exports so as not to incur criticism
from foreign countries as to dumping."

[144] *Nihon Keizai* (February 23, 1976).

[145] The *Japan Metal Bulletin* reported (April 10, 1976) that Japanese steel export prices "are
not enough to cover the cost and proper profits."

[146] Looking back on the industry's 1976 export drive, the Industrial Bank of Japan commented
that "The steel industry at the beginning of fiscal 1976 was faced with an urgent need to pull itself
out of the severest recession since the end of World War II. . . . We must concede in all fairness
that the industry got over its worst period by propping itself up with exports and with the
markups of [domestic] product prices. . . . Looking more closely at exports, the source of the
thrust for recovery, we note . . . in terms of prices, that the weighted average of products, which
hit bottom at $270 per ton in February 1976, recovered to $309 per ton in September 1976, but
that the prices even at this level proved considerably lower than the average prices at the peak
in the past. Such a differential indicates that the export increase in the first half of 1976 was in
volume rather than value." *Quarterly Survey of Japanese Finance and Industry* (October-
December, 1977), pp. 2-3.

[147] Japan Iron and Steel Exporters' Association, "Iron and Steel Exports," in *Japan's Iron and
Steel Industry 1977*, p. 60.

[148] *Metal Bulletin* (December 26, 1976).

between the EC and Japan had diverted Japanese steel exports from the EC to the U.S. market.[149] In early 1977 Gilmore Steel, a small U.S. producer based in Oregon, filed an antidumping action against five Japanese producers of carbon steel plate. Shortly thereafter the American Iron and Steel Institute published a study charging the Japanese mills with practicing price discrimination between domestic and export markets (to which the Japanese industry responded with a sharp rebuttal).[150] In September, U.S. Steel filed the largest antidumping action ever brought under the antidumping law, alleging that Japanese mills were dumping at "distress sale" prices. In October, the Treasury Department, having made a preliminary determination in the Gilmore case that Japanese producers were dumping plate in the U.S. at margins of 32 percent, required them to post bond equal to the amount of the dumping margin.

The Japanese mills increased their share of the U.S. market substantially, from 5.1 percent in 1974 to 7.9 percent in 1976, the highest annual import penetration any nation has achieved in the U.S. steel market in the postwar era.[151] In the antidumping investigation conducted by the Treasury Department in the Gilmore case, and in a subsequent investigation by the U.S. International Trade Commission, U.S. government investigators found that increased Japanese market penetration was achieved to a substantial degree through aggressive Japanese pricing, and in the instance of plate, through dumping.[152]

---

[149] 41 F.R. 45628, October 15, 1976. The investigation was discontinued on January 30, 1978 because of insufficient evidence that the surge in Japanese steel exports to the U.S. was attributable to the EC-Japan agreement. 43 F.R. 3962, January 30, 1978.

[150] Putnam, Hayes and Bartlett, Inc., *Economics of International Steel Trade: Policy Implications for the United States* (Newton, Mass: Putnam, Hayes and Bartlett, Inc., 1977); Japan Iron and Steel Exporters' Association, *U.S.-Japan Steel Trade: Basic Views on Current Issues* (Tokyo: Overseas Public Relations Committee, 1977).

[151] American Iron and Steel Institute.

[152] In the Gilmore case, *Carbon Steel Plate from Japan*, the U.S. Treasury Department found, after investigation, that the Japanese mills had been dumping plate in the U.S. market during this time period, and the U.S. International Trade Commission found that Japanese pricing was the principal factor underlying the increase in Japanese share of the U.S. plate market. Similarly, in a 1979 investigation of the impact of imports on steel competition in the western United States the Commission found that aggressive Japanese pricing tactics had occurred during 1975-77 in a number of the steel product areas under investigation, which included hot and cold-rolled sheets, plate, bars, angles, and welded pipe. The Japanese producers undercut U.S. firms' prices by "indexing"– informing their customers that they would undersell any U.S. producer price by a fixed percentage, regardless of whether the U.S. firms increased or decreased prices. U.S. International Trade Commission, *Carbon Steel Plate from Japan* U.S.I.T.C. Pub. No. 882, April 1978, pp. A-25, A-26; 43 F.R. 2032, January 13, 1978. U.S.I.T.C. Pub. No. 1004, September 1979, *Conditions of Competition in the Western U.S. Steel Market Between Certain Domestic and Foreign Steel Products.*

There was evidence that such practices were one direct cause of the major dislocations which occurred in the U.S. steel industry during these years.[153]

The penetration of the U.S. market achieved in 1976 proved to be a high water mark for the Japanese mills. The antidumping actions brought by Gilmore and U.S. Steel against the Japanese producers led to an abatement of the pressure on the U.S. market from Japanese steel exports.[154] In 1978, the U.S. government implemented the Trigger Price Mechanism, principally a device designed to deter Japanese dumping in the U.S. market.[155] From 1978 onward, the Japanese producers seeking to expand their U.S. presence confronted an array of actual and prospective U.S. trade policy measures, and as a result their export volume to the U.S. diminished.[156] Between 1978 and 1981, two successive Trigger Price Mechanism regimes (based on monitoring of Japanese costs) served to hold dumping in check; in 1982, when Japanese penetration of the U.S. market again began to increase, the American Iron and Steel Institute and a number of individual companies brought another action against Japan pursuant to Section 301 of the Trade Act of 1974.[157] In 1983, following a surge of low-priced Japanese pipe exports to the U.S., the U.S. government imposed antidumping duties on Japanese pipe and tube products.[158] In the fall of 1984, the U.S. government concluded a voluntary restraint arrangement with Japan, effective for five years, which established quantitative restrictions on Japanese steel exports to the U.S.

The trade dispute with the U.S., which saw a succession of cases brought against the Japanese mills, was one of several factors which induced them to modify their export patterns after 1978, when they increasingly sought outlets for their surpluses in the Soviet Union, China and the Middle East.

---

[153] In the *Carbon Steel Plate* case, the U.S.I.T.C. found that dumped imports from Japan had injured the U.S. steel industry in this sector. The Commission found that the industry's capacity utilization rate had fallen to 45% in 1976, the year in which Japanese import penetration peaked at 13 percent, and that the ten U.S. producers surveyed had suffered a cumulative operating loss in 1975-77, during the same period that price undercutting and deeper market penetration by Japanese producers was occurring. Based on these factors, the Commission concluded that the U.S. carbon steel plates sector had been materially injured by imports from Japan. *Carbon Steel Plate from Japan* (final), U.S.I.T.C. Pub. No. 882, April 1978.

[154] The preliminary margins imposed in the Carbon Steel Plate case were a substantial deterrent to shipments to the U.S. market. See Hugh Patrick and Hideo Sato, "The Political Economy of United States-Japan Trade in Steel," in *Policy and Trade Issues of the Japanese Economy*, ed. Kozo Yamamura, p. 209.

[155] John Jay Range, "The Trigger Price Mechanism: Does It Prevent Dumping by Foreign Steelmakers?" in 5 *N.C. Journal of International Law and Commercial Regulation* 279, 291 (Spring 1980).

[156] For a description of U.S. trade policy measures in steel, see chapter 7.

[157] Petition of the American Iron and Steel Institute, filed December 16, 1982.

[158] *Certain Steel Pipes and Tubes from Japan*, 48 F.R. 1206, January 11, 1983.

RESTRUCTURING EFFORTS 1975-1988

The global structural crisis in steel has caused the Japanese mills to undertake rationalization and restructuring efforts since the early 1970s, with mixed results. Encouraged by MITI, the Japanese industry has placed a considerable emphasis on technological adaptation to new global competitive circumstances, primarily through intensive research and development efforts, upgrading the quality of its physical plant, reducing the breakeven operating rate, and moving its product mix toward higher value added steel products.[159] The Japanese producers made relatively little progress in the areas where cartelization of the Japanese market has reduced competitive incentives to restructure, most notably the reduction of the capacity surplus which underlies most of the industry's present difficulties. Japanese gross crude steelmaking capacity actually continued to grow after 1974, from 138 million tons in that year to a peak of 162 million metric tons in 1983. While it is forecast to decline to approximately 143 million metric tons in 1988, this level is still higher than that at the beginning of the structural crisis.[160] While some capacity cuts were undertaken beginning in 1978, notably by Nippon Steel, these were small in proportion to the size of the Japanese surplus. Major Japanese capacity reduction efforts did not begin until 1986, twelve years after the onset of the structural recession, and it remains unclear how significant the Japanese capacity cuts will be.

Government policies have played an important, but low visibility role, in both the successful and unsuccessful aspects of the Japanese restructuring effort. The government has provided fiscal and other incentives for R&D, equipment modernization, and product diversification, but more importantly, continued to play a role in building a consensus with the industry that such initiatives were desirable and necessary. On the other hand, with respect to capacity cuts, the de facto exemption which the Japanese mills enjoy from the Antimonopoly Law has served to undercut closing of facilities on a scale which MITI and many industry executives recognize is necessary.

Reducing the Breakeven Operating Rate

In the mid-1970s, the fact that the Japanese industry's breakeven operating rate was averaging about 80 percent of capacity placed it in a very precarious position. Unless the massive Japanese facilities could be operated at a high rate, they would be uneconomical -- but such high levels of output had resulted in the export drive of 1975-77, which created major foreign relations difficulties for Japan. This problem proved soluble through an industry-government

---

[159] In 1988, the U.S. International Trade Commission reported that the ratio of researchers to total employment in the Japanese industry is nearly four percent, far higher than most other world steel industries. U.S.I.T.C., *Steel Sheet and Strip Industry*, pp. 9-15.

[160] Marcus and Kirsis, Core Report BB.

effort.[161] Beginning in 1977 the Japanese producers began to reduce their dependency on borrowed funds, one of the principal factors contributing to their high fixed costs.[162] The Japanese government began to step up the volume of its direct loans to the steel producers for capital investment; between 1975 and 1979, at least $600 million was loaned by government banks to the industry.[163] A substantial portion of these loans were devoted to the installation of more energy-efficient equipment.[164] The Japan Development Bank encouraged steel producers to convert from oil to coal energy with a program of low interest loans.[165] These efforts had a dramatic impact on the cost structure of the Japanese industry. The industry's continuous casting ratio grew from 21 percent in 1973 to 93 percent in 1986; yields improved from 84 percent to 92 percent between 1973 and 1983; and dependency on imported oil was substantially reduced.[166]

The Changing Product Mix

Since the early 1970s, at MITI's urging, the major Japanese steel producers have sought to shift the balance of their product mix toward higher value added commodities, and to diversify into entirely new businesses and product areas.[167]

---

[161] MITI's Director of the Iron and Steel Division said in 1979 that "Despite a production capability of more than 150 million tons, the industry has been operating at around 70% of capacity for quite some time now. . . . Storage yards have been overflowing with raw materials brought to the mills under long term contracts on the basis of earlier industry expectation of continued expansion. . . . Against this background of fluctuating demand, the industry finally came to realize that reform was imperative. No matter how long the producers waited, there was little hope of a recovery in demand sufficient to pull the industry out of its difficulties. The only way to guarantee profitability was to implement a tough rationalization campaign." *Japan's Iron and Steel Industry 1979*, pp. 71-72.

[162] Investments in 1977 and 1978 were cut to about half 1976 levels, and the Japanese mills began shifting to financing their new investments, to an increasing degree, out of their own depreciation funds (which were substantial, given the heavy investments of the prior decade). *Japan's Iron and Steel Industry 1979*, pp. 71-72.

[163] *Tekko Nenkan* (FY 1975, 1976, 1978, 1979).

[164] For example, Japan Development Bank loans were made to the leading steel producers to promote adoption of furnaces using low fuel consumption, heat exchange (recycling) equipment, dehumidifying and duct equipment, equipment to recapture waste pressure, waste heat boiler facilities, facilities for use of waste gas, and heat insulation equipment. The loans were usually matched by contributions by recipient firms. *Tekko Nenkan* (FY 1982).

[165] *Tekko Nenkan* (FY 1982).

[166] U.S. International Trade Commission, *Steel Sheet and Strip* (1988), pp. 9-17.

[167] In 1973, MITI's Industrial Structure Council issued a report on "The Steel Industry in the 1970s and What its Policy Should Be." One of the most significant recommendations was that "The industry will change direction to [emphasize] . . . high-quality goods, such as high value-added goods which have been produced through condensation of skillful knowledge and techniques." Steel Subcommittee Draft Report reproduced in *Tekkokai* (August 1973). See also *Nihon Keizai* (January 7, 1972).

This has involved a greater emphasis on higher value-added steel products, such as pipes and tubes, and entry into non-steel activities, including the development and production of new materials, electronics and even travel agencies.[168]

The steelmakers' rapid shifts in product mix have sometimes led to the same sequence of rapid capacity expansion, followed by surpluses and dumping, that occurred in the standard steel product lines. In seamless pipe, a particularly profitable product line during the oil exploration boom of the 1970s, four Japanese producers undertook an intensive expansion effort which actually accelerated after the world market for this product collapsed in 1982.[169] In a familiar pattern, Japanese producers sought to boost domestic prices through a series of concerted production cuts[170] while disposing of their surpluses overseas, an approach which led to dumping of seamless pipe in the U.S. market.[171]

Capacity Reduction Efforts

Since the early 1970s the Japanese government and the steel producers have shared a recognition that the Japanese industry possessed too much capacity and needed to be reduced in size.[172] Sharp cuts in capacity would reduce the industry's dangerous overdependence on exports and permit the industry to increase its operating rate. In practice, however, capacity cuts have proven extraordinarily difficult to implement, and Japan's "overhang" of surplus capacity has persisted since the onset of the structural crisis. That fact is sometimes attributed to steelmakers' reluctance to lay off workers. The real root of the problem, however, is the "cooperation structure" itself, which has insulated Japanese firms from competitive pressures that would otherwise have made capacity reduction necessary, rather than merely desirable.

The dynamics of capacity reduction in the 1970s and 1980s have to some extent mirrored those of capacity expansion in the 1960s. Each individual

---

[168] *Purometeusu* (September-October 1985); *Jihyo* (April 1986); *Jidosha Gijutsu* (August 1985); *Zaikai Tembo* (December 1985).

[169] *Japan Economic Journal* (April 20, 1982); *Japan Metal Bulletin* (May 23, 1978; December 10, 1981).

[170] *Japan Economic Journal* (April 20, 1982).

[171] Japanese seamless pipe export prices began falling sharply in 1982, and Japanese trading companies' U.S. subsidiaries were reportedly burdened by enormous inventories of unsold seamless pipe. *Nihon Keizai* (November 18 1982); *Nikkei Sangyo* (April 4, 1983). In 1983 the U.S. Department of Commerce found that the Japanese mills had been dumping several varieties of seamless pipe in the U.S. market. *Certain Steel Pipe and Tubes from Japan: Final Determination of Sales at Less Than Fair Value*, January 11, 1983 (48 F.R. 1206).

[172] As early as 1971, MITI was pressing the Japanese mills to adopt a policy under which new facilities would be built only if a corresponding amount of older capacity were also scrapped. This initiative was designed to "help solve the industry's current controversial problem of overequipment." MITI's policy was elegantly expressed as "mandatory on all steelmakers on a voluntary agreement basis." *Japan Economic Journal* (June 8, 1971).

producer has been reluctant to reduce capacity because by so doing, it jeopardizes its market share, and the system of production restraints reduces

Table 4-6. MITI Survey of Japanese Capacity, 1980-84

Type Facility	1980 Units	1980 Capacity (000 tons)	1984 Units	1984 Capacity (000 tons)	Increase(Decrease) 1980-84 Units	Increase(Decrease) 1980-84 Capacity (000 tons)
Blast Furnace	66	134,330	66	118,102	-	(16,228)
Converter	94	129,812	90	127,800	(4)	(2,012)
Electric Arc Furnace	388	28,665	353	29,110	(35)	445
Large Structurals	27	19,090	28	20,152	1	1,062
Small Structurals	222	42,240	130	34,877	(92)	(7,363)
Wire Rod	26	11,109	22	11,917	(4)	808
HR Sheet	23	67,151	22	70,424	(1)	3,273
Plate	27	22,877	22	21,827	(5)	(1,050)
Tinplate	13	2,388	13	2,388	-	-
Seamless pipe	19	4,248	22	6,269	3	2,021
Foreweld pipe	282	11,370	278	12,657	(4)	1,287

Source: MITI Statistics, reported in *Japan Metal Bulletin* (December 14, 1985).

the economic incentives to eliminate surplus production capability.[173] In the 1980s, Nippon Steel has led the way in implementing capacity cuts, but its competitors have followed only sluggishly, and Nippon Steel has seen its market

---

[173] *Nihon Keizai* commented on September 16, 1976 that "the iron and steel companies are no longer interested in new investments so greatly as they were before the occurrence of the oil shock. Nevertheless, they still seem to have a sound sense of shares at heart, with the exception of Nippon Steel, which maintains a somewhat negative view on future expansion of demand for iron and steel."

share eroded.[174]   Many "rationalization" programs have featured gradual reduction of employees rather than closure of facilities,[175] and facility "closings" have often consisted of mothballing, rather than demolishing, steelworks.[176]

Although the capacity surplus was the basic structural factor underlying many of the Japanese industry's difficulties after 1970, significant restructuring efforts did not really begin until 1978, when Nippon Steel implemented its first "rationalization program."[177]   This effort featured closure of older mills, a gradual work force reduction, and a reduction of crude steel capacity from 47 million metric tons per year (tpy) to 36 million metric tpy in 1980. A second rationalization program undertaken during the recession of 1982 cut crude steel capacity to 32 million metric tpy, and a third, begun in 1984, reduced capacity to 27 million metric tpy in 1986.[178]   Finally in January 1987, Nippon Steel announced its fourth rationalization program, which would mothball 5 of its remaining 12 blast furnaces and cut crude steel capacity to 24 million metric tpy.[179]

These cuts, while not inconsequential, were criticized by some of the company's own executives as inadequate,[180] and the other Japanese producers, particularly Nippon Kokan and Kobe Steel, were slower to follow with corresponding capacity cuts. Industry analysts concluded in 1987 that the plant closures which had occurred or been announced to date were insufficient to restore the industry to profitability.[181]   In mid-1987, MITI's Basic Industries Bureau concluded after a study that in light of falling demand, Japan's capacity surplus would actually worsen unless substantial further domestic reductions

---

[174] Nippon Steel's Fourth Rationalization Program, implemented in early 1987, was designed to be implemented at a pace sufficiently slow to preserve that company's domestic market share of 27 percent. *Metal Bulletin* (February 17, 1987).

[175] *Gekkan Koran* (April 1986).

[176] Nippon Steel, for example, announced plans in 1987 to take five blast furnaces out of operation, but insisted that "plant is simply being taken out and not scrapped completely." *Metal Bulletin* (February 17, 1987).

[177] *Metal Bulletin* (January 27, 1984).

[178] *Metal Bulletin* (January 10, 1984).

[179] *Metal Bulletin* (January 14, February 17, 1987).

[180] *Metal Bulletin* (January 10, 1984).

[181] Jardine Fleming Securities in *Metal Bulletin* (May 12, 1987). Kobe Steel announced in early 1986 that it would cut its work force to 22,000 by March 1989, from a level of 27,970 in 1985, largely through attrition or redeployment of employees to non-steel divisions. Its closure plans were limited to a "re-examination" of the production of pig iron at its Amagasaki works. Nippon Kokan was reported as early as 1987 to be contemplating a reduction of its workforce by one third by 1990, closure of a welded pipe mill, a seamless pipe mill, and possibly one blast furnace. By these standards Kawasaki's announced closure plans were aggressive -- two coke batteries, a slabbing mill, a plate mill, a hot strip mill, and a steelmaking shop -- but even Kawasaki's measures were relatively minor in relation to the size of Japan's capacity surplus. *Metal Bulletin* (December 2, 1986; February 20, 1987).

were implemented.[182] However, Kawasaki Steel announced in mid-1987 that in light of improved market conditions, it would postpone certain aspects of its restructuring plan, reducing the number of planned employee cuts.[183] In 1988, Nippon Steel indicated that the closure of one of the blast furnaces announced in 1987 might be postponed until the end of 1988, and Sumitomo and Kobe indicated they would restart furnaces which had been taken out of service for refurbishing.[184] Kobe indicated in 1988 that it would actually expand steelmaking capacity, raising its monthly hot-rolling capability to 20 thousand tons.[185]

The Japanese producers have been gradually reducing employment levels in the industry since 1970, and employment has fallen from 474 thousand in that year to 338 thousand in 1986.[186] The Japanese government has taken measures to cushion the impact of the work force reductions which have occurred. In 1982, the integrated steelmakers were reportedly granted "depressed" status by the Ministry of Labor, making them eligible for funding to finance layoffs, retraining, or loaning of workers to other companies.[187] In 1986, the steelmakers began placing some employees on "extended leave," during which they received 80 percent of their normal pay, and the government reimbursed the steel firms for 66 percent of this amount.[188]

Capacity reduction efforts in the electric furnace sector have been a particularly dramatic failure -- capacity actually expanded. This sector had suffered from a large capacity surplus from the early 1970s onward, and lapsed into a pattern of increasingly prolonged formal cartels, often accompanied by aggressive export drives of bars and rods, their principal products.[189] In an effort to address the problem of this and other industrial sectors which had become "structurally depressed," the Diet passed a succession of laws designed to facilitate capacity reduction, work force retraining, and structural rationalization.[190] For industries designated as "structurally depressed," the laws authorized government financial benefits for the disposal of excess facilities and

---

[182] *Metal Bulletin* (June 5, 1987).

[183] *Metal Bulletin* (July 27, 1987).

[184] *Metal Bulletin* (February 1, 1988).

[185] *Japan Economic Journal* (June 18, 1988).

[186] *Japanese Year Book of Labour Statistics.*

[187] *Metal Bulletin* (September 24, October 1, 1982).

[188] U.S.I.T.C., *Steel Sheet and Strip Industry,* pp. 9-21.

[189] *Nihon Keizai* (July 24, 1981); *Japan Metal Bulletin* (December 19, 1981).

[190] The Law on Temporary Measures for the Stabilization of Specified Depressed Industries in 1978. It was superseded by the Designated Industrial Structure Improvement/ Extraordinary Measures Law in 1983.

exemptions from the Antimonopoly Law to permit development of joint facility disposal plans, mergers and tie-ups.[191]

In 1978 the electric furnace sector possessed 21 million metric tons of steelmaking capacity. Under the industry's first Basic Stabilization Plan, the producers disposed of 2.7 million metric tons of capacity, but simultaneously continued to invest in upgrading the productivity of their remaining facilities, with the result that by March 1981, the industry's capacity had actually increased by 2.8 million metric tons, to 23.8 million metric tons.[192] The Second Basic Stabilization Plan, launched in 1981, was an even worse failure -- capacity increased again, to 26.7 million metric tons, and MITI warned that by 1988, despite implementation of a Third Basic Stabilization Plan, capacity could increase still further, to 28.0 million metric tons.[193] The basic problem was simply that each producer sought to maintain its market share by preserving, and if possible, expanding capacity, and had relatively little incentive to shut facilities down.[194]

The "Cooperation Structure"

An American observer of Japan's restructuring difficulties might well argue that the most rational way to achieve capacity cuts would be to allow the market to operate more freely, with the result that the less efficient facilities would eventually be forced by competitive pressures to close. Such a result, however, has not occurred, and given Japan's traditions of industrial organization and behavior, is unlikely to occur. Instead, the "cooperation structure" established after the formation of Nippon Steel has mitigated competitive pressure on the Japanese mills and enabled all of them to survive each recession with their capacity more or less intact. At each recessionary interval since 1971, the joint implementation of production restraints by the steel producers has stabilized prices. Cooperation has brought other benefits; the steelmakers have been able

---

[191] The original law directed MITI to a "Basic Stabilization Plan" for each industry designated as "structurally depressed." The Plan is a "recommendation" which must be negotiated with the industry. The Plan must be reviewed by the JFTC, but the law contemplated that collaborative agreements concerning facilities reduction, mergers, production curtailments and other joint actions will be reached by the industry pursuant to the Plan.

[192] *Nikkan Kogyo* (May 13, 1982); *Tekkokai* (November 21, 1981). The industry's commitment to capacity reduction was less than wholehearted. The Industrial Structure Council's 1981 Report complained that 40 percent of the "eliminated" facilities had simply been closed up, not demolished.

[193] In fact, by 1986 capacity had grown to 29.2 million tons. Marcus and Kirsis, *Steel Strategist 14*; *Tekko Kaiho* (August 21, 1983); *Japan Economic Journal* (July 19, 1983).

[194] *Nihon Keizai* commented on February 4, 1983 that "it can be said to be difficult to obtain the consensus of [electric furnace] industry circles on a concrete way of pushing the disposition of facilities."

to avoid closing entire mills by dividing up orders according to product type and distributing them among various mills.[195]

Such division of production (which would be illegal in the United States) not only reduced unit costs of production through greater economies of scale, but served to reduce the propensity for competition among the producers.[196]

The abiding strength of the Japanese steel cartel is perhaps best illustrated by the occasional challenges which have been mounted to it, generally by upstart firms seeking to win a larger share of the market. In 1982-84, for example, a Japanese electric furnace producer, Tokyo Steel, decided to challenge Nippon Steel's established position in structurals ("H-beams"), building a new mill and refusing to accede to Nippon Steel's demands that it reach an agreement concerning appropriate price and production levels.[197] There followed the so-called "H-beam Wars," in which Nippon Steel slashed the price of the structurals produced by Tokyo Steel, driving that firm into a loss position. Tokyo Steel ultimately was forced to accede to Nippon Steel's demands.[198] Its President complained that

> *Nippon Steel wants to control us. In the first war, Nippon Steel tried to make an agreement with us over our pricing and production policies but we refused to make such an arrangement. Now that our plant is built, Nippon Steel still wants to control our prices and distribution. Nippon Steel says: "The pie is limited. Nippon Steel cuts the pie. I give you your portion. Now keep silent!"*[199]

MITI has on occasion intervened directly to prevent such maverick firms from disrupting efforts to maintain a steel cartel. In 1977 Japanese rebar producers formed a cartel under the Medium and Small Scale Industries Law,

---

[195] A MITI official commented that "the drastic measure of shutting down an entire steelworks is out of the question because of the effect on the local economy. Various types of production are allocated appropriately among the most efficient facilities in all the mills." *Japan's Iron and Steel Industry 1979*, p. 75.

[196] In 1977, for example, two producers of steel angles (Tokyo Steel and Tokyo Kotetsu) concluded an agreement to eliminate competition between them. Tokyo Steel agreed to produce angles of 10 x 90 mm and larger, but to refrain from producing angles of less than 10 x 90 mm. Tokyo Kotetsu in turn agreed to produce angles of less than 10 x 90 mm but no larger. Each firm agreed to procure the steel angle which it did not produce from the other firm. *Japan Metal Bulletin* (September 6, 1977).

[197] Nippon Steel reportedly warned "Kyushu's small fabricators that they could not expect Nippon Steel's 'support' in the future if they supplied products for Tokyo [Steel's] new mill." *Metal Bulletin* (July 10, 1984). One Japanese trading company complained that "Tokyo Steel ignored [Nippon Steel's] request to reduce production, and announced the price reduction which will cause great price confusion in the market. It is an unfaithful act to us." *Nihon Keizai* (May 22, 1984).

[198] At one point Tokyo Steel's operating rate was driven down to 30 percent. *Nikkei Sangyo* (April 27, 1983); *Nihon Keizai* (May 23, 1984).

[199] *Metal Bulletin* (July 10, 1984).

which authorized MITI to impose sanctions on firms which refused to join. MITI cracked down on mavericks, setting production quotas for them and monitoring their sales to verify compliance. It issued an "Order to Align with the Cartel," directing all rebar producers to cut production by 35 percent, or a fine would be imposed.[200] Tokyo Steel resisted these pressures; Asahi later reported:

> *The two-year-and-eight month humiliation for Mr. Masanari Ikeya, the president of Tokyo Steel, called the "outsider to the electric furnace industry," was still fresh in his memory. It was the period for resisting MITI's obstinate approach to align with the cartel." When I heard the alignment order, I thought at first, 'That cannot be!' and gradually, I was furious with anger. After making the decision that I had no alternative but to join the cartel, I was exhausted and disheartened. ... Though the industry is supposedly suffering from a structural recession ... our firm was healthy. Can a healthy person be forcibly hospitalized? Can this occur in a free enterprise economy?*

A significant change in the "cooperation structure" would be difficult to effectuate given Japan's tradition of cooperative business behavior and weak antitrust enforcement, and also because it has proven extraordinarily beneficial over the years for the Japanese steel industry. On some occasions, as the economy has recovered from recession, the prolongation of production curtailments has sent prices soaring and enabled the producers to extract premium prices from consumers. This phenomenon has never been more evident than in the period following the onset of the "Yen Shock" in 1985, when the Japanese mills were able to salvage a catastrophic market situation and restore their profitability by extracting premium prices from consumers.

YEN SHOCK 1985-1988

The sharp appreciation of the yen against the dollar which began in late 1985 precipitated a severe crisis for the Japanese steel producers.[201] Japanese domestic steel demand stagnated because of the fall in demand for exports of Japanese end-products incorporating steel -- such as automobiles and consumer durables. The industry was particularly vulnerable in export markets, where "shadows [were] appearing over our competitive power with semi-advanced nations, such as ROK, in the field of costs."[202] In 1986 the steelmakers "grimly" resisted sharp increases in export prices, but this resulted in a drastic reduction

---

[200] *Japan Metal Bulletin* (June 21, August 18, August 20, October 6, November 29, December 1, 1977; April 20, 1978).

[201] While Japanese companies in other industries, such as electronics, could respond to the problem by shifting production to other countries, the steel industry's production capacity was not comparably mobile.

[202] Nippon Kokan President Yamashiro in *Sankei* (March 5, 1986).

in income.[203] The cost savings which the steelmakers realized as a result of the lower cost of imported raw materials was wholly insufficient to offset these factors and, as a result, in 1986 the Japanese producers suffered their worst losses since the end of World War II.[204] The shift in exchange rates, coupled with low operating rates, made the Japanese steel industry one of the highest cost producers in the world in dollar terms, much higher than industries in the United States, the U.K., France, Taiwan, and South Korea.[205]

The Japanese government's response to the crisis in the steel industry did not place a heavy emphasis on direct subsidies, as in many other countries. Some electric furnace steel firms hurt by the strong yen did receive government subsidized loans.[206] Far more significant, however, was a combination of measures designated to cut the steelmakers' costs, stimulate domestic demand, and raise domestic prices.

With respect to costs, on May 15, 1987, MITI approved a proposal by the Electricity Enterprise Council pursuant to which the nation's gas and utility companies would refund 57 billion yen ($438 million) in gas and electric bills to the steelmakers representing "windfall profits" reaped by the utilities as a result of the shift in exchange rates.[207] In December 1986, following complaints from steel producers that these cuts were "not sufficiently helpful," MITI approved a proposed rate reduction in utility bills which would save the steelmakers an estimated $415.4 million in utility charges in fiscal 1987.[208] Finally, MITI agreed to an arrangement whereby the steelmakers would phase out their traditional practice of purchasing a small proportion of their coal needs (about 5 percent) from domestic sources, permitting them to procure all of their needs through imports, which were less costly.[209]

---

[203] Japan's two largest export markets, China and the U.S., paid for steel in dollars, China through a dollar-linked pricing formula. *Far Eastern Economic Review* (November 13, 1986).

[204] The interim settlement of accounts for fiscal 1986 by the five integrated producers had suffered losses of about 184 billion yen ($1.4 billion at 130:1), if profits from the sale of stocks were excluded from the calculation. *Asahi* (November 12, 1986).

[205] Marcus and Kirsis, Core Report BB.

[206] *Japan Metal Bulletin* (March 6, 1986). The eligible firms received "low interest government-subsidized loans" at a rate of 5.5 percent.

[207] *Japan Metal Bulletin* (May 17, 1986). "To the major steelmakers, the bonanza represents a 0.5 percent extra gain on their overall sales of steel items, and will serve a significant relief on their plight caused by the recent upsurge of the yen. . . ." A number of other major industrial sectors received similar refunds. *Ibid.*

[208] *Japan Metal Bulletin* (December 9, 1986).

[209] For years domestically produced coal has been far more expensive than imported coal (the differential was 3:1 in 1985). During the past two decades the Japanese government spent an estimated $5.5 billion to narrow the price differential between the domestic and imported product, but the domestic variety was still far more costly. The government maintained a ceiling on domestic coal production but required that domestic consumers buy all of the coal produced. In 1986 the steel producers jointly stated that they could no longer pay this sort of premium.

More significant than such measures, however, was the government's public spending program. In 1986 the Diet enacted a $2.1 billion supplementary budget package designed to counteract the impact of the strong yen through government spending on public works projects. The steel industry calculated that this program would directly create demand for 1.6 million metric tons of steel, compensating for about half of the losses it had incurred on export sales.[210] MITI Minister Tamura assured the steel producers in November 1986 that the government "would implement the public works projects without delay and that due considerations will be given to areas which are depressed hardest, such as steel works."[211] One manifestation of this program was a MITI proposal advanced in early 1987 to replace guardrails on medium class highways in Japan with thick gauge steel plate, and to substantially increase the total mileage of highway in Japan which was lined with guardrails.[212]

The Japanese government had utilized government procurement as an instrument to counteract steel recessions on prior occasions, but never on this scale.[213] By the spring of 1987, the government's measures had resulted in "booming construction works," and an increase in demand for many types of steel.[214] By summer, shortages of structurals were being reported, with prices climbing from $363 to $415.[215] The price of reinforcing bars climbed so dramatically that MITI intervened to attempt to stabilize the market.[216]

After extended negotiations between the steel and coal industries (brokered by MITI) a compromise was reached whereby (a) the unit price of domestic coal would be reduced by 1,000 yen/ton [$5.93/ton], (b) the steelmakers would purchase some coal (1.7 million tons) in 1986, and (c) this volume would be progressively reduced through fiscal 1990, when steel industry purchases of domestic coal would cease. *Asahi* (October 25, 1986); *Yomiuri* (October 29, 1986); *Nihon Keizai* (August 22, 1986).

[210] *Japan Metal Bulletin* (July 12, September 25, 1986). Nippon Steel Chairman Takeda commented in *Nihon Keizai* (January 8, 1987) that "We want to expect Government measures for expanding internal demand, for the time being. Internal demand for iron and steel is dominated by that for engineering works and construction. If demand in this sector appears, it will have a big effect on industry circles."

[211] *Japan Metal Bulletin* (November 18, 1986).

[212] *Japan Metal Bulletin* (May 12, 1987).

[213] Between 1977 and 1981, MITI purchased rebars from depressed electric furnace makers and gave them away free to developing countries. The program was instituted to "mitigate the hardship of these steelmakers." $$25 million was committed to this program in 1979-80 and $20.8 million in 1981. *Japan Metal Bulletin* (December 6, 1977, September 2, 30, October 14, 1978; July 8, 1980; March 20, 1982).

[214] *Japan Metal Bulletin* (April 28, 1987).

[215] *Japan Metal Bulletin* (August 6, 1987).

[216] MITI asked the producers of bars to increase their production volume; sought to reduce scrap prices by asking the big 5 steelmakers to release scrap from their inventories; and by holding an "extraordinary meeting" with 13 trading companies, asking them to "refrain from speculative moves" in order to stabilize bar prices. *Japan Metal Bulletin* (October 22, November 2, 1987).

Alarmed by spreading shortages of construction materials, construction firms appealed to the government to rectify the situation, while construction workers rallied in September to protest the inadequacy of the government's actions.[217]

Underlying these developments was not only the new demand stimulated by the government spending measures, but the fact that the Japanese producers were jointly restraining production of construction steel products like structurals and bars in order to raise prices -- or, as the construction workers phrased it, "cornering the market."[218] MITI was obviously concerned that the emergency stimulative measures were becoming too much of a good thing, and it was increasingly compelled to intervene in the market on a day-to-day basis.[219] MITI officials pressed the steelmakers to increase production and warned that "no attempt should be made to raise market prices unreasonably due to supply shortage."[220] An interministerial conference was established to monitor the situation, which included a representative of the JFTC.[221]

In September MITI issued instructions to producers of structurals and bars to increase their production volume to stabilize the market.[222] This move sent the price of steel scrap (the basic raw material used by the electric furnace producers to make these products) soaring -- up 20 percent -- and raised the prospect of scrap shortages. The bar producers therefore requested that MITI moderate its "official request" for increased production.[223] Instead, MITI "requested" that the five major integrated steelmakers release part of their own scrap inventories -- 100,000 tons -- to the electric furnace mills.[224] MITI called an "extraordinary meeting" of trading companies in November, requesting that they "abstain from any speculative moves, so that prices of steel bar may be stabilized soon."[225] In early November, MITI requested that the integrated steelmakers make emergency shipments of slabs to the electric furnace mills to

---

[217] *Japan Metal Bulletin* (September 26, 1987).

[218] *Japan Metal Bulletin* (September 26, 1987). *Metal Bulletin* reported on September 17, 1987 that "though the demand for construction steel is undoubtedly strong, the price hikes have resulted largely from production cutbacks among the mini-mills -- a consequence of reduced shifts, and in some cases, temporary "holidays" for line employees."

[219] *Metal Bulletin* reported on October 12, 1987 that "the increases have put MITI into a quandary. On the one hand, it must support any move which helps the financially ailing steelmakers -- and especially the chronically ill electric sector -- regain what they've lost through the yen's appreciation. But on the other, it is also concerned about the impact the increases will have on consumers such as fabricators and construction companies."

[220] *Japan Metal Bulletin* (September 19, 1987).

[221] *Japan Metal Bulletin* (September 26, 1987).

[222] *Japan Metal Bulletin* (September 19, October 22, 1987).

[223] *Japan Metal Bulletin* (October 31, 1987).

[224] *Ibid.*

[225] *Japan Metal Bulletin* (November 7, 1987).

provide additional raw material for bars.[226] By February 1988 these measures had produced a drop in the price of scrap and an increasing supply of rebars, causing rebar prices to weaken; the rebar producers reportedly responded by jointly implementing 10 to 15 percent production cuts.[227]

The phenomenal increases in demand for construction steel were only the most dramatic manifestation of the government's stimulative measures. The construction boom resulted in a surge in orders for trucks and building machinery, which triggered a sharp increase in demand for sheets and plate. By the third quarter of 1987, the integrated mills' sales to the motor industry had increased by 4.7 percent, and to the machinery industry by 17 percent over the comparable period in 1986.[228] As a result of these unusual developments, quite unexpectedly, the Japanese mills finished 1987 in a profit position. *Metal Bulletin* commented on September 14, 1987

> *The strong demand (and self-imposed "production restraints") for some rolled products has helped push prices up. And while the most spectacular increases have been largely for mini-mill products like reinforcing bars, the prices of integrated mill products like H-shapes have also been pulled up in tandem. The net result is that all the five major blast furnace operators are expected to end the fiscal year in considerably better financial shape.*

EXPORT PATTERNS 1978-1988

The U.S. antidumping actions brought against the Japanese mills in 1977, and the prospect of antidumping duties, led to a curtailment of their efforts to expand their overall U.S. market share, although intense pressure continued in individual product lines; after 1985, Japanese exports to the U.S. were restrained pursuant to a formal voluntary restraint arrangement. Japanese exports to the EC were restricted pursuant to successive agreements on volume and minimum prices. After 1978, while Japanese steel surpluses were still exported in large quantities and at very low prices, they were directed primarily at markets like the Soviet Union, China and the Middle East, where domestic production was unable to satisfy demand. However, such exports do not represent a long-term solution to Japan's massive capacity surplus -- China, the Soviet Union and a number of Middle Eastern countries (Saudi Arabia, Iraq, Algeria, Qatar) are rapidly expanding their own domestic steelmaking capability, a development which will progressively foreclose these export outlets. Ultimately Japan must find still other outlets, or take meaningful steps to curtail its capacity surplus.

---

[226] *Japan Metal Bulletin* (November 10, 1987). The integrated mills agreed to release 60,000 tons of slabs to the electric furnace mills. *Japan Metal Bulletin* (November 17, 1987).

[227] *Metal Bulletin* (February 15, 1988).

[228] *Far Eastern Economic Review* (December 24, 1987).

The European Arrangements

By 1977 a history already existed of attempts by Japan and its principal export competitor, the EC, to divide world export markets and stabilize prices. Japan had entered into an export restraint arrangement with the European Community in 1971; at that time MITI presided over an export cartel of the leading steelmakers designed to limit export volume to the Community to 1,150,000 metric tons per year. This arrangement continued through the end of 1974, but lapsed at the beginning of 1975.[229] During 1975, with no restrictive agreement in effect, Japanese export volume to the Community soared, exceeding in the first six months the volume shipped in all of 1974.[230] In mid-1975, at the request of the Community authorities, Japan agreed to reinstate a quota ceiling of 1,220,000 metric tons, effective through the end of 1977. Japan and the EC also reportedly reached agreements designed to restrict Japan-EC competition in third country markets.[231] *Handelsblatt* reported on October 29/30, 1976, that a market division agreement was also reached:

The Japanese were ceded markets in third countries in the expectation that they would then "as little as possible" disrupt the EC market. This little-publicized agreement worked reasonably well until sometime in the first half of 1976.

In mid-1976, the Japan-EC arrangement came under strain. European producers were irritated by prices quoted by second-rank Japanese electric furnace mills in the EC market.[232] The Europeans retaliated by making offers undercutting Japanese prices in Southeast Asia, Korea and Taiwan -- traditional Japanese export markets.[233] However, Japanese mills curtailed their exports to the EC in early 1977 to levels substantially below those of 1976; at the end of 1977 the Industrial Bank of Japan commented that

In terms of regions, the main absorbers of Japanese exports were the United States, Eastern Europe including the USSR, and countries on

---

[229] The export ceiling was raised to 1,220,000 metric tons in 1973 to reflect the accession of Ireland and Denmark into the Community.

[230] *Nihon Keizai* reported on July 1, 1975 that "as domestic demand for iron and steel is sluggish, the various blast furnace companies are trying to find a way out in exports . . . the exports are concentrated in the . . . EC market." Japanese steelmakers told MITI in a Monday Club meeting that "our exports to the EC have become unprofitable recently." *Ibid.*

[231] *Metal Bulletin* (February 10, 1976)

[232] *Handelsblatt* (October 29/30, 1976). The electric furnace producers had not been party to the export cartel established by the big integrated mills. The electric furnace producers had formed a depression cartel in 1976 and were mounting an export drive to dispose of their surpluses. *Technocrat* (November 1976).

[233] *Metal Bulletin* (December 24, 1976).

the outer fringes of Europe, such as Spain and Greece, while in contrast Japanese steel mills had to impose "voluntary" quotas on exports to the European Economic Community. . . .[234]

In early 1978, the Japanese and the EC concluded a much more comprehensive bilateral agreement. The Japanese agreed not only to restrict their exports to a fixed tonnage, but also to observe minimum price levels in exporting to the EC market.[235] The minimum price agreement all but foreclosed sales of Japanese steel in the Community; by 1981, Japanese exports to the EC totaled only 205 thousand tons, or less than one-fifth the volume of the first six months of 1975, when no restrictions were in effect.[236] The new agreement reportedly provided for the division of export markets between the EC and Japan into respective "spheres of influence" to reduce price competition in these markets.[237]

The Japan-EC export arrangements of the late 1970s were disrupted by the large scale entry of developing country producers into export markets in the early 1980s. That phenomenon, coupled with the recessionary conditions that developed after 1981, resulted in a price collapse in Japan's traditional East Asian export markets.[238]

---

[234] *Quarterly Survey of Japanese Finance and Industry* (October-December 1977), p. 3.

[235] The minimum prices were pegged to the European producers' prices and were designed to ensure that Japanese exports to Europe did not disrupt the Community producers' attempts to increase their internal steel prices.

[236] The *Japan Metal Bulletin* observed on November 26, 1981 that the volume ceilings on Japanese exports to the EEC were nominal since export volume was far below the ceiling, reflecting "the weak competitive power of Japanese steel products on the EC market."

[237] The Japanese "sphere of influence" was said to embrace coastal East Asian markets, India and Pakistan. Market prices were to be established by Japan in this sphere and followed by the Europeans, who were also to observe volume restrictions. The European sphere consisted of the markets west of Suez and the Mediterranean basin; the Europeans were to exercise price leadership in this zone, while the Japanese observed quantitative restrictions. The Middle East, Eastern Europe and China were not restricted with respect to volume, but it was agreed that the Europeans would set prices in China. Any significant deviation from agreed prices and volumes was to be the subject of immediate consultations. The minutes of the March 17-18, 1978 meetings which established this arrangement, together with an exchange of correspondence between the EC Commission and the Japanese government confirming the arrangement, were submitted to the Office of the U.S. Trade Representative in a confidential petition by the American Iron and Steel Institute on December 16, 1982. See also Industrial Bank of Japan, *Quarterly Survey of Japanese Finance and Industry* (January-March 1979), pp. 31, 37-38.

[238] *Nikkei Sangyo* (December 11, 1981; May 24, 1982). Korea's Pohang Iron and Steel Company began undercutting Japanese export prices in the Philippines, Southeast Asia, and South America in 1980, forcing the Japanese mills into defensive price cuts. In 1981, the Japanese reportedly had abandoned efforts to match POSCO's pricing in Southeast Asia, stating that "we will not rise to POSCO's challenge and be drawn into a destructive price war." *Metal Bulletin* (July 18, October 28, November 4, 1980; July 1981).

The United States

In 1978, concurrently with the U.S. government's implementation of the Trigger Price Mechanism, which was designed to provide a quick response to Japanese dumping, Japanese import pressure on the U.S. market slackened. This change was not based on a formal commitment of any kind to the U.S., but was "the consequence of a general consensus within the industry and a fear of antagonizing competitors."[239] Reflecting this self-restraint policy, between 1978 and 1984 Japanese exports accounted for a steady 5.5-6.8 percent of U.S. consumption, at a time when U.S. imports from other sources (notably the developing countries) were increasing dramatically. New outbreaks of dumping in particular product lines were met with trade actions by U.S. producers.

In the fall of 1984, following the announcement of President Reagan's new steel import program, the U.S. Government indicated that it wanted "some kind of agreement" with Japan beyond the informal arrangement already in place.[240] In late 1984, Japan agreed to restrain its exports to the U.S. for five years, limiting sales to 5.8 percent of U.S. consumption, and a formal agreement was signed in early 1985 with quotas established covering sheet and strip, structurals, bars, pipe and tube, and wire.[241] MITI chaired a round of meetings among the Japanese producers to agree on a sharing out of the U.S. export quotas using each company's past shipments to the U.S. as a benchmark.

Under the current voluntary restraint arrangement, the Japanese mills do not confront the prospect of antidumping actions by U.S. producers. In the absence of an agreement, however, the underlying conditions which gave rise to dumping and trade litigation in the 1970s -- Japanese overcapacity and cartelization -- remain present and could result in a new period of trade friction with the U.S. In the interim, Japanese producers have undertaken a substantial amount of direct investment in the U.S. steel industry, which is seen, in part, as a way of circumventing trade restrictions. Kawasaki Steel and a Brazilian firm jointly own California Steel, which processes imported slabs into flat-rolled products. Nippon Kokan has acquired a 50 percent interest in National Steel, and numerous joint ventures have been established in the U.S. between Japanese and U.S. producers.[242]

---

[239] Hugh Patrick and Hido Sato, "The Political Economy of United States-Japan Trade in Steel," in Kozo Yamamura, ed., *Policy and Trade Issues of the Japanese Economy* (1982), p. 227.

[240] *Metal Bulletin* (October 26, 1984).

[241] *BNA International Trade Reporter* (May 22, 1985).

[242] Nisshin Steel and Wheeling-Pittsburgh have a joint venture galvanizing line in West Virginia, and Sumitomo and LTV have a joint venture electrogalvanizing line in Ohio. Nippon Steel and Inland Steel agreed in 1987 to jointly construct a continuous cold-rolling tandem mill. U.S.I.T.C., *Steel Sheet and Strip Industry*, pp. 9-14.

Other Export Markets

The reduction of export volume to the U.S. and Europe would have posed a far more serious dilemma for the Japanese mills in the late 1970s and early 1980s had they not been able to expand their sales to other markets, particularly China, the Middle East, and the Soviet Union. The fact that Japanese access to these markets may be curtailed during the coming decade raises the prospect that Japanese steel could be diverted to other makrets, including the U.S. By 1983 China had become Japan's leading export market, absorbing 7.2 million tons of Japanese steel (as opposed to 4.6 million tons for the U.S.). Prices to China and the USSR were generally lower than on Japanese domestic sales -- in effect, Japanese mills were dumping in these markets. Japanese industry spokesmen told the U.S. International Trade Commission staff in 1987 that they were losing money on export sales to China, and that the price to China was only about two-thirds the average export price to other markets.[243] To the extent that exporting surpluses at prices covering incremental costs remains an element of the Japanese industry's strategy, its focus has shifted to markets where such practices did not provoke trade policy responses by foreign governments.[244] This shift in trading patterns has been facilitated by the Export-Import Bank of Japan, which provided extremely generous long-term low interest financing for Japanese steel export sales to the Chinese and Soviets.[245]

International Price Arrangements, 1986-1988

In the wake of the sharp appreciation of the yen which began in mid-1985, the Japanese mills' need for a general increase in export prices became more urgent, and the Japanese producers reportedly became more active in seeking international arrangements designed to ensure price stability and export price increases. In 1986 the Japanese rebar producers began sending "observers" to meetings of IREPAS, the International Rebar Producers Association, which periodically meets to agree on world rebar price levels and production

---

[243] U.S.I.T.C., *Steel Sheet and Strip Industry*, pp. 9-10.

[244] There were exceptions to this general pattern. Canadian producers complained in 1986 that the Japanese mills were dumping cold-rolled sheet in Canada and a Japanese firm reportedly was selling structurals in Britain at prices 10,000 yen/ton [$59.34/ton] lower than in the Japanese market. *Metal Bulletin* (May 7, November 7, 1986).

[245] In 1976, MITI arranged for the first Japan Export-Import Bank financing of steel exports to China. A loan (reportedly $50 million at 7.5 percent, with a 3-4 year grace period) was granted to finance export of seamless and line pipe for a new Chinese petrochemical complex. In 1981, the Soviets purchased 700 thousand tons of large caliber steel pipe from Japanese firms, a sale worth over $360 million in revenue. The purchase was financed by a loan from the Japan Export-Import Bank at a rate of 8 percent over a 5 year period. (These terms undercut the so-called "consensus rate" -- a minimum interest rate agreed by OECD nations for such export financing packages, which at the time was 9.25 percent). *Japan Metal Bulletin* (October 21, November 28, December 3, 1981). The Japan Export-Import Bank was soon granting extraordinarily generous financing terms to clinch steel sales to the Soviet Union.

volume.[246] In mid-1987, press accounts began appearing to the effect that the Japanese and European mills had entered into a "conspiracy" to raise export prices worldwide, citing in particular joint actions on cold-rolled sheets and hot coil.[247] In early 1987 MITI approved the formation of an export cartel for the four producers of seamless pipe, designed to stabilize export prices for this product at about $800 per ton.[248] At the same time, *Metal Bulletin* reported (February 6, 1987) that seamless pipe prices were recovering, and that this was not attributable "to a firmer market:"

> *It is understood that a number of meetings have taken place between European, Japanese and Latin American producers, resulting in the current higher price levels. The Japanese made the first move, raising their export prices for seamless tube by $100 a ton, and European mills, it is understood, will be taking similar action.*

Until Japan substantially reduces its current capacity surplus, the potential remains for a relapse into the countercyclical exporting pattern, involving widespread dumping, which characterized the 1960-78 period. Japan possesses a capacity surplus which is larger in 1988 than it was in 1975-77, when the most massive exports to the U.S. occurred, and the cartelized domestic market makes dumping feasible. Significantly in this regard, the Japanese integrated mills continue to practice the two-tier pricing strategy (high domestic price, lower export price) in a number of major world markets. In 1986 Japanese pipe producers expressed their "grave concern" that Japanese hot-rolled sheet was being exported to Korea at a price lower than the Japanese domestic price, giving Korean pipemakers a major advantage,[249] and in 1987, the Japanese mills put a cap on their export volume to China because they wanted to reserve capacity for more profitable domestic sales.[250] During recessionary periods in the 1980s, the electric furnace producers have continued to export their products at prices substantially below domestic levels, usually in conjunction with joint production curtailments.[251] Japanese dumping in the U.S. market has occurred

---

[246] *Japan Metal Bulletin* (April 17, 1986).

[247] *Metal Bulletin* (June 16, 1987).

[248] *Asahi* (March 18, 1987).

[249] *Japan Metal Bulletin* (January 30, 1986).

[250] "The steelmakers will have to stand by the policy of more profits on the limited production, and in this sense, their voluminous exports of steel products at comparatively low prices to China should have certain limitations." *Japan Metal Bulletin* (February 26, 1987).

[251] *Nihon Keizai* observed on August 6, 1981 that as rebar production curtailments were implemented by the electric furnace mills pursuant to a formal cartel, export prices declined in "inverse proportion" to the rise in domestic prices, as the steelmakers found an "outlet" for their surpluses. In June 1981-82, the Japanese rebar producers found a formal production cartel, implementing joint production cuts to raise domestic prices. This triggered a surge in Japanese rebar exports, which was felt all over the world -- plunging Japanese rebar prices were reported

in some steel product lines, such as seamless pipes.[252] Finally, the recent shifts in exchange rates make it increasingly difficult for Japanese mills to export to the U.S. market at prices which cover their cost of production -- in effect, to sell in the U.S. market without dumping.

in China, the Soviet Union, Saudi Arabia, the United States, and Southeast Asia. *American Metal Market* (May 21, June 8, 1982); *Metal Bulletin* (June 15, 1982). In June 1982 the export price of Japanese rebars was falling so rapidly that one trading company suspended trading until market prices stabilized. *Metal Bulletin* (June 15, 1982). In October 1982 the ASEAN nations petitioned Japan to restrict its rebar exports "because the ASEAN markets are hit by a surge of imports of Japanese small bar at lower prices than the Japanese market prices." *Japan Metal Bulletin* (October 9, 1982).

[252] *Certain Steel Pipe and Tubes from Japan*, January 11, 1983 (48 F.R. 1206).

5

The Developing Countries

Prior to 1960, total annual raw steel capacity in all of the developing countries combined was only about 10 million metric tons. During the decade of the 1960s, several developing countries, notably Brazil, Mexico, India and South Korea, made serious efforts to expand their steelmaking capacity. Nevertheless, by 1970 even these countries remained wholly unable to satisfy their domestic steel needs.[1]

Beginning in the early 1970s, however, an extraordinary burst of steelmaking capacity expansion took place throughout the developing world. Many developing countries had accumulated significant amounts of capital as a result of rising world prices for industrial raw materials, energy and agricultural products. Large amounts of additional capital became available as investors in developed countries began to increase their debt and equity participation in developing country industrialization. Using this new wealth, many developing countries launched steelmaking expansion efforts which were both qualitatively and quantitatively far more ambitious than anything previously undertaken. As the Central Intelligence Agency noted at the end of the 1970s,

> LDCs [developing countries] began purchasing large-scale, fully integrated steel plants incorporating modern steelmaking technology. Unlike the 1950s and 1960s, associated engineering and training services also were purchased, helping to ensure optimum utilization of plant capacity. Thus, the LDCs installed large chunks of steelmaking capacity capable of producing products that could be competitive in global markets.[2]

---

[1] U.S. Central Intelligence Agency, National Foreign Assessment Center, *The Burgeoning LDC Steel Industry: More Problems for Major Steel Producers* (Washington, D.C.: CIA, 1979).

[2] *Ibid.*

By the late 1970s, over 50 developing countries possessed steelmaking facilities and over two dozen had constructed integrated steelworks. By 1986, the volume of developing country raw steel capacity reached 122 million metric tons, almost triple the level that existed in 1970. While the capacity expansion was concentrated in only a handful of developing countries, it was significant enough that the developing countries as a group possessed capacity in excess of domestic consumption requirements by the early 1980s (figure 5-1).[3] The technological level of many developing countries' steel facilities was superb; they often featured production equipment acquired from suppliers in the industrialized countries. By 1986, a number of developing countries (which had little or no continuous casting capability in 1973) were able to raise their continuous casting ratio to a level higher than that of the industries of the United States, Canada, and a number of European countries.[4]

Virtually all of this growth resulted from the initiatives of developing country governments.[5] The steel projects undertaken in the 1970s were too vast, too costly, and far too unlikely to produce a satisfactory return on investment to have been attempted by private entrepreneurs. Governments provided capital, planning, and infrastructure for the establishment of new facilities, and provided the guarantees needed to attract large foreign debt and equity investments in the new projects. As the new plants came on stream, governments took the measures needed to ensure their continued operation, providing protection from imports, subsidies to offset operating losses, successive injections of new capital, and incentives to promote export competitiveness.

Government Financial Assistance

The ambitious steelmaking expansion projects launched by the developing countries in the 1970s could never have been financed by domestic entrepreneurial capital. Even in nations such as Brazil where the private sector possessed substantial resources, no private investor or group of investors would have been willing to commit hundreds of millions of dollars to projects which entailed such high risks as the establishment of a greenfield

---

[3] In 1986, seven countries accounted for two-thirds of all steel capacity in the developing world: Argentina, Brazil, India, Korea, Mexico, Taiwan and Venezuela.

[4] Taiwan, Korea, Venezuela, and Argentina.

[5] As Venezuela's Marcelino Barquin, President of that country's Metallurgy and Mining Industry Association, put it in 1976, "When we speak of producing 15 million tons of steel we are implying that we have to invest 50 billion bolivares [$11.7 billion], train 48,000 workers who will work directly in the industry; that industry generates indirect employment for 960,000 workers and that, therefore, concrete plans must be devised to provide housing, water, energy, education, sanitation and transportation. To do all this over a period of 10 to 15 years involves a titanic effort that can only be achieved if there is a centralizing body with sufficient authority to plan and coordinate the development of the country's steel and iron industry." *El Universal* (August 8, 1976).

Figure 5−1: Developing Countries' Raw Steel Capacity and Consumption, 1960−1986

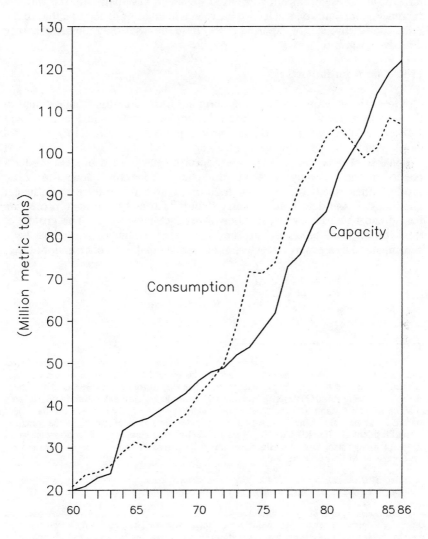

Source: Capacity data, see figure 2−3; consumption (in ingot equivalents) from table 2−4.

integrated steel mill.[6] Accordingly, in every developing country, the state was required to assume the primary role of provider of capital.

Once the steel plants became operational, developing country governments undertook a wide variety of measures to ensure that their steel exports were price-competitive internationally. The most common measures included the provision of subsidized government loans to cover the cost of steel produced for export, tax exemptions for exported steel, and devaluation of the national currency, sometimes on a selective basis, in a manner designed to enhance the price-competitiveness of exported steel. In many cases operating losses were directly subsidized.[7]

Protection from Imports

Government protection from imports has formed an essential element in the growth of steel industries in the developing countries in the 1970s and 1980s. Because steel products are basic commodities essential to industrial development, no developing country can restrict steel imports altogether; national steel industries can never produce the entire array of steel products needed by the economy. Instead, protection is generally extended to those product lines which the national industry is able to produce in sufficient quantities; as the developing country steel industries have grown, protection has spread to an increasing number of product categories.[8] The growth of steel production capability in the developing countries has thus been accompanied by a progressive closure of markets that were once major outlets

---

[6] Brazil's 1972-75 Phase II expansion plan, for example, was financed by the state steel companies themselves, by the government, and by the World Bank. Private investors were not seriously considered because the chronically poor financial history and prospects of the state-owned firms made them unattractive investments. Even the World Bank refused to participate in South Korea's Pohang Iron and Steel Project, which it regarded as an investment that would not prove commercially viable. On October 11, 1979 *American Metal Market* noted the comment of the President of SIDERBRÁS, Brazil's state steel holding company: "Why do we insist on creating the large steelworks? he asks, rhetorically. The large mill is so expensive only the state has the means to finance it, he said."

[7] See *El Universal* (March 28, 1984); *Metal Bulletin* (February 7, 1984) (Venezuela); *Metal Bulletin* (December 6, 1983) (Zimbabwe), and the country studies in this section.

[8] For example, in 1981 Taiwan's state-owned China Steel Corporation (CSC) developed the capability to produce certain high-grade steel slabs and rods. The Taipei *China Post* reported on August 24, 1981 that "it is expected that after the firm begins producing such products locally, the government will probably impose import restrictions on similar products from abroad." As CSC's hot-rolling and cold-rolling facilities came on stream, the Taiwanese government imposed import licensing requirements on hot coil and cold-rolled sheets that amounted to a virtual ban. *Metal Bulletin* (September 25, October 5, 1982).

for steel produced by developed nations.[9]   As one Japanese newspaper commented in 1983,

> Steel material import restrictions on such items as rods have spread among Southeast Asian countries. Over the last year and this year, Korea, Taiwan, Malaysia and Indonesia, one after another, have hammered out strict import restriction policies. Because of the worldwide economic depression, they are attempting to protect their own steel manufacturing companies from the offending import products. With their increasing ability to supply their own needs from new facilities, and the lack of foreign currency in developing countries, import restrictions have had a tendency to spread to even oil producing countries like Nigeria and Mexico. . . . The President of the Tokyo Steel Co. said that among Southeast Asian countries, the only market to which we can export is Singapore.[10]

Protection has generally been implemented through a government authority which screens all proposed import transactions, usually in consultation with the national steel producers. In Brazil, for example, imports considered "superfluous" are prohibited altogether and all other imports are subject to the discretionary grant of import licenses by CACEX, the foreign trade department of the Bank of Brazil.[11] Proposed steel imports must be approved by SIDERBRÁS, the state-owned holding company that controls

---

[9] *Metal Bulletin* reported on March 16, 1979 that as Brazilian steelmaking capacity came on stream, Japan was losing its export market in Brazil, product line by product line. "In Brazil, steel imports are limited to products which are not produced locally. . . . In the case of heavy plate . . . Brazil is itself an exporter. HR sheets can also be supplied from local sources with imports of the latter product only needed on an *ad hoc* basis when supplies are tight. . . . ACESITA has recently installed plants to produce [stainless steel sheet and electrical sheet] and therefore imports are likely to fall as domestic capacity is brought into the market." As Nigeria's President Shagari opened the nation's first steel mill in 1982, he proclaimed that "Nigeria would no longer be a dumping ground for the cheap steel products of other countries. . . . As soon as our steel products [are] ready for the market, policy measures on steel imports, pricing and distribution [will] be put into effect to safeguard the interests of the nation. . . ." Kaduna *New Nigerian* (January 30, 1982).

[10] *Nikkei Sangyo* (April 2, 1983); see also *Nippon Kogyo* (August 12, 1982); *Nikkei Sangyo* (May 24, 1982). Malaysia imposed an "indefinite ban" on imports of steel bars on November 25, 1982; *Metal Bulletin* reported (November 30, 1982) that a government spokesman indicated the ban was necessary "to ensure the healthy development of the domestic steel industry, which had been threatened by 'dumping' on the part of major foreign producers."

[11] Brazil's government policy toward steel imports has consistently been one of maintaining "prudent protective measures in the case of imports." Minister of Industry and Commerce, in *O Globo* (May 25, 1971). SIDERBRÁS possesses the authority to prohibit "unnecessary" steel imports. Steel importers cannot seek Central Bank authorization of a proposed import transaction without obtaining prior clearance from SIDERBRÁS.

much of Brazil's steel production.[12] Thus, in Brazil as in many other developing countries, the domestic steel industry effectively controls access to its own home market.

Developing Country Governments and Foreign Assistance

During the 1970s and 1980s the industrialized nations have poured tens of billions of dollars in capital into the expansion of steelmaking in the developing countries, and have provided them with modern equipment, technical assistance, and training. Developing country governments and their foreign aid benefactors have developed mutually reinforcing relationships which have facilitated this process (table 5-1). Governments have sought capital and equipment from foreign lenders and suppliers, who have in turn sought assurances that the government will provide guarantees for their investment, in the form of matching government equity investments, loan guarantees, subsidized credit, protection from imports, infrastructural improvements, and competent government oversight of the industry's operations.[13]

Export Financing. When the world steel recession developed in 1974, a number of leading steel producers in the industrialized nations began to see the export of production equipment to the developing countries as a means of offsetting the slackening demand for steel products. Competition among Western nations to sell such equipment to the developing countries intensified, and export financing by national export-import banks played a critically important role in determining which nation would win a particular bid.[14] The developing countries found that they could secure extraordinarily favorable financing for new steel plants simply by playing off Western countries' export financing institutions against each other.

Between 1977 and 1980, an estimated $7.8 billion in export credits were advanced by Western government institutions to finance steel projects in the developing countries, and in the 1980s, virtually every major steel project in the developing countries has involved export credit financing, usually on

---

[12] In addition to those measures, Brazil has imposed a 25 percent "financial operations tax" on imports and temporary tariff increases, to a maximum of 205 percent *ad valorem*.

[13] As one observer commented in the *Southeast Asia Iron and Steel Institute Quarterly* (April 1980): "Such government measures have made investments in LDCs considerably more attractive, in many cases, than investment in the United States. Very often governments, both national and provincial, will be in there bidding with tax holidays, infrastructure provision, favorable power and freight rates, protection against imports, preferential government purchasing policies and the like. . . ."

[14] France, for example, has been aggressive in offering favorable terms for financing steel equipment exports. Japanese steelmakers, who have competed with the French for some projects, reportedly complained of the French that "the President rushes in, carrying a bag filled with funds." *Nihon Keizai* (June 18, 1981).

extremely favorable terms to the buyer. While the OECD maintains "consensus" interest rates designed to fix minimum rates for export financing, those rates have been undercut in practice in the intense competition to win export contracts -- thus enabling developing countries to obtain capital for expansion projects at far below market rates.[15]

Table 5-1. Role of Developing Country Governments and Foreign Institutions In Establishing Steel Industries

	Developing Country Government	International Development Banks	Foreign Private Commercial Banking Syndicates	Foreign Export-Import Banks	Foreign Equipment Suppliers
Equity Capital	Provides equity contribution	Seeks assurances of government equity contribution	——	——	Occasional participation
Domestic Loans	Provides low interest loans	Seeks assurances of government loans	——	——	————
Foreign Loans	Guarantees loans	Provides loans and helps arrange private financing	Provides loans	Export Financing	Occasional loans in connection with equipment financing
Protection from Imports	Provides protection	Benefits from protection	Benefits from	Benefits from protection	protection
Infrastructure	Provides needed Improvements	May provide loans	May provide loans	————	May assist with infrastructure improvements
Steelmaking Equipment	May subsidize purchases of domestically made equipment	————	————	Export financing for equipment	Provide equipment
Export Subsidies and incentives	Provides subsidies and incentives	May seek incentives to ensure repayment	May seek incentives to ensure repayment	May seek incentives to ensure repayment	————
Planning and Technical Aid	Provides central planning for industry	Seeks coordinated government planning	————	————	Provide technical and planning assistance

Development Banks. International development banks, notably the World Bank, played an important role in financing the expansion of developing country steelmaking capacity, particularly in Latin America. Prior to 1983 the World Bank had extended slightly over $1 billion in loans to finance 54 iron

---

[15] The Export-Import Bank of Japan (a nation with low domestic interest rates and inflation) long offered rates beneath the OECD consensus rates. Thus when the consensus rate was 10.7 percent in 1983, Japan's rates were about 8.1 percent. Moreover, in the international competition to obtain contracts, the Japanese rate is itself often undercut.

and steel projects in the developing countries, loans which were frequently co-financed by international lenders which usually extended far larger sums than the World Bank (tables 5-2 and 5-3).[16] By providing limited amounts of financing for such projects and by acting as a catalyst for lending from other sources, the international development banks have been an important stimulus for lending by the developed countries to the developing countries.[17] These banks have also reinforced the role of national governments in the planning and financing of their steel industries, although the role of the banks has at times been so great that they have been accused of infringing on the sovereignty of recipient countries.[18]

In the late 1970s, the World Bank's appraisal of its own lending practices led to a reappraisal of its policies. The structural recession and the commissioning of many new steelworks had produced global oversupply and declining prices, and many of the steel projects financed by Bank loans were "poorly managed, underutilized," and in some cases, "shut down" entirely. In the early 1980s, the Bank shifted its emphasis away from discrete project lending toward technical and advisory support and the design of long-term steel strategies for developing nations.[19] In 1988, however, in another major policy shift, the Bank approved a $400 million loan to Mexico to finance the

---

[16] As of June 30, 1987, the World Bank had $1.4 billion in loans outstanding to developing countries for iron and steel projects; approximately half of these loans were made in Latin America. World Bank *Annual Report* 1987, p. 216. The U.S. International Trade Commission observed in 1988 with respect to steel projects that "by concentrating on helping developing countries acquire funds from other private and multilateral agencies, the World Bank tries to mitigate its funding limitations. These types of activities are time consuming as World Bank staff members must convince financiers of the soundness of the recommended policies and coordinate lending objectives and approaches." U.S.I.T.C., *Steel Sheet and Strip Industry*, pp. 4-10.

[17] The Inter-American Development Bank (IDB) is an international financial institution that provides development financing in Latin America. Between 1971 and 1985 the IDB made loans totaling $451 million to steelmaking projects in Mexico, Argentina, Brazil and Venezuela, representing about 4 percent of all lending involved in the projects supported. Like the World Bank, the IDB's principal role is one of a catalyst to increase confidence of other lenders. U.S.I.T.C., *Steel Sheet and Strip Industry*, pp. 4-16, based on interviews with IDB staff.

[18] In 1976, the World Bank charged Brazil's National Iron and Steel Company (CSN) with delaying its expansion plans. Shortly thereafter, the company's leadership was reshuffled for "administrative reasons," provoking charges that the Bank might have influenced this decision. Brazilian Senator Itamor Franco, government deputy leader, rejected this charge, stating that "The Brazilian government does not accept foreign interference in domestic affairs." *Brasilia Domestic Service*, 22:00 GMT, September 3, 1976, Foreign Broadcast Information Service. See also *O Estado de São Paulo* (May 29, 1977).

[19] U.S.I.T.C., *Steel Sheet and Strip Industry*, pp. 4-10, based on interviews with World Bank officials.

restructuring of its steel industry, and indicated it would consider loans to any other country with an approach similar to Mexico.[20]

Table 5-2. World Bank Loans to Steel Projects in Developing Countries

Year	Country	Capacity (million metric tons)	Bank Loan (million $)	Total Investment Costs (million $)
1972	Brazil	1.30	64.5	785.0
1972	Brazil	1.40	64.5	998.3
1972	Brazil	1.50	63.0	898.4
1972	Turkey	0.90	76.0	433.3
1973	Mexico	1.00	70.0	962.8
1974	Rumania	0.15	70.0	174.4
1975	Brazil	2.20	95.0	2,714.8
1976	Brazil	1.10	60.0	2,208.6
1978	Turkey	0.50	95.0	150.0
1979	Rumania	0.25	40.0	137.4
1980	Egypt	0.30	64.0	98.9
1981	Egypt	0.75	165.3	769.0
Total		11.35	927.3	10,330.9

Source: World Bank, "Bank Operations in Steel (1970-87)," cited in U.S. International Trade Commission. *U.S. Global Competitiveness: Steel Sheet and Strip Industry*, U.S.I.T.C. Pub. No. 2050, January 1988.

---

[20] *Metal Bulletin* (March 17, 1988). The Mexican government made commitments to decontrol domestic steel prices, liberalize trade restrictions, and eliminate indirect subsidies to the steel industry. The World Bank document addressing the loan acknowledged the risk that the Mexican government "might delay or shelve measures on complete price decontrol and return to higher protection." *Ibid.*

Table 5-3. Planned Financing of SICARTSA's Stage II Project, 1976
(million U.S. dollars)

	Phase A[1]	Phase B[2]	Total
Equity			
Mexican Government Capital Increase	$1,040.7	$ 77.0	$1,117.7
SICARTSA Cash Generation	851.1	159.8	1,010.9
Loans			
World Bank	95.0	—	95.0
Inter American Development Bank	95.0	—	95.0
Bilateral Export Credits	1,158.3	363.1	1,521.4
Mexican Government Nafinsa (Government Development Bank)	409.6	637.5	447.1
Total	$3,649.7	$637.4	4,287.1

Source: World Bank
[1] Installation of all steelmaking and hot-rolling capacity and one-half of ironmaking capacity. Completion planned for 1979.
[2] Installation of remaining ironmaking capacity, cold-rolling and finishing facilities. Completion planned for 1983.

Commercial Banks. A substantial proportion of the developing country steel industry development of the 1970s and 1980s has been financed by syndicates of private commercial banks in the U.S., Western Europe, and Japan. The oil price increases following the oil crises of 1974-75 and 1979-80 generated huge trade surpluses for oil exporting countries, who deposited a substantial portion of these surpluses in commercial banks in the West. A highly competitive lending environment developed as these institutions sought borrowers for the "petrodollars."[21] Such loans were facilitated in the 1970s by the innovation of "floating" interest rates. The loans were particularly attractive to lenders because the developing country government concerned guaranteed repayment.[22] Lenders offered developing countries virtually unlimited credit, often with only a cursory examination of the industrial investments contemplated.[23]

The Debt Crisis

The heady, even feverish lending environment of the late 1970s collapsed in the early 1980s. The rising energy costs, interest rates, and inflation that accompanied the second oil crisis in 1979-80 had a severe effect on the economies of the developing countries. Dollar interest rates rose sharply, dramatically increasing the debt burden of developing countries that had borrowed at floating interest rates. The non-OPEC developing countries were forced to borrow additional billions, often at floating interest rates, to finance imports of energy products.[24] By 1981 the external debt of some developing countries was reaching critical levels; nevertheless, a number of these nations opted to continue with their heavy investment programs, usually financed by additional borrowing, hoping that completed industrial projects

---

[21] U.S. International Trade Commission, *Developing Country Debt-Servicing Problems*, p. 1. On February 20, 1978 the Rio de Janeiro *O Globo* reported that "FRANCEFI, an entity established by the [French] government to regulate the participation of French public and private banks in international lending, is currently operating with Brazil on an unlimited credit basis. [A French banker] claimed that the same procedure had been adopted by a large number of European bankers, who are even vying for participation in the pools or making isolated bids. . . ." According to one French banker, Brazil enjoyed "unlimited credits in Europe and facilities for obtaining loans for any development project." Jacques Miot in *O Globo* (February 20, 1978).

[22] D.P. Dod, "Bank Lending to Developing Countries," in 67 *Federal Reserve Bulletin* 647 (September 1981). In 1981 the U.S. General Accounting Office noted with respect to Brazil's plan to establish a new greenfield integrated steelworks, AÇOMINAS, that would become the largest in Latin America, "The project is being financed with full and unconditional guarantees of the Federative Republic of Brazil. Such a guarantee is probably essential to attract foreign financing because of the unlimited risks involved in such a huge venture." Government Accounting Office, *New Strategy Required for Aiding Distressed Steel Industry* (Washington, D.C.: GPO, January 8, 1981), pp. 5-21.

[23] Geoffrey Bell, President of Geoffrey Bell & Co., commented that "600 banks who had little or no experience in international lending joined the international syndicated credit market in the 1970s. Now, to say that their knowledge of the borrowers was modest would give them a great deal of the benefit of doubt. Most of them didn't know where the countries were within a radius of several hundred miles. . . . Regulators say 'you lent money to Venezuela, where is your country risk assessment?' When you open the file you say 'There is a clipping from *The Economist*, there is something from Citibank, something from *Forbes* magazine, there's our country risk assessment.'" *American Metal Market* (April 11, 1984).

[24] Dod, "Bank Lending to Developing Countries."

would enable them to produce goods for export and generate foreign exchange with which to service their debt.

In 1982 the world entered into a severe recession -- just as many of the new steel facilities in the developing countries were becoming operational. The domestic economies of countries such as Argentina, Brazil and Mexico experienced a sharp fall in steel demand at the same moment that they possessed new, underutilized production facilities, a steel surplus, and in many cases, a huge foreign debt. The only logical recourse appeared to be to use the new mills to export steel, generating foreign exchange to service their debts. *American Metal Market* reported on July 31, 1983 that

> *Latin American steelmakers served notice . . . this week that despite growing "protectionism" in developed countries they intend to maintain or increase their exports to these critical markets in order to help pay off their staggering foreign debts. . . . With such nations as Mexico and Brazil groaning under a total foreign debt of about $175 billion, most of this to banks in industrialized nations, the "gloves are off" when it comes to pushing Latin American steel products overseas.*

The surge of steel exports from developing countries into Western markets which occurred after 1981 was seen by many observers as evidence of a fundamental shift in "comparative advantage" in steelmaking away from the industrialized countries to the developing world; this shift was seen as a reflection of lower labor costs and the proximity of deposits of high quality coal and iron ore, which, when combined with modern production equipment, would result in an unbeatable cost advantage. A closer examination of the steel industries of the developing countries, however, reveals that this perspective is simplistic.

Some developing country producers, such as South Korea's POSCO and Taiwan's China Steel, are highly productive and efficient by world standards. Many other developing country steel producers, however, have lurched from one crisis to the next, plagued by mismanagement, civil disorders, labor unrest, corruption, high energy costs, and seemingly endless operating losses. Poorly sited and ill-conceived steel projects have become "white elephants, monsters which gobble up lots of money and at best simulate usefulness."[25] Such crisis-ridden producers, which account for much of the total steelmaking capacity in the developing world, have been able to survive and establish a presence on the international market only through massive and sustained government support -- domestic and export subsidies, and protection from imports. They are not "competitive" as that term is generally understood in market economies, and certainly do not enjoy a competitive edge. Thus, ironically, while some analysts decry the imposition of countervailing and antidumping duties by the EC, Canada, and the United States as "protectionist" rear guard

---

[25] *Suddeutsche Zeitung* (February 10, 1984).

measures to preserve "noncompetitive" industries, developing countries defend their own protectionist policies on the grounds -- in many cases accurate -- that if restrictions were lifted, the domestic steel industry "just [could not] face the fight,"[26] and would "certainly [be] wiped . . . off the map."[27]

BRAZIL

The expansion of Brazil's steel industry over the past two decades is the largest yet implemented in the developing world. Planned and largely financed by government agencies, which borrowed heavily abroad to raise the needed funds, the Brazilian effort in steel involved the investment of tens of billions of dollars in the construction of three greenfield integrated facilities and the expansion of three existing state-owned integrated mills. Between 1973 and 1987, Brazilian crude steel output more than tripled, from 7.1 million metric tons to 22.2 million metric tons per year. In the 1980s, as Brazilian capacity has grown, domestic steel demand has not kept pace; apparent consumption of steel in 1986 amounted to less than 14.5 million metric tons. Nevertheless, Brazil's new National Steel Plan, announced in late 1986, visualizes the expansion of capacity to 50 million metric tons by the year 2000.

The Brazilian economy has been mired in a protracted crisis since 1980-81 as a result of the nation's foreign debt, which currently exceeds $112 billion. Having borrowed heavily to finance industrial growth in the 1970s, Brazil desperately needs to expand exports in order to improve its balance of payments position. The steel industry, now producing large annual surpluses, is a natural source of export earnings. Driven by the need to continue operation of their plants, by an array of government export subsidies, and by successive currency devaluations, the Brazilian steelmakers have entered world markets aggressively and established a major presence which, if anything, is likely to expand further in the next decade.

The Brazilian steel export drive has little or nothing to do with *laissez faire* competition, as that notion is generally understood in the West. The Brazilian state steel producers could not survive without continuing injections of government funds and could not continue their aggressive export pricing without the assurance of state backing. The Brazilian steel export effort reflects a series of past decisions -- on the part of the government, to overinvest in steel expansion, and on the part of foreign lenders, to finance that overinvestment. Now the only way out of Brazil's dilemma appears to be the use of its new plants to expand exports "whatever the cost."

---

[26] *Maeil Kjongje Sinmun* (May 2, 1986) (South Korea).

[27] *Review of the River Plate* (June 23, 1978) (Argentina).

264

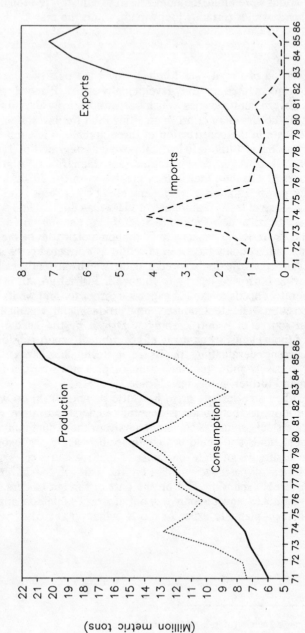

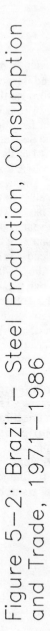

(Million metric tons)

Figure 5-2: Brazil — Steel Production, Consumption and Trade, 1971–1986

Source: International Iron and Steel Institute, Steel Statistical Yearbook, 1981, 1987. Production and Consumption refer to crude steel; Exports and Imports refer to semi-finished and finished steel.

The Expansion of the Brazilian Steel Industry

Brazil is a "mixed" economy with a long tradition of government intervention, driven by Brazilian nationalism, national security concerns, and aspirations to greatness and self-sufficiency. While it has been governed alternately by military regimes and civilian governments with both "left" and "right" predilections, all segments of society have embraced the notion that the state should actively promote economic growth. Recognizing the need for a private business sector, the Brazilian government has established state enterprises primarily in "empty" sectors such as integrated steelmaking and oil, which were deemed essential to national development but in which investment, if left to the private sector, would not have occurred.[28]

The National Steel Plan. By the mid-1960s Brazil already possessed an established integrated steel industry, dominated by three large state-owned enterprises, COSIPA, CSN, and USIMINAS. However, a combination of government-imposed price controls and mismanagement had left these firms in a weak financial position when, in the late 1960s, it became apparent that a major expansion of the existing steel production base would be required if the government's ambitious development plans were to be achieved.[29] In 1968, the Consultative Council for the Steel Industry (CONSIDER) was formed in an attempt to rectify some of the industry's most severe problems. It was charged with studying the national steel market, defining a steel policy suited to that market, and providing the technical support necessary for the expansion of the industry.[30] Five years later, the government consolidated the state-owned enterprises in one holding company, Siderurgia Brasileira (SIDERBRÁS).[31]

---

[28] Jorge I. Domínguez, "Order and Progress in Brazil," in *Ideology and National Competitiveness*, George C. Lodge and Ezra Vogel, eds. (Boston: Harvard Business School Press, 1987), pp. 256-257.

[29] T.J. Trebat, *Brazil's State-Owned Enterprises* (Cambridge: Cambridge University Press, 1983), pp. 227-228.

[30] F. Magalhães, *História da Siderurgia no Brasil* (São Paulo: Editora da Universidade de São Paulo, 1983), p. 383.

[31] *Ibid.* Brazil's state-owned steel enterprises currently account for approximately 70 percent of the nation's crude steel output. SIDERBRÁS exercises operational control over numerous steelmaking subsidiaries, including Brazil's five largest integrated steel producers, CSN, COSIPA, USIMINAS, CST and AÇOMINAS. *Siderurgia Latinoamericana* (April 1987) ("Desarollo de Recursos Humanos y Technologías Domésticas: La Experiencia de la Industria Siderúrgica Brasileña"), p. 44. A few additional companies are in the hands of government entities other than SIDERBRÁS. For instance, the state-owned Bank of Brazil owns an 82 percent share of ACESITA, a special steels producer (*Metal Bulletin* (July 30, 1985)) and the National Economic and Social Development Bank holds a controlling interest in the Nossa Senhora Aparecida steelworks. *Metal Bulletin* (September 7, 1987).

In 1970, CONSIDER developed a comprehensive National Steel Plan, pursuant to which the government undertook a major capacity expansion program. [32] This so-called "Phase II" effort focused primarily on upgrading the existing facilities of the three major state-owned firms. Private capital markets were disregarded as sources of funds for this project because the public steel sector had a poor financial record and the prospects for an adequate return were poor.[33] Much of the funding was therefore provided by BNDES, the National Bank for Economic and Social Development.[34] In a pattern that was to become familiar in subsequent years, the cost of Phase II greatly exceeded projections and the government, which had originally envisioned a contribution of around $300 million, was eventually forced to provide nearly half the funding, close to $1 billion.[35] Phase II was plagued by delays and by a progressive worsening of the financial condition of the three state-owned companies as they borrowed to raise funds to support the expansion effort.[36]

Notwithstanding the financial infirmities of the state steel enterprises, in the mid-1970s the Brazilian government launched an extraordinary steelmaking capacity expansion drive -- dwarfing the "Phase II" effort in a burst of intensive investment and construction, "one of the most ambitious of its kind ever undertaken,"[37] that enabled Brazil to increase its crude steel output at a rate of over one million tons per year every year between 1975 and 1980.[38] Brazil's basic growth strategy called for both the major expansion of existing

---

[32] *Siderurgia Latinoamericana* (May 1985) ("Informe de la Subcomisión Especial de Siderurgia de la Cámara de Diputados del Brasil"), p. 23.

[33] Trebat, *Brazil's State-Owned Enterprises*, p. 228.

[34] The BNDES, funded from the state treasury and public pension funds, extends medium-term credit at below market rates to public and private sector steelmakers to finance expansion projects and to provide working capital. Between 1970 and 1980 BNDES loaned approximately $6.5 billion to the steel industry. *Siderurgia Latinoamericana* (September 1982), pp. 40-42. As a result of BNDES' concessionary lending policies, the Bank lost $178.4 million in 1987 -- equivalent to 7 percent of its total lending in that year. *Gazeta Mercantil* (January 12, 1988). In addition, BNDES' Special Agency for Industrial Finance (FINAME) program provides low-interest loans to finance purchases of domestically-produced steelmaking equipment. Interest rates on FINAME loans ranged from 1 to 22 percent at a time when the Brazilian prime rate was between 52 and 62 percent. Business International Corp., *Investing Licensing and Trading Abroad: Brazil* (December 1980); Morgan Guaranty Trust, *World Financial Markets*.

[35] Trebat, *Brazil's State-Owned Enterprises*, p. 229. The balance came from international development banks, supplier credits and steelmakers' cash flow. *Ibid*.

[36] *O Estado de São Paulo* (May 29, 1977).

[37] *Latin America Weekly Report* (December 1981), pp. 8-9.

[38] By 1975 Brazil's expansion planning was based on the forecast that Brazil would consume 40 million tons of steel in 1985. *O Globo* (April 17, 1975). Brazil's actual consumption in 1985 was less than twelve million tons. International Iron and Steel Institute, *Steel Statistical Yearbook 1987*.

steelworks and the construction of a number of new "greenfield" plants. The government planned an expansion in successive stages of the facilities of the established state firms, CSN, COSIPA, and USIMINAS, which would nearly double their output by 1984.[39] Three entirely new integrated steelworks, AÇOMINAS, Mendes Júnior, and CST would also be constructed. Major improvements in the nation's infrastructure, including its railroad network,[40] port facilities,[41] and electrical generating capability,[42] were planned to support the industry's growth.[43] The U.S. Embassy in Brazil commented in 1977 that the "Brazilian Steel expansion program . . . is of truly vast dimensions, perhaps unparalleled in the developing world. . . ."[44]

Financing the Expansion. Between 1977 and 1980, the steel industry's expansion effort absorbed over $10 billion in investment funds (table 5-4). SIDERBRÁS, a primary source of funding, borrowed heavily from foreign sources and channeled the funds so raised into the producing enterprises in the form of additional purchases of "equity capital."[45] In the four years from 1977 to 1980, the government pumped $1.6 billion in new equity into the three largest state steel producers. Similarly, BNDES undertook a heavy lending program to support the industry's growth efforts; in 1977, loans to the iron

---

[39] SIDERBRÁS President Cavalcanti, in *Metal Bulletin* (March 13, 1979).

[40] One of the most ambitious infrastructure projects was the construction of a "steel railway" (Ferrovia do Aço) to carry iron ore from Jaceaba, Minas Gerais, to CSN's integrated steel mill at Volta Redonda. Begun in 1975, this project had absorbed $1.3 billion in government funds by mid-1983. American Consulate General, Rio de Janeiro, "Brazil's Iron and Steel Industry 1983," August 31, 1983; *Revista Bancaria Brasileira* (March 1980).

[41] For instance, three state-owned companies – CVRD, SIDERBRÁS and PORTOBRÁS – together invested $400 million in the construction of a facility to handle steel, coal and iron ore for the steel industry at Praia Mole near the new CST steel mill. *Siderurgia Latinoamericana* (February 1985) ("Informativo Regional"), p. 18.

[42] To foster the development of an iron and steel industry in the Amazon, Brazil constructed the fourth largest hydroelectric plant in the world at Tucurui. *Ibid.*, pp. 18-19.

[43] *O Globo* (April 9, 1975).

[44] U.S. Embassy, Brasilia, "Brazil's Steel Industry – Status at Mid-Year," August 31, 1977.

[45] COSIPA's *Relatório* for 1979 commented (pp. 13, 29) that "There has been an effective participation of the Federal Government through SIDERBRÁS, which contributed with capital investments on the order of 3 billion cruzeiros [$111.5 million], destined for the implantation of expansion projects. . . . The necessary resources for that expansion will be substantially obtained from [SIDERBRÁS] and from loans obtained from the National Bank for Economic Development, BNDES, and the Special Agency for Industrial Finance, FINAME." Finsider of Italy and Kawasaki Steel of Japan also became major equity participants in CST. *American Metal Market* (April 21, 1988).

Table 5-4. Brazilian Investments in Steel 1977-1986
(million U.S. dollars)

	SIDERBRÁS	INDUSTRY
1977	969.0	1607.0
1978	1877.5	2668.5
1979	2566.6	3089.5
1980	2407.5	2712.8
1981	2550.6	2881.9
1982	1803.0	2224.4
1983	1226.0	1521.0
1984	283.0	508.9
1985	363.4	473.2
1986	386.3	515.5
TOTAL	14,432.9	18,202.8

Source: CONSIDER, *Statistical Yearbook 1987*

and steel industry accounted for 19 percent of BNDES' total budget.[46] In addition, government loan guarantees enabled Brazilian steel producers to borrow heavily from foreign financial institutions.[47] These guarantees were significant in light of the fact that the progressively deteriorating operating results of the Brazilian producers eventually rendered them uncreditworthy to private investors.[48]

International development banks were another important source of financing for Brazil's expansion effort. Since 1972 the World Bank has provided $347 million in loans for Brazil's steel industry.[49] The International Finance Corporation, a World Bank affiliate dedicated to supporting

---

[46] *O Globo* (April 6, 1978). SIDERBRÁS periodically paid off some of the producing enterprises' debt to BNDES; such payments were treated as "advances" by SIDERBRÁS to the enterprises "in anticipation of future capital increases." COSIPA 1981/82 *Financial Statement*, p. 5; CSN 1981/82 *Financial Statement*, 1981/82.

[47] COSIPA noted in its 1980 *Relatório* (p. 9) that "Loans for the expansion plan are guaranteed by the National Treasury, SIDERBRÁS and BNDES." The USIMINAS *Relatório* for 1980 noted (p. 27) that foreign currency loans for the expansion plan are "guaranteed by surety bond issued by SIDERBRÁS. . . ."

[48] In 1982 USIMINAS attempted to sell $43 million in bonds in Japan without a Brazilian government guarantee. Japanese investors were not interested because they "did not expect a reasonable return on the investment." *Metal Bulletin* (May 11, 1982).

[49] U.S.I.T.C., *Steel Sheet and Strip Industry*, pp. 4-10. It also provided $304.5 million for the Carajás iron ore mining project in the Amazon. International Bank for Reconstruction and Development, *Annual Report* 1983, pp. 116-117.

nongovernmental development activities, invested $79 million in the stock of COSIGUA, a subsidiary of Brazil's largest private steel producer.[50] In addition, the Inter-American Development Bank has provided $228 million in loans to the Brazilian steel industry since 1971.[51]

The Brazilian government also implemented a variety of tax incentives to facilitate the steel expansion program. Pursuant to a special decree, the steelmakers began receiving rebates on Brazil's value-added tax; the rebates were placed in a fund earmarked for the financing of steel expansion projects.[52] In addition, several special decrees provided for an 80-100 percent exemption from customs duties and value-added taxes for imported steelmaking equipment.[53]

The Brazilian expansion program was plagued by a lack of coordination and central direction. The beginning of Phase III of Brazil's steel expansion plan was poorly meshed with the completion of Phase II -- capacity came on stream in an uncoordinated fashion, creating bottlenecks and gross imbalances in particular plants.[54] Difficulties in arranging financing led to long delays in the CST, Mendes Júnior and AÇOMINAS greenfield projects. Moreover, by the early 1980s, despite heavy government financial assistance, the Brazilian steel industry was experiencing mounting financial difficulties. (table 5-5). Losses on the sale of steel products depleted the state enterprises' internal resources, and they were forced into increasingly massive borrowings to

---

[50] *Siderurgia Latinoamericana* (May 1985) ("Informativo Regional"), p. 11. In February 1985 the IFC announced an additional $3 million investment to aid that company's modernization and expansion plans. *American Metal Market* reported on April 6, 1988 that SIDERBRÁS was seeking an $80 million loan from the IFC to purchase mill equipment.

[51] U.S.I.T.C., *Steel Sheet and Strip Industry*, pp. 4-16.

[52] Decree Law 1547 (April 1977). The Tax on Manufactured Products (IPI) is a value-added tax imposed on domestic sales in 14 industrial sectors, including steel. The steel companies collect this tax for the government; until 1980, the producers received a 95 percent rebate on this tax from the government which was deposited in a special account in the Bank of Brazil, to be applied to steel expansion projects. Pursuant to Decree Law 1843 (December 1980) the government now rebates 95 percent of the tax directly to SIDERBRÁS which funnels it into the state steel producers in the form of equity infusions. *Certain Carbon Steel Products from Brazil*, C-351-021 (final), April 18, 1984, and administrative review dated January 9, 1987. Between 1977 and 1987, the rebate generated $2 billion for the steel industry; President Sarney renewed the program for another ten-year period in 1987. *Siderurgia Latinoamericana* (March 1987) ("Informativo Regional"), p. 38.

[53] The Industrial Development Council (CDI) until 1979 administered a program pursuant to Decree Law 491 (March 5, 1969) as amended by Decree Law 1428 (December 2, 1975) authorizing reduction of the duty and IPI tax on equipment "of companies with export programs and which assume export commitments."

[54] *O Estado de São Paulo* (May 29, 1977); U.S. Embassy, "Brazil's Steel Industry," pp. 4-5.

Table 5-5. Brazilian Steel Industry -- Net Income 1977-1986
(million U.S. dollars)

	Net Income	% of Revenues
1977	129	3.1
1978	171	3.8
1979	(294)	(5.7)
1980	67	1.2
1981	(294)	(5.7)
1982	(1,034)	(20.0)
1983	(629)	(14.6)
1984	(81)	(1.5)
1985	(1,971)	(33.1)
1986*	(382)	(21.2)

Source: CONSIDER, *Statistical Yearbook 1987*
*March-June only.
Converted to U.S. dollars at average annual exchange rate given by International Monetary Fund.
Conversion: 1977: 14; 1978: 18; 1979: 27; 1980: 53; 1981: 93; 1982: 180;
1983: 577; 1984: 1,848; 1985: 6,200, 1986: 13,840.

finance continued expansion.[55] Thus, although Brazil managed to double steelproduction between 1973 and 1980, the rapid rate of growth placed the entire sector under severe strain.

The Brazilian Economic Crisis. As the decade of the 1980s began, it was clear that the entire Brazilian national industrial program was in trouble. Triple-digit inflation, the rising cost of oil imports following the second oil crisis, and an increasingly heavy burden of foreign debt, made considerably worse by rising interest rates, began to foster misgivings within the government over the scale of Brazil's expansion goals. CONSIDER announced in December 1980 that work on new facilities in the steel sector would be

---

[55] Brazilian producers blamed these losses, in part, on government price controls imposed on domestic steel sales.

restricted to projects already under way.[56] In 1981 the government imposed
economic austerity measures and reduced the flow of funds to major public
industrial projects.[57] These measures, coupled with continuing losses on steel
sales and sharply falling domestic demand, produced acute liquidity problems
for the state-owned producers. SIDERBRÁS, the parent company, could offer
little help; by 1982, it was one of the most heavily indebted steel enterprises
in the world, and needed $800 million a year merely to service its debts.[58]
Nevertheless, work on the major expansion projects went forward through
1982 and 1983; SIDERBRÁS alone made further investments of $3 billion in
those two years (table 5-4). In mid-1983, the government approved new
investments of approximately $800 million for SIDERBRÁS for the coming
year,[59] and announced that BNDES would receive equity shares in
USIMINAS, CSN and COSIPA in payment of the large debt owed by these
firms to the national bank.[60]

By early 1984, only two of the greenfield projects undertaken by
SIDERBRÁS were actually producing steel, CST, with a capacity of 3 million
tons, and Mendes Júnior, with a capacity of 720,000 tons.[61] The third
greenfield project, AÇOMINAS, was stalled for lack of funds; in February, the
construction contractors ceased work and announced that they would not
resume until they were paid.[62] In fact, SIDERBRÁS managed to invest only
$283 million in 1984; still, the company was determined to complete
AÇOMINAS. The government finally came up with funds to resume

---

[56] *O Estado de São Paulo* (December 17, 1980).

[57] International Bank for Reconstruction and Development, *Brazil: Industrial Policies and
Manufactured Exports* (Washington, D.C.: World Bank, 1983), p. 47.

[58] *Metal Bulletin* (March 16, 1982).

[59] *O Estado de São Paulo* (June 15, 1983); *Gazeta Mercantil* (April 21/22, 1983).

[60] American Consulate, "Brazil's Iron and Steel Industry 1983." By mid-1983, SIDERBRÁS'
external foreign currency debt had grown to $7.5 billion, about 8 percent of Brazil's total foreign
debt, and the company owed another $2.2 billion to domestic government development banks.
American Metal Market (September 7, 1983).

[61] *Siderurgia Latinoamericana* (May 1984) ("Informativo Regional"), p. 13. Mendes Júnior
is an interesting example of the role played by the state in fostering the development of "private"
steelmaking capacity. The mill was first planned as a private facility to produce 150,000 tons of
steel. CONSIDER, however, urged that the project be expanded ten times, to 1.5 million tons
of nonflat products, with SIDERBRÁS to provide the additional funds. Because the National
Steel Plan reserved non-flat steel production for private producers, the majority of the voting
stock in Mendes Júnior remained in the hands of private investors, while SIDERBRÁS took a
preferred stock interest. The mill, which ultimately was scaled back to 720,000 tons, cost $725
million to complete. *Ibid.*

[62] *Financial Times* (February 23, 1984).

construction, and several foreign banks provided additional financing. AÇOMINAS produced its first ton of steel in early 1985, four years behind schedule and $2.5 billion over budget. However, the mill's blast furnaces still had not been fired and its production was limited to the rolling of slabs brought in from other plants.[63] SIDERBRÁS invested $8.5 billion between 1980 and 1985; nevertheless, by 1985 AÇOMINAS, while producing some steel, was still incomplete and major expansions at the CSN and COSIPA plants were behind schedule. If completed, these projects would add 4 million tons of unneeded steel-making capacity at a cost, according to SIDERBRÁS estimates, of $1.6 billion.[64]

The Brazilian inflation rate reached 224 percent in 1984,[65] and 62 percent of Brazil's export earnings in that year were required merely to service the country's huge foreign debt.[66] Faced with these serious economic and social problems, the new government of President José Sarney froze public sector spending, banned further lending by BNDES, and curtailed hiring by state enterprises.[67] The government then issued a new development plan intended to halt further industrial investments by the state.[68] Ministers were directed to identify those industrial projects that should be frozen or cancelled due to "long maturation and/or dubious return," and AÇOMINAS was placed on the short list of projects to be considered for cancellation.[69]

Renewed Expansion 1985-88. The state steel industry quickly mobilized to fight any cutback of its expansion plans. SIDERBRÁS' new President, Amaro Lanari -- heralded by his predecessor as one of the "creators" of the AÇOMINAS project[70] -- insisted that the AÇOMINAS and COSIPA projects

---

[63] *Financial Times* (February 28, 1985).

[64] *Siderurgia Latinoamericana* (August 1985) ("Informativo Regional"), p. 33.

[65] *Siderurgia Latinoamericana* (October 1985) ("La Siderurgia Brasileña en 1984-85 y sus Perspectivas"), p. 2.

[66] U.S.I.T.C., *Developing Country Debt-Servicing Problems*, p. 51.

[67] *Metal Bulletin* (March 29, 1985).

[68] The Plan stated that "Industrial development finds itself in a phase of consolidation, by reason of an excess in installed capacity in some sectors, and does not require more allocations of financial resources from the public sector. There is no need, today, for public investments in plants for the production of basic inputs for industry." *Siderurgia Latinoamericana* (August 1985) ("Informativo Regional"), p. 33.

[69] *Siderurgia Latinoamericana* (September 1985) ("Informativo Regional"), p. 19.

[70] *Siderurgia Latinoamericana* (June 1985) ("Informativo Regional"), p. 21.

were nearly complete and that they should be brought to a conclusion.[71] In this fight, SIDERBRÁS had powerful allies. In February 1984 the Brazilian Parliament created a Steel Subcommission, to "study means in the legislative context, destined to favor the financial restoration of the [steel] companies. . . ."[72] A 1985 Subcommission report concluded that SIDERBRÁS' incomplete projects should be given priority in the budget process, "considering that to leave them incomplete would implicate a higher cost for the nation than to complete them." It also urged a series of measures to return the state enterprises to "self-sufficiency," including recapitalization of the industry's debt, an increase in domestic steel prices, expanded government incentives to develop the charcoal industry, and preferential electrical rates for iron ore producers.[73]

In April 1985, Lanari announced that SIDERBRÁS' financial problems could be resolved if the country showed the "political will to invest;"[74] by year's end it appeared that what the country lacked was the will not to invest. In October, an additional $170 million was budgeted for the AÇOMINAS project.[75] SIDERBRÁS obtained further financing through the sale/lease back of equipment to foreign banks and through the advance sale of AÇOMINAS' planned production.[76] By January 1986 the government had been convinced to continue the work at AÇOMINAS and the remaining "Stage III" projects at an estimated cost of $630 million.[77] In June SIDERBRÁS announced a new four-year investment plan to increase capacity by 4 million tons at a cost of $1.3 billion.[78] By late 1986, even the heavily criticized Steel Railway project had been reactivated in modified form, with $150 million in

---

[71] *Siderurgia Latinoamericana* (November 1985) ("Informativo Regional"), p. 18.

[72] *Siderurgia Latinoamericana* (February 1984) ("Informativo Regional"), p. 17.

[73] *Siderurgia Latinoamericana* (May 1985) ("Informe de la Subcomisión Especial de la Cámara de Diputados del Brasil"), pp. 22-32.

[74] *Siderurgia Latinoamericana* (April 1985) ("El Desarollo Tecnológico y el Momento Brasileño"), p. 62.

[75] *Siderurgia Latinoamericana* (October 1985) ("Informativo Regional"), p. 23.

[76] Manufacturers Hanover provided $95 million under one sale/lease back scheme. *Financial Times* (October 7, 1985). Another $380 million sale/lease back operation was financed by a pool of banks led by Chase Manhattan. *Metal Bulletin* (January 21, 1988). The Bank of Brazil agreed to pay half of the 21 percent interest charge demanded by foreign banks to finance the advance purchase of AÇOMINAS products. *Metal Bulletin* (October 8, 1985). INTERBRÁS, a division of the government-owned PETROBRÁS oil company, provided an additional $100 million through purchases paid in advance. *Metal Bulletin* (December 20, 1985).

[77] *Siderurgia Latinoamericana* (January 1986) ("Informativo Regional"), pp. 12, 14.

[78] *Siderurgia Latinoamericana* (June 1986) ("Informativo Regional"), p. 33.

funds to be provided by BNDES, SIDERBRÁS, private users, and the National Treasury.[79] In mid-1987, BNDES announced the release of $750 million to aid in the completion of the Stage III expansion.[80]

Although these moves served to revitalize the expansion effort, SIDERBRÁS remained in a state of financial crisis. By October 1986, the company's debt had climbed to $15.6 billion. Of this sum, $6.8 billion was owed to foreign banks; the balance was owed primarily to government entities.[81] In January 1987 the government agreed to assume $12.2 billion of SIDERBRÁS' debt, leaving the company to pay the balance itself.[82] BNDES and the newly-created National Development Fund would provide investment funds to the company.[83]

The Abortive "Privatization" Effort. Meanwhile, a government plan to privatize portions of the steel industry made little progress, underscoring the fact that steelmaking is not regarded as a particularly attractive investment in Brazil. The government's new Privatization Commission indicated in 1985 that six state-owned steel producers -- but not the four largest integrated producers -- would be sold to the private sector.[84] The Commission also hoped to obtain private participation in the larger state companies by offering minority interests on the stock exchange.[85] However, as SIDERBRÁS

---

[79] *Siderurgia Latinoamericana* (November 1986) ("Informativo Regional"), p. 21. The Steel Railway was widely criticized as an unnecessary and wasteful project. The former Transport Minister of the state of Minas Gerais, in which the railway was located, remarked that "in Minas Gerais, no one criticizes the paralysis of the Steel Railway because, given the economic situation, the work wouldn't have anything to transport, at least until the end of the decade." *Visão* (April 4, 1985). Sarney's planners agreed and they slated it for cancellation in 1985, after expenditures of $1.5 billion had been made. *Visão* remarked in the April 4, 1985 article that "the Steel Railway – whose works up to now completed are already falling to pieces – symbolizes the unpredictability, the bad planning, the megalomania and the interventionism of the State in questions of private initiative."

[80] *Metal Bulletin* (July 23, 1987).

[81] *Metal Bulletin Monthly* (October 1986), p. 45.

[82] This transaction was carried out by means of an "interministerial protocol." The protocol, which was drafted by SIDERBRÁS, declared that the debt to be assumed by the government was the result of price controls and of the government's failure to promptly deliver promised funds. *Siderurgia Latinoamericana* (April 1987) ("Informativo Regional"), p. 14.

[83] *Gazeta Mercantil* (International Weekly Edition) (February 2, 1987). The Fund's revenues are generated by a special tax on automobiles, gasoline, overseas air tickets, and other luxury goods. This tax is formally an "obligatory" loan; the public is to be repaid with shares of the state enterprises in three years' time. *Metal Bulletin Monthly* (October 1986).

[84] *Metal Bulletin* (August 20, 1985).

[85] *Metal Bulletin* (April 15, 1986).

president Lanari was quick to point out, the debts of most state steel companies exceeded the value of their assets. Accordingly, the purchase of shares in those companies would not be "inviting" to private investors,[86] This assessment proved accurate. Discussions between the government and Gerdau, a private steel company, for the purchase of SIDERBRÁS' Companhia Ferro e Aço de Vitória ("COFAVI") were initiated, but soon bogged down over COFAVI's $30 million debt to BNDES.[87] Gerdau eventually acquired another private producer instead.[88]

The following year, five other producers were targeted for privatization -- ACESITA, COSIM, Aços Finos Piratini, SIDERAMA, and USIBA.[89] Brazil's Planning Minister set a mid-1987 deadline for partial privatization of the companies.[90] However, not one of the companies had been sold by December 1987.[91] Of sixty-eight companies slated by Secretary of Privatization David Moreira for privatization or closing, only seven had been disposed of.[92]

The Second National Steel Plan. The troubles besetting the Brazilian steel industry have not deterred it from setting ambitious goals for the future. CONSIDER's second National Steel Plan, as sweeping as the first, is predicated on an eight percent annual increase in domestic demand through the year 2000. To satisfy this demand while maintaining exports at 25 percent

---

[86] Amaro Lanari, Jr., President of SIDERBRÁS, in *Siderurgia Latinoamericana* (September 1985) ("Informativo Regional"), p. 19.

[87] *Metal Bulletin* (March 12, 1985).

[88] *Siderurgia Latinoamericana* (April 1985) ("Informativo Regional"), p. 24.

[89] *Metal Bulletin* (August 20, 1985).

[90] *Metal Bulletin* (April 15, 1986).

[91] A document issued by the Private Steelmakers' Association in mid-1987 lamented that the competition between the state and private sectors was "unequal because the state enterprises don't confront risks and their eventual losses are transferred to society." *Siderurgia Latinoamericana* (July 1987)("Informativo Regional"), p. 28.

[92] In one instance, a company whose sole purpose was to build a bridge continued to generate expenditures thirteen years after the bridge was opened to traffic. Even the Minister of Planning, to whom Moreira submitted his resignation, expressed pessimism about the privatization process: "The program that we have today is only a mechanism for picking over cucumbers that the government received over the years, poorly planned or administered companies that no one wants to buy." *Veja* (December 18, 1987). In the spring of 1988, SIDERBRÁS announced "an ambitious, wide-ranging privatization plan." *American Metal Market* (May 12, 1988). Like the previous proposals, the plan calls for the sale of SIDERBRÁS' smaller producers and of minority stock shares in the integrated mills, beginning with USIMINAS. *Ibid.* Whether this plan will fare better than its predecessors remains to be seen.

of production, the Plan calls for a doubling of production to 50 million tons by the turn of the century.[93] The Plan, which would cost an estimated \$22.5 billion,[94] envisions the creation of four new "regional" mills, two for flat products and two for non-flats. Three of these mills would be built in areas of the country where little steel production presently takes place, such as the Amazon and the Center-West.[95] The Plan, which will not become official until approved by representatives of four government Ministries and by the Council on Economic Development,[96] has been criticized for grossly over-estimating Brazilian and world demand for steel.[97]

Nevertheless, the Plan has powerful supporters, including BNDES. The Bank asserts that Brazil will need 53 million tons of capacity by the year 2000, and that funding for the expansion will cost \$24.5 billion. BNDES itself proposes to provide \$1 billion per year towards the costs of this expansion,[98] and SIDERBRÁS' new strategic development plan would expand capacity at existing state-owned mills by 10 million tons, at a cost of \$10.8 billion.[99] On the political front, a Parliamentary Steel Group has formed to lobby for the Plan,[100] and the state governments are becoming involved; the government of Maranhão, in the Amazon, pledged funds in September 1987 to begin work on a projected 3 million ton plant in that state. "In January we will camp in Brasilia to guarantee Federal funds for USIMAR," announced Maranhão

---

[93] *Siderurgia Latinoamericana* (November 1986) ("Informativo Regional"), p. 19.

[94] *Siderurgia Latinoamericana* (June 1987) ("Informativo Regional"), p. 13.

[95] *Siderurgia Latinoamericana* (August 1987) ("Informativo Regional"), pp. 27-28.

[96] *Siderurgia Latinoamericana* (August 1987) ("Informativo Regional"), p. 27.

[97] "The critics judge that the Plan overestimates the market and that growth will not occur by leaps and bounds. If we arrive at 50 million tons without an internal market — they warn — exporting will not be an alternative, as it was in the recent past. It would be impossible to put nearly 40 percent of production on the external market, considering that the international picture favors protectionism. The existence of great idle capacity in the world contributes, furthermore, to depress prices, whose tendency is to remain low. In sum, it would be irrational to invest to export, simply comparing capital costs to prices, without speaking of other production costs." *Siderurgia Latinoamericana* (June 1987) ("Informativo Regional"), p. 13.

[98] *Siderurgia Latinoamericana* (August 1987) ("Informativo Regional"), pp. 26-27.

[99] *Siderurgia Latinoamericana* (July 1987) ("Informativo Regional"), p. 27.

[100] *Metal Bulletin* (September 7, 1987). The decision to decentralize steel production was a politically astute one. Not only did it provide a new *raison d'etre* for steel investments — the need to stimulate underdeveloped regions of Brazil — but it created a broader base of political support for the industry. The regional development rationale is developed in E. Manoel, "Las Empresas Estatales del Sector Siderúrgico en la Promoción del Desarollo Regional — Instrumento Compensatorio al Intercambio Desigual," in *Siderurgia Latinoamericana* (June 1987), p. 35.

Industry Minister Roberto Maceiro. Mr. Maceiro -- a cousin of President José Sarney -- was as good as his word.[101] On January 18, 1988, *Metal Bulletin* reported that the Federal government had provided an initial $150 million for the project, in spite of objections by SIDERBRÁS President Lanari that the market for steel did not justify construction of the plant.[102] Plans for other projects, such as a greenfield cold-rolling mill in Fortelaza and the doubling of CST's slab capacity, were also reported to be progressing.[103]

Meanwhile, the Brazilian steel industry's run of losses continued unbroken. For the first nine months of 1987, total losses amounted to nearly $1.5 billion, of which all but $270 million were attributable to state enterprises.[104] Industry losses were so high that the National Development Fund, established to bail out Brazil's state-owned steel and electricity industries, was itself running the risk of becoming "unviable," according to the head of the Secretariat for the Control of State Enterprises (SEST).[105] Nor is any short-term improvement likely; an investigation of COSIPA, conducted by the Ministry of Industry and Commerce after the firm reported continuing heavy losses, revealed that the company had invested nearly twice the sum budgeted it by the government. The report stated that

> *the company finds itself in a state of absolute financial, administrative and operational disorder. Conflict and confrontation between political groups carried the firm to a state of laceration that will demand a long time to heal.*[106]

---

[101] *Gazeta Mercantil* (September 30, 1987).

[102] *Gazeta Mercantil* (International Weekly Edition), May 11, 1987. Soviet and European interests have agreed to participate in the $3 billion plant, which is expected to produce hot-rolled products for export. *American Metal Market* (May 17, 1988).

[103] *Metal Bulletin* (January 18 and 21, 1988). In the spring of 1988, BNDES announced that it would provide $120 million for installation of a continuous caster at CST, and the company entered into talks with Japan's Eximbank for $1.5 billion in financing for the company's "Phase II" expansion. *Metal Bulletin* (April 7, 1988).

[104] *Gazeta Mercantil* (January 8, 1988). USIMINAS alone was expected to report a loss of $200-240 million for 1987. *Metal Bulletin* (March 14, 1988).

[105] *Gazeta Mercantil* (International Weekly Edition) (December 21, 1987). SEST was founded in 1979, in recognition of "the need to bring the increasingly large state companies within the discipline of a centrally determined fiscal and monetary policy." Trebat, *Brazil's State-Owned Enterprises*, p. 113. SIDERBRÁS resisted SEST's efforts -- in 1986, SIDERBRÁS President Lanari threatened to resign rather than submit to SEST's control. *Metal Bulletin* (October 24, 1986). Moreover, other state companies disregarded SEST directives. In 1985, the state enterprises exceeded the budget set by SEST three times over, and no punitive action was taken. As a result, "there is, among the enterprises, a conviction that the new [budget] determinations will not be followed and, once again, absolutely nothing will happen." *Visão* (August 5, 1987).

[106] *Gazeta Mercantil* (January 9, 1988).

Brazil's Foreign Trade in Steel

Brazil had borrowed heavily to finance industrial expansion projects in all priority sectors, and by 1987 its accumulated foreign debt exceeded $112 billion.[107] Many of Brazil's loans were contracted at floating interest rates, so that as rates rose in the late 1970s and in the 1980s the burden of servicing the debt increased rapidly. In February 1987, Brazil declared a moratorium on the payment of interest on the $67 billion it owed to foreign commercial banks. Only after difficult negotiations and the extension of new credits to Brazil did repayment resume.[108]

Given this situation, Brazil's government and its creditors agreed on one point -- the country needed to improve its balance of payments by curtailing imports and dramatically expanding its exports.[109] By 1982-83, exporting had become "a matter of life or death for the nation."[110] The steel industry, with its large new underutilized plants, was a natural instrument in what was seen as a struggle for national economic survival. As one Brazilian legislator commented in 1986,

The United States, the EEC and Japan must understand that they have to make room for our steel and not do as they have been doing up to now, refusing to see the relation between trade and debt. That is why they recommend that we put forward our claims against protectionism within the context of trade policy, without any reference at all to the debt problem. But that position is not correct for a simple reason: the relation between trade and debt is real. . . .[111]

Brazil became a net exporter of steel in 1978, and quickly emerged as one of the lowest-price exporters of steel in the world. As the debt crisis has deepened in the 1980s, the government exerted pressure on the state steel

---

[107] *Financial Times* (December 21, 1987).

[108] *Washington Post* (February 29, 1988).

[109] *O Estado de São Paulo* (March 31, 1982).

[110] *O Estado de São Paulo* (March 4, 1983); see also *Gazeta Mercantil* (February 23, 1983).

[111] Deputy Vinicius Pratini de Moraes, Chairman -- Parliamentary Steel Group, quoted in *Siderurgia Latinoamericana* (September 1986), pp. 49-50. Former Industry Minister Camilio Penna's assessment was similar: Foreign bankers "came knocking at my door offering money to buy a steel mill, using political and diplomatic pressure. We bought, and the only way I have to repay the debt is selling steel." *Washington Post* (February 21, 1984).

sector to expand exports "at any cost."[112] The government's direction to expand exports was given added impetus by a significant drop in domestic steel consumption, which induced Brazilian steelmakers, including those in the private sector, to sell their steel at a loss abroad.[113] Price controls in the domestic market provided a further stimulus to export.[114] In addition, the Brazilian government implemented a formidable array of financial incentives and outright subsidies to promote the export of industrial commodities such as steel.

Devaluations. One of the most important of these measures has been the progressive devaluation of the national currency, a measure which has had the effect of significantly reducing the price of Brazilian steel on the world market. The government undertook two maxidevaluations, in 1979 and 1983, in an effort to stimulate exports,[115] particularly of industrial products.[116] The effect

---

[112] *O Estado de São Paulo* (March 13, 1983); *American Metal Market* (December 29, 1981). *O Estado de São Paulo* reported that according to SIDERBRÁS President Cavalcanti, the government had, in the second half of 1981 "direct[ed] state companies to make an exceptional effort to export, a goal which was achieved, but sometimes at a cost of the deterioration of the economic health of those companies." [Although] Cavalcanti did not go into further detail on the matter, he meant to say that steel products were often exported at prices that were lower than desirable or even reasonable."

[113] *Metal Bulletin* reported on November 6, 1981 that one official from a private sector steel firm said that his company was "resorting to non-profitmaking exports in order to stave off a further cutback in production." Jorge Gerdau, President of Brazil's largest private steel producer, "recalled that, as regards exportation, its rise was the result of a coincidence between the growth in productive capacity and the fall in consumption. This situation left the mills with two alternatives -- operate with excess capacity and rising losses, or seek foreign markets for the excess not absorbed internally. . . . It happened that the international market was oversupplied and had low prices. . . ." *Siderurgia Latinoamericana* (December 1986) ("Informativo Regional"), p. 21. Even the rising world prices prevailing in early 1988 were inadequate to meet Brazilian costs. CST officials indicated that the company needed to sell slabs at $300 per ton, a sum well in excess of world market prices, to get a "reasonable return on investment." *Metal Bulletin* (April 7, 1988).

[114] Price controls were a source of constant complaint among Brazilian steel producers. According to one study, the real price of steel in the Brazilian market fell 50 percent between 1975 and 1982. *Siderurgia Latinoamericana* (April 1984) ("Informativo Regional"), p. 29. Therefore, foreign sales, even when made at depressed rates, "left a slightly better margin of contribution than the prices practiced internally." *Ibid.*, p. 28. In March 1986, the Brazilian government ordered SIDERBRÁS to reduce prices by 7 percent. In response, some mills actually suspended domestic sales. "A likely outcome," according to *Metal Bulletin* (March 18, 1986), "is that both state and private producers will try to offset the lower home sales by higher exports."

[115] U.S.I.T.C., *Developing Country Debt-Servicing Problems*, pp. 63-64. Brazilian Minister of Planning Delfim Netto said of the maxidevaluation that: "In depth measures such as maxidevaluations are proper measures that seek the right objective, which is to expand exports, thus increasing employment, and also to replace imports with locally manufactured goods. This too increases employment. You can see for yourself that in São Paulo there are industries that are laying off employees because they cannot export their goods while other industries are

of the maxidevaluation on Brazilian steel exports was soon apparent; CONSIDER indicated in late April, two months after the second maxidevaluation, that

> The expected export volume -- nearly 4 million tons -- will make our steel production goal of 14.5 million tons for 1983 viable. . . . The effects of the maxidevaluation of the cruzeiro have already been felt on the export performance of this sector.[117]

Since 1983, the Brazilians have maintained exchange rates favorable to exports by periodic devaluations of the cruzado under a "crawling peg" system.[118]

Export Subsidies. The government provided steel firms with subsidized credit for working capital needed for the production of goods for export, a measure which resulted in a major export subsidy on steel products. Under these programs, administered by the government Carteira do Comércio Exterior (CACEX) of the Bank of Brazil, Brazilian firms sign a commitment with CACEX legally binding themselves to export.[119] CACEX then issues a certificate which the firm can present to any commercial bank and obtain

---

rehiring personnel because they can export. You should not be worried by the maxidevaluation. Its objective is to increase employment." São Paulo *Radio Bandeirantes Network*, 16:00 6MT (February 22, 1983) (Foreign Broadcast Information Service).

[116] At the same time that the government devalued the cruzeiro, it imposed export taxes on primary products such as iron ore--thus, for foreign trade purposes, the effect of the measure was to devalue the currency selectively for purposes of stimulating industrial exports like steel, but not those of primary products. *Gazeta Mercantil* (February 21, 1983); *O Estado de São Paulo* (March 13, 1983).

[117] *Gazeta Mercantil* (April 21/22, 1983). SIDERBRÁS anticipated that the maxidevaluation would exacerbate the burden of its foreign debt but that it would "win something additional with the anticipated increase in its exports due to the stimulus of the maxidevaluation." *Gazeta Mercantil* (February 22, 1983).

[118] U.S.I.T.C., *Developing Country Debt-Servicing Problems*, p. 64. This policy continues to be effective. CONSIDER recently announced that, "due to recuperation of prices in the international market and to the devaluation of the cruzado in relation to the dollar," Brazilian steel production was on the rise. *Gazeta Mercantil* (December 17, 1987).

[119] Resolution No. 674, January 21, 1981, and Resolution No. 950, August 21, 1984.

loans at negative real rates of interest.[120] Export financing is also available directly from the Bank of Brazil[121] and CACEX[122] on favorable terms.

In addition, Brazilian steel exporters were made eligible for a variety of tax benefits and incentives designed to stimulate exports.[123] For instance, the profits of Brazilian firms attributable to exports were exempt from corporate income taxes.[124] Steel producers also benefit from accelerated depreciation on equipment used to produce goods for export,[125] a variety of local export promoting tax measures,[126] and an exemption from value-added and import

---

[120] The interest rate ceiling on Resolution 674 loans was 40 percent until mid-1983, at which time it rose to 60 percent. Given the rate of Brazilian inflation – 99.7 percent in 1982 – these loans were made at negative interest rates. In 1984 the U.S. Commerce Department found that such preferential credit was so advantageous to one state-owned Brazilian steel firm, CSN, that it gave rise to a 22.36 percent *ad valorem* subsidy on CSN's steel shipments to the U.S. *Certain Carbon Steel Products from Brazil* (final), 49 F.R. 17988, April 26, 1984. Perhaps as a result of such findings, Resolution 950 amended the scheme in August 1984 to provide capital at "market rates" through commercial lenders. However, the Bank of Brazil also agreed to pay the lender an "equalization fee" of up to 15 percent of total interest paid if the interest earned by the lender is less than 15 percent after inflation, thus allowing continued below-market loans. *Certain Heavy Iron Construction Castings from Brazil* (final), 51 F.R. 9491, March 19, 1986.

[121] Pursuant to CIG-CREGe 14-11, the Bank of Brazil has provided short-term loans at fixed, below-market rates to COSIPA and CSN. *Certain Carbon Steel Products*, pp. 12-13.

[122] The rate is variable. As of 1987, CACEX provided export financing at a rate of 8 percent for short-term credit; 7 percent for two-to-five year loans; and 6.5 percent for loans of 5 to 10 years. United States Trade Representative, *Foreign Trade Barriers (Washington, D.C.: GPO, 1987)*, p. 35.

[123] They have received cash reimbursements ("export premiums") of taxes paid pursuant to Brazil's value added tax (IPI) in connection with their steel exports. The U.S. Department of Commerce found in 1984 that as a result of IPI export credit premiums, the steel exports of COSIPA, CSN and USIMINAS had benefited from an *ad valorem* subsidy of 7.50, 10.78 and 8.71 percent, respectively. *Certain Carbon Steel Products from Brazil, op. cit.*, pp. 13-14. In 1985, the Brazilians agreed to eliminate this subsidy in exchange for the termination of an American countervailing duty investigation of Brazilian footwear. United States Trade Representative, *Foreign Trade Barriers*, p. 35.

[124] *Carbon Steel Plate from Brazil*, 48 F.R. 2573 (January 20, 1983). Decree Law 2391 purports to eliminate this exemption in 1988. As of December 1987, however, the government was considering a "gradual termination" of the exemption. Pinheiro, *Doing Business in Brazil* (New York: Matthew Bender, 1987), Supp., December 1987, p. 5.

[125] Decree Law 1137, (Article 1(d)).

[126] In July 1982 "SIDERBRÁS' Henrique Brandeo Calvalanti pointed out . . . that the first five months' [strong export] performance was largely attributable to favorable local tax measures. . . ." *Metal Bulletin* (July 6, 1982).

taxes on machinery, parts and inputs necessary for the production of export goods.[127]

Brazil's various export subsidies and incentives had a pronounced impact on its steel exports, which in 1987 reached 7.3 million tons[128] and accounted for nearly one-third of all Brazilian steel output.[129] This surge of low-priced Brazilian steel into the international market caused trade friction on a global scale. A SIDERBRÁS official conceded that Brazil had "jammed" 500,000 tons of steel into the EC during a five month period in 1981 and 1982,[130] and in 1982, the EC imposed antidumping duties on Brazilian cold-rolled sheet,[131] followed in 1983 by antidumping duties on hot-rolled sheet and plate and countervailing duties on Brazilian cold-rolled sheet.[132] In Canada, producers brought successful antidumping actions against Brazilian sheet, wire and pipe.[133] And in Asia, Japanese producers complained that Brazilian steel pricing was causing "chaos" in their export markets.[134]

For most of this decade, however, Brazil's most important steel export market has been the United States.[135] Brazilian penetration of the U.S. market has been significant. Despite falling U.S. domestic demand, the volume of U.S. imports of Brazilian steel jumped from 540 thousand net tons in 1981 to almost 1.5 million net tons in 1984. The U.S. Commerce Department found in 1984 that Brazilian producers were dumping steel at margins which in one

---

[127] Decree Law 2324 (March 30, 1987). *Metal Bulletin* reported on August 24, 1987 that Gerdau, Brazil's largest private steelmaker, has entered into an agreement with the Brazilian government, under which Gerdau has committed to export $330 million over the next ten years in exchange for $44 million in tax relief.

[128] *Gazeta Mercantil* (December 17, 1987).

[129] *Metal Bulletin* (January 28, 1988). Weak domestic demand in early 1988 pushed this figure up to 35 percent. *Metal Bulletin* (February 8, 1988).

[130] *American Metal Market* (May 25, 1982).

[131] *Metal Bulletin* (May 18, 1982).

[132] *Official Journal*, L. 131 (May 18, 1983), No. L 45 (February 14, 1983); *Metal Bulletin* (August 6, 1982). The Europeans suspended these penalties after Brazil agreed to limit exports to 190,000 tons in 1985. *Metal Bulletin* (March 12, 1985). The quota was raised to 212,000 tons in 1986. *Metal Bulletin* (April 17, 1987).

[133] *Metal Bulletin* (August 31, 1984; March 19, August 2, 1985; December 6, 1986).

[134] *Metal Bulletin* (January 28, 1983).

[135] *Metal Bulletin* (October 1, 1983).

case exceeded 100 percent.[136]   Brazilian price-cutting was so aggressive that
many other foreign producers, themselves subsidized, refused to match them.
In 1983, commenting on what seemed to be unnecessarily extreme Brazilian
discounting on the West Coast, one U.S. steel buyer said that "either the
Brazilians know something that we don't or their market intelligence isn't that
good. On the other hand, maybe they need the money so bad that they can't
risk losing any business at all to other mills."[137]   Brazilian penetration of the
U.S. market for hot-rolled plate was particularly pronounced -- by 1983
Brazilian plate accounted for 4.1 percent of all U.S. consumption of this
product. A U.S. steel executive charged that the shipment of 700,000 [net]
tons of Brazilian steel -- mainly plate -- had "literally destroyed" pricing in the
Gulf Coast region.[138]   Perhaps not surprisingly in light of such events, in the
spring of 1983 the U.S.I.T.C. found that Brazilian plate imports had materially
injured the U.S. steel industry, noting that in all cases of lost sales by the U.S.
industry, the reason was the low price of Brazilian steel, which was reported
to be as much as $80 to $250 per ton below the U.S. domestic price.[139]   Low-
priced Brazilian steel exports to the U.S. continued despite the imposition of
antidumping and countervailing duties:

> Market sources report that large quantities of Brazilian-made steel
> may be en route to the United States despite the countervailing duty
> and antidumping actions against products from that country which
> have stemmed the flow on individual product lines. 'First it was plate,'
> one source said. 'Then it was wire rod. Now they've been stopped on
> those two products and we hear that large amounts of sheets are being
> shipped here. . . .' 'There's an awful lot of unrest over the extremely
> low prices that are being offered in the market right now,' one official
> said. 'Unless prices firm pretty quickly we could have some major
> problems on our hands.'[140]

In early 1984, faced with steep duties on some products and pending trade
complaints on numerous others, Brazil negotiated a voluntary restraint

---

[136] *Certain Flat-Rolled Carbon Steel Products from Brazil* (final), 49 F.R. 3102, January 25,
1984; *Certain Carbon Steel Products from Brazil*, (final), 49 F.R. 28298, July 11, 1984.

[137] *American Metal Market* (January 28, July 27, 1983).

[138] *American Metal Market* (July 14, 1983). A SIDERBRÁS official conceded in 1983 that
Brazil's plate exports to the U.S. had been conducted in a "disorderly" fashion. *American Metal
Market* (May 25, 1983).

[139] *Hot-Rolled Carbon Steel Plate from Brazil*, No. 701-TA-87 (final) March 1983, p. 506.

[140] *American Metal Market* (July 15, 1983).

agreement with the United States.[141] The five-year VRA, which was signed on February 28, 1985, restricted Brazilian exports of finished steel products to the United States to 0.8 percent of the American market. For 1985, this amounted to roughly 800,000 net tons. Semifinished products, which did not fall within the VRA, were subject to a fixed 700,000 ton quota.[142]

Import Protection. The Brazilians have been harshly critical of "protectionist" measures in the U.S. and the EC. However, Brazil itself imposes far more restrictive controls on the importation of foreign products, including steel. Prospective importers of steel products must obtain a license from the Foreign Trade Department of the Bank of Brazil (CACEX),[143] which may limit or proscribe imports at its discretion.[144] Import licenses may be denied if "comparable" products are available from Brazilian producers, and in any event may be subject to delayed approval.[145] Steel imports are subject to tariffs which range from 15 to 65 percent,[146] and to a "financial operations

---

[141] *Metal Bulletin* (March 2, 1984). By late 1984, thirteen dumping and countervailing duty cases had been filed against Brazilian steel producers in the United States, *Siderurgia Latinoamericana* (March 1985) ("Informativo Regional"), p. 28, and the Department of Commerce had repeatedly held that Brazilian steel products were being subsidized and/or dumped on the American market.

[142] The special quota for semifinished products was the result of Brazilian "downstream" participation in the American steel industry. In November 1983, after years of work and an enormous investment, CST's new plant came on line. *Siderurgia Latinoamericana* (February 1984) ("Informativo Regional"), p. 15. The mill was scheduled to produce 2.4 million tons of slabs in 1984 -- however, the home market could absorb only 800,000 tons. *Metal Bulletin* (March 2, 1984). Faced with resistance in world markets, the Brazilians adopted an innovative approach -- they bought an American rolling mill to provide an export market for their slabs. *Financial Times* (July 18, 1984). As a result, SIDERBRÁS had a "virtually captive" market in the U.S. for its excess CST production. *Siderurgia Latinoamericana* (October 1984) ("Informativo Regional"), p. 13. As one magazine observed, "the mechanism of investing in protected markets is well-known to the Brazilians, by their own experience, since it was to overcome [Brazilian] protectionist barriers that the majority of transnationals that operate in Brazil came to install themselves among us." *Siderurgia Latinoamericana* (November 1984) ("Informativo Regional"), pp. 17-18.

[143] CACEX Communiqúe No. 154 of December 5, 1986.

[144] Pinheiro, *Doing Business in Brazil*, 6.102-6.103.

[145] U.S.I.T.C., *Developing Country Debt-Servicing Problems*, p. 65. In 1986, a brief surge in domestic demand, accompanied by production problems and heavy export commitments by Brazilian steel mills, necessitated the import of 690,000 tons of steel. *Metal Bulletin* (February 17, 1987). However, delays in the issuance of import licenses were so severe that by February 1987, only 25 thousand tons had actually been imported.

[146] *Tarifa Aduaneira do Brasil*, 73.06 -- 73.27 (1987).

tax," which can run as high as 25 percent.[147] Nor are these restrictions likely to be eased in the near future. The Brazilian Parliament's Steel Subcommission has argued that import controls should continue, "given the abnormal conditions of oversupply in the international market and the artificial practices applied by other producing countries."[148]

Future Prospects. Although the U.S. VRA has limited the ability of Brazil to expand its American market share over the past few years, the Brazilians have not abandoned their plans to become major international suppliers of steel. In 1987 Brazil had a trade surplus of $1.8 billion in steel products.[149] The second National Steel Plan calls for the export of 25 percent of Brazil's projected 50 million tons capacity by the year 2000.[150] Thus, even if Brazil's optimistic prediction of eight percent annual growth in domestic consumption is realized, the country will have to sell 12.5 million tons of steel in world markets by the turn of the century. The projected 3 million ton USIMAR plant is intended primarily as an exporter; in fact, the great distance between its Amazon location and the major consuming centers of the southeast of Brazil render it suitable for little else.[151]

Brazil in recent years has relied on third world markets to absorb excess production, often on a barter basis. However, in light of its continuing debt problems, the country is unlikely to remain satisfied with exchanging its steel for Chinese rice and Malaysian rubber,[152] and can be expected to return to the North American market -- "unquestionably the best market of any."[153] As the President of a Brazilian steel company replied when asked if there was a "clear tendency of dislocation" of steel production from developed countries

---

[147] Pinheiro, *Doing Business in Brazil*, 6.105; Office of the United States Trade Representative, *Foreign Trade Barriers*, p. 30.

[148] "Relatório Final de la Subcomisión Especial de Siderurgia del Parlamento Brasileño," in *Siderurgia Latinoamericana* (May 1985).

[149] *Metal Bulletin* (March 24, 1988).

[150] *Siderurgia Latinoamericana* (November 1986) ("Informativo Regional"), p. 19.

[151] *Metal Bulletin* (March 31, 1988).

[152] *Metal Bulletin* (October 4, July 2, 1985). In late 1985, SIDERBRÁS President Lanari noted that the companies earnings would be 20 percent lower than in 1984 "due to the large volume of sales to China, which had absorbed part of the steel diverted from the USA but at lower prices." *Metal Bulletin* (December 20, 1985).

[153] *Siderurgia Latinoamericana* (December 1984) ("Informativo Regional"), p. 14.

toward countries such as Brazil, "I see this trend clearly . . . the train has already started in this direction and it cannot any longer be detained."[154]

Such statements are incongruous in light of the Brazilian experience in steel. While Brazilians may view their country's growth as a steel exporter as inevitable, Brazil has yet to demonstrate that it can sustain a viable integrated steel industry. The Brazilian industry has been built up by means of massive subsidies and extraordinary levels of debt, much of which may never be repaid. Brazilian losses in steel have been enormous, and the industry continues to be plagued with administrative and management problems. While the country has become a major steel exporter, it has done so through levels of dumping and subsidization which have few equals even in an industry where these practices are endemic. In the end, the decisive factor may not be Brazilian competitiveness but Brazilian economic nationalism. As *Jornal do Brasil* commented with respect to Brazilian export subsidies on June 13, 1978:

> *Exports are decisive for the survival of some enterprises and for the success of our foreign trade strategy. . . . Is Brazil granting subsidies? It is. But who does not? . . . Brazil is willing to play for high stakes in defense of its interests -- as the other international trade partners do, with greater or lesser reasons than Brazil.*

SOUTH KOREA

In a relatively short period, South Korea has established what some observers regard as the most competitive steel industry in the world. The Korean industry, grouped around the state-owned Pohang Iron and Steel Company (POSCO), enjoys modern production facilities, low costs, and strong management. By 1986 Korea had become the world's seventh largest steel exporter, and was continuing to expand its steel production facilities despite global overcapacity. Korean steel has rapidly displaced the Japanese mills in many East Asian markets and has made dramatic inroads throughout the Pacific basin; Korea is now the United States' fourth largest source of steel imports after the EC, Japan and Canada. While many accounts of the spectacular ascent of Korean steel attribute its rise solely to entrepreneurial talent and the zeal of its management and workers, a far more important factor has been the industrial policies of the Korean government, without which Korea could not have emerged as a major international competitive force in steel.

At the beginning of the 1960s, Korea was a resource-poor, low-income developing country whose population still primarily depended on agriculture for its livelihood.[155] General Park Chung Hee assumed the Presidency after

---

[154] P. Schmithals, President of Mannessman, S.A., quoted in *Siderurgia Latinoamericana* (September 1986), p. 54.

[155] U.S.I.T.C., *Foreign Industrial Targeting*, p. 121.

(Million metric tons)

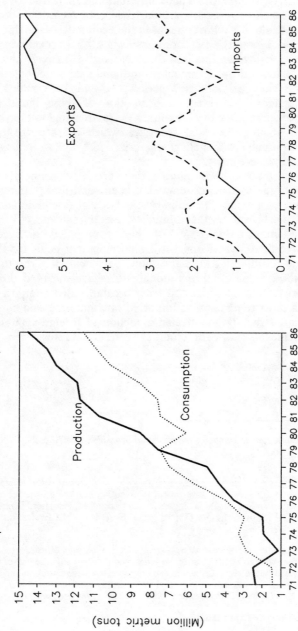

Figure 5-3: South Korea — Steel Production, Consumption and Trade, 1971–1986

Source: International Iron and Steel Institute, Steel Statistical Yearbook, 1981, 1987. Production and Consumption refer to crude steel; Exports and Imports refer to semi-finished and finished steel.

a military coup in 1961, and imposed a developmental strategy of ambitious modernization on the country. In the following decades the nation was propelled into the status of a major international industrial power through the implementation of government industrial policy measures noteworthy for the "prominent role of the government in the economy, the boldness of policy changes, and, not least, the extraordinary results."[156] Korean industrial policy measures are roughly divisible into three phases: a "takeoff" phase between 1961 and 1973, featuring government promotion of export-oriented industries; a "heavy and chemical industry" period between 1973 and 1979, which emphasized extensive government promotion of these industries; and a "liberalization" phase after 1980, featuring the gradual and uneven curtailment of the more overt government measures which characterized the earlier periods, but which was still characterized by substantial government intervention in the economy.[157]

Through all three of these phases, the Korean government's role in the development of the national economy has been pervasive.[158] Industrial policy was implemented pursuant to military standards of discipline and efficiency that were "transferred to the administrative bureaucracy."[159] The State Economic Planning Board (EPB) has formulated a succession of comprehensive Five Year Plans, setting development goals for the nation's industries and coordinating the acquisition and allocation of resources needed to achieve those goals.[160] Promotional tools have included the setting of annual export targets; subsidies and other fiscal incentives; import protection, coupled with tariff remissions on imported raw materials and equipment for designated industries; the controlled induction of foreign capital; and most importantly, allocation of bank credit at preferential rates.

---

[156] World Bank, *Korea: Managing the Industrial Transition* (1987), p. 29.

[157] *Ibid.*, p. 31.

[158] One observer commented in 1982 that "It could be argued that the Korean model, if it demonstrates anything, shows that government intervention into the private sector has been as profound, pervasive, and all-encompassing as in many socialist economies." D. Steinberg, *The Economic Development of Korea; Sui Genesis or Sui Generic?*, A.I.D. Evaluation Special Study No. 6, January 1982.

[159] During and after the Korean War, large numbers of Korean officers attended U.S. staff schools where they studied administration, logistics, and planning. By the end of the 1950s, the Korean military had "more highly trained management skills, better discipline, and higher morale than the government bureaucracy or any other group in Korean society." Vincent S.R. Brandt, "Korea," in Lodge and Vogel, *Ideology and National Competitiveness*, p. 220.

[160] *Korea's Economy* (April 1983).

Preferential Credit Allocation

Far and away the single most significant industrial promotion tool used by the Korean government has been the preferential allocation of credit to favored industries and firms. Until the early 1980s the government owned controlling interests in four of the five nationwide commercial banks and indirectly controlled the fifth; it held majority interests in Korea's six specialized banks and wholly owned the Korea Development Bank (KDB), by far the largest single financial institution in Korea, as well as the Export-Import Bank.[161] The commercial banks were completely dominated by the government; a Western observer commented in 1982 that "the monetary system is run like a military unit."[162]

The Korean government has always controlled the interest rate on loans by government and commercial banks. The official rates are extremely low, and, in light of Korea's rate of inflation, they have actually been negative for extended periods, particularly in the 1970s (table 5-6). In addition to the official rates, until 1982, the government fixed a wide variety of special, extremely low rates for so-called "policy loans" to achieve a variety of industrial policy objectives, such as the acquisition of equipment to be used in export industries and to finance production for export.[163] The ceilings on interest rates naturally created an excess demand for credit, and the government controlled the rationing of this credit to designated industries. As an official of the Korean Institute of Development Financing commented in 1979, "our financial policy supports an extremely low rate of interest for the targeted industries."[164] *Korea's Economy* observed in September 1983 that

Through ownership and directives, the government controlled the allocation of bank credit by sector, and even by individual firms, during 1963-81. All bank loans were made at administered interest

---

[161] The Korea Development Bank is the largest source of long-term financing for industry. Most foreign loans to Korean industry have been made through the KDB and another government bank, the Korea Exchange Bank. *Far Eastern Economic Review* (April 26, 1984).

[162] *Asian Wall Street Journal* (June 9, 1982).

[163] "The bank loan rate of interest has been controlled by the government at a rate always below the curb market rate. . . . This controlled rate provided an effective way to channel resources in favor of export industries, through subsidized loans." Y. Lim, *Government Policy and Private Enterprise: Korean Experience in Industrialization* (Berkeley: Center for Korean Studies, Korea Research Monograph, 1981), p. 31.

[164] Chong Hyun Nam, *Characteristics of the Iron and Steel Industry and its Supply and Demand Structure* (Berkeley: Center for Korean Studies, June 30, 1979); U.S. Embassy, Seoul, "Great Expectations: A Tale of the Steel Industry in Korea," Airgram dated June 23, 1983.

rates well below market-clearing rates. . . . Bank credit was allocated to promote desired investment, output and exports.[165]

Firms and individuals that could not qualify for loans at the government-controlled rates were forced onto the private credit or "curb" market, where rates frequently ran 3-4 times higher than the government-controlled rates.[166]

Table 5-6. South Korean Nominal and Real Interest Rates

Year	Nominal Rate	Real Rate
1971	23.0	10.9
1972	17.0	2.2
*1973	15.5	2.3
*1974	15.5	(14.1)
*1975	15.5	(9.2)
*1976	16.5	(1.2)
*1977	17.3	1.0
*1978	17.7	(2.9)
*1979	19.9	(0.6)
1980	20.0	(5.6)
1981	16.5	0.6
1982	10.0	2.9
1983	10.0	7.0
1984	10.0 - 10.5	6.2 - 6.7
1985	10.0 - 11.5	5.9 - 7.4
1986	10.0 - 11.5	7.7 - 9.2

* Asterisks denote approximate years of the heavy and chemical industries industrialization drive. Source: Bank of Korea, *Economic Statistics Yearbook* 1986

The government supplemented the financial resources of both the government-owned KDB and the private deposit money banks with funds appropriated directly from the state budget and from special government funds

---

[165] Similarly, a 1982 staff paper by the International Monetary Fund commented that "Bank interest rates in Korea are under official control. As a result of selective credit policies, a large number of preferential interest rates to support activities accorded priority by the Government have emerged over the years." International Monetary Fund, *Korea: Recent Economic Developments*, April 9, 1982.

[166] The curb market is a source of capital for small businesses, large corporations and individuals -- in effect, any borrower that cannot secure all of its needed funds by means of government-directed low interest credit. In 1976 the "curb" interest rate was 40.5 percent. The government controlled rate was 17.5 percent; and the short-term rate for exports was 8 percent. Lim, *Korean Experience in Industrialization*; *Korea Herald* (May 9, 1982); *Asian Wall Street Journal* (June 9, 1982); Economic Planning Board, *Economic Bulletin* (May 26, 1982); *Korea's Economy* (September 1983).

such as the National Investment Fund (NIF).[167] The government directed the depository banks with respect to both the allocation of these government funds and the banks' own resources to particular priority sectors and projects.[168] Loans were made in accordance with government priorities rather than commercial considerations.[169]

These fiscal policies played a central role in the expansion of the Korean steel industry. In 1973 the Korean government shifted its industrial policy emphasis from one of general export promotion to the rapid expansion of the heavy and chemical industries (HCI), in which steel was the dominant sector in terms of investment requirements. The single most important aspect of the HCI phase was the preferential allocation of credit, usually at negative real rates of interest, to designated HCI industries. The World Bank estimated in 1987 that the cost of borrowing for HCI sectors between 1973 and 1979 was 20-35 percent below that for light industries during the same period; for the steel industry, which borrowed at extremely low rates, the margin was higher than that (table 5-7). The National Investment Fund loaned nearly two- thirds of its portfolio to HCI projects; the real impact of this bias was its "announcement effect" on commercial bank lending practices with respect to government priorities.[170] The HCIs received a number of other government

---

[167] The NIF is a government fund established to provide subsidized medium-term credit to designated industrial sectors. In 1983 it accounted for approximately one-third of the KDB's total borrowing to finance its domestic operations.

[168] The Korea Development Bank IV, *Korea: Staff Appraisal Report*, November 20, 1980 (Report No. 3106-KO) (hereafter, *"Staff Appraisal"*) W. Hong described how the loans were allocated: "All the KDB loans and 30 to 40 percent of the total DMB loans [deposit money banks] were so-called 'policy loans' which were allocated according to the government investment and financial plan. The remaining 60-70 percent of DMB loans were allocated in accordance with the Regulation on the Use of Loan Funds. Since the Regulation is fairly vague with respect to actual loan management, there existed, at least in theory, some room for discretion by bank officers. In practice, however, even the distribution of non-policy loans was heavily influenced by the government investment policies and various other non-economic considerations." Wontack Hong, *Trade Distortions and Employment Growth in Korea* (1979), p. 163.

[169] As the KDB indicated in its 1982 *Annual Report* (pp. 18-19), "The investments of the KDB have been made with major emphasis on the national economy, rather than profitability, in conformity with the purpose of its establishment, which is to expedite the reconstruction of industries and the development of economy."

[170] In 1976 the Korean government Heavy and Chemical Industry Promotion Council commented that" The Fund [NIF] will provide capital needed beyond the equity and foreign loan investment to construct the planned heavy and chemical industries so that there will be no problems during the construction period. . . . Since long term funds at low interest are necessary for the construction of heavy and chemical industries because profits cannot be expected over the short term and the construction period will be relatively long, the plan is for the Fund to supply low interest loans by combining the fund sources of private savings induced at market rates with capital subscribed by the government at no interest. The mix of this interest free capital subscription with resources raised through issuance of Fund bonds allows the Fund to make loans to the heavy and chemical industries at lower rates of interest." Heavy and Chemical Industry Promotion Council, *Heavy and Chemical Industry* (Seoul: 1976), p. 18.

Table 5-7. Average Cost of Borrowing by Selected Korean Industries, 1973-84 (percent interest)

	1973	1974	1975	1976	1977	1978	1979	1980	1981	1982	1983	1984
Steel	5.93	7.93	7.77	7.85	7.28	6.63	9.67	11.36	15.00	11.23	10.52	12.47
Construction	2.28	11.70	12.90	15.00	11.80	15.30	17.20	18.40	19.50	16.10	15.40	13.55
Chemicals, Petroleum, Coal	9.36	13.23	13.11	13.34	12.34	15.30	17.31	23.58	20.58	18.12	13.91	17.45
Paper & Printing	11.65	14.44	14.99	16.59	17.08	16.96	18.76	20.99	20.09	19.17	13.92	12.21
Fabricated Metal Products	8.62	12.11	10.61	11.66	12.32	11.51	13.46	19.71	17.51	15.69	13.08	13.98
W&R Trade, Hotels	11.18	12.00	14.70	15.80	16.40	16.70	20.30	23.70	24.80	18.40	16.30	17.19
Nonmetallic Minerals	10.39	8.33	11.54	10.37	11.34	10.56	13.34	15.72	17.54	16.06	14.69	13.59

Source: World Bank, *Korea: Managing the Industrial Transition*, Vol. II, 1987, p. 124.

benefits, including a five year tax holiday, accelerated depreciation, and investment tax credits, at a time when other Korean industries faced higher taxes. Reflecting these policies, between 1977 and 1979, the HCIs accounted for nearly four fifths of Korean industrial investment.[171]

The Expansion of the Korean Steel Industry

The promotion of a modern steel industry had begun several years before the HCI drive placed steel at the center of the nation's economic priorities. In the late 1960s South Korea's steel industry consisted largely of a few antiquated open hearth furnaces and rolling mills engaged in finishing operations that were largely dependent upon imported semifinished steel to compensate for Korea's comparative lack of integrated steelmaking capability.[172] During the Second Five Year Plan (1966-1971), President Park Chung Hee determined to give the development of a modern steel industry the highest priority because of its defense implications. Park appointed retired General Park Tae Joon as Chairman of the Committee for the Development of the Steel Industry in 1967 and charged him with planning and arranging funding for the construction of a modern integrated steelworks in Korea. The Pohang Iron and Steel Company (POSCO) was formed in 1968 under government majority ownership to undertake this project. The POSCO project encountered a major initial obstacle when various foreign lending agencies refused to help finance the project on the grounds that it was not commercially feasible, and the Korean government itself provided the necessary capital, using Japanese war reparations funds.[173]

POSCO was organized as a quasi-governmental entity. The government and the government-owned Korea Development Bank held a majority of the equity ownership and the rest of the firm's stock was held by government-

---

[171] World Bank *Annual Report* 1987, Vol. I, pp. 39-42.

[172] The industry suffered from poor integration, inadequate scale economies and superannuated equipment, and was unable to satisfy more than about one-fourth of South Korea's domestic steel demand. Korea Development Bank (KDB), *Industry in Korea* (1976), pp. 52-53; *Korea News Review* (November 12, 1983), p. 13.

[173] Suk Tai Suh, "Statistical Report on Foreign Assistance and Loans to Korea (1945-75)," Monograph 7602, Korean Development Institute, September 1976, p. 5. The International Bank for Reconstruction and Development and the International Economic Consultative Organization for Korea "rejected the feasibility of an integrated steelworks in Korea, reasoning that Korea would find it difficult to repay foreign credits due to its rising foreign debts." *Korea Herald* (February 18, 1981). In 1973 the World Bank still refused to loan money to the POSCO project, considering it impractical. *Wall Street Journal* (May 13, 1981). As Pohang's first steelmaking capacity came on stream in the early 1970s, international lending institutions continued to counsel that expansion of POSCO was inadvisable. However, "President Park Chung Hee, eager to take South Korea on one giant leap towards industrialization, overrode the advice of the World Bank and the U.S. Eximbank against the POSCO project." *Far Eastern Economic Review* (February 13, 1981).

controlled Korean banks. All management-level positions and policy decisions were subject to government approval, with daily operations (including pricing and marketing) left to company management.[174] The initial phase of construction of the Pohang works resulted in the completion of production capacity capable of producing 1.0 million tons of crude steel per year in 1973, when the HCI drive began. Thereafter, as a succession of accelerated expansion plans were implemented, POSCO's capacity increased by an average of 1 million tons per year through 1981 (table 5-8).

Direct and indirect government financial support remained instrumental in this expansion, including a variety of fiscal, transportation, and resource benefits available under the 1970 *Steel Industry Promotion Act*.[175] The government made periodic equity injections into POSCO during the 1970s despite the fact that the company did not pay dividends on its stock.[176] In the late 1970s the Korean government borrowed $131 million from the Japanese government and reloaned the sum to POSCO at an interest rate of 3.5 percent per year repayable over the period 1979-1996.[177]

However, the government's single most important contribution came during the heavy and chemical industrialization drive (1973-79) when it used its complete control over the Korean financial system to channel low interest loan capital to POSCO to finance its intensive building program.[178] As a World Bank study concluded in 1987, POSCO's development was attributable

---

[174] U.S. Embassy, Seoul, "Great Expectations," *op. cit.*

[175] Law No. 2181, January 1, 1970, amended by Law No. 3179, December 28, 1979 and Presidential Decree No. 5366, October 20, 1970, amended by Presidential Decree 10002, August 23, 1970. According to a former executive of the Korea Development Institute, pursuant to this law, "not only can the government invest in a steel mill (with capacity exceeding 1 million tons), it can also provide the manufacturer with long term low interest loans using fiscal funds as well as various means of administrative support. The government can also provide various SOC facilities in addition to the discounts on railway rates (up to 30 percent), harbor rental (up to 50 percent), water rates (up to 30 percent), electricity rates (up to 50 percent) and on gas rates (up to 20 percent). Furthermore, a supplier of iron ore to a domestic steel mill is treated like an exporter of ore." Hong, *Trade Distortions*.

[176] In 1979 POSCO's capital was increased from 300 million shares to 450 million shares with a par value of $2.07 per share. The shares were purchased by POSCO's shareholders in rough proportion to the existing percentage of equity ownership, although the government's total share increased by 0.5%. POSCO's 1979 *Financial Statement* indicated (p. 26) that "no dividend has been paid since the date of the establishment of the company."

[177] POSCO 1978 *Financial Statement*. The U.S. Commerce Department held that this loan was not a countervailable subsidy because it was made from Japanese war reparations funds.

[178] The Korea Development Bank commented in 1976 that "thanks to the government's various supports, the large-scale capital goods industries such as iron and steel . . . were industrialized more rapidly." KDB, *Industry in Korea*, p. 16.

Table 5-8. Expansion of the Pohang Iron and Steel Company (POSCO)

Year	Item	Total Installed Crude Steel Capacity (million metric tons)
1968	POSCO Incorporated	——
1970	First Stage Project Construction Begins	——
1973	First Stage Project Completed; Second Stage Begins	1.0
1976	Second Stage Project Completed; Third Stage Begins	2.6
1978	Third Stage Project Completed	5.5
1979	Fourth Stage Project Begins	5.5
1981	Phase 1 of Fourth Stage Completed	8.5
1982	Site Preparation for Second Integrated Plant at Gwang Yang Begins	8.5
1983	Phase II of Fourth Stage Project Completed, Kwangyang Stage One Construction Begins	9.1
1986	Kwangyang Stage Two Construction Begins	9.1
1987	Kwangyang Stage One Completed	11.8
1988	Kwangyang Stage Two Completed	14.5
1989	Kwangyang Stage Three Construction Begins	14.5
1991	Kwangyang Stage Three Construction Completed	17.2

to "highly subsidized capital."[179] The industry was formally designated as a priority sector for lending by Korea's largest bank, the government-owned Korea Development Bank;[180] the POSCO project was specifically singled out as a priority for KDB loans;[181] and by 1978 the KDB was POSCO's largest single domestic creditor.[182] As a result of its priority designation, POSCO also received low interest loans from private commercial banks.[183] In 1976, of the $217 million in low interest industrial loans extended by the government National Investment Fund (NIF), nearly 10 percent ($20.7 million) was allocated to POSCO.[184]

In addition to directing domestic credit, the Korean government controlled the allocation of foreign investment capital to specific industries and projects, including POSCO. On the basis of actual and *de facto* government guarantees,[185] POSCO was able to raise about one half of the capital needed

---

[179] World Bank, *Annual Report* 1987, Vol. I, p. 45.

[180] KDB, *Staff Appraisal*, The *Korea Herald* reported on December 14, 1982 that the KDB would provide a total of $2.5 billion in "policy funds" to designated sectors in 1982. The funds were to be raised by the KDB through foreign borrowing, issuing bonds, and borrowing from the National Investment Fund. The steel and shipbuilding industries were to receive $170 million in KDB funds.

[181] *Korea Herald* (October 3, 1981); KDB, *Staff Appraisal*, p. 25. The KDB's Policy Statement provides that the KDB shall not normally extend financial assistance to a single entity in excess of either 25 percent of its own equity or 65 percent of the total assets of the enterprise. As of December 31, 1979 the KDB had exceeded these limits in 15 cases amounting to $7.3 billion – an amount representing 57 percent of the aggregate loan, investment, and guarantee portfolio of the largest financial institution in Korea. Two companies – Korea Electric Co. and Pohang Iron and Steel Co. – accounted for 68 percent of the exceptions. *Staff Appraisal*, Annex B, p. 7.

[182] POSCO *Financial Statement* 1978.

[183] POSCO *Financial Statement* 1978. The Korean government stood as guarantor of loans made at its behest; a World Bank staff paper indicated that "the Government agreed to relieve KDB of the financial risk pertaining to such loans." KDB, *Staff Appraisal*, p. 69.

[184] Planning Office, Heavy and Chemical Industry Promotion Council, *Heavy and Chemical Industry* (1976), p. 19. A significant feature of Korea's interest rate policy is the fact that reductions in the government controlled interest rate apply to the interest on outstanding loans, as well as on new loans, resulting in substantial benefits to sectors that had been major beneficiaries of controlled domestic credit – in effect, the firm's overall financing charges were reduced by government fiat. Thus, when the government of Korea reduced the controlled interest rate on commercial loans from 14% to 10% in mid-1982, the Ministry of Commerce and Industry announced that "The state-run Pohang Iron and Steel Co. and the country's nine other steelmakers . . . will save 107 billion [US$146 million] in 1982 interest payments." *Korea Herald* (July 9, 1982).

[185] POSCO's foreign creditors secured covenants in their loan agreements requiring the Korean government at all times to maintain majority equity ownership in POSCO, effectively guaranteeing the repayment of the loans. POSCO *Financial Statement* 1978, p. 26. Lim, in *Korean Experience in Industrialization*, commented (pp. 33-34) that "More than 90 percent of

for its expansion efforts from foreign banks despite the fact that a number of international lending institutions had concluded that the project was not commercially feasible.[186] A number of foreign export-import banks agreed to extend favorable equipment financing to the Pohang project -- even the U.S. Eximbank ultimately entered the fray, providing $75 million in equipment financing in 1975-77.[187]

Efforts at Liberalization

Beginning around 1980, with the implementation of Korea's Fifth Five Year Plan, the government began a cautious process of disengagement from some of its more overt market intervention policies.[188] This change in direction reflected the fact that the growing complexity of Korea's economy was making it more difficult for the government to manage, and a recognition that far too great a proportion of the nation's resources had been channeled into heavy industry in the 1970s, resulting in major distortions in the economy. In finance, liberalization efforts were manifested in the sale of some government-owned banks to private investors; the progressive consolidation of the various "policy loan" interest rates into a few unitary rates; and an effort to reduce and eventually phase out the policy of credit rationing to particular sectors. In trade, formal import restrictions were slowly reduced or eliminated.

---

foreign loans [to Korean industry] were in the form of supplier's credits. Foreign lenders were willing to lend money, encouraged by repayment guarantees provided either by the Bank of Korea or by the government."

[186] As of 1981 domestic investments totalling $1.3 billion had been made in the Pohang mill; foreign capital contribution through that point had totalled $1.96 billion. *Korea Herald* (February 19, 1981). A joint study by Harvard University and the Korea Development Institute observed that "the most glaring examples of misallocation appear to have been the cases where government was heavily involved in arranging large packages of foreign and domestic financing for projects of questionable profitability, such as the steel mills. . . . Although interest rates, cost-benefit ratios, and internal rates of return may have been given lip service at the time of project appraisal, they were actually irrelevant to the final decision, which was made by government on grounds of international defense or prestige." D.C. Cole and Y.C. Park, *Studies in the Modernization of the Republic of Korea, 1945-78* (1983).

[187] U.S. Export-Import Bank staff and *Supplement to the Annual Report 1975*, p. 29. The *Korea Herald* commented on February 18, 1981 that as a result of such bank lending competition, "Quality facilities could be obtained at relatively low cost as a result of international competitive biddings. . . . It should not be overlooked that although the world monetary mart has entered a high-interest age, as can be seen in 17 percent LIBO and 20 percent Prime Rate . . . POSCO introduced foreign credits bearing an annual average interest of 8 percent, thanks to close contact maintained with foreign capital." *Korea Herald* (February 18, 1981).

[188] Economic Planning Board, *A Summary Draft of the Fifth Five Year Economic and Social Development Plan*, September 1981.

These changes, while significant, did not herald an abrupt end to Korea's traditional industrial policies; the World Bank commented in 1987 that "the actual reforms witnessed so far have involved mainly changes in the objectives pursued and the overtness of policy tools."[189] Privatization of government-owned banks was "nominal," with banks still operating as *de facto* arms of the government's industrial policies and lending primarily to well established industrial groups favored by the government.[190] The official interest rates, while unified, were still artificially low, and "would soar if decontrolled." As a result, in 1988, low interest credit was still being allocated, with "bank managements better attuned to politics than economics."[191] In addition, large business and trade associations were formed to monitor implementation of past government policies; these entities expected continued government intervention and criticized the government for its occasional perceived lack of activism.[192]

POSCO has continued to enjoy a favored position in the new industrial environment that has evolved since the beginning of the 1980s. POSCO receives special treatment on price and credit terms for its raw materials since it is the institution through which the government controls the price of a basic industrial material, steel.[193] POSCO enjoys a domestic monopoly on a number of basic steel products, and while it maintains relatively low prices, it enjoys a substantial degree of price stability in its domestic market. POSCO was completely exempt from corporate income taxes until 1982, and the entire Korean steel industry continued to benefit from favorable tax treatment after 1982.[194]

---

[189] World Bank, *Annual Report* 1987, Vol. I, p. 55.

[190] The *Far Eastern Economic Review* commented on April 24, 1984 that "The government sold off the last bank, Choheung Bank, to private owners in March last year but South Korean banks are still operating as arms of Seoul's industrial policies, lending to well-established borrowers at rates well under those charged on the kerb [private market]." See also *Asian Wall Street Journal* (March 28, 1983). Similarly, the Federation of Korean Industries (FKI) indicated in 1984 that "the available financial resources of the bank are focused on very limited sectors according to government-set priorities. Such "government preferred borrowers" include a very limited number of key industries. . . ." *Business Korea* (June 1984).

[191] *Far Eastern Economic Review* (February 11, 1988). Overt use of policy loans by the commercial banks was ended in 1982, but the practice of policy loans continued in government financial institutions like the KDB and the NIF. *Business Korea Yearbook* (1987), p. I-47.

[192] World Bank, *Annual Report*, Vol. I, p. 55.

[193] *Business Korea Yearbook* (1987), p. III-415; *Far Eastern Economic Review* (May 21, 1987).

[194] *Korea Herald* (October 28, 1983). Steelmaking is designated as a "basic industry with military implications and export promotion aspects" for purposes of the Tax Exemption and Reduction Control Act (effective January 1, 1982). Within the designated sectors, deductions equivalent to a 100 percent depreciation rate or up to 5 percent of total business assets are available. *East Asian Executive Reports* (March 15, 1982); *Business Asia* (February 5, 1982). *East*

The Korean government has restricted wage levels for POSCO's workers, with the result that the Company has one of the lowest labor costs per ton of any integrated steel mill in the world.[195] POSCO is not unionized; employee relations are handled by a "labor/management coordinating committee," made up of representatives of labor and management. Labor unrest shook 18 Korean steel companies in 1987, although most of these disputes were reportedly settled peacefully through labor-management negotiations. POSCO's workers received one pay increase in 1987 and will receive another in 1988; increases which, with bonuses, will bring monthly wages to about $820, or one third the wage levels of Japanese steel workers.[196]

The Kwangyang Project

Reflecting the progressive expansion of the Pohang facility, South Korea's domestic steel production exceeded domestic consumption for the first time in 1979 -- and by 1982 was resulting in an annual surplus of over 4 million metric tons.[197] Nevertheless, despite growing surpluses and a stagnant world market, POSCO has pressed ahead in the 1980s with ambitious plans to establish a massive new greenfield integrated plant at Kwangyang Bay. The Kwangyang facility would produce basic steel items with the most advanced technology, while POSCO's older Pohang facility converted to the production of a variety of advanced steel product types.

Stage One of the Kwangyang project, completed in 1987, brought 2.7 million metric tons of new steelmaking capacity on stream, and the completion of Stage Two at the end of 1988 would boost Kwangyang capacity to 5.4 million metric tons, giving POSCO overall capacity of 14.5 million metric tons by the end of the decade of the 1980s and making it one of the largest steel producers in the world. Moreover, in late 1987, POSCO announced a Stage Three expansion effort at Kwangyang, which would add another 2.7 million metric tons of capacity by 1992. The Kwangyang facilities featured a

---

Asian Executive Reports commented on March 15, 1982 that "the new tax changes are part of Korea's efforts to focus on certain major industries and expand its global market share in those areas."

[195] In 1982 the Korean government indicated to the U.S. Commerce Department that there are no mandatory wage controls for any industry in Korea, and that the government does not control or influence POSCO's wage levels. The Commerce Department accepted this statement *Certain Steel Products from Korea*, 47 F.R. 57539. However, the *Korea Times* reported on February 23, 1982 that "the government has decided to allow 23 state-run enterprises to raise their wages by an average of 6-10 percent this month. . . . The first group of 14 enterprises . . . has been permitted to raise pay scales by between 6 and 8 percent while the other group has been authorized to raise the wage levels by between 8 and 10 percent. The government plans to level the pay scale of all the state-run enterprises gradually."

[196] U.S.I.T.C., *Steel Sheet and Strip Industry*, pp. 10-5, 10-8.

[197] International Iron and Steel Institute, *Steel Statistical Yearbook 1987*.

continuous casting and extensive use of automation and computerization.[198] Expansion at Kwangyang has been paralleled by extensive new investments by POSCO at its original Pohang site.

Financing this expansion required a massive investment. A Korean source estimated that in 1986 the nation's steel producers would invest $1.6 billion, about half of which was earmarked for Kwangyang.[199] While POSCO has financed over half of the cost of Kwangyang from its own resources,[200] its status as a state-owned and supported firm has clearly proven beneficial in enabling it to sustain this effort. In 1987 POSCO's management opposed a proposed privatization initiative floated by the government, arguing that the sale would be "coming too early, while the company is still engaged in massive investment."[201] In 1987,

> *An executive at one of the other big eight [Korean] steel companies complained of POSCO's preferential treatment, calling it "the hand of the government reaching down into the depths of this industry."*[202]

POSCO was also greatly aided in financing its expansion through concessional export financing of the equipment purchased from western suppliers. The Export-Import banks of the supplying countries rushed to extend concessional financing offers to POSCO, enabling the Koreans to play one off against the other to obtain financing at far below market rates.[203] Government funds also helped to establish the necessary infrastructure for Kwangyang; government funds of approximately $290 million were allocated to cover construction costs of basic groundwork for the mill, including roads,

---

[198] *Maeil Kjongje Sinmun* (February 27, 1987); *Business Korea* (January 1988); *Korea Business World* (December 1987).

[199] *Maeil Kjongje Sinmun* (April 12, 1986).

[200] *Korea Times* (February 21, 1987).

[201] *Far Eastern Economic Review* (May 21, 1987). This proposal was designed in part to "help quash allegations that POSCO's success is due to government support." *Metal Bulletin* (November 7, 1986).

[202] *Far Eastern Economic Review* (May 21, 1987).

[203] Austria, for example, announced in 1983 that it would offer 6.25 percent financing for any and all exports of equipment to Kwangyang, triggering a flurry of interest rate reductions by other nations. The United States Eximbank disapproved of this bidding war and refused to enter into it; its Chairman commented in 1984 that the Bank would not make any more loans or guarantees that had the effect of subsidizing steelmaking capacity. *American Metal Market* (April 24, 1984).

29.1 kilometers of new railroad line, loading and unloading port facilities, and electric and communications facilities.[204]

Private Steel Producers

While POSCO is the dominant entity in Korean steel, Korea supports a number of privately owned steel firms which have become important international competitors. Most of these firms belong to large Korean industrial groups (*chaebol*) which provide them with a substantial financial backing, and a few are POSCO affiliates or subsidiaries. Many of the private Korean mills engage in downstream processing of products (such as pipes and tubes and cold-rolled and galvanized sheets) from intermediate products manufactured by POSCO.

The private firms have not received the same degree of public assistance as POSCO, but they benefit indirectly from the government support given to POSCO, which is manifested in part through low domestic steel prices, as well as the government's various steel industry support schemes, import protection, and export incentives. In addition, the Korean government has intervened in a number of instances to bail out these firms when they have encountered financial crisis. Inchon Iron and Steel, a manufacturer of structurals and Korea's second largest steel producer, encountered financial difficulties in the 1970s; these were "ironed out" by the Korean Development Bank and the firm was acquired by the Hyundai *chaebol*.[205] Ilssin Steel went bankrupt in 1982, and its assets were acquired by POSCO through a newly-established subsidiary, Dong Jin Steel.[206] Union Steel's *chaebol* collapsed in 1985; a rescue plan for Union was devised by creditor banks and the Korean government in which the top management of the company was taken over by POSCO executives.[207]

Import Protection

During its industrialization drive, Korea pursued an import substitution trade policy with respect to steel; as the domestic industry became capable of producing a particular product, import restrictions would be imposed on it. Steel products manufactured by Korean firms were placed on the list of "restricted import items," which meant that the product could only be imported if approved by the Ministry of Commerce and Industry and on the

---

[204] *Yonhap*, 11:00 GMT, March 5, 1982 (Foreign Broadcast Information Service).

[205] *Business Korea* (July 1987).

[206] *Certain Cold-Rolled Carbon Steel Products from Korea*, 49 F.R. 47284 (final), December 3, 1984.

[207] U.S.I.T.C., *Steel Sheet and Strip Industry*, p. 10-7.

recommendation of the Korean Iron and Steel Association, which represents South Korea's steel manufacturers. The proportion of steel items on the restricted list jumped from 28 percent in 1967 to 75 percent in 1978 as Korean steelmaking capability developed.[208] In 1979 an official of the Korean Institute of Development Planning commented that

> *trade liberalization is not an adequate solution to the problem [of unmet domestic steel demand] due to its various side effects. . . . By letting our iron and steel demand remain at the mercy of external forces, we will become susceptible to the possible ills experienced in other countries, thus allowing our economy to fluctuate at their whims.*[209]

In the late 1970s the Korean government began removing many of Korea's formal barriers to imports of many products, including steel, and between 1984 and 1988, all steel products were removed from the "restricted list." The domestic steel industry opposed these moves; on May 2, 1986 *Maeil Kjongje Sinmum* summarized comments reportedly submitted to the government by the steel industry:

> *Under present circumstances, the domestic industry just cannot face the fight. Aside from product quality, the domestic industry is far inferior in price competition. . . . Domestic supply far exceeds demand. If a foreign product is added to this, the impact on the domestic industry will be significant. In order to help settle the domestic steel industry, the open market should be postponed at least until after 1988.*

Korea retained high tariffs on most steel products, ranging from 10 to 20 percent, prompting criticism by Taiwan that Korea was "limiting steel imports." In late 1987, the Korean government, responding to this charge, lowered tariffs on a variety of steel products, but only for a limited time period and for limited quantities; tariffs were reduced, for example, to 10 percent from 50 percent for high carbon HR coil, but only for 5,200 tons. *Metal Bulletin* reported on September 14, 1987 that "despite the reductions, few importers seem to have taken advantage of the relaxations."

---

[208] World Bank, *Annual Report*, Vol. I, pp. 57-58; *Nikkei Sangyo* (April 2, 1983). While Korea also maintained tariffs on steel imports, Korea has relied primarily on quantitative restrictions rather than tariffs to protect indigenous producers.

[209] Nam, *Characteristics of the Iron and Steel Industry.*

Korean Steel in World Markets

POSCO's Third Stage Project was completed in late 1978 -- doubling its annual crude steel capacity to 5.5 million metric tons -- and in 1979, South Korea for the first time produced a steel surplus and became a net exporter of steel. The volume of Korea's steel export surpluses has progressively increased since that time -- in 1982 Korea exported over half of its total production, 5.9 million metric tons (figure 5-3).[210] South Korea's emergence as a major steel exporter in the midst of a protracted worldwide slump in demand generated widespread trade friction, a fact attributable in part to the aggressiveness with which the Koreans pursued the expansion of their export market.[211]

Japanese steel producers, which had previously dominated East Asian steel markets, were the first to be severely affected by South Korea's rapidly expanding steel exports. Korean steel penetrated the Japanese market (often through clandestine channels) with a greater degree of success than steel from any other source.[212] In East Asia, as the *Japan Economic Journal* reported on December 8, 1981,

> *Aggressive advances of steel products from ROK . . . are sharply eroding Japanese steelmakers' footholds in Southeast Asian markets. . . . Hot coils manufactured by Pohang Iron and Steel started muscling into [Japanese] markets as from last fall and are rapidly pushing Japanese products out of the ring.*[213]

---

[210] Moreover, under current expansion plans, Korea's capacity is projected to more than double in the decade between 1980 and 1990 -- a buildup which portends a significantly higher volume of exports.

[211] A large proportion of South Korea's steel exports are handled by Korean General Trading Companies (GTCs) noted for their price competitiveness. Professor Cho Dong-Sung of South Korea's Seoul National University International Business School of Management has criticized the GTCs for their "predatory dumping" tactics. He notes that these tactics are "closely related" to the fact that Korea's "monopolistic and oligopolistic enterprises . . . tend to go by a dual standard, pricing their products high on the home market while dumping them on export markets." *Business Korea* (November 1983), p. 37.

[212] See chapter 4.

[213] POSCO began undercutting Japanese hot coil prices in Southeast Asia, the Philippines, and South America in 1980 following the completion of a new hot strip mill with a 3.2 million tons/year capacity. The Japanese were forced into defensive price cuts to retain their traditional markets, but their hot coil export volume still fell by 30 percent in 1980 as a result of Korean competition. By 1981 the Japanese had abandoned attempts to match POSCO's pricing in Southeast Asia, declaring that they "will not rise to POSCO's challenge and be drawn into a destructive price cutting war." *Metal Bulletin* (July 18, October 28, November 4, 1980; July 31, 1981); *Nikkei Sangyo* (December 11, 1981; May 24, 1982).

The emergence of Korea was felt all around the Pacific rim.   In 1981,
Australia's John Lysaght, Ltd. brought an antidumping action against POSCO
with respect to cold-rolled sheets, complaining that

> *disastrously low import prices for Korean steel would generate
> continuing pressure and ensure that [John Lysaght's] share of the
> stagnant market continues downward.*[214]

In 1982, Canadian producers of welded steel pipe filed dumping charges
against South Korea, alleging sales below the cost of production, and in 1983
the Canadian government found that 100 percent of the Korean wide-flanged
beams imported into Canada had been dumped at margins averaging 34.9
percent.[215]

Korean steel made dramatic inroads into the U.S. market, where it rose
from 0.9 percent of U.S. consumption in 1978 to 2.4 percent in 1984.
Although this share had fallen to 1.5 percent in 1987, following
implementation of President Reagan's steel program, Korea remains the
fourth largest exporter to the U.S. after Japan, the European Community and
Canada. Korean penetration of the U.S. market was particularly pronounced
in pipes and tubes and wire nails, where the Korean share of the U.S. market
reached a startling 34 percent in 1984, the last year before the VRA.[216]
Korean penetration of the U.S. market prompted a spate of antidumping and
countervailing duty complaints against Korea by U.S. producers between 1982
and 1985. Affirmative findings of dumping were entered against Korean mills

---

[214] *Metal Bulletin* (October 16, 1981). The Koreans agreed to a major increase in the export
price of their steel to offset these charges. In 1983 Australia imposed a 20 percent duty on
imports of South Korean wire, which had previously entered duty free due to Korea's developing-
country status. The 20 percent rate was still lower than the general rate of 30 percent but
"reflects concern that imports of Korean wire, especially wire rope, may be causing injury to
domestic producers." *Metal Bulletin* (October 11, 1983).

[215] *Metal Bulletin* (April 20, 1982; July 26, 1983).

[216] Korean steel has been marketed in the U.S. with an aggressiveness that recalls Korean
penetration of the Japanese market through clandestine channels. In 1983 Korean firms, along
with Brazilian mills, were cited as the "price leaders driving down the market" in a number of
product areas." *American Metal Market* (December 23, 1983). In 1982 a U.S. company pleaded
guilty in Texas to a charge of conspiracy with Daewoo International, a Korean trading company,
to import steel pipe by means of false statements at prices below former Trigger Price levels.
American Metal Market (April 4, 1984). In 1984 a two year federal investigation of Daewoo and
its U.S. subsidiary resulted in a 32-count indictment against Daewoo and nine of its employees
charging them with criminal conspiracy to evade the U.S. antidumping laws with respect to steel
pipe, through a variety of rebate or discount schemes. *Wall Street Journal* (March 26, 1984).

in plate, rectangular pipe and tube, circular pipe and tube and wire nails.[217]

The price-aggressiveness of the South Koreans in international markets is attributable in significant part to Korean competitive strategy. Steel facilities are operated at a high rate of utilization, substantially reducing unit costs, while surpluses are exported at low prices with the assistance of government export promoting measures.[218] The *Japan Economic Journal* commented on December 8, 1981 that one of the primary reasons underlying the "exceptionally strong competitive power of the Pohang steelworks" was the fact that

> *the steelworks operates at full capacity at all times and . . . export prices are held down to very low levels because of the ROK government export promotion policy.*[219]

This mode of operation inevitably gives rise to intense Korean export pressure during downturns in Korean domestic consumption levels, since the surplus available for export becomes much larger -- this phenomenon was cited as one reason for the surge of low-priced Korean exports in 1980 and 1981 which disrupted Japanese markets in Southeast Asia.[220] The *Korea Herald* reported on January 22, 1981 that

> *Korea's exports of steel products amounted to $1,940 million in 1980, an increase of 45.2 percent over the previous year and $500 million over the 1980 export target, despite the worldwide economic recession. . . . Business sources attributed the sizeable increase in*

---

[217] *Circular Welded Carbon Steel Pipes and Tubes from Korea*, 49 F.R. 9926, March 16, 1984; *Certain Steel Wire Nails from Korea*, June 24, 1982 (47 F.R. 27492); *Carbon Steel Plate from Korea*, June 29, 1984 (49 F.R. 26774); *Rectangular Welded Carbon Steel Pipes and Tubes from Korea*, March 16, 1984 (49 F.R. 9936).

[218] There is some evidence that this strategy contemplates export sales at prices substantially below domestic levels. For example, the *Korea Herald* reported on February 17, 1981, that Inchon Iron and Steel's new H-beam rolling mill would produce 100 thousand tons for the domestic market, enabling Korea to save $60 million in foreign exchange which it had paid to import the product; "the company plans to export the remaining 200 thousand tons to earn another $90 million a year." *Ibid.*

[219] *American Metal Market* noted on March 3, 1983 that POSCO operates the Pohang facility at 100 percent capacity utilization.

[220] Korean apparent consumption of steel (crude steel equivalent) fell from 6.9 million tons in 1979 to 5.2 million tons in 1980. Export volume increased from 3.1 million tons to 4.5 million tons over the same period. International Iron & Steel Institute. *Metal Bulletin* (July 31, 1981) reported that according to one South Korean observer, "One major factor keeping [export] prices low in mid-1981 is the current recession affecting Korea's home steel market. When this with its attendant high inflation blows over, possibly sometime next year, South Korea's steel export prices may rise due to increasing home demand. . . ."

steel exports primarily to Korea's efforts to seek new export markets
and develop new products because of dwindling domestic sales.

The Korean government has encouraged this countercyclical strategy by setting higher steel export targets during periods when slack demand is anticipated.[221]

The aggressive pricing of the Korean steelmakers in international markets reflects in part the fact that the South Korean government has undertaken a number of measures to enhance the price competitiveness of designated export industries, including steel.[222] Perhaps the most important measure has been the provision of preferential financing for export enterprises.[223] Prior to 1982, under Korea's Export Financing Regulations, exporters could receive short-term financing from commercial banks at preferential rates. In 1982, the rate for export loans was changed to the official interest rate for all commercial loans, although as a practical matter loans to exporters were still favored because the Bank of Korea established rediscount rates to the commercial banks which were more favorable for export than domestic loans.[224] Exporters also received a variety of tax incentives, including a variety of reserves for export activities which are not subject to corporate tax,[225] and

---

[221] The *Korea Herald* reported on February 23, 1980 that "The government has set the reinforcing bar export goal for this year at 181,000 tons with shipments scheduled to be made entirely in the first half of this year, a period of slack demand for the nation."

[222] *Yonhap*, 3:10 GMT, February 1, 1984 (Foreign Broadcast Information Service); *Far Eastern Economic Review* (April 26, 1984).

[223] As a Korean analyst commented in 1980, "Through its control of the domestic financial structure, the government has established a broad range of short, medium and long-term financial instruments which offer preferential terms to Korean exporters, as opposed to firms which produce only for the domestic market." S.H. Song in *East Asian Executive Reports* (December 1980).

[224] *Certain Cold-Rolled Carbon Steel Products from Korea*, 49 F.R. 47284 (final), December 3, 1984. The *Far Eastern Economic Review* reported on May 10, 1984 that "Currently, the Bank of Korea encourages exports by rediscounting bills of credit brought to them by the domestic banks for 70 percent of the value of the exports, giving the banks a healthy 5 percent yield. South Korean banks typically rely on this export-credit business for around half of their profits – as much an indication of the low profitability of other transactions as it is a sign of the high returns on export finance, which are effectively subsidized by the central bank."

[225] Under Article 22 of the Act Concerning the Regulation of Tax Reduction and Exemption, a corporation may establish a reserve of one percent of foreign exchange earnings, or 50 percent of net income, whichever is smaller; if certain export losses occur, they are offset from the fund. Under Article 23, a corporation may establish a reserve fund equal to one percent of foreign exchange earnings; expenses incurred on developing markets overseas are offset from the fund. Article 24 permits establishment of reserves equal to five percent of the book value of the products which will be exported by the close of the business year, which may be used to offset losses incurred through the fluctuation of prices for imported goods. *Ibid.*

special 30 percent additional depreciation allowances for firms which earn over 50 percent of their total proceeds from foreign exchange.[226]

The Korean government views its various export-promoting measures as a means of offsetting rising domestic costs in order to maintain international competitiveness.[227] In addition, while South Korea's foreign debt -- over $45 billion by 1986 -- does not pose as severe an economic problem as that of Brazil, it remains an important factor underlying the government's export-promoting measures.[228]

MEXICO

The Mexican steel industry emerged as the result of a concerted government policy designed to foster import substitution. After the Mexican Revolution, the government protected domestic producers by means of high tariffs and nontariff measures; in addition, it took over failing private producers and established new state-owned producers alongside them. By the mid-1970s, the industry was quantitatively able to cover most of Mexico's domestic needs; however, it was not internationally competitive in many product lines with regard to either cost or quality. Further, although the government was willing to fund the continued expansion of capacity based on the optimistic demand forecasts generated by the oil boom, strict price controls made it difficult for the industry to generate the revenues necessary to improve the productivity of existing mills and the quality of their products.

With the collapse of world oil prices and the onset of a severe economic crisis in 1982, domestic demand tumbled. Saddled with large debts, low productivity and slack demand, the Mexican industry attempted to maintain revenues by selling its products at low prices in world markets. Although exports increased dramatically, revenues remained inadequate to cover costs and the Mexican government was forced to assist by injecting equity and assuming debt. In the mid-1980s, the government began to rationalize the steel sector and to loosen both price and import controls; these measures were

---

[226] *Ibid.*

[227] *Yonhap* reported on May 29, 1981 that "At a monthly export promotion meeting chaired by President Chon Tu-Whan, [Finance Minister] Yi said that inflation at home weakened the competitive power of Korean exporters, and that the current government subsidy scheme should be continued to tide over such difficulties. As short-term actions, Yi said the government should support the floating system of foreign exchange rates, and extend the 12 percent prime rate for export loans until the end of the year. . . ." 01:17 GMT, Foreign Broadcast Information Service.

[228] *Korean Times* (December 17, 1986). *Far Eastern Economic Review* reported on February 13, 1981 that "Earning foreign exchange will be a priority for POSCO in the months ahead as it must repay large overseas credits incurred during the plant expansion and to pay for raw material imports. Of US $3.4 billion invested over the past 11 years of POSCO's operation, US $2 billion is in the form of supplier's credits involving purchases of such items as a blast furnace from Mitsui and sintering mills, continuous casting mills and cold-rolling mills from Austria's Voest-Alpine." POSCO's debt accounted for about five percent of Korea's total foreign debt.

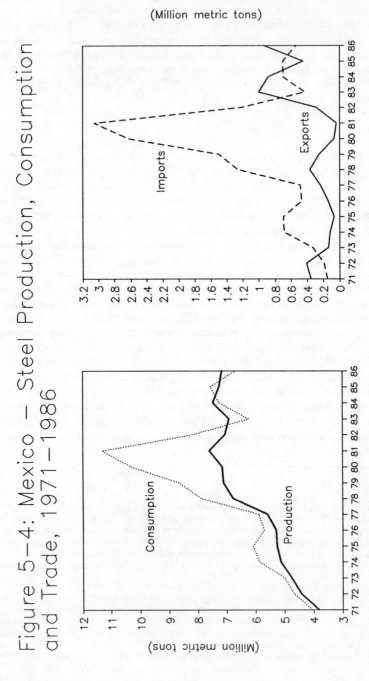

Figure 5–4: Mexico – Steel Production, Consumption and Trade, 1971–1986

(Million metric tons)

Source: International Iron and Steel Institute, Steel Statistical Yearbook, 1981, 1987. Production and Consumption refer to crude steel; Exports and Imports refer to semi-finished and finished steel.

intended to force the industry to compete while allowing it the revenues necessary for that purpose. However, the government still provided assistance to the sector and continued to consider plans for a significant expansion of the nation's capacity.

Decades of Expansion

Unlike the steel industries of many developing countries, the Mexican industry initially was dominated by private producers. Compañía Fundidora de Fierro y Acero de Monterrey (Fundidora), founded in 1900, was the first integrated steelmaker in Latin America;[229] Hojalata y Lámina, S.A. (HYLSA) was established in the 1940s. After the Mexican Revolution, the state assumed a more active role in the development of Mexico's basic industries, both through direct investment and through fiscal and trade policies designed to encourage private initiative.[230] In 1941 the government established Altos Hornos de México, S.A. (AHMSA), now Mexico's largest integrated steelmaker, and in 1976 the government took control of Fundidora. The following year a new state-owned company, Siderurgia Lázaro Cardenas-Las Truchas, S.A. (SICARTSA), began production. In 1979 the state producers were brought together under the control of a single holding company called SIDERMEX.[231]

The consolidation of the Mexican steel industry in the hands of the state occurred during a period of rising domestic demand for steel. During the 1970s, Mexico undertook an aggressive steel industry expansion program, increasing theoretical capacity by approximately 50 percent between 1975 and 1979 (table 5-9). This capacity expansion received substantial government support; from 1970 to 1978, Federal expenditures for the steel industry

---

[229] D. Kendrick, A. Meerhaus & J. Alatorre, *The Planning of Investment Programs in the Steel Industry* (Baltimore: Johns Hopkins University Press, 1984), p. 45.

[230] M. Torre & Y. Mercado, *El Sector Siderúrgico Paraestatal* (Mexico City: Centro de Investigación y Doencia Económicas, 1983), pp. 6-8. The Revolution had a great impact in increasing state participation in economic affairs. As one author explained, "In the name of the Revolution, the new state ... claimed the right to oversee all economic and social activities. With the partial exception of the Porfiriato, the state has always been regulative and entrepreneurial, chartering businesses but competing with them through its own economic activities. But the vast scope of the revolutionary state's social and economic intervention was new. The state went beyond charters to create its own directly productive enterprises, running steel mills, oil wells, farms, and even supermarkets. The norm would be market-shaping, not just market-conforming, policies." J. Domínguez, "Revolution and Flexibility in Mexico," in C. Lodge & E. Vogel, *Ideology and National Competitiveness*, p. 276.

[231] Torre and Mercado, *Sector Paraestatal*, p. 50. The new company represented approximately 60 percent of the nation's steel making capacity. *Ibid.*

Table 5-9. Mexico - Theoretical Crude Steel Capacity (million metric tons)

	SIDERMEX	Private Sector	Total
1975	3.560	2.822	6.383
1977	6.130	3.000	9.130
1979	6..130	3.533	9.663
1981	6.130	3.798	9.928
1983	6.750	3.798	10.548
1986	5.250*	3.798	9.048

* This drop in capacity reflects the closing of Fundidora in 1986.
Source: International Bank for Reconstruction & Development, "Staff Appraisal Report -- Mexico Steel Sector Restructuring Project," February 8, 1988, Annex 2-1, p. 2.

amounted to almost $1.8 billion.[232]   Yet just as Mexico seemed to be approaching self-sufficiency in steel, the unexpected happened: Mexico discovered enormous reserves of oil.   By 1981, as these reserves were developed, steel consumption had climbed to unprecedented levels, and further strong growth appeared likely.

The discovery of oil generated immense optimism about the future of the Mexican economy.   In 1979, the government issued a 5-year National Industrial Development Plan, intended to harness the nation's oil revenues for national development. The Plan identified steel as a "priority" industry entitled to special consideration with regard to economic incentives and import protection.[233] The Plan forecast that Mexican steel demand would soar to 26-28 million metric tons by 1990, three times existing levels,[234] and called for the

---

[232] Torre and Mercado, *Sector Paraestatal*, table 25. Federal aid to state-owned companies was a notable feature of the Mexican economy in the 1970s. In 1975, state subsidies for economic activities constituted 61 percent on all Federal expenditures; as a result, the public sector deficit reached 8.5 percent of GDP in that year. The deficit was financed by domestic borrowing and money creation, generating serious inflationary pressures. U.S.I.T.C. *Developing Country Debt-Servicing Problems*, pp. 19-20.

[233] U.S.I.T.C., *Foreign Industrial Targeting*, pp. 180-181.

[234] *Siderurgia Latinoamericana* (December 1979) ("Situación Futura de la Industria Siderúrgica Mexicana"), p. 71.

expansion of the Mexican industry to meet this demand. SIDERMEX alone was to increase capacity to 21 million metric tons by 1990, at a cost of $17.2 billion, and private companies were also expected to do their share.[235]

The SICARTSA project, a greenfield plant to be built on the isolated Pacific coast of Mexico was the foremost example of the Mexican government's commitment to expand the nation's steel industry. It was to be constructed in four stages; the first stage of the project would produce 1.3 million metric tons of crude steel for non-flat products; upon completion of the fourth stage of the project, in 1995, SICARTSA would be a megamill with an annual capacity 10-11 million metric tons.[236] The World Bank provided $70 million in loans for the first stage, which was completed roughly on schedule in 1977.

The government's principal institutional mechanism for promoting the industry's growth has been Nacional Financiera (Nafinsa), the state's main industrial bank, which finances industrial development programs pursuant to government directives. Nafinsa provides funding for industries "into which private banks just won't go. . . . We run risks that private sector banks are not willing to take."[237] Nafinsa has provided most of the Mexican government's loans to the steel industry;[238] periodically purchased blocks of stock in government-owned and private steel companies;[239] and negotiated loans for the steel industry with national and international lending institutions.[240] Between 1977 and 1982, Nafinsa injected approximately 19.7 billion pesos in equity into AHMSA and Fundidora alone.[241] The government provided additional

---

[235] For example, HYLSA was expected to double capacity, to 3.0 million tons. *Siderurgia Latinoamericana* (September 1980) ("México '80: Panorama Siderúrgico"), p. 6.

[236] Torre and Mercado, *Sector Paraestatal*, p. 19. In addition to SICARTSA, SIDERMEX planned to build another greenfield mill, Siderúrgica III, with an annual capacity of 5 million tons, and to increase AHMSA's production to 4.5 million tons. *Siderurgia Latinoamericana* (February 1980) ("Informativo Regional"), pp. 35-36.

[237] *Institutional Investor* (January 1982).

[238] Nafinsa provides short and long-term debt financing for companies engaged in priority industries at interest rates less than those for commercially available loans. *Certain Carbon Steel Products from Mexico*, February 10, 1984 (49 F.R. 5142).

[239] *El Mercado de Valores* (March 19, 1976); *Nafinsa Annual Report* (1982).

[240] *El Mercado de Valores* (April 11, 1977).

[241] Nafinsa, AHMSA and Fundidora *Annual Reports*, 1977-82.

financial support to the steel industry in the form of various tax and excise concessions and benefits.[242]

The expansion effort was troubled. Although demand was strong in the late 1970s and early 1980s, Mexican producers were unable to take full advantage of the strong market because of a strict system of price controls,[243] while at the same time, they were expected to commit resources to the capacity expansion effort. As a result, private producers in particular were placed under severe financial strain. Fundidora's ambitious $200 million expansion plan, completed in 1976, proved too much for the company.[244] With the nation's oldest steelmaker on the verge of failure, the government had little choice but to step in and assume control of the company.[245] Government aid was also provided to sustain the Alfa Group, owner of HYLSA, Mexico's largest remaining private producer.[246] In addition to pricing and financial problems, the industry suffered from bottlenecks that kept production below theoretical capacity, a weak distribution system, shortcomings in infrastructure and a lack of product specialization among producers. The consolidation of the nation's state-owned steelmakers into SIDERMEX in 1979, and the

---

[242] Steel producers received a 100% duty reduction for certain steelmaking equipment; a 100% credit on stamp tax for postage used in connection with steel production; accelerated depreciation on equipment investments; a 20 percent tax credit for new investments; a 5-15 percent tax credit for the purchase of Mexican capital goods used for expanding or building a plant; and a reduction of as much as 30 percent on gas and electricity charges. *Siderurgia Latinoamericana* (March, November, 1977; July, 1978); Secretary of Commerce and Industrial Development, *Industrial Development Plan 1979-1982-1990* (1979); *Certain Carbon Steel Products from Mexico*, February 10, 1984 (49 F.R. 5142).

[243] This system of price controls has been characterized as a "price-subsidy" to encourage the development of steel-consuming industries. The failure of the government to approve price rises sufficient to keep up with inflation, combined with supply shortages, gave rise to a black market in steel products. Torre and Mercado, *Sector Paraestatal*, p. 32.

[244] The company's "third stage" expansion plan was intended to raise capacity to 1.8 million tons of steel per year. *Siderurgia Latinoamericana* (August 1976) ("Informativo Regional"), p. 19; May 1976 ("Nuevas Metas Logra Fundidora en su 76° Aniversario"), p. 28; February 1976 ("Informativo Regional"), p. 19.

[245] President Lopez Portillo explained that "The old Fundidora, the result of private initiative, with an old history of successes and a recent [history] of painful failures, has, because of its situation, necessarily gravitated to the State to protect it, as happens with many failures in the private sector. On many occasions we have said that for the necessities of the country, the parastatal sector is a security for inefficiency of the private sector. When important companies fail, the State has to protect them for the role they have in development and employment. This is the case of Fundidora." *El Mercado de Valores* (October 29, 1979), p. 928.

[246] The government-owned Public Works Bank (BANOBRAS) loaned Alfa $285 million, and the government bought $204 million of preferred stock in Alfa to help HYLSA maintain its steel investment program; approximately $239 million was specifically designated for steel investments. *Latin American Weekly Report* (August 14, 1981), p. 5; (October 30, 1981), p. 5.

recapitalization of the companies of the group, was an effort to confront these problems in a systematic fashion.[247]

Crisis and Adjustment

Mexico was fortunate in the early phases of the steel crisis. While most other nations, including Mexico's Latin American neighbors, were confronting major crises as a result of excess capacity and falling demand for steel, the Mexican economy was experiencing an oil boom. Encouraged by rising oil prices and falling interest rates, foreign banks willingly loaned Mexico money to finance its budget and current account deficits.[248] However, oil prices began to slide in 1981, and interest rates on Mexico's outstanding debt rose sharply. With foreign loans drying up and the public sector deficit rapidly spiraling out of control, the government turned to the International Monetary Fund for help. Draconian austerity measures were imposed, the peso was devalued, and strict import controls were put in place.[249] Although conditions have varied somewhat through the 1980s, the Mexican economy has remained stagnant, characterized by slow growth and high inflation. Mexican steel consumption has not subsequently approached its peak period of 1980 and 1981.

The steel industry was severely affected by Mexico's economic crisis. One particularly serious problem was the industry's massive debt. Like other sectors of Mexican industry, the steel industry borrowed heavily abroad, and the devaluation of the peso had a "devastating" impact on the steel industry's financial costs.[250] By 1986, interest payments for SIDERMEX and HYLSA amounted to an appalling 50 percent of sales.[251] The inability of the steel sector to generate enough revenue to meet its financial obligations was not solely a function of slumping sales and overborrowing; the Mexican

---

[247] Torre and Mercado, *Sector Paraestatal*. The recapitalization provided the constituent companies with $1.8 billion to remedy their financial difficulties and to undertake further expansion. *Ibid.*, p. 53.

[248] Mexico's foreign debt leaped from $42.8 billion in 1979 to $85.8 billion in 1983, 75 percent of which was at variable interest rates. U.S.I.T.C., *Developing Country Debt-Servicing Problems*, p. 21.

[249] See "Mexico's Foreign Trade in Steel" below.

[250] By 1984, 80 percent of the industry's debt was owed to foreign banks. *Siderurgia Latinoamericana* (February 1984) ("Informativo Regional"), p. 19; (October 1984) ("Informativo Regional"), p. 22. For example, Fundidora in 1981 arranged a $300 million loan from a syndicate led by the Bank of America, and AHMSA borrowed $175 million from Citibank and the Bank of America. *Siderurgia Latinoamericana* (February 1981) (Informativo Regional"), p. 13; (August 1981) ("Informativo Regional"), p. 24.

[251] E. Maza, "Study Recommends Measures to Restore Steel Industry," in *Proceso* (February 10, 1986).

government's refusal to allow price increases consonant with inflation also played a major role.[252]

Although conditions in the steel industry were extremely difficult by 1982, the industry was slow to accept the need for long-term adjustment. Industry leaders resisted plant closings and lay-offs, apparently in the belief that the downturn was only temporary and that production could be maintained through increased exports.[253] In fact, the steel industry remained optimistic about the prospects for growth. "Start[ing] from the premise that the short-run economic problems would be satisfactorily resolved," the Mexican steel industry had in progress 34 investment projects involving $572 million for internal investment and $762 million for external purchases as of October 1984.[254] Among the projects was SICARTSA II, a 1.5 million metric ton plate mill.[255] Rapid expansion also continued in the area of tubular products, for

---

[252] According to officials of the National Chamber of the Iron and Steel Industry (CANACERO), the government allowed price increases of only 37 percent in 1985, while inflation rose at a rate of 63 percent. *Siderurgia Latinoamericana* (July 1986) ("Informativo Regional"), p. 35.

[253] The chief of SIDERMEX explained in a 1984 interview that "the situation of the Mexican steel industry is that of a depressed market. In this it is no different from the rest of the world. Nevertheless, unlike what is happening in other countries, particularly those countries with a high degree of development such as the United States and the European Economic Community, unemployment has not been created as a consequence.... We continue forward with our production, and with the policy of President de la Madrid to conserve and maintain employment and productive plant.... It is a fact that, when internal demand falls notably, as has happened in 1982 and 1983, excess steel production must be placed in foreign markets...." Interview with Miguel Alessio Robles, reported in *Siderurgia Latinoamericana* (April 1984) ("Informativo Regional"), p. 35.

[254] *Siderurgia Latinoamericana* (October 1984) ("Informativo Regional"), pp. 21-22. This in spite of the fact that GDP had declined 4.7 percent over the past year and that demand for steel was down 50 percent from 1981. *Ibid.* The figure relating to internal investment was converted from pesos to U.S. dollars at an average annual exchange rate of 167.83:1.

[255] SICARTSA II has had a checkered history. The original plan for a sheet and coil mill was suspended by the government during the crisis that accompanied the take-over of Fundidora. However, the project was later resurrected as a 2 million metric ton direct reduction facility and 1.5 million ton plate mill. *Metal Bulletin Monthly Supplement* (October 1985), p. 15. The World Bank withdrew a previous offer to provide funds for the project because market demand analysis for the new product was considered insufficient. International Bank for Reconstruction and Development, "Staff Appraisal Report - Mexico Steel Sector Restructuring Project," February 8, 1988, p. 2. However, the Inter-American Development Bank provided $95 million for the project. *Siderurgia Latinoamericana* (December 1976) ("Informativo Regional"), p. 43. Construction was begun in 1984. *Siderurgia Latinoamericana* (December 1984) ("Informativo Regional"), p. 18. As of December 1986, $1.89 billion had been invested in the project, of which $899 million was appropriated by the Federal government. *Siderurgia Latinoamericana* (August 1987) ("Informativo Regional"), p. 34.

which a strong demand from the petroleum industry was expected.[256] In all, Mexico planned to increase capacity to 12.75 million metric tons by the end of 1985.[257] During this period the government continued to inject new capital into the state steel enterprises.[258]

After 1984, market realities began to become more apparent to decision-makers. Alfa group, owner of HYLSA, struggling under $2.6 billion in debt, dropped plans to expand flat products capacity by 500 thousand tons in early 1985.[259] Work on SICARTSA II was temporarily suspended a few months later,[260] and in January 1986 an independent consultant presented the government with a gloomy assessment of the state of the steel industry. The report harshly criticized the government for its price control policies, as a result of which both private and public companies faced a "financial crisis threatening their very survival."[261] It criticized "the low productivity of the state-owned companies, the unwieldiness and inaccessibility of their operations, and the relative shortage of raw materials."[262] The report recommended that the government provide funds to improve productivity, assume the industry's debt, reorganize SIDERMEX and, most radically, close Fundidora, whose financial situation appeared hopeless.[263]

---

[256] The most ambitious oil country tubular goods expansion project was undertaken by a private producer, Tubos de Acero de México, S.A. The company doubled its capacity of seamless tubes (*Metal Bulletin Monthly Supplement* (October 1987), p. 7) with the construction of a new industrial complex, Tamsa II, at a cost of $830 million. *Siderurgia Latinoamericana* (June 1987) ("Informativo Regional"), pp. 24-25. Tamsa's President remarked at the inauguration of the facility that "investments of this magnitude by the private sector . . . are only possible with the help of concerted policies between the private sector and the Federal Government. . . . *Ibid.* p. 25. And Productora Mexicana de Tubería, a joint venture between Nafinsa, SIDERMEX and a number of Japanese companies, opened a $130 million facility capable of producing 300 thousand tons of pipe. *Siderurgia Latinoamericana* (April 1986) ("Informativo Regional"), pp. 32-34; *Metal Bulletin Monthly Supplement* (October 1985), pp. 15-16.

[257] *Metal Bulletin* (March 8, 1985).

[258] *Excelsior* (January 19, 1984); *Apendice Estadistico*, Vol. I, Presupuesta de Egreso de la Federacion (1984).

[259] *Metal Bulletin* (March 12, 1985).

[260] *Metal Bulletin* (October 22, 1985).

[261] E. Maza, "Study Recommends Measures to Restore Steel Industry," in *Proceso* (February 10, 1986).

[262] *Ibid.*

[263] *Ibid.*, pp. 6-9. The report indicated that the parastatal steel industry had "approximately half the productivity level" of comparable steel plants in similar countries. *Ibid.* According to the World Bank, Mexican non-flat steel is generally competitive with international norms, but the quality and cost of the country's flat product lines is seriously deficient. International Bank for Reconstruction and Development, "Staff Appraisal Report - Mexican Steel Sector Restructuring Project," February 8, 1988, p. 8.

The government adopted the latter suggestion, shutting down Fundidora in the spring of 1986.[264] In addition, the government undertook to resolve the industry's debt problem, assuming responsibility for nearly $1 billion of SIDERMEX debt.[265] It also implemented a reorganization plan for SIDERMEX,[266] and instituted a program of trade liberalization involving the reduction of tariffs and nontariff barriers on steel products. Most importantly, perhaps, the government agreed to a bimonthly adjustment in steel prices at 95 percent of inflation.[267]

In 1988 the Mexican government formalized its restructuring program. As a condition for the approval of a $400 million loan from the World Bank,[268] the government issued a "Steel Sector Policy Letter." The letter committed the government to a multiple point plan involving (a) the modernization of facilities; (b) the closing of inefficient and obsolete plant; (c) the liberalization of trade in steel; (d) the decontrol of steel pricing; and (e) the phasing out of government subsidies. The letter indicated that the government would halt further intervention in the industry's financial situation, and would focus on modernization rather than capacity expansion.[269]

---

[264] The decision was a difficult one, for it involved the elimination of 9,000 jobs. International Bank for Reconstruction and Development, "Staff Appraisal Report - Mexico Steel Sector Restructuring Project," February 8, 1988. However, it was almost inevitable, for Fundidora lost $228.5 million in 1985 alone and had a foreign debt of $390 million. *Metal Bulletin* (July 4, 1986). The government also closed one of AHMSA's blast furnaces for rehabilitation. *Excelsior* (September 12, 1986).

[265] *Siderurgia Latinoamericana* (December 1986) ("Informativo Regional"), p. 23. This debt assumption was undertaken pursuant to a "Financial Rehabilitation Agreement," under which the government assumed and converted to equity $883 million in SIDERMEX obligations. International Bank for Reconstruction & Development, "Staff Appraisal Report - Mexico Steel Sector Restructuring Project," February 8, 1988, p. 15. The government also suspended payments on the debt of bankrupt Fundidora. *Siderurgia Latinoamericana* (August 1987) ("Informativo Regional"), p. 32.

[266] The Plan called for the sale of many SIDERMEX's non-steel subsidiaries, which had interests in hotels, maritime transportation, and concrete enterprises. *Siderurgia Latinoamericana* (August 1987) ("Informativo Regional"), p. 32.

[267] *Siderurgia Latinoamericana* (November 1987) ("La Siderurgia Mexicana en 1986-87 y sus Perspectivas"), p. 45.

[268] The $400 million would be used as follows: $100 million would finance raw material and steel product imports during the period of adjustment to trade liberalization; $225 million would be invested in the modernization of AHMSA plant and SIDERMEX mining operations; and $75 million would be used to modernize HYLSA's flat products facility. The funds would be repayable over 15 years, with a three-year grace period. Compliance with the price and trade elements of the restructuring plan was a covenant of the loan agreement. International Bank for Reconstruction and Development, "Staff Appraisal Report - Mexico Steel Sector Restructuring Project," February 8, 1988.

[269] The letter, titled "Lineamientos de Política para la Industria Siderúrgica Paraestatal" is dated January 15, 1988. It may be found at annex 4-4 to the World Bank "Staff Appraisal Report."

If implemented, Mexico's steel restructuring plan could restore a degree of rationality to the country's steel industry. In essence, the plan was calculated to restore the industry to viability and then to make it responsive to the competitive pressures of the marketplace by lowering trade barriers, withdrawing subsidies, scaling back capacity expansion programs and returning to market pricing. However, it remains to be seen whether the Mexican government would implement measures consistent with the spirit of the plan. The government's commitment to eliminate subsidies "in the long-term" was somewhat indefinite,[270] and the industry has vociferously opposed the government's trade liberalization measures. Perhaps the critical test related to SICARTSA II and the industry's steel expansion plans; in light of existing demand, completion of the SICARTSA II project would be a questionable decision, yet industry leaders continued to press for the implementation of the project.[271]

Mexico's Foreign Trade in Steel

Mexico was traditionally a net importer of steel products. Throughout the 1970s and the first years of the 1980s, the country pushed forward with capacity increases in an effort to keep pace with or exceed rapidly rising demand and achieve self-sufficiency in steel. To cope with the fall in steel demand after 1982, the steel industry fell back on a program of exports and import substitution.[272] The program, aided by a government policy of devaluations, import controls, and export incentives, resulted in substantial net exports in 1983, 1984 and 1986; total exports for 1987 remained stable at

---

[270] The plan's goals with regard to subsidies were inconsistent. The letter stated that "The Mexican government's intention for the long-term is not to intervene financially in the parastatal steel sector any further than is provided for in the Financial Rehabilitation Agreement," and the World Bank's "Staff Appraisal Report" indicated that "the total elimination of direct subsidies and government transfers is also expected to occur in a relatively short time." (p. 11) Yet the report also stated that further financial restructuring measures would be needed in the future (pp. 15, 17), and indicated that the AHMSA project would be supported by the government, "including adequate annual budgetary authorizations and when required, additional equity contributions. . . ." (p. 28) The World Bank estimated that direct government budgetary transfers to the state-owned steel industry averaged $75-100 million per year. *Ibid.* at 10.

[271] The "Staff Appraisal Report" indicated that "The completion of SICARTSA II may lead to excess capacities, particularly in plate production. Therefore, discussion with SIDERMEX and the government led to the understanding that alternatives to SICARTSA II would be considered on their merits. . . ." Yet as recently as November 1987, CANACERO anticipated that SICARTSA II would add 2 million tons of steel capacity, more than offsetting the closure of Fundidora. *Siderurgia Latinoamericana*, November 1987 ("La Siderurgia Méxicana en 1986-87 y sus Perspectivas"), p. 42.

[272] As *Siderurgia Latinoamericana* noted in April 1985, "Last year was the second consecutive year in which the export of steel products has been a determining factor for the evolution of marketing of steel in Mexico, since although it was certainly true that exports were considered as surplus not consumed on the domestic market until 1982, now they are and will be from 1983 on a primal factor in order that there is no slowdown in the steel sector."

around 1 million tons.[273] The most aggressive exporters were the pipe and tube producers, whose ambitious expansion plans turned Mexico from a major importer to an exporter over the course of the 1980s.[274]

The government's exchange rate policy was critical to the success of Mexican steel exports. After several years of appreciation, a major devaluation of the peso in 1982 stimulated exports. A second devaluation was implemented in 1985 to preserve the benefits of devaluation;[275] as of 1988, an undervalued peso continued to encourage exports.[276] The government also promoted export through loans from FOMEX, a trust established by the Mexican government, to steel exporters and U.S. importers at discounted rates.[277] Mexico's export efforts in steel led to friction with its trading partners. After the Department of Commerce found in 1984 that its export stimulating programs constituted countervailable subsidies,[278] Mexico entered into a Voluntary Restraint Agreement with the United States, under which it agreed to limit its exports to 0.3 percent of the U.S. market.[279] In 1987 and

[273] *Metal Bulletin* (September 21, 1987, February 15, 1988). In 1986, Mexico exported $320 million in steel products, $93 million of which was non-flat products, $88 million flat products and $62 million tubular goods. *Siderurgia Latinoamericana* (November 1987) ("La Siderurgia Mexicana en 1986-87 y sus Perspectivas"), p. 44.

[274] TAMSA, Mexico's sole producer of seamless pipe, exported 50 percent of its production in 1987, and hoped to increase that figure to 60 percent in 1988. PMT, a welded tube producer with capacity of 290 thousand tons, exported 90 percent of its production in 1987, and HYLSA exported 45 percent. *American Metal Market* (April 12, 1988).

[275] U.S.I.T.C., *Developing Country Debt-Servicing Problems*, p. 30. The benefits of the devaluation were enhanced by a dual exchange rate which, according to a Nafinsa report, "greatly favor[ed]" exports. *Siderurgia Latinoamericana* (October 1982), p. 25; *El Mercado de Valores* (June 13, 1983), supp., p. 163.

[276] *Financial Times* (April 14, 1983).

[277] FOMEX loans involved short-term financing in U.S. dollars to Mexican steelmakers for exports of steel products at an interest rate of 6 percent at a time when market rates were between 14 and 18 percent. U.S. customers buying Mexican steel also received 180-day loans at 6 percent. February 10, 1984 (49 F.R. 5142).

[278] See *Oil Country Tubular Goods from Mexico*, 49 F.R. 47054, November 30, 1984; *Bars and Shapes from Mexico*, 49 F.R. 32887, August 17, 1984; *Certain Carbon Steel Products from Mexico*, 49 F.R. 5142, February 10, 1984 (preliminary).

[279] *Siderurgia Latinoamericana* (February 1985) ("Informativo Regional"), p. 23; (January 1984) ("Informativo Regional"), p. 25; (August 1984) ("Informativo Regional"), p. 19. In 1987, after American producers complained that Mexican stainless steel was being sold in the United States at as much as $150/ton below domestic prices, a VRA was negotiated for those products as well. *Metal Bulletin* (March 27, 1986); *Siderurgia Latinoamericana* (March 1987) ("Informativo Regional"), pp. 42-43. The United States in 1988 allowed a one-time increase of 12.4 percent in Mexico's steel quota. *Metal Bulletin* (January 7, 1988).

1988, the European Economic Community imposed steep antidumping duties on Mexican sheet, plate and coil.[280]

Mexican export promoting measures were accompanied by a number of protectionist measures, including import licensing, quotas, tariffs, official reference prices for customs valuation, and discriminatory government procurement policies, which were calculated to ensure that domestic producers obtained the largest possible share of the domestic market.[281] In 1985 the government began implementation of a trade liberalization policy in preparation for admission to the GATT. In spite of industry complaints that it would be "seriously damaged" by the policy,[282] the Mexican government dismantled many of the import barriers that shielded the domestic industry from its foreign competition.[283] At the same time, the government enacted antidumping legislation apparently designed to serve as a GATT-consistent safeguard against unfair competition.[284]

The Mexican government traditionally protected and fostered its domestic steel industry in an effort to become self-sufficient in an important basic product. In the late 1980s, however, the government began to question whether the direct cost to the government and the indirect costs imposed on consumers -- including exporters of goods for which steel is an input -- might

---

[280] The Europeans imposed the duties on sheet and plate after an investigation revealed that Mexico had taken 3.5 percent of the European market in those products and that they were being sold at a weighted averaged margin of 37.7 percent below fair market value. *European Report* (November 28, 1987). Provisional duties were imposed on coil after a finding that the product was being dumped by SIDERMEX at a weighted average of 22.2 percent and by HYLSA at a weighted average of 15.8 percent below fair market value. *European Report* (January 27, 1988).

[281] U.S.I.T.C., *Foreign Industrial Targeting*, pp. 181-187. The study points out that government "Buy Mexican" procurement practices were potentially very significant in a nation where public sector expenditures amounted to 45 percent of GNP. *Ibid.* at 187.

[282] *Siderurgia Latinoamericana* (July 1986) ("Informativo Regional"), p. 36. CANACERO recognized that by opening the doors to foreign competition, the government would force Mexican industry to improve quality and prices; "It is lamentable, nevertheless, that in the case of steel the indiscriminate opening to imports constitutes a serious danger. The present disorder in the international market for steel products will generate serious disadjustments. It is a fact that today steel has two prices in any country in the world: the domestic price and the export price. Regularly export prices are substantial inferior to domestic prices." *Ibid.* As a result, CANACERO has continued to fight the government's proposals. *Siderurgia Latinoamericana*, (July 1987) ("Informativo Regional"), p. 32.

[283] The World Bank, which made implementation of steel import liberalization a condition of its steel sector restructuring loan, reported that Mexico reduced steel tariffs to 0-15 percent (from 40 percent for finished nonflats and 25 percent for flat products), eliminated official reference prices (under which duties were levied based on an inflated "official" price rather than the actual transaction price) and abolished all quantitative restrictions on steel imports. International Bank for Reconstruction and Development, "Staff Appraisal Report, Mexico Steel Sector Restructuring Project," February 8, 1988, p. 12. That substantial liberalization has been carried out was confirmed by the United States Trade Representative. See United States Trade Representative, *Foreign Trade Barriers*, pp. 217-221.

[284] *Siderurgia Latinoamericana* (February 1987) ("Informativo Regional"), pp. 24-25.

not outweigh the benefits. The Mexican steel industry could not supply its own market without protection, nor could it export without government subsidies. The industry was not pleased with the prospect of losing its privileges; as one commentator remarked, "Mexican business most fears being cast adrift from the helping hand of government and being left to face the rigors of competition on its own."[285] Whether the government is willing to stay the course and force its steel industry to compete may well be the critical question for the sector in the 1990s and beyond.

TAIWAN

Although Taiwan's steel industry is comparatively small, its emergence has been one of the most widely noted of that of any developing country industry. The growth of Taiwan's steel industry reflects, in large part, the success of a series of government policies undertaken in the 1970s and 1980s to promote the industry -- heavy government investments, protection from import competition, major government improvements to the infrastructure, and government financial aid, including the extension of subsidized credit. Government funding made possible the establishment and expansion of the China Steel Corporation (CSC) integrated mill when sufficient private capital could not be attracted, and has assisted smaller Taiwanese producers to upgrade and rationalize their facilities. Protection from imports has enabled CSC to stabilize domestic prices at levels higher than those prevailing internationally, although it offers special discounts to "downstream" consumers, including steel firms, which produce finished products (such as pipes and tubes) for export.

While government assistance has enabled CSC to establish one of the most modern integrated mills in the world, this facility must operate at near full nominal capacity to break even. As a result, during periods of domestic recession, CSC has continued to operate at full capacity, disposing of its surplus production in export markets at prices significantly below those prevailing in the domestic market. Low-priced Taiwanese steel exports have made substantial inroads in traditional Japanese markets in East Asia, and have led, in several instances, to the imposition of antidumping penalties on Taiwanese steel firms by the U.S. government.[286] At present, CSC is in the midst of a major new capacity expansion program and is contemplating establishment of a second greenfield integrated mill, an indication that Taiwan's industry will become an increasingly significant factor in the international steel market in the next decades.

---

[285] Domínguez, "Revolution and Flexibility," p. 287.

[286] *Carbon Steel Plate from Taiwan*, 44 F.R. 29734, May 22, 1979; *Certain Welded Carbon Steel Pipes and Tubes from Taiwan*, 49 F.R. 9931, March 16, 1984.

(Million metric tons)

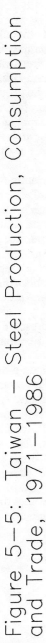

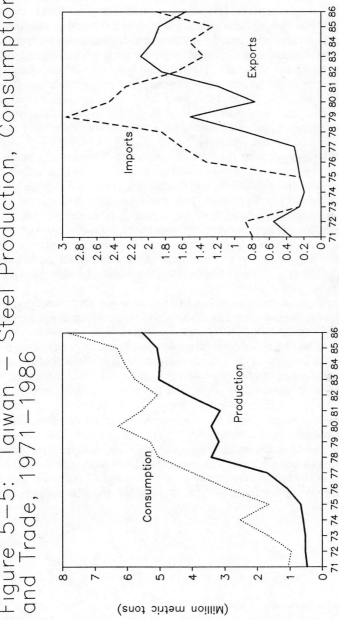

Figure 5-5: Taiwan – Steel Production, Consumption and Trade, 1971–1986

Source: International Iron and Steel Institute, Steel Statistical Yearbook, 1981, 1987. Production and Consumption refer to crude steel; Exports and Imports refer to semi–finished and finished steel.

Expansion of the Taiwanese Steel Industry

Much of Taiwan's economy has traditionally been dominated by family-run enterprises suspicious of state regulation and intervention. The Nationalist state, however, has imposed a substantial degree of government planning and direction on this base, particularly in the large, capital-intensive industries. After 1949, the Nationalist government broke up large private accumulations of wealth and took over the banking system, and large private financial groups have only recently begun to emerge in Taiwan. As a result, while family firms operate numerous small enterprises, they have often proven incapable of achieving world-class competitive power in strategic industries, and the development of capital-intensive sectors has required a major role by the government and by foreign investors.[287]

The steel industry reflects these characteristics of Taiwan's economic life. The industry was traditionally dominated by several hundred small, family-run mills, which still produce a substantial proportion of Taiwan's steel, operating a variety of electric furnace, pipe-and-tube, specialty steel and rolling facilities. The state established CSC to provide large-scale integrated steel making capability needed to support Taiwanese industrialization. More recently, the government, private Taiwanese financial groups, and large investors have engaged in joint "triangular" arrangements to establish new enterprises to enhance Taiwan's finished steel capability, notably the An Feng cold-rolled sheet mill.

The "mixed" public-private structure of the Taiwanese economy resembles that of many developing countries. The government Council for Economic Planning and Development (CEPD) develops overseas and national industrial policy, which is spelled out in long-term plans, and reviews progress on major projects and the budgets of the various ministries. The Ministry of Economic Affairs handles the day-to-day administration of the economy, the development of sector-specific plans, and the implementation of measures such as tax, tariff and financial incentives to ensure that plan goals are met. The Taiwanese banking system is dominated by the government, and two government-owned banks, the Bank of China and the Bank of Communications (a national development bank), make loans to designated priority industries and projects. The government has promoted the growth of favored sectors (including steel) through a wide range of tax, fiscal and duty drawback incentives pursuant to the Statute for the Encouragement of

---

[287] See generally Edwin A. Winckler, "Statism and Familism on Taiwan," in *Ideology and National Competitiveness*, ed. George C. Lodge and Ezra F. Vogel.

Investment (table 5-10).[288] State-owned enterprises dominate certain large industrial sectors such as energy, shipbuilding, integrated steelmaking and specialty steel, where capital requirements are large, risk is comparatively high, and the prospect for a return on investment is relatively poor.

Prior to 1970 all of Taiwan's steel was imported or produced by one of the many small family-run mills, which were heavily dependent upon imported billets and scrap for raw materials. These small producers suffered from high costs and generally low quality in their output and engaged in periodic, debilitating price wars.[289] Moreover, these firms could not produce the high-quality flat-rolled products needed by Taiwan's growing shipbuilding and auto industries.[290] However, while the Taiwanese government studied the establishment of a large, modern integrated steel mill throughout the 1960s, such a project faced uncertain prospects and was not attractive to private capital:

> *The integrated steel project calls for a huge amount of capital investment and highly developed techniques but shows a very low initial rate of return. For this reason, government agencies will continue to confer with related parties to deliberate on the establishment of an optimal steel plant.[291]*

In 1971, the government announced the formation of the China Steel Corporation (CSC), which was to construct an integrated mill initially capable of producing 1.1 million metric tons of steel per year (beginning in 1975) at Kaohsiung, the port which was the principal site of Taiwan's shipbuilding

---

[288] This statute was promulgated in September 1960 and was repeatedly amended thereafter, reflecting the evolution of the Taiwanese economy and the government's shifting industrial development priorities. It was enacted "for the purpose of encouraging investment and accelerating economic development" (Chapter 1, Article 1). The Executive Yuan periodically issues decrees setting forth categories of enterprises eligible for benefits under the statute, with the intended effect of encouraging such enterprises. For example, the Executive Yuan issued Decree No. Tai(71) Tsai-0156, *Categories and Criteria of Productive Enterprises Eligible for Encouragement*, on January 7, 1982 providing, among other things, for "tax holidays" for producers of steel plates "limited to those which have a minimum annual production capacity of 100,000 M/T." (Category VI(4)).

[289] *Geppo* (July 1983). The China Council for International Economic Cooperation and Development commented in 1969 that "At present, the steel manufacturers are faced with a number of difficulties. They are equipped with obsolete facilities of small capacity, conducive to high unit production costs, and they rely too heavily for raw material on imported steel scrap, which fluctuates in price and makes it very difficult to control production costs and product quality. The situation has become even worse because some steel plants have undergone expansion too rapidly and find it difficult to develop export markets. They have been cutting prices to meet keen competition in the domestic markets with the result that they are finding it very difficult to run their businesses successively." *Fifth Four Year Plan for Economic Development of Taiwan*, February 1969.

[290] International Commercial Bank of China, *Economic Review* (July-August, 1979).

[291] *Fifth Four Year Plan*, p. 173.

Table 5-10. Special Financial and Tax Benefits Available to Taiwanese Steel Producers Under the Statute for Encouragment of Investment

Section of Statute	Item	Comment
Article 15	Preferrential Income Tax Ceilings	Special 22 percent ceiling on annual income tax
Article 6	Accelerated Depreciation	If depreciable life of assets is 10 years or more, may accelerate 5 years. If less than 10 years, may accelerate by half. Applies to producers of sheet, plate, seamless pipes.
Article 6	Tax Holidays	One to four year deferral of taxes after an enterprise begins to market its products
Article 10	Tax Credits for Investments	5 to 20 percent tax credit for investment in machinery and equipment.
Article 21	Exemption from Tariff on Imported Equipment	Applies to equipment purchased to establish or expand production capacity
Article 84	Preferential Long Term Loans	Long term loans from government Bank of Communications to important productive enterprises (includes steel industry)

Sources: Taiwan Industrial Development and Investment Center, *Categories and Criteria of Productive Enterprises Eligible for Encouragement* (March 1985) and *Criteria for Encouragement of Establishment or Expansion of Industrial and Mininig Enterprises* (June 1985); Response of Board of Foreign Trade of the Republic of China in *Small Diameter Welded Carbon Steel API Line Pipe from Taiwan*, No. C-583-503 (September 20, 1985).

industry.[292] The construction of the integrated steel mill was the most costly of the so-called "Ten Major Projects," a group of major long-term government construction projects launched in 1971 to spur Taiwan's economic growth.[293]

CSC was originally capitalized at $80 million, with the Taiwanese government contributing 80 percent of the amount and Voest-Alpine, the Austrian steelmaker, subscribing to the remaining 20 percent.[294] Voest-Alpine was to contribute a loan of $50 million to the project and the Taiwanese pledged to raise an additional $192 million in debt capital, which was expected to be forthcoming from a European consortium.[295] The mill was to be built in a special industrial zone to be established by the government for a steel-shipbuilding complex at Kaohsiung.[296] Construction began in 1972, and proceeded on an expedited basis reflecting the Ministry of Economic Affairs' desire to "get Taiwan's first integrated steel mill to start production far ahead of schedule."[297]

It soon became apparent that the original 1975 completion date was unrealistic, as was the government's desire to finance the project predominantly through private investment. Following the devaluation of the dollar in 1972-73, Voest-Alpine began demanding that CSC pay higher interest rates on the equipment financing loans which Voest was extending to the project. CSC refused, and Voest-Alpine pulled out of the venture altogether. USS Engineers and Consultants, a U.S. Steel subsidiary, agreed to take over construction of the mill (for completion in 1977), but U.S. Steel did not invest in CSC,[298] and other sources of private capital proved difficult to locate.[299]

Thereafter the government's role in the project became more prominent.[300] While maintaining the position that the government's participation in the project was to be a minority interest, the government appropriated

---

[292] *Free China Weekly* (October 31, 1971).

[293] Most of the Ten Major Projects involved efforts to establish the basic infrastructure for a manufacturing economy -- harbors, roads, railroads, and a power grid. *Free China Weekly* (June 27, 1971; June 27, 1976).

[294] The Taiwanese share was to be split between the government ($36 million) and the China Development Corp. ($28 million), representatives of the government, the Taiwanese private sector, and Voest-Alpine. *Free China Weekly* (November 7, 1971).

[295] The 9-man board of directors was divided equally by representatives of the government, the Taiwanese private sector, and Voest-Alpine. *Ibid.*

[296] *Free China Weekly* (March 10, 1972).

[297] *Free China Weekly* (May 13, 1973).

[298] *Free China Weekly* (August 19, 1973).

[299] Premier Chiang Ching-Kuo's *Report on the Fiscal 1977 General Budget Bill to the Legislative Yuan*; *Free China Weekly* (August 19, 1973).

[300] CSC was "primarily capitalized with government funds after failing to attract investment from the private sector." *Free China Journal* (June 30, 1985).

progressively larger sums to the project -- in late 1974 the government was reportedly planning to invest $742 million to complete the CSC Kaohsiung mill.[301] By 1976 the government owned 45 percent of the stock of CSC with the remaining 55 percent "reserved for private investors;"[302] in fact, the government had "to advance capital for the private shares yet to be subscribed and the advanced procurement of raw materials."[303] Private investors were deterred by the fact that the cost of the CSC project was far exceeding original estimates -- by 1976 the total projected cost of the first stage of construction had risen to over $1 billion.[304] At length, in July 1977, the idea of attracting private investors was abandoned and CSC became a wholly "state-owned enterprise."[305]

In addition to the actual construction of the integrated mill, other government efforts contributed to the establishment of a supporting infrastructure and the securing of raw materials to support steel production. The Kaohsiung harbor, the site of the CSC mill, was expanded and deepened.[306] The Taiwanese government oversaw the construction of a network of railroads and highways to support the Kaohsiung industrial zone,

---

[301] *Free China Weekly* (December 15, 1974). Much of the "private sector" investment was actually drawn from quasi-official sources. Part of the "private sector" contribution came from the Sino-American Fund for Economic and Social Development, a fund established in 1965 (largely with loans from the United States) whose expenditures were allocated to Taiwanese development projects by the government Economic Planning Council. *Free China Weekly* (March 23, November 23, 1975). These loans bore an annual interest rate of 6 percent. CSC *Annual Report* 1980, p. 22. In addition, a number of government banks, including the Central Trust of China, guaranteed Japanese yen loans made to finance the first phase of CSC's expansion. *Ibid.*

[302] *Free China Weekly* (June 27, 1976). The state budget drawn up in the fall of 1976 for completion of the Kaohsiung steel mill allocated $14.8 million in government funds to the project and indicated that no private investment had been forthcoming. Economic Planning Council, Executive Yuan, *Six-Year Plan for Economic Development of Taiwan*, October 1976, Appendix 6. One non-government source of funding did materialize in 1979; the U.S. Export-Import Bank extended $212.5 million in export financing to the Kaohsiung project. *American Metal Market* (October 26, 1979).

[303] *Free China Weekly* (June 27, 1976).

[304] *Geppo*, July 1983. As Premier Chiang Ching-Kuo reported in 1976, "The money [for the 10 major projects] will come from both government and private sources. Because it is not easy to obtain private capital for the China Steel Corporation and the China Shipbuilding Corporation, additional government investment must be temporarily substituted for the planned share of private investment." *Report on the Fiscal 1977 General Budget to the Legislative Yuan.*

[305] Premier Chiang's *Report to the Legislative Yuan on the Central Government's General Budget Bill for Fiscal 1978.*

[306] *Free China Weekly* (January 11, 1976). By 1973 Kaohsiung Harbor was inadequate to handle existing cargo requirements and was characterized by numerous bottlenecks and delays. *Industry of Free China* (April 1979), p. 10.

financed by the Taiwan Provincial Government.[307] The Kaohsiung Shipyard, another of the Ten Major Projects, began producing "huge ore ships" for CSC which carried coke and iron ore from foreign sources (South Africa, Australia, India and Latin America) to the Kaohsiung mill, compensating for Taiwan's dearth of indigenous raw materials for steelmaking.[308]

The Ten Major Projects were given priority in the allocation of Taiwanese government budget funds and other resources;[309] as a result the projects "proceeded without a hitch despite the economic buffeting" that occurred to the Taiwanese economy during the world recession following the First Oil Crisis.[310] CSC production began in late 1977 as the first phase of construction came to a close. At a cost of approximately $971 million -- the greater portion contributed by the government of Taiwan -- CSC had installed facilities capable of producing 1.5 million metric tons of steel per year, including semifinished products, plate, wire and wire rods.[311]

As the Ten Major Construction Projects approached completion, the Taiwanese government announced the inauguration of the so-called "Twelve New Development Projects," which included the second-stage expansion of the CSC integrated steelworks at Kaohsiung.[312] The CSC second-stage expansion, launched in January 1978, was designed to boost Taiwan's capacity to 3.25 million tons per year by 1981 at an estimated cost of $1.4 billion. Among other things, the second stage expansion was designed to enable CSC to

---

[307] Three government agencies supervised the improvements in the Kaohsiung infrastructure -- the Ministry of Economic Affairs, the Taiwan Highway Bureau and the Taiwan Railway Administration. *Free China Weekly* (September 15, 1974).

[308] The ore ships were operated by the government-owned China Merchants Steam Navigation Co. *Free China Weekly* (December 15, 1974).

[309] Premier Chiang's *Report on Administration to the First Meeting of the 59th Session of the Legislative Yuan* (February 25, 1977). Chiang indicated that the government would "give priority to funds for export enterprises, the Ten Major Construction Projects and agricultural development." The *Free China Weekly* reported on May 19, 1974 that "all central and provincial government agencies have listed the Nine Projects as their prime administrative objectives." (The ten major projects were sometimes referred to as nine, depending on the inclusion or exclusion of a nuclear power project).

[310] Premier Chiang Ching-Kuo's *Report on Administration to the First Meeting of the 60th Session of the Legislative Yuan.*

[311] *Free China Weekly* (November 6, 1977).

[312] Premier Chiang's *Presentation to the Legislative Yuan of the Central Government's General Budget Proposal for 1979*, April 7, 1978. Premier Chiang reported in 1978 that "The Ten Projects and subsequent 12 are multi-purpose, multi-benefit public engineering projects and the required capital must be invested if our country is to attain the developed status. In FY 1979 these projects require a total capital of NT 60,951 million [$1.68 billion], for which most arrangements have been carefully made. Expenditures have been calculated practically and budgeted by the central and local governments."

produce hot-rolled and cold-rolled sheets.[313] This effort, which was completed in 1982, was paralleled by a $3 billion shipbuilding program, a principal objective of which was to provide ore ships to supply raw materials for CSC.[314]

Phase Three of CSC's expansion was launched in 1984, designed to add another 2.4 million metric tons of crude steel capacity at a cost of $1.4 billion, raising its raw steel capacity to 5.65 million metric tons. The government provided 45 percent of this amount, ($624 million) the largest industrial investment undertaken by the government in 1984.[315] The balance of the investment was provided by eighteen foreign financial institutions and six Taiwanese banks,[316] and the equipment has been furnished by a wide range of foreign suppliers. CSC is reportedly planning a fourth phase expansion; "it's only a question of when."[317]

The Private Sector

Although the greater portion of the government's efforts in the 1970s were directed toward the establishment of a modern integrated steel mill, the government also attempted to put the nation's numerous small and medium-sized mills on a sounder economic footing.[318] These firms, which numbered nearly 300 by the mid-1970s, had long been "encouraged to merge or otherwise cooperate through a division of labor,"[319] and when CSC's capacity began coming on stream, the Ministry of Economic Affairs issued an order prohibiting further entry into the industry.[320] The government offered new incentives to the small firms either to merge into entities with specific minimum capacities or to expand their existing capacities. Merging firms

---

[313] *China Post* (January 7, 1980); *Free China Weekly* (November 6, 1977). Planned additions included another blast furnace, sintering plants, and two continuous casters. Reports of the estimated capacity which would be operational at the end of the second stage expansion varied from 3.25 to 6 million tons. *Taiwan Enterprise* (April-May 1978).

[314] Under this plan, six 125,000 DWT ore carriers were to be constructed to deliver raw materials to CSC, covering 70 percent of its raw materials requirements. *Free China Weekly* (February 10, 1980).

[315] *Free China Journal* (April 7, 1984).

[316] *Free China Journal* (March 25, 1984).

[317] *Metal Bulletin Monthly* (December 1986).

[318] In addition to CSC, one producer, Taiwan Steel, possessed a blast furnace, although only with 54 thousand tons of annual capacity. The government-managed Tang Eng Iron Works possessed two 30-ton electric furnaces and one 20 ton furnace; Tosei Steel, Nanho Steel and Daiei Steel each possessed 20 ton electric furnaces. Most of the other producers were engaged in electric furnace steelmaking with similar furnaces and hot-rolling (166 companies). About a dozen firms produce pipe, the largest being Tokosho Steel. *Geppo* (July 1983).

[319] Economic Planning Council, Executive Yuan, *Six Year Plan*, p. 58.

[320] *Taiwan Enterprise* (April 1978).

received an exemption from business income taxes, investment tax credits for the installation of new equipment, increased electricity supplies, lower tariffs on raw materials imports and lower taxes on related commodities.[321] While many of the small firms are troubled by aging equipment and other problems, several have emerged as low-priced exporters, such as Kao Hsing Chang Iron & Steel (CR sheet and pipe) and Yieh Hsing Co. (CR strip and tube).[322]

In the mid-1980s several important new Taiwanese steel firms have emerged, reflecting "triangular" alliances between the government, Taiwan's financial groups and foreign investors. An Mau Steel, formed in 1984, produces pipe and tube products and cold-rolled sheets. An Mau's ownership is divided between two Taiwanese investment groups, Australia's CRA, and two Japanese firms, Yodogawa (a producer of sheets) and Toyomenka (a trading company).[323] An Feng Steel was reportedly being formed in 1987 to produce hot-rolled strip; its investors would be the Bank of Communications (the government development bank) with a 25 percent share, several Taiwanese financial groups, and possibly Japanese trading companies.[324] The Evergreen Superior Alloy Corporation was reportedly being formed in 1987 to produce tool steel, alloy steel and other types of special steel, with government entities holding 28 percent of the firm's equity.[325]

The growth of these new competitors reflects the fact that government policies implemented to foster the steel industry have made investment in steel more attractive -- An Mau, for example, enjoys a four-year tax holiday in some product areas,[326] and the An Feng venture has been attractive, in part,

---

[321] *Metal Bulletin*, November 6, 1981. The enterprises were made eligible for benefit under the Statute for the Encouragement of Investment by a series of decrees by the Executive Yuan which specified, among other things, minimum capacities for eligibility (*e.g.*, 30,000 annual tons of seamless pipes, 60,000 annual tons of coated flat products). "Categories and Criteria for Special Encouragement of Important Productive Enterprises," Decree No. Tai (70) Tsai - 15404, October 27, 1981; *Decree* No. Tai (71) Tsai-0156, January 7, 1982. *American Metal Market* commented on October 7, 1983 that "The government has been trying to pursue those mom-and-pop operations to merge but traditional Taiwanese independence has so far stymied such efforts."

[322] *Metal Bulletin Monthly* (December 1986).

[323] An Mau's chairman is a member of Taiwan's Legislative Yuan and the company is said to be "well connected" in Taiwan, which has enhanced its attractiveness to investors. *Metal Bulletin* (May 8, July 9, 1987); *Metal Bulletin Monthly* (December 1986).

[324] The Taiwanese investors included An Mau Investment and Kuo Tung Investment, which had been principal investors in An Mau Steel. They reduced their share substantially (to 7.5 percent each) through sales to Japanese investors. *Metal Bulletin* (July 9, 1987).

[325] The new venture was encouraged by the government's Industrial Technology Research Institute (ITRI), which will reportedly take a 6 percent equity stake in the project, for its "technical support." The government Bank of Communications holds another 22 percent. *Metal Bulletin* (October 26, 1987).

[326] *Metal Bulletin Monthly* (December 1986).

because of the import protection which the government provides in hot coil.[327] In addition, these firms have moved into market niches which CSC cannot or will not occupy, either because it does not possess the production capability or because, as the state-owned producer, "China Steel is very sensitive to criticism, and for that reason is not aggressively competitive [in the domestic market]".[328] CSC's lack of aggressiveness, coupled with import protection, has provided a competitive milieu in which these firms have flourished.

The Taiwanese Steel Industry in International Competition

CSC and several Taiwanese producers of finished steel products have emerged as significant low-priced steel exporters. Their performance reflects low labor costs,[329] a solid infrastructure, protection from import competition, continuing government financial assistance, and, in the case of CSC, state-of-the-art equipment and a *de facto* monopoly on domestic sales of many flat-rolled products. CSC's facilities were a "showcase of the most advanced technology and equipment the world had to offer" and its continuous casting ratio is 100 percent.[330] While in many countries installation of such equipment has proven costly, because it cannot be operated at full utilization rates, in Taiwan a highly restrictive system of import protection and a domestic monopoly on a number of products have diminished this risk factor substantially.

Government Financial Support. CSC has continued to enjoy the extensive government financial backing which made its expansion possible. CSC benefited from a special government program designed to channel credit to selected enterprises at below-market rates -- with the discount subsidized,

---

[327] *Metal Bulletin* (May 8, 1987).

[328] *Metal Bulletin Monthly* (December 1986).

[329] Strikes are illegal in Taiwan; activist labor organization is prohibited, and labor's interests are represented by docile, government-dominated unions whose role is largely limited to promoting good relations between labor and management. Winckler, "Statism and Familism on Taiwan," pp. 189-90.

[330] *Metal Producing* (March 1980).

where necessary, by the Central Bank of China.[331] The *China Post* reported on October 10, 1982 that

> The Central Bank of China has raised the rediscount level for the state-run China Steel Corp. (CSC) from NT$2.5 billion [$63.9 million] to NT $4 billion [$102.2 million]. CSC can now go to any local banks and ask for the discount on loans up to that amount, using bills as promissory notes, bills of exchange, and banker's acceptance. The maximum term for discounts provided in this way is 180 days. The banks are then able under the new regulation to request a rediscount with the appropriate bills from the Central Bank. The maximum time for this is 90 days. Previously, CSC could apply for discounts of up to NT $1,250 million [$31.9 million] from both the First Commercial Bank and the Cooperative Bank of Taiwan.

Moreover, CSC benefited from major direct government financial infusions when rising costs placed it under financial strain.[332] CSC and many other Taiwanese steel producers were exempt from import duties, harbor dues and surtax on raw materials used to produce steel for export, and were exempt from business taxes, stamp taxes, sales taxes and education taxes on revenue generated by export sales.[333] Finally, Taiwanese steel firms benefitted from several government export incentives, including the provision of low interest

---

[331] In 1977 the Cabinet adopted a program designed to stimulate Taiwanese capital investment; pursuant to this program "Banks will be requested to extend certain credit lines for manufacturers in accordance with their export and production records as well as their business plans if they can produce guarantees in advance. The manufacturers thus can draw the amount within the credit lines by producing their letters of credit -- Banks shall be encouraged to accept the bills and provide customers with discount services. The Central Bank of China will refinance such discount services if necessary." *Taiwan Enterprise* (September 1977); *China Post* (October 22, 1982). *Geppo* reported in January 1984 that Taiwanese steel producing enterprises could borrow funds to finance production of goods for export at an annual rate of 12 percent on the security of a letter of credit drawn on the government. In addition to subsidizing credit, the Central Bank of China has occasionally granted extensions on loan repayments to steel producers "to help them tide over current financial difficulties." *China Post* (March 12, 1982).

[332] *Metal Bulletin* reported on March 17, 1981 that: "Taiwan's China Steel Corp. is reported to have hit serious problems with its ambitious expansion plans. Soaring oil prices, high inflation and the need for a further 127 hectares of land have forced the Taiwan government to inject an extra NT $4,466 [about $112 million] in to finance its expansion." The new injection was approved by the Council for Economic Planning and Development. China News Agency, November 29, 1980, 2:39 GMT (Foreign Broadcast Information Service).

[333] Response of CSC to the Antidumping Questionnaire of the U.S. Department of the Treasury, April 30, 1980, Item B-9; Statute for the Encouragement of Investment, Section 3, Article 29.

government export financing loans.[334] In 1983, a spokesman for the Japanese steel industry estimated the margin of subsidization on Taiwanese steel exports at 10-20 percent.[335]

Protection. CSC is effectively insulated from competitive pressure in the domestic market. Government-administered import controls virtually eliminate competition from this source; CSC enjoys a *de facto* domestic monopoly on many steel products, and, as the dominant producer, "sets local prices" in product areas which it does not monopolize.[336] CSC maintains a two-tiered price structure to Taiwanese steel consumers, with a lower price charged for steel used for products destined for export, including finished steel products.[337] While CSC does not exploit the market power inherent in its position to extract excessive prices from consumers, it is assured of a substantial degree of price stability in its home market throughout the business cycle, a significant international competitive advantage.[338]

Taiwan remains a major importer of steel products simply because the domestic steel industry does not produce many of the varieties of steel products needed by the country's burgeoning economy, or does not produce them in sufficient quantity.[339] However, the government controls imports of products which do compete with locally produced goods, and import permits for such products must be issued on a case-by-case basis by the Board of Foreign Trade (BOFT).[340] In the case of steel,

---

[334] The Central Bank of China permits exporters to secure low-interest loans which cover up to 85 percent of the value of an export transaction. Under the Statute for Encouragement of Investment, exporters can establish an export loss reserve of up to one percent of the prior year's export earnings to be used to offset export losses. Exporters treat the loss reserve as a business expense, deducting it from taxable income in one year, then settle the account and carry the reserve funds forward as taxable income for the next year. *Oil Country Tubular Goods from Taiwan*, 51 F.R. 19583, May 30, 1986.

[335] Hiromoto Toda in *Far Eastern Economic Review* (November 17, 1983).

[336] *Metal Bulletin Monthly* (December 1986).

[337] *China Post* (November 29, 1982); *Welded Carbon Steel Line Pipe from Taiwan*, 50 F.R. 53363, December 31, 1985 (final). CSC's prices are subject to the approval of the Ministry of Economic Affairs.

[338] Several recent investigations by the U.S. government have revealed that CSC's prices in Taiwan are at or above world prices for comparable steel products. *Oil Country Tubular Goods from Taiwan*, 51 F.R. 19583, May 30, 1986 (Final).

[339] Taiwan is a major importer of coated steel products, alloy steel, billets and structurals.

[340] Josephine Wang, "A General Overview of Import Regulation" (Taiwan) in *East Asian Executive Reports* (May 1986). Two Taiwanese scholars commented in 1978 with respect to Taiwan's import policies that "Imports are controlled mainly for protective purposes. Control signifies the granting of import licenses only if comparable goods are not produced domestically. . . . The principle that domestic availability justifies import control is an important part of the protective system in Taiwan as in many other developing countries." K.L. Liang and C.H Liang, "Incentive Policies for Import Substitution and Export Expansion in the Republic of

If someone would like to import a product that CSC can make, the importer must first receive CSC's written permission before the product may be imported. This gives state-run CSC veto power over imports, and many complain that CSC has too much power.[341]

The government's policy has been to encourage import substitution, with the result that as CSC's capacity to produce various steel products came on stream, the Taiwanese government imposed restrictions, in the form of licensing requirements, on the import of these products.[342] *Metal Bulletin* observed on October 5, 1982 that as CSC began a "concerted effort to expand its export markets ... import restrictions are helping to protect the Taiwanese home market for the new mill's output." Japanese producers had traditionally supplied much of Taiwan's hot coil demand; however, in June 1982 CSC's hot strip mill commenced operations and the Taiwanese government concurrently imposed import licensing requirements on hot coil that amounted to an outright ban.[343] Similar restrictions followed the start-up of CSC's cold-rolling mill. *Metal Bulletin* reported on September 28, 1982 that

Taiwan is to institute a system of import licensing for CR coil, a move which Japanese steel industry circles think will amount to a more or less strict ban on imports of the product. This follows the start-up last July of the new CR mill at Taiwan's China Steel Corp. which should work up to a production rate of 20,000 tpm by October. Taiwan has a similar import licensing system for HR coil. Japan has been exporting some 400,000 tpy of CR coil to Taiwan, and this trade will most likely be lost, it is feared, following the loss of the 400-600,000 tpy of HR coil the Japanese used to send Taiwan before the import controls on this product were introduced last July. China Steel's hot strip mill was commissioned last June.

Protection has posed some problems for CSC's users; its various expansion projects have disrupted production runs at its existing facilities, reducing supplies of some products to end users and making spot imports necessary. CSC's refusal to permit wire rod imports prompted major complaints by

China" in International Commercial Bank of China, *Economic Review* (November-December 1978), p. 11.

[341] Unclassified Department of Commerce Cable No. R-2181352, July 1983 (Taipei).

[342] *China Post* (August 24, 1981).

[343] *Metal Bulletin* (September 28, 1982). In the spring of 1982, in anticipation of these developments, "At the export business negotiation for the quarter of April through June, some [Japanese] companies were told by [Taiwanese hot coil] users that this was the final business transaction." *Nikkei Sangyo* (May 24, 1982).

domestic users when a shortage of this product developed in 1983.[344] In 1986-87, CSC was "in the throes of expanding hot strip rolling capacity," with the result that deliveries of hot coil to users were being disrupted.[345] The Board of Foreign Trade acknowledged this problem and granted import permits for hot coil, the "first time [importers were] able to buy coil outside China Steel in years."[346] The formation of An Feng Steel (to produce hot coil) was in part a response to CSC's hot coil delivery shortfalls; observers warned, however, that An Feng's "position would remain strong so long as present arrangements effectively controlling imports are maintained," but would deteriorate "if pressure from Taiwan's trading partners to open its markets filters down to the semifinished steel sector."[347]

In addition to outright protection, CSC strengthened its hold on the Taiwanese domestic market by developing an extremely close relationship with "downstream" producers of finished steel products, which both guaranteed these producers a supply of low-priced steel and ensured CSC of a domestic outlet for its products.[348] CSC took steps in 1983 to establish a "reciprocal production-sales system with downstream processors," providing 2,000 downstream enterprises with management assistance on the condition that "80 percent of the factory's materials must be procured from the CSC."[349] CSC offers special price discounts to "export oriented processors" which are "designed to enhance their export competitiveness."[350]

Exports. Because of its high continuous casting ratio and highly-leveraged financial position, CSC can only break even if its facilities are operated at a very high rate all of the time.[351] CSC undertook its initial expansion projects on the assumption that domestic demand would absorb 90 percent of its output, an assumption which has proven overly optimistic. CSC and other domestic Taiwanese mills have pursued a countercyclical approach to exports

---

[344] Unclassified U.S. Department of Commerce Cable No. R2181352 (July 1983) (Taipei).

[345] *Metal Bulletin* (April 17, 1987).

[346] *Metal Bulletin Monthly* (December 1986).

[347] *Metal Bulletin* (May 8, 1987).

[348] *China Post* (July 20, 1981). In an example of one such arrangement, CSC entered into a joint project with the Chun Yu Works, Co. to make polished steel bars for export; CSC provided the necessary steel to Chun Yu, which processed it and paid CSC out of the export proceeds. The *China Post* observed on December 8, 1981 that "This both increases [CSC's] sales and boosts exports of processed steel. [A CSC official said] "This is one of the best ways for the whole local steel industry to ride out the current low demand in sales and production."

[349] *China Post* (October 4, 1983).

[350] *China Post* (November 29, 1982).

[351] *Geppo* indicated in July 1983 that "Because of the financial structure . . . CSC needed the over 100 percent operation rate to reach the breakeven point." See also *China Post* (May 25, 1983).

to sustain a high operating rate when domestic demand has been inadequate to absorb such a high proportion of total output. In 1982, Taiwan's domestic steel demand fell sharply just as CSC's new second stage capacity was coming on stream. CSC found that it could dispose of only about half of its production locally,[352] and it began to incur substantial losses.[353]

During this period CSC maintained a high rate of operation -- actually utilizing its facilities at more than 100 percent of nominal capacity -- and disposed of its surpluses by exporting them at prices substantially below domestic price levels.[354] Expanding export sales, even at discounted prices, enabled CSC to operate at full capacity and reduce its unit costs of production.[355]

The Taiwanese mills' export practices have given rise to periodic friction with Taiwan's principal trading partners. In 1978, CSC sought to dispose of a massive surplus of plate by aggressive pricing in Japan and the U.S.,[356] and in 1979, the U.S. government found that CSC had been dumping plate in the

---

[352] *China Post* (January 1, 1982). The Taiwanese government requires that CSC give priority of sales to domestic buyers. This leads to the periodic suspension of export shipments when local demand increases. *China Post* (September 10, 1980). Conversely, as the *Free China Weekly* observed on December 5, 1982, "While the steel mill was originally geared mainly to supplying the domestic market, it managed to export the surplus whenever the demand was slack."

[353] The *China Post* reported on February 8, 1983 that "Since the second stage started to join the operation line last July, due to recession and other factors, the CSC was in the red continuously. From July to December in 1982 the company suffered a total deficit of NT $830 million [$21.2 million]." Taiwan's smaller electric furnace producers were even more severely affected by the slump -- in 1983 over 100 of these enterprises suspended production altogether. The Taiwan Iron and Steel Association proposed a 40 percent cut in output for 1984 to stabilize domestic prices. *Metal Bulletin* (December 23, 1983). These firms suffered in part from government restrictions on the import of scrap plate, which were imposed to protect CSC's new plate mill, but which had the effect of raising scrap prices. The government's concern was that the scrap plate was being resold in competition with CSC's plate rather than rerolled. *Metal Bulletin* (February 17, 1980); *China Post* (October 2, 1980).

[354] In early 1980, CSC was quoting prices for steel plate of "NT $14,950 [about $414.59] a ton for domestic sales and NT $12,700 [$352.19] for exports." *Metal Bulletin* (March 14, 1980.) On April 3, 1984, the *Free China Journal* reported that "Many [Taiwanese] steel companies have encountered overproduction problem . . . local steelmakers have been exporting their products without profits." The *Free China Weekly* reported on July 11, that "Previously, as much as 80 percent of production was used in Taiwan, but because of the recession reducing local demand, exports have been boosted. [CSC Chairman T.K. Liu said] that China Steel sells large quantities of steel to Japan, because export prices are 15 percent lower even after a 5 percent duty is added on. China Steel is currently producing 10 percent more than design capacity to make the highest export sales possible. Because the international price of steel is significantly lower than the domestic price, the facility must produce more to make a profit, he said."

[355] *China Post* (July 29, 1982).

[356] *Metal Bulletin* (December 29, 1978); *Japan Metal Bulletin* (December 14, 1978).

U.S. market by a weighted average margin of 34 percent.[357] Several "downstream" Taiwanese producers, who purchase CSC steel at discounts and process it into finished pipe-and-tube products, have been major exporters to the U.S. market. In early 1984 a number of these firms were reportedly receiving a 20 percent discount from CSC for hot coil to be used to produce pipes for export.[358] These firms have priced very aggressively.[359] In March 1984 the U.S. Commerce Department determined that Taiwanese welded pipes had been dumped in the U.S. market at substantial margins;[360] in 1986 it found that Taiwanese oil country tubular goods had been dumped in the U.S. market at margins of 26 percent;[361] and in 1986 it found that Taiwanese pipe fittings had been dumped in the U.S. market at margins as high as 87 percent.[362]

Taiwan has refused to enter into a voluntary restraint arrangement with the United States under President Reagan's steel program, and in 1986, U.S. imports from Taiwan more than doubled over 1985 levels, from 224 thousand short tons to over 500 thousand tons. Concerned over possible U.S. reactions to this surge, Taiwanese steel exporters began to exercise some collective restraints on their exports to the U.S. in 1987, and U.S. imports from Taiwan fell to 263 thousand tons in that year.[363]

Conclusion

The growth and successful export performance of Taiwan's steel industry demonstrates how a sustained government promotional effort can produce an efficient, export-oriented steel industry. Government investment enabled CSC to acquire a modern facility and to acquire an infrastructure to overcome the handicap of insufficient local resources. Stringent protection from imports has

---

[357] *Carbon Steel Plate from Taiwan*, 44 F.R. 9639, February 14, 1979. The U.S. International Trade Commission noted that "When questioned at the Commission's public hearing on whether China Steel intended to price its steel plate at or above fair value in the future, the company's vice president . . . and counsel . . . were evasive or noncommittal." 44 F.R. 29735.

[358] *Geppo* (January 1984).

[359] *American Metal Market* reported on July 20, 1982 that "One of the greatest discounts from former trigger prices remains electric resistance welded pipe from Taiwan and South Korea in diameters up to six inches. Taiwanese pipe has been reported for third quarter shipment at about $450 per ton in schedule 40 blank plain end, 2 inches in diameter."

[360] The margins for the three largest sources of Taiwanese pipe (which accounted for 95 percent of U.S. imports of this product) were Tai Feng Industries, 43.7 percent; Yieh Hsing Enterprises, 38.5 percent; Kao Hsing Chang Iron Steel Corp., 9.7 percent. Tai Feng subsequently became insolvent. *Certain Welded Carbon Steel Pipes and Tubes from Taiwan* (Final), 49 F.R. 9931, March 1984.

[361] *Oil Country Tubular Goods from Taiwan*, 51 F.R. 19371, May 29, 1986 (Final).

[362] *Carbon Steel Butt-Weld Pipe Fittings from Taiwan*, 51 F.R. 37772, October 24, 1986 (Final).

[363] U.S. International Trade Commission; *Metal Bulletin* (September 2, 1986).

enabled CSC to stabilize prices, operate at a high rate of capacity and to dispose of its surplus steel in the export market at low prices. Government-subsidized credit, and the assurance of continuing government financial injections, has further reduced costs and enabled CSC to map out and implement a carefully phased expansion program. All of these factors are likely to make Taiwan a significant factor in international steel competition in the late 1980s and 1990s -- and to pose a dilemma for those that do not enjoy comparable government backing.

ARGENTINA

The Argentine steel industry's growing presence in world markets reflects that nation's chronic economic crisis. The industry, which was founded with government assistance to meet the "strategic" requirements of the nation's military, was originally expected to displace foreign steel imports in the domestic market. Unfortunately, the increase in national steelmaking capacity coincided with the collapse of demand for steel in the domestic economy in the late 1970s, and burdened by an overvalued currency, low productivity and erratic government policies, the industry was forced to retrench. Despite rationalization efforts, however, steel capacity continued to exceed consumption and utilization rates remained low. In the mid-1980s the government, faced with an enormous foreign debt and a severe shortage of foreign exchange, devalued the national currency and promised that it would implement a set of consistent policies for the promotion of non-traditional exports, including steel. The steel industry, assisted by government export subsidies, has responded with an unprecedented export drive, converting Argentina into a significant net exporter of steel.

The Expansion of the Argentine Steel Industry

Argentina traditionally exported agricultural commodities and relied upon foreign sources for most of its manufactured products. Beginning in the 1930s, however, periodic world business cycles and a general downward trend in commodity prices led Argentina to undertake an import-substitution policy intended to lessen the impact of such forces on the local economy.[364] Self-sufficiency in steel was an important aspect of that policy. The government's steel program relied upon a combination of public and private enterprise. On the one hand, the government created state-controlled companies that were expected to participate directly in the production process. SOMISA, now the

---

[364] International Bank for Reconstruction and Development, *Argentina: Economic Memorandum* (1985), p. 159.

largest steelmaker in Argentina, was founded by the government in 1947.[365] Because self-sufficiency in steel was considered essential to the national defense, SOMISA was placed under the authority of the Dirección General de Fabricaciónes Militares (DGFM).[366] In addition to SOMISA, the government created a second integrated producer, Altos Hornos Zapla, and an iron ore producer, HIPASAM, both of which were also placed under military control. The military, one of Argentina's most powerful institutions, has continued to play a key role in the development of the Argentine steel industry up to the present day.

The government also undertook to promote private investment in the steel sector. Toward this end, it eliminated tariffs on imported capital goods, provided loans and loan guarantees for the implementation of investment plans, and built a system of investment incentives into the tax system.[367] As a result of these promotional activities, a significant private sector steel industry soon emerged in Argentina. Although state producers dominated the production of raw steel and flat products, two private companies, ACINDAR and SIDERCA, became the leading producers of non-flat and tubular products, respectively. Both state and private producers benefitted from tariffs and other import barriers designed to protect and stimulate domestic production, and from export incentives designed to maintain production in times of slack domestic demand.

The Argentine Steel Plan. In 1974, with steel consumption still well in excess of domestic production, the Argentine government developed an ambitious "Argentine Steel Plan."[368] The Plan foresaw the quintupling of Argentine steel production by 1985 to 14 million metric tons. To achieve this goal, SOMISA would undertake to expand capacity to 4 million metric tons, while a new state-owned producer, SIDINSA, would construct a greenfield integrated mill with an initial capacity of 3.8 million metric tons.[369] Private

---

[365] L. Randall, *An Economic History of Argentina in the Twentieth Century* (New York: Columbia University Press, 1978), p. 138. SOMISA, the Sociedad Mixta Siderúgica Argentina, was technically a mixed public-private company. The government, however, put up 80 percent of its capital, and each government share had ten votes, in contrast to one vote per private share. *Ibid.*

[366] General Oscar Gallino, Director General of DGFM, explained in 1980 that the goal of producing more steel internally was the only way to ensure that the country would never lack steel for the production of arms. "The country must produce at least all the steel necessary for its Defense," he declared. *Siderurgia Latinoamericana* (June 1980) ("Informativo Regional"), p. 33.

[367] Randall, *Economic History*, p. 163; *Siderurgia Latinoamericana* (August 1979) ("Argentina: Políticas de Comercio Exteriór Siderúrgico"), pp. 75-76.

[368] Decree No. 619, *Official Bulletin* (March 4, 1974).

[369] SIDINSA was founded by the DGFM and the Banade (National Development Bank) in 1975, and was headed by an Argentine general. *La Prensa* (May 4, 1977); *Telam* (November 18, 1978).

producers such as ACINDAR and SIDERCA would also make large new investments.[370]   The first stage of this expansion, which would increase production to 6.1 million metric tons by 1977, was expected to cost $1.1 billion.[371]   Although SOMISA would have been deemed uncreditworthy if it were a private firm, government equity infusions, loans, loan guarantees, certain tax exemptions and a variety of other forms of assistance provided it with the capital to support this effort.[372]

The timing of the expansion program proved unfortunate. Argentina entered a serious economic slump in 1975, when a world recession coincided with the closure of important foreign markets for the nation's agricultural products. Inflation skyrocketed to 1000 percent in 1976, the public sector deficit rose to 16 percent of GDP and the nation's trade balance swung into deficit. As the economic crisis deepened, the Argentine military overthrew the civilian government of President Juan Perón. The new government slashed the public sector deficit by cutting spending and raising taxes, causing a further contraction in the economy.[373]   Steel consumption fell nearly 25 percent, and never returned to its 1974 peak (figure 5-6).

Despite the crisis, the steel industry did not abandon its expansion plans. SOMISA continued to aim for a capacity in excess of 4 million metric tons[374] and, although it became increasingly clear that that goal would not be reached as quickly as planned, the company had installed 2.8 million metric tons of capacity by 1979.[375]   SIDINSA continued in that year to plan a facility that would by itself produce more steel than the nation's apparent consumption,[376]

---

[370] Brigadier General Joaquín de Las Heras, Director of Development, DGFM, in *Siderurgia Latinoamericana* (January 1976) ("Analizó las Perspectivas de la Siderurgia Argentina"), pp. 14-16.

[371] *Latin American Economic Report* (April 26, 1974).

[372] In 1984 the U.S. Department of Commerce determined that in view of SOMISA's poor financial performance, the firm had been uncreditworthy between 1978 and 1982, and unequityworthy between 1977 and 1983. The government invested $80 million in SOMISA during this period; the company secured an additional $25 million loan from the Banco de la Nación on the basis of a guarantee from the State Secretariat of Finance. *Cold-Rolled Carbon Steel Flat-Rolled Products from Argentina*, April 26, 1984 (49 F.R. 18006).

[373] U.S.I.T.C., Pub. No. 1950, *The Effect of Developing Country Debt-Servicing Problems on U.S. Trade*, March 1987, pp. 80-82.

[374] SOMISA's 1975 *Annual Report* notes that, despite the rapid collapse of the domestic market, "The company is conscious of the fundamental contribution that it makes to the development of the country and of the need that its expansion plans reach their pre-fixed goals." Five years later, in its 1980 *Annual Report*, the company remained optimistic: "Because this is a serious situation but a temporary one, according to all forecasts. . . . SOMISA is continuing to aggressively pursue its expansion plan, a significant contribution that will enable our country to have a reasonable supply of domestic steel by the end of this decade."

[375] *Siderurgia Latinoamericana* (September 1979) ("Informativo Regional"), p. 87.

[376] *Siderurgia Latinoamericana* (May 1979) ("Informativo Regional"), p. 32.

Figure 5-6: Argentina — Steel Production, Consumption and Trade, 1971–1986

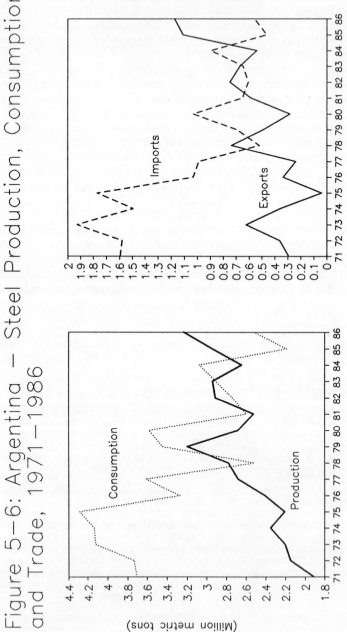

(Million metric tons)

Source: International Iron and Steel Institute, Steel Statistical Yearbook, 1981, 1987. Production and Consumption refer to crude steel; Exports and Imports refer to semi-finished and finished steel.

and in September 1976 the government approved the expansion programs of 5 private producers. The most ambitious of these projects was the construction by ACINDAR of Argentina's largest private-sector integrated steel mill, which was completed in 1978 with considerable government assistance.[377] SIDERCA, the nation's leading producer of seamless tubes, also integrated its facilities and expanded capacity with the help of the Argentine government.[378]

The Industry in Crisis. By the end of the decade, Argentina had neared its long-sought goal of self-sufficiency in steel.[379] However, the financial condition of the producers was precarious, and the industry was plagued with an enormous overhang of unutilized capacity; the nation's theoretical raw steel capacity was 6.9 million tons,[380] or approximately double its total apparent consumption. Industry leaders implored the government to take actions to reactivate domestic demand;[381] however, the government was committed to a restrictive monetary policy that was unlikely to satisfy the industry's

---

[377] The plant, which uses direct reduction technology, has a capacity of 600,000 tons of raw steel. It cost $265 million, $82 million of which was provided by the state-owned National Development Bank. A further $70 million was provided by the Inter-American Development Bank. *Siderurgia Latinoamericana* (March 1979) ("ACINDAR Inauguró su Nueva Midiaceria Integral"), p. 14.

[378] SIDERCA installed direct reduction capability, new coke ovens, and continuous casting machines. Much of the funding consisted of long-term loans from foreign financial institutions, which were guaranteed by the National Development Bank. *Siderurgia Latinoamericana* (March 1977) ("Dalmine Siderca Está en Pleno Proceso de Expansión"), p. 14.

[379] In 1978, production exceeded apparent consumption by 250,000 tons (figure 5-6), an achievement that resulted from a combination of low domestic demand and steadily increasing production. *Siderurgia Latinoamericana* noted in June 1979 that "The low level of the internal Argentine market, united with the increased supply at the basic level (primary iron and steel) has modified in notable form the relative panorama of supply and foreign demand, changing the normally negative figure (more imports than exports) to a positive one. . . ." Although Argentina's overall theoretical capacity was more than sufficient to meet the nation's demand for steel, several factors caused Argentina to slip back into net importer status in the early 1980s. First, the industry was faced with bottlenecks in its production capability -- most notably in the area of slabbing -- which forced it to import certain products. Hogan, *World Steel in the 1980s*, p. 170. The situation was aggravated by government liberalization and revenue measures, which lessened somewhat Argentina's import barriers and temporarily eliminated tax rebates on exports. By 1983, however, production once again exceeded apparent consumption, and in the mid-1980s the margin of production over consumption widened significantly (figure 5-6).

[380] *Siderurgia Latinoamericana* (June 1979) ("Expectativas Del Mercado Argentino de Acero en 1979"), p. 40.

[381] The Treasurer of the Centro de Industriales Siderúrgicos complained that "This decline in sales, which have not managed during the course of the year to recuperate to the levels of previous years, constitutes a very worrisome situation that we have raised repeatedly with the national authorities, conscious of the need to undertake adequate measures to avoid a continuation of this tendency, which could represent irreparable losses for the steel industry and for the State." *Siderurgia Latinoamericana* (March 1979) ("Informativo Regional"), p. 20.

demands.[382] Furthermore, the government embarked on a trade liberalization program that, although only partially applied to steel, exerted downward pressure on domestic prices and led to an import surge.[383] SOMISA's losses were offset by repeated government injections of equity capital;[384] however, other less fortunate companies were forced to retrench or even to close their doors.[385] As a result, while overall steelmaking capacity declined somewhat, it remained greatly in excess of consumption.[386]

Argentine Steel in the 1980s

The fortunes of the Argentine steel industry in the 1980s have been mixed. On the one hand, the nation's severe economic crisis, which was aggravated by the Falklands War with Britain in 1982, dealt a blow to the industry's expansion plans. SOMISA discontinued negotiations with the Japanese for the

---

[382] *Siderurgia Latinoamericana* (January 1980)("Informativo Regional"), p. 4; U.S.I.T.C., *Developing Country Debt-Servicing Problems*, p. 85.

[383] Imports increased by more than 50 percent in 1980 before falling back the following year. In 1980 General Rivera, President of SOMISA, stated that "I support adequate protection for our domestic steel industry because, aware of the international steel situation, I consider that some temporary measures ought to be adopted. Among them, it is necessary to slow down the rate of decreases in tariffs to avoid serious failures and even the possible annihilation of the industry." SOMISA *Annual Report 1979-80*. In fact, imports were a threat because Argentine steel prices exceeded those of Europe and America by as much as 20 percent. SOMISA *Annual Report 1976-77*. General Rivera believed that foreign steel was being subsidized or sold at a loss, and that "to attempt to establish comparisons [between Argentine and foreign steel prices] under these circumstances, ignoring other distorting factors ... [such as] different cost structures between economies in different stages of development, is very difficult and dangerous." *Siderurgia Latinoamericana* (August 1980) ("Informativo Regional"), p. 46. In 1980 the Argentine government responded to these concerns by undertaking a dumping investigation against certain U.S., Japanese and Brazilian steel products. *Siderurgia Latinoamericana* (March 1980) ("Informativo Regional"), p. 29; *Quarterly Economic Review: Argentina* (Fall 1980), p. 12.

[384] SOMISA *Annual Reports*, 1979-80, 1980-81, 1981-82.

[385] In 1980 a private producer, Gurmendi S.A., laid off 700 of its 2,000 workers and closed down one of its electric furnaces. *Siderurgia Latinoamericana* (September 1980)("Informativo Regional"), p. 16. Eventually, Gurmendi merged with ACINDAR and another private firm in a major consolidation of the industry. *Siderurgia Latinoamericana* (June 1982) ("Informativo Regional"), p. 26. Aceros Ohler, a specialty steels company controlled by DGFM, was forced to shut down altogether due to the shrinking domestic market and lower tariff protections. Ohler was offered for sale to the private sector, but no one was interested in buying it. *Siderurgia Latinoamericana* (May 1979) ("Informativo Regional"), p. 32.

[386] Data regarding the extent of these capacity reductions is inconsistent. The American embassy reported in 1983 that Argentina had reduced its steelmaking capacity to 5 million tons from 6.6 million tons in 1979. American Embassy, *ARGENTINA: Sectoral Review 1982-83* (1983). However, *Siderurgia Latinoamericana* noted in July 1983 that "Steel production capacity has remained stable in the last few years, with a weak downward tendency because although there have been some adjustments that have expanded capacity and reactivated installations, others have been temporarily or permanently shut down," and it reported in May 1985 that Argentine theoretical crude steel capacity exceeded 7 million tons in 1984.

purchase of a $200 million hot strip mill,[387] which was to have been the first phase of the oft-delayed SOMISA "four million ton plan."[388] However, by 1983 expansion plans had been reactivated at a number of firms; SOMISA planned to invest $500 million in the 1983-89 period,[389] and SIDERCA began implementation of a $600 million expansion and modernization program.[390] Even ACINDAR, which was beset by financial difficulties, undertook a major modernization plan.[391]

Privatization Efforts. In recent years a number of efforts have been made, for the most part abortive, to reduce the role of the Argentine government in the steel sector. In 1980 the military government adopted Law No. 22177, which set out guidelines for the sale of state enterprises.[392] In 1983, the process received a boost when the military government, which suffered a serious blow to its prestige as a result of the Falklands War, was replaced by the civilian government of President Raúl Alfonsín. Alfonsín transferred control of the state-owned steel mills from the military to the civilian Ministry of Defense[393] and announced plans to sell SOMISA to the private sector.[394]

---

[387] Although the Argentines "postponed for two years" their plan to purchase such a facility from Japan, they requested that the Japanese invest in SOMISA anyway. The Japanese declined. *Japan Economic Journal* (August 17, October 12, 1982). In light of SOMISA's precarious financial position, Nippon Steel even withdrew its technicians from a remodeling job it was performing on one of SOMISA's blast furnaces. *Japan Economic Journal* (September 28, 1982).

[388] *Latin American Regional Reports: Southern Cone*, April 10, 1981.

[389] *Siderurgia Latinoamericana* (June 1983) ("Informativo Regional"), p. 22. The journal reported that "Steel production in the first months of 1983 reveals that the slowdown observed in the last five years continues. . . . Industrial demand remains stagnant, and construction is suffering from one of its worst crises. Exports, on the other hand, maintain only part of the level achieved in 1982. In spite of the circumstances above signalled, the firms' concerns remain concentrated on expanding capacity and perfecting production." *Ibid.*

[390] *Siderurgia Latinoamericana* (April 1986) ("Informativo Regional"), p. 23. The investment program, which was financed in part by a $40 million loan from the Inter-American Development Bank, was entering its final stage by late 1987. *Metal Bulletin* (October 19, 1987). The United States opposed the IDB loan on the grounds of "doubtful economic and financial viability due to global overcapacity." National Advisory Council on International Monetary and Financial Policies, *Annual Report to Congress 1986*, p. 40. The Argentine government also provided financing at subsidized rates. *Wall Street Journal* (May 31, 1988). SIDERCA reported a loss of $21.2 million in 1986-87, as a result of a "marked decline in the sale of seamless tubes in the domestic market and low prices in the external market." *Siderurgia Latinoamericana* (November 1987)("Informativo Regional"), p. 25.

[391] *Latin American Commodities Report* (October 29, 1987).

[392] Business International, *Investing, Licensing and Trade Abroad: Argentina* (November 1982), p. 5. The Director General of DGFM remarked that privatization should take place "to the extent that private capital has reached the interest to continue the work of production of basic materials for the defense." Oscar Gallino, in *Siderurgia Latinoamericana* (June 1980) ("Informativo Regional"), p. 33.

[393] *Siderurgia Latinoamericana* (March 1984) ("Informativo Regional"), p. 23.

The announcement provoked sharp opposition; the labor unions, the Peronists, the Communists and the military all spoke out against privatization.[395] More fundamentally, a serious question existed as to whether any investor would want to buy the company, and at what price.[396] Although the government did succeed in selling one small pipe producer to the private sector,[397] plans to privatize SOMISA were abandoned.[398]

Continuing Financial Difficulties. Meanwhile, the economic condition of Argentina's steelmakers has been variable at best. Although the severe losses of the early 1980s had turned to substantial profits in 1982-83, the trend once again reversed itself by 1984-85 (table 5-11). Argentine producers suffered from weak demand and government price controls; in late 1984 producers complained that steel prices were lagging behind input prices by 40 percent, and the producers began to accumulate inventories of steel for which the cost of production exceeded official sales prices.[399] The situation had improved little by 1987.[400]

ACINDAR was among the worst hit of Argentine steel producers. The company, which was responsible for roughly one-third of the nation's steel production, suffered losses of $70 million in the 1985-86 fiscal year.[401] In 1987 the firm refinanced $250 million of its $342 million debt; repayment would be made over twelve years with a 3-year grace period. Some foreign creditors, however, apparently concluded that ACINDAR would never be able to pay back its obligations; *The Economist* reported on March 12, 1988 that

---

[394] *Financial Times* (February 26, 1986).

[395] The Secretary General of the General Confederation of Labor, Saul Ubadini, warned the "dark minds" planning privatization that "the workers' movement will continue fighting on every front without fear of slander or lies," and workers at SOMISA staged rallies and strikes. *Buenos Aires Herald* (April 3, 1986). The Perónists and the military objected that the sale would threaten the national interest. *Latin America Weekly Report* (February 28, 1986); *The Economist* (March 8, 1986). From the standpoint of the military, an element of self-interest may also have been involved; *Quarterly Economic Review: Argentina* remarked in the winter of 1982 that DGFM "amongst other things provides well paid jobs for retiring army officers."

[396] SOMISA's losses in 1985 amounted to 15 percent of sales. *Siderurgia Latinoamericana* (April 1986) ("Informativo Regional"), p. 25. The firm's president indicated in June 1986 that, although the net worth of the firm was $800 million, its replacement value was approximately $4.6 billion. *Siderurgia Latinoamericana* (June 1986) ("Informativo Regional") p. 30.

[397] SIAT, a producer of welded pipe, was privatized in early 1986. *Siderurgia Latinoamericana* (March 1986) ("Informativo Regional"), p. 24.

[398] *Latin American Commodities Report* (October 29, 1987).

[399] *Siderurgia Latinoamericana* (January 1985) ("Informativo Regional"), p. 24.

[400] *Siderurgia Latinoamericana* (March 1987) ("Informativo Regional").

[401] *Mercado* (May 28, 1987).

ACINDAR had bought back $100 million of its foreign debt at 20 percent of face value.

Table 5-11. Financial Results of the Argentine Steel Industry 1980-1985 (million U.S. dollars)

	Sales	Income	Income/Sales (%)
1980-81	950	(251)	(26.4)
1981-82	1,156	(176)	(15.2)
1982-83	1,331	380	28.6
1983-84	1,334	141	10.6
1984-85	1,134	(76)	(6.7)

Source: Agostino Rocca, "Ventajas Operativas y Rentabilidad de la Siderurgia Argentina," reprinted in *Siderurgia Lationoamericana* (January 1986), p. 11.

Argentina's Foreign Trade in Steel

Argentina's pattern of trade in steel has resembled that of many newly industrialized countries. Traditionally a net importer of steel, Argentina sought and achieved self-sufficiency by the early 1980s as the result of a government policy of import substitution, which depended in good part on the imposition of stringent controls on imports. During periods of slack demand, comparatively stable production levels were maintained by exporting surplus steel, often at very low prices. The Argentine export drive resulted in antidumping actions by the EC[402] and the U.S.[403] However, the most recent export drive exceeded all such previous export surges by a large measure; net

---

[402] The EC imposed antidumping duties on Argentine hot coil imports in 1983. *Metal Bulletin* (April 6, 1983).

[403] Argentine export pricing has been aggressive. In 1984, the United States Department of Commerce found that SOMISA was dumping cold-rolled sheet at margins of 242.5 percent and that ACINDAR was dumping carbon steel wire rod at margins of 119 percent. *Cold-Rolled Carbon Steel Flat-Rolled Products from Argentina*, 49 F.R. 48588, December 13, 1984; *Carbon Steel Wire Rod from Argentina*, 49 F.R. 38170, September 27, 1984. A dumping margin of more than 100 percent indicates that the fair market value of the product is more than double its sales price. The following year the Department found that SIDERCA was dumping oil country tubular goods at a margin of 61.7 percent. *Oil Country Tubular Goods from Argentina*, 50 F.R. 12595, March 29, 1985. The Department found the following year that margins on this product had dropped to *de minimis* levels. *Oil Country Tubular Goods from Argentina*, 51 F.R. 20240, June 3, 1986.

steel exports amounted to over half a million tons in 1985.[404] In 1987, exports reached 1 million metric tons, or about one third of Argentina's total production.[405] The recent surge in exports is attributable to Argentina's greatly expanded steel production capacity, continued depressed domestic demand and its urgent need for foreign exchange to service its large foreign debt.[406] *Metal Bulletin Monthly* observed in October 1985 that "Argentina's need for foreign currency is so great, and the steel industry's search for markets so desperate, that exporting is all they can do for their own and their country's survival."

Export Subsidies and Incentives. The steelmakers' export efforts and pricing reflect a series of special government measures undertaken with the object of stimulating exports. Successive Argentine governments have implemented a bewildering array of export-stimulating (and import-deterring) measures, often replacing one package with another within a relatively short time, in response to the conflicting demands for decreasing the public sector deficit, controlling inflation, maintaining employment, generating foreign exchange and encouraging the efficient allocation of resources. These measures have included currency devaluations,[407] export tax rebates,[408]

---

[404] In 1985 domestic demand plummeted 800,000 tons from 1984's depressed levels and exports rose dramatically. *Siderurgia Latinoamericana* noted in August 1985 that "The critical situation of the Argentine internal market, with a severe decline in public and private investment, has reaffirmed the need to increase exports. . . . Producing companies have visualized as an alternative spilling their excess and productive capacity toward the external market, so as to cover in part their costs and to continue producing." Two months later, the magazine asserted that "While the domestic steel market is experiencing one of its most recessive periods. . . . SOMISA has reached unprecedented production levels in recent years with the putting into operation of blast furnace no. 2. This apparent paradox is explained in that the export volumes carried out by the firm compensate for the decline of the internal market. The strategy of the firm responds to the political decision to achieve a high rate of utilization of its productive capacity. On the other side, it aims to favor the earning of foreign exchange. . . . The combination of depressed demand and low prices stemming from price controls makes internal sales unprofitable, while the export route barely covers costs." *Siderurgia Latinoamericana* (October 1985) ("Informativo Regional"), p. 17.

[405] *Metal Bulletin* (March 7, 1988).

[406] ACINDAR's President, Arturo Acevedo, remarked in 1985 that, unlike previous export drives by Argentine producers, "We have to commit ourselves to foreign markets. These markets have to be developed and then maintained - which in the past has been a great problem." *Metal Bulletin* (August 30, 1985).

[407] In the area of exchange rates, as with other economic policies, Argentine government policies have vacillated. In the late 1970s steelmakers complained that the peso was overvalued. *Siderurgia Latinoamericana* (March 1977) ("Informativo Regional"). In fact, the real value of the peso appreciated rapidly between 1977 and 1980. U.S.I.T.C., *Developing Country Debt-Servicing Problems*, p. 90. However, the government devalued the peso dramatically in 1981, causing SOMISA to report in its 1980-81 financial statement that "the current situation, although gloomy, is different from the one in the preceding period because the adjustment of exchange rates has kept down steel imports and has made possible the export of steel products, although at a low profit margin." The government promised in 1984 that it would "maintain an exchange rate policy which will help to generate a large trade surplus," *Quarterly Economic Review of Argentina*

preferential export financing programs[409] and duty drawbacks.[410] The Minister of Foreign Trade, announcing an export promoting program, stated that "The system, whose technical aspects were drawn up by an institute that functions within the economic cabinet, establishes the application of direct subsidies to the iron and steel [sector]. . . . During the first year of the system, the iron and steel industry that produces plate products would receive a subsidy of $359 million, while the firms that produce non-plate products would receive some $364.8 million."[411] While the various export incentives changed constantly, their underlying policy rationale remained the same -- without them, Argentine steel would find it extremely difficult to compete in the world market.   General Diego Uricariet, Argentina's Director of Military Manufacturing, told a banquet in 1978 that

> *The sum of higher costs in Argentina generates domestic [steel] prices that are higher than those in the United States, Japan, and other countries by approximately 30 percent. . . . In order for enterprises to be able to export surpluses that cannot be sold on the domestic market due to a decline in demand, reimbursements should be set at levels that at least make up for the taxes paid in the process.*[412]

Import Restrictions. The Argentine government's export promoting measures coincided with strict controls on steel imports.   Although Argentina's military government pursued an anti-inflation economic policy in

---

(1st Quarter 1984), a goal which the government has continued to pursue through periodic currency devaluations. U.S. Department of Commerce, *Foreign Economic Trends: Argentina* (January 1988), p. 5.

[408] The *"reembolso,"* first created in 1971, is intended to reimburse exporters for indirect taxes paid on export goods. The rebate, calculated as a percentage of the f.o.b. value of the exported product, varies depending on the product -- the maximum rebate was reduced from 40 percent in 1976 to 10 percent in 1982. International Bank for Reconstruction and Development, *Economic Memorandum: Argentina* (1985), p. 184. The Austral Plan eliminated the *reembolso* as a revenue measure, *Siderurgia Latinoamericana* (August 1985) ("Informativo Regional"), p. 31, but it was quickly reinstated and amounted to between 10 and 12.5 percent on steel products in 1987. *Siderurgia Latinoamericana* (October 1986), p. 18. In addition, companies with no established export history were entitled to 12-15 percent reimbursements under the Special Export Program. Consejo Técnico de Inversiones, *Tendencias Económicas 1986*, p. 209.

[409] In 1986, the government announced a new export financing program which provided funds at 1.5 percent below LIBOR and guaranteed prefinancing for certain products. *The Review of the River Plate* (August 29, 1986).

[410] Import duty drawbacks were available for parts and materials used in the manufacture of steel products for export. Eligibility for these benefits was conditioned on a finding that the imports were either not being produced by domestic steel producers or were in short supply. *Siderurgia Latinoamericana* (August 1979) ("Argentina: Política de Comercio Exterior Siderúrgico"). The program was reinstated in 1987. *Metal Bulletin* (June 19, 1987).

[411] *La Prensa* (November 26, 1981).

[412] *La Nación* (December 22, 1978).

the 1976-81 period that sought to liberalize the country's economy through periodic tariff reductions, this policy was only partially extended to steel. The government entities in charge of overseeing and approving the steel industry's expansion plans, DGFM and the State Secretariat of Industrial Promotion, jointly controlled the grant of import certificates for specific transactions and the implementation of the tariff reduction regime on steel products.[413] As a result, in 1982, after four years of import liberalization, tariffs on finished steel products still remained at 48 percent *ad valorem* levels.[414] Moreover, those import transactions which were permitted pursuant to "liberalization" measures depended on a finding either that the steel product in question was not being manufactured by the domestic industry or that there was an insufficient domestic supply.[415]   The basic concern, expressed by a steel industry spokesman in 1978, was that "the government's gradual freeing of imports, if applied to steel, would certainly wipe the Argentine industry off the map."[416]As of early 1988, all steel imports remained subject to approval of DGFM, which could refuse to provide a license if the product was available domestically,[417] and efforts to liberalize the import regime continued to draw fierce resistance from industrialists.[418]

The frequent changes in Argentine industrial and trade promoting measures should not obscure the broader patterns which have emerged in the

---

[413] *Siderurgia Latinoamericana* (August 1979) ("Argentina: Política de Comercio Exteriór Siderúrgico"), p. 76.

[414] *Siderurgia Latinoamericana* (June 1982) ("La Siderurgia Argentina en 1980-81 y sus Perspectivas"), p. 24. This result was predicted as early as 1979 -- *Latin American Weekly Report* remarked on November 30 of that year that "The Armed Forces are unlikely to tolerate any moves that tend to weaken sectors of manufacturing industry which they consider vital to the smooth and independent functioning of their supply companies. The steel industry, for example, has remained an exception to the tariff liberalisation programme."

[415] *Siderurgia Latinoamericana* (June 1982) ("La Siderurgia Argentina en 1980-81 y sus Perspectivas").

[416] *Review of the River Plate* (June 23, 1978).

[417] For example, the government reserves 48 percent of the oil country tubular goods market to domestic producers. SIDERCA, the only significant Argentine manufacturer of these products, takes advantage of its guaranteed market share by charging Argentine customers more than $50 per meter for standard pipe that it sells in world markets for $22. *Wall Street Journal* (May 31, 1988).

[418] The government announced in February 1988 that it would lower tariff barriers on steel and petrochemical imports from a maximum of 53 percent to 20 percent and would eliminate import licensing on those products, as part of a renewed liberalization of the economy. *Mercado* (February 25, 1988); *Financial Times* (February 21, 1988). Despite the assurances of government officials that measures such as favorable exchange rates and strict enforcement of dumping legislation would accompany the liberalization, the future of the scheme remains in doubt -- *Mercado* reported that "If the birth has taken place, the 'baby' is premature and is in the incubator together with a great number of unmade decisions." *Mercado* (February 25, 1988). One steel producer threatened to close its steel mill if the government went through with its plans. *Wall Street Journal* (May 31, 1988).

past decade. As a result of Argentina's steelmaking expansion efforts, which have been encouraged and partially funded by a succession of governments, the Argentine steel industry is today burdened with substantial excess capacity.[419] That fact, coupled with Argentina's large foreign debt burden, has led the industry to expand its export sales -- a phenomenon which has been encouraged by various Argentine administrations through a variety of subsidies and currency manipulation policies. Given Argentina's current balance of payments difficulties, it is likely that the steel sector will continue to rely on exports in the years to come.

VENEZUELA

In the 1970s Venezuela seemed an ideal location for the establishment of a successful steel industry. Although Venezuela had the highest per capita steel consumption in Latin America, the nation imported more steel than it produced domestically. With a government prepared to commit its substantial oil revenues to remedy this situation, and abundant supplies of iron ore and energy to supply new steel mills, it seemed that the industry's prospects for expansion were good.

However, Venezuela attempted to achieve too much too fast, seeking to expand its production fifteen-fold in two decades. The country's broad industrial policy goal was to diversify the economy by channeling oil revenues into new industries. Towards this end, government agencies financed an enormous expansion of the Siderúrgica del Orinoco steel producer (SIDOR) and developed plans for two new producers of comparable size. Like Mexico, however, Venezuela overestimated the extent and duration of the oil boom. By the early 1980s, oil income was shrinking and domestic demand for steel also declined. Moreover, SIDOR's rapid expansion, which would have been a daunting task for even the most experienced producer, proved beyond the company's ability. Its costly plant, which used new and largely unproven direct reduction technology, developed serious problems and never approached its rated capacity. The survival of the debt-encumbered company was only ensured by the massive and repeated intervention of the state.

In the late 1980s, the condition of the industry stabilized somewhat. After almost a decade of losses, SIDOR -- relieved of most of its debt by the state -- began to turn a profit, and the Venezuelan government, after years of uncertainty, cancelled the nation's other proposed greenfield plants. Domestic demand nevertheless still fell far short of projections and SIDOR remained reliant on export markets as outlets for its excess steel production.

---

[419] *Metal Bulletin* reported on March 7, 1988 that Argentine domestic demand for steel remained weak and that producers were seeking increased exports to keep their production rates up.

350

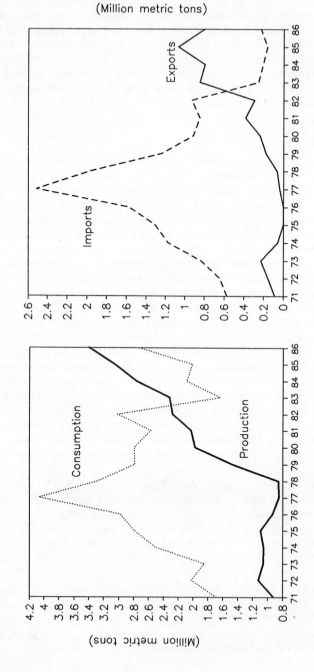

(Million metric tons)

Figure 5–7: Venezuela – Steel Production, Consumption and Trade, 1971–1986

Source: International Iron and Steel Institute, Steel Statistical Yearbook, 1981, 1987. Production and Consumption refer to crude steel; Exports and Imports refer to semi-finished and finished steel.

Expansion

In 1955, the Venezuelan government signed a contract for the construction of a steel plant at Matanzas, near the confluence of the Orinoco and Caroni rivers in the state of Guayana. Five years later, the newly-created Corporación Venezolana de Guayana (CVG), a regional development corporation established by the Venezuelan government, took charge of construction. The plant, which utilized the country's abundant hydroelectric energy for its electric furnaces, initially produced seamless pipes for the emerging Venezuelan oil industry; operation of the plant was entrusted to SIDOR, which was jointly owned by the CVG and the Venezuelan Investment Fund (FIV), a government body charged with investing half of the nation's oil revenues abroad and utilizing the proceeds for development projects. In two subsequent phases of expansion, SIDOR increased its crude steel production capacity to 1.2 million tons and added substantial flat-rolling capability.[420]

Although the new SIDOR mill represented a quantum leap forward for the Venezuelan steel industry, it did not come close to satisfying domestic demand for steel. As a major producer and exporter of iron ore, it seemed to many Venezuelans that the nation had a natural competitive advantage in steel production that ought to be exploited. In 1974, the President of the Republic announced the creation of a National Iron and Steel Council, whose primary task would be to study the possibilities for the development of the steel industry and to draft a National Iron and Steel Plan,[421] and in that year the Council adopted an ambitious proposal for a steel industry with a capacity in excess of 15 million tons.[422] Underlying this Plan was the goal of creating a diversified industrial economy that did not rely heavily on oil exports.[423]

The National Iron and Steel Plan was to be implemented in three stages. The capacity of the existing SIDOR plant was to be increased dramatically to

---

[420] *Siderurgia Latinoamericana* (March 1980) ("Plan IV de SIDOR: La Respuesta a un Desafío"), p. 21; *Metal Bulletin Monthly* (November 1978) ("SIDOR: Giant of the Orinoco"), p. 9.

[421] *El Nacional* (April 30, 1974).

[422] *Siderurgia Latinoamericana* (March 1980) ("Plan IV de SIDOR: La Respuesta a un Desafío"), p. 21.

[423] Venezuela was aware that its almost total dependence on oil earnings for foreign exchange was a potentially dangerous situation, and it hoped to use its oil revenues to develop alternative economic bases. The President of the Association of Metallurgy and Mining Industrialists explained that "Developing the country's iron and steel industry with all the mining, energy and economic wealth it has is a task for the present generation. The public and private sectors must recognize this fact; otherwise we will miss the only tangible opportunity to diversify the country's economy. . . ." Interview with Dr. Marcelino Barquin, in *El Universal* (August 8, 1976).

nearly 5 million tons of steel by 1979.[424]   Next, a new greenfield mill of comparable size would be constructed in the state of Zulia, with completion scheduled for 1990.[425]   A third mill would be built later.   The cost of the expansion would be enormous;[426] much of the financing was to come from the FIV.[427]

SIDOR's new facilities employed direct reduction plants to feed the mill's electric furnaces.[428]The decision to use this new and relatively untried technology was based on the country's special conditions: it had ample supplies of the iron ore, natural gas and hydroelectric power required to run a direct reduction-based mill, but lacked the domestic reserves of coal and scrap required by traditional blast furnaces.[429]   By 1980 construction of the expanded SIDOR facilities had been largely completed,[430] at a cost estimated by one source of $9.9 billion,[431] a significant portion of which was provided by foreign banks.[432]

Unfortunately, it proved very difficult for SIDOR to operate its new facilities.   In 1978 SIDOR predicted that it could raise its utilization rate to full capacity by 1983 as it gained experience with the new plant;[433] yet by 1980 it had fallen seriously behind its production schedule.[434]   The principal difficulty involved SIDOR's HYL direct reduction units, which developed severe operational problems, running at a disastrous 22 percent of capacity in

---

[424] *Metal Bulletin* (January 17, 1978); *Siderurgia Latinoamericana* (September 1976) ("Dinámico Impulso Muestra Proceso de Expansión Siderúrgica Venezolano"), pp. 41-42; *Latin American Economic Report* (February 21, 1975).

[425] *El Universal* (January 8, 1976).

[426] The President of SIDOR estimated in 1978 that Venezuela would invest $35 billion in its steel industry and related infrastructure by the year 2000. *Siderurgia Latinoamericana* (January 1979 ("Informativo Regional"), p. 28.

[427] *El Universal* (April 24, 1975);   *Latin American Economic Report* (February 21, 1975) ("Rapid Progress in Venezuela's Steel Plans"), p. 29. The FIV was committed to provide the external financing for large projects in a number of priority sectors, including steel. Venezuelan Investment Fund, *Operating Policies* (July 1975).   By 1976, the FIV had over $5.1 billion in foreign assets. Interview with Dr. Constantino Quero Morales, in *El Universal* (January 8, 1976).

[428] *Latin American Economic Report* (February 21, 1975).

[429] *El Universal* (July 15, 1977); *El Nacional* (July 11, 1977).

[430] *Metal Bulletin* (June 12, 1981).

[431] *American Metal Market* (September 8, 1982). Another source put the cost of the SIDOR expansion, including finance charges, at $5 billion. *Siderurgia Latinoamericana* (March 1980) ("Plan IV de SIDOR: La Respuesta a un Desafío"), p. 27.

[432] European and American banks provided $2 billion in loans for the SIDOR project. *Forbes* (June 3, 1985).

[433] *El Universal* (November 19, 1978).

[434] *Metal Bulletin* (April 3, 1980).

1982.[435] SIDOR blamed the contractor who had supplied the equipment for the problems, rescinded the contract and initiated arbitration proceedings.[436] SIDOR's electric furnaces suffered from a shortage of sponge iron.[437] Quality was so low that many consumers preferred to buy more expensive imported steel,[438] and productivity per worker was abysmal.[439] Worker morale was extraordinarily poor -- SIDOR experienced a 25 percent annual work force turnover, with 50 percent of the departing personnel leaving through "unsolicited resignation."[440]

Crisis in the Steel Industry

Although SIDOR gradually resolved its production difficulties, it faced a more fundamental problem of weak domestic demand. After years of steadily rising domestic consumption, Venezuela's demand for steel began to decrease in 1978. Although steel producers believed that this situation would not long continue,[441] the government's restrictive fiscal and monetary policies -- aggravated in later years by a fall in oil revenues -- in fact resulted in a

---

[435] Metal Bulletin (May 6, 1983).

[436] Metal Bulletin (January 31, 1984; May 6, 1983). Although SIDOR's operational problems may have been caused in part by the faulty implementation of a relatively untested technology, there were also allegations of mismanagement. One report complained that "There is no cohesive management team with clear goals and objectives in the administration of the business. There are no continuous programs designed to improve production techniques, reduce costs, develop management personnel and promote employees, control inputs and the purchase of parts, and supervise inventories." Report of the Engineers, Architects and Professionals for the Social Christian Party, in El Nacional (April 27, 1980). This criticism may have been partially motivated by party rivalries; in any event, SIDOR's management team was replaced in 1980. Metal Bulletin (June 6, 1980).

[437] Metal Bulletin (November 12, 1985).

[438] Resumen (May 11, 1980).

[439] SIDOR required 23 man-hours to produce a ton of steel in 1981, far short of the company's 11 man-hours target. Latin American Regional Reports: Andean Group (April 3, 1981). SIDOR did not approach this goal until 1986. Metal Bulletin Monthly (October 1986), p. 57. In 1979, economic consultant Peter West had warned that Venezuela's shortage of skilled manpower, coupled with the problems inherent in implementing a new technology, would likely cause production difficulties, and that cashflow problems would emerge as interest payments came due on the faltering projects. Accordingly, he urged Venezuela to slow down the pace of development. Metal Bulletin (April 3, 1979).

[440] Resumen (May 11, 1980). The SIDOR plant was located in the Guyana region "in which daily existence is basically a hardship." Ibid.

[441] Metal Bulletin reported on July 17, 1979 that "The slight slackening in demand [in 1978] is, however, expected to be only temporary." And Dr. Edgar Marshall, the President of SIDOR, remarked in early 1980 that SIDOR would guarantee the supply of steel to the internal market in 1981 and 1982 when a "steel scarcity crisis" was expected to occur. Siderurgia Latinoamericana (January 1980) ("Informativo Regional"), p. 34.

sustained contraction of the domestic market;[442] consumption in 1986 was only two thirds of its 1977 peak. One response open to Venezuelan producers was to sell their excess steel abroad;[443] however, low productivity and saturated world markets made this course difficult. Further problems were caused by government price controls, which SIDOR claimed were forcing the company to absorb rising production costs.[444]

The combination of a shrinking domestic market and serious production difficulties placed SIDOR in a precarious position by the late 1970s. Hobbled by debts incurred during the expansion process, the company suffered substantial and increasing losses. (table 5-12). By 1981 SIDOR's position had deteriorated to such an extent that it was demanding additional government funds simply to remain in operation.[445] The FIV agreed to capitalize $745.4 million of SIDOR's debt and to inject an additional $698.8 million in equity, on condition that the Venezuelan Treasury also capitalize $190.3 million in debt.[446] Additional state funds were pumped into the company in 1982 and 1983.[447] Nevertheless, the company's condition showed few short-term signs of improvement.[448] The company finally reported a profit in 1986, after the Venezuelan government again relieved SIDOR of its debt and injected further capital.[449]

---

[442] *Metal Bulletin* (April 25, 1980).

[443] *Metal Bulletin Monthly* (August 1983) ("Fall in Consumption Hits Venezuela"), p. 39. For a discussion of Venezuela's export drive, see "Venezuela's Foreign Trade in Steel."

[444] *Latin American Regional Reports: Andean Group* (April 3, 1981); *El Nacional* (August 21, 1979).

[445] *Latin American Regional Reports: Andean Group* (April 3, 1981).

[446] *Siderurgia Latinoamericana* (May 1981) ("Informativo Regional"), p. 23. In 1981-82 one dollar was equal to 4.2925 bolivars. International Monetary Fund, *International Financial Statistics* (May 1988), p. 540. After 1983 the conversion of bolivars into dollars was complicated substantially by the fact that Venezuela implemented a system of multiple exchange rates depending on the nature of the transaction. In those cases where the authors have converted sums from bolivars to dollars, the market rate of exchange has been used. The impact of this system on the steel industry is discussed in "Venezuela's Foreign Trade in Steel."

[447] In 1982 the government agreed to write off SIDOR's $888.9 million accumulated losses, and FIV agreed to provide another $433.3 million in equity. *Metal Bulletin* (May 24, 1983); *Metal Bulletin Monthly* (August 1983), p. 41.

[448] By 1984, despite the capitalizations, SIDOR owed more than $855 million, *El Universal* (March 28, 1984), and the company President reported that 1/3 of the company's revenues were required merely to service the debt. *Inter Press Service*, July 11, 1984.

[449] *VenEconomy Monthly* (October 1986), p. 4; *Siderurgia Latinoamericana* (August 1986) ("Informativo Regional"), p. 28. In fairness to SIDOR, it should be noted that the government frequently promised a great more than it delivered. For instance, an 817 million bolivar capitalization approved in 1981 had still to be implemented in 1986. *Ibid.*

Table 5-12. SIDOR -- Net Income 1977-87
(million U.S. dollars)

Year	Net Income
1977	(93)
1978	N/A
1979	(100)
1980	(298)
1981	(419)
1982	(185)
1983	(104)
1984	(151)
1985	(57)
1986	70
1987	27

Sources: *Metal Bulletin* (June 6, 1978; July 7, 1981; September 14, 1982; February 7, 1984; March 5, 1985); *Metal Bulletin Monthly* (October, 1986); *Financial Times* (March 26, 1987; January 28, 1988); *Latin American Regional Report* (April 3, 1981).
Converted to U.S. dollars at average annual exchange rate given by the International Monetary Fund. Conversion: 1977-1984: 4.2925, 1984: 7.0175, 1985: 7.5, 1986: 8.0833, 1987:14.5.

Meanwhile, a protracted political struggle took place over the other elements of the National Steel Plan. The most furious dispute related to the planned SIDERZULIA complex. This 5 million ton plant, which unlike SIDOR was to use indigenous coal deposits in Zulia state, was expected to generate a "new phase in the history of Zulia."[450] As the condition of SIDOR declined and world steel consumption slackened, financing for the project became increasingly problematic.[451] Nevertheless, the government would not abandon the project, for the Zulia state was an electoral stronghold of the ruling COPEI party.[452] In spite of criticism by the President of FIV,[453]

[450] *El Universal* (January 8, 1976).

[451] *Metal Bulletin* (June 6, 1978).

[452] *Metal Bulletin* (August 10, 1979). As one commentator pointed out, Zulia had 700,000 votes on which COPEI had traditionally relied. But the party's support in the region was waning, and cancellation of SIDERZULIA would be the "coup de grace." *Zeta* (September 5, 1982).

[453] *Metal Bulletin* (April 28, 1981). FIV took issue with the optimistic demand forecasts prepared by CORPOZULIA, the regional development corporation which was to be a major participant in the project and was one of its strongest supporters. *Metal Bulletin* (August 18, 1981).

legislation authorizing the project was passed in 1982.[454] In 1985, however, as Venezuela's struggle to service its enormous foreign debt became increasingly difficult,[455] the government finally shelved the project.[456]

To a great extent, the story of SIDOR is the story of the Venezuelan steel industry, for the company is overwhelmingly the country's dominant producer, but there are other national producers. SIVENSA, a minimill operator that is Venezuela's largest private steel company, has remained generally profitable in spite of the crisis, in part by exporting excess production.[457] Other producers, however, have not fared so well. SIDEROCA, a Zulia producer of tubular products, was driven to the edge of bankruptcy and its experience remains one of the worst corporate disasters in the nation's history.[458]

Venezuela's misfortunes in steel have not dampened its enthusiasm for further expansion. Although the massive projects of the past have for the moment been set aside, SIDOR officials still dream of the day when Venezuela will turn all its own iron ore into steel.[459] Heartened by profitable years in 1986 and 1987, the first in this decade,[460] SIDOR announced plans for

---

[454] The legislation anticipated an expenditure of $2.3 billion for the first stage of the project, which was to include infrastructure and coal developments as well as steel mills; much of the money was to be borrowed abroad. *Metal Bulletin* (September 14, 1982). One newspaper, reporting on the hail of criticism directed against the project, noted that the Presidential candidates and their parties "put themselves forth as the most deserving of the Venezuelans' votes, but with their recent behavior and their 'consensus' they are assuring us that the errors that have brought us to the brink of this economic, political and social abyss will continue to be repeated until a collapse is achieved, as is happening now in Mexico. Such is the case of the 'Coal-Steel' project of Zulia, and the scandalous show of irresponsibility and demagoguery in the passage of the bill authorizing the Executive to place the republic in debt for 10 billion bolivars [$2.3 billion] and to compromise the future, in an enterprise whose plans estimate a cost of 30 billion [$6.9 billion]. In view of the precedents established by other, similar projects, it is not unreasonable to assume that it will cost five times more. The law was passed knowing that this project will be a drain, as SIDOR is today." *Resumen* (September 12, 1982).

[455] According to government figures, the nation's foreign public sector foreign debt was almost $28 billion by 1983, of which 30 percent was incurred by state enterprises. Simply to service the debt would have required 77 percent of Venezuela's total export earnings. *El Universal* (March 4, 1984). Accordingly, the government desperately sought to renegotiate the debt. *El Nacional* (March 28, 1984).

[456] *Metal Bulletin* (January 25, 1985).

[457] *VenEconomy Monthly* (July 1986).

[458] SIDEROCA undertook an over-ambitious expansion scheme at the Proacero pipe mill, which was constructed between 1975 and 1979 at a cost of $116.5 million (much of which was provided by the government) and which closed in 1981. *Metal Bulletin* (October 18, 1983). The company has been characterized as a "corporate cripple," struggling under nearly $111.3 million in debt, including $45 million in foreign obligations. The company's restructuring plan would require the government to recapitalize the firm's debt; however, SIDOR is reputed to covet the company's assets and to oppose the rescue plan. *VenEconomy Monthly* (November 1986).

[459] E.g., Cesar Mendoza, President of SIDOR, in *Latin America Commodities Report* (January 24, 1986).

[460] *Financial Times* (March 26, 1987).

$1.23 billion in investments in the 1988-1991 period.[461] However, although domestic demand strengthened somewhat in 1986, SIDOR's management conceded that domestic demand was likely to remain stagnant in the period 1988-1990 as a result of the nation's continuing economic crisis,[462] so that hope for the resumption of the steel industry's stumbling expansion program rested on Venezuela's efforts to become a major steel exporter.

Venezuela's Foreign Trade in Steel

Until the early 1980s, Venezuela's role in the world steel market was that of purchaser rather than seller. However, since the 1970s Venezuela has sought to transform herself from a provider of raw materials such as oil and iron ore to a producer of higher value manufactures, including steel. The President of CVG explained this goal in 1973:

> *Venezuelan policy is to not export any more iron ore and to refine completely in Venezuela ore mined here. So there is already discussion of building another large metals plant [in addition to SIDOR] which could be in operation by 1980 and which, to give only a preliminary rough estimate, could have a capacity of 6 million tons of steel for export.*[463]

The country's ambitious expansion plans reflected extreme (and, in retrospect, misplaced) optimism regarding the strength of world demand for steel.[464] By 1981, Venezuela recognized that the world steel boom had failed to materialize, a factor underlying the abandonment of the SIDERZULIA

---

[461] *Financial Times* (February 12, 1988). SIDOR's plans include expansion of its direct reduction capacity and hot-rolling mill. *Metal Bulletin* (November 12, 1987); *Siderurgia Latinoamericana* (September 1987) ("El Proyecto de Modernización de la Fábrica de Tubos de C.V.G. Siderúrgica del Orinoco, C.A. -- SIDOR, de Venezuela"), p. 9. Yet the goal of 4 million tons of crude steel capacity is still less than the company had planned to achieve with its previous expansion program.

[462] *Siderurgia Latinoamericana* (March 1987) ("Informativo Regional").

[463] Dr. Argenis Gamboa, President of CVG, in *El Nacional* (April 17, 1974).

[464] Dr. Marcelino Barquin, President of the Association of Metallurgy & Mining Industrialists, remarked in 1976 that "The worldwide scarcity of iron and steel is already irreversible. Its magnitude is directly related to the degree of world industrialization. The truth is that the countries with a capacity to produce steel and metal components will be in the same privileged position now enjoyed by the oil-producing countries. The production of 15 million metric tons of steel and iron products is equivalent to annual exports of 200 million barrels of oil at today's prices. . . . In a world that consumes 1 billion metric tons of steel a year, it is not idealistic to speak about exporting 4 million metric tons." *El Universal* (August 8, 1976). This optimism was not universally shared. Reviewing Venezuela's expansion plans, *Metal Bulletin Monthly* remarked in November 1978 that "It is questionable whether the Venezuelan market will grow fast enough to absorb all the extra capacity, or whether the export market can take what the domestic market cannot."

project.[465] Despite this scaling back of expansion plans, and although the effective capacity of SIDOR's new facilities was scarcely half theoretical capacity by 1983, SIDOR's gradually increasing output, coupled with stagnant or falling demand in the home market, still left the company with a substantial surplus. This had to be exported to pay interest on SIDOR's debt.[466] A SIDOR executive explained in 1982 that "a deliberate policy of exporting the surplus had been undertaken with the development of a liberal export policy."[467]

SIDOR's situation mirrored that of the nation as a whole, which, by the early 1980s, was staggering under an almost insuperable debt crisis.[468] To surmount the crisis Venezuela had to increase its non-oil exports, and resorted to a variety of export-stimulating measures.[469] Perhaps the single most significant measure for promoting exports was a multi-tier exchange rate system. Under this system, the exchange rate varied depending on the entity and purpose for which foreign exchange was bought or sold. Qualified debtors could purchase foreign exchange to make payments to creditors at much less than the free market rate,[470] and manufacturers such as SIDOR could buy dollars cheaply from the Central Bank to purchase foreign inputs, while they were allowed to exchange dollars earned on exports for many more bolivars in the free market.[471] In addition, Venezuelan exporters of nontraditional products were entitled to "fiscal credits" based on the

[465] SIDERZULIA was initially planned as a steel exporter; when the world steel market collapsed, it was reoriented toward the domestic market. SIDOR, unenthusiastic about competition in a market which was already well-supplied with steel, became an opponent of the project. *Latin American Regional Reports: Andean Group*, April 3, 1981.

[466] SIDOR's Corporate Planning Manager, Jovito Martinez, noted that as a result of the weak domestic market, SIDOR had been forced "to completely revise our thinking on our markets. We now have to look for firm markets internationally." *Business Week* (April 19, 1982).

[467] *Metal Bulletin* (May 21, 1982).

[468] As of 1981, the nation's foreign debt was $26.2 billion, and public officials were calling for drastic action to remedy the situation. *Resumen* (September 12, 1982). In 1984 Venezuela failed to make interest payments as they came due, *El Universal* (February 29, 1984), and entered into negotiations with foreign banks to refinance its obligations. *El Nacional* (March 28, 1984).

[469] As one Venezuelan businessman remarked, "If we don't increase nonoil exports during the oil recession, we will drown and be unable to pay the debt." Raúl Lopez Perez, Vice President of the Confederation of Chambers of Commerce, in *Forbes* (June 3, 1985).

[470] For a detailed explanation of this system, see International Monetary Fund, *Exchange Arrangements & Exchange Restrictions: Annual Report 1987*.

[471] *Metal Bulletin* (May 24, 1983). In 1985 steel producers could buy dollars for 7.5 bolivars and sell them for 12.5. *Forbes* (June 3, 1985). Although Venezuela still maintains a multiple exchange rate system, as of December 1986 exporters are no longer permitted to repatriate earnings at the free market rate of exchange. Office of the United States Trade Representative, *Foreign Trade Barriers* (1987), p. 329.

Venezuelan value-added of the product.[472] These incentives had a favorable impact on SIDOR's troubled finances[473] and stimulated a rapid rise in steel exports, which nearly tripled between 1982 and 1983.[474]

Venezuela's steel export drive generated trade friction with a number of countries. Neighboring Colombia blamed the depressed state of its own steel industry in part on the import of 50,000 tons of "contraband" steel from Venezuela.[475] Business Week reported on April 19, 1982 that SIDOR was exporting steel at less than half its domestic sales price; this report was confirmed when the United States Department of Commerce found SIDOR to be dumping steel wire rod at margins of 40 percent.[476] In 1984 the United States indicated its desire to enter into a VRA with Venezuela. Although Venezuela initially resisted the imposition of a VRA and threatened retaliation against American exports if one was imposed,[477] a preliminary ruling that Venezuelan wire rod had been subsidized at a rate of 70.98 percent *ad valorem* and the pendency of additional unfair trade practices actions against Venezuelan producers led Venezuela to accept a VRA in the summer

---

[472] Decree No. 881, April 29, 1975. The decree applied to all exports except, *inter alia*, petroleum and its byproducts, unprocessed or nontransformed minerals and coffee. Of course, petroleum and minerals were traditionally Venezuela's only significant exports. In 1986 the Venezuelan Senate was considering strengthening this system with a new "Law to Encourage and Promote Exports." *Siderurgia Latinoamericana* (October 1986) ("Informativo Regional"), p. 28; *VenEconomy Monthly* (June 1986) ("Export Promotion Bill Misses the Mark"), p. 9.

[473] *Siderurgia Latinoamericana* (March 1984) ("Informativo Regional"), p. 30; *Metal Bulletin* (February 7, 1984).

[474] *Metal Bulletin* (October 28, 1983). *Metal Bulletin* commented on May 24, 1983 that "By permitting SIDOR to sell its foreign exchange earnings at the high free rate, the government has considerably bolstered the company's financial prospects. The new measure will also reinforce the company's resolve to boost the volume of export sales this year to offset declining local demand."

[475] Bogota *El Siglo* (August 10, 1982).

[476] *Carbon Steel Wire Rod from Venezuela* (final), 47 F.R. 58329, December 30, 1982. The International Trade Commission subsequently found that the imports had not caused injury to American producers. *Carbon Steel Wire Rod from Venezuela*, 5 I.T.R.D. 1163 (February 1983).

[477] *Washington Post* (April 10, 1985); *Metal Bulletin* (March 15, 1985); *Siderurgia Latinoamericana* (February 1985) ("Informativo Regional"), p. 24.

of 1985.[478] A similar arrangement was concluded with the EC (which had imposed antidumping duties on Venezuelan steel) in 1987.[479]

Venezuela also took steps to limit steel imports to the greatest extent possible. In the late 1970s, with strong domestic demand and limited capacity, imports consistently exceeded domestic production.[480] As SIDOR's new facilities came on stream, however, local steel replaced imports, which fell dramatically. Consumers had little choice but to switch to domestic production where available, for SIDOR itself had a monopoly on the importation and marketing of foreign steel.[481] Imports were further restricted by high tariffs[482] and by the enforcement of a "Buy Venezuela" policy.[483] Thus, despite the fact that foreign steel was often less expensive[484] and of higher

---

[478] *Metal Bulletin* (June 14, 1985). The VRA, which allowed Venezuela to export an average of 183,000 tons of steel per year, was "front-end loaded," *i.e.*, it allowed greater than average shipments in the first years of the VRA, which were to be set off against lower than average shipments in later years. *Metal Bulletin* (June 18, 1985). The President of the Institute of Foreign Commerce remarked that "the results obtained exceeded the most optimistic expectations." *Siderurgia Latinoamericana* (August 1985) ("Informativo Regional"), p. 41.

[479] The European market for Venezuelan steel had been limited since 1982, when antidumping duties were imposed on Venezuelan steel products. *European Report* (June 14, 1987). In 1987 the European Community suspended the duties after Venezuela agreed to a 72,000 ton per year quota on steel sales in the Member States. *Latin American Commodities Report* (April 23, 1987).

[480] Imports accounted for 60 percent of the Venezuelan steel market in 1978. *Metal Bulletin* (July 17, 1979).

[481] *Metal Bulletin* (November 2, 1979). SIDOR complained that it was forced by government price controls to sell foreign steel at prices below what it paid for the products abroad. *Ibid.* However, the monopoly on importations allowed SIDOR to limit competition from imports by reducing its purchases of products that could be supplied domestically. *Siderurgia Latinoamericana* (July 1980) ("Informativo Regional"), p. 50; *Metal Bulletin* (May 16, 1980).

[482] The question of tariff rates occasioned a rift between Venezuela and the other members of the Andean Pact, a regional trading pact that applied common external tariffs. Venezuela, the only significant steel producer in the group, sought high tariffs, ranging from 25 percent for semifinished products to 40 percent for finished products. Venezuela also favored reference prices for steel imports. Other members, who did not have large domestic steel industries to protect, favored tariffs as low as 5 percent and opposed reference prices. *Metal Bulletin* (August 25, 1981; April 15, 1980). Venezuela ultimately went its own way and imposed tariffs ranging as high as 60 percent. *Arancel de Aduanas de Venezuela*, Chapter 73 (September 4, 1986).

[483] Acting Finance Minister Hermann Luis Soriano explained in 1982 that "special emphasis will be given to the reduction of imports by the government. The 'Buy Venezuela' Decree will be rigorously enforced for this purpose, and any foreign purchases that are not strictly necessary to increase or improve the production of goods and services and to guarantee regular supplies of essential goods, will be eliminated. In this manner, the country's balance of payments situation will be improved, and demand will be channeled toward the domestic productive apparatus, contributing to its strengthening and expansion." *El Universal* (October 8, 1982).

[484] *Metal Bulletin* (August 25, 1981).

quality[485] than the domestic product, Venezuelan steel imports had plummeted by the mid-1980s.

Although Venezuela's efforts to develop a major steel industry have been plagued with a succession of operational and financial crises, the country has not abandoned its goal of becoming a major steel exporter. In April 1988, CVG announced tentative plans to construct a 1 million ton slab mill targeted for the United States market, and to add another 1 million tons of capacity at a later date.[486] If the past is any guide, the government is likely to take the measures necessary to ensure that Venezuelan steel retains a presence in export markets.

OTHERS (INDONESIA, TURKEY, CHINA)

Indonesia. Indonesian steel production is dominated by a 100 percent state-owned integrated steel firm, Krakatau Steel. Krakatau has a history of political upheaval, alleged mismanagement and corruption, and chronic financial crises, but has emerged in the mid-1980s as a potentially significant factor in international steel trade. In 1962, Indonesia's Sukarno regime launched a plan to establish a national integrated steel industry at Cilegon, a seaside site on the island of Krakatau, with assistance from the Soviet Union. This effort came to a halt in 1966 when Indonesia's new military government severed ties with the Soviets after the Communist coup attempt, and was not resumed until 1972. At that point, the state oil company, Pertamina, joined with the government to establish Krakatau Steel. With West German assistance, a facility for producing long products was established on the Cilegon site.[487] In 1975, however, Pertamina became embroiled in a series of financial scandals, and its role in Krakatau was ended.[488]

A new government management team decided to completely overhaul the original Krakatau expansion plan. The new plan called for scrapping of some of the facilities under construction, renegotiation of construction contracts, and a phased increase in capacity that would enable Krakatau to produce several types of long products by the end of the 1970s, and, in the early 1980s, to produce an increasingly sophisticated range of primary rolled products. Finishing operations (such as cold-rolled strip, tinplate and pipe production) would be reserved for the private sector or undertaken by Krakatau with a private sector partner.[489] Krakatau would stress use of direct reduction of iron

---

[485] *Resumen* (May 11, 1980).

[486] *Metal Bulletin* (April 14, 1988). The project will cost an estimated $1 billion. *Ibid.*

[487] Krakatau Steel was jointly capitalized by Pertamina and the Ministry of Finance. Kuala Lumpur *Business Times* (March 9, 1977).

[488] *Metal Bulletin Monthly* (July 1982); *Suara Karya* (December 23, 1976).

[489] *Business Times* (March 9, 1977); *Metal Bulletin Monthly* (July 1982).

(DRI) technology to capitalize on Indonesia's abundant supplies of natural gas.

Most of the capital for Krakatau's expansion was reportedly provided by the Indonesian government.[490] The effort was assisted by many foreign engineering firms, including Ferrostaal, Hoogovens and Klöckner, and benefitted from extensive financing from foreign commercial syndicates and export credits.[491] Downstream facilities (such as sheet rolling mills) were established by joint ventures capitalized by foreign lenders and various state-owned Indonesian firms, including Krakatau.[492]

Krakatau was plagued with operational and financial difficulties as its expansion proceeded. It lost money every year of its existence through 1985, and its losses in the four years ended in 1980 reportedly totaled $400 million.[493] While the size of Krakatau's debt burden remained a guarded secret, it was admitted by the government to be "rather large", with some reports placing it at just under $480 million.[494] Critics charged that Krakatau was inefficient and badly sited, and that it would "never repay the large sums that have been invested in it."[495]

Support from the Indonesian government was instrumental in enabling Krakatau to grapple with such problems. By 1985, Krakatau had incurred "crushing" losses for over a decade; in that year, the government covered these losses and its large debts, converting them into additional capital in the company, in which it already held a 100 percent equity interest. Government capital injections in the form of "PMP" (government participation capital) not only helped to finance the continuation of the expansion effort but enabled Krakatau to borrow additional funds.[496] "After the burden of the debts had been lifted and more PMP had been contributed to the company, this state-owned company was able to breathe again and to improve management."[497] Krakatau reported its first profit in 1986.[498]

---

[490] *Kompas* (July 3, 1983). Krakatau and the government have remained secretive, however, about the levels of funding involved.

[491] *Harian Umum Ab* (May 21, February 5, 1979).

[492] *Kompas* (July 1, 1983).

[493] *Kompas* (February 11, 1987); *Merdeka* (April 30, 1986); *Metal Bulletin* (January 10, 1984).

[494] *Merdeka* (November 30, 1984). The Minister of Industry, questioned by reporters on the level of Krakatau's debt, responded: "I don't know what the exact figure is." *Ibid.*

[495] *Metal Bulletin Monthly* (August 1986).

[496] Krakatau's President has refused to divulge the amount of PMP received by the firm but admits that they have been an important source of the firm's strength. *Kompas* (February 11, 1987). "The condition of Krakatau Steel was strengthened by the action of the government, which took over the Company's debts as a form of subsidy." *Sinar Harapan* (August 12, 1986).

[497] *Kompas* (February 11, 1987)

[498] *Sinar Harapan* (August 12, 1986).

Government assistance was also instrumental in Krakatau's emergence as an international competitor in steel. In 1981, by government decree, Krakatau became the sole authorized importer of a wide range of steel products, enabling it to regulate access by its foreign competitors to its home market. Domestic steel price levels were fixed at levels designed to enable it to cover its production costs.[499] The industry received export incentives in the form of so-called Sertificat Ekspor (SE certificates), which provided for rebates, upon export, of import duties and import taxes paid on imports used in production.[500] Steel exports received additional impetus from a series of substantial devaluations in the national currency.[501]

The rapid expansion of Indonesia's steel industry was not accompanied by an increase in domestic demand; in fact, demand fell substantially in the mid-1980s, resulting in "a huge oversupply" of some products, such as bars and rods.[502] Reflecting the growing gap between supply and demand, the Indonesian industry expanded its export activity. Krakatau's first significant exports occurred in 1985, and the firm rapidly emerged as a significant regional competitor.[503] Krakatau maintained a three-tiered price structure, with domestic consumers paying the highest prices, domestic manufacturers producing finished products for export an intermediate price, and foreign steel consumers the lowest price.[504] The principal markets for Indonesian steel were China and other Southeast Asian markets, and the United States. The U.S., which did not import any steel from Indonesia in 1984, reported marginal import levels in 1985 and 1986 (10 and 40 thousand tons, respectively), which increased dramatically, to 235.6 thousand tons in 1987.[505]

Krakatau's long-range plans call for continued expansion, particularly in flat products and high quality long products. In 1988 it announced a $400 million modernization and expansion plan, featuring enhanced hot strip and wire rod capability. Krakatau plans to cover $240 million of the investment cost, with export credits from Western countries supplying the new equipment; additional funds will be obtained through local and overseas borrowing. Krakatau has indicated it would be prepared to repay its loans with steel products "in kind" as well as cash.[506]

---

[499] *Metal Bulletin Monthly* (July 1982, August 1986).

[500] Jakarta *Business News* (June 19, 1985).

[501] Jakarta *Business News* (January 23, 1985).

[502] *Metal Bulletin* (June 13, 1986).

[503] *Antara News Bulletin* (July 22, 1985); *Kompas* (December 3, 1985); *Metal Bulletin* (June 6, 1986).

[504] *Metal Bulletin* (June 6, 1986).

[505] U.S. Department of Commerce.

[506] *Metal Bulletin* (February 1, 1988).

Turkey. The modern Turkish steel industry was founded by the nationalist leader Kemal Ataturk, who established an integrated steelworks after World War I at Karabuk, an inland location separated by mountains from the Black Sea, where it would be safe from enemy attack. A second integrated mill was established in the 1960s at Eregli on the Black Sea Coast, funded by the largest financing ever paid by the U.S. Agency for International Development for an industrial project. Further expansion of the Eregli facility was funded by joint loans from the World Bank and the U.S. government in 1972. A third integrated mill was established in the early 1970s at Iskenderun on the Mediterranean coast, financed and equipped by the Soviet Union. The Karabuk and Iskenderun works are wholly owned and managed by the Turkish government through its national steel concern, TDCI, and produce long products. The government holds a majority interest in the Eregli mill, which produces flat products and is operated by ERDEMIR, the Eregli Iron and Steel Corporation.[507] The three operational state firms produce about 65 percent of Turkey's steel; the remainder is made by the privately-owned electric furnace sector (largely concentrated around Izmir).

The Turkish state steel sector has produced "textbook cases of government insistence in a developing country on setting up large-scale heavy industry with little or no regard for market values."[508] The Kabaruk mill, for example, was secure behind its mountain barrier from enemy attack, but the remote location imposed high raw material and transportation costs, and "now threatens its future in a way that invading armies never did."[509] Despite such problems, the government is pressing forward with the establishment of a second inland mill at Sivas in central Anatolia; "just why it is going ahead, no one seems to be able to explain -- but the reasons seem to have more to do with voters and with politics than with anything else."[510] The industry is further disadvantaged by Turkey's electricity costs, which one producer in 1986 called "the highest in the world."[511] A 1980 World Bank Study calculated that Turkish investment costs per ton of steel produced were twice as high as those of internationally competitive mills, and concluded that "the development of the Turkish steel industry suggests a losing effort to achieve economic viability."[512]

---

[507] Bertil Walstedt, *State Manufacturing Enterprise in the Mixed Economy: The Turkish Case* (Baltimore and London: Johns Hopkins University Press, 1980), pp. 157-63; *Metal Bulletin Monthly* (February 1986); *8 Days* (June 20, 1981).

[508] *Financial Times* (July 22, 1987).

[509] *Metal Bulletin Monthly* (February 1986).

[510] *Financial Times* (July 22, 1987). The Sivas project has been a source of political controversy in Turkey for over a decade. Critics cited its prospective dependence on imported raw materials and stressed the need to focus on economic, not political facilities.   Istanbul *Hurriyet* (October 11, 1976).

[511] *Metal Bulletin Monthly* (February 1986).

[512] Walstedt, *The Turkish Case*, p. 161.

The Turkish government has helped its industry surmount its international competitive shortcomings through a combination of import protection and export subsidies. Protection is administered through a system of import duties and taxes; in 1987 Turkish import duties on rebars were reportedly "prohibitive" unless the steel was designated for a specific project.[513] Steel exports have been subsidized through a system of tax rebates which have run as high as 17.5 percent of the f.o.b. price of exported steel.[514] The import tariffs and export rebates are reviewed and modified annually, a fact which has been a source of continuing controversy and turmoil within the Turkish steel industry.[515] The government has recently been seeking to reduce the level of protection and export subsidies, but complete phaseout seems unlikely because without them the Turkish steel industry would confront severe difficulty in competing internationally. Even with respect to the most efficient segment of the industry, the electric furnace sector, "it does seem clear that if the electric sector is to have a sound financial future some form of government action is going to be needed. Either a reduction in their electricity costs, or more export incentives or more protection from imports."[516]

Despite the Turkish industry's problems it has expanded rapidly in the 1980s. By 1985 Turkey possessed 6 million tons of raw steel capacity, and the government had set targets of 8 million tons by 1989 and 10 million tons by the mid-1990s.[517] All of Turkey's major electric furnace mills undertook major expansion efforts,[518] and according to one estimate Turkey's electric furnace output could increase to 4 million tons per year by 1989.[519] Most of this expansion has taken place at Aliaga, near Izmir on the Aegean, an industrial development zone established with government tax incentives which was

---

[513] *Metal Bulletin* (September 10, 1987). *Metal Bulletin* reported on October 29, 1985 that "with imports subject to the duty and taxes, [Eregli] has little difficulty in selling to the home market."

[514] If the value of a company's exports exceeds 30 percent, the percentage reimbursable by the government increases. *Metal Bulletin Monthly* (February 1986).

[515] Protection has created periodic shortages of semifinished steel, to the consternation of the producers of finished products. The state mills were criticized by the private sector for their chronic failure to deliver ingots and slabs; it was charged that the state producers were inefficient, and covered for their failure to deliver by repeatedly raising the price of semifinished steel so that "home market prices are higher than world prices." *Cumhuriyet* (October 23, 1984); *Milliyet* (August 16, 1986); *Dunya* (March 7, 1983).

[516] *Metal Bulletin Monthly* (February 1986).

[517] Of the 8 million tons projected for 1989, about 2.5 million would be accounted for by the private electric furnace sector, the remainder by the state sector. *Metal Bulletin* (October 29, 1985).

[518] *Dunya* (September 23, 1986).

[519] *Metal Bulletin* (November 8, 1985)

touted as "Turkey's Brescia."[520] Expansion in the state sector was financed by credits from the government Public Partnership Authority.[521]

By 1987, iron and steel products accounted for 10.8 percent of Turkey's total exports.[522] Until very recently Turkey's steel exports centered heavily on Iran and Iraq, which accounted for 82 percent of all exports in 1984.[523] However, the expansion of Turkish capacity in the mid-1980s has been accompanied by a spectacular increase in its export volume to the United States, which jumped from 43.9 thousand tons in 1984 to 407.4 thousand tons in 1987.[524] A spokesman for U.S. producers of wire rod complained in 1987 that Turkish capacity had expanded well beyond domestic needs, and that "the surplus can only go out of Turkey." He said that the traders handling Turkish rod "aren't showing any restraint at all. If they aren't attacked now, the import levels are just going to get enormous."[525] A U.S. trade official commented that "it is frustrating for us . . . for [Turkey] to substantially increase its exports to us during a time when others are exercising restraint."[526]

China. China's principal significance in the world steel market to date has been as a huge market for exported steel. Chinese apparent consumption of crude steel in 1986 was 75.7 million metric tons, more than twice that of West Germany, but its production was only 51.9 million metric tons. The longstanding gap between Chinese production capability and demand has created the largest national export market in the world outside of the United States, and in 1986, Chinese imports of finished and semifinished steel products actually exceeded U.S. imports slightly, 18.47 million metric tons compared to 18.38 million metric tons for the United States.[527] During the structural crisis, China has absorbed a substantial portion of the western world's surplus production (particularly that of Japan) and by so doing, has partially mitigated the severity of the recession. The fact that China is

---

[520] *Metal Bulletin* (March 13, 1987).

[521] In 1987, for example, the Sivas project received a $40.8 million credit from the authority. *Metal Bulletin* (December 24, 1987). The government also made clear that "credit facilities" offered by European countries and Japan to finance equipment acquisition were essential to the expansion. *Metal Bulletin* (October 29, 1985).

[522] *Metal Bulletin* (April 21, 1988).

[523] *Dunya* (May 28, 1986). These exports were sold at prices substantially below Turkish home market prices, a source of chronic disgruntlement for Turkish steel consumers, who confronted not only higher prices but occasional shortages. *Cumhuriyet* (October 23, 1984); *Milliyet* (August 16, 1986).

[524] U.S. Department of Commerce.

[525] *Metal Bulletin* (February 3, 1987).

[526] *Metal Bulletin* (May 6, 1987).

[527] IISI, *Steel Statistical Yearbook 1987*, table 8.

embarked on an ambitious drive to become self-sufficient in steel has serious implications for the longer term, since it will progressively foreclose this export outlet and force its major suppliers (particularly Japan) to seek other markets.

China is a centrally planned economy in which investment, prices, allocation of resources, and foreign trade are controlled by the state. However, since the Communist Party took power in 1949, the country has been disrupted by periodic political upheavals which have brought the economy to a standstill. The period of the First Five Year Plan (1953-57) was characterized by increased centralization of economic decisionmaking, but the so-called Great Leap Forward, launched in 1958 to accelerate the transition to communism, disrupted the Second Five Year Plan and resulted in economic chaos. The decade-long Cultural Revolution (1966-76) saw many producing enterprises virtually cease operations; the legal system was abolished; the university system was virtually destroyed; management was taken over by revolutionary committees, and concern for production, technology, efficiency and profitability were condemned. "Allocation decisions became more and more arbitrary and subjective as central management became increasingly ineffective." As a result, true central planning, involving the centrally coordinated application of resources to achieve designated goals, has been practiced relatively infrequently since the 1950s,[528] and the country has only embarked on a truly systematic program of modernization during the past 15 years.

The belated evolution of China's steel industry reflects the deleterious effects of decades of revolutionary turmoil. China's steel production, negligible at the time the Communists came to power in 1949, was increased with Soviet assistance to 18.7 million metric tons by 1960. However, a significant portion of China's iron was produced in primitive "backyard" furnaces that were established during the Great Leap Forward. This effort involved recruiting millions of peasants to become steelworkers virtually overnight under the slogan "all people joining steel production;" by October 1958, 50 million people, or 18.8 percent of China's work force, were engaged in steelmaking, producing steel of such poor quality that much of it was useless.[529] The withdrawal of Soviet assistance in 1961 following the Sino-Soviet rift and the disruption of the Chinese economy during the Cultural Revolution dealt a severe setback to Chinese steel development; output levels fell sharply, and in 1970 were still lower than in 1960.[530] Plans to establish

---

[528] World Bank, *China: Socialist Economic Development* (Washington: World Bank, 1983), Vol. I, pp. 46-47.

[529] U.S. International Trade Commission, *China's Economic Development Strategies and their Effects on U.S. Trade* (Washington: U.S.I.T.C., February 1985).

[530] Hogan, *World Steel in the 1980s.*

more modern facilities at Wuhan in the early 1970s were "greatly delayed by obstruction from the Gang of Four."[531]

In 1978 the Central Committee of the Chinese Communist Party rejected Mao's thought and launched the country on a more pragmatic course under Deng Zaiopeng. The government announced a plan to expand steel production from 31.8 million metric tons per year to 60 million metric tons by 1985, with output eventually slated to reach 160 million metric tons by the year 2000. Under the original plan, the government would build ten iron and steel facilities at new or existing sites, eight coal mines, ten oil and gas fields, thirty power stations, six trunk railways, and five harbors. The plan would be implemented with massive Japanese and other foreign assistance valued at $20 billion over an eight year period.[532]

At the time this effort was launched, China's largest steelmaking facility was at Anshan in Liaoning Province, China's "capital of steel." The Anshan complex and another major works at Wuhan were principally equipped with Soviet equipment and were in need of modernization; the Chinese plan called for upgrading of these facilities as well as those at eight other existing sites and the construction of a number of entirely new plants with Japanese and other Western assistance, most notably a 6 million metric ton integrated mill at Baoshan on the Yangtze River, and a second integrated mill of 10 million metric tons capacity in Hopeh Province.[533]

The steel industry expansion program was part of a larger government Ten Year Plan launched in capital-intensive projects; implementation of this plan proved impracticable and far too expensive, and in 1979, the government abruptly implemented the so-called "Three Year Adjustment Plan," pursuant to which the budgets of the heavy industrial sectors were slashed and many projects suspended or scrapped.[534] Plans for the Baoshan complex were drastically scaled back; while work was eventually resumed, plans for a second stage of construction, which would boost capacity from 3 to 6 million metric tons per year, were cancelled.[535] Resources which had been channeled by the government into heavy industrial development were diverted into the light and textile industries to foster their development.

However, the economic reforms implemented in the 1980s under Deng resulted in the rapid growth of the Chinese economy and the sharp increase in steel demand. By the mid-1980s, China's continuing dependency on imported steel, which required use of foreign exchange urgently needed for other purposes, had "become one of the important factors restricting the

---

[531] *Kyodo* (December 7, 1978).

[532] Hogan, *World Steel in the 1980s*.

[533] Hogan, *Ibid.*, pp. 156-57.

[534] *Kyodo* (March 13, 15, 1979).

[535] *Nihon Keizai* (June 18, 1981); *Kyodo* (January 22, 1981). Loss of contracts in connection with Baoshan reportedly cost Japanese firms $1.5 billion. *Metal Bulletin* (February 13, 1981).

development of the national economy."[536] Accordingly, one of the principal objectives of the Seventh 5-year plan was the expansion of Chinese steel production to 60 million metric tons by the end of the plan period, and 80 million tons by 1995.[537] The government indicated that one of the key priorities in the plan would be the doubling of Baoshan's capacity from 3 to 6 million tons per year, and the government indicated it might seek to expand Baoshan's capacity to 10 million metric tons by 1993.[538] In addition, modernization and expansion efforts would be undertaken at most existing sites, including Anshan and Wuhan, and a 3 million metric ton greenfield mill would be established on the coast.[539]

China's long-range objective was to eliminate its status as a major steel importer and to develop its industry's export capability. An official commenting on the current expansion effort indicated in 1988 that import substitution achieved through new steel capacity would enable China to save $2 billion in foreign exchange each year, and that a significant proportion of the new capacity wuld be dedicated to exports to secure additional foreign exchange.[540] These developments, should they occur, will have a major impact on patterns of steel trade throughout the Pacific basin.

[536] *Jingji Guanli* No. 2 (1987).

[537] *Dongbei Jingji Bao* (March 14, 1987). China also reportedly plans to expand capacity to 90 million metric tons by the year 2000. *American Metal Market* (June 20, 1988). Other reports have placed China's target at 80 million metric tons by the year 2000. *Metal Bulletin* (December 31, 1987).

[538] *Metal Bulletin* (April 18, 1986).

[539] *Ching-Chi Tao Pao* No. 38-39 (October 1, 1986); *Metal Bulletin* (April 25, August 12, 1986).

[540] *American Metal Market* (June 20, 1988).

6

Other Industrialized Countries

Outside of the EC, Japan and the United States, a sizable group of industrialized countries exists which has a major impact on world steel competition. These "other" industrialized countries include the Soviet Union and its satellites, European countries on the periphery of the Community, and several present or former members of the British Commonwealth which have achieved advanced stages of development. In all of these countries the state has played a substantial, if not pervasive, role in steel.

THE PERIPHERAL EUROPEAN COUNTRIES

The EC is surrounded by a number of industrialized states which have developed significant steelmaking capability, and two of these countries, Spain and Sweden, are major steelmaking countries. The "peripheral" European states share a number of common problems: their domestic markets are generally too small to permit the achievement of optimum scale economies, and they are both dependent on the Community as a market for their exports as well as vulnerable to competitive pressure from the large, heavily-subsidized EC mills. The peripheral states have adopted a variety of competitive strategies in steel; Spain and Portugal, which have joined the Community, are urgently seeking to restructure their steel industries to enable them to remain viable when they are integrated into the Common Market; the Nordic producers have attempted to rationalize production and marketing in Scandinavia through the establishment of a variety of transnational reciprocal arrangements; and Austrian firms have developed markets in the Soviet bloc, placed a heavy emphasis on steel engineering projects in developing countries and Eastern Europe, and substantially diversified out of steel. In virtually all of the peripheral states, the principal integrated producers are state-owned, and the government of each country has provided substantial aid to the steel industry.

Spain

The Spanish steel industry offers a striking illustration that competitive factors such as efficiency and productivity are not necessarily the ultimate determinants of international performance. The condition of the Spanish industry deteriorated dramatically after 1974, and its integrated steel producers became increasingly dependent on large injections of government aid to avoid collapse. However, as the financial and operational condition of the Spanish steel industry became progressively more critical, Spanish export volume increased rapidly, and the crisis-ridden Spanish industry emerged as one of the world's leading steel exporters. Spain's incongruous rise as a major exporter is solely a reflection of government support -- domestic and export subsidies, and import protection -- which has enabled it to expand and sustain a position in the international market.

The Years of Growth. The Spanish steel industry was originally entirely privately owned and fragmented among numerous comparatively small producers. The largest firms were grouped in an oligopolistic structure dominated by the major integrated producer, Altos Hornos de Vizcaya (AHV), whose main facilities were located in Spain's Basque region. In the 1950s the Spanish government established a state-owned steel producer, Empresa Nacional Siderúrgica (Ensidesa) as a counterpoise to the private steel sector. By the mid-1970s Ensidesa had emerged as the industry leader, possessing more than twice the production capacity of AHV -- a fact which reflected in part Ensidesa's absorption of the second-largest private producer, Uninsa, in 1973-74.[1]

The Franco government provided the primary impetus for the rapid expansion of the Spanish steel industry in the 1960s and 1970s. In 1964, when Spanish steel output was 3.15 million metric tons per year, the government launched its first Concerted Action Plan (1964-73)[2] to expand the industry,

---

[1] Ensidesa *Memoria*, 1974. Ensidesa's stock was held by the Instituto de Industria Nacional (INI), a state holding company formed by the Franco regime in 1941 to create new enterprises in sectors where private investment was unlikely. Over time, INI's role has broadened considerably — it has acquired control over failing enterprises and taken partial equity interests in other firms. It has been criticized as a "hospital for enterprises." *La Vanguardia* (April 27, 1979). INI's President Basagoitia commented in 1979 that "Because there isn't a specific institution charged with saving or restructuring floundering firms, as there is in other countries, INI has been entrusted, perhaps too often, with this sort of task. . . . Engaging in this sort of activity gives the public the impression of inefficiency, unjustly harming INI's reputation." *Ibid.*

[2] The Concerted Action Plans were adopted by Spain's Ministry of Industry in order to upgrade and expand a number of Spanish industrial sectors including steel, shipbuilding, coal mining, and pulp and paper. The Plans provided tax and fiscal incentives to firms that entered into commitments to take certain actions stipulated by the government, such as expansion of capacity, improvement of technology, and merger into larger competitive units. See Unesid, *La Acción Concertada en la Siderurgia Española* (December 1973); Unesid, *La Industria Siderúrgica Española y la Acción Concertada* (Madrid: 1969).

featuring a combination of low-interest government loans to public and private producers and equity injections into Ensidesa.[3] By 1973, Spanish crude steel output had more than tripled over 1964 levels, to 10.8 million metric tons per year.[4] Pleased by these results, the Spanish government in 1974 unveiled a second Concerted Action Plan (1974-82)[5] for the steel industry. The Plan, which fixed as its goal an output of 16.7 million metric tons of steel by 1982, provided substantial benefits for public and private steel producers willing to commit themselves to a major capacity expansion effort.[6]

One of the most important single expansion projects was the construction of a greenfield integrated steelworks at Sagunto (near Valencia) by Altos Hornos del Mediterráneo (AHM), a firm created in 1973 in which AHV held the largest equity interest. AHV already possessed some old blast furnace and finishing facilities at Sagunto; it was decided to establish alongside these an entirely new integrated plant capable of producing 6 million metric tons per year, a facility which would provide a major impetus for the development of the Valencia region.[7] The first stage of this plan, a cold-rolling mill with 1.3 million metric tons per year capacity, was completed in 1976.[8]

The Spanish Steel Industry Crisis. The expansion effort launched under the Second Concerted Action Plan proved to be inopportune. The Spanish producers committed themselves to acquiring expensive new equipment and to expanding their work forces just as the domestic and international steel markets were on the verge of a severe and protracted recession. Spanish domestic demand began falling sharply in the fall of 1974, the beginning of a progressive erosion in demand that did not bottom out until 1978. Although declining demand called into question the advisability of a major expansion effort, by early 1976 a large number of firms had entered into individual concerted action agreements with the government which, together with AHM's Sagunto project, were expected to expand Spain's crude steel output by 10

---

[3] *La Acción Concertada en la Siderurgia Española* (1969), pp. 43-47, 50. INI assisted Ensidesa through direct equity injections, assistance in placing securities on private capital markets, and by helping to raise foreign loans. *Ibid.*

[4] IISI, *Steel Statistical Yearbook 1987.*

[5] Decree No. 669/74, March 14, 1974.

[6] Benefits extended under the Plan included official credits for up to 40 percent of non-liquid investments at a 6.5 percent interest rate, repayable in 10 installments over a 14-year period; "forced expropriation" of land needed for plant expansion, right-of-way for access routes, transportation lines, pipelines, and power lines; a 95 percent reduction in customs duties on imported equipment; and a variety of tax and fiscal measures designed to stimulate investment. Decree No. 669/74, March 14, 1974, Article Sixth, Eleventh Precept.

[7] Instituto de Promoción Industrial, *Repercusiones.*

[8] *ABC* (September 8, 1983).

million metric tons per year, a level nearly double the 1974 total of 11.5 million metric tons.[9]

The steel producers' decision to expand capacity in the face of falling demand was in part an outgrowth of the "paternalistic"[10] attitude of the government toward the industry under Franco; it was generally felt that the government would continue to make credit available to the industry and cover the losses of producers that encountered serious financial difficulties.[11] Franco's death in 1975 resulted in a change in the government's attitude, but the industry was slow to recognize it.[12] As a result, in the late 1970s, the Spanish steel industry slid into a crisis of survival, characterized by mounting losses and increasingly insistent calls by the producers for injections of state aid that were not immediately forthcoming.

The depression in the Spanish steel market worsened dramatically in 1976-78; by 1978 Spanish steelmaking capacity had grown to approximately 15 million metric tons, but domestic consumption was little more than 7 million metric tons (figure 6-1). With the domestic market glutted, a series of intense price wars erupted.[13] To compound the industry's difficulties, the Franco-era ban on labor unions had been removed -- labor's demands became more organized and insistent, and a series of labor disputes ended in costly settlements.[14] Stringent domestic employment security laws and the growing strength of unions had the effect of virtually precluding short-term layoffs of personnel.[15] As a result, the Spanish producers continued to operate at a high rate of capacity utilization and exported their mounting surpluses, often at

---

[9] *Metal Bulletin* (February 17, 1976).

[10] The term was used by Minister of Industry Sahagún in *Ya* (August 27, 1978).

[11] *Financial Times* (January 5, 1981). Minister of Industry Sahagún referred to this phenomenon as the "traditional policy of nationalization of losses under the previous system when there was sufficient political and social pressure." *ABC* (December 21, 1978).

[12] *Financial Times* (January 5, 1981).

[13] *Metal Bulletin* (January 27, February 17, November 9, December 3, 1976; January 7, September 20, 1977). As one producer complained in 1977, "We are making steel, we are selling it, but no cash goes in the bank." *Metal Bulletin* (September 20, 1977).

[14] *El País* (December 20, 1978). *Actualidad Económica* noted on October 4, 1977 that unions in the iron and steel sector were among the nation's most "highly belligerent"; it commented with respect to union demands that "except for the peculiarities of each of them, the common denominator is obvious; high demands, many of which cannot be met, companies in crisis, general antagonisms and in the background, the economic crisis." Between 1975 and 1979 wages in the steel industry rose to a level higher than those of Britain and Italy, labor costs increased from 15 percent to 30 percent of turnover, and worker productivity declined dramatically. *Financial Times* (January 5, 1981).

[15] L. Albertson and J. Zaragoza, "Estructura y Política Siderúrgica -- de la Acción Concertada a la Política de Reconversión," in *Información Comercial Española* (November 1982), p. 78.

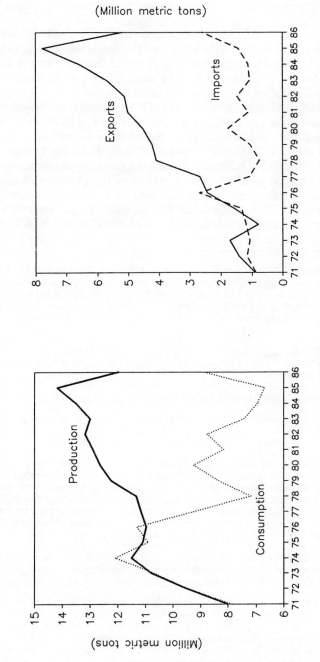

Figure 6–1: Spain – Steel Production, Consumption and Trade, 1971–1986

(Million metric tons)

Source: International Iron and Steel Institute, Steel Statistical Yearbook, 1981, 1987. Production and Consumption refer to crude steel; Exports and Imports refer to semi–finished and finished steel.

"ruinous" prices.[16] All of the major Spanish producers incurred substantial operating losses beginning in 1977 and were reportedly suffering from extreme cash flow problems.[17]

The post-Franco Spanish government reacted sluggishly to what was clearly a growing crisis in the Spanish economy; major plans dealing with steel were delayed so long in preparation and approval that they had to be rewritten, having been rendered obsolete by events.[18] Government spending was restricted, reflecting anti-inflation measures and a desire to curb benefits to "privileged" industrial sectors,[19] and the low-interest government loans that were to be made pursuant to the Concerted Action Plans were frozen, to the dismay of the steel producers.[20] Restrictions on official credit drove up interest rates, so that by 1978 the steel firms' financing charges were 10-11 percent of their total billings.[21] Finally, the government maintained rigid price ceilings on steel products, which prevented the producers from recovering their rapidly rising costs and exacerbated their operating losses.[22]

By early 1978 it was evident that despite the government's reluctance, urgent government measures would be required to avert the "collapse of the

---

[16] *Metal Bulletin* (February 20, 1976). *Metal Bulletin* reported on July 13, 1976 that in 1975 "Ensidesa made a great effort throughout the year to maintain its production levels to avoid laying off too many men. This entailed an effort to increase exports and to open new markets abroad." According to Ensidesa's Managing Director, the company conducted some of these operations at a loss. *Metal Bulletin* (January 9, 1976). See "Spanish Foreign Trade in Steel" below.

[17] In 1977 the operating losses of the three major integrated producers were reportedly $210.6 million, a "deficit . . . never before reached." *ABC* (February 5, 1978); *Actualidad Económica* (February 4, 1978).

[18] *Financial Times* (January 5, 1981).

[19] Curbs on government spending were imposed pursuant to the so-called "Moncloa Pact," a two-year economic program agreed to by the government and major opposition parties designed, among other things, to curb inflation. *ABC* (October 22, 1977).

[20] The government Banco de Crédito Industrial, which was supposed to provide the promised credits to the steel industry, continually delayed doing so. The concerted action financing programs (which also existed in other industries) were widely criticized as "privileged" financing arrangements which should be ended. Unesid Head Miguel Salis charged in 1977 that the credit restrictions were "an almost insuperable problem" for steel concerns which were already in debt and had begun capital investment programs backed by the state. *Metal Bulletin* (October 18, November 3, 1977).

[21] *Ya* (June 16, 1977); *ABC* (February 5, 1978); *El País* (December 17, 1978). By 1981, the Spanish producers' financial costs were the highest in Europe, exceeding 20 percent of turnover. *Financial Times* (January 5, 1981).

[22] Pursuant to a series of decrees issued in the early and mid-1970s the Spanish government maintained official ceilings on steel prices which the domestic producers complained were too low. Increases in costs could not be compensated with parallel price increases without prior government approval. Decree Law 12/1973, November 30, 1973; Decree No. 690/1975, April 5, 1975; Royal Decree No. 2730/1976, November 26, 1976. Widespread discounting frequently prevented producers from realizing even these prices.

Spanish integrated steel industry."[23] Although complete nationalization was discussed, the government wished to avoid a takeover of the entire integrated steel sector, and nationalization of AHV, centered in the Basque region, was considered politically unacceptable.[24] The ailing AHM, however, confronted the government with a problem for which nationalization appeared the only alternative to insolvency. AHM was heavily indebted and in 1978 it stopped meeting its payroll.[25] In December 1978 the government enacted the Law for Urgent Measures in Support of the Iron and Steel Sector[26] and a series of decrees[27] which placed AHM under the complete control of INI and provided extensive state aid to the industry.[28] In contrast to some past aid programs, most of the amounts provided for in the Law for Urgent Measures were actually disbursed to the steel companies.[29] In addition, INI guaranteed a series of loans from commercial banks to Ensidesa at a time (1979-82) when the company was uncreditworthy (according to the U.S. Commerce Department).[30]

---

[23] *Metal Bulletin* (March 31, 1978).

[24] *Metal Bulletin* (February 10, 14, 24, 28, 1978). AHV was so heavily indebted to the government — owing, among other things, unpaid taxes and social security contributions -- that it was regarded as "virtually nationalized." *Financial Times* (January 5, 1981). The plight of AHV was part of a larger problem facing the Spanish government. The economy of the Basque region was excessively dependent upon the steel industry, and with the world steel recession, the Basque country had become severely depressed. Economic problems exacerbated the region's chronic separatist tendencies, which were periodically manifested in acts of armed violence. *El País* (July 27, 29, 31, 1979).

[25] *ABC* (September 18, 1983).

[26] Law No. 60/1978, December 23, 1978.

[27] Ministry of Economy Order Dated December 26, 1978; Royal Decree 3089, December 1978 (Ministry of the Treasury).

[28] Pursuant to this plan, INI acquired complete control over AHM and injected $52.1 million in new equity into the ailing firm. *Ya* (August 26, 1978); Law No. 60/1978, Article 1st(1); Article 3rd. Ensidesa received an equity infusion of $143.5 million, Law No. 60/1978, Article 2nd (1), and the government was authorized to capitalize AHV's long-term debt to the government Banco de Crédito Industrial. Law No. 60/1978, Article 5th(4). Low-interest loans totalling $306.5 million from the Spanish Treasury were authorized for the three producers in 1978-79 to finance new investments and working capital. Law No. 60/1978, Article 5th(3). The equity injections and loans were particularly important because, given their string of operating losses, the Spanish producers could not raise funds from other sources. AHV commented in its 1979 *Memoria Ejercicio* that "every avenue of capital financing has been explored, and the means whereby it might proceed with restructuring are lacking in both the financial and industrial sectors."

[29] Ensidesa *Memoria*, 1978; AHM *Memoria*, 1979; Spanish Embassy, "General Answers, Countervailing Duty Questionnaire, Certain Steel Products from Spain," June 21, 1982.

[30] *Carbon Steel Wire Rod from Spain*, May 8, 1984 (49 F.R. 19551).

While the steel companies welcomed the Law for Urgent Measures, it was clearly only an emergency stopgap measure.[31] In fact, although domestic consumption rose slightly in 1979 and 1980, the industry's condition continued to deteriorate; all three producers suffered record-breaking operating losses in 1980. By early 1980 AHV, the remaining major private-sector producer, faced the "gravest crisis in the company's history" -- the firm's continuing losses forced it to borrow heavily, increasing its financing charges to 16-17 percent of sales, and the firm was encountering difficulty meeting its payroll and paying for raw materials.[32] By late 1980 the integrated steel sector once again was in desperate need of assistance .

In May 1981 the Spanish government enacted a massive new aid program for the steel industry, "Reconversion Measures for the Integrated Iron and Steel Industry."[33] Under this measure, the government, the unions and the companies made commitments to a "Reconversion Plan" entailing salary reductions for labor, financial contributions by the government, and restructuring measures by the companies. INI was authorized to inject new capital into Ensidesa ($108.3 million) and AHM ($86.7 million) and to guarantee loans to the ailing AHV of up to $368.3 million in 1981.[34] The debt of all three major producers was to be refinanced on extremely generous terms.[35] INI was authorized to grant credits to Ensidesa totaling $146.4 million between 1981 and 1985 at 8 percent interest through 1985.[36] In March 1982 the principal and interest on certain outstanding INI loans to Ensidesa were converted to capital in the company.[37]

---

[31] AHV commented in its 1978 *Memoria Ejercicio* that "The passing of this [Urgent Measures] law in itself is not an absolute guarantee for the survival of AHV in the private sector, but it allows a margin of time to come up with a definitive solution."

[32] *Metal Bulletin* (February 19, 1980). AHV commented on its mounting losses in its 1979 *Memoria Ejercicio* (p. 25): "It is essential to note that the crisis, which has affected the steel industry everywhere on a worldwide level, has caught AHV without the necessary reserves. Thus a situation has arisen which surpasses AHV's capacity to react to it. . . . Under these conditions the Company finds itself particularly disqualified from seeking help on the capital market . . . and its operational possibilities are reduced to a minimum."

[33] Royal Decree 878/1981, May 8, 1981.

[34] Royal Decree 878/1981, Chapter 11, Article Five (one)(e).

[35] Pursuant to the 1978 Urgent Measures legislation, AHM's repayment obligations for certain government loans granted in the 1970s were deferred until 1985, and "exceptional credits" were granted to Ensidesa ($184.1 million), AHM ($30.3 million) and AHV ($88.8 million) to pay off all debt principal which had matured or would mature between 1981 and 1985. These credits were granted at an 8 percent interest rate with a five-year grace period on repayment. Royal Decree 878/1981, Chapter II, Article Six.

[36] INI's standard rates would apply after 1985. Royal Decree 878/1981, Chapter II, Article Five(a).

[37] *Carbon Steel Wire Rod from Spain*, May 8, 1984.

While the Spanish producers blamed their financial plight on the government's price ceilings, the removal of those ceilings in 1981 and the adoption of measures to control price competition demonstrated that the industry's problems were more fundamental; the producers continued to suffer heavy losses (table 6-1). Measures taken pursuant to Royal Decree 878/1981

Table 6-1. Losses Incurred by Spain's Integrated Producers 1980-86 (million U.S. dollars)

	ENSIDESA	AHV
1980	(218)	(165)
1981	(226)	(113)
1982	(190)	(78)
1983	(188)	(38)
1984	(153)	(34)
1985	(104)	(31)
1986	(103)	(103)

Sources: Company Annual Reports; *Metal Bulletin*; *Financial Times*; *El País*.
Converted to U.S. dollars at average annual exchange rate given by International Monetary Fund.
Conversion: 1980: 71.7, 1981: 92.3, 1982: 109.9, 1983: 143.4, 1984: 160.8, 1985: 170, 1986: 140.

eliminated the ceilings and implemented a pricing system comparable to that of the EC, establishing a mechanism through which the leading producers could raise prices through collusive interfirm arrangements.[38] The new measures provided that actual domestic prices should conform to producers' published list prices, which constituted not only maximum but also minimum prices. The stability of list prices and the conformity of market prices to list

---

[38] Royal Decree 878/1981 delegated to the Minister of Industry and Energy the authority to implement the ECSC pricing system, which was done through a Ministerial Order dated September 17, 1981. The order abolishing ceilings required conformance to a system of published list prices similar to that prevailing in the ECSC.

price were subsequently ensured through meetings of the major producers.[39] Price stability was reinforced by a four-year market-sharing agreement to reduce competition between the traditional leading rivals, Ensidesa and AHV.[40]

The financial assistance and price increases made possible by the Reconversion Plan did little to resolve the industry's financial crisis. Spanish domestic consumption remained stagnant in 1981-82, and the three major producers suffered a cumulative loss in 1982 of $307.7 million.[41] Despite the massive government aid measures undertaken in 1981 and supplemental measures in 1982,[42] the industry complained that government aid levels were inadequate and that the government had delayed the disbursement of funds.[43]

The Restructuring Dilemma. The principal problem faced by the Spanish producers was the fact that by 1982 Spain possessed over 17 million metric tons of effective crude steel capacity, but consumed less than 9 million metric tons of steel products. This capacity overhang forced producers either to operate at uneconomically low rates,[44] or to operate at higher utilization rates and export their surpluses at what was generally a loss. Under the circumstances, a wholesale restructuring, featuring major capacity cuts, was clearly warranted. However, by the 1980s, with much of the industry nationalized, decisions with respect to the steel industry were increasingly dominated by political rather than economic considerations, and an industry-government-labor consensus on restructuring proved elusive. The government, while willing to countenance closure of a few marginal facilities, was reluctant

---

[39] AHV noted in its 1982 *Memoria Ejercicio* (p. 12) that "The application of the ECSC price system to the Spanish steel market on October 18, 1981 was accomplished by orders in the framework of Royal Decree 878/1981, concerning the restructuring of the integrated steel industry. The proper application of this legislation, guaranteed by means of periodic meetings of the three large integrated steel companies, has brought about the well-known recovery of domestic steel prices. . . . The increase in the list prices which was made, which has been satisfactorily accepted by the market, has made it possible to bring the relative situation of prices to terms it occupied in 1979. . . ."

[40] Royal Decree 878/1981, Article Thirteen (One) provided for the establishment of production and distribution quotas by the Coordination Committee.

[41] *Actualidad Económica* (February 1983).

[42] Law No. 33/1982, July 1, 1982, authorized interest-free government loans to Ensidesa ($91 million) and AHM ($72.8 million).

[43] One steel official complained in 1983 that "as of now there has been no industrial conversion but rather a mere restoration in terms of liabilities, finances and labor problems and that was probably a necessary step although insufficient. . . . The sector that needs more emergency measures in the area of investment is the integrated steel industry where we are losing $278.9 million per year. . . . " *Actualidad Económica* (February 1983).

[44] In mid-1981 AHM's cold-rolling mill at Sagunto was reportedly operating at a "highly unsatisfactory" 15 percent of full capacity. *Metal Bulletin* (August 11, 1981).

to press for widespread capacity cuts.[45]   The producers sought to continue their own expansion projects while calling for cutbacks by other producers, and the labor unions tended to oppose any cuts adamantly.   The impasse was further exacerbated by Spain's traditional regional conflicts -- each region sought the upgrading of its own steel facilities and felt that any cuts should be made in other regions.

In October 1982, against a background of widespread unemployment and deepening economic crisis, the Socialist Party came to power in Spain, having made a campaign promise to create 800,000 new jobs.   However, the new government was immediately confronted with the problem of the steel industry, which was burdened with excess capacity and personnel, whose restructuring effort had been drifting, and whose growing losses were placing an increasing strain on the national treasury.[46]   The Socialists quickly found that the proposed closure of even a small increment of the most obsolete capacity was an explosive political and social issue.   Attempting to confront the capacity issue, in February 1983 the government announced plans to close the nation's most obsolete and uneconomic steelworks, the AHM blast furnace operation at Sagunto, triggering the so-called "Drama of Sagunto," one of the most volatile domestic controversies faced by the new government.[47]

The Sagunto Crisis.   AHM's Sagunto mill posed a particularly difficult problem.   Because the original 6 million metric ton per year greenfield facility contemplated for Sagunto had never been completed -- a casualty of the steel crisis -- the Sagunto works consisted only of a modern 1.3 million ton per year cold-rolling mill and a hopelessly obsolete blast furnace facility.   Lacking a hot-rolling mill, AHM was forced to ship ingots from its blast furnace facility to other mills for processing into hot-rolled coils which were then returned to Sagunto for treatment in AHM's cold-rolling mill, a procedure that was uneconomic.[48]   Analyses of the Sagunto works recommended that a hot-rolling mill be constructed to complete the processing cycle; however, the construction of a new hot-rolling facility was vehemently opposed by other producers and regions on the grounds that Spain was already burdened with

---

[45] Minister of Economic Affairs Leopoldo Sotelo in *Metal Bulletin* (February 13, 1981).

[46] *Mercado* commented on April 8-14, 1983 that "Last year the losses of these entities [AHV, AHM and Ensidesa] amounted to about $455 million, and they have increased in recent years; which proves that the measures adopted (or not adopted) by the administration have been futile. Herein lies the crux of what confronts the Socialist cabinet: How to prevent that constant increase?"

[47] *El País* (March 6, 1983); *Metal Bulletin* (December 3, 1982).

[48] *El País* (February 17, 1983).   In 1983 Spain's Minister of Industry and Energy commented that AHM had the most antiquated and least competitive installations in Spain, and that "out of every 100 pesetas [$.70] produced, Sagunto loses 36.5 [$.25]. . . ."   The Minister noted that Ensidesa lost $.13 and AHV $.11 per $.70 produced. *El País* (April 15, 1983).

overcapacity, and alternatively, that any new hot-rolling facility should be established in a region of the country other than Sagunto.[49]

The Socialist government's proposed closure of the Sagunto facility, coupled with a planned redirection of steel investments toward the more modern facilities in Asturias and the Basque region, triggered a political uproar and a general strike in Valencia.[50] In February 1983 an estimated 30-35 thousand demonstrators, joined by numerous local politicians, marched through the streets of Sagunto shouting "Government listen, the people ask for a hot-rolling mill."[51] In March Sagunto steelworkers defied a management order to curtail production of cast iron due to surplus stocks in Spain, triggering a boisterous demonstration of 20,000 people.[52] At length, intensive lobbying by Valencia area officials led to suspension of the proposed Sagunto closure, stalling the entire Spanish restructuring effort.[53]

In July 1983, after four months of futile negotiations between representatives of the government, the unions, and AHV, AHM and Ensidesa, Minister of Industry and Energy Solchaga issued a decree providing for comprehensive measures for the entire steel industry. Solchaga announced that the old Sagunto blast furnace would be shut down and that the hot-rolling mill would not be built. In exchange, the government agreed to finance major new investments by the three leading steel companies and to bring new

---

[49] In 1982 a study of the Spanish steel industry by the Japanese producer Kawasaki recommended, among other things, that a new hot-rolling mill be constructed at Sagunto and many facilities of Ensidesa and AHV be closed. The report triggered a heated controversy in Spain. *Actualidad Económica* reported in February 1983 that "The report set off an explosion and both AHV and Ensidesa, but especially the latter, raised a ruckus. All public intervention now became engaged in demagogy. In many cases, this situation only managed to get everybody all stirred up, and that applies not only to the workers but also the public opinion. The bitter debate was kept going in spite of the fact that the report was withdrawn. . . . Everybody demands the installation of the TBC [hot-rolling mill] for himself and the dialectical battle has been revived."

[50] Defenders of the Sagunto mill charged that "At a time when part of the Spanish steel industry has to be shut down, the government has not dared to take on Altos Hornos de Vizcaya, in the Basque Country, where the Basque Fatherland and Liberty Group (ETA) could step up its violence; nor Ensidesa in Asturias, where the PCE's [Communist Party's] power is well known. . . . That is why it chose Sagunto." *ABC* (September 30, 1983).

[51] *El País* (February 17, March 6, 1983).

[52] The workers saw the order as the first step toward closure. The demonstrators surrounded AHM headquarters, cornering the company's president for 10 hours until he rescinded the order to cut production. *El País* (March 22, 1983).

[53] *Mercado* commented on April 8-14, 1983, that "The restructuring of the iron and steel sector has confronted [Minister of Industry and Energy] Solchaga with a difficult commitment. They must achieve the maximum amount of profitability, and this leads to personnel cuts and even the closing of plants. Nevertheless, in the test begun at Sagunto, his besieging received a response from an entire town, and he has to back down, for the moment. . . . Under the Socialist sky, the dense smoke from the high stacks of the Spanish blast furnaces continues to dim the broad bases for hope that had been established two years ago, when the sector's restructuring was planned."

industry to Sagunto. However, AHM's announcement that it would begin shutting down the Sagunto blast furnace in September prompted further violent worker protests and strikes in defiance of management.[54] The unions collected 585,000 signatures opposing Solchaga's July decree in an attempt to induce the Cortes (parliament) to derogate the decree; Solchaga indicated that he would resign if this occurred.[55]

Intensive negotiations between INI, union officials and the AHM works council finally resulted in an agreement in April 1984 concerning the Sagunto closure. Pursuant to the agreement, the blast furnace operation was closed in October 1984, although the cold-rolling mill remained operational, and INI provided worker rehabilitation aid.[56] Thus thirteen months of extraordinary political confrontation, punctuated by strikes, demonstrations and sporadic violence, had been required to reach an agreement on the retirement of approximately one million metric tons of the most obsolete raw steel production capacity.

Accession to the European Community. The European Community, in anticipation of Spain's accession, placed heavy pressure on Spain to curb its aid to the steel industry. The President of the EC Council of Ministers, Leo Tindemans, indicated in 1982 that Spain's steel plans were inconsistent with the EC's restructuring program and that therefore no date could be set for that country's admission to the Community.[57] The following year, the Spanish Minister of Industry and Energy bluntly warned the industry that restructuring was proceeding too slowly,[58] and that once Spain became a member of the EC,

---

[54] *El País* (September 17, 1983). A "pitched battle" between steelworkers and the National Police occurred in February 1984, accompanied by a 24-hour general strike which "entirely paralyzed" Sagunto and the surrounding region. Thousands of workers and Sagunto residents traveled by car and bus to Madrid to protest the closing at the negotiations between Sagunto workers and the government. *El Alcázar* (February 10, 1984).

[55] *Ya* (September 27, 1983); *El País* (September 27, 1983).

[56] *Metal Bulletin* (April 13, 1984).

[57] *Metal Bulletin* (January 15, 1982).

[58] "Let's consider first the steel supply in Spain. . . . I must say to you, between us, that I am not satisfied with the progress of reconversion; that the progress is too slow, that I don't yet see sufficient structure in some sectors, that I don't yet see that we are adjusting our production capacity to our needs, that I don't yet see sufficiently rapid progress in investments, that I don't yet see the adjustment in staff to the necessary level." Minister of Industry and Commerce don Carlos Solchaga, at the annual meeting of Unesid, reported in *Información Siderúrgica* (July 1984), p. 9.

the Commission would be able to exert greater control over the industry than could the Spanish government.[59]

Spanish steel exports to the EC had been subject to quotas since 1978,[60] and Community producers feared that Spanish overcapacity would exacerbate existing problems in the Community, a concern which was hardly assuaged by statements of the President of AHV that Spain's restructuring plans assumed access to the EC market.[61] In fact, those plans hardly contemplated any net capacity reductions -- cuts of 1.7 million metric tons in the integrated steel sector would virtually be offset by increases in the special steel and electric furnace sectors, leaving Spain with 22 million metric tons of capacity in 1988.[62] The Spanish government, skeptical that EC producers could phase out subsidies by the 1986 deadline, offered "parity" on subsidies; that is, it would renounce state aid to the steel industry to the extent other EC nations were able to do so.[63] The Community, however, continued to insist that Spain reduce its capacity to 18 million metric tons before it entered the EC.[64]

In late 1984, the negotiators finally agreed to a formula for Spain's accession to the EC. Under the Treaty of Adhesion, signed in June 1985, Spain would enter the Community in 1986, and would gradually dismantle its tariffs on EC imports over a seven-year period.[65] Protocol No. 10, which dealt specifically with the steel industry, allowed Spain 3 years to complete its steel industry restructuring plan and to restore the industry to "viability." In the

---

[59] *Ibid.* The Minister's warning was not overlooked -- it did not, however, draw the expected response. Recognizing that EC membership could result in capacity restrictions, the government of Asturias urged INI to proceed with the Ensidesa investment plan -- which anticipated expansion at the Avilés facility in that province -- before it was too late. *Metal Bulletin* (September 4, 1984).

[60] *Metal Bulletin* (April 25, 1978).

[61] *Metal Bulletin* (October 2, 1984).

[62] *Metal Bulletin* (October 2, 1984).

[63] *Metal Bulletin* (October 9, 1984). Industry and Energy Minister Solchaga believed that Italy and Spain would be "natural allies" in the struggle to continue subsidies to their steel industries, because their restructuring plans would not be completed by the 1986 deadline. *Información Siderúrgica* (July 1984), p. 12.

[64] *Metal Bulletin* (November 30, 1984).

[65] *Official Journal*, L.302 (November 15, 1985). Spain was required to dismantle its tariffs on EC goods and to adopt the common EC tariffs on third-country goods over a seven-year period ("El Desarme Arancelario," in *Información Siderúrgica* (May 1986), p. 7) and to eliminate import licensing. "Nueva Regulación del Comercio Exterior Español," in *Información Siderúrgica* (March 1986), p. 25. It was also required to replace the existing indirect taxes, from which exporters were exempt, with a VAT, from which they were not. AHV President Juan Luis Burgos predicted that the introduction of the VAT would cost the industry $117.6 million per year (*Metal Bulletin* (August 30, 1985)) and noted that "it will affect the operating levels of the firms and perhaps impede the export of some products, that with the cited reduction would not cover their variable costs." *Información Siderúrgica* (March 1985), p. 7.

interim, Spain could continue to subsidize its steel industry; however, Spanish steel exports to the Community would remain under quota. At the close of the three-year transition period, Spanish steelmaking capacity could not exceed 18 million metric tons and all subsidies would cease.[66]

Restructuring in the Integrated Steel Sector. In July 1983, at the height of the Sagunto crisis, the Spanish government asked the three leading steel companies to draw up investment and job reduction proposals; the government would provide a massive $4 billion to implement the plans.[67] Ensidesa's record breaking 1983 loss of $188.4 million, together with dismal forecasts for the 1984-86 period, caused INI to reconsider Ensidesa's entire investment program.[68] This hesitation provoked a wave of unrest in Asturias, the site of Ensidesa's facilities,[69] however, and the investment program was reinstated.

In March 1984, the Spanish cabinet approved a comprehensive financing package for the restructuring of Spain's integrated steelmakers, providing $2.7

---

[66] Spanish steelmakers were not entirely pleased with the terms of accession. Unesid President Burgos identified a number of factors which he considered "worrisome:" a dismantling of tariffs on EC steel products which exceeded those imposed on Spanish products; the elimination of certain tax advantages for exporters; and a "lack of reciprocity" on import controls during the three-year transition period. Juan Luis Burgos, "La Siderurgia Española Ante La CEE", in *Información Siderúrgica* (April 1985), p. 6. And the director of the Independent Steelmakers Association warned that "far too much importance was being given to deadlines" in the restructuring program. *Metal Bulletin* (October 15, 1985). Consumers, on the other hand, looked forward to Spain's entry into the EC, which they hoped would slow down increases in the price of steel. *Metal Bulletin* (June 4, 1985). Prices were maintained at artificially-high levels by means of market-sharing agreements, which were encouraged by the Spanish government. In the mid-1980s such agreements extended to special steels and to rebars. *Metal Bulletin* (January 6, 1984; January 17, 1986). As Minister of Industry and Energy Solchaga explained, "I believe that there is no sense to a competition between firms that lowers prices." *Información Siderúrgica*, June 1985, p. 9. The Spanish government in 1983 established minimum import prices to insure that these agreements would not be undercut by inexpensive imports. Ministry of Economy and Finance, Order of July 7, 1983.

[67] *Metal Bulletin* (July 15, 1983).

[68] *Metal Bulletin* (January 31, 1984). A Spanish government report, leaked to the press in January 1984, forecast the following losses for Ensidesa: 1984, $143 million; 1985, $129.4 million; 1986, $171.4 million. *Metal Bulletin* (January 17, 1984). INI's investments in and loans to the steel industry were described in 1983 as "state subsidies with no foreseeable return." *El País* (October 8, 1983).

[69] *Metal Bulletin* reported on December 23, 1983, that "INI's top management seems concerned mainly because it will have to underwrite Ensidesa's losses, and it would like a clearer idea of when it will be able to stop doing so. The new uncertainty over Ensidesa's modernization has given rise to a furor in the northern province of Asturias where Ensidesa's works are sited. Trade unions issued a demand for the industry ministry immediately to approve the program and arrange financing and set a timetable. A 48-hour strike has been threatened to back up the demand for a decision on the new melting shop before the end of this year. Meanwhile the President of the Asturias regional government, Pedro Silva, stated that financing has already been arranged for the start of work on building the new steelmaking shop."

billion in aid for investments and financial restructuring between 1985 and 1988.[70] The aid would be provided by means of capital increases, loans from INI and the Banco de Crédito Industrial, and subsidies.[71] In addition, the state undertook to guarantee $802.4 million in loans. As part of the restructuring program, the integrated producers agreed to cut capacity by 1.4 million metric tons and to reduce employment by 9,629 workers by 1990.[72] Major new investments would be undertaken to improve productivity and quality of production.[73] Despite this restructuring program, there remained widespread skepticism that the integrated steel sector would be viable by 1989.[74]

Restructuring in the Electric Furnace Sector. The Spanish electric furnace industry was fragmented among 17 sites, mostly located in the Basque country. The steep decline in domestic steel consumption had thrown many of these companies into financial difficulties by 1984.[75] Rather than undertake serious restructuring, however, this sector simply exported its surpluses; in 1985, the Spanish minimills, with a combined capacity of 5 million metric tons, exported 3.1 million metric tons.[76] The Minister of Industry and Energy expressed his dissatisfaction with the situation in the summer of 1985:

The common steel sector continues fundamentally spineless. It continues without sufficient controls in its politics of raw material and energy inputs, absolutely essential to move ahead; without a system of transparency regarding its levels of production, and I say this not

---

[70] Ensidesa, *Annual Report 1984*, p. 7. Private banks were required to lend a certain portion of their funds to industrial reconversion programs – these loans were guaranteed by the state. Ministry of Economy and Finance, Order of January 2, 1985.

[71] *Ibid.* For 1985, the rate of interest on loans from the Banco de Crédito Industrial for the implementation of approved reconversion plans was 9 percent.

[72] *Ibid.*

[73] Royal Decree 2586/1985 eliminated tariffs on the import of certain capital goods required by the mills for their restructuring effects. Both Ensidesa and AHV were granted authority to take advantage of these tariff breaks. General Directorate of Foreign Commerce, Resolutions of June 30 and September 1, 1986.

[74] Ensidesa's directors were reputed to doubt that the firm's investment plan could restore the company to profitability by 1989. *Metal Bulletin* (August 6, 1985). Ensidesa's President, Fernando Lozano, remarked in 1987 that "The INI and the government are amply meeting their commitments with regard to ENSIDESA. However, the company itself still has not been capable of arriving at a situation where competitiveness would be achievable by 1989." Ensidesa, *Annual Report 1986*, p. 3.

[75] Several minimills shut down in 1984 (*Metal Bulletin* (August 10, 1984)) and a number of others found themselves in need of financial assistance from the government. *Metal Bulletin* (December 4, 1984).

[76] Francisco Rubiralta, President of Celsa, in *Metal Bulletin* (March 14, 1986).

because I am interested from the economic point of view, but to order competition and supply in the marketplace; without a suitable and united system of foreign marketing; and without a clear idea as to levels of production, specialization of facilities, and reduction of the most obsolete facilities or those whose financial possibilities of survival are more doubtful.[77]

In late 1985, the first steps were taken toward consolidation in this sector, when the Spanish government conditioned the allocation of $17.6 million in aid to the ailing Galician firm Sidegasa on the company's formation of links with other producers.[78] In the first quarter of 1986, as minimill exports plummeted almost 40 percent,[79] the sector accelerated its restructuring plans. In April, four troubled Basque producers formed a joint "rationalization" company to study restructuring options.[80] In June, the Independent Steel Federation urged that the government develop a plan to cut capacity by 1 million tons and reduce employment in the sector by 30 percent.[81] The Federation believed that government pressure would be necessary to convince private competitors to close;[82] the government, however, after its experience in the Sagunto crisis, showed a marked hesitation to select the victims itself.[83] Finally, in December 1987, two days before the EC's deadline for approving state aid for closures, the government issued a plan providing for the closure

---

[77] Don Carlos Solchaga, in *Información Siderúrgica* (June 1985), p. 9.

[78] *Metal Bulletin* (October 1, 1985).

[79] *Metal Bulletin* (June 27, 1986). The fall was attributable in part to the elimination of tax incentives for exporters. See "Spanish Foreign Trade in Steel" below.

[80] *Metal Bulletin* (April 25, 1986). The steel crisis had badly shaken these companies. In November 1985, minimill Nervacero warned that it faced closure after employees rejected a recovery plan that would have laid off nearly a quarter of the work force (*Metal Bulletin* (November 26, 1985)), and in April 1986 Esteban Orbegozo suspended payments to creditors. *Metal Bulletin* (April 11, 1986).

[81] *Metal Bulletin* (April 26, 1986).

[82] *Metal Bulletin* (February 6, 1987).

[83] According to the Minister of Industry and Energy, "The permanent efforts at cost reductions should be accompanied . . . by a redimensioning downward of production levels over the medium term, that permits it to attend in a profitable manner to the domestic and certain foreign markets; in this diagnosis we all agree. There exist, however, disparate opinions over how to carry out this inevitable adjustment process. In my opinion, only an initiative by the companies -- which I understand is already in progress, in particular in non-integrated common steels -- that designs a business and productive structure, can serve as a base so that the new government that emerges after the upcoming election can study . . . the possibility of a request to the EC for complementary means. Don Juan Majó, in *Información Siderúrgica* (June 1986), pp. 8-9.

of 5 plants. In order to avoid confrontations with regional governments, the plan would close one plant in each major steel-producing region.[84]

Restructuring After Accession. The Spanish restructuring plan approved by the EC Commission involved substantial additional state aid. The government agreed to pay companies approximately $121 per ton for the closure of capacity.[85] To facilitate lay-offs, the government agreed to finance early retirement programs for workers over sixty years of age and to provide comparable aids for younger workers affected by restructuring.[86] It renegotiated debts owed by steel companies to public entities[87] and provided subsidies for export financing.[88] In all, the government in 1987 obtained approval from the EC for an additional $1.8 billion, on top of the $4.3 billion previously provided to aid in the restructuring process.[89] In exchange for Commission approval of the additional aid, Spain committed to reduce its capacity to 17.25 million metric tons of steel by 1989.[90] However, in 1986, some observers were expressing concern that Spain might not achieve its capacity reduction goals.[91]

Militant reaction by workers to proposals for plant closures and layoffs did not diminish after the "Drama of Sagunto". In the fall of 1987, the minimill company Celsa announced plans to close Sidegasa,[92] a small Galician mill burdened with a debt of $81 million.[93] In response, a thousand workers took to the streets of La Coruña.[94] The next day, 200 of the most militant protestors cut the national highway.[95] The demonstrations continued in the weeks to follow, with demonstrators cursing and throwing eggs at local

---

[84] *Metal Bulletin* (January 14, 1988). The estimated cost of the plan is $123.5 million.

[85] *Metal Bulletin* (May 3, 1987); *El País* (September 14, 1987). The funds would be used to reduce debts, or in the case of complete closure, to pay off creditors. *Ibid.*

[86] Ministry of Labor and Social Security, Orders of April 9, 1986 and May 5, 1987.

[87] *Información Siderúrgica* (April-June 1987), p. 8.

[88] Royal Decree 322/1987.

[89] *Financial Times* (April 25, 1987).

[90] The EC agreed to provide Spain with $102 million to help workers affected by restructuring. *Metal Bulletin* (August 10, 1987); *European Report* (September 23, 1987).

[91] Adolf Faber of the EC Commission remarked in 1986 that although Spain had eliminated 4.2 million metric tons of obsolete capacity between 1981 and 1986, it had added similar amounts in new projects. *Metal Bulletin* (August 29, 1986).

[92] *Metal Bulletin* (September 10, 1987).

[93] *El País* (August 21, 1987).

[94] *Ibid.*

[95] *El País* (August 11, 1987).

government officials who they believed were not doing everything possible to save the plant.[96]

In 1987, Forjas y Aceros de Reinosa, an INI-owned producer of special steels, announced a restructuring plan that would require a reduction of 463 workers.[97] The government appropriated $64.8 million to ease the restructuring process;[98] nevertheless, the workers' response was angry. In July, 2,000 protestors descended on INI and the Ministry of Industry in Madrid, chanting "Reinosa wants to live" and "No more layoffs."[99] A few days later, workers cut all rail and road access to Reinosa, dumping beams, rafters and tons of dirt on highways and railroad tracks.[100] A general strike was set for July 21.[101] Not until September was the matter settled -- 222 workers over the age of 52 received early retirement, while 186 would draw a salary from the "fund for the promotion of employment" until they reached age 55, at which time they too would receive early retirement.[102] The intensity of the social strife generated by these relatively minor restructuring programs helps explain the government's hesitancy to choose other targets for restructuring, but it remains altogether unclear how, and whether, Spain will be able to achieve the Commission's capacity reduction targets.

Spanish Foreign Trade in Steel. During the past decade Spain has emerged as one of the world's most important steel exporters. In 1985, its best export year, Spain sold nearly 8 million metric tons of steel products abroad, making it the world's eighth largest steel exporter. Spain's export performance, however, has been more a reflection of the depressed condition of the Spanish domestic market and of its huge "overhang" of surplus capacity than of the industry's international competitiveness; in fact, the industry is

---

[96] *El País* (September 5, 1987).

[97] *El País* (July 11, 1987).

[98] *Financial Times* (April 25, 1987).

[99] *El País* (July 3, 1987).

[100] *El País* (July 11, 1987).

[101] *El País* (July 14, 1987).

[102] *El País* (September 27 and 30, 1987). *El País* noted on September 27, 1987 that the attempt to cut employment at Foarsa "gave rise, over the last seven months, to innumerable disturbances of a social character in the district, including the death of the worker Gonzalo Ruíz, tens of injuries and fifty arrests, as well as producing large material losses to Renfe [the national railroad] due to the blockage of its communications." In addition to these disturbances, in 1986 Ensidesa lost over 90,000 working days -- roughly five days for every man and woman employed by the company -- to strike actions. Ensidesa, *Annual Report 1986*, p. 34.

plagued by high costs and low productivity.[103] Indeed, the growth in Spanish export volume through 1985 serves as a virtual benchmark of the industry's deepening crisis. As the Spanish producers' financial and operational difficulties mounted, so did the volume of Spanish steel exports. Only in the late 1980s, as foreign trade barriers increased and an EC-mandated elimination of tax incentives for exports took effect, did Spanish steel exports decline.

From the onset of the steel crisis through 1985, Spanish steel producers operated their facilities at a comparatively high rate of utilization and exported their surpluses, which grew larger as Spanish domestic demand deteriorated.[104] Exports were, in effect, an alternative to capacity cuts and layoffs that could trigger explosive social unrest. However, while exports helped to maintain utilization rates, employment levels, and political and social stability, they were often uneconomic. Due to high costs and the depressed condition of the international market, exported Spanish steel was frequently sold below cost, contributing significantly to the industry's mounting losses.[105]

---

[103] *Le Monde* observed on March 19, 1981 that "Spain, which was exporting only 4.5 percent of its steel production in 1970 had increased its foreign sales tenfold by 1979. But the slump plaguing the entire European iron and steel industry, coupled with the protectionist reaction it triggered in EC countries, has made export operations difficult, especially as the Spanish steel industry is not very competitive; the value added per person in that sector is only 69 percent of the average value added in the ECSC countries." Fernando Lozano, President of Ensidesa, lamented that: "In an objective examination of ENSIDESA today, we discover a failure to adapt the company structure to the modern competitive integrated iron and steel industry. The obsolence [sic] of many plants, the lack of equity finance, the structure of its organization, behavioral standards, staff imbalances, etc.; these aspects are blatantly obvious and add up to cost and quality levels unsuitable to modern iron and steel industries." Ensidesa, *Annual Report* 1984, p. 3.

[104] According to Don Carlos Solchaga, Minister of Industry and Energy, Spanish steelmakers were exporting 65 percent of their production by June 1985. *Información Siderúrgica* (June 1985), p. 6. *Metal Bulletin* commented on February 15, 1980 that "Up to now, Spanish steel makers have been unable to adapt supply to home demand, notably because of the strict labor laws which virtually ban short-term layoffs. This meant that exporting was the only solution in the face of crumbling home demand." Luis Guereca, Director-General of Unesid, acknowledged this dilemma in 1985: "The labor market was less flexible in our country than in the EC, and therefore the adaptation of employment to the [steel] crisis only began in 1983, while in the ECSC it had already begun in 1975. As a result, the only adjustment that remained to Spanish steel to face the crisis was to export." *Información Siderúrgica* (December 1985), p. 6. The President of AHV explained in 1985 that "As a consequence of the decline in domestic steel consumption . . . the excess production caused by the necessity to maintain installations at the levels of activity indispensable to support the volume of employment and fixed costs must be directed toward export in conditions which, as we have said, are becoming increasingly more difficult. Interview with don Juan Luis Burgos, in *Información Siderúrgica* (March 1985), p. 4.

[105] *El País*, commenting on the steel crisis in the Basque region (site of AHV's main works) noted on July 29, 1979 that the steel crisis "forced the Basque industry to curtail its production rate, which now amounts to 70 percent of its potential; and this [rate] is due to some amazing figures on exports which, in many instances, have been made at a loss." AHV President Claudio Boada remarked in 1979 that "AHV has been obliged to overcome increasingly strong resistance from governments in the USA and the EC, with selling prices which have been unprofitable but

Spanish steel export prices were generally considerably lower than domestic prices.[106] Price differentiation between the home and foreign markets was made possible by a combination of collusive pricing arrangements, barriers to imports and subsidies for exports.[107] The adoption of the EC pricing system and the abolition of government price ceilings in 1981 enabled Spanish producers to collude to increase domestic price levels. To prevent foreign producers from undercutting these arrangements, the Spanish government imposed a regime of import licensing[108] and minimum import prices.[109] The government also subsidized exporters through a variety of means, including short-term working capital loans for exports[110] and exemption of export sales from indirect taxes.[111]

The high volume of low-priced Spanish steel exports embroiled Spain in a series of bitter disputes with its principal trading partners. During the first years of the steel crisis, Spanish exports to its neighbors in the EC provoked

---

necessary to have access to world markets where competition was intense. [The alternative to unprofitable exports was] not to export, which would oblige us to cut further our capacity with thousands of layoffs and an increase in costs." And Minister of Industry and Energy Don Juan Majó noted that, although Spain had racked up record exports in 1985, they were made at prices which were "little or not at all remunerative." *Información Siderúrgica* (June 1986), p. 5.

[106] *Metal Bulletin* reported on January 31, 1984 that "The domestic market-sharing agreement between the major integrated steel companies meant that Ensidesa was obliged to export as much as 30% of its output last year, at prices lower than those ruling on the Spanish market [Ensidesa President] Lucia said." And on February 7, 1984, *Metal Bulletin* reported that Ensidesa exported 38 percent of its production in 1983. By requiring Ensidesa to export such a large percentage of its products, "the agreement on market sharing has reportedly caused Ensidesa to suffer losses of more than 4 billion pesetas [$27.9 million] in 1983."

[107] Price discrimination between the home market and foreign markets was tacitly acknowledged by the government in Royal Decree 878/1981, Chapter III, Article Ten (c), which provides that exchanges of semifinished products between Spanish producers "will be carried out at international prices when the products are to be exported and at domestic prices when the products are to be used for domestic purposes."

[108] U.S. industry sources charged that the import licensing system was so difficult to understand that it rendered importing uneconomical. Steel Advisory Committee, *State of the U.S. Steel Industry*, September 7, 1984. In 1988, several EC steel producers and Spanish steel importers complained that the government was using delays in issuance of permits for tube imports "as an import barrier." *Metal Bulletin* (February 18, 1988).

[109] Ministry of Economy and Finance, Order of July 7, 1983.

[110] Under the Privileged Circuit Exporter Credit Program (PCECP) the government required commercial banks to make loans to "privileged" sectors for exports (including steel) at below market interest rates. *Carbon Steel Wire Rod from Spain, May 8, 1984.*

[111] Industry figures believed that this tax exemption, the "Desgravación Fiscal a la Exportación," was essential to their export drive. *Información Siderúrgica* (July 1984), p. 20.

widespread protest and trade complaints within the Community.[112]   In April 1978, Spain agreed to limit its exports to the Community to 900 thousand tons per year.[113] The agreement, which was renewed annually, limited the extent to which Spanish producers could dispose of their growing surpluses in the EC. As a result, Spanish exports to other nations began to increase substantially.

Spanish penetration of the U.S. market progressively increased from the onset of the Spanish steel industry crisis until a voluntary restraint agreement was signed in 1985. In 1984, Spanish exports of steel to the United States more than doubled from the previous year, to nearly 1.4 million tons, making Spain the sixth largest provider of steel to the United States market.[114] Between 1982 and 1988, no less than sixteen affirmative findings of dumping and subsidization were made by the U.S. government with respect to Spanish steel exports to the U.S., more than were made against any other steel producing nation during this period. Findings of dumping and subsidization have been made with respect to Spanish structurals, plate, hot and cold-rolled sheet, PC strand, wire rod, stainless wire, oil country tubular goods, galvanized sheets, hot-rolled bars, cold formed bars, stainless CR strip and sheet, stainless bars and stainless wire.[115]

The extent to which Spain's expanded export presence resulted from government intervention, rather than efficiency, was amply demonstrated in 1986 when Spain, now a member of the EC, came under severe pressure from EC steel no longer subject to Spanish tariff restrictions.   Even before January 1, 1986, Spain's formal date of entry into the Community, EC producers were underselling Spanish producers in their home market -- despite complaints that Spain was no longer a "third country," but a member of the EC, and that the low prices being quoted were therefore illegal.[116] In February 1986, the Union of Spanish Steel Producers demanded relief from

---

[112] Spain's export surge prompted the Community to impose antidumping duties on Spanish structurals and sheets and plates. *Official Journal*, L. 37 (February 13, 1979); L. 53 (March 3, 1979).

[113] *Metal Bulletin* (April 25, 1978). Notwithstanding this accord, trade frictions continued. In 1979 the Community imposed antidumping duties on steel sheets, plates and structurals originating in Spain but entering the Community through third countries. *Official Journal*, L.117 (May 12, 1979); L.135 (June 1, 1979). In 1984 the Community accused three Spanish companies of illegally shipping 200 thousand tons of bars (one-fourth of Spain's 1983 quota) into the Community by using third-country intermediaries. The Spanish exporters admitted to fraudulent practices (with the exception of Ensidesa, which denied accusations of involvement in fraudulent sales) and Spanish and EC officials entered into a new accord designed to "prevent the continued invasion of concrete bars from Spain into the EC." *Ya* (February 7, 1984).

[114] American Iron and Steel Institute, *Annual Statistical Reports*.

[115] U.S. Department of Commerce, *Summary of Steel Cases Since January 1, 1981* (as of June 15, 1988).

[116] *Metal Bulletin* (November 1, 1985).

an "invasion" of low-priced steel,[117] and in March the EC Commission agreed to impose quotas on EC steel sales in the Spanish market under the "safeguard" clause of the Treaty of Adhesion.[118] These quotas protected Spanish steelmakers in a number of product lines; however, producers complained that the pressure was shifting to those products as yet uncontrolled.[119] In addition, exports fell drastically in 1986, an eventuality which the Union's Director General blamed in part on the changing tax laws, which eliminated export subsidies.[120] In any event, invocation of the "safeguards" clause did no more than buy the industry some breathing space -- as a member of the EC, Spain would not be allowed to protect its steel industry indefinitely. The experience of 1986 drove home the fact that the Spanish mills were unable to compete unassisted in the world market.

On balance, Spanish government policies cannot be credited with having produced a viable, competitive steel industry, but they have certainly played a direct role in Spain's emergence as a major steel exporter. Government aid -- and promises of more aid -- induced the rapid expansion of Spanish capacity to a level approximately twice that needed to supply Spanish domestic demand. Government labor policies and the politicization of the steel industry virtually precluded major cutbacks, and continuing government aid injections made possible a policy of producing large steel surpluses and exporting them at a loss. Spanish tax incentives for exporters further encouraged exports. In sum, the growing volume of low-priced Spanish steel exports is a reflection of such policies and of the political pressures which underlie them, rather than an indicator of the competitiveness of the Spanish industry.

---

[117] *Metal Bulletin* (February 14, 1986).

[118] Article 379 of the Treaty of Adhesion provides that "Until December 31, 1992, in case of grave and persistent difficulties in a sector of economic activity and of difficulties that could result in the grave alteration of a regional economic situation, a new member state may request the authorization to adopt means of safeguard that permit it to reequilibriate the situation and to adapt the interested sector to the economy of the Common Market."

[119] *Información Siderúrgica* (March 1986), p. 3. Similarly, Spain reinstituted a licensing and quota system for imports from third countries. Ministry of Economy and Finance, *Resolution* of January 23, 1987; *Metal Bulletin* (April 3 and 16, 1987).

[120] Don Luis Guereca, in *Información Siderúrgica* (June 1986), p. 16. Ensidesa remarked that "A major contribution to the reduction in [1986] turnover was the modifications [sic] made to the tax structure on January 1, 1986 with the introduction of VAT and the disappearance among others, of the export tax credits." Ensidesa, *Annual Report 1986*, p. 22. And it lamented the passing of "The constant increase in exports for more than twelve years thanks to a policy of subsidies, in this case basically via tax credits, that has now been cut back to the level of 1981-1983. . . ." *Ibid.*, p. 9. Exporters continued to push for a complete exemption from the VAT. *El País* (July 11, 1987).

Sweden

The experience of the Swedish steel industry dramatically illustrates how massive government intervention in the market can alter international competitive outcomes. By the mid-1970s, the Swedish steel industry had become noncompetitive internationally due to its high costs, poor structure and obsolete equipment. Had the Swedish state simply allowed the market to operate in the years after 1975, most of the nation's steel industry would have disappeared. Instead, regarding such a result as politically and socially unacceptable, a succession of Swedish governments poured subsidies into the industry to cover its mounting operating losses and to finance its acquisition of modern production equipment. The carbon steel industry was nationalized and a thorough government-supervised restructuring effort was undertaken, designed to reduce competition between Swedish firms and to eliminate surplus capacity and employees. By the early 1980s, the Swedish steel industry, which had been on the verge of extinction only a few years before, had emerged as a major exporter, a phenomenon that gained added impetus from several devaluations of the Swedish krona.

Sweden's government in the mid-twentieth century has been dominated by the Social Democratic Party, whose programs have placed a great emphasis on equalizing incomes, maintaining employment, and providing a wide range of public services and social "safety net" programs. The country's "mixed" economy, featuring state ownership of many enterprises, did not evolve by design, but through successive government interventions in crisis sectors whose collapse was considered unacceptable for social, political, or national security reasons.[121] The state is thus tended to be regarded less as an entrepreneur than as an "emergency ward."[122] During the 1970s this process accelerated as a number of major Swedish industries experienced severe financial crises simultaneously, most notably steel, specialty steel, and their principal customer, the shipbuilding industry. Most of the carbon steel and shipbuilding enterprises were nationalized in 1977-78.

While state ownership of Swedish enterprises may have grown more through happenstance than design, once it has acquired control, the government has not hesitated to use such enterprises to achieve a variety of national goals. The operations of many of the state industrial enterprises (including steel) have been directed by a government holding company, the

---

[121] R. Henning, *Staten som Foretagere*; L. Waara, *Den Statliga Foretagssektorns Expansion* (1980).

[122] *Dagens Nyheter* (February 7, 1984). "In Sweden the State has never acquired or established enterprises as a conscious step in a nationalization of industry. . . . In certain cases, it is considerations of employment or regional development policy which have resulted in the State assuming direct responsibility for ownership of an enterprise. This is no new phenomenon. . . . it was not unusual even during the 1920s and 1930s for the State to have to take over enterprises which were insolvent." Per Skold in *Skandinaviska Enskilda Bankens Quarterly Review* (January 1982), p. 6.

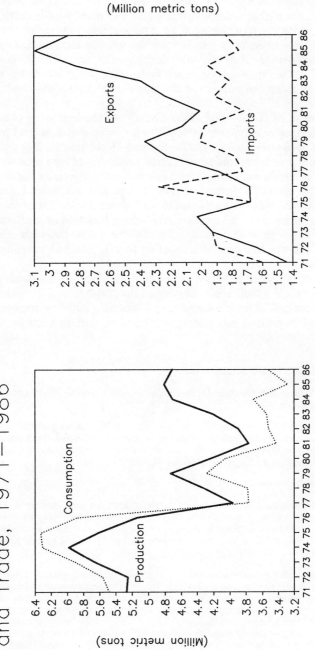

(Million metric tons)

Figure 6-2: Sweden – Steel Production, Consumption and Trade, 1971–1986

Exports

Imports

Consumption

Production

(Million metric tons)

Source: International Iron and Steel Institute, Steel Statistical Yearbook, 1981, 1987. Production and Consumption refer to crude steel; Exports and Imports refer to semi-finished and finished steel.

Statsforetag Group, which was established by the Government in 1970 in order to make the state enterprises more effective instruments of industrial policy. Sweden is distinguishable from virtually all other developed countries "by the extraordinary lengths to which it has gone to hold down unemployment,"[123] and the state holding company's growing role in Swedish industry has reflected a mix of employment and regional development, as well as commercial concerns.[124] The state-owned steel firm, SSAB, for example, has been characterized as an "instrument of the State's social responsibility."[125]

Background of the Swedish Steel Crisis. At the beginning of the 1970s, the Swedish steel industry consisted of three principal carbon steel producers, Norbottens Jarneverk (NJA), Oxelosund and Domnarvet, a large number of specialty steel producers, and several small producers of long products.[126] One carbon steel producer, NJA, was state-owned. Specialty steel products accounted for about 20 percent of Sweden's production volume, but around 50 percent of the total value of output and about 80 percent of the value of Sweden's steel exports. The nation had a long tradition of steelmaking and was richly endowed with iron ore, but by the 1970s the high cost of ore extraction, and the low cost of competing foreign ore had virtually nullified this advantage.[127]

The Swedish steel industry confronted significant structural problems before the world steel crisis developed in 1974-75. The industry was excessively dependent upon a single steel consuming industry, shipbuilding, for its sales, and its product mix was heavily concentrated on a few product lines

---

[123] Barry P. Bosworth and Alice M. Rivlin, *The Swedish Economy* (Washington, D.C.: The Brookings Institution, 1987), p. 6.

[124] Statsforetag has been charged by the State with solving "various political problems such as employment and regional policies" through its operation of nationalized companies. R. Henning, *Staten som Fortagare: En Studie au Statsforetag AB's Mal, Organisation och Effectivitet* (1974) pp. 168-69; *Svenska Dagbladet* (January 29, May 19, 1978).

[125] *Svenska Dagbladet* (May 19, 1978).

[126] Specialty steel was dominated by a group of medium-sized firms, most notably Uddeholm, SKF, Fagersta, Avesta, Nyby, and Sandvik. In addition, about 20 small specialty steel mills were operating in central Sweden, "many of them producing a bucket of one steel quality, others of another, and so on *ad infinitum*. It has increasingly become a kind of general store business." *Dagens Nyheter* (October 7, 1976).

[127] By the mid-1970s, the state-owned iron ore producer, Luossavaara-Kiirunavaara Corporation (LKAB), was in serious financial trouble. The decline in ocean freight rates, and development of lower-cost overseas ore deposits in the developing countries, had eliminated the traditional advantage of Swedish ore -- its proximity to Western Europe. In addition, Swedish ore possessed a high phosphorous content which was less desirable to most steelmakers, and in some cases "no longer worth mining." LKAB also suffered from high production costs and the high cost of rail transportation within Sweden. Sweden was forced to import most of its coking coal. Lulea *Norrskensflamman* (October 12, 1976); *Dagens Nyheter* (February 12, 1977).

designed to meet the needs of ship producers.[128] The specialty steel producers were dangerously dependent upon exports.[129] The steel industry as a whole was suffering from rapidly rising costs; none of the carbon steel producers were large enough to achieve optimum economies of scale in crude steel production, most of them possessed outdated equipment, and their wage levels had risen rapidly in the early 1970s. Virtually all ordinary and specialty steel producers produced their own iron and steel from iron ore, and given the high cost of domestic ore, the industry's ore-based steel production was rapidly losing competitiveness to scrap-based mills.[130]

Probably the weakest single producer was the state-owned NJA, which was unable to operate profitably even in the boom years of 1973 and 1974. In an effort to reverse the firm's sagging fortunes, NJA's management mapped out a long-range strategic plan which dominated public debate over steel through most of the 1970s, but which did nothing to resolve the company's problems. NJA's Lulea steelworks was located at the maritime outlet for much of Sweden's iron ore. As the ore itself became less competitive internationally, NJA sought to develop the capability to process the ore to the semifinished steel stage on a large scale for export to the steel producers of the European Communities -- in effect, developing a new way to maintain an export outlet for Swedish ore. The plan, the controversial "Stalwerk 80" project, called for the establishment of a giant steelworks in Lulea to produce semifinished steel for export.

At the time of its inception, Stalwerk 80 was the most expensive industrial investment ever undertaken in Sweden, and it became a highly charged political issue.[131]   Stalwerk 80 was to be financed by a combination of government equity injections, government regional development grants, and government-guaranteed loans. The net effect of the project, which was ultimately abandoned, was the diversion of NJA's management and financial resources into a commercially unsound, but politically expedient project at a time when many more pressing problems needed to be addressed. The director of the state holding company, Statsforetag, later complained that the

---

[128] In the mid-1970s Sweden possessed the second largest shipbuilding industry in the world after Japan. This industry absorbed about 50 percent of the steel produced by Swedish firms for domestic consumption. *Dagens Nyheter* (May 28, 1984) Ship plate for the Scandinavian market was practically the only product of Granges' Oxelosund works, one of the three principal carbon steel enterprises in Sweden.

[129] In mid-1970s exports accounted for 70-80 percent of Swedish specialty steel producers' sales. *Metal Bulletin Monthly* (August 1978).

[130] *Dagens Nyheter* (April 16, 1977); Tony Hagstrom, *1977 ars Specialstalutredning Del I* (Industri-Departmentet, 1977).

[131] Stalwerk 80 was to be located in Norbotten County -- politically an expedient decision since the county had the highest unemployment rate in Sweden -- but economically questionable since the port was icebound 4-5 months per year. As a result, NJA was required to invest in icebreaking vessels which added an estimated $2.70 to the cost of producing each ton of steel. *Svenska Dagbladet* (September 2, 1976); *Metal Bulletin Monthly* (July 1974).

Stalwerk 80 project was "unrealistic in market and economic terms," and that Parliament had failed to adhere to its commitment to provide Statsforetag with adequate "compensation for commercial sacrifices."[132]

NJA's expansion plans were matched by most of Sweden's other steel producers during the boom years of 1973 and 1974. Investments were made to expand capacity even for products, such as bar, where surplus capacity existed even during the boom in demand.[133] All of the Swedish producers, therefore, were in a vulnerable position when, in late 1974, demand began to fall precipitously in the wake of the First Oil Crisis. Swedish producers' costs, high already, rose still further, not only in absolute terms but in relation to costs in other nations.[134]

The full effect of the global recession was not fully reflected in Swedish domestic steel demand until early 1977. In part this was because of backlogged orders in the steel sector's largest consuming industry, shipbuilding, which continued producing vessels which had been ordered prior to the oil crisis until the first months of 1977.[135] However, a more significant factor was the government's decision to treat the steel crisis as a cyclical problem; it launched a major program to encourage a continued high level of steel output, with the surplus production placed in government subsidized stockpiles to be liquidated when the expected business upturn occurred in 1977.[136] In addition, through mid-1978, the Swedish government paid 75

---

[132] *Skandinaviska Enskilda Banken Quarterly Review* (January 1982). Statsforetag was unenthusiastic about the project, the impetus for which came from Parliament and from NJA management. As the unfeasability of the original concept became more apparent, the plans for the new works were modified. Joint ventures would be established in Sweden (one of them with Krupp) to process the semifinished steel into heavy sections and sheet. Krupp pulled out of this arrangement and "profound disagreement" was reported between Statsforetag and NJA. In 1976 NJA's Managing Director resigned because of "lack of support" from Statsforetag for the project. *Metal Bulletin* (August 1978).

[133] *Dagens Nyheter* (April 16, 1977).

[134] Between 1974 and 1976 Swedish industry's costs rose "an alarming 40%." (*Metal Bulletin Monthly* (August 1978). The Swedish "cost crisis" was the subject of extensive comment and debate in Sweden in the 1970s. See, *e.g., Svenska Dagbladet* (February 2, 1977; January 29, 1978). The Stockholm *Expressen* commented on February 4, 1977 that "What happened, however -- and this we cannot get away from -- was that the costs of Swedish enterprises suddenly, beginning in 1975, increased very rapidly, while at the same time the costs of our competitors increased less rapidly than formerly."

[135] Once ordered, production of Swedish ships took between one and three years to complete. C. Himiltor, *Public Subsidies to Industry: The Case of Sweden and its Shipbuilding Industry* (World Bank Staff Working Paper No. 566, 1983), p. 9.

[136] As a result of this policy, "which remained in effect from mid-1975 to mid-1977 . . . a large proportion of Sweden's production of finished steel products was stockpiled during the crisis." *EFTA Bulletin* (July-September 1982). Several other basic industries also benefited from the stockpiling subsidies. The *Neue Zürcher Zeitung* commented on September 11-12, 1977 that "A total of 1.2 billion kroner [$267.8 million] in state funds have been made available to the companies, which build up their inventories instead of reducing production. This stimulating

percent of the wages of redundant workers who were kept on the payroll of steel companies.[137]

Despite reasonably stable domestic steel demand in 1975 and 1976, however, the Swedish industry's condition deteriorated rapidly. Most Swedish producers were heavily dependent upon exports, and steel export demand and prices were severely depressed. That fact, coupled with their rapidly escalating costs, threw most producers into a loss position in 1975 and 1976. Moreover, by early 1977, it became clear that the anticipated business upturn was not going to occur -- in fact, with shipbuilding activity falling as the last backlogged orders were filled, domestic steel demand began falling dramatically.[138] By this time the steel industry possessed "enormous" stockpiles of steel as a result of the government's countercyclical program, and in late 1977, the producers began unloading the surplus in export markets at prices which one producer, NJA, admitted were "substantially cut."[139]

NJA, financially weak even in the best of times, was on the verge of insolvency by the end of 1975, and its losses were so heavy that they were placing a strain on Statsforetag, the state holding company.[140] In 1976 NJA suffered a "staggering" loss of $179.9 million,[141] and its future prospects were grim.[142] Granges, the private company which operated the Oxelosund

---

injection began to take effect in mid-1975, when the inventories from the previous year's boom were emptied. The natural inventory buildup expected in this situation was augmented by the artificial to such an extent that losses will occur in the clearance necessary in the end. . . ."

[137] E. Hook, "Steel and the State in Sweden," in 51 *Annals of Public and Cooperative Economy* 504 (December 1980).

[138] In Sweden, as in Japan, the steel crisis of the mid-1970s was, to an unusually significant degree, linked to the parallel crisis of the shipyards. See E. Hood, "Cyclical and Structural Problems in the Swedish Steel Industry" in *Skandinaviska Enskilda Bankens Quarterly Review* (March-April 1978).

[139] In mid-1977 the industry held stockpiles of steel valued at $321.2 million. NJA alone held 200,000 tons. *Metal Bulletin* (September 16, 1977). Prime Minister Falldin commented in 1977 that "It is true that many industries have large stocks. We have contributed to the policies that have increased the stocks. . . . We should not sell off the stocks in any kind of panic." *Expressen* (February 4, 1977).

[140] Statsforetag estimated in mid-1976 that it would suffer a decline in net profitability of $137.7 million between 1975 and 1976, principally as a result of NJA's losses. *Svenska Dagbladet* reported on June 16, 1976 that "It is the collapse in the state of the steel market which is affecting Statsforetag above all. And it is NJA above all which is bearing the brunt. . . . The state-owned steel plant in Norrbotten is threatened this year with losses which are expected to be greater than 1975's record: 180 million kronor [$41.3 million]."

[141] *Financial Times* (March 18, 1977).

[142] In late 1976, the Managing Director of Statsforetag, Per Skold, delivered a report to the Minister of Industry of NJA's condition: "As Skold's report unfolded, the Industry Minister sank deeper and deeper into his office chair. According to substantiated forecasts, unless urgent measures were taken, NJA's losses in the coming two years would be in the billions." Bengt Ericson, *Huggsexan* (Stockholm: LT, 1979).

steelworks, was in equally desperate condition by the end of 1976 -- its losses for the year, $64.3 million, were far higher than expected, and by the beginning of 1977, with shipyard orders falling rapidly, the firm was on the verge of insolvency.[143] Similarly, by late 1976 the Swedish specialty steelworks were "threatened with extinction."[144]

Throughout 1976 and early 1977, a heated debate raged in Sweden over what was to be done about the deterioration of the steel industry, although the continuing controversy over NJA's Stahlwerk 80 project tended to deflect attention from more basic underlying problems.[145] The government ordered two major studies of the steel industry by commissions headed by Lars Nabseth and Tony Hagstrom, which investigated the carbon steel and specialty steel sectors, respectively.[146] Before either study was completed, however, the ruling Socialist party was ousted by a center-right coalition headed by Thorbjorn Falldin, bringing to power Sweden's first non-socialist government in 44 years. The new government inherited a disastrous economic situation. The shipbuilding sector was on the brink of insolvency, and other steel-consuming industries, such as engineering, were also severely depressed.[147] The government confronted the prospect of the simultaneous collapse of most of Sweden's shipbuilding, steel, and specialty steel industries, with the loss of

---

[143] "Oxelosund's ironworks now seemed to threaten the existence of the entire Granges concern. In a letter to the Government dated February 2, 1977, Ian Wachmeister had explained the situation: 50% of the customers of the ironworks consisted of shipyards. The crisis in the dockyards had now resulted in some heavy reduction of the tonnage of the sheet metal for ships and no new customers were in sight. Certain crisis measures have been taken already, e.g., employment and vacation freezes during four weeks of July. But that would not go far enough: during the first six months of the enterprise estimated gross losses to be 304 million kronas [$67.8 million] per week." Ericson, *Huggsexan*.

[144] *Dagens Nyheter* reported on October 7, 1976 that "Prices were forced down and profits gradually approached zero, where they now remain for many companies. Head of the Office of Iron Affairs, Eric Hook, who is now directing coordination within the industry, says: "Approximately 8 billion kronor [$1.8 billion] are invested in specialty steel and the normal liquidation payment on this amount ought to be 800 million kronor [$183.6 million]. However, after write-offs, the total yield is not far from zero."

[145] The government approved a massive injection of capital -- $344.4 million -- into Statsforetag to finance Stalwerk 80; Granges, feeling that because of the project it was being left out of the development of the carbon steel sector, reportedly made a direct approach to the minister for industry, Rune Johansson, offering the government participation in its Oxelosund steelworks in addition to its mining and railway interests to assist in rationalization.

[146] *Dagens Nyheter* (March 7, 1977).

[147] *Svenska Dagbladet* (September 23, 1976; April 17, 1977).

tens of thousands of jobs and a severe impact on regional economies throughout Sweden.[148]

The Falldin government quickly made it clear that despite its center-right political orientation, it intended to intervene extensively in Sweden's troubled heavy industrial sectors, assuming ownership, where necessary, so "that the future becomes secure for essential basic industries."[149] In steel, soon after taking office, the government extended a series of stopgap subsidies to prevent the collapse of individual steelworks until the government could devise a more comprehensive rescue plan. A massive $401.6 million infusion was approved to keep NJA's steel enterprise alive.[150] In March 1977 the government extended $7.1 million to Uddeholm's Storfors steelworks; the Minister of Industry stated that "with this decision the government wishes to guard the Storfors division's opportunity to survive."[151] In the spring of 1977, the Falldin government began implementing a series of sweeping relief measures to salvage the collapsing steel, specialty steel, and shipbuilding industries.

Shipbuilding. The condition of the steel industry's principal consuming sector, shipbuilding, was most critical and relief for this industry was the government's first priority. The industry had engaged in what, retrospectively, had proven to be an extremely ill-advised expansion effort in the 1960s and early 1970s; it now confronted the prospect that it would have virtually no

---

[148] *Expressen* commented on February 4, 1977 that "Thirty, forty, fifty thousand persons in Sweden are threatened by loss of jobs or furloughing. Enterprise after enterprise gives warning of curtailment of production or shutdowns. Fifty thousand persons, a whole city. A spirit of hopelessness is spreading in the economy. Is it possible at all to do anything about this increasing stream of bad news?"

[149] Minister of Industry Nils Asling in *Dagens Nyheter* (April 20, 1977). Prime Minister Falldin said in early 1977 that "In industries having problems . . . the state should be prepared to intervene." *Expressen* (February 5, 1977.) Ironically, the three parties which formed the coalition had for years -- as opposition parties -- expressed their "extremely dubious" view of state ownership of enterprises. Looking back on the 1977-78 period, Social Democratic Minister of Industry Reine Carlsson commented on how "unbelievable it was that a number of shipyards and steel companies, among others, were added to the state companies during the nonsocialist period." *Svenska Dagbladet* (April 2, 1983).

[150] The NJA Stalwerk 80 project had been severely criticized in the election campaign, and the Falldin government shelved it indefinitely. *The Economist* (April 25, 1977).

[151] *Dagens Nyheter* (March 7, 1977). *Dagens Nyheter* commented with respect to Uddenholm's Storfors pipe mill and its Degerfors stainless plate works on March 6, 1977, "If one demands normal profits, none of these industries could probably be justified. . . . The capital once invested in these industries can from the point of view of the stockholders be regarded as lost." Uddeholm ultimately received 600 million Kronor [$133.9 million] in government "contingency loans" in the years 1977-78. Ericson, *Huggsexan*, Appendix.

orders after 1977.[152] To the extent ships were being sold at all on the world
market, they were being ordered from countries other than Sweden.[153] The
shipyards were undertaking massive cutbacks of production capacity and
employment, but there was no guarantee that such measures would save
them.[154] Moreover, the collapse of the shipbuilding industry would pull down
with it large segments of the steel and other supplier industries.[155]

By early 1977 the State had already acquired sole or partial ownership of
eight of Sweden's thirteen major shipyards, reflecting a succession of
acquisitions of failing enterprises.[156] The government now separated these
enterprises from Statsforetag, the state holding company, and merged them
into a new state entity, Statsvarv AB. This entity received an unprecedented
volume of government subsidy funds designed to tide the industry over a 3-
year period, pending a restructuring program and phased reduction of capacity
and manpower levels. *Svenska Dagbladet* reported on April 19, 1977 that

> *The 3 years of grace won't be cheap. In order to finance the new
> shipyard concern, the state will issue shares for 900 million kronor
> [$200.8 million]. . . . In order to strengthen solidity and liquidity,
> Statsvarv will also get a stockholder subsidy of 375 million [$83.6
> million] and 800 million [$178.5 million] to cover the losses in
> inventory production 1977-78. The latter subsidy will take the form of
> value guarantees. It can be considered doubtful that the money will
> be enough to clear up [ship producer] Gotaverker's books especially.
> . . . All in all shipyard subsidies will cost the state about 3 billion*

---

[152] *Dagens Nyheter* commented on May 24, 1984 that "Construction of a ship provides jobs
in everything from steel mills to cabinetmaking shops and the electronics industry. . . . In Sweden,
the government contributed to the building of the Uddevalta Shipyard's giant dock, Kockums
expanded to be able to build a supertanker every 40 days . . . giant gantry cranes went up to
handle the heavy lifting that would be required by future super construction jobs. The jobs
never came. The oil crisis made the overcapacity noticeable in a flash. Demand for shipping
dropped, and fjords and protected harbors were soon filled with idle ships."

[153] *The Economist* (April 23, 1977). Sweden produced comparatively unsophisticated types
of ships. Countries like Japan, Taiwan and Korea could build ships of equal or greater
sophistication at a much lower cost. World Bank Staff Working Paper No. 566, p. 10. *Svenska
Dagbladet* commented on January 19, 1978 that "There is no future in welding plate together to
make standard boats. Other countries can do it cheaper."

[154] *Dagens Nyheter* (October 30, 1976).

[155] Although the shipbuilding sector was ultimately saved from complete shutdown, the steel
producers were severely affected by the fall in demand from the shipyards. Dagens Nyheter
recalled on May 28, 1984 that "the demand for steel fell because shipyards were ordering less ship
plate, and the steel industry, which had expanded to meet the expected demand, entered a slump.
It asked for, and got, government subsidies." *Dagens Nyheter* commented on October 30, 1976
that "Those most severely affected by such cutbacks [in shipbuilding] are the supplying
enterprises. These are large enterprises, such as NJA (vessel sections), Oxelosund Iron Works
(metal plate). . . ."

[156] *Svenska Dagbladet* (April 18, 1977); *Dagens Nyheter* (March 19, 1977).

kronor [$669.4 million] up to and including 1979. According to one study made by Statsvarv it would cost a sum equally as great to cover losses in the next 5-year period.

In addition to such outright subsidies, the government set aside another massive sum to finance "inventory production" -- production of ships for which there was no present demand or outstanding order. The government offered $446.2 million in loan guarantees to pay the costs to the shipyards of such vessels, which otherwise would never have been built. The state also sought to stimulate actual demand for ships by providing that Swedish shippers who ordered ships between July 1977 and June 1978 would receive government-guaranteed loans for up to 70 percent the contract price.[157] Finally, another 4.85 billion kronor ($1.1 billion) in government loan guarantees were made available to the shipyards -- an important benefit since the yards had long since ceased to be reasonable credit risks. Cumulative state subsidies for the years 1977-79 were estimated by one Swedish source at $2.3 billion.[158]

The bailout of shipbuilding not only preserved the steel industry's principal source of domestic demand, but also provided massive subsidies for the construction of ships for which no customers existed -- in effect creating a larger outlet, through state funding, for Swedish steel. Metal Bulletin reported on April 26, 1977, following announcement of the subsidies, that

Swedish government measures last week to aid the shipbuilding industry will enable sales of ship plate sections, and other steel products to increase somewhat.

Carbon Steel. After shipbuilding, carbon steel was the next crisis industry on the government's list. The Nabseth report on the ordinary steel industry -- commissioned under the prior government -- was released in April 1977, and had a powerful influence on subsequent government industrial policy in this

---

[157] *Svenska Dagbladet* (March 19, 1977). This measure proved extremely costly over the long run. *Helsingin Sanonmat*, a Finnish newspaper, reported on March 15, 1983 that "Statsvarv is left with ships on its hands that have either been stored due to a lack of orders or otherwise remain unpaid for and whose value has tumbled. The value of about 30 ships has dropped by over a billion kronor [$223.1 million] since they were built and, in light of the prospects for selling them, what they have on the shelves has primarily scrap value."

[158] *Svenska Dagbladet* (April 18, 1977). Svenska Dagbladet observed on February 22, 1977, the creation of the "Statsvarv AB colossus" would require "such billion-crown spending that the Stahlwerk 80 project will be over shadowed." The World Bank subsequently estimated that in the 1978-79 fiscal year, the volume of government subsidies flowing ot this industry was 52 percent higher than the industry's total value added.

sector.[159] Nabseth offered an extraordinarily pessimistic view of the industry's condition and prospects. He indicated that because of the glut of cheap steel in the international market, Sweden would be required to find an outlet for its non-special steel primarily within the Nordic countries. However, steel demand in this region could not be expected to grow significantly in the future, leaving Sweden with a substantial overhang of surplus capacity, much of it tied up in obsolete, high-cost facilities.[160] He concluded that

> to maintain the present level of employment in the sector would require permanent subsidization of the ordinary steel sector in view of the limited scope available for expansion.[161]

Nabseth's study recommended a number of major reforms, most notably the consolidation of facilities within the industry around the most productive plants, and closure or scaling back of the remainder, with the objective of improving scale economies and making the industry competitive in the domestic market in a few product areas of particular concentration.[162] Steelmaking capacity was to be reduced to 3.2 million metric tons per year and the work force cut by 25 percent by 1985.[163] The release of the Nabseth report triggered an intensive series of negotiations between the government, the steel producers, and the steelworkers' unions; Nabseth himself was appointed the government's "chief negotiator." Given the report's emphasis on rationalization and consolidation of facilities, and the desperate financial condition of the producers, it was evident that the carbon steel producers would have to be merged, with the state holding at least a part interest in the consolidated entity.[164]

---

[159] Lars Nabseth, *Handel Stalindustrin infor 1980-talet* (1977). Although the Nabseth study had been initiated by the Social Democrats, its conclusions -- calling for rationalization of the industry, plant closures and job cuts -- were strongly supported by the center-right coalition's Minister of Industry, Nels Asling. The study made possible the development of a consensus on the measures needed; Dr. Nabseth was the head of the Swedish Federation of Industry, and the study was generally in line with what the steel companies themselves envisioned as potential rationalization moves. *Dagens Nyheter* (April 16, 1977); Ericson, *Huggsexan*.

[160] The principal conclusions Nabseth report are summarized in SSAB's *Annual Report* 1978 and *Metal Bulletin Monthly* (August, 1978).

[161] *Metal Bulletin Monthly* (August 1978), p. 19.

[162] Specifically, Nabseth recommended shutting down all of Sweden's ore-based crude steel plants except the NJA plant at Lulea and Granges' works at Oxelosund. Flat-rolled steel production was to be limited to two locations, Domnarvet and Oxelosund, and Lulea would be the only site of heavy section production. Industry output should be diversified away from shipbuilding-oriented products to product lines needed by the automobile, machine, building, and engineering industries. Nabseth, *Handel Stalindustrin*.

[163] *Metal Bulletin Monthly* (August 1978), p. 19.

[164] Ericson, *Huggsexan*.

Protracted bickering followed over the value to be placed on the private steelmakers' assets which were to be transferred to the new entity, highlighting the fact that carbon steelmaking was no longer regarded as an economically viable proposition in Sweden -- the assets had little real market value.[165] The state holding company's representative complained that Stora was asking much too high a price for steelmaking facilities "which nobody would have given anything for under normal circumstances."[166] Granges complained, however, that if it accepted the state's proposed purchase price, it would have to write off facilities with a book value of 1.2 billion kronor [$267.8 million], and would be "forced to liquidate immediately."[167] Moreover, the private firms became extremely concerned when the state disclosed that it expected them to retain a partial ownership interest in the new state enterprise.[168] The companies subsequently insisted that if they were to retain an interest, the government should be the majority owner, and the firm would have to be structured to protect the companies against the potential for ill-conceived, government-initiated projects -- "a new Stalwerk 80 and the like."[169]

Agreement was finally reached in the fall of 1977. A new company would be formed, Svensk Staal AB (SSAB), which would acquire control of the steelmaking facilities of NJA, Granges and Stora, as well as the latter two firms' ore mining and railroad operations. The state would own 50% of the equity stock; Granges and Stora would each hold a 25% interest, which they agreed to retain for at least five years. Each 25% share was valued at $156.7 million; Granges, Stora and the state holding company received their share in return for the assets of their steelworks and other facilities, and the state

---

[165] "Granges and Stora were overjoyed [at the prospect of state takeover] -- all operations were clearly losing concerns with little possibility for survival. At the same time, the companies wished to appear businesslike in this situation. Therefore the enterprises demanded an unbiased appraisal of the facilities, something Nabseth agreed to.... Two consultants were called in.... The task was to calculate after-acquisition value of the steel industry with allowances for depreciation and obsolescence -- i.e., what would it cost to build up a new adequate industry (A clearly theoretical question -- nobody could think of such a silly idea)." Ericson, *Huggsexan*. This exercise proved futile -- the two consultants produced inconsistent estimates -- and Stora and Granges began negotiating directly with the government on the sale price.

[166] *Ibid.*

[167] *Ibid.*

[168] When Stora's representative heard this proposal, "He became very excited. "We cannot discuss the organization here, it is completely impossible to continue," he exclaimed, and left the room." *Ibid.*

[169] Ericson, *Huggsexan*. Stora and Granges wanted to retain the right to leave the joint enterprise in the event of a disagreement with the government. The Ministry of Industry proposed that Stora and Granges might be given the right to compensation "based upon actual losses caused by decisions which would be in conflict with the economic criteria of the enterprise." This proposal, however, provoked a furor; Statsforetag "worked itself up into a rage over the Industry Ministry's questioning of its ability to make economically correct decisions for the enterprise." *Ibid.*

acquired another 25% share through a $156.1 million government equity injection into SSAB. The state paid added compensation to Granges of $76.5 million.[170] In addition, the state agreed to provide SSAB with so-called "conditional" or "reconstruction" loans, designed to cover operating losses ($401.6 million), and "structural" loans ($290 million) for new investments.[171]

Although the Swedish government was committing, at the outset, over $892.5 million to the new state steel enterprise, there was little pretense that this represented a commercially viable investment.[172] In fact, a projected balance sheet for SSAB's first five years of operations showed that it was not expected to show a profit until 1982, and even this would occur only under the most optimistic assumptions. However, the primary purpose of the state's investment in SSAB was not commercial; the government sought to maintain domestic employment levels and preserve regional economies. Thus, it was

> Agreed that insofar as the government requires SSAB to pursue policies against its commercial judgment for social reasons, the state will pay.[173]

Specialty Steel. Specialty steel represented a third crisis sector. Fragmented among over 20 independent firms, this industry suffered from facility and employee redundancies, financial weakness, and inadequate scale economies.[174] The center-right coalition, having presided over the

---

[170] Granges needed additional funds to avoid bankruptcy if assets with a book value of $267.8 million were sold to SSAB for stock valued at $156.1 million. Thus the government agreed to remove a small railroad subsidiary of Granges, TGOC, a chronic money-losing concern, from the original pool of Granges assets valued at $156.1 million being transferred to SSAB. TGOC was then sold to the government separately for an additional $75.8 million.The Minister of Industry "groaned audibly" the first time he heard of this proposed arrangement. "They will be paid twice for the same item. Is there really no other solution?" Ericson, *Huggsexan*. See also *Certain Carbon Steel Products from Sweden.*

[171] *Ibid.* The "conditional" or "reconstruction" loans were interest free for three years, after which interest of 9.5 percent was charged. The "structural loans" were interest free for three years, after which interest of 5 percent would be charged. SSAB *Annual Report*, 1978; *Certain Carbon Steel Products from Sweden*, 50 F.R. 3375, August 19, 1985 (final).

[172] SSAB's vice president in charge of the Oxelosund steelworks said in 1978 that "SSAB will lose a lot of money in 1978 and will not be making profits for many years." *The Engineer* (June 22, 1978). The opposition Social Democrats, citing SSAB's projected massive losses, complained in Parliament that the agreement establishing SSAB was "in conflict with sound business principles, and that the government had not looked after, in a satisfactory manner, the interests of the State in the agreement. . . . The taxpayers would carry the entire burden of the necessary financial reconstruction, while the private shareholders would receive full compensation. . . . The property contributed [*e.g.*, the steelworks] had a negative investment value, and therefore the value set at 700 million kronor [$154.9 million] was in conflict with sound business principles." *Riksdagens Arsbok 1977-78*, pp. 392-393.

[173] *Metal Bulletin Monthly* (August 1978).

[174] *Dagens Nyheter* (February 8, March 6, 1977).

nationalization of shipbuilding and carbon steel, had no desire to take over a third major industrial sector, and sought instead to promote the consolidation of the industry, offering subsidies as an incentive for mergers.[175] While some consolidations took place, for the most part the initial restructuring effort foundered because of the spirit of independence prevailing in the industry and the government's unwillingness to become a shareholder in any merged entity.[176] The impasse was papered over temporarily through the late 1970s by disbursements of government loans to ailing specialty steel firms, who were "screaming for state support."[177]

Thus in the two year period 1977-78 the Swedish state had become sole owner of the nation's shipbuilding and ordinary steel sectors (with the exception of several small barmaking firms) and had embarked on a major effort to guide the restructuring of specialty steel.[178] In the years after 1978, the full implications of this expansion of state power would be manifested as the government deployed massive resources to restore its crisis sectors.

Restructuring. In the years between 1978 and 1984 the Swedish steel industry underwent a dramatic transformation. Obsolete plants were shut down, the work force was gradually cut back, and intensive investments in state-of-the-art production equipment were undertaken. Net steelmaking capacity was reduced, but the efficiency and productivity of the remaining facilities was upgraded. By 1984 Sweden had a continuous casting ratio of 80 percent. The Swedish steelmakers, who in the 1970s had found they were rapidly losing competitiveness internationally, were becoming embroiled in an increasing number of trade disputes because of their aggressive behavior in export markets. A Swedish analyst commented in 1982 that "few periods, relatively speaking, are likely to present a more radical transformation of the industry than that which has occurred since 1974/75." [179]

The sweeping overhaul of the Swedish steel industry could not have even begun, much less been carried out, without massive state support. The government provided survival aid to SSAB and other firms to enable them to continue operations despite heavy losses. Additional government funds were

---

[175] A $334.7 million "Special Steel Restructuring Fund" was established by the government as an inducement to consolidation; "it was clearly stated that money was to go to those who wanted to make new efforts and cooperate." *Dagens Nyheter* (March 4, 1978); *Metal Bulletin Monthly* (August 1978).

[176] *Metal Bulletin Monthly* (August 1978).

[177] *Dagens Nyheter* (March 4, 1978); *Metal Bulletin* (February 21, 1978; June 5, 12, 22, 1979).

[178] The Oslo *Aftenposten* commented on December 17, 1978 that "The concentration of power in the Swedish economy has continued at undiminished strength during the most serious crisis since the 1930s. . . . It is the State that through the takeover of enterprises such as Svenskvarv and Svensk Stal AB [SSAB] and others, and hit by the crisis, has increased its ownership share and thereby strengthened its control of the economy."

[179] Erik Hook in *EFTA Bulletin* (July-September 1982).

used to help finance investments in modernization. Finally, the government sought to induce a series of consolidations and rationalization measures that served to reduce competition in the domestic market between Swedish firms but to enhance Swedish competitiveness in international markets.

Survival Aid. Perhaps the most important aspect of the restructuring effort was simply to keep Sweden's steelmaking enterprises from collapsing pending implementation of longer term reforms, which required major government subsidy injections, most notably for SSAB. SSAB's annual reports show that the firm suffered a cumulative net loss of over $149.8 million between 1978 and 1983, including a massive $142.4 million loss in 1981 alone (table 6-2). These reported results understate the severity of SSAB's losses since they count as revenue to the company some of the subsidy grants made by the state.[180]

These losses, however, were more than made good by periodic new injections of state aid. The $398.3 million in government "reconstruction loans" authorized in 1978 had been designed to cover SSAB's operating losses; however, by 1981 this fund had been exhausted, and SSAB's management appealed to its owners -- Stora, Granges and the State -- for new capital. Minister of Industry Asling put together a $908.4 million aid package to cover SSAB's losses and support its "ambitious capital spending plans."[181] The government also undertook to induce the private co-owners, Stora and Granges, to match its own investments; Granges was effectively forced to contribute $74 million in new equity to SSAB,[182] but Stora took this opportunity to abandon its stake, selling its entire 25% interest to Granges for

---

[180] In addition, the company realized substantial interest cost reductions when in 1981 and 1982 the government converted some of its outstanding loans to SSAB into additional equity -- a move which, in all probability, no commercial investor would have taken, given SSAB's poor financial condition. If the subsidy and interest savings are removed from SSAB's results, a better picture of its actual results can be obtained -- the company probably lost over $187.2 million in the years 1978-83, with an annual average negative return on investment of nearly 6 percent.

[181] *Metal Bulletin* (July 31, 1981). In addition, in 1979 the Swedish Parliament voted to authorize an additional $174.9 million in "structural loans" to SSAB for new investments and working capital. *Ibid.*

[182] Minister Asling blocked a proposed government procurement deal between Granges and the state electricity company "until the private shareholder in SSAB releases funds for the steelmaker." *Metal Bulletin* (July 31, 1981) The arrangement was sweetened for Granges, however, by legislation in which the government agreed to pay Granges $172.8 million for its shares in SSAB in 1991, if Granges decided to sell them -- in effect guaranteeing Granges a 9.5 percent annual return on its investment. *Certain Carbon Steel Products from Sweden* (1985).

a nominal $.20, who promptly resold this 25% block of equity to the State, also for $.20.[183]

Table 6-2. SSAB Financial Results, 1978-1983
(million U.S. dollars)

	SSAB * Reported Profit (Loss)	State Grants	State Debt-Equity Conversion Amount	Interest Savings	SSAB Profit(Loss) Minus Grants and Interest Savings
1978	(18.6)	12.6			(31.2)
1979	(6.9)	6.3			(13.2)
1980	(35.2)	2.9			(38.1)
1981	(144.3)	4.5	110	5.5	(154.2)
1982	23.4	3.5		4.4	15.6
1983	3.9	3.5		3.6	(3.1)

* Bottom line financial result reported in SSAB financial statement.
Source: SSAB *Annual Reports*
Converted to U.S. dollars at average annual exchange rate given by International Monetary Fund.
Conversion: 1978: 4.5; 1979: 4.3; 1980: 4.2; 1981: 5.0; 1982: 6.3; 1983: 7.7

The Swedish government, now 75 percent owner of SSAB, proceeded to inject $108.6 million in new equity into the company -- in effect, purchasing additional shares of the stock to which Stora had assigned an investment value of zero -- and converted $122.7 million in outstanding debt to still further equity.[184] These new state investments were made at a time when "knowledge of the prospects of SSAB indicated that a reasonable return could not be

---

[183] *Metal Bulletin* (August 25, October 6, 1981). As part of the settlement the government provided that Granges could sell hydroelectric power to the State Power Board. Granges remained a reluctant partner in SSAB; in 1981 it was "actively working to withdraw as soon as possible from responsibility for Swedish Steel [SSAB]." *EFTA Bulletin* (April-May, 1981) *Metal Bulletin* (October 6, 1981); SSAB *Annual Report*, 1981.

[184] SSAB indicated in its 1982 *Annual Report* (p. 9) that the new government equity was intended to cover that portion of SSAB's operating losses that had not been met by the $398.3 million reconstruction loan. Additional government loans to SSAB were authorized. SSAB reported in its 1982 *Annual Report* that by the end of that year the government had committed $875.4 million to the enterprise since its inception in the form of new equity and loans. The breakdown was equity capital, $290.5 million; reconstruction loans, $316.9 million; structural loans, $241 million; and debenture loans, $23.9 million. SSAB *Annual Report* 1982, p. 9.

expected on any new equity investment in SSAB."[185] In addition to the sums expended on SSAB, the specialty steel sector also received a substantial volume of state financial aid in the years after 1977.[186]

Such massive aid infusions reflected the politicization of economic decisionmaking which followed from the government's increasing involvement in the affairs of industry.[187] The operating subsidies to SSAB (and to the shipbuilding sector) were a way to maintain employment; in effect, they were adjuncts to Sweden's social welfare system, which was seen as inadequate to deal with the crisis in the national economy which developed after 1976. Subsidies to steel in the period 1977-79 corresponded to about 40 percent of the industry's wage bill.[188] A subsequent Ministry of Industry attributed such subsidies to an "unholy alliance of labor, business and local authorities,"[189] and complained that in recent years Sweden's "industrial policy had been synonymous with a defensive subsidization policy."[190]

Although SSAB reported net profits in 1982, 1983 and 1984, the margins were extremely narrow; its president indicated that SSAB's profits were "way below the level needed for long term survival . . . and below the profit required to accumulate capital for long term investment."[191] SSAB suffered a net loss in 1985, and its future prospects remain uncertain.[192]

Modernization. Restructuring between 1978 and 1984 involved a sweeping modernization of Swedish steelmaking facilities. A number of obsolete facilities were shut down completely, and extensive investments were undertaken to upgrade efficiency and productivity at the remaining sites. All

---

[185] *Certain Carbon Steel Products from Sweden* (1985).

[186] One source estimated in 1982 that the specialty steel industry had received "about 2 billion kronor [$318.3 million] from the State" since 1977. *Svenska Dagbladet* (November 5, 1982).

[187] *Svenska Dagbladet*, looking back on this period, commented on February 8, 1984 that over two-thirds of all government financial aid had "gone to crisis-ridden industries, especially shipbuilding and steel: 'Injections of capital, performed at the emergency ward, were sometimes preceded by pressure that verged on political blackmail.' [Minister of Industry] Nils G. Asling wrote in his book that 'Business leaders would approach the government, followed by the trade union chairman, often by the Social Democratic head of the local government, and in many cases by the region's representative in parliament and the governor of the county.' During the years that billions were pumped into unprofitable companies, the trade unions, the Social Democratic opposition, and local public opinion agreed that the government always had to do more."

[188] Bo Carlsson, "Industrial Subsidies in Sweden: Macro-Economic Effects and an International Comparison," in 32 *Journal of Industrial Economics 1* (September 1983).

[189] *Dagens Nyheter* (February 7, 1984).

[190] *Svenska Dagbladet* (March 6, 1984).

[191] *Metal Bulletin* (August 31, 1984).

[192] SSAB *Annual Report* 1985.

of Sweden's open hearth furnaces were closed.[193] Net Swedish steelmaking capacity shrank from 7.3 million tons per year in 1975 to 5.3 million tons in 1984. Sweden's continuous casting ratio increased from 25 percent in 1975 to 80 percent in 1984.

The merger of all of Sweden's integrated steel producers into one entity, SSAB, facilitated this process. The merged firm's resources could be concentrated on specific, non-duplicative investments, with a "division of labor" between the three principal sites. All of SSAB's scrap based production was concentrated at one site, Domnarvet, which was equipped with continuous casters, and the site's blast furnaces were shut down. Domnarvet specialized in flat-rolled sheet and strip and it received state-of-the-art hot and cold-rolling equipment -- SSAB's so-called "Band 82" project.[194] Lulea and Oxelosund continued ore-based production, were equipped with continuous casters and specialized in sections and plate, respectively.[195]

SSAB's new facilities were largely financed through government aid. Its principal source of investment funding was the government's so-called "structural" loans, which were interest free for three years, then bore a relatively low interest rate.[196] In addition to the structural loans, some "reconstruction loans" -- normally designed to cover operating losses -- were also granted to finance SSAB investments in new plant and equipment, with a three year grace period.[197] By 1982 the Riksdag had authorized $318.3 million in "structural" loans alone to the state steel enterprise; the total cost of SSAB's restructuring investments was estimated at about $391.2 million as of 1984.[198] The government also funded efforts to encourage Swedish steelmakers to shift their emphasis toward more sophisticated, high value added steel products and production techniques, supporting a variety of

---

[193] Between 1975 and 1981, eleven open hearth furnaces were shut down, and crude steel production was phased out altogether at four locations. In addition, a number of bar and section mills, cold-rolling mills, and sintering and pelletizing plants were closed. At the same time, between 1978 and 1981 seven modern rolling mills, two new electric furnaces, five continuous casting plants, and three modern AOD and LD converters became operational. *EFTA Bulletin* (July-September 1982).

[194] "Band 82" featured the installation of a strip mill capable of producing 450 thousand tons of hot strip and 650 thousand tons of cold rolled strip per year. The cost to SSAB was $315.9 million. *EFTA Bulletin* (April-May 1981); *Metal Bulletin Monthly* (January 1984).

[195] *Metal Bulletin Monthly* (January 1984).

[196] SSAB *Annual Report* 1978, p. 5. In 1981 $108.6 million in outstanding structural loans were converted by the government into new equity in SSAB. The U.S. Department of Commerce concluded in 1985 that the conversion had been "inconsistent with commercial considerations." *Certain Carbon Steel Products from Sweden* (1985).

[197] *Certain Carbon Steel Products from Sweden.*

[198] SSAB *Annual Report* 1982, p. 9; *Metal Bulletin* (August 31, 1984).

research and development programs aimed at improving steelmaking techniques and developing new products.[199]

Steel industry work force reduction was achieved comparatively smoothly in Sweden, in contrast to other European countries.[200] A 25 percent reduction in net work force was achieved without the riots and other civil disturbances that accompanied restructuring efforts in Spain and the EC. In part, this was due to extensive government unemployment, retraining and reemployment programs.[201] At the time of the formation of SSAB, the government promised that it would shoulder 75 percent of the cost of ensuring that the new firm would pursue "socially acceptable personnel policies," and that if this proved insufficient, additional conditional loans would be granted for this purpose.[202] The government subsidized the retention of surplus employees by SSAB for interim periods to cushion the impact of capacity curtailment.[203] In addition to the six-month lead time for layoffs required by Swedish law, "SSAB was requested by its state owner to extend the time of notice for supernumerary personnel by 24 months;" much of the cost of this measure was covered by reconstruction loans.[204]

Reduction of Domestic Competition. A high priority of the Swedish restructuring effort was the reduction or elimination of competition among domestic steelmakers, and in some cases government aid was tied to a commitment to eliminate "duplicative" activities.[205] The formation of SSAB

---

[199] Government R&D funds were (and are) channeled through the National Swedish Board for Technical Development (STU), an umbrella R&D agency subordinated to the Ministry of Industry, to two research institutions supported by the Swedish steel industry association, Jernkontoret, The Institute for Metal Research in Stockholm and The Metallurgical and Metal Working Research Plant (MEFOS). These institutes have conducted joint R&D projects (funded by the government and industry) as well as contract R&D for individual firms. *Teknik I Teden* (Autumn, 1983); *Steel Times* (November 1983).

[200] SSAB has 18,000 employees in 1978, and it planned to reduce these to 14,650 by 1987. *Dagens Nyheter* (June 1, 1978).

[201] Swedish unemployment benefits were comparable to the national "average daily wage." The government spent $1.81 per year on job provision, training, and job creation ("Preparedness Work"). *Frankfurter Rundschau* (May 5, 1985).

[202] Ericson, *Huggsexan.*

[203] One Swedish analyst commented with respect to SSAB that "Up to now the Company has been reducing its personnel at a slower rate than was planned. This can be partly explained by the fact that the enterprise was instructed by parliament to carry out the restructuring 'in socially acceptable forms.'" J. Waingelin in *EFTA Bulletin* (April-May 1981).

[204] Answers of SSAB to Countervailing Duty Questionnaire, *Certain Carbon Steel Products from Sweden* (1985), p. 15.

[205] Fagersta's chairman said in 1978 that "Swedish steelmakers will have to stop competing among themselves. . . . It is our foreign competitors we shall fight." *The Economist* (March 11, 1978).

did much to advance this objective; because the merger had incorporated all of Sweden's major carbon steel producers, SSAB enjoyed a domestic monopoly on production of all flat-rolled steel product lines, heavy sections, and a number of other products. Despite a bilateral agreement with the EC which limited imports from the Community to "traditional" levels of trade, SSAB still confronted intense competition from foreign steel, and it devoted substantial effort to winning back the domestic market.[206] By the early 1980s SSAB held only 40 percent of the domestic market for ordinary steel, with imports accounting for most of the remainder.[207] SSAB moved to strengthen its domestic market position, aiming initially at achieving a 60 percent share, by extending its control over most of Sweden's steel distribution system. These moves attracted the attention of Sweden's Monopolies Ombudsman, which, after investigation, secured an agreement from SSAB in 1986 that it would sell its stake in one stockholder, Edstrang, "as soon as it could without making a loss," although it would continue to control about 70 percent of Sweden's wholesale steel trade.[208] By the end of 1985 SSAB had acquired partial or complete control of companies which, taken together, accounted for about 90 percent of Sweden's steel wholesale trade.[209]

In the specialty steel sector, reduction of interfirm competition through rationalization measures was inhibited by traditional interfirm rivalries and dispersal of many of the producers' works.[210] Nevertheless, after 1977 a series of mergers and other tie-ups occurred which enabled the specialty steel producers to eliminate areas of product overlap.[211] Typically, in 1982, Fagersta and Uddeholm set up a jointly-owned venture to which each transferred its

---

[206] See following section, "Sweden's Foreign Trade in Steel."

[207] *Svenska Dagbladet* (November 5, 1982).

[208] *Metal Bulletin* (February 10, 1987).

[209] SSAB *Annual Report* 1985, pp. 20-21. SSAB acquired Tibnor, Sweden's largest steel wholesaler (it distributed 50% of Sweden's steel not sold directly to users by producers) in 1979, a move which was "in line with SSAB's objective of winning a larger part of its domestic market." In January 1981 SSAB entered into a joint venture with Axel Johnson, another distributor forming the "Axel Johnson Steel Wholesaling Company." *Metal Bulletin* (August 31, 1979); Johnson controlled 70% of Sweden's wholesale steel trade. *EFTA Bulletin* (April-May 1981) Tibnor acquired control over Fagersta's steel distribution in late 1981. *Metal Bulletin* (December 1, 1981). In 1985, SSAB acquired a 29 percent stake in Broderna Edstrand, Sweden's third largest steel stockholder. *Metal Bulletin* (February 10, 1987).

[210] Swedish specialty steelworks tended to be scattered among a number of *"bruks"* — small industrial towns often dependent on a single industry. By the mid-1970s the specialty steelmakers had "a 20-year history of product swaps, takeovers and rationalization measures" designed to reduce interfirm competition. However, the Falldin government criticized such measures as "too hesitant." *Metal Bulletin Monthly* (August 1978).

[211] The most common form of tie-up was the establishment of a joint venture to which the partners would transfer ownership of their facilities for producing a particular product or products. The joint venture would then shut down redundant facilities and concentrate investment resources on the most efficient plants.

facilities for producing high speed steel. Production tasks were then divided up among the two firms' various plants.[212] The most dramatic consolidation occurred in early 1984, when Sweden's four stainless steel enterprises were combined to form a single large industrial group, creating an entity with a monopoly on the domestic production of stainless steel.[213] In 1986, Finland's specialty steel producer, Ovako, merged with Sweden's SFK Steel, a move designed to "strengthen the competitiveness" of Nordic steel in light of the restructuring underway in the European Community.[214]

One group of Swedish steel firms, the small producers of bars and rods, had been left out of the 1977-78 restructuring effort. At that time overcapacity in this sector was estimated at as much as 50 percent,[215] and the heavily-subsidized SSAB also produced bars and rods, placing the barmakers in the unenviable position of competing against a firm backed by the State treasury. The government suggested that the smaller firms might benefit from agreements to reduce or eliminate interfirm competition.[216] Following a series of industry-government talks in late 1978, SSAB promised to restrain its competitive pressure on the bar producers,[217] who were urged by the

---

[212] The main advantages of the merger, according to Fagersta deputy managing director Dan Johansson, will be the concentration of research and production facilities and the elimination of unnecessary duplication of activities. In addition, domestic competition will be reduced. . . ." *Metal Bulletin* (July 6, 1982).

[213] Department of Industry Press Release 1984-01-10 No. 2184; *Metal Bulletin* (January 13, 1984). The government had been pressing for a consolidation of this sort since late 1982; the stumbling block was the ailing Nyby Uddeholm, which was in a "serious crisis." Nyby Uddeholm had received $149.6 million in government loans, and was seeking a whole or partial write-off of those loans. The other three producers were reluctant to enter into a merger with Nyby Uddeholm until the issue had been resolved. At length the government broke the deadlock by agreeing to write off loans totaling $71.6 million. *Svenska Dagbladet* (November 5, 1982).

[214] The merger created SSAB's largest competitor in bars and rods in the Nordic region, and was opposed by SSAB. The merged firm's principal product areas were bearings, alloy steel bars, wire rod and tube, as well as some carbon steel products. *Metal Bulletin* (April 11, 22, October 17, 1986).

[215] *Metal Bulletin* (December 19, 1978).

[216] Industry Minister Asling commented in 1977 that "We will have to see how they are affected by this big giant [SSAB]. None of the small plants will be included in the big merger. They have their distinctive character, and they have nothing to gain from such a merger. What may happen is that the products will be divided up among them, and they may receive help toward cooperating with each other in the area of production." *Dagens Nyheter* (October 7, 1977).

[217] SSAB agreed not to expand its capacity to produce the types of bars made by the smaller mills, and "not to use its state aid to eclipse the smaller producers." *Metal Bulletin* (January 9, 1979).

government -- with financial aid as an inducement -- to "explore further possibilities for coordination and product exchanges."[218]

The bar firms established a joint sales office, Basta, in 1984, which featured a commitment to "orderly marketing" in Scandinavia and interfirm agreements on price levels and market shares.[219] This arrangement collapsed, however, when the largest firm, Halmstad, withdrew, and subsequent talks on capacity reduction and resumption of the joint marketing arrangements were inconclusive.[220] SSAB has continued to seek "rationalization," pursuing acquisition of one or more of the Swedish rebar mills,[221] closing several of its own long product facilities, and seeking to foster cooperation and price increases in the sector.[222]

Thus, reflecting a long series of combinations encouraged by the government, competition between Swedish steel producers was significantly reduced, although not eliminated entirely. Given the trends toward "rationalization" already under way, it is not unlikely that Sweden will eventually have only one producer of each major steel product type.[223]

The 1986 Restructuring. In 1986, with SSAB reporting an operating profit, the Swedish government announced a major reorganization of the company's structure designed to give SSAB an ownership structure which would be more active in taking strategic decisions about the future of the Swedish steel industry. Granges, the "sleeping partner," which was "interested only in sitting

---

[218] Industry Minister Erik Huss in *Metal Bulletin* (January 9, 1979). Subsequently, SSAB and the small producers worked out "a general rationalization of production, with SSAB concentrating on larger sizes of bars and each of the independent mills specializing to some extent." *Metal Bulletin* (June 19, 1981).

[219] *Metal Bulletin* (November 22, 1985).

[220] The result was a "rebar war" in which the competition between the Swedish mills spilled into Norway, prompting a retaliatory move into Sweden by Norwegian rebar mills which had previously "agreed to keep out of the Swedish market." A truce was called in early 1986, when Sweden's Halmstadt and Norway's Norsk Jernwerk signed a "technical cooperation agreement" and simultaneously implemented price increases of $16.85 per ton. *Metal Bulletin* (November 22, 1985; February 11, 1986).

[221] *Metal Bulletin* (October 17, 1986). No agreement could be reached on acquisition terms. The Managing Director of one of the bar mills, however, was named SSAB's Chairman and Chief Executive Officer in 1987. *Metal Bulletin* (May 29, 1987).

[222] *Metal Bulletin* (February 17, 1987).

[223] Swedish steel executive Wilhelm Eckman commented on this phenomenon at an industry association meeting in 1984. *Metal Bulletin* reported (September 4, 1984) that "[Eckman] noted that product rationalization had been given priority and that there remain generally only one or two producers per product. But Eckman said there was still room for improvement to boost profitability. He suggested that SSAB transfer its rebar production to the independent Halmstad Company, and that a new special steel company be formed to take over production of tool and high speed steel, and stainless non-flat products. Ekman's ideas, if adopted, would virtually eliminate competition between Swedish steel companies."

out" the years until it could unload its stake in SSAB in 1991, was authorized to sell its 25 percent share to the government. Granges' shares plus a block of SSAB shares were sold to a group of private financial institutions, and LKAB, the state-owned iron ore producer, paid $98.3 million for bonds convertible into a 22 percent stake in SSAB by the early 1990s. The reorganization reduced the state's share in SSAB from 75% to 67%, and the government indicated it would "like to float the company on the stock exchange," although this would not occur for five or ten years.[224]

Sweden's Foreign Trade in Steel. Sweden has traditionally been both a major importer and exporter of steel -- its ratio of both imports-to-consumption and exports-to-production are among the highest of any major steel producing nation in the world. Sweden enjoys some import protection in steel as a result of its bilateral arrangement with the EC, but in crisis sectors like steel and shipbuilding, government has employed massive domestic subsidies as an alternative to import protection to preserve domestic industries suffering international competitive pressure.[225] While SSAB has urged the government to adopt a more restrictive regime (*e.g.,* a system of import quotas), to date the government has not done so.[226]

In steel, despite the EC agreement, Sweden has experienced an extraordinarily high import penetration ratio -- imports accounted for between 38 and 48 percent of Swedish domestic steel consumption in the years 1968-74, a figure which rose to 65 percent by 1980.[227] In significant part the high penetration ratio reflected the fact that Sweden's relatively small industry did not make all of the product types required by domestic consuming industries. However, a substantial portion of the imports represented lost sales, and SSAB's primary initial marketing strategy, therefore, has been to regain control of the Swedish domestic market, counting on its restructuring effort

---

[224] *Metal Bulletin* (November 18, December 16, 1986); Answers of SSAB to Administrative Review Questionnaire, *Certain Carbon Steel Products from Sweden*, No. C-401-401 (May 15, 1987).

[225] A 1981 World Bank study explained Sweden's preference for subsidies over protection as primarily attributable to the export-orientation of Swedish industry. Crisis sectors like shipbuilding were hurt by depressed export demand and stood to gain little from protection of the comparatively small domestic market. At the same time, import restrictions might have invited retaliation which would have played havoc with Swedish exports. World Bank Staff Working Paper No. 494, *Patterns of Barriers to Trade in Sweden: A Study in the Theory of Protection,* October 1981, p. 21.

[226] Response by the Government of Sweden to Countervailing Duty Questionnaire, *Certain Carbon Steel Products from Sweden*, No. C-401-401 (1985). SSAB President Henry Lundberg in *Svenska Dagbladet* (November 5, 1982). Lundberg complained that "I am entirely in favor of free trade but other nations use invisible trade barriers and completely open regulations which cause the competition to become lopsided." *Ibid.*

[227] *EFTA Bulletin* (April-May 1981).

and increasing control over the distribution system to roll back the import tide.[228]

In the export market, the posture of Swedish steel has undergone a transformation as a result of the 1978-84 restructuring. In the mid-1970s, the Swedish producers were rapidly losing their position in the international market -- they were often required to export their products at prices below the cost of production in order to retain market position.[229] Six years (and millions of dollars in subsidies) later, the Swedish producers, equipped with new government-supplied facilities, were eagerly seeking to expand their export sales. The Swedish press, which had extensively reported the decline of Swedish steel in the 1970s, was by the early 1980s criticizing other countries' attempts to restrict Swedish steel exports.[230]

While much of the Swedish producers' expanded export presence is attributable to the restructuring and rationalization of production, they were also substantially assisted by several devaluations of the krona, most notably a 16% devaluation in 1982.[231] *Dagens Nyheter* commented on March 10, 1984 with respect to the nation's growing trade surplus that

The Swedish export success depends largely on the fact that prices for Swedish goods have been lower, compared to the prices of the principal competing nations. Which was, after all, precisely the objective of the devaluation.

---

[228] Imports would probably have taken over virtually the entire Swedish market for carbon steel products in the years 1977-81 had the government not kept the industry alive with subsidies.

[229] *Svenska Dagbladet* reported on January 28, 1978 that steel "exports rose by six percent last year, but this was actually not a bright spot either, according to [steel industry association spokesman] Folke Gustavson. The ironworks had liquidity problems, which forced the necessity of sales." With respect to specialty steel, *Dagens Nyheter* commented on October 7, 1976 that "During the last few decades a number of specialty steel mills have been constructed in the United States, Japan, and on the continent, but they have concentrated on a few products and larger series, thereby manufacturing steel more cheaply than Sweden."

[230] *Svenska Dagbladet* reported with respect to the U.S. government's imposition of restrictions on specialty steel imports in 1983 that "It is simply a protectionist measure . . . designed for an industrial sector unable to assert itself in the face of healthy competition from abroad. This is true of Swedish exports, of specialty steel to the United States. . . . The Swedish specialty steel industry's primary goal has been to retain its market position while at the same time making production more efficient and cheaper. . . . You would think that U.S. steel plants could work with the same objectives rather than pressing for trade barriers." *Svenska Dagbladet* (July 8, 1983).

[231] *Dagens Nyheter* noted on April 26, 1984 that "When the kronor was depreciated in terms of other currencies, the export firms were able to lower their prices and still increase their profits. The boost in exports is to a large extent the result of lower relative prices. . . . In effect what the government has done is to redistribute resources from households to the export industry." (A 10% devaluation had already been implemented in late 1981.) *Metal Bulletin* (September 18, 1981).

Sweden's National Industrial Board estimated in 1987 that the combined effect of the two devaluations (subtracting the cost of price increases for imports) on Swedish industry was a 17 percent improvement in its international competitive position.[232] With their adverse position of the late 1970s reversed, the Swedish producers began to mount increasing pressure on the European market, one of their principal traditional outlets, as well as on the U.S. market.[233] Between 1976 and 1986, Swedish imports into the U.S. market increased dramatically, from 106,510 net tons in 1976 to a peak of 670,820 net tons in 1985. U.S. imports from Sweden in 1986 were 548,068 net tons. For the three year period 1984-1986, total U.S. imports from Sweden were 1,858,239 net tons compared to 459,614 net tons in the 1976-1978 period, an increase of over 300 percent.[234]

The Swedish industry's aggressive re-entry into the international arena resulted in substantial friction with a number of Sweden's trading partners. The West Germans, in particular, were incensed over what they saw as "Sweden's unbridled aggression" in the German market,[235] and German objections made it substantially more difficult for the Community to conclude a steel trade agreement with Sweden in 1986.[236] Sweden refused to enter into a VRA with the United States under President Reagan's steel program, arguing that a VRA would be contrary to GATT principles.[237] U.S. carbon steel producers brought a countervailing duty action against Swedish hot and cold-rolled sheets in 1985,[238] and U.S. specialty steel producers brought a succession of actions, including countervailing duty cases and a complaint

---

[232] *Dagens Nyheter* (March 24, 1987).

[233] Since 1978 steel trade between Sweden and the Community has been governed by a bilateral agreement which does not expressly establish quantitative limits, but seeks to maintain "normal patterns of trade." In early 1984 West Germany delayed its approval of the renewal of this agreement to express its unhappiness with import levels. In July, reports appeared in the press in Germany and Sweden to the effect that SSAB was undercutting minimum prices by selling prime product as nonprime, and increasing shipments of steel products not covered by the agreements. The Swedish producers, noting the high level of German steel exports to Sweden, said that "we have as much to complain about as the Germans." *Metal Bulletin* (April 3, July 24, 1984). *Metal Bulletin* reported on August 31, 1984 that SSAB "wants an early return to free trading in steel on the European market so that it can capitalize on having undertaken restructuring in advance of most of its competitors. . . ."

[234] Import data from American Iron and Steel Institute, *Annual Statistical Report*, various years.

[235] The Germans charged that the Swedes were not respecting ECSC Article 60 price rules with respect to their deliveries to the Community. *Financial Times* (August 21, 1984); *Metal Bulletin* (March 14, 1986).

[236] *Metal Bulletin* (March 21, April 4, April 22, 1986).

[237] *BNA International Trade Reporter* (January 1, 1986); *Metal Bulletin* (April 25, 1986).

[238] *Certain Carbon Steel Products from Sweden*, 50 F.R. 33375, August 19, 1985 (final). The margin of subsidization against SSAB was 8.77 percent.

under Section 301 of the Trade Act of 1974.[239] The relationship between SSAB's penetration of the U.S. market and the subsidies which it had received was underscored by the U.S. countervailing duty action, which resulted in a final affirmative determination of subsidization of 8.77 per cent. SSAB officials complained that "We don't have the sales margins to remain competitive should this duty be imposed. . . ." In effect, measures offsetting the subsidy benefit would make it impossible for SSAB to compete in the U.S. market.[240]

Conclusion. The Swedish experience demonstrates how a sustained government commitment to a failing industry can dramatically reverse that industry's fortunes. The Swedish government determined in the late 1970s that the loss of its indigenous steelmaking capability was unacceptable, and poured billions of dollars into the industry to enable it to restructure, and within a comparatively short period, the industry emerged as a major exporter. The "fall and rise" of the Swedish steel industry, and the emergence of a nationalized steel enterprise that has proven virtually impervious to losses, underscores the importance of the state as a critical, and perhaps decisive determinant to competitive outcomes in this industry.

Finland

Finland possesses a steel industry with a reputation for competent management, efficiency, high employee morale, and high product quality. The existence of this industry today reflects government decisions taken over a span of three decades to establish such an industry and assist it to remain competitive. The government founded the nation's principal steel enterprises, Rautaruukki Oy and a specialty steel plant operated by Outokumpu Oy, because private industry would not undertake such investments. Since their founding these two firms have received regular government equity injections, which, by 1990, will be made on an annual basis in amounts equal to ten percent of each firm's fixed asset investments. Both firms have benefited from the government's fiscal policies and subsidies to downstream steel consuming enterprises, and Outokumpu received interest free government loans and interest subsidies to finance the construction of its principal steelworks.

Finland is a "mixed" economy in which approximately 15-20 percent of the nation's industrial output is accounted for by state-owned industrial

---

[239] The U.S. specialty steel industry filed a Section 301 action but withdrew it in early 1986 after the Office of U.S. Trade Representative (USTR) told the Swedish government that it sought a VRA on Swedish steel. Disgruntled by the failure to secure a VRA, the U.S. industry refiled its Section 301 action in August 1986, prompting a new round of bilateral talks. The talks failed to produce an agreement, and USTR then rejected the Section 301 complaint, stating that the industry should seek relief under the countervailing duty law. *Metal Bulletin* (March 21, September 5, October 24, 1986).

[240] *Financial Times* (August 16, 1983).

enterprises, primarily in basic sectors like steel, oil refining, chemicals and mining. These enterprises' equity capital consists primarily of appropriations from the state budget and their operations are subordinated to the Minister of Trade and Industry, who "wields supreme power at company meetings."[241] As in many mixed economies, the Finnish government has established state-owned enterprises primarily in those sectors where investment would not otherwise have occurred if left to the private sector, such as the production of flat-rolled and specialty steel.[242] While the Finnish government has stressed that state-owned companies should be managed on a profitable basis, like private firms, these enterprises have frequently pursued policies and undertaken investments that would not have occurred had they been under private management.[243]

With government encouragement, the Finnish steel industry has been structured so that its producers "have grown and developed with no internal competition of any size to worry about [which] has obviously helped with the planning of added capacity as the home market is relatively assured."[244] No two producers in Finland make the same steel product. The principal producer, the state-owned Rautaruukki Oy, produces all of Finland's flat-rolled carbon steel products as well as welded pipes and beams, and is the principal supplier of plate and sheet to Finland's shipbuilding industry. The diversified state-owned firm Outokumpu Oy, has emerged as a major producer of threaded steel and stainless steel products. The privately-owned Ovaku Oy, formed through the merger of a number of smaller firms in 1979, produces Finland's long products (bars, rods, light structurals), and a number of

---

[241] *Helsingin Sanomat* (November 25, 1986).

[242] The state-owned companies have gone "into businesses which private capital has either not wanted or been able to handle." *Helsingin Sanomat*, (November 25, 1986). "In most cases state enterprises have been set up to meet a national need which could not be met through private financing. Examples are . . . [steel producers] Outokumpu and Rautaruukki." State-Owned Companies Advisory Board ("SOCAB"), *State-Owned Companies in 1982*.

[243] SOCAB, *State-Owned Companies in 1974*, p. 5. Finland's Deputy Head of the Department of Trade and Industry commented in 1979 that "The State did not establish companies merely to be able to invest its capital at the highest possible rate of return, but rather to promote the development of our national economic structure. . . . In the event of the State requiring a company to take other important matters, such as regional policy or employment, into consideration in its operations, the point of departure is that an effort to compensate the company for the excessive costs thus incurred." Markku Markinen in SOCAB, *State-Owned Companies in 1979*, p. 4.

[244] *Metal Bulletin Monthly* (August 1981). The *Norwegian Journal of Commerce and Shipping* commented on this arrangement on November 13, 1980: "The Finnish authorities have since the 1960s cooperated with the steel industry in expanding steel production in the plate and thread sector, etc. to meet the needs of their yards and to expand their exports to other areas. The structure of production was altered so that the producers of steel did not compete against each other."

(Million metric tons)

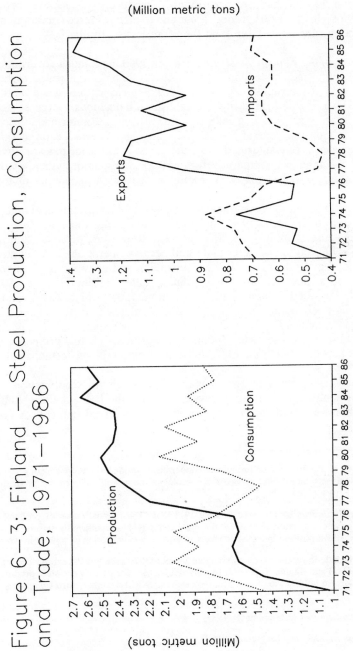

Figure 6–3: Finland – Steel Production, Consumption and Trade, 1971–1986

Source: International Iron and Steel Institute, Steel Statistical Yearbook, 1981, 1987. Production and Consumption refer to crude steel; Exports and Imports refer to semi-finished and finished steel.

processed products such as bolts, springs and screws.[245] The absence of domestic competition has enabled Finnish producers to achieve better economies of scale in various product areas and to plan resource commitments and production runs on a stable (and therefore less costly) basis.[246]

Expansion of the Finnish Steel Industry. In 1960 the Finnish government created Finland's leading steelmaker and only producer of flat-rolled carbon steel products, Rautaruukki Oy, as a 98.9% government-owned entity. Rautaruukki was created primarily to establish an indigenous source of steel plate for Finland's shipbuilding industry, and reflecting Rautaruukki's close ties with that industry, several Finnish shipbuilding concerns acquired (and retain) token shares of Rautaruukki's stock.[247] The firm's principal works was established at Raahe in a comparatively undeveloped region of Finland on the Gulf of Bothnia, and has played a dominant role in the economy of that region.[248]

Rautaruukki began the construction of a greenfield integrated steel mill on the Raahe site in the early 1960s and began ironmaking there in 1964. It commenced steelmaking in 1967, when two LD converters, three continuous casters and a 700,000 ton per year plate mill became operational. A hot strip mill was added in 1971 and in 1972 a cold-rolling and galvanizing plant was established at a new site at Hameenlinna, near Helsinki.[249] In 1973, Rautaruukki launched its ambitious "Programme 1500," which was designed to increase its steelmaking capacity to 1.7 million metric tons per year and its sheet and plate capacity to 1.3 million metric tons per year, making Finland self-sufficient in these products. Intensive investments on this project were undertaken between 1973 and 1977, and a new pipe mill was established at Oulainen.[250]

Rautaruukki's expansion was financed through a combination of government equity injections and heavy borrowing, the latter made possible through Finland's system of credit allocation to preferred enterprises (see

---

[245] The state and private sector producers "cooperate on production and marketing . . . to give Finnish steel consumers better service and consolidate the position of domestic products." *Finnish Trade Review* (June 1978), p. 8.

[246] *Metal Bulletin Monthly* observed in June 1978 that "The rationalization of production between the private and state sectors of the steel industry has significantly improved the industry's competitive position in export markets as well as in endeavoring to replace imports."

[247] These include the state-owned shipbuilder Valmet Oy (0.2%) and the private firms Oy Wartsila Ab (0.1%) and Rauma-Repula Oy (0.3%). Finland's other state-owned steel producer, Outokumpu Oy, also holds 0.4% of Rautaruukki's shares. SOCAB, *State-Owned Companies in 1983*, p. 47.

[248] *Helsingin Sanomat* (November 29, 1977).

[249] *Metal Bulletin Monthly* (September 1982).

[250] SOCAB, *State-Owned Companies in 1976*.

below). The Finnish government periodically increased Rautaruukki's capital through purchases of new equity with funds appropriated from the state budget (table 6-3). These investments, which totaled more than $75 million

Table 6-3. Finnish Government Equity Injections into Rautaruukki and Outokumpu, 1968-1986 (million U.S. dollars)

	Rautaruukki Oy	Outokumpu Oy
1968	13.8	4.3
1969	3.6	4.3
1970	8.3	0.0
1971	7.1	0.0
1972	0.0	0.0
1973	7.9	0.0
1974	7.9	21.1
1975	8.1	10.8
1976	0.0	12.8
1977	7.5	1.2
1978	0.0	3.0
1979	0.0	6.3
1980	9.4	10.0
1981	6.9	5.7
1982	0.0	5.1
1983	0.0	4.4
1984	0.0	0.0
1985	4.0	5.0
1986	10.0	8.7

Source: Advisory Committee on State-Owned Companies, *State-Owned Companies in Finland* (various issues)
Converted to U.S. dollars at average annual exchange rate given by International Monetary Fund. Conversion: 1968: 4.2; 1969: 4.2; 1970: 4.2; 1971: 4.2; 1973: 3.8; 1974: 3.8; 1975: 3.7; 1976: 3.9; 1977: 4.0; 1978: 4.1; 1979: 3.9; 1980: 3.7; 1981: 4.3; 1982: 4.8; 1983: 5.6; 1985: 6.2; 1986: 5.0

between 1968 and 1981, were made despite the fact that Rautaruukki paid negligible dividends on its stock during those years.[251] This phenomenon,

---

[251] Rautaruukki paid no dividends in the years 1968-71 and 1977-83. It paid token dividends ($25 thousand) in 1972 and 1973, and small dividends in 1974, 1975 and 1976 (a total of $1 million, $1.6 million and $1.06 million, respectively). SOCAB, *State-Owned Companies*, various issues.

common to the state-owned enterprises in Finland, has been criticized as the grant of "free money" by the state to these concerns.[252]

Finland's other state-owned steelmaker, Outokumpu Oy, was a mining concern in which the state acquired a majority interest in 1932.[253] In 1973 the government encouraged Outokumpu -- by then an enterprise with interests in many mining and metal fields -- to become a producer of specialty steel products through the establishment of a greenfield integrated steelworks at Tornio. Financing of the project was made possible through a combination of government equity injections, interest-free government loans, and government interest subsidies.[254] The Treasury established a fund from which Outokumpu could draw funds on an interest free basis to finance various stages of Tornio's construction.[255] Government equity injections into Outokumpu totaled $45.2 million in the three years 1974-76 (table 6-3).[256] The Tornio works became operational in 1976, at a total construction cost of $155.4 million.[257]

In the mid-1980s, the Finnish government adopted a proposal to provide each government-owned firm with a regular annual injection of new equity which would increase each year in order to improve the enterprises' international competitiveness.[258] The objective was to progressively raise the

---

[252] Finland's Minister of Trade and Industry complained in 1981 that "certain [state-owned] companies have been frugal in the distribution of dividends, and the share capital invested in them has thus been branded "free money." Now it is high time to forget the myth of free money and to set clear profitability targets for investment." Esko Ollila in *State-Owned Companies in Finland in 1981.*

[253] At present the government owns 80.9% of Outokumpu's stock. The remainder is held by Finland's Social Insurance Institutions. SOCAB, *State-Owned Companies in 1983.*

[254] "The decision to build a stainless steel works at Tornio was reached by the [Outokumpu] Supervisory Board in February, after the financing had been arranged. In accordance with the decision of Parliament, the financing of the works will be covered by raising the Company's share capital by 150 million markkaa [$39.2 million] and a budget loan of 75 million markkaa [$19.6 million] from the Treasury. For additional financing, an interest subsidization law was passed on June 15, 1973, according to 225 million markkaa [$58.8 million] will be met by the Treasury for a maximum of 20 years." SOCAB, *State-Owned Companies in 1973*, p. 52.

[255] SOCAB, *State-Owned Companies in 1974.* Outokumpu also benefited substantially from foreign export credits granted to encourage Finnish procurement of steelmaking equipment. In 1974 Outokumpu received $51.4 million in preferential export credits to finance acquisition of equipment for Tornio. *Ibid.*

[256] SOCAB, *State-Owned Companies,* various years.

[257] SOCAB, *State-Owned Companies in 1976.*

[258] Minister of Trade and Industry Seppo Lindblom stated in 1983 that "In order to improve real competitiveness in the 1980s, Finland's state-owned companies must also make investments to increase and improve research and development, marketing, and management and other occupational skills. . . . Over the long run . . . the aim should be for the increase in state-owned companies' share capital to average about ten percent a year in relation to investments in fixed and intangible assets. . . . The Advisory Committee on State-Owned Companies has discussed

volume of equity injections in the 1988-90 period so that by the turn of the decade each annual contribution would equal 10 percent of the firm's fixed asset investments.[259] Under this scheme, the government's contributions to Rautaruukki and Outokumpu increased sharply in 1986.[260]

The government's regular contributions to the equity of these firms cannot be characterized as an investment based on normal commercial considerations;[261] rather, "share capital investments in the state-owned companies are viewed primarily as an industrial policy measure."[262] The profits of both firms have been consistently very low, generally less than one percent of annual turnover; Rautaruukki's best year since 1977 was 1979, when operating profits were 2.35 percent of sales (table 6-4). In 1977 Rautaruukki was the biggest money-losing enterprise in Finland,[263] and between 1980 and 1986, both firms barely broke even.

For the Finnish steelmakers borrowed funds have been a more important source of financing than new equity. By 1980, shortly after completion of its "Programme 1500" expansion, Rautarukkii's long-term debt exceeded its share capital by a ratio of over three to one.[264] Outukumpu's long-term liabilities have generally exceeded equity and reserves by a ratio of over two to one,[265] and both firms carry a substantial additional burden of short-term liabilities.[266] The Finnish steelmakers' ability to finance much of their expansion through borrowing was attributable in part to the fact that because of State ownership,

---

the issue of increasing state-owned companies' share capital and has come to the conclusion that the state should strive to place state-owned companies' share capital on the required level by substantially increasing budget funding." *State-Owned Companies in Finland 1983.*

[259] *State-Owned Companies in Finland 1986*, p. 6.

[260] After years of paying token or no dividends to the State for its investments, Rautaruukki began paying dividends in 1985. *State-Owned Companies in Finland 1986.*

[261] President U. Raade of Neste Oy, a Finnish state-owned company, commented in 1967 that "State enterprises are considered to enjoy a measure of advantage in the capital markets which are not open to private enterprise. This is principally in the form of investment of funds collected through state taxation in these enterprises." "Definition of the Areas in Which Governments Should Involve Themselves Directly by Ownership in Industry" in Third Nordic Conference *Papers and Proceedings*, May 19, 1967.

[262] *State-Owned Companies in Finland 1986*, p.6.

[263] *Helsingin Sanomat* (April 25, 1978).

[264] Rautaruukki's long-term debt was $428.9 million in that year; equity share capital was $141.5 million. Rautaruukki carried another $161.3 million in short-term liabilities. Rautaruukki Oy *Annual Report 1980.*

[265] *State-Owned Companies*, various issues.

[266] An analyst for the Ministry of Trade and Industry commented in 1976 that "the recent development of state-owned companies' indebtedness is really rather alarming." Matti Purasjoki in *State-Owned Companies in 1976.*

Table 6-4. Financial Results of Rautaruukki and Outokumpu 1977-1986
(million U.S. dollars)

| | Rautaruukki Oy | | Outokumpu Oy | |
	Profit (Loss) For Financial Year	Profit (Loss) as a Percent of Sales	Profit (Loss) For Financial Year	Profit (Loss) as a Percent of Sales
1977	(27.8)	(9.45%)	1.7	0.48%
1978	8.8	2.06	2.0	0.47
1979	12.6	2.35	2.6	0.45
1980	7.0	1.13	3.1	0.43
1981	(0.2)	0.00	3.4	0.44
1982	0.3	0.06	(3.1)	(0.46)
1983	0.2	0.04	2.7	0.42
1984	3.8	0.07	10.0	1.39
1985	4.4	0.08	16.2	2.18
1986	6.2	0.09	(1.5)	(0.18)

Source: Advisory Committee on State-Owned Companies, *State Owned Companies in Finland* (various issues)
Converted to U.S. dollars at average annual exchange rate given by International Monetary Fund. Conversion: 1977: 4.0; 1978: 4.1; 1979: 3.9; 1980: 3.7; 1981: 4.3; 1982: 4.8; 1983: 5.6; 1984: 6.0; 1985: 6.2; 1986: 5.0

loans to these firms were virtually risk free.[267] In addition, government-directed fiscal policies helped the steel firms to obtain a high volume of funds at attractive rates despite a shortage of capital in the Finnish economy and a chronically high domestic rate of inflation.

---

[267] "In a market economy, the fate of a company that does not do well is to have to file for bankruptcy in an extreme case. . . . Otherwise state company losses are nationalized, that is, the taxpayers are made to pay for them. Protection against bankruptcy granted the state companies would in practice mean that banks, goods suppliers and customers behave differently toward the state companies." *Helsingin Sanomat* (November 25, 1986).

In Finland, both individuals and firms must rely largely on domestic commercial banks for investment funds.[268] The government has strictly controlled borrowing from foreign sources, limiting Finnish firms' ability to resort to this form of financing -- although given the government's fiscal policies, domestic borrowing was usually more attractive anyway.[269] The government of Finland has traditionally maintained rigid ceilings on interest rates for bank loans, holding rates so low that, given Finland's high rate of inflation, funds were often loaned at negative real interest rates.[270] This naturally led to an excessive demand for loans and normalized the practice of credit rationing by Finnish banks.[271]

The central monetary authority in Finland is the Bank of Finland, which has traditionally been the only source of liquidity for domestic commercial banks.[272] The Bank of Finland has borrowed very heavily abroad -- at prevailing international interest rates -- and reloaned to the commercial banks, which are the principal source of financing for Finnish industry, at controlled domestic rates.[273] The extraordinarily low domestic interest rates have made domestic borrowing for investment highly attractive to Finnish companies.[274]

Predictably, the low -- even negative -- cost of borrowed money in Finland produced a chronic, excessive demand for loans by Finnish industry. As in

---

[268] Finland has virtually no short-term capital market, and the long-term capital market is comparatively undeveloped.

[269] "Finnish firms may take foreign credit only with the permission of the Bank of Finland. Every foreign financing credit requires the approval of the Bank of Finland. In this sense the Finnish money market is completely closed." H. Koivisto, "The Importance of Real Rates of Interest" in *Kansallis-Osake-Pankke Economic Review* (First Quarter 1977), p. 3.

[270] At times Finland's real interest rate has been as low as negative 10 percent. *Kansallis-Osake-Pankke Economic Review* (First Quarter 1977), p. 5.

[271] A. Creutzberg, "The Demand for Money in Finland Revisited," *Economic Planning Centre Report 9* (Helsinki 1983).

[272] The Bank of Finland traditionally maintained monetary quotas for each commercial bank, with the two largest commercial banks particularly favored. The banking system in Finland has frequently been characterized as "oligopolistic." Creutzberg, *Ibid.*; *Kansallis-Osake-Pankki Economic Review* (Fourth Quarter 1974). As in Japan, the commercial banks tended to "overloan" to preferred customers, becoming more dependent on the Bank of Finland for funds. *Liiketaloudellinen Aikakauskirja* Second Quarter 1977), p. 187.

[273] *Ibid.*

[274] The *Kansallis-Osake-Pannki Economic Review* (Second Quarter 1982, p. 15) described this system in 1982: "A special feature of government borrowing in Finland has been the large share of external debt. This has been a trend which became particularly conspicuous in the late 1970s and the early 1980s. . . . The rigid interest rate policy pursued has kept domestic interest rates at a low level, and with the high rates prevailing abroad, this has maintained and widened the difference between the rates payable on foreign and domestic credits. Understandably the private sector has been reluctant to import foreign capital, and has focused its demand mainly on domestic sources of finance. In these circumstances government capital imports have been a means of supporting domestic demand and ensuring the necessary liquidity.

other countries with similar interest rate policies, loans were "rationed" by the commercial banks, reflecting the guidance of the Bank of Finland, to preferred industries and companies.[275] Firms unable to obtain regular commercial financing at the controlled rates borrowed funds on the so-called "grey market," where interest rates were substantially higher than the official rate.[276]

Despite their poor earnings records, both Rautaruukki and Outokumpu were favored by Finnish commercial banks and the Bank of Finland for the extension of credit.[277] Both firms' borrowing peaked in the years 1974-77, when each was engaged in an intensive expansion of steelmaking facilities, during a period when the Bank of Finland was enforcing a tight money policy, maintaining strict ceilings on the total volume of domestic loans in order to curb inflation. In effect, the steel firms were able to multiply the volume of their borrowings at the very point that the allocation of domestic credit was being most strictly controlled.[278] This appears to reflect a policy, expressed by the Minister of Commerce and Industry in 1972, that the government would impose "demands" on the state-owned companies and at the same time "provide the prerequisites for the compliance with these."[279]

Finland and the World Steel Recession. Rautaruukki and Outokumpu brought their new steelmaking capacity on stream in the mid-1970s, at the

---

[275] The *Kansallis-Osake-Pannki Economic Review* commented in 1977 that "The quantitative monetary policy pursued in Finland has signified in a way the rationing of investments through the credit decisions of the banks. It has been possible to direct this rationing only by issuing general guidelines. It has been necessary, it is true, to satisfy a part of the demand for credit by raising foreign loans because of the need to finance the deficit on current account. These loans are dependent on Bank of Finland approval, and in this way it has retained the control of rationing, *i.e.*, of selecting the enterprises to be financed." (First Quarter 1977).

[276] The source of grey market loans was primarily other Finnish firms. Creutzberg, "The Demand for Money," p. 4.

[277] One factor in such firms' favor was the likelihood that the government was unlikely to allow state enterprises to go bankrupt. The President of one state-owned firm, Neste Oy, commented in 1967 that "It must be admitted that even when a State-owned Company for some reason or other is unsuccessful, it is almost impossible to dissolve it." U. Raade, Third Nordic Convention, *Papers and Proceedings*, May 19, 1967.

[278] *Hufvudstadsbladet* (June 11, 1976); *Suomen Kuvalehti* (March 19, 1976).

[279] "The coordination of the administration of and collaboration between the state-owned companies should be developed by strengthening the position of the Bank of Finland, the Ministries of Finance and of Commerce and Industry, by channeling communications between the companies and by dove-tailing their operations more closely than before." *State-Owned Companies in 1972.* The "specialty" of the Minister of Commerce and Industry in 1976, Eero Rantala, was "directing the flow of capital." In an interview in *Suomen Kuvalehti* (January 2, 1976) he stated that he wished the Cabinet to acquire a greater degree of control over the activities of the Bank of Finland: "We need an opportunity to direct the flow of capital and investments truly effectively. . . . I would like to emphasize the importance of directing investments. . . . I consider increased opportunities for the Government to influence the Bank of Finland a very important matter." *Ibid.*

same time that the world steel market was entering a severe recession. Finnish steel demand began falling in 1976 and by 1978 was severely depressed. Finnish steel consumption in the 1980s has remained stagnant, showing virtually no increase over demand in the 1973-75 period. Partly as a result, Rautaruukki and Outokumpu have experienced consistently poor or negative profitability between the mid-1970s and 1986.[280]

The ability of the Finnish producers to avert financial disaster during this period was attributable to several factors. Rautaruukki's plant had been established relatively recently, and the company had adopted modern production methods rapidly, including continuous casting and other energy-saving techniques. The Finnish mills could cushion the impact of sharply rising raw materials and energy costs through a form of barter trade with the Soviet Union made possible by a unique Finnish-Soviet trade agreement.[281] The Soviet connection was particularly important to the steel industry because Finland lacked indigenous sources of coal, coke, and oil, and had only very limited iron ore deposits.[282] It gave the Finns access to low cost oil and other raw materials at a time when these commodities had become much more costly on the world market. "That is what helped us over the decline in Western markets in the wake of sharply rising oil prices."[283]

An important factor in sustaining the Finnish steel industry was the fact that they could maintain sales to Finland's domestic steel consuming industries which, although frequently depressed, nevertheless received sufficient state support that they continued to constitute a comparatively stable source of steel demand. Rautaruukki's largest source of domestic demand was the shipbuilding industry, which concentrated on "niche" markets like icebreakers, arctic multipurpose vessels, and oil drilling vessels; Rautaruukki in turn concentrated on developing steel products, such as polar quality steel for

----

[280] *Metal Bulletin Monthly* (September 1982).

[281] Under the Finnish-Soviet trade agreement, each nation pays for imports from the other in its own currency, without any money actually flowing between the two countries. The central banks of each country keep accounts of the markkas or rubles owed by each country and regularly balance accounts. For the Soviets, this arrangement is advantageous because they can acquire Finnish manufactured products without paying hard currency; the Finns benefit by their ability, in effect, to pay for raw materials such as coal, ore, and oil with goods and labor rather than currency. More recently, the Finns have become concerned over the imbalance in accounts in this system, with the Soviets importing more Finnish goods than they are able to "pay" for with raw materials, a phenomenon whch may cause the breakdown of this arrangement. *Helsingin Sanomat* (December 15, 1981; January 30, 1982); *Hufvudstadsbladet* (December 18, 1986; January 8, 1987).

[282] The Soviets and a Finnish consortium have established an iron ore pelletizing plant just inside the Soviet border adjacent to Rautaruukki's Raahe mill, as well as a rail line from the pellet plant to Raahe. *The Economist* (September 29, 1979).

[283] *Hufvudstadsbladet* (December 19, 1986).

icebreakers, which were needed by the shipbuilders.[284] Although the Finnish shipbuilding industry avoided the worst effects of the worldwide recession which occurred in that industry in the 1970s, it was severely depressed, and ultimately required government financial support to remain viable. In the mid-1970s the government began subsidizing the cost of the industry's employment and granting subsidies to cover part of the cost of individual shipbuilding projects.[285] Exports accounted for about 80 percent of Finland's ship production, and the government's "K-guarantee" program enabled Finnish producers to purchase "Export Inflation Insurance" from the government.[286] In addition to the K-guarantees, the steel-consuming industries -- most notably shipbuilding -- received extensive export financing from Finnish Export Credit

---

[284] One of Finland's four shipbuilding firms, Valmet Oy, is state-owned. *Kansallis-Osake-Pankki Economic Review* (First Quarter 1982), p. 12; *Helsingin Sanomat* (November 29, 1977). The government has overtly urged a "buy Finnish" attitude on the part of Finnish industry, although given the close ties that already exist between Rautaruukki and the shipbuilders, such exhortations are probably unnecessary. An official of the Ministry of Commerce and Industry stated in 1972 that "Technical collaboration has . . . taken place between certain companies, *i.e.,* . . . Valmet and Outokumpu and Rautaruukki. Cooperation over purchases would be an excellent form of collaboration. In this connection more attention should be paid to finding domestic sources of supply for state-owned company purchases. Successful measures of this nature could facilitate the balance of payments deficit and improve the employment situation. This factor should be given special consideration where company decisionmaking is concerned as Finland cannot afford to discriminate against domestic industry." *State-Owned Companies in 1972,* p. 12.

[285] In 1977-78 a committee was appointed, consisting of representatives of the government, the Bank of Finland, the shipping companies and the unions to examine ways to address the shipbuilding recession. In addition to direct subsidies, preferential financing and a "buy Finnish" policy were recommended: "The committee anticipated . . . that the Finnish shipbuilding industry would be forced to cut back sharply. Fortunately, that did not happen. . . . [The Committee] examined ways of steering domestic orders to the Finnish yards (without resorting to coercive measures) and what could be done to facilitate financing." *Kansallis-Osake-Pankki Economic Review* (First Quarter 1982).

[286] If the domestic cost of labor and materials used to produce items for export increased above fixed levels, the added cost was rebated to the producer by the government. (The scheme is described in *Papermaking Machines from Finland,* 44 Fed. Reg. 10451, Feb. 20, 1079 and OECD Economic Surveys, *Finland* (December 1982, p. 39.) Finnish shipbuilders -- among the principal beneficiaries of this scheme -- denied that it was an export subsidy, labeling it "insurance." Wartsila General Manager Tor Stolpe, in *Kansan Uutiset* (March 6, 1983.) However, in contrast to ordinary commercial insurance, the "K-guarantees" resulted in constant drain on the state treasury as funds were "rebated" to exporters. *Hufvudstadsbladet* (June 11, 1976.) The K-guarantees were primarily employed to subsidize exports of the "metal industry," which embraced not only shipbuilding but machinery and other steel-consuming sectors. *Ibid.*

Ltd. (FEC), a government majority-owned company established to promote Finnish exports.[287]

These government subsidies and support measures had the net effect of maintaining for Rautaruukki (and, to a lesser extent, Outokumpu and Ovaku) a stable source of domestic steel demand for which no significant competition existed through the years of crisis. Rautaruukki was also able to sustain its position because of its production of a wide range of "downstream" fabricated steel products. Here, too, Rautaruukki received state help; in 1983, for example, the Finnish government provided a subsidy of $12.5 million to Rautaruukki to construct a plant to produce rail cars for the Soviet Union.[288] By 1988 Rautaruukki was expected to be delivering 1,900 cars annually from this facility to the Soviets.[289]

A final factor enabling the Finnish steel industry to surmount the global structural recession comparatively well was its ability to penetrate niche markets for specialized types of steel, such as ice-resistant steel for arctic vessels. This has required a sustained commitment to research and development by the Finnish steel producers. The Finnish government has reinforced these efforts through R&D conducted by the Valton Teknillinen Tutkimuskiskus (VTT), the technical research center of Finland,[290] and through contributions to Sweden's Stiftelson for Metallurgisk Forskning (MEFOS), an industrial research institute open to metallurgical firms in Nordic countries.[291]

Finland's Foreign Trade in Steel. Finland became a net exporter of steel in 1977, following completion of Rautaruukki's "Programme 1500," and has

----

[287] As of 1983 FEC, which is jointly funded by the government, the Bank of Finland, and a number of commercial banks, had $484.7 million in loans outstanding which had been used to finance Finnish ship exports, and another $484.7 million which had financed exports of other Finnish steel-consuming industries. The loans were generally made at OECD consensus interest rates. In 1983, the consensus rate for ships was 8 percent. The bulk of FEC's funds were raised through the sale of subordinated debentures to the government of Finland (the largest single subscriber), the Bank of Finland, and the commercial banks. FEC *Annual Report 1983.*

[288] The project entailed fixed asset investments of about $82.5 million. *Helsingin Sanomat* (June 24, 1983). *Helsingin Sanomat* reported on April 30, 1983 that "The members of the government's ministerial economic policy committee were unanimous on granting Rautaruukki a subsidy to cover interest costs on Friday." The purpose of the subsidy, in part, was to maintain Rautaruukki's employment levels following the closure of several of its mines. Construction on the project began in June 1983. *Helsingin Sanomat* (April 30, June 24, 1983).

[289] *Helsingin Sanomat* (August 13, 1987).

[290] The VTT is a government research agency with a staff of 1,500 which concentrates Finland's R&D resources on particular areas of industrial technology. Metals R&D generally has received financing from the state budget matched by industry contributions which are twice as large. *Valton Teknillinen Tutkimuskiskus Annual Review*, various issues.

[291] *Steel Times* (November 1983).

maintained an export surplus in every subsequent year. All three of the Finnish producers export a major portion of their total production.[292]

Like many other steel producing nations, Finland turned to increased exports to offset the decline in domestic steel consumption which occurred in the mid-1970s. Finnish domestic steel consumption began declining sharply in 1977, bottoming out in 1978 and remaining stagnant in 1979.[293] Rautaruukki's "Programme 1500" facilities became operational in 1977, and Finnish steel production hit an all-time high in 1978, the year that domestic consumption was most severely depressed. The surpluses were exported. Finland's steel export volume was higher in 1978 than in any prior or subsequent year (figure 6-3). The Finnish government conceded in 1978 that exports during this period had been made at prices below the cost of production: "Domestic steel sales had also diminished as a result of the depressed state of investment activity and the decreasing demand for steel plates by shipyards. It has been necessary to export a large proportion of the increased output at unprofitable world market prices."[294]

Import Restrictions. Finland does not produce many types of steel needed by its domestic economy, and imports have generally accounted for about 40 percent of Finnish consumption.[295] While in the past the Finnish government refrained from formally restricting steel imports,[296] it has secured a variety of forms of import restraint from its European neighbors. The Finnish bilateral agreement with the EC obliges the parties to keep their steel exports within "traditional patterns of trade," and the Finns have made it clear that the agreement prohibits sharp surges in EC exports to Finland.[297] Similarly, in the spring of 1984, the government imposed restrictions on imports of steel from the Soviet Bloc countries, which were threatening the Finnish domestic price

---

[292] About 51 percent of Rautaruukki's sales consist of exports. Rautaruuki Oy *Annual Report* (1987). Ovaku Oy has traditionally exported around 50 percent of its total production, and Outokumpu exports about 70 percent of its stainless steel production. *Metal Bulletin Monthly* (August 1981).

[293] In most other industrialized nations the slump in steel demand began to be felt in late 1974. In Finland, however, a substantial portion of steel demand is attributable to shipbuilding. Because ships take 1-3 years to complete, the effect of diminished orders for ships was not felt immediately.

[294] Government of Finland, *A Survey of the Prospects for the Finnish Economy and State Finances in the Years 1980-1982* (Helsinki: 1978), p. 18.

[295] *Metal Bulletin Monthly* (January 1984).

[296] Imports of certain designated steel products were subjected to "surveillance licensing,"but approval was usually automatic. The system was reportedly designed to monitor rather than restrict imports.

[297] In 1988, the Finns opened consultations with the EC authorities after a surge in EC rebar exports to Finland which, in the Finns' view, was inconsistent with the terms of the agreement. *Metal Bulletin* (February 4, 1988).

structure.[298] Rautaruukki and Ovaku complained that "Cheap steel imports from countries such as Poland, Rumania and East Germany [were] flooding the home market."[299] Following the imposition of import restrictions in the spring, in mid-1984 Finland secured voluntary restraint agreements with the Soviet Bloc nations to reduce Finnish steel imports by 32 percent.[300] In an interview with *Hufvudstadsbladet* (March 30, 1984) an official from Finland's Foreign Ministry Trade Policy Department commented on the new policy:

Q: What have the reactions been?

A: They have reacted in the same way that we would have reacted -- they think this is an extremely dirty trick by Finland.

Q: Is this not protectionism?

A: It is a form of protectionism. But today Finland is the only open market in Europe and we do not think that we alone should bear the burden for Europe. This is the only opportunity for keeping our own steel production going in Finland. Price wise we are unable to compete with the CMEA countries.

The United States. Finland's principal traditional steel exports to the United States have been plate and hot-rolled sheets produced by Rautaruukki; in 1983 Finland began exporting significant quantities of cold-rolled sheets to the U.S. market as well. Between 1979 and 1982 the volume of U.S. imports from Finland did not exceed 150,000 net tons in any given year. In 1983 however, U.S. import volume increased to 196,000 tons, and in the first 10 months of 1984, the volume of U.S. imports from Finland had reached an annual rate of 304 thousand tons -- by far an all-time high. Imports of hot-rolled sheets were running at about 1983 levels, which represented more than a 100 percent increase over 1982 levels. In December, 1984, the U.S. Department of Commerce determined, after investigation, that Rautaruukki was dumping steel plate in the U.S. market. In 100 percent of the sales surveyed, the Finnish domestic price for plate exceeded the price at which Finnish plate was being sold in the U.S. market, by margins ranging from 4.6 to 45.9 percent. The weighted average Finnish dumping margin was 12.3 percent.[301] Moreover, in December 1984, Bethlehem Steel filed a complaint

---

[298] *Hufvudstadsbladet* (March 30, 1984); *Metal Bulletin* (April 13, 1984).

[299] *Metal Bulletin* (March 2, 1984). The Finnish producers were particularly concerned over COMECON shipments of "sensitive" products, including HR and CR sheet, bars, wire rods, and structurals. *Metal Bulletin* (August 14, 1984).

[300] *Ibid.*

[301] *Carbon Steel Plate from Finland*, No. A-405-401, 49 F.R. 48781 (final), December 14, 1984.

charging Rautaruukki with dumping hot and cold-rolled sheets in the U.S. market.[302]   In early 1985, Finland entered into a voluntary restraint arrangement with the U.S. pursuant to President Reagan's steel program, and the U.S. industry's antidumping actions were terminated.[303]   Finland's export volume to the United States has declined from 199 thousand short tons in 1984, the last year before the VRA, to 175 thousand tons in 1987.

Others (Austria, Portugal, Norway)

Austria.   Austria has a long and proud steelmaking tradition; the basic oxygen furnace (BOF) and many other advances in steelmaking technology originated in Austria. Austria's principal steel producers are Voest-Alpine, a state-owned bulk steel and engineering firm, and its subsidiary, Vereinigte Edelstahlwerke (VEW), which produces specialty steel.   Austria's technological leadership in developing the BOF gave its steel industry major cost advantages in the 1950s and 1960s, and provided the basis for the large scale export of steel mills.   Voest has been active in steel engineering projects all over the world, including many Eastern bloc countries, and in the 1960s was installing about one third of all oxygen furnaces built worldwide.[304]   Voest diversified out of steelmaking to such an extent that steel accounted for only 16 percent of its total revenues in 1985 (compared with 42 percent in 1974).[305] In the 1970s and 1980s, however, the industry sank into a protracted crisis, and became increasingly dependent on injections of government funds to sustain itself.

The Austrian steel industry was nationalized after World War II.[306]   The industry's importance to the national economy made it a perennial bone of contention between the nation's two leading political parties, the socialist SPÖ and the conservative ÖVP, which forestalled the development of a coherent industrial strategy for the industry.   After 1974, Austria's nationalized industries, and particularly steel, were expected by the government to support full employment through actions taken for social as well as economic

---

[302] *Ibid.*

[303] 50 F.R. 3948, January 29, 1985.

[304] Peter J. Katzenstein, *Corporatism and Change: Austria, Switzerland, and the Politics of Industry,* (Ithaca: Cornell University, 1984).

[305] By 1986 Voest had built 444 individual plants in 65 countries. *Metal Bulletin Monthly* (February 1986).

[306] Nationalization of steel and many other enterprises was not a reflection of ideology; it was undertaken to defend national sovereignty over key firms which had been German assets and had been taken over by Soviet occupation authorities. *Financial Times* (March 10, 1983).

reasons.[307] With the onset of the structural recession in 1974, the industry "accepted losses in productivity rather than employment, even when this required selling below cost."[308] Both Voest and VEW began suffering a succession of severe operating losses, and were forced to turn to the state for assistance.

There was a general consensus within Austria in both political parties that neither VEW nor Voest could be allowed to fail, even if this required state intervention. State aid was provided by the Österreichische Industrieverwaltungs-Akteiengesellschaft (ÖIAG), the state holding company. The steel sector's losses were initially covered by financial measures taken within the ÖIAG, pursuant to which profits from other nationalized firms were transferred to steel -- "simply, oil profits paid for steel losses."[309] But steel's losses were so large that they eventually threatened to drag down the entire nationalized sector, and the government was compelled to intervene with direct subsidies in the form of funds raised by the ÖIAG on the capital markets.[310]

At the beginning of the 1980s, VEW was in severe financial straits, and Voest was losing $54 on every ton of steel sold. VEW received approximately $231.9 million in financial aid from the ÖIAG in the late 1970s and early 1980s, and in 1981 Voest appealed for state help.[311] It received an injection of $125.5 million in 1981-82 for "structural improvement,"[312] and in 1983 it received another $334 million; VEW concurrently received $144.7 million.[313] The U.S. Embassy in Vienna estimated that between 1970 and 1983 the nationalized sector of the steel industry had received $947 million in government financial aid.[314]

Despite such assistance the condition of both companies continued to deteriorate, leading to a growing public furor. Another $144.9 million in "restructuring" aid was extended to Voest in 1985, as the company's losses mounted. Voest lost $555.8 million in 1985 and indicated it would need

---

[307] Voest and VEW were Austria's two largest employers, and account for about 12 percent of all Austrian industrial employment. In some localities, they provided virtually the only source of employment, reflecting the fact that during World War II, a number of mills had been sited deep in remote mountain valleys to secure them from enemy attack. Oskar Grunwald, "Steel and the State in Austria," in 51 *Annals of Public and Cooperative Economy* 477 (December 1980).

[308] Kalzenstein (1984); *Neue Zürcher Zeitung* (October 19/20, 1983).

[309] *Ibid.*, p. 208.

[310] *Ibid.*

[311] *Metal Bulletin* (August 1, November 10, 1981).

[312] *Law* 602/1981; *Bundesgesetzblatt* (December 19, 1981); *Certain Carbon Steel Products from Austria*, 51 F.R. 33369 (final), August 19, 1985.

[313] *Law* 589/1983; *Bundesgesetzblatt* (December 13, 1983); *Metal Bulletin* (October 21, 1983).

[314] Unclassified Cable No. R612372 (December 1984).

subsidies of $517.1 million through 1989 in order to break even in that year. The entire Voest management resigned as forecasts of the company's losses were continually revised upward; the opposition party called for a vote of censure for the Minister for Nationalized Industries.[315] Austrian Chancellor Franz Vranitsky indicated his desire to privatize Voest, because "the government cannot continue to pour subsidies into state companies which are unable to improve their performance."[316]

In 1987 Voest and VEW were reporting disastrous losses, and asked for $2.4 billion in subsidies to cover accumulated losses through 1990.[317] The two firms' difficulties were paralleled by an aggressive export drive in 1987-88; producers in the EC sharply criticized VEW's sales of tool steel in the Community at "abnormal" prices, and in 1988 the Commission began an antidumping investigation against Voest in seamless tubes.[318]

Portugal.   Portugal's only integrated steel producer is the state-owned Siderurgia Nacional, which was nationalized following that country's revolution in 1974. This firm was in a precarious financial condition even before the structural crisis began, and its situation deteriorated dramatically thereafter. Siderurgia Nacional received government capital injections and other financial support, but this aid was criticized because it was extended without a commitment from the firm to achieve designated national goals.[319] In 1978, Siderurgia Nacional launched a major expansion effort, financed by government capital infusions and loans from foreign banks; this effort was shelved in 1982 following repeated delays due to inadequate funding, political disruptions and a downturn in the economy, and Siderurgia Nacional was saddled with substantial unutilized new equipment.[320] A more modest modernization program was announced in 1987, involving $106.5 million in government financial support, part of which was to be raised from proceeds of the sale of the equipment purchased for the prior plan.[321] In 1987 the government began to show interest in eventually privatizing Siderurgia Nacional, but in the words of the Prime Minister the company was in the

---

[315] *Metal Bulletin* (December 6, 1985; September 30, 1986).

[316] *Metal Bulletin* (September 30, 1986).

[317] *Metal Bulletin* (February 20, July 30, 1987).

[318] *Metal Bulletin* (July 23, 1987; February 8, 1988).

[319] Domestic production only satisfied about half of Portugal's domestic needs by the late 1970s. By 1977 Siderurgia Nacional's debt was approximately $195.9 million. Lisbon *Expresso* (July 16, 1977).

[320] *Metal Bulletin Monthly* (January 1986).

[321] *Metal Bulletin* (September 17, 1987).

category of concerns "in no fit state to have their shares quoted on the stock market at present."[322]

Portugal's steel industry was exempted from the EC's general prohibition on subsidies for a period of five years after Portugal joined the Community; in return, Portuguese steel shipments to neighboring EC countries were restricted after accession.[323] In 1988 the Portuguese government implemented a restructuring program for Siderurgia Nacional, pursuant to an agreement with the Commission, which was designed to be completed by 1990, the cutoff date for subsidies.[324]

Norway. Norway's steel market is very small (about 1.5 million tons) and highly fragmented, requiring small quantities of many types of steel, a fact which, by the late 1970s, was giving rise to fundamental structural dilemmas for the country's principal producers, the state-owned Norsk Jernwerk and the private Elkem-Spigerverket. Sufficient domestic demand to sustain a mill on the basis of domestic sales alone existed only in rebars. Norsk Jernwerk, which operated Norway's only integrated steelworks at Moi Rana, was compared with some of the best mills in Europe, but suffered from high costs reflecting its small scale, its location in northern Norway, and its excessive dependence on exports.[325] The two companies' one area of product overlap was rebars; they generally sought to "cooperate to avoid mutually destructive competition."[326] As a practical matter, this meant "price control agreements" on rebars and efforts to "divide the market up between them."[327] In addition, Norsk Jernwerk worked out a variety of reciprocal marketing arrangements with producers in neighboring countries (Denmark, Sweden).[328]

Both Norsk Jernwerk and Norway's private sector firms have received government financial assistance for many years.[329] In early 1983, Norsk Jernwerk asked the Norwegian government for $274 million to pay off its debts and fund new investments. The government balked at providing the full amount of aid requested, but in 1984 it agreed to provide the company

---

[322] *Ibid.*

[323] Protocol 20 of the Portuguese Treaty of Accession provided that state aid would be granted for restructuring of the steel industry through the end of 1990. Portugal was assigned a quota on its exports to the Community which was raised annually, with total integration set for 1992. *European Report* No. 1352 (October 18, 1987) and No. 1368 (December 24, 1987).

[324] *Metal Bulletin* (January 7, 1988).

[325] *Metal Bulletin* (November 6, 1981). Norsk Jernwerk's principal products were structurals and bars, many of which were exported.

[326] *Metal Bulletin* (March 21, 1980).

[327] *Metal Bulletin* (September 28, 1984).

[328] *Metal Bulletin* (July 31, 1979; March 21, 1980).

[329] Oslo *Arbeidersbladet* (November 9, 1977).

with $94.3 million in public funds, with more aid possible contingent on the success of the company's restructuring plan. In 1985, Norsk Jernwerk and Elkem-Spigerverket agreed to merge their steelmaking operations, creating the Nordic region's third-largest steel producer, and the combined firm began discussions with Sweden's SSAB on further joint marketing opportunities.[330] Despite the fact that the merger concentrated 95 percent of Norway's domestic rebar capacity in one enterprise, a rebar price war broke out in 1985 when reciprocal marketing arrangements with neighboring Swedish producers collapsed.

The Norwegian mills possessed substantial surplus capacity, particularly in rebars and structurals, and their pursuit of export outlets for these products embroiled them in a series of trade disputes in the 1980s. West Germany complained in 1984 that Norway was "flouting" the so-called triple clause in its bilateral arrangement with the Community, which required exporters to spread out their exports across the Community, across the product range, and throughout the year; Germany's specific grievance was that Norway was concentrating a disproportionate amount of its exports on the German market, and on two products, rebars and wide flanged beams. British producers similarly were "very dissatisfied with the level of rebar imports from Norway."[331] In 1985, the U.S. Department of Commerce determined that Norwegian producers were dumping structurals in the U.S. market at a weighted average margin of 13.7 percent.[332]

PRESENT AND FORMER BRITISH COMMONWEALTH COUNTRIES

A second group of "other" industrialized countries consists of present and former members of the British Commonwealth which have achieved a high degree of development: Canada, Australia, South Africa and New Zealand. With the exception of New Zealand, all of these countries possess substantial deposits of the resources needed for steelmaking; with the exception of Canada they are geographically remote from other major foreign competitors. All of these countries embrace the principles of private enterprise and *laissez faire* competition, while at the same time undertaking a substantial degree of public intervention in strategic sectors, including steel.

South Africa

For decades the goal of South African industrial policy has been to ensure that the country could survive economic isolation in the event of Western sanctions. In steel, government policy has emphasized the need to establish

---

[330] *Metal Bulletin Monthly* (April 1986).

[331] These difficulties eventually led to the establishment of separate quotas for Norwegian long product exports to West Germany. *Metal Bulletin* (June 8, July 27, 1984; April 19, 1985).

[332] *Carbon Steel Structural Shapes from Norway*, 50 F.R. 42975, Final, October 23, 1985.

and preserve sufficient steelmaking capacity to supply all of the country's requirements in the event of embargo. This has entailed installation of capacity sufficient to meet the nation's needs even during periods of peak demand, resulting in substantial surplus capacity at other points in the demand cycle.[333] During such periods South African mills have traditionally turned to exports to absorb their surpluses, and engaged in extensive low-priced export sales after the onset of the structural crisis. While the economic sanctions imposed by numerous Western countries in 1986 foreclosed direct exports to many major markets, sanctions do not appear to have significantly curtailed net South African exports; rather, they have simply made South African steel export destinations increasingly difficult to monitor.

The South African government publicly endorses the principles of free enterprise, while playing an interventionist role in the development of basic industries seen as necessary to national survival. Railroads, harbors, airlines, broadcasting, electricity and iron and steel production have been operated either by ventures owned by the state ("parastatals") or as state-controlled utilities; in addition, the South African government Industrial Development Corporation (IDC) has launched industrial ventures in paper, textiles, energy, rubber and minerals. Import restrictions have been imposed to protect certain high-cost manufacturing sectors, including steel.

The South African steel industry is dominated by a state-owned enterprise, Iscor, which produces about 75 percent of the nation's steel and accounts for roughly the same proportion of the nation's exports. Iscor was founded in 1928 by the government, which held 99 percent of its stock; its first integrated mill was established at Pretoria in the 1930s and a second was opened at Vanderbijlpark near Johannesburg in the 1940s and 1950s.[334] By 1970 Iscor possessed the capacity to produce 4 million metric tons of crude steel per year.[335] While Iscor is by far the leading producer, South Africa has several important privately-owned producers, notably Highveld Steel and Vanadium (an integrated steelmaker), the Union Steel Corporation (USCO), the Dunswart Iron and Steel Works and several privately-owned producers of pipes and tubes.[336]

---

[333] *Metal Bulletin Monthly* (May 1984).

[334] These two mills were well positioned to supply the Rand, the mineral-rich region which was the center of South Africa's mining and manufacturing industries. Iscor developed its own iron ore and coal mines to supply its mills with raw materials, and remains a major producer and exporter of coal and ore.

[335] J.B. Coetzee, "South Africa's Steel Industry and its Economic Potential-Consolidation" in *Symposium on South Africa's Steel Industry and its Economic Potential* (Johannesburg: Engineer's Association of South Africa, March 20, 1970).

[336] USCO is controlled by Iscor, although ownership is shared with private firms. Until recently the private firms' output was limited largely to bars and structurals. Highveld has in recent years installed a plate mill and hot-rolling facilities.

440

(Million metric tons)

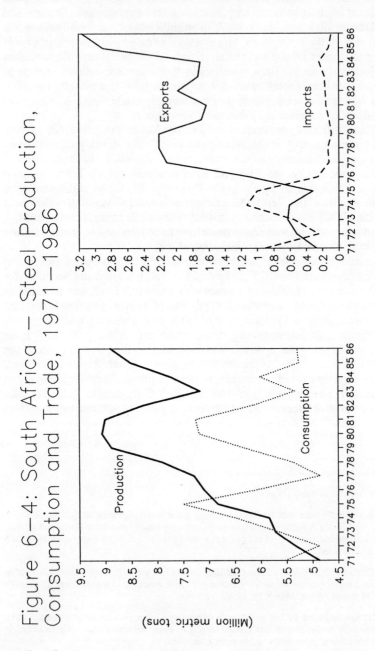

Figure 6-4: South Africa – Steel Production, Consumption and Trade, 1971–1986

(Million metric tons)

Source: International Iron and Steel Institute, Steel Statistical Yearbook, 1981, 1987. Production and Consumption refer to crude steel; Exports and Imports refer to semi-finished and finished steel.

Iscor's Expansion Drive of the 1970s. In 1969 the Ministry of Economic Affairs announced to the South African Parliament that Iscor would launch a major capacity expansion effort during the next decade. Both the Pretoria and Vanderbijlpark mills were to be expanded, and an entirely new greenfield steelworks would be established at Newcastle in Natal; taken together, these projects were initially designed to double Iscor's crude steel capacity to 8 million metric tons by 1980.[337] These plans were subsequently expanded.[338] Primarily reflecting Iscor's intensive investment efforts, South African steel output increased dramatically during the 1970s. Iscor's Newcastle mill became operational in 1978, adding 3.5 million metric tons per year of raw steel capacity,[339] and a number of additional facilities came on stream at Pretoria and Vanderbijlpark. By early 1978 Iscor possessed a crude steel capacity of 7.8 million metric tons per year.[340] South Africa, which had been forced to import substantial quantities of steel to meet its domestic needs in 1974 and 1975, produced a surplus in every year after 1976.

Iscor, which suffered major operating losses between 1974 and 1979, financed its expansion effort through a combination of government equity injections (table 6-5), suppliers' credits, and government-guaranteed foreign and local loans. Government equity contributions, which were made on an annual basis throughout the 1970s, played an important role in enabling Iscor to finance its expansion; in addition to providing funds for capital investment, these contributions, which totaled around $900 million between 1972 and 1980, enabled Iscor to maintain a better debt-equity ratio and to increase its level of borrowing.[341] Iscor was forced to raise all of its equity capital through sale of stock to the government because of the universal skepticism of private

---

[337] Coetzee, "South Africa's Steel Industry."

[338] The *Financial Mail* reported on March 17, 1972 that Iscor was "pressing on urgently with its expansion plans for a huge increase in steel and finished products." Pursuant to a "first phase comprehensive extension programme" Iscor's crude steel capacity was to be expanded to 6.5 million tons per year by 1976 at a capital cost of $1.4 billion. Iscor *Annual Report*, 1972. A second phase "extension programme" was to boost Iscor's crude steel capacity to an estimated 11.3 million tons per year by 1983-84 Iscor *Annual Report*, 1973.

[339] Iscor *Annual Report*, April 1978.

[340] *Metal Bulletin Monthly* (April 1978).

[341] Iscor noted in its 1972 *Annual Report* that "In terms of an existing arrangement with the Government a further 10 million B shares of R2 each were issued at par to the State President on March 30 1973. Further such increases in issued share capital will take place in the future in terms of the same arrangement. These contributions on the part of the Government do not only constitute an important source of financing, but also result in the Corporation's ratio of loan capital to total assets remaining within acceptable limits. "In 1975 Iscor's chairman said that the company needed "more investment by government, since our gearing is all wrong -- our loans are too high compared with equity". This request was heeded; Iscor received approximately $533 million in government capital contributions in the three years 1975-77. *Financial Mail* (June 6, 1975).

investors "who did not believe in the viability of a local iron and steel industry."[342] Iscor's managing director, J.P. Coetzee, commented in 1978 that

> *This negative attitude was one of the main reasons why the state even today controls all Iscor's shares.*[343]

Table 6-5. Government Equity Injections into Iscor in the 1970s (million U.S. dollars)

Year	Profit(loss)*	Profit(Loss) as a % of Net Sales Revenue	Government Equity Injections
1973	5.5	1.1	28
1974	(56.4)	(8.5)	45
1975	(50.2)	(6.0)	182
1976	(34.6)	(3.9)	219
1977	(56.5)	(5.3)	138
1978	(84.2)	(6.5)	58
1979	(45.8)	(2.7)	126
1980	100.8	4.1	98

* Based on current cost accounting methods used by Iscor.
Converted to U.S. dollars at average annual exchange rate given by International Monetary Fund.
Conversion: 1973: 1.4; 1974:1.5; 1975:1.4; 1976:1.15; 1977:1.15; 1978:1.15; 1979:1.2; 1980:1.3

The government continued to purchase new equity shares in Iscor despite the fact that the company stopped paying dividends on its common stock in 1972

---

[342] *Metal Bulletin Monthly* (April 1978).

[343] *Ibid.* Coetzee noted that the original act of Parliament establishing Iscor "provided for 500,000 'A' shares to be subscribed for by the government and 3,000,000 'B' shares to be offered to the public. Owing to poor reaction from the public and the financial squeeze preceding the depression of the early 1930s, the government had no choice but to take the remaining 'B' shares; this resulted in complete ownership by the state of all the 'A' and 'B' shares. *Ibid.*

and did not pay them for the remainder of the decade.[344] The *Financial Mail* reported on November 21, 1975 that

> *Iscor either has to borrow on overseas or local capital markets (underwritten by government) or government puts more and more money into the Corporation by taking up further equity. At present government's shareholding (that means taxpayers') stands at R 324.7m [$443.6 million], and it is committed to take up a further R 100m [$136.6 million] of B shares before March 31. And with Iscor making huge losses in the past two years, government has had to waive its dividends.*

The government guaranteed a substantial proportion of the loans Iscor obtained abroad, loans which often carried interest rates significantly lower than were attainable locally.[345] The government itself provided loans on favorable terms.[346] By 1978, Iscor had accumulated approximately $2.3 billion in fixed period debt, much of it borrowed abroad; however, the government paid $80.5 million of Iscor's financing charges in that year, reducing the company's annual charges to $72.4 million.[347]

---

[344] *Carbon Steel Wire Rod from South Africa*, 47 F.R. 30559, July 14, 1982. The government's waiver of its dividend was linked to the financial burden which its price ceilings placed on Iscor. The company commented in its 1973 *Annual Report* that "On the occasion of the latest steel price increase, the Government, as the holder of all the issued A and B shares in Iscor, restricted the domestic selling price of steel to an absolute minimum in order to make an effective contribution towards combatting inflation and for that reason decided to waive, in respect of the 1972/73 financial year, its requirement of the payment of a dividend to the amount of R 7.5 million [$9.7 million] on the A and B shares. . . . This arrangement very clearly illustrates the close and hearty cooperation between Iscor and the Government in matters of national interest."

[345] The *Financial Mail* reported on June 6, 1975 that "the fact that the Corporation is running at a loss apparently has not adversely affected its position in overseas capital markets (its borrowings are guaranteed by the government)." Reporting on one such foreign loan, the *Financial Mail* commented on March 17, 1982 that "financing of these massive projects will be largely on the overseas money markets. Iscor has just clinched a loan of DM 100m (about R 23m)[$41.2 million] in the West German capital market -- the loan documents were signed a week yesterday -- at the satisfactory interest rate of 7 percent. Iscor doesn't expect to be able to raise much loan capital on the local market, and certainly not as cheaply as this."

[346] The *Financial Mail* reported on January 3, 1975 that because of Iscor's difficulty in raising loans, "government itself has had to step in with favorable loans (6.5%)." Iscor's Managing Director Coetze said in 1978 that "From time to time, Iscor expands, its board requests the Cabinet to provide more capital as equity or even in the form of loans." *Metal Bulletin Monthly* (April 1978).

[347] *Financial Mail* (November 17, 1978). Iscor commented in its 1978 *Annual Report* that "over the past four years, the Government has contributed appreciable amounts in share capital to augment Iscor's redemption needs; in the past financial year this contribution came to R50 million [$57.5 million]. It was nevertheless necessary for the Government to contribute a further R70 million [$80.5 million] in order to bring some relief to the Corporation with regard to its financing cost, which amounted to R134 million [$154.1 million] in respect of the year under review."

Iscor suffered losses in every year between 1973 and 1983 with the exception of fiscal 1980 and 1981, when it reported a slender profit. Its chronic losses, widely attributed to government-imposed steel price ceilings, were a subject of widespread public concern, and in 1979, with Iscor's management reportedly demoralized by the firm's losses, the government appointed a committee to investigate the firm's problems.[348]

Iscor's financial picture was somewhat clouded, however, by its system of cost accounting. Since 1952 Iscor has used replacement cost accounting to determine its operating results; that is, it calculates its annual depreciation expense on the basis of the current cost of replacing an asset, rather than on the historical cost of that asset.[349] Because during periods of high inflation the replacement cost of fixed assets is substantially higher than historic cost, this accounting method greatly increases a firm's depreciation expense, and has been cited by Iscor as the principal reason for its "book" operating losses. In fact, Iscor has been able to exploit the fact that it keeps two sets of books to manipulate domestic and foreign policy decisions. When dealing with domestic price control authorities, Iscor denounced South Africa's steel price ceilings, citing the severity of its operating losses (which it blamed on the ceilings) using replacement cost accounting.[350] Conversely, when U.S. steel companies brought countervailing duty actions against Iscor in 1982, charging that government equity investments in Iscor had been inconsistent with commercial considerations, Iscor told Commerce Department investigators that the company had been profitable in every year since 1962, except 1974

---

[348] The Chairman of the Committee concluded that the company's return on capital was too poor to permit the sale of the company to private investors. The Chairman told the *Financial Mail* on July 6, 1979 that "A return on capital employed of 8.5% and even 10%, which is what we hope to achieve [for Iscor] will not be attractive to the private sector. A private investor would need about 20% to 25% for his investment to be worthwhile. I personally can't see this happening...."

[349] Iscor calculates depreciation on a normal straight line basis but adds a separate charge based on South Africa's inflation index to provide for the increased replacement costs of fixed assets. The funds which cover the added replacement cost of fixed assets." In effect this reserve forms an element of cash flow similar to that of normal depreciation.

[350] On July 15, 1979 its representatives told the Johannesburg *Sunday Times-Business Times* that "By refusing to accept a programme for the decontrol of steel prices, the Government is misusing more than R3,000 million [$3.5 billion] worth of public assets. It is distorting one of the most crucial -- indeed strategic -- markets in the country. And it is shackling scarce management and technical binding in a straightjacket which will always prevent them from achieving reasonable profits. "*The Star* (Johannesburg) reported on January 3, 1978 that in 1977 "[Iscor's] net losses grew to R49.1 million [$56.4 million].... [Iscor's chairman said] 'It means that the higher costs hoisted on us in less than 18 months have added R75 million [$86.2 million] a year to our production costs.' We simply cannot go without better prices." In 1978 Iscor's managing director told the *Financial Mail* (January 6) that government- permitted price increases were "unlikely to be enough to make up for rising production costs or compensate for Iscor's financial losses." The *Financial Mail* commented on August 25, 1978 that without a price increase "and a goodly one at that, government will have to continue pouring money into Iscor."

and 1975, using historic cost accounting.[351] The real state of Iscor's financial condition has been a subject of debate, although Iscor's management reportedly has brushed off the argument successfully used with the Commerce Department that on an historic cost basis the firm has been profitable.[352]

Direct government financial aid to Iscor largely ended in the 1980s as the state steel producer entered into a period of consolidation, modernization, and somewhat lower levels of capital investment.[353] The government has discussed "privatization" of Iscor for many years, and in 1988, announced that it had decided "in principle" to privatize the company. By "privatization," the government meant that it would continue to hold at least 51 percent of Iscor's equity stock and sell the remainder to private investors. No timetable was set for the sale.[354]

The Controlled Market. The South African government has collaborated with the steel industry in maintaining a system of market control measures which enabled Iscor (and other South African producers) to obtain substantially higher steel prices than would have been possible in a fully competitive market. These measures have probably done more to strengthen South African steel firms than direct government financial aid. The South African system of steel market controls has two basic elements, import protection and measures to stabilize domestic prices. Import protection, coupled with the comparative lack of domestic price competition, enabled producers to raise prices without significant competitive constraints. Government price controls, in effect until 1985, prevented the producers' resulting market power from being wielded with such vigor that domestic consuming industries were jeopardized, but were nevertheless administered in such a way as to permit liberal price increases after 1978. The removal of price controls in 1985 was followed by steep price increases, prompting an outcry from South African steel consumers.

Import Protection. Prior to 1975, international steel prices were higher than domestic prices, and South African trade policy was designed to mitigate

---

[351] The Commerce Department accepted this argument. See Iscor Post-hearing Brief. *Certain Steel Products from South Africa*, August 5, 1982; 47 F.R. 39379, September 7, 1982.

[352] The *Financial Mail* reported on November 17, 1978 that Iscor "maintains that if it employed the same accounting methods as other steel producers it would have declared a profit of R6.4m. Behind the scenes, however, Iscor men discount this and are adamant that unless government adopts a more liberal steel pricing policy, and takes over the corporation's liabilities, this year's appalling performance is bound to worsen in times ahead."

[353] Iscor halted further major expansion efforts in 1980 to consolidate its operations. *Metal Bulletin,* (January 25, 1980). In 1982 Iscor began closing down some obsolete facilities, converting its old Pretoria works to an electric furnace operation, and beginning to establish direct reduction (DR) units, *Financial Mail* (February 5, 1982); *Metal Bulletin* (November 12, 1982, October 11, 1983); Iscor *Annual Report*, 1983.

[354] *Metal Bulletin* (February 11, 1988).

this price differential.[355] The onset of the structural recession, however, saw a sharp decline in world steel prices and raised the prospect of an influx of low-priced imports into the South African market. In early 1975 the government Director of Imports de Villiers wrote to steel users warning them not to import steel at "dumped" prices. His assistant explained that the letter was intended to "put the fear of God in anyone contemplating coming in through the back door."[356] The *Financial Mail* reported on June 13, 1975 that

> *Imports of cold-rolled steel products require a specific permit, while hot-rolled products do not. They require only a general import permit. So theoretically there's nothing stopping users from importing the latter. What would happen to them if they do? The Department would "take a jaundiced view," says [his assistant] ominously. Is the Department aware of any transgressions? None as yet. And it doesn't seem likely since, as one user told the FM [Financial Mail] "It would be more than my future supplies are worth. . . ." The request is to be backed by the iron fist of Customs and Excise which is "arranging to monitor all imports of steel and steel products being imported contrary to the declared policy." It's clearly a case of cooperate or else.*[357]

After 1975, with South African steelmakers producing surpluses every year, import volume shrank to negligible proportions; South Africa imported under five percent of its domestic consumption, and these imports consisted in

---

[355] Iscor purchased steel abroad at higher prices, reselling it on the domestic market at the lower domestic prices. The higher cost of imported steel was financed by a special levy collected by steel producers from users on each ton of steel sold domestically and paid into an import levy fund. The fund was used to compensate South African steel producers who had imported steel on behalf of users at higher prices. Despite periodic increases in the levy, the fund was continually in the red, and financing of the scheme was finally taken over by the government in 1974. Payments were made thereafter out of the levy fund to producers to liquidate the large debit balances they had accrued in the early 1970s. Iscor *Annual Report*, 1972, 1973, 1974, 1975.

[356] *Financial Mail* (June 13, 1975).

[357] According to Cornelius Kleu, Chief Industrial Adviser to the Department of Industries, the government relied on pressure on users, rather than more formal controls because "we have to tread carefully. We don't want to offend GATT by imposing protection." *Financial Mail* (June 13, 1975.) The government demonstrated that it was prepared to take more forceful measures when jawboning of users proved insufficient. In 1977 South African pipe and tube producers complained that a "tidal wave of cheap imports . . . are now being dumped in the Republic." The imports were coming in despite a 15 percent duty and licensing requirements. Accordingly, Director of Imports de Villiers imposed a total ban on imports of steel pipe until the end of 1977; the South African producers commented that this measure "is a step in the right direction. It shows that the government has our welfare at heart." *Financial Mail* (June 17, 1977).

significant part of specialty steels that could not be produced in sufficient quantities locally.[358]

In 1983, the South African government began considering a limited liberalization of steel imports to reduce inflationary pressures in the economy, to mitigate international criticism of its closed market and to "appease the GATT."[359] Domestic steel producers protested this initiative("Iscor doesn't want anybody to import anything"[360]) but the government permitted them to draft the new import rules which would cover the majority of steel products.[361] The new system abolished quantitative restrictions based on import permits, and established a system of trigger prices. Base tariffs of 5 to 20 percent *ad valorem* were set for imports sold at or above trigger prices, and a formula was devised for imports below trigger prices which assessed duties equal to the spread between the trigger price and the import price.[362] The system was carefully devised to permit some import competition in the less industrialized coastal areas, but with little impact in the main South African industrial markets in the Transvaal, where the combination of tariffs and high railroad freight rates to the interior would prevent significant import inroads.[363] The new system became effective in August 1985. Despite misgivings expressed by South African producers, an import influx did not materialize.[364]

Pricing. Between 1964 and 1985, the South African government maintained a system of price controls on the domestic sale of steel, designed to buffer the inflationary effect of steel price increases on the economy as a whole.[365] Steel price increases have been agreed upon by the nine primary steel producers who meet in an industry association, the South African Rolled Steel Producers' Association. Prior to 1985, if the agreed increases exceeded allowable ceilings, they were presented to the Department of Industries, Commerce and Tourism for approval. The Price Controller (an official of this

---

[358] *Financial Mail* (February 18, 1977). *Metal Bulletin* reported on December 9, 1983 that "At present there is a blanket ban on all imports of those steel products which South Africa itself produces. . . ."

[359] *Financial Mail* (August 2, 1985).

[360] *Metal Bulletin* (December 13, 1983).

[361] *Metal Bulletin Monthly* (May 1984).

[362] *Metal Bulletin* (March 6, 1984).

[363] One South African trader observed in May 1984 that "The Government has certainly done its homework on prices. The new duties will allow some import business to be done so the door will be opened just wide enough for Iscor to feel a slight draught, but without any effect being felt on Iscor's own doorstep in the Transvaal." *Metal Bulletin Monthly* (May 1984).

[364] *Financial Mail* (October 31, 1986).

[365] Price Control Act, 1964 (Act 25 of 1964).

department) ruled on the amount of the allowable increase based on an investigation of producers' costs.

South African steel prices were held by the government at levels which were (for Iscor) uneconomically low throughout the early and mid-1970s. However, beginning in early 1978 the government began to relax its ceilings significantly.[366] A succession of major increases in ceilings followed; between 1978 and 1981 the average domestic price of South African steel increased by 57 percent, exceeding the general rate of inflation.[367]

In August 1985, government price controls on steel were eliminated concurrently with the changeover in the South African import regime from quantitative restrictions to tariffs.[368] The Rolled Steel Producers Association thereafter announced a series of price increases which prompted an outcry from South African steel consumers, who charged that the Association was a "cartel" that had implemented effective price increases of 50 percent since decontrol; they complained that South African steel was being exported at prices substantially below domestic levels. In a telex to the South African Competitions Board, an association of wire convertors complained that

We would be better off moving our factories to Europe or Asia where we could buy cheap Iscor steel subsidized by South African industry. Steel is being delivered overseas 20% cheaper than in Cape Town.[369]

Even in the absence of a producers' group to fix prices, the structure of the South African steel industry would limit the degree of internal competition. Iscor traditionally has enjoyed a domestic monopoly on the major flat-rolled steel product lines such as hot and cold-rolled sheets and galvanized sheet.[370] Moreover, while Highveld has pursued a policy of installing capacity which duplicates that of Iscor in certain product lines where demand is highest, a "cream skimming" tactic which has been a chronic irritant to the state

---

[366] In January 1978 steel price increases averaging 13.5 percent (flat-rolled products) were authorized. *Financial Mail* (January 6, 1978). Later that year the rolled-steel producers met with the Minister of Economics and convinced him — somewhat to their own surprise — of the need for another 10 percent price increase. *Financial Mail* (September 22, 1978). In fact, the price increase was greater for many steel users, in part because of "extras" Iscor was able to tack on for factors such as higher quality. *Financial Mail* (October 6, 1978).

[367] *Financial Mail* (December 4, 1981).

[368] *Financial Mail* (November 1, 1985).

[369] *Metal Bulletin* (September 16, 1986).

[370] In 1975 Iscor was the only producer of plate, hot and cold-rolled sheets, and galvanized sheets. The other South African producers' output was limited to bars and structurals. *Financial Mail* (July 11, 1975).

producer,[371] the intrusion of Highveld into a number of product areas has not for the most part been accompanied by significant price competition. Both producers have used the export market to dispose of their surpluses rather than engage in intensive domestic price-cutting.[372]

The Export Outlet. Since the mid-1970s many observers have regarded South Africa's steel production capacity as excessive to meet the country's domestic needs. However, "the country's delicate position in the world trading community means its steel industry will continue to be too large."[373] As a result, the South African mills have used the export market as an outlet for their surplus production, enabling them to run their facilities at a relatively high rate without intensifying domestic price competition. The *Financial Mail* observed on December 4, 1981,

> *In recent years local production has surpassed demand. The surplus is disposed of abroad at prices below domestic ones to help recoup capital costs. Imports appear to be negligible except for small quantities of special steel not made here. SA steel marketing strategy is thus similar to that of most other producers: namely, to sell at production-related costs at home, to check imports wherever possible, and to cut the competition to ribbons abroad. Local steelmen claim it could not be otherwise. . . . "At present you can safely say that anyone who sells on international markets is dumping."*

The importance of the export outlet to domestic price stability was underscored by the fact that South Africa's first steel price war "in decades" occurred during a four-month period between October 1982 and

---

[371] In the 1970s Highveld installed a plate mill, entering a product area where Iscor could already supply the market, and established capacity to produce beams and sections in competition with Iscor. In 1982 Highveld announced plans to install a hot strip mill, although Iscor possessed sufficient capacity to supply the domestic market. *Financial Mail* (February 12, 1982); Johannesburg *Sunday Times - Business Times* (July 15, 1981). Iscor commented in its 1982 *Annual Report* that "the duplication of capacity by other organizations of overcapacity already existing at Iscor is a problem. The creation of hot strip capacity will have a substantial influence on our future profits."

[372] Highveld has been able to capture sales from Iscor through its ability to supply local customers on short notice and because local consumers do not want to "put all of their eggs in one basket" by procuring solely from Iscor. One observer commented that "Iscor is a faceless giant . . . [it] loses sales opportunities because orders get tied up in bureaucratic red tape." *Financial Mail* (July 17, 1981). The principal effect of Highveld competition has apparently been to force Iscor into disposing of larger percentages of its steel abroad, at international prices, and to reduce "sales of Iscor's more profitable lines," forcing it to "keep under-utilized plant in commission to make relatively small amounts of specialized products ignored by its rival. This has a considerable impact on costs." *Financial Mail* (February 12, 1982).

[373] *Metal Bulletin Monthly* (May 1984).

February 1983, when export markets were unusually stagnant.[374] The
Financial Mail reported on October 8, 1982 that Iscor and other producers
had been accused of

> *dumping on the domestic market in competition with merchants
> because they cannot meet export targets in soft overseas markets.*

The advantage of producing surpluses for sales overseas, even at heavily
discounted prices, was, in Iscor's words, that it enabled it "to utilize the
Corporation's production units to the optimum extent."[375] Operation at or
near full capacity utilization lowered the unit cost of all steel produced, and
significantly improved domestic profit margins, provided that the surpluses so
produced could be kept out of the domestic market. While the objective in
export pricing was to cover at least production-related (marginal) costs, South
African steel exports have sometimes reportedly been made at loss.[376] Iscor's
marketing general manager complained in 1981 that

> *in times of oversupply, private sector companies concentrate on the
> more lucrative local market, leaving the burden of exporting at
> uneconomic prices to Iscor.*[377]

The South African government has facilitated the use of the steel export
outlet through a series of export incentives and subsidies. The government,
which operates the nation's railroads, maintains a rate schedule for steel
shipments destined for export that is approximately 50 percent lower than

---

[374] *Financial Mail* (October 8, 1982); Highveld *Annual Report*, 1983. During the price war
domestic prices dropped to about 12-1/2% below the government's ceilings. *Metal Bulletin*
(December 13, 1983). One steel merchant commented that "I have never seen such a dramatic
fall in the market in my 25 years." *Financial Mail* (October 8, 1982).

[375] Iscor *Annual Report* 1976 (p. 3). Iscor commented in its 1978 *Annual Report* that "Iscor's
net earnings in respect of its steel exports were inevitably much lower than average domestic
sales yield. . . . Mainly on account of its high fixed-cost structure in the steelmaking industry, it
is a fact that if exports were discontinued, production consequently cut and manufacturing
equipment taken off-stream, losses would mount and further adjustments to local steel prices
would become necessary."

[376] The Johannesburg *Sunday Times - Business Times* observed on December 18, 1977 that
"Iscor . . . has exported about 1.5 million tons of steel this year at sub-economic prices. But Iscor
considers it more advantageous to export steel at lower prices than withdraw expensive
equipment from production and retrench skilled employees. . . . Iscor's export manager
commented in 1979 that 'nobody exports at a profit.' *Metal Bulletin* (February 13, 1979).

[377] *Financial Mail* (July 17, 1981).

domestic rates.[378]   A further benefit was obtained through the so-called "Central Government Rebate" of up to 25 percent of the railroad charges on products shipped on open railway cars for export.[379]   In addition, the government Department of Industries, Commerce and Tourism maintains a four-part general export incentive program, several aspects of which have been used by South African steel producers.[380]

The fact that the South African domestic price of rolled steel was higher than the international price posed a potential dilemma for South African producers of finished steel products, such as pipes and structural sections, who used domestically-made flat-rolled steel to produce finished steel for export -- and thus incurred the higher cost of domestic sheet products. Accordingly, the government has established the so-called "Iron/Steel Export Promoting Scheme" (ISEPS) administered by Iscor, pursuant to which the nine primary steel products contribute a fee on each ton of steel sold domestically into an account managed by Iscor which is utilized to grant rebates to firms exporting finished steel products. In early 1984 the rebate granted to exporters out of this fund was 19.5 percent of the f.o.b. value of the exported products.[381]

---

[378] The U.S. Department of Commerce has on several occasions found this rate differential to be a countervailable subsidy, but on the basis of representations from the South African government, concluded that the differential rate was not used after April 1982. The Commerce Department learned in 1984 that ISCOR was still receiving preferential rail rates, and preliminarily determined that the rate differential gave rise to an *ad valorem* subsidy ranging from 1.07 percent (plate) to 9.09 percent (HR sheet).

[379] The Commerce Department found that these rebates gave rise to *ad valorem* subsidies ranging from 1.0 to 2.4 percent, depending on the producers and the products. *Certain Steel Products from South Africa.*

[380] Category A of this program consisted of a tax credit equal to the duty that would have been paid on imports of raw materials used to manufacture a product for export, whether or not the raw materials were actually imported. Category B was a tax credit of 10 percent of the value-added component of exported merchandise if there is a South African import duty on the manufactured product. Category D was a tax deduction of 200 percent for initial expenditures made for export market development. In 1983 these three programs were found by the U.S. Commerce Department to constitute countervailable subsidies on South African steel pipe and tub exports, at a combined *ad valorem* rate of 7.27 percent (Tubemakers of South Africa, Ltd.) and 2.14 percent (Brollo Ltd.). *Steel Pipe and Tube Products from South Africa* (final), 48 F.R. 40928, September 12, 1983. Category C of this program (terminated in 1982) provided a tax-free rebate to firms which increased the value of their exports of manufactured goods; the rebate was equal to 25 percent of the interest cost of financing exports and was held to provide an *ad valorem* subsidy of 1.2 percent (Iscor) and 1.9 percent (Highveld). *Certain Carbon Steel Products.*

[381] On October 18, 1981, *American Metal Market* reported with respect to this scheme that "Iscor is increasing by 30% the rate of assistance payable to exporters under its steel export promotion scheme for all export shipments undertaken on or after October 1. Iscor's new largesse is seen as yet another move to aid the local steel product manufacturers in their export drive. 'Our steel products markup is very low, profits are marginal, and we labor under the disadvantage of having to compete at exceptionally low prices internationally' [said one executive of a firm producing structural sections]. 'Any aid and incentives from Iscor will only help get our products to the market at lower and therefore more competitive prices.'"

Foreign Trade Relations.   South African steelmakers began producing significant surpluses in 1976, and the volume of South African steel exports increased significantly in that year. With the world steel market suffering from stagnant demand and excess production capacity, South African export prices were generally significantly lower than domestic levels.[382] While steel dumping was widespread throughout the world after 1975, South African producers were sufficiently aggressive in this environment to enable the nation to expand its export volume in a declining world market. The *Financial Mail* observed on December 4, 1981 that

> *SA is apparently holding its own in this cut-throat business [dumping]. Japan, which has cut back production, is losing some sales of its exported surpluses to SA. Locally-made steel is also finding its way into the U.S. where producers are working at only 70% capacity.*

Canadian producers charged that South African firms had dumped pipe in Canada in 1982, allegedly forcing domestic price reductions of 24-40 percent,[383] and Iscor made major inroads into traditional Japanese markets in East Asia.[384]

One of South Africa's traditional major export markets was the EC; however, in 1977 European producers charged that the South Africans were dumping steel in the Community, and the British government imposed stiff

---

[382] Iscor's General Works Manager F. Kotzee commented in 1977 that "We export to the UK, Europe, the Middle East and to America. We sell to them at below SA prices and generally at below their own steelmaking prices." *Financial Mail* (June 17, 1977). *Metal Bulletin* reported on November 27, 1979 that according to Iscor's planning and development manager, in 1978 Iscor's 1.8 million tons sold abroad earned $385 million in revenue, but if this tonnage had been sold at domestic prices, Iscor would have earned an additional $200 million. The *Financial Mail* commented on February 5, 1982 that "SA steel producers have been exporting their surpluses for some years at low prices. They found it less costly and less disruptive than closing down plants." Iscor's 1976 *Annual Report* noted that "As a result of the recession in the local market, Iscor was obliged to sell 282,100 tons of steel products, or about 8 percent of the tonnage sold, on the overseas market during the year at prices that were lower than domestic prices."

[383] *Metal Bulletin* (September 17, 1982).

[384] *Metal Bulletin* reported on April 28, 1981 that "Japan's export markets in SE Asia have come under attack from Iscor of South Africa and Australia's BHP. . . . CR sheet is offered [in Taiwan] at prices 50-60% below those quoted by Japanese mills. Iscor's prospects in Indonesia seem to be bright, and its price of $390 a ton C&F for CR sheets compares with $397 f.o.b. asked by the Japanese producers. *Metal Bulletin* reported on November 17, 1981 that "Iscor has frequently underbid Japanese steelmakers for sales contracts, and in our case, was reported even to have undercut South Korean steelmaker Pohang Iron & Steel Co.'s prices. A year later, *Metal Bulletin* reported that "Japanese exporters are finding that they are having to cut prices for almost all steel exports. . . . The Japanese cut the price of broad-flange beams to South East Asia to $345 a ton C&F to meet strong European competition, only to be undercut by South Africa's Iscor, which has offered Singapore broad-flange beams at $334 a ton C&F."

antidumping duties on South African merchant bars.[385] At the request of the EC, South African steel exports were voluntarily curtailed, with the result that "alternative markets had subsequently to be found in a hurry."[386] The financial editor of the Johannesburg newspaper *The Star* commented on February 14, 1977 that

> *I understand that the [EC] dumping charges may in fact be quietly dropped in talks behind the scenes -- but a package deal may possibly end in SA producers agreeing to voluntarily slow down its export tonnage to Western Europe. This in turn will mean trying to find wider inroads into alternative markets -- Japan and the United States -- with the handicap of being awfully quiet about it to avoid attracting the attention of home market producers there too.*

In fact, U.S. import volume from South Africa surged dramatically in 1977, increasing from a *de minimis* level of 21 thousand net tons in 1976 to 463 thousand net tons in 1977. South Africa established a strong presence in the U.S. market in 1977 which it maintained in every subsequent year until the imposition of sanctions in 1986.[387]   South African penetration of the U.S. market ultimately prompted a series of trade complaints against South Africa producers across a broad range of product lines. Actions were brought with respect to the major flat-rolled product lines, as well as galvanized sheets and bars;[388] wire rods;[389] pipes and tubes;[390] and prestressed steel wire strand.[391]

In May 1984, faced not only with a pending antidumping complaint but also with the prospect of U.S. import quotas pursuant to a pending import relief action, the South African government announced that it had unilaterally decided to limit the volume of South African steel exports to the U.S. to 1979-

---

[385] *The Star* (Johannesburg) (February 14, 1977).

[386] Iscor *Annual Report*, 1977, p. 11.

[387] The *Financial Mail* reported on July 29, 1977 that "Iscor's canny negotiators are quietly pulling a commercial coup in the cut-throat international steel market. . . .   A small but significant order comes from the U.S. west coast-gulf region dominated by the Japanese for a decade. Last year, SA sold a meager 1,800 tons in this area but US speculation is that Iscor (and possibly other local steelmakers) will ship in upwards of 50,000 t this year. . . . SA's foreign steel sales will not, naturally, make the same percentage contribution to revenue as domestic sales as export prices are pared to the bone. Pared even more so, if that's possible, to help (along with steelmakers from South Korea, Taiwan, Australia, New Zealand, the Philippines and soon Mexico) break Japan's west coast-gulf grip on what was virtually its home ground."

[388] *Certain Steel Products from South Africa*, 47 F.R. 39379, September 7, 1982; *Certain Carbon Steel Products Imported from South Africa* (filed February 10, 1984).

[389] *Carbon Steel Wire Rod from South Africa* (final), 48 F.R. 42396, September 27, 1982.

[390] *Steel Pipe and Tube Products from South Africa* (final) 48 F.R. 40928, September 12, 1983.

[391] *PC Steel Wire Strand from South Africa* (final), 47 F.R. 33310, August 2, 1982.

81 levels.[392] By its action, South Africa consolidated the market position which it had won in the U.S. after 1977. This market, however, and others in the EC, Japan, and Canada were lost in 1986 when the prospect of economic sanctions finally became a reality.

The Imposition of Sanctions. In the mid-1980s, growing civil disorders within South Africa over the nation's racial policies gave rise to international sentiment in favor of economic sanctions against South Africa. In the summer of 1986, the U.S. Congress overrode a Presidential veto and imposed a ban on U.S. imports of a wide range of South African products, including steel products, and Japan, Canada and the EC imposed sanctions which banned imports of most South African steel products. These moves "severely jolted" South African steel producers, who had been using exports as a means of maintaining viability during a current slump in domestic sales,[393] and some observers predicted that the sanctions would have dire consequences for the steel industry.[394]

However, South African industry had been preparing for sanctions for a long time, and the steel producers quickly began developing alternative outlets for their exports.[395] Iscor indicated its intention to seek new markets in Asia,[396] but little public information was available on specifics, since the steelmakers had pulled into the "no comment laager on the sanctions issues."[397] Iscor Chairman Kotzee simply indicated that "alternative markets had been developed and will be utilized to advantage."[398]

By mid-1987, the Johannesburg *Business Day* was reporting that there was "no indication that international sanctions [were] having any effect on SA steel exports." Iscor "declined to deny" that it had concluded a deal to supply Turkey with 50 thousand tons of rails.[399] "Eyebrows were raised" over reports

---

[392] Import relief was being sought by Bethlehem Steel and the United Steelworkers of America pursuant to Section 201 of the Trade Act of 1974.

[393] Johannesburg *Business Day* (September 23, 1986).

[394] *The Citizen* (October 14, 1986); *Business Day* (September 15, 1986).

[395] The Johannesburg *Business Day* reported on October 9, 1986 that according to one analyst, at the time of the imposition of sanctions, 54 percent of South Africa's export trade was already "semi-clandestine," meaning no data was available on the country of origin. "Analysts said manufacturers had various ways of issuing false certificates of origin."

[396] *Business Day* (September 23, 1986).

[397] *Metal Bulletin Monthly* (December 1986). Iscor indicated that in light of the sanctions, it would no longer publish detailed information about its earnings. Highveld also placed "harsh curbs on information contained in its annual report." *Financial Mail* (March 20, 1987); *Metal Bulletin* (November 7, 1986).

[398] *Metal Bulletin* (November 7, 1986).

[399] *Business Day* (June 3, 1987).

of increased Turkish purchases of semifinished steel from South Africa, which were possibly being re-rolled in Turkey for export to embargoing countries; an "informed U.S. source. . .expressed concern that Turkey may now be exporting to the USA pipe and wire rod rolled from South African steel."[400] Discussions were reported between South Africa and Taiwan to supply that country with billets.[401] Brazil was cited as a major source of demand for South African steel slabs and stainless steel plates, given shortages in that country and annoyance at the EC for the import quota levels allotted to Brazilian steel.[402] Reports in the European press indicated that Israel had established a "low profile" company in Geneva to "launder Israeli steel imports from South Africa."[403]

Thus, while South Africa would at first glance appear to have been eliminated as a competitive force in Western steel markets, the reality is more complex. The South African mills appear to be sustaining a substantial presence on the world market, although it is far more difficult to ascertain the extent and nature of that presence.

Others (Canada, Australia, New Zealand)

Canada. Canada's three principal integrated steel firms, Algoma, Dofasco and Stelco, are all privately owned companies based in southern Ontario. Three other important firms, Sysco, Sidbec-Dosco and IPSCO, are located outside Canada's principal industrial zone in Ontario and are wholly or partially owned by provincial governments.

In the 1950s the Canadian steel industry was small, inefficient, and relatively noncompetitive. Beginning in the 1950s, however, the industry, working informally with the government, dramatically improved its competitive position, emerging by the early 1970s as highly competitive on a world scale. The government flexibly applied Canada's antitrust ("anticombine") laws to permit domestic producers to divide and allocate product markets, achieving improved economies of scale. Canadian tax policy permitted complete depreciation of steel facilities in approximately two years (versus 15 years in the U.S.), encouraging investment in new facilities. The industry did not overbuild, as occurred in much of the rest of the world; capacity was established to serve the Canadian market in product areas which Canadian firms could expect to dominate, with the rest of the market left to imports. This permitted maintenance of relatively high operating rates throughout the demand cycle; during downturns, domestic mills could continue to run at a

---

[400] *Metal Bulletin* (May 12, 1987).

[401] *Metal Bulletin* (September 23, 1986).

[402] *Business Day* (June 17, 1987).

[403] *Metal Bulletin* (August 27, 1987). Israeli sources denied these reports.

high rate, and their output used to displace imports in the domestic market, "facilitated by the government's purposeful application of the trade laws."[404]

In the mid-1970s, however, Canadian producers undertook a series of expansion programs, with the result that the industry developed a capacity surplus in some product areas. The motives for this effort included a desire to exploit Canada's perceived natural resource advantage through a more explicit industrial policy, competition between the provinces to expand capacities, public concern over periodic steel shortages, and a desire to foster steel as an export industry.[405] The federal and provincial governments stimulated this expansion with a variety of public assistance schemes, although these were generally modest by comparison with those under way outside North America.[406] There were several exceptions, notably the subsidies provided to the two firms wholly owned by provincial governments, Sysco and Sidbec-Dosco.

The Sydney Steel Corporation (Sysco), an integrated firm whose principal product is rails, was acquired by the Province of Nova Scotia in 1967 after its private owners had decided to shut it down. "Despite massive infusions of public funds, Sysco has been unable to show a profit in any year since 1974 when its records were first made public."[407] By 1986 Sysco had cost the federal and provincial governments over $719.6 million since 1968, and had incurred long-term debts of over $287.8 million (table 6-6).[408] By the end of 1986, a Toronto-based investment analyst commented that the company was not worth saving:

> *Economically, there's no question: Sysco should not continue. Politically, I don't know. But it's a stupid attempt to keep jobs, irrelevant of costs. Last year it had sales of C$65 million [$47.6 million] and losses of C$83.5 million [$61.1 million], with manufacturing costs of C$69.4 million [$50.8 million]. Its debts at the end of March were C$410 million [$300 million]. I've never seen figures like these in 20 years as an investment analyst.*[409]

However, the federal and provincial governments opted for new measures designed to keep Sysco afloat. In 1987 Nova Scotia and the federal government approved a joint investment of $157 million in Sysco (table 6-7)

---

[404] Barnett, *Steel: Upheaval in a Basic Industry* (1983), pp. 219-24.

[405] *Ibid.*, pp. 224-27.

[406] A number of these programs are summarized in *Oil Country Tubular Goods from Canada*, 51 F.R. 15037, final, April 22, 1986.

[407] Algoma Steel Corporation, *Impact on Algoma Steel and Others of the Proposed Additional Subsidization of the Sydney Steel Corporation* (1987).

[408] *Metal Bulletin* (December 2, 1986).

[409] Jay Gordon in *Metal Bulletin* (December 2, 1986).

to modernize its facilities. In addition, the Canadian National Railroad agreed to purchase 80 percent of its requirements for most types of rail from Sysco,

Table 6-6. Canadian Federal and Provincial Government Subsidies to the Sydney Steel Corporation for Modernization 1987 (thousand U.S. dollars)

Sysco Modernization Program	Estimated Cost	Federal Share	Provincial Share
Capital Work Projects			
(a) Steelmaking	65,198	45,639	19,560
(b) Ladle Refining	11,418	7,993	3,425
(c) Caster and Transfers	11,765	8,235	3,529
(d) Bloom Reheat Furnace	7,685	5,379	2,305
(e) Rolling Mills	21,252	14,876	6,376
(f) Services	1,078	755	324
(g) Public Information and Evaluation	113	79	34
Total	118,509	82,956	35,553

Source: Algoma Steel Corporation
Converted to U.S. dollars at average annual exchange rate given by International Monetary Fund.
Conversion: 1987: 1.326

in effect closing off much of this substantial market to Algoma, Sysco's principal domestic competitor, and to foreign firms. A Sysco spokesman commented that "this gives us some assurance of a home market, but we will rely on a considerable amount of export sales to fill the order book."[410] These moves "prompted outrage" in other parts of Canada; Algoma pointed out that its own operations had been adversely affected by the continuing subsidization of its principal rival, and that the cost per job of public aid to Sysco was $845,400.[411]

---

[410] *Metal Bulletin* (February 17, 1987).

[411] Algoma Steel Corporation, *Memorandum Re: Sydney Steel Corporation* (1987).

Sidbec-Dosco is an integrated producer owned by the provincial government of Quebec. Sidbec lost money in every year between 1974 and

Table 6-7. Sydney Steel Corporation: 10 Year Summary of Results (million U.S. dollars)

	Sales	Operating Loss[1]	Net Loss[2]	Govt. Funding[3]
1977	73.6	14.5	43.6	21.4
1978	73.2	20.9	48.9	31.7
1979	99.9	25.9	54.5	61.7
1980	137.2	25.7	60.8	10.3
1981	141.4	4.3	45.9	3.8
1982	108.5	17.2	62.1	102.2
1983	63.8	13.8	56.7	23.8
1984	62.8	10.3	46.6	45.6
1985	76.0	4.8	47.2	36.8
1986	46.8	16.4	60.2	12.9
Total	883.2	153.8	526.5	350.2
Average/ year	88.3	15.4	52.7	35.0

[1] Before depreciation and financial charges
[2] Before operating grants
[3] Operating grants plus capital grants plus other assistance

Debt at March 31, 1986 - $297 million
Equity at March 31, 1986 - $155 million negative
Unfunded pension liability at March 31, 1985 - approximately $35 million

Source: Algoma Steel Corporation
Converted to U.S. dollars at average annual exchange rate given by International Monetary Fund.
Conversion: 1977: 1.0635; 1978: 1.1407; 1979: 1.1714; 1980: 1.1692; 1981: 1.1989; 1982:1.2337; 1983: 1.2324; 1984: 1.2951; 1985: 1.3655; 1986: 1.3895

1985, and the province periodically provided substantial injections of public funds to cover operating losses, retire debt, and fund the purchase of new equipment. Sidbec's losses, covered by the province, totalled roughly $771.5 million between 1974 and 1985.[412] Sidbec's losses stemmed in substantial part from its 50.1 percent equity ownership in Sidbec-Normines, a financially troubled iron producing venture established in 1976. While the government periodically considered divesting the company of this drain, political pressures prevented disposal of Sidbec's interest until 1984. The company reported a profit in 1986, and the Premier of Quebec indicated that Sidbec would "have to be self-financing from now on."[413]

IPSCO Inc., the largest producer in Western Canada, is a producer of sheets, plate and pipes and tubes in which the Provincial government of Saskatchewan, and Steel Alberta, a corporation linked to the Provincial government of Alberta, each hold substantial equity positions. IPSCO has received grants for steel facilities under the Industrial and Regional Development Program, the General Development Agreement and the Canada Saskatchewan Subsidiary Agreement on Iron, Steel and Other Related Metal Industries, as well as loans from the provincial government of Alberta.[414]

Canada emerged as a net exporter of steel in 1976; the bulk of its steel exports were destined for the U.S., which, because of its geographic proximity, Canadian firms regarded as "part of their home market."[415] Canada did not enter into a VRA with the United States under the Reagan steel program which began in 1984, and Canadian penetration of the U.S. market increased from 2.4 percent in the years immediately preceding the Reagan program to 3.8 percent in 1987, at a time when imports from other developed countries were declining.

Australia. Australia's principal significance for the world steel industry is as a source of cheap, high quality iron ore and coking coal; however, it also supports a significant steel industry. Australian steel production is dominated by the privately-owned Broken Hill Proprietary Company (BHP), which operates all of Australia's three integrated plants and accounts for over 80 percent of domestic steel consumption.[416] BHP's subsidiary, John Lysaght Ltd. (JLA), operates rolling mills which process BHP steel into finished products. BHP is a diversified firm that produces iron ore, coal, aluminum, and oil and gas.

With the onset of the steel crisis, BHP and its subsidiary JLA found that their costs were rising and their domestic market position increasingly eroded by imports. Plants were neither as large nor as technologically advanced as

---

[412] U.S.I.T.C., *Steel Sheet and Strip Industry*, p. 64.

[413] *Metal Bulletin* (June 29, November 23, 1982; August 12, 1986; April 10, August 27, 1987).

[414] U.S.I.T.C., *Steel Sheet and Strip Industry*; IPSCO *Annual Reports*, 1980, 1981, 1982, 1983; *Oil Country Tubular Goods from Canada*, 51 F.R. 15037, final, April 26, 1986.

[415] U.S.I.T.C., *Steel Sheet and Strip Industry*, p. 6-23.

[416] BHP owns or controls major reserves of iron ore and coking coal in Australia as well as a coastal shipping fleet.

those being installed in Japan and elsewhere.[417] In order to respond to these developments, BHP embarked on a restructuring effort, closing down some of its older facilities and seeking to modernize the others. This led to layoffs which, by Australian standards, were substantial and which had a pronounced impact in the affected regions.[418] In 1982, "steel workers and coal miners stormed the steps of Parliament demanding job protection."[419]

In March 1983, a Labor government came to power under Prime Minister Bob Hawke, and later that year it entered into a tripartite steel pact with BHP and its labor unions. Under the plan, the government established a "trigger mechanism" under which it had the power to impose import quotas if import penetration levels exceeded 20 percent in any of about 80 product lines; the quotas would be imposed by a newly established Steel Industry Authority (SIA). Imports from developing countries, the principal source of Australia's increased imports, were to be restricted to an average of the five years preceding 1983. In addition, the government promised to pay "bounties" of up to $64.6 million per year to customers who purchased Australian steel products.[420] In return, the unions agreed to limits on wage increases, productivity targets, and strict adherence to established grievance-settlement procedures. BHP agreed to undertake $722 million in productivity-enhancing investments, to provide job security for the existing work force, and to maintain operations at all three of its integrated sites (Newcastle, Port Kembla and Whyalla).[421]

The Australian plan worked reasonably well. BHP adhered to its commitments to maintain job security, keep all three integrated plants open, and undertake $722 million in investments. Productivity reached the target level set by the plan. The government paid out less under the bounty scheme than envisaged, and perhaps worse from the industry's perspective, permitted a surge in CR sheet and galvanized sheet imports in 1984-85 (principally from South Korea) which caused the domestic share of CR sheet to fall well below the 80 percent threshold for over a year.[422] However, by mid-1986, Australian firms held an 89 percent share of the domestic market, reflecting a weakening of the Australian currency and an array of antidumping cases filed against foreign producers.[423]

---

[417] Australia Industries Assistance Commission, *Iron and Steel Industry* (Report No. 249), SGPS, (Canberra: 1980).

[418] The Ilawara region lost an estimated 16,500 jobs in steel and related support industries. *Sydney Morning Herald* (July 27, 1983).

[419] Melbourne *The Age* (August 12, 1983).

[420] Minister for Industry and Commerce, *News Release* (August 11, 1983).

[421] *The Age* (August 12, 1983).

[422] The government's response--suspension of GSP tariff treatment for South Korean steel--proved ineffective. The government did not impose quotas.

[423] *Metal Bulletin* (July 15, 29, 1986).

New Zealand. In the late 1970s the government of New Zealand began developing plans with the country's principal steel producer, the privately-owned New Zealand Steel, pursuant to which the company would undertake a major expansion of its capacity. In 1981 the government adopted the plan. Stage 1 of this effort would increase New Zealand Steel's raw steel capacity fivefold, to 750 thousand tons; Stage 2, to be completed by 1986, would give the firm 550 thousand tpy of hot and cold-rolling capacity. The arrangement was one of the government's "most favorable deals granted to a privately owned company."[424] The government pledged to provide 30 percent of the capital cost of the expansion; loan guarantees; tax credits; a complete ban on imports of all products made by New Zealand Steel through 1989; infrastructural improvements, including roads, railroads, worker housing and training; and raw materials assistance.[425] The company expected to export half of its output, raising concern in neighboring Australia that it would compete in a market that was already "overserved."[426] There were "strong doubts from the first among official advisers about the value of the project."[427]

The cost of New Zealand Steel's expansion wildly exceeded the original projections of $11.6 million a year; by 1981 costs had risen to $183.5 million a year and by 1983, to $590 million, "by far the worst of all the major projects approved by the National Government."[428] The government found that it was forced to guarantee all loans to the company, since to do otherwise would suggest to lenders that it had changed its mind; however, by 1984, after a new government took office under David Lange, the government began casting about for a way to extricate itself. At length, the government agreed to take over $658.3 million in debt which had been run up by New Zealand Steel, and acquired an 81.2 percent equity interest in the company, but indicated that it would no longer be bound by the prior government's other commitments to the company. The government believed that there was a "very real risk that the cash flow from the expansion would not service the expansion debts without excessive and continuing state aid," so the government would "take its loss up front" rather than prop up the project indefinitely.[429] The government made clear it would try to cut its losses by selling its shares as soon as possible. However, as the *New Zealand Herald* observed on December 23, 1985, "it is safe to say that no one will be injured in a rush for [the shares] . . .

---

[424] *New Zealand Herald* (December 24, 1984).

[425] *Ibid.*

[426] *Metal Bulletin* (May 17, 1985).

[427] *New Zealand Herald* (December 23, 1985). The Treasury warned that subsidies granted to the company would subject its exports to the U.S. to the application of the U.S. countervailing duty law. *Ibid.*

[428] *New Zealand Herald* (December 24, 1984).

[429] *New Zealand Herald* (December 23, 1985).

and potential buyers will be well aware of the bargain they should be able to drive."

New Zealand Steel's financial problems substantially delayed the start-up of its new facilities, but by 1987, they were beginning to come on stream. Steel production was forecast to reach 420 thousand tons in 1988, and 750 thousand tons by 1992, and new pipe mills and hot and cold strip mills were scheduled to become operational in 1987. In late 1987, the government announced that it had sold its stake in New Zealand Steel to Equiticorp, a group of New Zealand investors, for $193.6 million, or about one-sixth the estimated $1.2 billion it had invested in the company by 1988.[430]

THE SOVIET BLOC

The Soviet Union and its Eastern European affiliates in the Council for Mutual Economic Assistance (CMEA) collectively have a much higher rate of steel production and consumption than any Western nation or bloc. They are significant, from a Western perspective, both as a huge market absorbing a substantial portion of the noncommunist world's surpluses, and as a source of periodic, unpredictable surges of low-priced steel exports into Western markets, often concentrated within a very narrow product range.

Steel has enjoyed an important place in the industrial policies implemented by government central planners in the CMEA countries. Since World War II national resources have been marshalled and deployed in most of these countries to promote the expansion of the steel industry, and major steel production bases have emerged in the Soviet Union, Poland, Romania, East Germany and Czechoslovakia. Although the Soviet Union is the world's largest producer of steel (161 million metric tons of crude steel in 1986), the Soviet steel industry has proven chronically incapable of meeting the nation's steel needs, in terms of quantity, quality, and product range,[431] and Soviet officials, "glum-faced with downcast eyes, state bluntly that [the steel distribution] system is a nightmare and change is much needed."[432] This has required the Soviets regularly to import large quantities of steel from its Eastern European satellites and from the West;[433] the ability of producers in Japan, West Germany and other nations to sell large quantities of these

---

[430] *Metal Bulletin* (October 26, 1987). Equiticorp estimated the value of the company's assets at $1.2 billion. The government was happy to be rid of the company, which it regarded as a "potential drag on the economy."

[431] Much of the Soviet steel industry was built just before and just after World War II; despite the presence of some new plants (many built with Western equipment), much of the industry is burdened with obsolete equipment. In 1986, 53 percent of the country's crude steel was still produced by the open hearth method. Yields were low and Soviet production methods wasteful, resulting in chronic overconsumption of energy and raw materials. Kiev *Economika Sovetskoy Ukrainy*, No. 9 (September 1986); IISI, *Steel Statistical Yearbook 1987.*

[432] *Metal Bulletin* (April 7, 1988).

[433] *Metal Bulletin Monthly* (August 1985).

products to the Soviets has helped to alleviate trade friction in the West in the late 1970s and 1980s by removing surpluses from the market. Initiatives now under way in the Soviet Union, East Germany and other CMEA countries to achieve *autarky* (self-sufficiency) in steel may result in the gradual curtailment of this Western outlet over the next decade.

The Soviet satellites of Eastern Europe have established a much larger presence in Western steel markets than the Soviet Union itself. All of these countries have achieved significant penetration of the Community and the United States, and most of them have been cited repeatedly for dumping. The inroads made by these countries in Western steel markets are no reflection of the competitiveness of CMEA producers, which are generally outmoded, inefficient, and poorly managed, a fact which analysts in these countries occasionally concede.[434] In centrally-planned regimes, exports are not seen as an end in themselves, but simply as one instrument to be employed in achieving the overall national plan -- and the role assigned to exports almost inevitably fosters dumping. The state foreign trade organizations (FTOs), which monopolize foreign trade in the CMEA countries, are instructed to export at high prices and earn the maximum foreign exchange possible, but profitability is only one of a number of objectives which the FTOs must accomplish. They are also required to achieve predetermined export targets under quarterly and annual export plans, and to acquire foreign exchange.[435] Dumping can result from FTOs' efforts to meet these targets; from the disposal of surplus inventories; in response to "cyclical shortages of foreign exchange" which require an FTO to export certain products quickly; and from countertrade transactions designed to secure needed imports without using scarce foreign exchange.[436]

Two of the leading CMEA exporters to the United States, Poland and Romania, have among the least efficient steel industries in the industrialized world. The history of these industries since 1975 is largely a chronicle of bad investment decisions, bad management, and worker malaise and unrest. The expansion of steel exports achieved by these countries during this period can

---

[434] With respect to Bulgaria, see *Ikonomicheski Zhivot* (February 5, 1986) and *Pogled* (November 17, 1986); Poland, *Polityka* (January 10, 1987); Hungary, *Nepszabadsag* (February 29, 1984); Romania, *Revistà Economicà* (October 26, 1979); Czechoslovakia, *Hospodarske Noviny* No. 30 (1986), p. 7, and No. 21 (1987), p. 2.

[435] Profitability, while desirable, is not, as in capitalist countries, the ultimate determinant of enterprise survival. This is underscored by the fact that in Romania, for example, the government must exhort FTOs to perform basic tasks, such as the collection of payment for exported goods, which any private enterprise would be required to do to remain solvent. See *Revistà Economicà* (June 25, 1982).

[436] Josef Wilcynski, cited in E.N. Botsus, "Patterns of Trade" in *Eastern Europe in the 1980s*, ed. S. Fisher-Galati (Boulder and London: Westview Press, 1981); *Revistà Economicà* (June 25, 1982); Paul Marer, "U.S. Market Disruption Procedures Involving Romanian and Other CPE Products, with Policy Recommendations," in *New Horizons in East-West Economic and Business Relations*, ed. M.R. Jackson and J.D. Woodson (New York: Columbia University Press, 1984), pp. 128-129.

only be attributed to government planners' determination to utilize such exports to achieve broader national goals.

Romania[437]

While numerous foreign governments have channeled subsidies and other resources into their steel industries, few have enjoyed the virtual total command of the national economy possessed by Romanian central planners, or have placed such a disproportionate emphasis on the expansion of the steel sector. In the years after 1965, Romania, originally an agrarian nation, committed approximately 10 percent of the nation's total investment capital to expansion of the steel industry in an effort to transform itself into an industrial power. By the early 1980s Romania had become the world's 12th largest steelmaking nation, producing more steel per capita than such traditional leaders as Germany, the United States, Sweden and the Soviet Union. However, as *Reuters* reported in 1984,

> *Romania has paid a heavy price for its steel industry. "The building of a giant steel industry is an achievement that has helped to break the back of the Romanian economy and pauperize the population," one Western expert said. . . . A huge export drive mounted in 1980-82 ended with Bucharest being accused of dumping in the United States and the European Community by selling steel at 35 to 41 percent below Romanian production costs.[438]*

While Romania's massive steel industry expansion effort has become a symbol of national independence, the domestic resource, energy and infrastructural bases for a large steel industry did not initially exist and have not subsequently been developed. As a result, Romania has been forced to import a large proportion of the coal, ore and energy needed to sustain the industry, which has placed severe drain on the entire domestic economy. These problems have been compounded by widespread mismanagement, inefficiency, bottlenecks, and excessive bureaucracy within the industry which have contributed to its repeated failure to achieve the goals set by government planners.

The Apparatus of State Control. The Romanian steel industry, like all major Romanian industries, is owned and centrally administered by the state. All major decisions affecting the industry are made by the Ministry of Metallurgy, which exercises control over all steel producing enterprises, as well as four metallurgical technical research institutes and a variety of construction, fabricating, and scrap metal enterprises. Based on goals fixed in a mandatory national economic plan, the Ministry designates physical (*e.g.*, production),

---

[437] This section is adapted from Thomas R. Howell, "Steel and the State in Romania," in *Comparative Economic Studies*, Vol. XXIX, No. 2 (Summer 1987).

[438] *Reuters North European Service*, May 16, 1984.

465

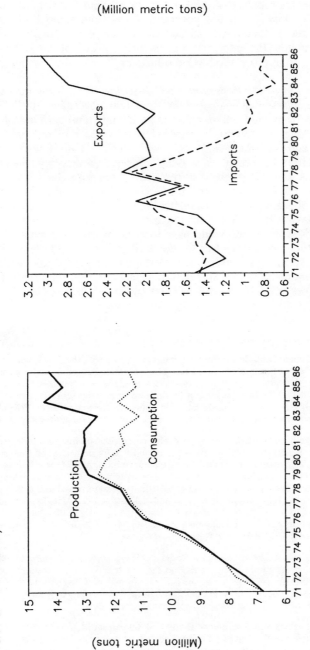

(Million metric tons)

Figure 6-5: Romania — Steel Production, Consumption and Trade, 1971-1986

Exports

Imports

Production

Consumption

Source: International Iron and Steel Institute, Steel Statistical Yearbook, 1981, 1987. Production and Consumption refer to crude steel; Exports and Imports refer to semi-finished and finished steel.

financial and operational targets for the enterprises under its jurisdiction, which they are required to implement. Investment decisions are made at the national level by the leading government and Communist Party officials and incorporated in long-term and annual national development plans.[439] As a practical matter, the enterprise management's principal role is the narrow one of seeking to improve production efficiency.[440]

Expansion of the Romanian Steel Industry. The Romanian Communist Party, which assumed control of the Romanian government in 1947, sought to transform Romania from an agrarian nation into a modern industrial state by concentrating investments in several key capital and technology-intensive sectors, one of which was iron and steel. The industry, which was comparatively undeveloped in 1950,[441] received a disproportionate share of Romania's slender investment resources,[442] and by 1960 its capacity had increased to 1.8 million metric tons from 555 thousand metric tons in 1950. However, because the government's long-range industrialization goals called for the massive expansion of the machine-building industry, it was evident that Romania's steel output would have to grow by several orders of magnitude. In 1960, the Party's directives for the 1960-65 Six Year Plan set a steel output target of 3.3 million metric tons by 1965, a level needed to sustain a planned 120-percent increase in Romania's machinery output. The centerpiece of the entire effort would be the construction, over a ten-year period, of a greenfield

---

[439] Investment funds derive from a number of sources, with the largest portion of industrial investment funds being appropriated directly from the state budget. In addition, enterprises are credited -- in their account in state banks -- with depreciation and "retained profits" from the sale of their products, and investments can be financed from these sources. In addition to these sources, bank credit has been made available to finance investments since 1970, although bank loans may only be made to support projects consistent with state-approved plans.

[440] Marketing and distribution of producing enterprises' products is conducted by separate enterprises; in steel, separate ministries are responsible for domestic and foreign distribution. Romanian steel exports are handled by Metalimportexport, an FTO which deals directly with foreign steel importers, negotiates prices and delivery terms, and ultimately delivers the steel to the customers. In conducting negotiations, Metalimportexport consults with the steel producing enterprises concerning appropriate price and delivery terms. Metalimportexport is jointly subordinated to the Ministry of Foreign Trade and the Ministry of Metallurgy. "Memorandum of Metalimportexport on the Determination of Fair Market Value" in *Carbon Steel Plate from Romania*, A-435-006, March 1, 1982; *Bulletinul Official* (July 20, 1981).

[441] Integrated steelworks existed at Resita and Hunedoara, and a handful of rolling mills and other finishing mills were scattered around the country. While the country possessed some deposits of iron ore and coking coal, the nation's raw materials base was inadequate to support large-scale steel production. A. Radoi, "The Industrial Geography of Romania in the First and Second Five Year Plans," in *Natura* (September-October 1956).

[442] Steelmaking, which accounted for 5.1 and 4.0 percent of gross industrial output in 1950 and 1955, respectively, received 6.7 and 8.7 percent of Romanian industrial investment in those years. Tsantis and Pepper, *Romania: The Industrialization of an Agrarian Economy under Socialist Planning* (Washington, D.C.: World Bank, 1979), p. 598.

integrated steelworks at Galati which would eventually produce over 4 million tons per year.[443]

The Galati steelworks was not only the flagship project of Romania's industrialization drive of the 1960s but a major symbol of Romanian nationalism and the catalyst for the dispute between the Soviet Union and the Romanian Communist Party which eventually led to Romania's estrangement from the Soviet bloc. The Soviets, and their industrialized partners in East Germany and Czechoslovakia, opposed the Galati project, arguing that Romania lacked the resource base for a steel industry, and that its role within the Soviet bloc should remain primarily a supplier of foodstuffs and oil, while serving as a market for manufactures from the more industrialized states within the bloc. Romania rejected these views since they would tend to perpetuate Romania's underdeveloped status. Despite Soviet refusals to provide credits for the project, Romania persisted in proceeding with it, lining up equipment and credits from Western countries.[444]

During the following decade, under the 1960-65 Six-Year Plan and the subsequent (1966-70) Five Year Plan, Romania channeled an unprecedented volume of investment resources into expansion of the steel industry.[445] Steel investment rose to over 10 percent of the nation's total industrial investment,[446] while the percentage of investment directed to less favored sectors, such as petroleum extraction, declined dramatically. Not surprisingly, the steel industry grew more rapidly than most other sectors.[447] Crude steel output increased to 6.5 million metric tons in 1970 and to 11.4 million metric tons in 1976, making Romania one of the leading steelmaking nations in the world.[448]

---

[443] Monthias, *Economic Development in Communist Romania* (Cambridge, Mass.: MIT Press, 1967), p. 202.

[444] G. Ionescu, *Communism in Rumania 1944-62* (1964); D. Gloyd, *Rumania: Russia's Dissident Ally* (1965).

[445] *România Libera* (December 2, 1977).

[446] *Metal Bulletin Monthly* (January 1979).

[447] Romanian Party and government officials repeatedly stressed that the steel industry's rapid growth was directly attributable to the priority accorded to the sector by the government in its allocation of investment resources. The Deputy Minister of Metallurgy observed in 1976 that "Because priority was given to the metallurgy industry within the framework of a sustained pace of development of the whole economy, substantial investment funds have continued to be allocated to create the material base for an accelerated growth of production both in terms of quality and quantity. This made it possible, by the end of 1976, to place Romania 14th in the world among steel producers." *România Libera* (December 2, 1977). See also *Metalurgia* (August, 1969).

[448] By the mid-1970s a broad heavy industrial base had been established in Romania, and per capita productivity and standards of living had significantly increased. Some observers have attributed the government's subsequent rigidity in reacting to the economic crisis that developed in the late 1970s to its reluctance to abandon a system that had fostered such a sustained pattern of growth. P. T. Knight, *Economic Reform in Socialist Countries* (Washington, D.C.: World Bank, 1983), p. 27.

However, while by the early 1970s the Romanian steel industry had achieved a significant expansion of net capacity, problems were beginning to become evident which would hamper the industry's operations in the future. Despite the increased volume of output, the industry still could not fully keep pace with steel demand from Romania's rapidly-industrializing economy.[449] Moreover, the domestic extractive and recycling industries were demonstrating their growing inability to supply the domestic mills with adequate quantities of iron ore, scrap, and coking coal, forcing Romania to import progressively greater quantities of these raw materials.[450] Finally, as the industry grew in scale, its operations were hampered by inefficiency, spot shortages of raw materials and equipment, and poor coordination between and within the enterprises.[451]

Despite such problems, capacity expansion efforts -- and the nation's commitment to steel -- intensified in the 1970s.[452] Under the 1976-80 Five Year Plan, Romania launched its most ambitious steel industry expansion drive to date -- the Minister of Metallurgy called the new plan the "Five Year Plan of Metallurgical Investments."[453] A target of 17-18 million tons of steel output was fixed for 1980, and the Minister of Metallurgy made grandiose, and wholly unrealistic, predictions of expanding steelmaking capacity to 28-30 million tons by 1980. The new plan entailed allocation of a proportion of

---

[449] Minister of Metallurgy N. Agachi in *Era Socialista* (November 21, 1973).

[450] By 1973, Romania was importing over 75 percent of its coking coal. Minister of Metallurgy Agachi commented in 1973 that "in the entire 1975-80 period there will be a shortage of coke in Romania." Cadres were urged to seek methods to reduce coke consumption, and a significant portion of the metallurgical research institutes' R&D efforts were devoted to identifying ways to increase the volume of coke production from "inferior" Romanian coal. *Ibid.*; *Scînteia* (January 4, 1975); *Metalurgia* (September 1972).

[451] Accidental stoppages at Galati's slabbing mill resulted in more than 100 hours of lost production time in 1973 (*România Libera*, December 12, 1973). The Minister of Metallurgy noted in 1974 that many of the steel finishing enterprises were operating on an unprofitable or low profitability basis, a reflection of their aging production equipment. *Scînteia* (January 4, 1974).

[452] The 1971-75 Five Year Plan featured the construction of a greenfield integrated specialty steelworks at Tirigoviste which would supply advanced steel products to the Romanian machinery industry. After Galati, the Tirigoviste project received the largest portion of capital invested in the steel industry (23 percent); it was built largely with West German equipment and technology. *România Libera* (January 8-9, 1976); *Metal Bulletin Monthly* (January 1979).

[453] *România Libera* (January 8-9, 1976). The Draft Directives of the new Plan provided that "By improving the structure of the production and expanding advanced processes, we will increase the degree of utilization of metal, so that in 1980 the value of rolled steels obtained from one ton of steel ingots will be approximately 10 times higher than in 1975." *Draft directives of the 11th Romanian Communist Party Congress on 5-Year Plan*, reproduced in *Scînteia* (August 3, 1974).

industrial investment to the steel sector which was, on the whole, even higher than that of the 1971-75 period.[454]

The Romanian Economic Crisis. The Romanian economic crisis that began at the end of the 1970s had multiple elements.[455] It was apparent by this point that Romania was simply unable to supply its growing industrial base with sufficient quantities of raw materials or energy; it was even forced to import oil, of which it had once been a leading exporter.[456] At the same time, Romania's efforts to offset its growing trade imbalance through exports were frustrated by stagnant economic conditions in the West.[457] Romania had borrowed heavily in the West to finance the import of production equipment and raw materials, and had enormous amounts of capital sunk in half-completed industrial projects.[458] Its foreign debt problems were exacerbated by rising energy costs and interest rates. In 1981 Romania was unable to roll over its short-term debt and was forced to seek a rescheduling agreement with the IMF and creditor countries and banks.[459]

Internally, the centralized economic system, which had proven effective as a means of increasing quantitative industrial output, was acting as a drag on economic performance as the economy became more diversified and complex. Individual enterprises suffered from raw materials and energy shortfalls, inability to convert from oil-fired production, bottlenecks, poor coordination and sheer bureaucratic inertia.[460] A new round of "decentralization" measures in 1979 did little to alleviate these problems.[461]

---

[454] Another greenfield integrated steelworks was to be established at Calarasi, incorporating state-of-the-art Western technology. Modernization and expansion of the Galati, Resita, Tirigoviste, Hunedoara and other existing works was also planned. *România Libera* (January 8-9, 1976).

[455] The Yugoslav journal *Borba* commented on November 10, 1983 that "Generally speaking, the word 'crisis' cannot be heard in Romania when economic problems are discussed. It is used reluctantly, and in order to describe the situation one uses terms like 'uncoordinated development of individual economic branches' and 'contradictions and deviations in the implementation of adopted policy.'"

[456] *Era Socialista* commented on March 25, 1983 that "In the process of industrial production on the whole, a certain disproportion between the processing industry and the base of energy and new materials has appeared."

[457] House Ways and Means Committee, Subcommittee on Trade, *Report on Trade Mission to Central and Eastern Europe*, 98th Cong., 2d Sess., March 29, 1984, p. 57.

[458] *Revistà Economicà* (September 7, 1979; June 19, 1981); *România Libera* (February 18, 1982).

[459] Ways and Means Committee, *Report on Trade Mission*, pp. 57-58.

[460] See, *e.g.*, *Revistà Economicà* (February 18, 1983) ("Delays in 1983 Investment Plan Implementation Analyzed"); *România Libera* (May 20, 1983) ("Failure to Deliver Supplies to Energy Construction Sites Deplored").

[461] *Die Presse* (April 20, 1982).

The steel industry, like other major Romanian industrial sectors, began to experience severe difficulties in the late 1970s.[462] The industry was increasingly dependent on imported raw materials and energy to support its operations; by 1980 the industry was forced to import over 80 percent of its iron ore and to pay for much of it with valuable hard currency.[463] Because of the acute shortage of coking coal the government urgently sought to promote conservation of this commodity by the steel producing enterprises, although with limited success.[464] A major related problem was growing energy shortages and periodic interruption in the power supply at individual steelworks, which caused production lines to shut down and reduced yields and productivity.[465]

The industry was also plagued by mismanagement, personnel problems, and poor coordination and distribution between the various producing enterprises. The steel mills, particularly those producing flat-rolled, specialty and other processed products, were dependent upon other enterprises for their inputs, and the chronic inability of enterprises to deliver as planned had negative ripple effects through the industry.[466] Worker errors and mounting undiscipline impeded productivity, prompting the economic and party journals to call for improved training programs.[467] Numerous instances of inadequate "technological discipline" by mid-level management were cited; when problems arose, it was charged,

Instead of closely examining each problem for basic resolution, often there are ad-hoc approaches, with scores of experts and executives

---

[462] *Scînteia* reported on August 30, 1979 that "President Comrade Nicolae Ceausescu criticized the nonfulfillment of the production plan in the case of steel, rolled goods and other products and recommended that firm and responsible action should be taken to recoup lags and completely fulfill this year's tasks."

[463] Economist Intelligence Unit, *Quarterly Review of Romania, Bulgaria and Albania* (Third Quarter 1981). In the late 1970s the government launched ambitious programs to increase recovery and utilization of scrap, but the country did not possess enough scrap processing facilities to support a major expansion in scrap utilization.

[464] *Revistà Economicà* (September 7, 1979); *Scînteia* (November 27, 1980); *România Libera* (August 4, 1983).

[465] *Revistà Economicà* (September 7, 1979).

[466] *Scînteia* (November 27, 1980); *Revistà Economicà* (March 23, 1979); *România Libera* (August 4, 1983).

[467] *Munca de Partid* complained in July 1978 that "Serious violation of work discipline continued to occur -- absenteeism, leaving facilities unsupervised or operating them incorrectly, leaving them unattended, introduction and drinking of alcoholic beverages, pilfering. Such situations, which occurred against the backdrop of serious manifestations of undiscipline, disorder and lack of supervision were also found at . . . Galati Metallurgical Combine [and] Cimpia Turzii Metallurgical Combine." See also *Scînteia* (August 30, 1979); *Revistà Economicà* (March 23, 1979).

from various departments in enterprises, centrals, and the ministry almost totally limiting themselves to control work.[468]

The steel industry's difficulties continued despite repeated efforts at reform in the 1980s. While new investments were planned -- most notably a massive new coke oven at Galati -- implementation of the investments fell far behind schedule in the metallurgical (as well as other) branches.[469] While profit-and-loss data for the Romanian steel producing enterprises is not available, it is evident that by the 1980s the industry was operating on an unprofitable basis.[470] Reuters reported in 1984 that:

While output capacity grows apace, output itself is likely to fall short by ever greater amounts, the experts said. Output targets went underfulfilled even during the past decades of growth, while capital investment for the targets was being pumped in as planned. This had compounded overall nonprofitability and sent Romanian steel production costs soaring, they said. Deficits were due not to slackening production capacities but raw materials handicaps and low productivity, they added. The gap between capacity and output is widening. Capacity use fell from 88 percent in 1980 to 72 percent in 1982.[471]

Romania's massive commitment to steel had thus produced an industry which, in comparison with the nation's size, was enormous, which consumed huge quantities of energy and raw materials which Romania could not produce domestically and could import only at great cost to the economy, and which repeatedly proved unable to operate efficiently. A less likely candidate to achieve a major export presence could hardly be found. Yet since the late 1970s Romania has become one of the world's major steel-exporting nations, shipping more net export tonnage in 1981 than nations such as Sweden and Brazil. This phenomenon does not reflect any comparative advantage achieved by the Romanian industry -- if anything, the reverse is true. As the contradictions in the Romanian economy multiplied, the volume of its steel

---

[468] *Revistà Economicà* (March 23, 1979). At the Tirigoviste specialty steelworks management was chided for "Insufficient technological discipline, in the failure to provide appropriate technical assistance for all shifts, in maintaining some equipment in inoperable condition, inappropriate maintenance and lengthening of the time needed to repair certain equipment, irregular supply of certain items to work sites, poor cooperation with raw materials and materials suppliers, and so forth." *Revistà Economicà* (October 26, 1979).

[469] The principal problem was the failure of suppliers to deliver the requisite equipment to the sites of the investment projects. *Revistà Economicà* (February 18, 1983).

[470] The industry's utilization of steel ingot remained chronically low and fell far below plan targets, a problem that was attributed to work stoppages and raw materials and energy shortfalls. *Revistà Economicà* (March 23, 1979).

[471] *Reuters North European Service*, May 16, 1984.

exports increased, and in fact a correlation appears to exist between these two phenomena; growing Romanian steel exports are not an isolated sectoral development, but one symptom of Romania's larger economic crisis and the efforts of government planners to cope with it.

Romania's Foreign Trade In Steel. Since 1978 Romania has been found to have dumped steel, or has been reportedly selling steel at low prices, in the United States, France, West Germany, Belgium, the Netherlands, Finland, the United Kingdom, and Japan, as well as the European Communities as an entity.[472] Such exports tended to occur in abrupt surges of a relatively small number of product types (most commonly plate and thick sheets produced by the Galati steelworks) into only a few Western markets.[473] These surges do not reflect Romanian enterprises' response to market opportunities. Rather they are attempts by Romanian planners to employ an unwieldy, highly centralized system to enhance export earnings on an urgent basis in a volatile and highly competitive international market.

Romanian planners have given several sectors, including steel, the principal task of achieving export earnings.[474] The designated export sectors and enterprises are given priority in the allocation of national resources such as energy and raw materials.[475] Such responses were sufficiently scarce that even the favored enterprises suffered from power brownouts and raw materials shortages, but the rest of the economy fared far worse -- in 1984 *Reuters* characterized the steel industry as a "drain on [imported] Romanian energy" which resulted in the "need to strictly limit electricity use by the nation's consumers."[476]

Traditionally Romanian foreign trade has been conducted on a "command" basis, with export pricing decisions being made based on factors such as a

---

[472] *Hot-Rolled Carbon Steel Plate from Romania*, No. 731-TA-51 (1982); *Metal Bulletin* (June 5, 1984); *American Metal Market* (January 27, 1982); *Certain Carbon Steel Products from Romania*, No. A-484-401 (1984). *Metal Bulletin* (February 3, 1978; March 11, 1980;August 11, November 24, 1981; May 14, 1982); *Japan Metal Bulletin* (January 19, 1984); *Kyodo*, 10:40 GMT, December 30, 1984 (Foreign Broadcast Information Service). *Official Journal*, L. 23 (January 28, 1978); *Official Journal*, L. 108 (April 22, 1978).

[473] *Revistà Economicà* acknowledged on December 6, 1985 that Romanian export pricing was "causing difficulties for many traditional western steel firms." In 1984 52 percent of Romania's exports of thick and medium sheets were concentrated on only three markets, the U.S., Japan, and West Germany, and 82 percent of its exports of thin and galvanized sheet were concentrated on the U.S., France and West Germany.

[474] In 1984 *Kyodo* reported that Romania's Deputy Minister of Light Industry had "singled out aluminum, steel, chemical products, consumer goods, furniture and agricultural products as possible high value added products for exports. Romania, suffering from international debts, is giving top priority to expanding exports and reducing imports." 04:13 GMT, August 14, 1984 (Foreign Broadcast Information Service). See also *Revistà Economicà* (November 30, 1984).

[475] *Revistà Economica* (April 13, 1984).

[476] *Reuters North European Service*, May 16, 1984; *Sudosteuropa* (May 1983).

government-mandated target amount of foreign currency to be earned or a target export volume to be achieved. In the late 1970s and 1980s, Romania made an effort to move away from stimulating exports "manually" in favor of government economic incentives to the FTOs and producing enterprises -- through use of devices such as export subsidies and other export-forcing practices commonly employed in Western countries.[477] In 1983 the government established a special fund in the Ministry of Foreign Trade "in order to promote and maintain export of products with assured sales on certain foreign markets." The fund consisted of revenues obtained by selling the same products domestically (or in certain foreign markets) at a higher price, and "other sources as well," apparently a reference to the state budget.[478] Another decree provided for

> *raising the level of profitability and profit from the export output at the expense of the profitability and profit from the output for domestic consumption . . . so that the profitability of the export output will be 80 percent higher than that of the output for domestic consumption.*[479]

While the state could employ a variety of export-stimulating measures to stimulate sales by enterprises, a far more difficult problem was the need to achieve a true economic profit on exports; that is, to secure a price that offset the cost to the national economy of producing the commodity, and provided a return element which could be used to service the debt. The export of products at prices which entailed a net loss to the economy was the constant despair of Romanian planners,[480] and the steel industry was one of the export

---

[477] *Revistă Economică* noted approvingly on May 29, 1981 that many nations were stimulating exports through mechanisms which "provide better conditions for production and foreign sales than those created for production and sales on the domestic market." It pointed out that it was "possible to perfect and diversify the use of such methods of stimulating exports as customs exemptions and aids granted for imports for export production, encouragement of export production through profits, granting credits for export production and marketing, use by the producer units of part of their above-plan foreign exchange collections, formation of special funds in the economic units to encourage the workers, etc. These methods can create a climate favorable to export activity and a use of economic forces and levers to stimulate that activity."

[478] The size of the export promoting fund was to be determined annually in conjunction with the preparation of the budget. Section B, Article 9, Decree of the State Council on *Incentives to Enterprises and Workers to Fulfil and Exceed Export Production*, reproduced in *Scînteia*, September 22, 1983; *Agerpres*, 11:10 GMT, September 22, 1983 (Foreign Broadcast Information Service).

[479] The state could manipulate the "profits" of the enterprises in this manner because these funds were, in effect, simply accounts in state banks which would be disbursed to the enterprises only with central government approval. Under this scheme enterprises would automatically be credited with higher "profits" on commodities produced for export production.

[480] *România Libera* (March 19, 1981); *Revistă Economică* (June 25, 1984).

industries chided for its failure to achieve exports at the level of remuneration set by planners.[481]

A series of administrative measures were implemented after 1980 designed to encourage profitability in export sales, but below-cost Romanian exports continued.[482] The FTOs faced a difficult task in attempting to achieve prices which resulted in "profitability" on the international market; Romanian production of commodities such as steel entailed production costs that were out of proportion to their real sale value on the international market, and under such circumstances, the FTO had to choose between unprofitable sales or no sales at all. Moreover, the Romanian system was poorly adapted to react quickly to developments and changes on the international market, a problem that preoccupied Romanian commentators.[483] The result of such rigidities was the implementation of production according to a plan, culminating in the production of commodities for which little international demand existed and ultimately, dumping in the international markets.[484]

Other instances of dumping reflected the entrepreneurial zeal of individual FTO officials, who were able to exploit the disorganization and complexity of the foreign trade bureaucracy for personal gain.[485] Moreover, some government measures designed to increase profitability actually led to increased sales of low-priced Romanian goods on the international market. Thus, in a drastic attempt to improve the balance of payments, the Romanian government in 1981 decreed that each FTO's operations must become self-

---

[481] *Revistă Economică* reported on December 11, 1981 that "For some goods in the export program contracts were not concluded at the levels called for in the export plan. . . . Such situations, especially noted for steel and iron products [and six other sectors] led to the failure to fulfill the export plan."

[482] These include allowing the enterprises to retain, as a bonus, revenues which represent prices obtained above "standard" international prices, sharing by the FTOs of a percentage of revenues obtained from trade with the producing enterprises, requiring the FTOs to cover their costs out of their own trade incomes, and payment of bonuses to managers and workers for "outstanding export achievements." While some of these incentives existed prior to 1980, most of them were instituted through Law No. 12 of 1980, the *"Law Designed to Strengthen the Working People's Self-Management and the Economic, Financial and Foreign Exchange Self-Administration in Foreign Trade and International Economic Cooperation Activities."*

[483] *Revistă Economică* (March 30, August 21, September 21, 28, October 26, 1984).

[484] A Romanian economist admonished enterprises in 1984 that "The planning of extra merchandise for exportation, according to law, must be based on concluded international sales contracts having guarantees of fulfillment." I. Georgescu in *Revistă Economică* (September 21, 1984).

[485] *Scînteia* commented on August 19, 1982 that "Because of the irresponsibility and dishonesty of certain foreign trade cadres, which in some cases were compounded by deficient goods quality and nonobservance of contract terms Romanian products showed losses in international markets. Certain Romanian products . . . were marketed at lower than international prices, which inflicted great losses on the national economy. . . . Due to the incompetence or corruption of certain foreign trade cadres, clearly disadvantageous contracts were accepted offhand and dubious price concessions were made against the interests of our national economy."

sustaining with respect to foreign currency -- that is, any foreign exchange used by the FTO for imports had to be derived from the proceeds of the individual FTO's export sales.[486] This rule led to a significant increase in countertrade transactions, with the Romanians pressing their Western trading partners, as well as their creditors, to accept Romanian commodities -- frequently of very poor quality -- in direct exchange for Western goods or in satisfaction of Romanian debt.[487] Ultimately, the Romanian commodities were then disposed of somewhere in the world, usually at a discount.[488]

The immediate causes of Romanian dumping thus may vary from transaction to transaction -- the reason may be an urgent need for hard currency, corruption of individual FTO officials, a countertrade deal, the existence of surplus inventories, or simply the poor marketing skills of the FTOs. All of these factors, however, are ultimately manifestations of a system in which the state enjoys a pervasive role in the production, distribution and sale of industrial commodities.

Poland

In the 1970s the government of Poland financed a massive expansion of several key industrial sectors, including steel, drawing heavily on hard currency loans from Western banks. Poland's expansion drive was so poorly managed that the economy virtually collapsed in 1980-82, leaving the country saddled with a staggering burden of foreign debt, a trade deficit, and a variety of giant production facilities in various stages of completion, many of dubious economic value. The only way Poland could satisfy its foreign debt obligations was through an intensive expansion of exports, and the Polish government has implemented an extensive system of export incentives to achieve this purpose.

Low-priced Polish steel exports have caused intermittent disturbances in Western markets since the late 1970s. When Poland's expanded steelmaking capacity began to come on stream in 1977-79, a surge of low-priced Polish steel exports prompted the imposition of antidumping duties both in the European Community and the United States.[489] Shortly thereafter, the Polish steel industry was engulfed by Poland's growing economic and political crisis, culminating in the imposition of martial law and retaliatory trade sanctions by the U.S. government in 1982. Poland's steel exports to the West fell

---

[486] *Scînteia* (December 27, 1980).

[487] *Die Presse* (April 20, 1982).

[488] Countertrade transactions partially account for the surge of Romanian steel, predominantly plate, into the U.S. market which occurred in late 1984 and early 1985. At the end of 1984 a U.S. firm "imported Romanian steel plate through its [U.S. trading arm] under a 'complicated countertrade and barter arrangement' with Romania." Romanian plate imports into the U.S. totaled 158 thousand tons in 1984 and accounted for 12.2 percent of all imports of carbon steel plate under 6 inches in thickness, the second largest volume of this product from a single country. *American Metal Market* (March 21, 1985).

[489] *Certain Carbon Steel Plate from Poland*, 44 F.R. 23619, April 20, 1979.

(Million metric tons)

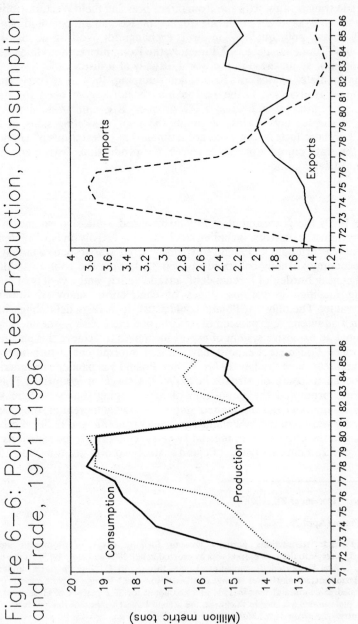
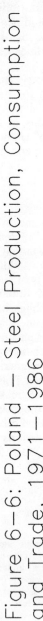

Figure 6–6: Poland – Steel Production, Consumption and Trade, 1971–1986

Source: International Iron and Steel Institute, Steel Statistical Yearbook, 1981, 1987. Production and Consumption refer to crude steel; Exports and Imports refer to semi-finished and finished steel.

substantially thereafter, but dumping recurred in a number of specific product sectors. Over the long run Poland is likely to remain a major exporter of steel to the West, if only because such exports represent an obvious means of reducing Poland's foreign debt.

As might be expected in a Soviet-style economy, the role of the state in directing the expansion of the Polish steel industry has been virtually absolute. The industry is state-owned and directly subordinated to the Ministry of Metallurgy and Machinery. Strategic decisions concerning the industry's growth and operations have been made pursuant to long, medium and short term government plans for the entire economy.[490] The government's pervasive control of the economy has enabled it to direct major concentrations of resources into those industrial sectors which it has deemed most important. After 1971-72, the expansion of the steel sector was a primary objective of Polish central planners.

The Gierek government, which came to power in late 1970, committed Poland to an intensive investment program designed to modernize industry, develop a strong export sector, and expand the availability of consumer goods. This program entailed heavy imports of Western production equipment, financed largely through heavy borrowing from Western banks. The basic Polish strategy was to employ the new equipment to produce export commodities that would then generate foreign exchange to repay the Western loans. Almost immediately, it became apparent that the underdeveloped state of the Polish steel industry constituted a major bottleneck in this plan.

In 1970 the Polish steel industry consisted of a large number of antiquated mills scattered through the former German territories in Silesia,[491] and several new plants constructed with Russian assistance after the war, most notably the Lenin steelworks in the Nowa Huta district of Krakow.[492] The technological

[490] After adoption by the Council of Ministers these plans have been refined and expanded at the ministerial and subministerial levels and passed down to the producing enterprises in the form of "plan directives" — in effect, obligatory commands to perform various economic tasks, such as the production of a given amount of steel. The investment, raw materials, energy and other resources necessary to achieve plan targets have likewise been channeled to the enterprise by government administrators, who also fixed the prices of raw materials and of finished steel products. Over time, the "command" style of economic administration has yielded to the increasing use of economic incentives to enterprises to achieve plan goals.

[491] Some of the Silesian mills dated back to the era of Metternich — in 1970, three of these plants were over 140 years old, and one of them, the Kosciusko mill, was the oldest continually operating steel mill in the world. *Zycie Gospodarcze* (September 2, 1979).

[492] *Wiadomosci Hutnicze* (November 11, 1979). After an initial intensive postwar investment program, Polish investments in steel had fallen off sharply. During the 1950-55 Six-Year Plan, investments in steelmaking accounted for 8.3 percent of total Polish investment. By 1966-70, this percentage had declined to 3 percent of total investments. *Zycie Warsawy* (October 6, 1973); *Wiadamosci Hutnicze* (May, 1979).

level and efficiency of the Polish industry was poor.[493] As Gierek's economic expansion program was implemented, the perceived need to expand Polish steelmaking capacity "became one of the most urgent problems facing economic planners."[494]

The Polish Capacity Expansion Effort. In 1971-72 the government launched a massive program to expand the steel industry in the 1971-75 period through an "enormous injection" of investment funds -- substantially increasing investment levels over prior periods (table 6-8).[495] The decision was made to place primary emphasis on the expansion at the more modern sites (Nowa Huta and Bierut) and the construction of a giant greenfield steel mill at Katowice. Construction of the Katowice steelworks (Huta Katowice) was Poland's largest single investment project of the entire 1970-80 decade.[496] The basic notion was that Huta Katowice would replace many of Poland's small open-hearth steelworks with a centralized melting plant, shipping semifinished slabs and blooms back to the smaller works (some of which would also be modernized) for rolling. This program would rationalize Poland's aging industry without the adverse social consequences entailed by widespread steelclosure of older mills.[497] Jointly planned by Polish and Soviet engineers, Katowice was to possess blast furnaces nearly as large (13 meters) as the largest Japanese facilities, and by 1980, upon completion of the first stage of its construction, was expected to produce 21 percent of Poland's national steel

---

[493] "We still run into old-fashioned steel plants and divisions that remind us of the 19th century." *Zycie Gospodarcze* (March 3, 1974). While the Lenin steelworks had two basic oxygen furnaces, and 13 electric arc furnaces had been brought into use in Poland, in 1970 over 80 percent of Poland's nominal capacity still consisted of obsolete Marten furnaces. *Wiadamosci Hutnicze* (June 1972), pp. 181-87.

[494] *Gospodarka Planowa* (July-August 1977), pp. 334-41. In 1975 alone, Poland spent 800 million dollars in foreign exchange to import metallurgical products, primarily iron and steel. *Nauka Polska* (November 1976). Poland's domestic steel production shortfalls were "the ball and chain of many investment projects . . . there is not enough reinforcing steel, pipes and sheet metal. This affects the construction, completion dates of residential sections, manufacturing plants, and research establishments." *Zycie Warszawy* (June 2, 1977).

[495] *Zycie Warszawy* (June 2, 1977); *Kurier Polski* (May 3, 1972). Because it is difficult to convert investment zlotys into a meaningful dollar equivalent, the figures showing the percent of national investment dedicated to steel give a better idea of the degree to which national resources were committed to this sector.

[496] *Zycie Warszawy* (June 2, 1977). In 1973 a longer range "Metallurgical Development Program" was adopted by the Presidium for the 1976-80 time frame, the primary feature of which was to be the further expansion of Katowice and the upgrading of many of the older mills. *Handel Zagraniczny* (November 1977), pp. 20-23.

[497] *Metal Bulletin Monthly* (December, 1987).

output, 4.5 million metric tons.[498] Upon completion of the "second stage" of its construction, this figure was to rise to 35 percent, or 9 million metric tons.[499] Production equipment for the mill was purchased both from westernations and the Soviet Union.[500] Construction of the Katowice mill was to be supplemented by a "vast expansion of the Lenin works" at Nowa Huta.[501]

Table 6-8. Polish Capital Investment in Steelmaking, 1966-80

	1966-70	1971-75	1975-80
Investment Outlays (Billions of Zlotys)	26.9	80.9	194.5
Steel Investments as a Percent of Total National Outlays	3.0	4.2	6.1
Steel Investments as a Percent of Total Industrial Investment	7.5	4.2	13.5

Source: Planning Commission attached to Council of Ministers in *Wiadomosci Hutnicze* (May 1979).

By the mid-1970s, at about the time that Katowice produced its first steel, it was becoming clear that the Gierek economic plan was in trouble. Poland's debts to Western banks were reaching alarming levels, but the export growth which, it had been hoped, would provide the means for repaying Poland's debts had not materialized -- Poland's balance of trade actually deteriorated as the 1970s progressed. When the giant investment projects had been undertaken, insufficient attention had been paid to such basic problems as the need to strengthen the transportation and energy infrastructure, with the result that the new plants suffered chronically from raw materials shortages,

---

[498] *Zolnierz Wolnosci* (May 1-2, 1976); *Nauka Polska* (November 1976). The plans for Katowice were drawn up jointly by the Polish Biprohut Metallurgical Design Institute -- which had been advocating the establishment of some form of large new "Centrum Plant" -- and the Soviet design organization GIPROMEZ. *Trybuna Robotnicza* (April 24-26, 1981).

[499] *Zolnierz Wolnosci* (May 1-2, 1976). The decision to build Katowice in two consecutive stages was based on the unacceptable strain which building the entire mill at one time would place on Poland's economy. *Gospodarka Planowa* (July-August 1977), pp. 334-41.

[500] *Trybuna Robotnicza* (April 24-26, 1981).

[501] *Zolnierz Wolnosci* (February 5, 1973).

brownouts, and power stoppages. The start-up of plants built with imported equipment was repeatedly delayed, and bottlenecks throughout the economy depressed output.[502]

The Katowice steelworks exemplified many of these problems, and it ultimately became a symbol of the "gigantism" and economic failures of the Gierek government.[503] Huta Katowice had been built in an area without the necessary transportation infrastructure.[504] The construction of the "first phase" of the Katowice project was plagued by delays, enormous cost overruns, and continuing controversy over the site chosen for the steelworks, which imposed unusually high transportation costs on raw materials delivered to the mill.[505] The original capital investment requirements projected for the first phase were $565.3 million -- an estimate which was "illusory and imprecise" at the time it was made and which, it was later suggested, should never have been made public.[506] By 1981 a total of $2.6 billion -- over five times the original estimated amount -- had been poured into the Katowice project, which was being blamed as a principal cause of Poland's economic crisis.[507] The Poles immediately faced "the need to repay the investment loans for the construction of the Katowice plant, as well as to pay the interest on these loans, which, in accordance with the regulations, burdens the production cost with the substantial sum of $58.6 million annually."[508]

As Huta Katowice's capacity became operational in the late 1970s and modernization measures were implemented at older mills, Polish steel production volume did increase dramatically, reaching an all-time high of 19.5

---

[502] As a Polish academic commented in 1983, Gierek's program "ended in disaster. Total collapse of market balance, huge foreign indebtedness, the considerable load of scattered and uncompleted investments, their faulty structure and gigantism, the strong dependence on imports from capitalist countries, the highly uncomplimentary, petrified structures -- led to the sudden drop of productivity of fixed assets and management efficiency." Juliusz Kolipinski in *Przeglad Techniczny* (June 19, 1983).

[503] *Wiadomosci Hutnicze* (October 1985).

[504] This move was apparently designed to help bind Poland to the Soviet Union economically and was attributed to decisions by "political authorities" rather than engineers. See *Polityka* (January 10, 1987).

[505] *Kurier Polski* (June 1, 1976); *Trybuna Robotnicza* (April 24-26, 1981).

[506] *Trybuna Robotnicza* (April 24-26, 1981).

[507] In a rather tepid defense of this expenditure, a Katowice official argued that the steelworks project alone could not be blamed for Poland's economic troubles: "The sum of 132.4 billion zlotys [$2.6 billion] is tremendous, accounting for about 9 percent of Poland's annual national income. But even such a huge sum was spent over the years 1973-88 (the expenditures during 1978-80 were relatively small) or in the course of five years (and perhaps there still remain some still unpaid debts in this connection) so that, in per annum terms, it accounted for 1.4 percent of the state budget. Comments are unnecessary. The construction of the Katowice Steel Plant could not tangibly shake the foundations of the nation's economy and hence the causes of the economic setback should be sought elsewhere . . ." *Trybuna Robotnicza* (April 24-26, 1981).

[508] *Ibid.*

million metric tons in 1980. Thereafter, however, the problems afflicting the Polish economy as a whole began to act as a serious drag on steel production. Energy and coal shortages led to drastic curtailments in output -- giving rise to "horrendous complaints" from the steel mills -- despite the fact that steel was one of the "areas deemed most important by the government program for emerging from the crisis."[509]   Finally, in late 1980, in an atmosphere of mounting economic chaos, the Polish government froze 15 major investment projects and curtailed work on 7 others, including Huta Katowice.[510]

The imposition of martial law by the Polish military at the end of 1981, and the widespread disorders that preceded and followed it, brought much of Poland's economy to a standstill, and resulted in a dramatic fall in steel production.[511] Some of the steel plants, such as Huta Katowice and the Lenin Works in Nowa Huta, were hotbeds of unrest.[512] Activity at the plants was hampered by absenteeism and the "struggle for every ton of raw material, for every component of a machine."[513]

---

[509] *Zycie Gospodarcze* (October 15, 1981). Zbigniew Szalajda, Minister of Metallurgy, commented that "At all such plants the good of the state is in collision with the good and interests of the individual plant; the problems ensue chiefly from the generally adopted principles for coal allocation. When the supply of coal, liquid fuels or energy is low, nearly everyone agrees that the quantity supplied to heavy industry should be reduced. This is logical, just, and easy to understand. But certain plants view this differently." *Ibid.*

[510] *Metal Bulletin* (February 3, 1981).

[511] The Ministry of Metallurgy -- widely blamed for the failures of the steel sector -- was by this time in a state of near paralysis. *Zycie Warszawy* reported on February 22, 1982 that "The relationship between the ministries and the enterprises is still in great flux and remains amorphous. The Ministry of Metallurgy and Machinery is still looking for a place for itself, for a new function to fulfill, and trying to distance itself from the current management, which is under such sharp criticism. . . . Everyone is feverishly looking for a place of his own under the new conditions, but no one has found it yet. . . . [Some plant managers] who are still attached to the old style of action and who have been thrown into the deep water of the reform and sucked up by the crisis, have become hangers-on at the Ministry . . . where they beseech assistance, support, or sometimes the removal of responsibility from their shoulders."

[512] The Polish Army reportedly had to intervene with tanks at Huta Katowice to restore order on December 23, 1981. *American Metal Market* (May 3, 1983) *Prano I Zycie* reported on September 24, 1983 with respect to the Lenin Steelworks that during the preceding 20 months workers at the plant had been arrested on numerous occasions for "offenses of a political nature," and that repeated interventions by militia had been required to maintain order. "Until now it was among the rolling plant workers where incidents of unrest most often occurred; various illegal activities usually started here. . . ."

[513] *Zycie Warszawy* (February 22, 1982). Polish Domestic Television Service reported on October 11, 1982 that "The work forces of the steelworks have not fulfilled the planned tasks in full. Less pig iron and steel was produced than planned. Meanwhile, the planned production of rolled steel products fell short by 2,500 tons. The main reasons for this state of affairs are the lack of railway cars to take away completed metallurgical products, which holds up production, and the cadre shortages. Today we visited the Jednoscz Steelworks in Siemianowice Slaskie. . . . Here too the cadre shortage is felt. If it were possible to ensure that there was a man at every work position, seven melts, instead of just six, could be completed during a shift." Foreign Broadcast Information Service (18:30 GMT).

By 1982 the state of the Polish steel industry was desperate. Raw materials and power shortages, labor strife, and the disordered state of Poland's economy seriously impeded production. Even the Katowice mill, from which so much had been expected, was grossly uneconomic to operate -- a consequence of its huge fixed costs, government-controlled prices, and the fact that additional major investments would be required before the mill could attain its planned production objectives.[514]

The Polish government was required to subsidize the steel industry's substantial losses, a fact which became public knowledge in 1982, when, as part of a 1983-85 plan to restore the economy through decentralization measures, the Jaruzelski government began calculating the financial performance of individual producing enterprises, noting that the lossmaking entities required subsidies from the state budget.[515] One of the principal industries to require an injection of subsidy funds to cover its losses was the steel industry; when the state budget was published in 1982, the government allotted funds to finance "losses and funds of enterprises of the metallurgy branch."[516] The Pokoj steelworks, one of the worst performers, lost money in every year after 1975, and by 1986, was losing $45.64 on every ton produced.[517] *Zycie Gospodarcze* complained on July 24, 1983 that

> *Of course, no reasonable person questions subsidies as an instrument of economic policy. . . . Let us subsidize economic activity, but completely openly and only motivated by truly important economic considerations. Such an important purpose is, let us say, subsidizing the consumption of milk, but it is not, for example, the subsidizing of iron metallurgy. Enterprises of this last trade received, however,*

---

[514] As a Katowice official observed in 1981, "And so we have a modern iron and steel plant which, in 1980, produced for the national economy. . .a loss of 11.6 billion zlotys [$262.3 million]. Should not this fact be regarded as unique? If viewed on the world scale the answer is certainly yes, because nowhere else in the world would production be modernized in such a way that, regardless of the huge investment outlays borne, the end result would be such enormous losses. But so far as this country is concerned, the answer is no, because here there exists so many other instances showing that the more modern a plant is, the more it operates in the red." *Trybuna Robotnicza* (April 24-26, 1981.) A Polish economist remarked caustically that "If all of society is to spend billions of zlotys on the construction of our giant [Katowice Steelworks] and who knows how many billions of zlotys annually to cover current deficits, then it would be well to consider whether it would not be socially more advantageous to abandon the further development of steelmaking in general." *Przeglad Techniczny* (June 19, 1983).

[515] It was reported that "2,600 economic units noted a negative financial accumulation in 1982. . . . It was necessary to subsidize enterprises with that much plus essential additions in the form of 'profits' from the budget, in order for them to operate by 'self financing' (it is difficult to hide that in this context both words sound grotesque)." *Zycie Gospodarcze* (July 24, 1983).

[516] Budget Law for 1983 of December 29, 1982, reproduced in *Dziennek Ustaw* (December 1982), item 288, pp. 761-808. The state budget allocated $422 million in expenditures to the Ministry of Metallurgy and Engineering, including "product subsidies" and funds for financial losses.

[517] *Trybuna Ludu* (April 10, 1987).

subsidies from the budget in the amount of around 32 billion zlotys [$349.5 million].[518]

By the mid-1980s, by the admission of Polish analysts, Poland's massive commitment to steelmaking had produced one of the least competitive steel industries in the industrialized world. "It is said in many Polish accounts that productivity of Polish mills, including the newest ones, is much lower than anywhere in the world. Some estimate it is several times lower."[519] Despite the fact that much Polish steelmaking plant was of relatively recent vintage, it was technologically backward.[520] Worker morale was so low that it led to a "mass efflux of manpower" from the mills,[521] making it difficult to maintain enough skilled personnel in "critical work positions";[522] at the same time, on a world scale, the industry was overmanned, and worker productivity was astonishingly poor.[523] In early 1988, strikes by workers at the Lenin Steelworks shook the Jaruzelski regime and threatened to ignite a more general wave of strikes across Poland.

Poland's commitment to steel arguably was irrational. The industry produced a low-quality product which was in surplus on international markets and for which hard currency prices were low; yet it depended for inputs on imported iron ore which required the use of scarce hard currency, and it consumed huge quantities of domestic coal which could otherwise have been exported. One Polish economist commented in 1987 that "As an economist, I would like to know, how much does one ton of steel of a specific grade cost us [to make]? As far as I know, no cost-effectiveness analysis was prepared in a credible way, either at the investment or the operating stage."[524] Because of the need to subsidize steel enterprises' losses and to invest in

---

[518] Poland's ferrous metallurgy sector had the lowest rate of capital accumulation of any Polish industrial sector in 1982. *Zycie Gospodarcze* (February 27, 1983). Polish journalist Piotr Cegielski commented that with the granting of subsidies "[enterprises] certainly find it easier to carry on with wasteful and expensive production and keep receiving their subsidy than to attempt to reduce their costs and improve their management efficiency." *Gazeta Olsztynska* (June 20, 1983).

[519] *Polityka* (January 10, 1987).

[520] Huta Katowice, for example, had been built without continuous casting technology. *Wiadomisci Hutnicze* (October 1985).

[521] *Rzeczpospolita* (December 30, 1986).

[522] The housing conditions for workers at the Lenin Steelworks were "detestable," and in late 1986, 4,000 workers at that mill were still waiting for their own housing. The Polish mills poured massive quantities of pollutants into the air, leading to frequent complaints by workers and residents. *Dziennik Polski* (October 9, 1986).

[523] A Polish analyst noted in 1985 that in the European Community the steel industry averaged 0.8 manhours per ton of steel, whereas Poland averaged over 20 manhours per ton. *Wiadomosci Hutnicze* (October 1985).

[524] Dr. Wawrzyniek Wierzbicki in *Polityka* (January 10, 1987).

modernization, every year the industry "consumed 20 billion zlotys [$75.4 million]." The same Polish economist exclaimed in 1987:

> *Let us not blunder along any further. The insatiable steelworks demon is devouring all of the funds allocated for investment and it is also gobbling up raw materials and energy. . . . Let us stop harassing Polish society to maintain such an outdated and inefficient structure.*

To rectify some of these deficiencies, since 1985 Polish planners deployed some of the country's limited resources to undertake the modernization of segments of the Polish steel sector, leading one analyst to comment that "this drama, or at least the tragedy of errors surrounding the Katowice Steelworks, is still going on."[525] Huta Katowice, which originally had been planned as a source of semifinished steel for other mills, began moving into downstream processing itself. It received a new coking plant and an automated rail hardening plant from the Soviets, the latter to be paid for on a barter basis with the export of its rails to the Soviet Union.[526] However, in early 1988, Poland shelved most of its modernization plans for the industry until after 1990, cutting planned investments back by more than two thirds.[527]

Poland's Steel Exports. The disordered state of Poland's steel industry has not resulted in a poor international trade performance. During the same period that the Polish economy was declining dramatically (1980-82), Poland was becoming, for the first time, a net exporter of steel, at least in volume. The 1981-82 crisis saw a slight drop in Polish steel export volume and a shift in export patterns away from the West, but this decrease was in no way commensurate with the wholesale disruption of Polish steel production during the period. In 1987 Poland won out against "stiff" competition from Japan, West Germany and Britain to make a massive sale of rails to Brazil.[528] Poland's continued strong export performance demonstrates the government's overriding determination to maintain a high level of exports, regardless of the condition of the steel industry and internal state of the Polish economy.

Government policy, rather than industrial efficiency, has always been the primary determinant of Polish export performance. Prior to 1982 Poland's domestic economy was largely insulated from the world market; the nation's international trade was primarily conducted by foreign trade organizations (FTOs) which bought goods for export from domestic producing enterprises at domestic prices. Export transactions by the trading organizations were conducted at world market prices -- there was no real relationship between the price which an FTO paid to a domestic producing unit for a commodity

---

[525] *Polityka* No. 44 (1986).

[526] *Rzeczpospolita* (December 5, 1985); *Trybunu Ludu* (October 9, 1986).

[527] *Metal Bulletin* (January 11, 1988).

[528] *Metal Bulletin* (August 6, 1987).

and the price realized by the trading unit for the commodity on the world market. Profits realized by the trading organizations on exports were transferred to the state budget, which also covered losses with so-called "price-equalization subsidies."[529] Export decisions were made pursuant to government-fixed targets made on a "material" basis -- that is, targets based on factors such as export volume and the totals of foreign currency to be earned -- not profitability.[530]

This "command" export structure was operating in 1977-78 when Huta Katowice first became operational and Poland was in a position to expand its steel export volume. Polish planners placed high hopes on Katowice to reduce the need for imports and to produce steel for export.[531] In fact, the activation of Huta Katowice in 1977 did result in an abrupt drop in the volume of Polish steel imports and a steady increase in the volume of exports through 1979. Polish exports increased significantly in 1977-78 despite depressed world demand and prices, and low-priced Polish steel exports quickly provoked a spate of antidumping actions against Poland by the European Communities.[532] In 1978 the Community and Poland entered into a bilateral agreement pursuant to which Poland agreed to quantitative limits on its steel exports to the Community; Polish exports to the Community were limited thereafter to quantities reflecting Poland's "traditional" share of the market. In the United States the 1978 volume of steel imports from Poland doubled over 1977 levels,

---

[529] Jan Giezgala, Deputy Director of Poland's Foreign Trade Institute, in "The Foreign Trade System in Poland," in Paul Marer, ed., *Polish-U.S. Industrial Cooperation in the 1980s* (Bloomington: Indiana University Press, 1981), p. 91.

[530] *Zycie Gospodarcze* commented on December 13, 1981, "we do not know whether our exports are profitable or not." *Handel Zagraniczny* observed on November 3, 1983, with respect to the pre-1982 foreign trade system that "Export deliveries were planned either from the viewpoint of the benefits derivable from a production task-related export [*e.g.*, the acquisition of foreign exchange] or as a result of the "pressure" put on by a particular plenipotentiary . . ."

[531] In 1976 Poland's Minister of Metallurgy indicated that Katowice was expected to supply all of Poland's demand for sectional products and sheets, and "periodic balance surpluses can be exported." *Nauka Polska* (November 1976). *Zycie Warszawy* commented on June 7, 1977, soon after Katowice produced its first steel, that "Construction of the Katowice Iron and Steel Works is the salvation, it will permit modernization of the steel industry and an amelioration of the unfavorable trade balance." Several months later Polish metallurgical industry leaders met and agreed that "A further improvement in the balance and effectiveness of foreign trade, particularly with the [Western nations] was recognized as one of the leading tasks this year. It is anticipated that the balance of turnovers of metallurgical products made with iron with these countries will improve by nearly 500 million foreign exchange zlotys, chiefly as a result of production undertaken by the Katowice Foundry rolling mill." (Conversion to U.S. dollars not available.) *Zycie Gospodarcze* (February 12, 1978).

[532] In early 1978 the European authorities imposed provisional antidumping duties on imports of Polish galvanized sheets. *Official Journal*, L.19 (January 24, 1978). They also commenced a more general investigation into alleged dumping of Polish steel products in the Common Market. *Bulletin of the European Communities* (January 1978), p. 55.

causing the U.S. Treasury Department to self-initiate an antidumping investigation which also resulted in the imposition of duties.[533]

Although the 1981-82 crisis saw a steep drop in steel production and the eruption of domestic steel shortages,[534] Stalexport, the Polish FTO handling steel, endeavored with considerable success to maintain the overall volume of Polish steel exports at or near pre-crisis levels,[535] although at a reduced per ton earnings level.[536] Trade sanctions imposed by the U.S. and other Western nations following the imposition of martial law disrupted Poland's trade with the West, and in 1982-83 much of Poland's steel export volume was shifted to the Soviet bloc, nonaligned nations, and developing countries;[537] Finland complained that in the first 8 months of 1982 it had been "hit by cheap imports" of Polish steel at triple the volume of the comparable period in 1981.[538] In 1986, Poland exported approximately 200 thousand tons to Western

[533] The Treasury Department found that 82 percent of the Polish steel plates imported into the U.S. had been sold at dumped prices, with margins ranging as high as 44 percent. *Certain Carbon Steel Plate from Poland*, 44 F.R. 23619, April 20, 1979.

[534] In October 1982 *Gospodarcza Materialowa* reported domestic shortages of bars, pipes, galvanized sheets, and black plates.

[535] The Warsaw network P.A.P. reported on February 22, 1982 that "in spite of unfavorable conditions, current plans of the foreign trade enterprise Stalexport provide for keeping this year's exports at last year's level. Capitalist countries are to receive one million tons of Polish steel . . ." 14:12 GMT, Foreign Broadcast Information Service.

[536] *Polityka* observed critically on January 15, 1983, that "we had to do with . . . an increase in the quantity of exports and drop in value. The negative difference in value was more than 8 percentage points and was greater than that of any of our other exports for that year. This resulted not so much from the unfavorable economic situation in the world steel market as from the products of the Katowice Metallurgical Plant. This plant produces simple products, *e.g.*, railroad rails, supplies them for export, and influences the selection of products exported by Stalexport; in this way it contributes to decreasing the foreign exchange prices converted to per ton of steel."

[537] In early 1982 an East Coast longshoreman's union boycott of all goods loaded at Polish ports resulted in a dramatic fall in U.S. steel imports from Poland — from 97 thousand tons in 1981 to 17 thousand tons in 1982. The U.S. government suspended Poland's most-favored nation status in October 1982, causing the U.S. duty on most Polish steel products to increase from 7 percent to nearly 23 percent. *American Metal Market* (May 3, 1983) On the other hand, following the imposition of martial law the Soviets began making good some of the raw materials shortages which had plagued the Polish steel industry — supplying substantial quantities of iron ore and pig iron. *Trybunu Ludu* (March 28, 1983). In 1983 the Poles planned iron and steel exports to the Soviet bloc of over 1.7 million tons — a nearly 100 percent increase over 1982 levels and an export tonnage approaching Poland's total steel product export tonnage (1.9 million tons) in the years preceding the crisis. *Zycie Gospodarcze* (December 12, 1982)

[538] *Metal Bulletin* (November 5, 1982). In 1984 the Finnish government announced it would impose restrictions on imports of steel from Eastern Europe. Finnish producers complained that "cheap steel imports from countries like Poland, East Germany and Romania are flooding the home market" and that import volume had reached 'intolerable' levels." *Metal Bulletin* (March 2, 1984).

markets, down from 800 thousand tons in 1979.[539] The drop in Polish steel exports to the U.S. market is an aberration reflecting the U.S.-Poland political impasse; a Stalexport official described the U.S. sanctions as a "curse" and indicated that

The success of our [steel] industry has been due in large part to our access to the American market. It was an MFN-oriented structure.[540]

The same official indicated that Poland would attempt to maintain some presence in the U.S. market despite sanctions, stating that "we are trying to sacrifice ourselves" -- that is, accept lower margins to compensate for the higher duty.[541] In 1983, "state-owned steel companies in Poland" were cited as among the most price-aggressive foreign sources of structural shapes sold in the U.S. market (along with South Korean and Spanish producers), a factor in what was termed the "complete collapse" of structural beam and channel pricing.[542] In June 1984 the Department of Commerce ruled that Poland was dumping wire rod in the U.S. market by a weighed average margin of 36.8 percent.[543] In 1985 Poland entered into a voluntary restraint arrangement with the U.S. under President Reagan's steel program.

In fact, over the longer term, Polish steel exports are virtually certain to resume a significant presence in Western markets, because of the continuing burden of Poland's debt to the West. The Poles recognize that "the only way out of the debt trap is through a rapid increase in exports."[544] However, they are also aware that because of the comparatively underdeveloped state of their industrial economy, a substantial increase in exports will have to occur, first of all, in "fuels and energy, industrial metals, and food," for which markets can be found in the West, rather than in more complex industrial product areas where Polish products are not competitive.[545] Steel products, for which the Poles now possess substantial production capacity, are likely export candidates.[546] The Rzeszow *Nowiny* observed on October 9, 1986 that

---

[539] Stalexport in *Metal Bulletin Monthly* (December 1987).

[540] *American Metal Market* (May 3, 1983).

[541] *Ibid.*

[542] *American Metal Market* (June 14, 1983).

[543] *Carbon Steel Wire Rod from Poland* (final), No. A-455-002, July 14, 1984.

[544] *Gazeta Krakowska* (May 10, 1983).

[545] *Handel Zagraniczy*, No. 1-2 (1982), pp. 9-10.

[546] Significantly, while the government has frozen many investment projects, it has permitted a number of steel modernization and expansion projects to go forward. In the Katowice district, "work will be resume soon on . . . 16 capital projects in the iron and steel and machine building industries. . . ." *Trybunu Ludu* (November 8, 1983).

> *Debt service will weigh on the country's development for a long time yet. In this situation the only way out is to intensify our exports, as the Stalowowalsk Steelworks is doing. Plans to the year 2000 call for a tripling of exports to [the Soviet bloc] and a quadrupling of exports to [Western nations].*

Polish Export Incentives. A fundamental strategic dilemma confronting Polish planners has been how to sustain an export presence at all in an industry with weak international competitiveness. The principal response has been the implementation of a variety of export incentives similar to the export subsidies used by many capitalist and mixed economies. In 1982, the government renounced the practice of stimulating exports "manually" in favor of a system which does so solely through the use of economic incentives to the enterprises -- devices such as subsidies, currency devaluation, and tax and other fiscal incentives.[547] This reflected an overriding governmental determination to expand exports as a national priority -- the government made it clear that if one set of incentives did not succeed in sufficiently boosting exports, another set would be tried.[548]

The most significant export promoting measure was a law which permitted producing enterprises to retain, in their own accounts for their own use, a percentage of the foreign currency revenues generated from their export sales.[549] These funds could be used to purchase Western raw materials, equipment, or other commodities.[550] Because of the devalued state of the zloty, the ability to secure, hold and use scarce foreign exchange without cumbersome administrative procedures was clearly a powerful incentive to

---

[547] These reforms are summarized in Polish Chambers of Foreign Trade, *Economic Reform in Poland* (Warsaw: The Chambers, 1982). As *Nowe Droge* expressed the change (April 1983, pp. 126-36), it meant rejection of the "belief that enterprises can be forced effectively to export by means of orders" in favor of creating "operating conditions that move them to export as much as possible."

[548] *Rynki Zagraniczne* (June 16, 1983).

[549] Law on Financial Regulations of State Enterprises, February 26, 1982, Dziennik Ustaw No. 7, item 54. Prior to this measure the producing enterprises received foreign exchange for their own use "largely by means of a hierarchical system of ministries and associations." *Handel Zagraniczny* No. 3 (1983). Foreign exchange "bonuses" were granted to enterprises that meet or exceed export targets, although in practice, the bonus payments frequently did not make it down through administrative channels to the enterprise.

[550] The percentage of foreign exchange which may be retained is fixed by the Ministry of Foreign Trade for each enterprise. In theory the percentage cannot exceed 50 percent of the enterprise's earnings, although in fact the rate may be increased in "exceptional cases." *Polityka* (March 20, 1982).

export -- if not an outright subsidy.[551] Stanislaw Dlugosz, assistant chairman of the Council of Ministers Planning Commission, commented in 1983 that

> *It is generally acknowledged that the most aggressive pro-export instruments are the foreign exchange allowance accounts, since they give enterprises access to the rarest asset that we have, and that is foreign exchange funds.*[552]

As of August 1982, of the 331 producing enterprises maintaining such accounts, the Katowice and Lenin (Nowa Huta) Iron and Steel Works were among the 9 largest users (both in terms of credits and expenditures from the accounts) -- an indicator that the foreign exchange retention scheme was proving advantageous to these enterprises.[553]

In addition, among the most controversial export-promoting measures taken by the government were a series of devaluations of the zloty against foreign currencies.

> *This was done to ensure the profitability of all our exports, so that the rate of exchange serves as an incentive for producer exporters to undertake more effective production. [Since the devaluation] the overwhelming majority of Polish exports have proven profitable ... the new rates of exchange have made it possible almost immediately to single out plants and even whole sub-branches working effectively, cheaply, and competitively in relation to foreign competitors.*[554]

---

[551] The U.S. Commerce Department recently held that this scheme did not constitute a countervailing subsidy, noting that "because there is no reasonable basis for quantifying such an advantage, such alleged benefits do not constitute a bounty or grant." *Carbon Steel Wire Rod from Poland*, February 16, 1984, p. 18. However, whether quantifiable or not, the ability to possess and use foreign currency in a society where access to that currency is regulated, and where the currency itself commands extraordinary buying power, is a significant export incentive. *Przeglad Techniczny* commented on March 20, 1983 that "Wherever the dollar is regular or exchangeable currency a citizen knows he can spend it on half a pack of cigarettes, a kilogram of fruit, two newspapers, or one-third of a cinema ticket. In Poland, mythology starts with a one-dollar bill, commonly known as a 'Washington,' which on the black market can buy 20 packs of cigarettes, almost a hundred newspapers, 150 bus tickets ... and ten cinema tickets." The black market dollar/zloty exchange rate was estimated at about 700:1 in early January, 1984, compared with an official rate of 99:1. *Forbes* (February 13, 1983)

[552] *Rynki Zagraniczne* (June 16, 1983).

[553] *Polityka* (August 21, 1982). By 1983, 1,621 manufacturing enterprises had opened these accounts, with a total balance of over $1 billion. Ministerstwo Handlu Zagranicznego letter to U.S. Department of Commerce Office of Investigations, January 12, 1984.

[554] *Zycie Warszawy* (June 30, 1982).

Initially, the zloty was devalued against both Western currencies and the Soviet bloc exchange currency, the transfer ruble.[555] Thereafter, however, "the rate of exchange of the dollar is changed in a fairly arbitrary manner compared with the real change value of the zloty"[556] -- in effect the zloty was periodically further devalued against the dollar when this was deemed necessary to ensure the continued profitability of 75-80 percent of Poland's exports to the West.[557] In an interview with *Rzeczpospolita* (July 1, 1983), Stanislaw Majewski, President of the National Bank of Poland, explained the system:

> *Q: The decision to devalue was probably dictated by our desire to increase exports to free-currency markets. ...*
>
> *A: Yes, that's exactly what we had in mind. The exchange rate level influenced the profitability of production destined for foreign buyers. By raising profitability, the devaluation of the zloty creates more favorable terms for exporting enterprises. It is a simple process. Let us assume that we sell a certain product abroad for 1000 dollars. As late as yesterday the value of such a deal, calculated in zlotys, amounted to 88,000 zlotys. From now on it will equal 95,000 zlotys. ... Improved terms for producers of exported goods should bear fruit in the form of increased foreign currency earnings. ...*

The government has adopted numerous additional export incentives. Enterprises producing for export receive priority in allocations of raw and other material supplies.[558] Tax exemptions, reductions and rebates were

---

[555] On January 1, 1982, the zloty was devalued against the dollar from a rate of 54:1 to 80:1, and against the "transfer ruble" -- an accounting unit used by CEMA nations in settling accounts -- from 44:1 to 68:1. *Rynke Zagraniczne* (March 2, 1982.) The goal was to "guarantee the profitability of export production for approximately 80 percent of the deliveries of processed products as well as all raw and other materials deliveries." *Nowe Drogi* (April 1983), pp. 156-36.

[556] *Ibid.*, pp. 125-36.

[557] *Rynki Zagraniczne* (June 16, 1983). The comparatively deeper devaluation of the zloty against the dollar had the practical effect of producing a greater incentive to export to Western nations than to the Soviet bloc. *Handel Zagraniczny* commented (No. 2, 1983, pp. 305) that "The dollar is established by the International Bank for Economic Cooperation in Moscow [at a rate of 1 dollar: 0.7 rubles]. In the meantime our rates for internal accounting have different mutual relationship (80:68). For that reason, in case of the export of the same goods for dollars and for rubles, the profitability achieved by the producer by virtue of the sale of rubles is considerably less."

[558] This priority was weakened somewhat in 1983 -- export production was reduced to third priority. Cabinet Statute No. 226, cited in *Handel Zagraniczny* No. 2 (1983).

granted to producing enterprises for exported items.[559]   The Minister of Foreign Trade maintained a "compensation fund" ($18.5 million in 1983) out of which "emoluments" are paid to foreign trade enterprises and producing units "as rewards for increases in exports."[560]

[559] Assistant Chairman Dlugocz commented in 1983 that with respect to tax measures as export incentives, "we are just learning about the effect of taxes on enterprise reform. Until 1982, taxes, for all practical purposes, were not of great significance in our economy." *Rynki Zagraniczne* (June 16, 1983).

[560] These measures were vestiges of the old export promoting system — under the "command" system emoluments had been paid to enterprises which met or exceeded export targets. *Handel Zagraniczne* (June 16, 1983).

7

The United States

It is perhaps appropriate that the United States is the last country to be addressed in a book on government policies in steel, since the U.S. government's relative passivity, in contrast to the government activism which has characterized this sector generally, has resulted in the United States becoming the principal residual market for steel surpluses generated elsewhere in the world. A U.S. representative to the OECD Steel Committee described U.S. industrial policy in the following terms in 1982:

> *We do have [an industrial policy]. It is simpler than some of the policies you have adopted. It requires no major public expenditure, no planning and no direction by government. Key decisions are left to those closest to the market -- the firms themselves. But our policy, which relies on the free play of market forces to ensure that structural change and adaptation take place regularly, is a true industry policy. . . .[1]*

While such a policy has merit in a domestic context, in a world market where government intervention is pervasive, the lack of a coherent trade policy -- other than reliance on the market and reaction to the practices of other nations -- has allowed foreign government actions to influence the shape of the U.S. steel industry. It should not be particularly surprising, under such circumstances, that the market position of the U.S. steel industry has eroded.

The fortunes of the U.S. steel industry have changed dramatically over the past three decades. The U.S. industry produced almost 60 percent of the western world's raw steel in 1950. By 1986, the share of raw steel output accounted for by the U.S. industry had fallen to just 17 percent (figure 7-1). U.S. production has declined absolutely since 1974 and raw steel capacity has shrunk significantly since 1977 (figure 7-2). The share of imports in domestic

---

[1] Telegram to U.S. Department of Commerce, available in *Certain Steel Products from the Federal Republic of Germany*, Department of Commerce Docket A-428-004, reproducing statement made July 21, 1982.

Figure 7–1: U.S. Share of Western World Steel Production, 1950–1986

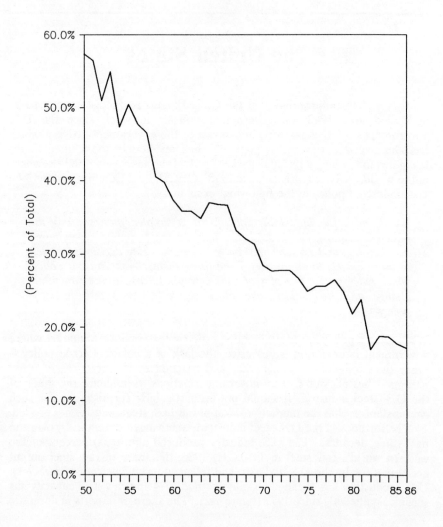

Source: Table 2–1.

consumption has increased from an average of 2.3 percent in the 1950s to an average of 21.7 percent in the 1980s. Today the United States is the sole major western steel producing nation that is a net importer of steel.

There have been many studies and accounts of the changing fortunes of the U.S. steel industry.[2] A host of factors have been presented to explain the problems the U.S. industry has faced over the past three decades, all subject to varying degrees of consensus and disagreement.[3] As discussed in chapter 2, the main factors accounting for the relative erosion in the share of world production accounted for by the U.S. steel industry have been the higher rates of growth in steel demand in other regions of the world combined with government-directed assistance to promote domestic production capability to meet this increasing demand, which in many cases led to overinvestment.[4] Rapid increases in steel consumption provide excellent opportunities for investment in greenfield steelmaking facilities and the adoption of new technologies. Over 45 new integrated steelworks were constructed in the

---

[2] Kiyoshi Kawahito, *The Japanese Steel Industry With an Analysis of the U.S. Steel Import Problem* (New York: Praeger Publishers, 1972); Federal Trade Commission, *Staff Report on the United States Steel Industry and Its International Rivals: Trends and Factors Determining International Competitiveness* (Washington, D.C.: U.S. Government Printing Office, November 1977); Council on Wage and Price Stability, *Prices and Costs in the United States Steel Industry*; Hans Mueller and Kiyoshi Kawahito, *Steel Industry Economics: A Comparative Analysis of Structure, Conduct and Performance* (New York: Japan Steel Information Center, 1978); Office of Technology Assessment, *Steel Industry Competitiveness*; AISI, *Steel at the Crossroads*; U.S. General Accounting Office, *New Strategy Required for Aiding Distressed Steel Industry* (Washington, D.C.: U.S. GAO, January 8, 1981); Bruce S. Old, Frederic A. L. Holloway and Michael Tenenbaum, *Brief Technology Assessment of the Domestic Steel Industry* (Bethlehem, Pennsylvania: Lehigh University, January 1981) reprinted by National Technical Information Service, Document No. PB81-153934; Crandall, *Recurrent Crises*; Adams and Mueller, "The Steel Industry;" Hogan, *World Steel in the 1980s*; National Academy of Sciences, *U.S. Steel Industry*; U.S. Department of Commerce, *The U.S. Primary Iron and Steel Industry Since 1958* (Washington, D.C.: U.S. Government Printing Office, May 1985); Kent Jones, *Politics vs Economics in World Steel Trade* (London: Allen & Unwin, 1986), ch. 4.

[3] These explanations have included (1) an erosion of cost competitiveness due to comparatively higher raw material and labor costs, (2) a slow adoption rate of new technology, (3) anemic growth in steel consumption, (4) unfairly traded imports, (5) worldwide excess steelmaking capacity, (6) managerial decisions, (7) foreign government ownership and control of steelmaking capacity, and (8) U.S. government controls and regulations, including tax policies that failed to provide for adequate capital recovery.

[4] The technology of steelmaking gives rise to three differentiable types of producers: (1) integrated producers using the hot metal route involving the blast furnace in combination with the basic oxygen furnace, (2) minimill or semi-integrated producers using the cold metal (scrap) route of the electric arc furnace, and (3) specialty producers using electric arc furnaces to make special alloy steels. Integrated producers also employ EA furnaces, accounting for approximately 50 percent of electric furnace capacity in the United States. In terms of shipment tonnage in 1986 the largest group was the integrated producers (32 companies) which accounted for 80.4 percent of total shipments, compared to 18.2 percent accounted for by minimill producers (45 companies) and 1.4 percent accounted for by specialty producers (11 companies). Marcus and Kirsis, *Steel Strategist 14*, exhibit F. Given the differences in the technology used for making steel, the competitive situation of each of these groups is different. Unless otherwise indicated, the discussion of the U.S. industry will be concerned primarily with the integrated producers.

Figure 7-2: U.S. Raw Steel Capacity and Production, 1950-1986

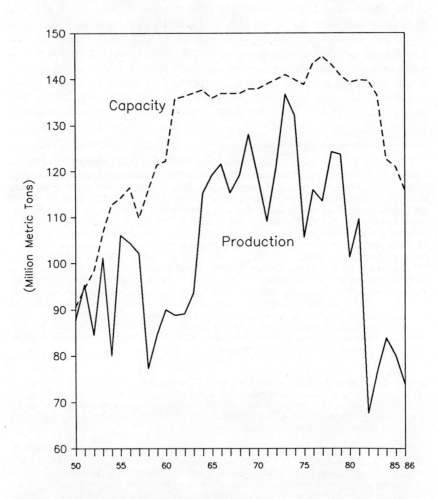

Source: Table 2-1 for production data; capacity data from American Iron and Steel Industry, <u>Annual Statistical Reports</u>, except for 1965-1974, which are from Marcus and Kirsis, <u>World Steel Dynamics: Core Report BB</u> (PaineWebber, Inc., January 1988).

western economies after 1950, with Japan alone accounting for half of the new capacity.[5] Because of slower growth in the U.S. market for steel products, only two of the new integrated facilities were built in the United States -- U.S. Steel's Fairless works and Bethlehem's Burns Harbor facility -- accounting for 3 percent of the new world capacity.

There has been considerable debate about the performance of U.S. integrated producers over the past three decades. Much of the controversy has focused on whether the U.S. industry, especially the larger firms in the industry, have lagged in the adoption of major steelmaking innovations such as the basic oxygen process[6] and continuous casting technology.[7] It is generally true that major process innovations, and many product innovations, can only be effectively realized with new investment in plant and equipment, sometimes involving whole new facilities (*i.e.*, greenfield plants), and this placed the U.S. industry at a distinct disadvantage relative to many foreign countries where almost all of their industry was constructed through greenfield investments after the commercial feasibility of innovations such as the basic oxygen process and continuous casting technology had been established. Nevertheless, the more recent studies on the subject have concluded that given the specific conditions U.S. integrated producers faced in the post war period, the U.S. industry in general, and larger integrated producers in particular, did not lag

---

[5] Old, Holloway and Tenenbaum, *Domestic Steel Industry*, table 7.

[6] The initial critique concerning the basic oxygen process was Walter Adams and Joel Dirlam, "Big Steel, Invention and Innovation," *Quarterly Journal of Economics* 80 (May 1966): 167-189. For an initial rebuttal to Adams and Dirlam and their reply, see Alan K. McAdams, "Big Steel, Invention, and Innovation Reconsidered," *Quarterly Journal of Economics* 81 (August 1967):457-474 and Walter Adams and Joel Dirlam, "Big Steel, Invention, and Innovation: Reply," *Quarterly Journal of Economics* 81 (August 1967):475-480. Another article that same year concluded that the U.S. industry did not lag the rest of the world in installing basic oxygen furnaces. G.S. Maddala and Peter T. Knight, "International Diffusion of Technical Change - A Case Study of the Oxygen Steelmaking Process," *Economic Journal* 77 (September 1967): 531-558. See also the critique provided by David R. Dilley and David L. McBride, "Oxygen Steelmaking - Fact vs. Folklore," in *Iron and Steel Engineer* 49 (October 1967): 131-152.

[7] For a critique of the industry see D. Ault, "The Continued Deterioration of the Competitive Ability of the U.S. Steel Industry: The Development of Continuous Casting," *Western Economic Journal* 11 (March 1973): 89-97; the critique of Ault is given in David A. Huettner, "The Development of Continuous Casting in the U.S. Steel Industry: Comment," *Economic Inquiry* (June 1974): 265-277.

in the rate of adoption of new technology.[8] One analyst has suggested that U.S. producers were making an optimal investment choice.

> *Early adoption of a (too small) basic oxygen converter may have been a mistake. Viewed from 1974, the industry may have rushed to install basic oxygen converters before technical progress slowed: that is, adopted prematurely. The abandonments of oxygen steelmaking after 1978 and continuing today suggest this view.*[9]

There is agreement among almost all studies of the U.S. steel industry that an important factor affecting the industry has been the relative erosion of the U.S. advantage of the 1950s in labor and raw material costs. Labor costs (wages and benefits) in the U.S. industry have outrun productivity increases (in part affected by work rule practices). The result was that unit labor costs for most American producers surpassed the level of the industry's major foreign rivals. This cost disadvantage has been a significant problem facing U.S. steel producers and still remains a major problem despite recent efforts by steel companies and the United Steelworkers of America to address it.[10] The U.S. advantage in raw material costs (primarily in iron ore and coking coal) generally shrank in the 1960s and 1970s with respect to foreign

---

[8] Rossegger's analysis of the results of "piecemeal innovation" (the strategy of upgrading existing production facilities through the introduction of major process innovations) by four large integrated producers is unique in its focus on the actual conditions faced by individual plants with respect to the decision on whether and when to adopt new technology. Especially noteworthy in Rossegger's analysis is the degree of empirical specificity as opposed to theoretical assumptions concerning adoption rates. For example, the discussion of the initial difficulties in the continuous casting of slabs as compared to the casting of billets and bars helps to explain the rate of adoption of this technology by integrated producers whose production was dominated by flat-rolled products. Gerhard Rossegger, "Adjustment Through Piecemeal Innovation - the U.S. Experience," in *Ailing Steel: The Transatlantic Quarrel*, ed. Walter H. Goldberg (New York: St. Martin's Press, 1986), pp. 307-337. Karlson provides further recent evidence that the largest integrated producers did not lag their smaller rivals in the adoption of BOP/EA technology by using a more complete and realistic model of innovation, disputing not only Adams and Dirlam, who argue that the U.S. industry lagged in the adoption of new technology, but also more recent work by Sumrall and Oster. Stephen H. Karlson, "Adoption of Competing Inventions by United States Steel Producers," *The Review of Economics and Statistics* 68 (August 1986):415-422; James B. Sumrall, "Diffusion of the Basic Oxygen Furnace in the U.S. Steel Industry," *Journal of Industrial Economics* 30 (June 1982):421-437; Sharon Oster, "The Diffusion of Innovation among Steel Firms: The Basic Oxygen Furnace," *The Bell Journal of Economics* (Spring 1982):45-56.

[9] Karlson, "Adoption of Competing Inventions," p. 421.

[10] Labor costs represent from 20 to 40 percent of the cost of producing a ton of finished steel. The labor intensity of steelmaking has been highest in maintaining primary steelmaking facilities and in operating the finishing processes. General Accounting Office, *Distressed Steel Industry*, pp. 7-13, and National Academy of Sciences, *U.S. Steel Industry*, pp. 57-59. The labor productivity of the U.S. steel industry generally remained competitive with that of its major rivals, but the difference in productivity no longer offset the relatively higher wage and benefit levels in the 1960s and 1970s.

steelmakers with deep-water port locations.[11] By the 1980s these plants could obtain iron ore, limestone, coal, and other raw materials at costs comparable to the best located inland plants in the United States.[12] Given that labor and raw material costs (including energy) represent 80 percent to 90 percent of steelmaking costs, these trends caused an erosion of the relative cost leadership of the U.S. steel industry.[13]

Despite this *relative* erosion, by the late 1970s, the U.S. industry remained one of the world's low cost producers, with costs "only moderately higher than those in Japan, widely believed to be one of the lowest-cost producers in the world."[14] In the U.S. market, where transportation costs imposed substantial penalties on foreign producers, U.S. firms generally enjoyed a cost advantage (which has substantially widened in the mid-1980s).

Under such circumstances, there has been considerable controversy over the reasons for the rapid increase in U.S. steel imports in the 1960s and 1970s, given the fact that costs in the U.S. were competitive with those of foreign rivals. Imports initially increased because of labor strife which disrupted domestic supply. However in the 1960s and 1970s imports increased because of their substantially lower price compared to domestic prices and the decision of U.S. producers generally not to match the low import prices.[15] The debate

---

[11] Federal Trade Commission, *United States Steel Industry and Its International Rivals* , ch. 3. Three factors, other than exchange rates, account for the loss of the U.S. industry's raw material cost advantage: (1) development of low cost raw material sources outside of the United States, (2) reductions in bulk ocean transportation rates, and (3) higher yields for steelmaking in countries like Japan. National Academy of Sciences, *U.S. Steel Industry*, pp. 59-60.

[12] Robert W. Crandall, "Investment and Productivity Growth in the Steel Industry: Some Implications for Industrial Policy," in *Ailing Steel*, p. 193.

[13] The discussion of cost competitiveness deals with the aggregate or average position of the entire U.S. industry. However, production costs vary significantly among individual producers and individual plants because of differences in the age and efficiency of facilities, plant location and management, local market conditions, and the product mix being produced. For a recent competitive assessment of major integrated plants see Marcus and Kirsis, *Steel Strategist 14*, exhibit U.

[14] National Academy of Sciences, *U.S. Steel Industry*, p. 48. See also Joel S. Hirschhorn, "Restructuring of the United States Steel Industry Requires New Policies," in *Ailing Steel*, pp. 209-210: "Widely fluctuating exchange rates and substantially different utilisation rates among nations continue to make international cost comparisons difficult. Nevertheless, on the whole, the US steel industry is cost-competitive in most domestic markets, and for some types of steel even cost-competitive in international markets where, of course, other factors such as exchange rates may still preclude market competitiveness."

[15] The decision to match lower-priced imports is a complex one. Not only must the firm calculate the lower revenue with respect to the sales that compete with imports but in addition the lost revenue from sales in the domestic market that could have been made without the price reduction (what Scitovsky has termed the "price variation cost"). Given equal marginal costs, the foreign exporter (or smaller, single product line producer) will generally be at an advantage in a price cutting situation compared to large domestic producers with numerous established product lines because the foreign exporter will have much lower price variation costs. Stegemann, *Price Competition and Output Adjustment*, pp. 23-29. U.S. companies have, in fact, tried to prevent import penetration by matching import price reductions, but with little success.

has centered on why import prices have been lower than U.S. domestic prices.[16]

One explanation commonly offered is that foreign producers have lower costs than U.S. producers and therefore can sell steel at lower prices. However, the *landed* cost of foreign steel almost never produced a cost edge for foreign producers. More fundamentally, as this study has examined in the preceding chapters, most foreign producers do not export steel at prices which cover costs. Some of the nations which have achieved major penetration of the U.S. steel market in the 1980s (Spain, Romania, Poland, etc.) support extremely high-cost, inefficient steel producers who cannot compete on a cost basis in world markets, a fact which has proven no obstacle to the establishment of a major export presence. In addition, even with respect to more efficient foreign producers, export prices have generally not reflected the full cost of production.[17] Exports are often priced to cover only variable costs of production, or some portion of variable costs, especially during periods of excess capacity like that which prevailed after 1974.[18] Such export pricing is facilitated by cartel arrangements, which foster dumping, and by government operating and export subsidies.

One effort, Armco's "foreign fighter" program, was implemented in the late 1970s to stem import penetration in the Gulf Coast region. Armco met the import prices in an attempt to prevent the erosion of its market for structurals from its Houston plant. However the mill suffered operating losses in almost every year and finally closed in 1982. Armco *1982 Annual Report*; U.S. International Trade Commission, "U.S.I.T.C. Investigation No. 731-TA-18/24," Testimony of Eugene L. Stewart, April 17, 1980, pp. 39-40. In the mid-1980s U.S. steel firms also reduced prices to meet import prices and maintain operating rates. Nevertheless, the end result was that prices fell, losses increased and capacity utilization for the industry as a whole did not change significantly. See David J.Cantor, "Steel Manufacturing in the United States: Can a Smaller Industry Be Profitable?," (Washington, D.C.: Congressional Research Service, July 31, 1987), pp. CRS-4 to CRS-6.

[16] National Academy of Sciences, *U.S. Steel Industry*, ch. 6; Jones, *World Steel Trade*, ch. 4.

[17] For example, a study by the Council on Wage and Price Stability concluded that for the period examined (1976 to 1977) the evidence was clear that EC producers were selling in the U.S. market below their cost of production and that Japanese producers were likely selling below production costs (a definitive conclusion could not be reached because of difficulties in assessing the effect of differences in product mix between export sales and domestic sales). The study concluded that "nothing in this chapter suggests, however, that the U.S. steel industry cannot compete with Japanese steel in U.S. markets." The study went on to state that until world demand for steel revived, "U.S. steel firms, like their foreign counterparts, will continue to suffer from aggressive price competition." Council on Wage and Price Stability, *Prices and Costs in the United States Steel Industry*, pp. 67-84.

[18] Economists refer to this as marginal cost pricing, because marginal cost depends only on variable costs and is independent of fixed costs. Note that this assumes that where price equals marginal cost average revenue is greater than average cost. Otherwise a loss will be made at this price and output level. It may still make sense, *in the short run*, to produce at this price and output level if the alternative of not producing is more costly. In the long run, unless firms have access to operating subsidies, fixed costs must also be covered or the capacity will be eliminated. In general terms, however, it is not appropriate to apply the microeconomic results of perfect competition to an oligopolistic industry like steel. For a different, but useful analytical framework, see Stegemann, *Price Competition and Output Adjustment*, ch. 2.

Another complicating factor is that changes in capacity utilization, exchange rates, input costs and other factors can lead to significant changes in relative costs among countries over time and even from year to year. As discussed in chapter 2, variations in the operating rates of U.S. and Japanese producers caused swings from year to year in the relative cost competitiveness of each industry. In one year the Japanese industry's average costs were lower than average costs in the U.S. industry. In the next year, the relative cost position was reversed.[19] Furthermore the level of imports itself affects costs by affecting the rate of capacity utilization. The U.S. market has historically been the most open major market for steel products in the world and thus has been the outlet for much of the world excess steel capacity.[20] U.S. producers have therefore been confronted with pressures on operating rates from both relatively stagnant domestic consumption and increasing imports. No other major steel producing country in the world is a net importer of steel and the industries in those countries have therefore not been subject to this dual pressure on operating rates.

The shrinkage of the U.S. industry's relative cost leadership, coupled with the effect of increasing imports and declining and/or slow demand growth on prices and costs (affecting utilization rates), has meant that steel industry profitability has generally been below the manufacturing average for the post war period (figure 7-3).[21] As a result net investment in structures was negative (disinvestment) every year from 1969 to 1980 while net investment in equipment has remained positive in most years (except for the 1971-1973 period) but generally declined from 1967 to 1981.[22]

THE STATE OF THE U.S. STEEL INDUSTRY IN THE 1980s

The U.S. steel industry suffered dramatically in the 1980s under the combined pressure of reduced consumption and rising imports which kept prices low, drastically reduced capacity utilization and thereby produced record financial losses. Over the five year period from 1982 to 1986 the industry lost $12 billion. Over 25 steel companies, including large steelmakers like LTV and Wheeling-Pittsburgh, filed bankruptcy proceedings. Capacity

---

[19] On the other hand, while *average* U.S. or Japanese steelmaking costs may be more competitive in any given year, plants with above average costs may not be able to compete. In the late 1970s a study of the U.S. industry indicated that up to 10 percent of plants had costs that were at least 15 percent above the average for the industry. National Academy of Sciences, *U.S. Steel Industry*, pp. 49-50. This again points to the need, in making conclusions based on cost comparisons, to be specific with respect to plant, location and product mix.

[20] Office of Technology Assessment, *Steel Industry Competitiveness*, p. 150.

[21] Profitability was also adversely affected by "jawboning" on price increases in the Truman, Kennedy and Johnson Administrations as well the price controls in the early 1970s during the Nixon Administration. Despite the poor profitability of the U.S. steel industry, it has consistently been more profitable than its major foreign rivals.

[22] U.S. Department of Commerce, *U.S. Primary Iron and Steel Industry*, pp. 29-34.

Figure 7—3: U.S. Steel Industry Profits (After Taxes) as a Percent of Stockholders' Equity Compared to All Manufacturing, 1950—1987

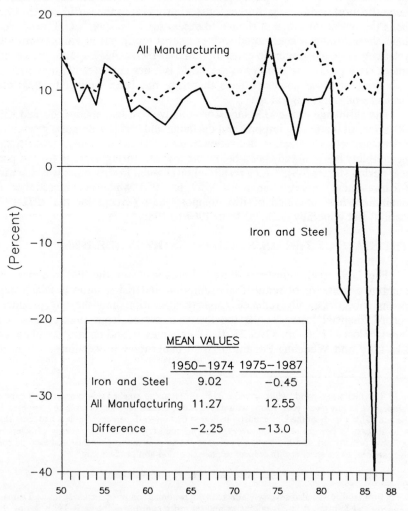

Source: Federal Trade Commission (1950—1981) and U.S. Department of Commerce (1982—1987) Quarterly Financial Report.

utilization reached a new low since the 1930s Great Depression of 48.4 percent in 1982 and has averaged less than 65 percent from 1980 to 1986.[23]

The disastrous operating results of the early 1980s were exacerbated by the sharp rise in the value of the U.S. dollar that added to the problems the U.S. industry was already struggling with because of the structural crisis of overcapacity in the world steel industry. Dollar appreciation adversely affected the steel industry in two ways. First because of the appreciating dollar, world export prices (denominated in dollars) fell sharply, providing a marked stimulus to U.S. steel imports (figure 7-4). Secondly, the dollar appreciation helped trigger a huge surge in net manufacturing imports, especially in steel intensive products like machinery, machine tools and automobiles.[24] This meant that U.S. producers lost sales not only directly, to imports of steel mill products, but also indirectly as their markets in U.S. steel consuming industries also lost sales to imports. In fact, the increase in steel imports from indirect steel trade has exceeded the increase in direct steel imports in the 1980s.[25]

With consumption stagnant, imports growing, prices depressed and capacity utilization low, U.S. steel producers were forced to undertake drastic adjustments. In six years U.S. steelmaking capacity was reduced by over a quarter (42 million tons), from 154 million tons in 1982 to 112 million tons by 1987. Employment was cut by 60 percent, from 399,000 employees in 1980 to 163,000 in 1987. Labor productivity increased significantly, from 9.92 man hours per ton (MHPT) in 1981 to 6.69 MHPT in 1987.[26] At actual operating rates, U.S. labor productivity is now the best in the world. The percent of steel continuously cast has risen from 20 percent in 1981 to 60 percent by 1987. This helped increase the crude steel to finished steel yield from 72

---

[23] Capacity utilization has a direct effect on production costs. As shown in figure 7-5, U.S. costs of production soared in 1982 because of the sharp decline in capacity utilization.

[24] Recent studies of the effects of the appreciation of the dollar on U.S. manufacturing industries indicate that primary metals and fabricated metal products were the most severely affected by the high value of the dollar. Eichengreen, *International Competition in the Products of U.S. Basic Industries*; William H. Branson and James P. Love, "U.S. Manufacturing and the Real Exchange Rate," NBER Working Paper (Revised, July 1987).

[25] In the eight year period from 1972 to 1979, direct steel imports averaged 16.6 million tons per year compared to an average of 19 million tons per year in the eight years from 1980 to 1987, an increase in the average annual import level of 2.4 million tons. Indirect steel imports from imports of steel containing manufactured products averaged 9.1 million tons in the 1972 to 1979 period compared to 13 million tons in the 1980 to 1987 period, an increase in the average annual import level of 3.9 million tons. The data and a further analysis of consumption trends is provided in Appendix A.

[26] Labor productivity at the more modern facilities is much greater. MHPT at Bethlehem's Burns Harbor facility is reported to be under 3. Marcus and Kirsis, *Steel Strategist 14*, p. 66. For a discussion of some of the factors accounting for the sharp gains in productivity see David J. Cantor, "The U.S, Steel Industry: Factors Influencing Gains in Industry Productivity," (Washington, D.C.: Congressional Research Service, June 10, 1987).

(Million metric tons)

Figure 7–4: United States – Steel Production, Consumption and Trade, 1971–1986

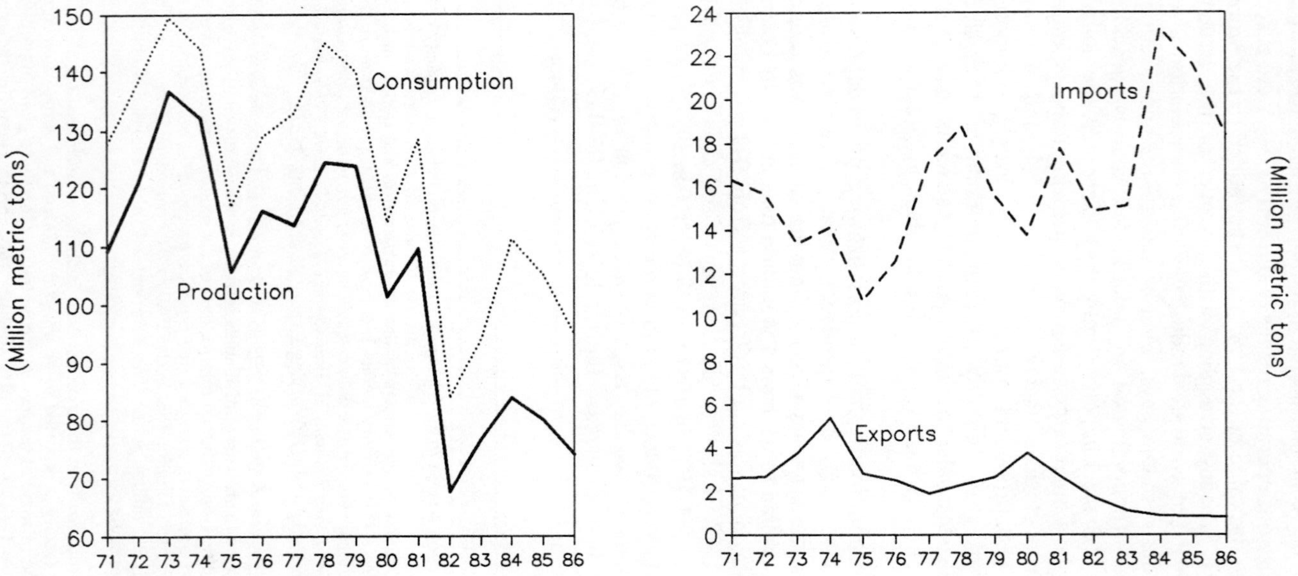

Source: International Iron and Steel Institute, Steel Statistical Yearbook, 1981, 1987. Production and Consumption refer to crude steel; Exports and Imports refer to semi-finished and finished steel.

Table 7-1. Estimated Pretax Costs for Major Steelmakers
(U.S. dollars per ton shipped)

November 1987

	U.S.	Japan	Germany	U.K.	France	Korea	Taiwan
Operating rate (%)	85%	60%	80%	80%	77%	101%	100%
Currency/U.S.$	1.00/$	Y136/$	DM1.67/$	£0.56/$	FF5.81/$	WON803/$	NT$29.91/$
MHPT	6.7	7.3	7.4	6.9	7.5	9.5	9.0
Wage/hour	24	23	24	16	20	5	8
Employment cost/ton	160	168	178	110	150	47	72
Material cost/ton	272	277	302	286	266	260	260
Operating costs	432	445	480	396	416	307	332
Financial costs	43	115	48	29	79	117	95
Pretax total	$475	$560	$528	$425	$495	$424	$427

Adjusted for Exchange Rate at end of April 1988

	U.S.	Japan	Germany	U.K.	France	Korea	Taiwan
Currency/U.S. $	1.00/$	Y124.85/$	DM1.668/$	£0.53/$	FF5.67/$	WON740/$	NT$28.61/$
Pretax total	$475	$610	$529	$449	$507	$460	$446
Duty, Freight and Handling	-	$77	$68	$68	$68	$77	$77
Landed cost in U.S. Market	$475	$687	$597	$517	$575	$537	$523

Source: Peter F. Marcus and Karlis M. Kirsis, *World Steel Dynamics: Steel Strategist 14*
(December 10, 1987), Exhibit D. April 1988 exchange rates from International Monetary Fund,
International Financial Statistics (June 1988). Entry costs into U.S. market include duty, freight,
handling, etc., estimated by Bethlehem Steel Corporation from U.S. Customs tapes.

percent in the late 1970s to 86 percent in 1987.[27]
    All of these adjustments had a significant effect on costs. By the end of
1987, average U.S. costs per ton shipped were $475, down 31 percent from the
peak of $684 in 1982. The combination of major industry adjustments -- which
not only reduced factor input costs but increased operating rates -- and the
depreciating U.S. dollar made the U.S. industry one of the lowest cost
producers in the world by 1987 (figure 7-5).
    Table 7-1 gives estimates of average pretax costs for major steelmakers as
of November, 1987. The November 1987 estimates have been adjusted for
exchange rate changes through the end of April 1988. This data does not
adjust for the cost reducing effects of current or past government subsidies.
The data show that U.S. producers are now more cost competitive in U.S.
dollars than producers in Japan, Germany and France. When delivery costs
to the U.S. market are added to the pretax costs, U.S. producers are cost
competitive with British, Korean and Taiwanese producers. A surprising
aspect of the table is that it depicts the United Kingdom as the world's lowest
cost producer, although, as discussed in chapter 3, this reflects not only cost
cutting adjustments, but also the high degree of recent past subsidies resulting
in very low current depreciation and interest costs. French producers'

---

[27] All data from American Iron and Steel Institute except data on MHPT, which is from
Marcus and Kirsis, *Steel Strategist 14*, pp. 42-43.

financial costs have also been substantially reduced through government writeoff of large levels of debt.

The turnaround in the cost competitiveness of the U.S. industry, combined with increased shipment levels in 1987 and early 1988, returned the industry to profitability in 1987 and caused some commentators to suggest that the steel industry in the United States had finally adjusted to the structural and competitive problems it has struggled with for over a decade.[28]   A recent *Business Week* article was headlined "Cancel the Funeral -- Steel is on the Mend."[29]   But even that article noted that significant adjustments were still required to keep steel out of the red in the years ahead, including further reductions in capacity.

While the U.S. industry is currently cost competitive, in large part due to restructuring and modernization efforts as well as the depreciation of the dollar, it still needs to modernize dated plant and equipment. A recent editorial in *Metal Bulletin* summed up the situation as follows:

> *The exchange rate factor, however, cannot gloss over the severe disadvantages U.S. mills face in having to compete with foreign rivals equipped with modern capacity. By most yardsticks, the U.S. steel industry is looking very long in the tooth and until there is a major effort to catch up technologically the long-term outlook must remain very uncertain. The Catch 22 situation is that until U.S. mills are earning reasonable profits they will not be in a position to invest in the new kit -- but without modern plant they are unlikely to make resonable profits. In a world of highly volatile currencies it is a risky business to count on a weak exchange rate to sustain an industry's competitiveness over the period of time steelmakers need to formulate a sound investment policy.[30]*

Some have concluded that despite the return to profitability in 1987 the major U.S. mills still face "terrible long-term threats."[31]   Others have argued that an additional 20 million tons of capacity must be retired to make the industry

---

[28] AISI reported net income of $1 billion for 1987 for the U.S. steel industry, the first year of profits since 1981. However, a large portion of the reported net income represented recovery of unused investment tax credits and other one-time items.

[29] *Business Week* (October 5, 1987), pp. 74-77.

[30] *Metal Bulletin* (February 25, 1988), p. 7.

[31] Marcus and Kirsis, *Steel Strategist 14*, p. 10.   Standard and Poor's Corporation, in reaffirming the debt rating of USX Corporation, stated the following: "Stronger-than-anticipated steel results are currently boosting USX's earnings.   Even so, profitability remains weak. Moreover, given the cyclicality of steel markets and the industry's persisting structural problems, the current level of earnings from steel operations isn't expected to be sustained long-term." *American Metal Market* (May 26, 1988), p. 3.

Figure 7–5: Pretax Costs of Major Steel Mills, By Country, 1978–1987 (actual operating rates)

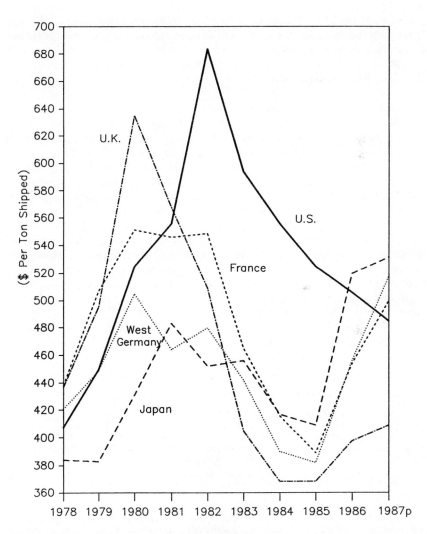

Source: Peter Marcus and Karlis Kirsis, <u>World Steel Dynamics: Steel Strategist 14</u> (PaineWebber, Inc., 1987), Exhibit O.

profitable by permitting firms to operate at 80 to 90 percent of capacity.[32] However events of late 1987 and early 1988 suggest that additional capacity reductions may be problematical at this time. Capacity utilization in the U.S. industry has averaged 90.4 percent through the first four months of the year. However prices, while recovering from the very low levels of the 1982 to 1986 period, are still below levels of the early 1980s. In fact, prices for steel mill products have increased less than prices for all manufactured products since 1981 (figure 7-6).

Whether the industry can maintain profitability and continue to modernize to stay abreast of its foreign rivals will depend not only on its own efforts but on future U.S. government policies toward steel.[33]

U.S. GOVERNMENT POLICIES

The U.S. Government has never implemented an industrial policy in steel, or, with few exceptions such as aviation, in any other industrial sector. The massive subsidy injections and other forms of direct state financial aid which are pervasive throughout the world steel industry have no U.S. counterpart.[34] Federal and state "buy American" laws have established bidding preferences for domestic products with respect to procurement by government agencies, but these laws affect only a small proportion of the U.S. steel market, historically have not prevented government procurement of foreign steel, and have been partially mitigated by U.S. accession to the GATT Procurement Code. The government has generally assumed the role of a neutral arbiter of the rules of competition in the marketplace, and a regulator of industry to safeguard employment, environmental and safety concerns. As many analysts have noted, U.S. Government policies affect the steel industry in many ways, some positive and some negative, but they are not implemented in a coordinated fashion to achieve any particular result. More dramatic interventions, such as President Truman's takeover of the industry during the early days of the Korean War, have been short-lived responses to immediate

---

[32] David J. Cantor, "Steel Manufacturing in the United States."

[33] The industry still faces the problem of capital availability due to its poor profit performance over the past decade. The lack of internally generated funds and the high cost and limited availability of outside financing have inhibited and substantially slowed the pace of modernization efforts. In addition the industry still must confront the problem of high exit costs in further reducing outdated capacity. Plant closings mean the burden of substantial liabilities for early retirement costs and other benefit-related liabilities to laid-off employees. These and other potential costs pose a significant problem for the future financial health of the industry.

[34] There have been a few isolated instances of government loan guarantees and grants being provided to U.S. steel firms under community assistance programs of the federal government (the Commerce Department's Economic Development Administration and the Urban Development Action Grant Program). The largest such action involved loan guarantees totalling $140 million to Whelling-Pittsburgh Steel Corporation in 1979 for a new rail mill. These loan guarantees were protested by other domestic producers. *Metal Bulletin* (September 7, 1979), p. 36.

Figure 7−6: Producer Price Index for All Manufactured Goods and Steel Mill Products, 1951−1987

(1982=100)

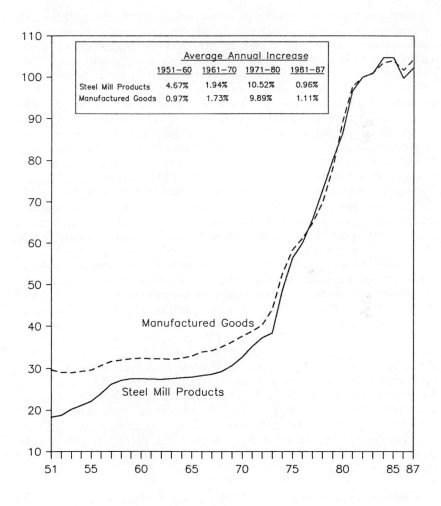

	Average Annual Increase			
	1951−60	1961−70	1971−80	1981−87
Steel Mill Products	4.67%	1.94%	10.52%	0.96%
Manufactured Goods	0.97%	1.73%	9.89%	1.11%

Source: U.S. Department of Labor, Bureau of Labor Statistics

crises, and have produced little in the way of lasting consequences. The only area characterized by substantial government policy measures has been trade, and even here, it is difficult to identify a consistent U.S. policy. The lack of a coherent steel trade policy in an environment where competitive outcomes are being shaped by other governments' policies has contributed substantially to the industry's erosion.

U.S. Trade Policies

Compared with the policies of other industrialized states, U.S. trade policies in steel are noteworthy for their short-lived and erratic character, their ineffectiveness in limiting import growth, and for the enormous public controversy which they have engendered. Japanese trade policies in steel have remained virtually unchanged in the twenty-five years since formal import restrictions were removed; domestic producers and traders have been allowed to control domestic distribution in a manner which has never let imports gain more than 5 to 6 percent of the market and, for many years, import penetration averaged less than one percent (figure 7-7). The European Community has maintained essentially the same system of import restrictions, based on VRAs, since 1978, and import penetration has remained constant, between 10 and 12 percent, since the inception of the system. In the EC and particularly Japan, protective measures are implemented with little public debate, and often with little or no transparency. While steel consumers occasionally protest such restrictions, protection is not particularly controversial, and is generally perceived as necessary to ensure the international competitiveness of the domestic industry.

In the United States, by contrast, steel trade policy has consisted virtually entirely of the administration of trade complaints filed by U.S. producers and a succession of *ad hoc* government actions taken in response to surges of imports which have created political crises (both domestic and international) for the Administration in office. The measures taken have sometimes produced short-term relief from import pressure, but have failed to prevent new import surges or a continuing erosion of the U.S. industry position over the longer term. The trade policy measures taken have proven extraordinarily controversial and have been denounced as "protectionist;" at the same time, by prevailing world standards, they have yielded relatively little protection. Between 1967, the year before the U.S. government first took steps to restrict steel imports, and 1984, when the current VRA program was announced, the U.S. steel import penetration ratio grew from 12.2 percent to 26.4 percent. After 1984, the import penetration ratio fell to 23 percent in 1986 and 21.3 percent in 1987 (figure 7-8).

The U.S. Trade Policy System. The United States government has no general mandate to structure U.S. trade or industry. The government's proper role has traditionally been seen as that of a neutral arbiter and enforcer of the rules of competition, ensuring only that various competing interests observe

Figure 7−7: Import Penetration of Steel Mill Products in the United States, Japan and the EC, 1960−1986

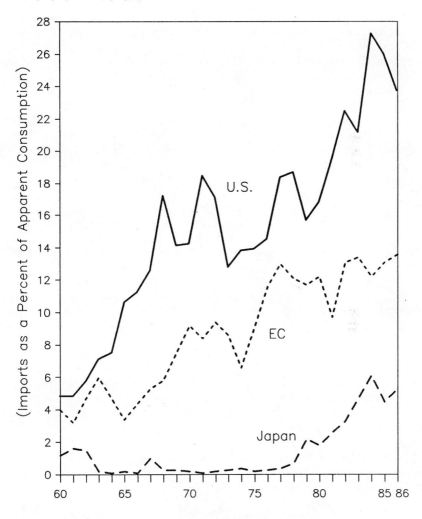

Source: United States (American Iron and Steel Institute); Japan (Organization for Economic Cooperation and Development); EC−9 (OECD for 1960 to 1979, Eurostat for 1980−1986).

Figure 7—8: U.S. Imports of Steel Mill Products as a Percent of Apparent Consumption, 1950—1987

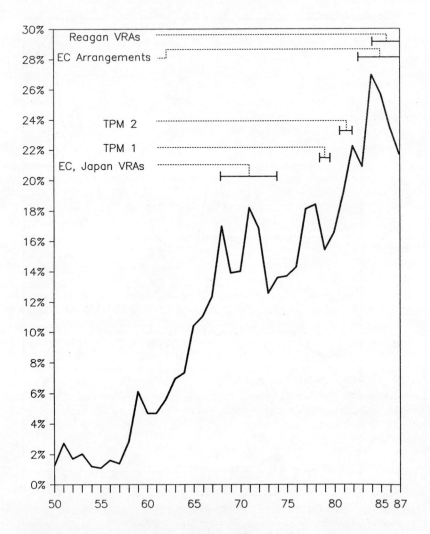

Source: American Iron and Steel Institute and the Office of the U.S. Trade Representative.

those rules. With a few exceptions like agriculture and some defense related industries, the government has not implemented comprehensive sectoral promotional policies of the sort so common elsewhere in the world. Trade policy is not viewed as an adjunct to a domestic program to enhance the competitiveness of a particular industry, simply because the U.S. government generally does not implement such programs. U.S. trade policy is generally designed to ensure that "unfair" trade practices do not distort competitive outcomes, rather than to influence such outcomes in favor of U.S. industries. "What is . . . dispensed is equity, not the promotion of an industry."[35]

The U.S. trade policy system is complicated by the Constitutional division of authority between Congress and the Executive branch. Congress possesses the residual authority to regulate foreign trade, but since the nation's unfortunate experience with the Smoot-Hawley Tariff, it has chosen to delegate trade and negotiating authority to the President. Successive Republican and Democratic Administrations have used this authority, in general, to pursue trade policies emphasizing the elimination of international barriers to trade and investment; "protectionism" has been regarded by every Administration since the 1930s as inherently abhorrent and to be avoided. At the same time, fearful that the Executive branch will compromise U.S. commercial interests, Congress has also enacted and refined an array of unilateral trade remedies which may be invoked by U.S. industries confronting "unfair" foreign practices.[36]

These institutional and ideological peculiarities combine to produce a trade policy system which is fundamentally reactive. The U.S. government responds to complaints by U.S. producers, processes trade cases, and applies or denies remedial relief with little or no connection to larger national industrial objectives. In some cases, including steel, a trade problem may become so severe that it creates political pressures for broader government intervention. Even in such cases, however, government action is virtually always taken reluctantly, in reaction to an immediate crisis, and is terminated when the political pressure abates. The activities of the American steel industry in approaching the Congress and the Executive branch to seek policy changes and the trade cases filed by U.S. steel firms are largely a consequence of the fact that in the United States, there is no powerful industry ministry with a broad mandate to formulate and implement fiscal, trade, and competition policies needed to ensure the industry's survival and competitiveness. Those policies must be sought by industry in the political arena and through administrative litigation.

---

[35] Alan Wm. Wolff, "International Competitiveness of American Industry: The Role of U.S. Trade Policy," in *U.S. Competitiveness in the World Economy*, ed. Bruce R. Scott and George C. Lodge (Boston: Harvard Business School Press, 1985), p. 304.

[36] See Alan Wm. Wolff, "Evolution of the Executive-Legislative Relationship in the Trade Act of 1974," 19 *SAIS Review* No. 4 (1975); Wolff, "International Competitiveness."

The Antidumping and Countervailing Duty Laws. While the U.S. government has generally refrained from implementing trade policy on a sectoral basis, it has made available to U.S. industries an array of quasi-adjudicative trade remedies which may be invoked against specific "unfair" foreign trade practices, the most significant of which in the steel context have been the antidumping and countervailing duty laws.[37] The antidumping law provides for the imposition of duties on imports which are sold, or likely to be sold, in the U.S. market at less than their fair value, which cause or threaten "material injury" to a U.S. industry.[38] The countervailing duty law provides for the imposition of duties when a subsidy is bestowed by a foreign country on the manufacture or production for export of a product which is subsequently imported into the United States.[39] Following the filing of a petition by an interested party, the Commerce Department investigates whether sales at less than fair value or subsidized imports have occurred, and the U.S. International Trade Commission determines whether such imports have materially injured, or threaten to injure, a U.S. industry. Duties may only be imposed if both the Commerce Department's and the Commission's final determinations are affirmative. Certain provisional measures may be taken if both the Commerce Department and the Commission make affirmative preliminary determinations of dumping or subsidization. The investigations conducted by Commerce and the Commission are thorough, involving detailed information requests directed at the companies or the countries under investigation, followed up by on-site verification by U.S. officials in the countries themselves.

While many countries provide for the imposition of antidumping and countervailing duties, the manner of the U.S. application of these remedies reflects the degree to which the government has placed a priority on the dispensation of equity rather than the promotion of domestic sectoral interests. Under the U.S. system foreign firms which are the subject of investigation are permitted to participate fully in the investigation, offering evidence and

---

[37] The signatories to the General Agreement on Tariffs and Trade (GATT) have developed agreements to deal with the issues of subsidies and dumping. Congress has modified the U.S. antidumping and countervailing duty laws to ensure that they are applied consistently with the GATT agreements, which are popularly referred to as the Antidumping Code and the Subsidies Code. 19 U.S.C. §1671 *et. seq.* and 19 U.S.C. §1673 *et. seq.*

[38] "Less than fair value" means imports sold either at prices below "foreign market value," which is determined by reference to the price in the home market, or, if these cannot be determined, below prices in third-country markets, or, if neither can be determined, below "constructed value" (the sum of the producer's cost of production, plus at least 10 percent for general expenses and 8 percent for profit). The law requires the use of constructed value to determine foreign market value if home market sales or third country sales have been made at less than the cost of production over an extended period of time and in substantial quantities, and at prices which do not permit reasonable recovery of all costs within a reasonable period of time in the normal course of trade. 19 U.S.C. §1677(b).

[39] Countervailing duties may be imposed on imports from countries which have signed the GATT Subsidies Code only if they are found to have caused material injury to a U.S. industry; duties may be imposed on imports from non-signatories without an injury finding. 19 U.S.C. §1671(b).

arguments, and enjoy a variety of other procedural safeguards. The officials who administer these laws are specialists who make their decisions by applying legal standards and economic methodology to the facts of each case. While foreign firms are not always satisfied with the outcome of antidumping and countervailing duty proceedings, they infrequently challenge the basic fairness and integrity of the system itself.

These remedies are also designed to ensure equity in a larger sense. Practices such as dumping and subsidization of exports are generally agreed to accord "unfair" competitive advantage to foreign sellers, thus unbalancing the "level playing field," upon which, at least in theory, private firms compete in the U.S. market. The antidumping and countervailing duty laws attempt to quantify the unfair advantage and offset it by an import duty equal to the margin of dumping or subsidization -- thus restoring the level playing field.

The U.S. steel industry has made extensive use of trade remedies available to it, particularly the antidumping and countervailing duty laws. More antidumping and countervailing duty actions have been brought in steel than any other industrial sector. Since the beginning of the structural crisis, by rough count, over 250 antidumping and countervailing duty investigations have been conducted into imports of various steel products, and a significant proportion of these investigations have resulted in findings of dumping and subsidization, often at substantial margins.[40] However, the fact that import penetration levels increased dramatically during this period, and that much of this import volume consisted, according to the Commerce Department's findings, of dumped or heavily subsidized steel, suggests that the antidumping and countervailing duty laws, by themselves, have constituted an inadequate policy response in sectors characterized by major market distortions. The recent history of U.S. steel trade suggests several reasons for this.

First, the trade remedies are reactive in character. They can only be invoked after "material injury" has occurred to a U.S. industry and sufficient evidence of such injury has accumulated to establish the fact of injury before the U.S. International Trade Commission.[41] Additional time is consumed preparing a case and in conducting the investigation once a petition is filed,

---

[40] Because so many of these cases were terminated, suspended, or revoked pursuant to agreements with the foreign country subject to investigation -- often prior to entry of a final affirmative or negative determination -- it is difficult to compile a meaningful tabulation of the total number of cases where dumping or subsidization was actually found. For a listing of steel cases since 1981 (which omits, however, many cases involving the EC), see U.S. Department of Commerce, *Summary of Steel Cases Since 1981* (as of June 15, 1988).

[41] Duties may legally be imposed on the basis of the threat of injury, rather than actual injury, but as a practical matter it has proven virtually impossible to establish to the satisfaction of the International Trade Commission that a threat of injury exists which is sufficiently "real and imminent" to warrant remedial action.

during which time injury may continue to occur.[42] If an industry succeeds in establishing dumping or subsidization, it does not receive any form of compensation for the economic injury which has already occurred -- the relief available is prospective in nature.

Another basic problem is inherent in the piecemeal way in which the antidumping and countervailing duty laws are applied, that is, to specific products from individual countries. These remedies have proven most effective when applied to trade problems involving imports of only a few products from one country. The antidumping actions brought against Japan in 1977, for example, played a major role in curtailing Japanese dumping in the U.S. steel market. In the 1980s, however, the U.S. industry has confronted what amounts to a rising tide of imports -- many products from dozens of countries. Duties have been imposed on one product line from an exporting country only to be followed by a surge of imports in another product line from that country,[43] and the establishment of numerous restraints on imports from a particular country has been followed by import surges from other countries.

The fact that dumped and subsidized steel imports tend to enter the U.S. market from many countries and in many product lines increasingly means that if the antidumping and countervailing duty laws are to be applied in a manner which restores the "level playing field," cases must be filed in large numbers. In 1982, for example, when an influx of imported steel from the Community and several developing countries occurred, the U.S. steel industry filed 132 antidumping and countervailing duty petitions. Such actions inherently elevate trade issues into major international political disputes. Ironically, in this context, the antidumping and countervailing duty remedies have sometimes proven potentially too effective to actually be applied by the U.S. government, since their application to the facts would in some cases have resulted in the virtual exclusion of steel from a country or group of countries from the U.S. market. Such a result has been regarded as unacceptable not only by foreign governments but also by successive U.S. administrations concerned over the impact of steel trade litigation in the broader context of U.S. foreign relations. Instead, various administrations have pressed the U.S. industry to withdraw its cases in return for alternative measures devised by the Executive branch.

Finally, it should be noted that the antidumping and countervailing duty laws do not offset all government measures that impart competitive advantage

---

[42] During a massive influx of low-priced structurals from the EC, a U.S. steel executive commented that "Structurals are at a 49 percent (increase) over July. As far as we can see they're at the highest level in history for August. Apparently the foreigners are bringing it in with reckless abandon. It's very disappointing to see it happen. From what we can see, the government won't be able to find injury until possibly February, by which time it won't do any good." *American Metal Market* (October 1, 1981).

[43] Typically in 1983, one U.S.observer commented on a rapid increase in imports from Brazil that "First it was plate. Then it was wire rod. Now they've been stopped on those two products and we hear that large amounts of sheet are being shipped here." *American Metal Market* (July 15, 1983).

to foreign producers. The Commerce Department has ruled, for example, that many domestic subsidies are not countervailable under U.S. law if they are available to a number of industries. Home market protection and the formation of cartels cannot be addressed under the antidumping and countervailing duty laws, and historically other U.S. legal remedies have proven incapable of offsetting such measures.

The First Voluntary Restraint Arrangements, 1968-74. The first significant U.S. trade policy measures in steel were undertaken in 1968. In the wake of a surge of steel imports from Japan and the European Community, which together accounted for about 90 percent of U.S. imports, Congress began considering legislation which would establish import quotas on steel. Confronting the likely prospect of passage of legislation regarded as too protectionist, President Johnson negotiated voluntary restraint agreements with Japan and the EC, effective through 1974, pursuant to which these countries agreed to restrain their exports to the U.S. to fixed tonnages. These arrangements functioned for two years; in 1970 both Japan and the EC exceeded their quotas (by 13 and 9 percent, respectively), requiring the U.S. government to renegotiate the accords, effective through 1974. Because of a world steel shortage and the imposition of wage and price controls in the U.S., import levels in 1973 and 1974 were substantially below quota levels, and the VRAs, apparently no longer needed, were allowed to lapse.

The 1976-78 Steel Dispute. The collapse in the world steel market in 1975 resulted in a substantial increase in foreign penetration of the U.S. market; imports from Japan grew from 5 to nearly 8 percent of U.S. consumption between 1974 and 1976, and EC penetration, after falling to 3 percent of U.S. consumption in 1976, rose to over 6 percent in 1977. By 1978, imports, which had accounted for under 13 percent of U.S. consumption in 1973, had risen to 18.1 percent.[44] A sharp fall in industry profitability in 1977 was accompanied by widespread plant closings and layoffs. The Alan Wood Steel Company went bankrupt, and major plant closings were undertaken by Kaiser, Jones and Laughlin, Bethlehem Steel and U.S. Steel.

The Carter Administration confronted substantial domestic pressure to deal with rising steel imports from Japan virtually from the moment it took office in early 1977. In the fall of 1976 the American Iron and Steel Institute had filed a petition against Japan and the EC pursuant to Section 301 of the Trade Act of 1974, alleging that a recently-concluded Japan-EC bilateral agreement had diverted Japanese steel from the EC to the U.S. market.

---

[44] During this period the "Europeans had persuaded the six major Japanese producers to limit voluntarily shipments of general steel products to the EC." The U.S. industry brought an action under Section 301 of the Trade Act of 1974, alleging that the restraint arrangement diverted Japanese steel from the EC to the American market. The Ford Administration did not seriously act on the petition, which was later dismissed for lack of evidence. Patrick and Sato, "Political Economy," p. 200.

Gilmore Steel, a small Oregon-based producer, filed an antidumping action against five major Japanese producers in February 1977, alleging dumping of carbon steel plate.[45] This was followed by an American Iron and Steel Institute study which charged that the Japanese mills were practicing price discrimination between the Japanese and U.S. markets, *e.g.*, dumping.[46] A clear consensus did not exist within the Carter Administration over how to deal with the issue, but it was eventually decided not to pursue policy measures that would involve quantitative import restraints.[47] Instead, the Administration gave the industry a "sincere (if not fully thought through) assurance" that it would enthusiastically enforce U.S. trade laws against dumped and subsidized steel imports.[48]

In September 1977, U.S. Steel filed an antidumping action against six Japanese companies, the largest antidumping action yet brought under the law, and in October, the Treasury Department determined in the Gilmore case that Japanese firms were dumping plate at margins averaging 32 percent. By late 1977 it was evident that European mills were dumping in the U.S. on a widespread scale, and by December 1977 a total of nineteen antidumping actions had been filed against Japan and various European countries, primarily by U.S. Steel. In the Congress, five bills had been introduced which would restrict steel imports, and the Chairman of the House Ways and Means Subcommittee on Trade warned the U.S. Trade Representative that "we simply can't wait for the administration to come up with a position while more steel mills throughout America close down and create problems of unemployment and havoc."[49]

The Trigger Price Mechanism. The Carter Administration quickly found that it did not possess the resources to handle large numbers of antidumping cases, and became increasingly concerned over the prospect of deteriorating relations with the EC arising out of massive steel litigation. "The early statements about enforcing the trade laws had to be discarded as being overly

---

[45] In July, the Japanese mills refused to provide cost-of-production data to the Treasury Department in the Gilmore case, increasing the prospect of a government-to-government confrontation.

[46] Putnam, Hayes & Bartlett, Inc., *Policy Implications.*

[47] Some in the Administration were reluctant to oppose relief for the steel industry because of their desire to win steel's support for the current round of Multilateral Trade Negotiations (MTN). On the other hand, quantitative restraints were opposed on the grounds that they would be inflationary. In addition, the Administration had just concluded an orderly marketing arrangement with Japan on color televisions, and there was a reluctance to provide similar relief in another major sector. Patrick and Sato, "Political Economy," p. 209.

[48] Wolff, "International Competitiveness," p. 312.

[49] U.S. Congress, House Ways and Means Subcommittee on Trade, *Hearings on World Steel Trade*, 95th Cong., Sept. 20, 1977, cited in Borrus, "The Politics of Competitive Erosion," p. 90.

simplistic."[50]   In September 1977, President Carter established a task force headed by Under Secretary of the Treasury Anthony Solomon to develop an alternative solution. In December 1977 the task force released the Solomon Report, which concluded that the antidumping laws were too cumbersome to provide adequate relief for the domestic industry from sudden import surges.[51]

The Solomon task force proposed to rectify this problem with the so-called Trigger Price Mechanism (TPM). The TPM was primarily a device to offset Japanese dumping.   U.S. producers felt they could compete successfully against the Japanese mills if their prices reflected their true costs. The TPM established a set of minimum "trigger prices" against which the U.S. government monitored the price levels of steel imports -- the government promised it would investigate any steel imports entering below trigger price levels and initiate its own expedited antidumping cases where appropriate. The trigger prices were supposed to reflect the minimum price at which steel could enter the United States and be above "fair value" as defined by the antidumping statute. They were determined by reference to Japanese steel production costs. The trigger prices were calculated in a manner roughly consistent with the methodology for determining "constructed value" under the U.S. antidumping statute -- that is, for determining what, given a producer's costs, a minimum fair market price for its products should be. The U.S. industry, under pressure from the Administration to accept the TPM as an alternative to continued prosecution of the dumping cases, agreed to withdraw the pending cases.[52]

It was generally acknowledged that the TPM would allow the European producers -- less efficient than the Japanese -- to sell in the United States below their own production costs. However, the U.S. government argued that while the TPM would not eliminate below cost sales by the Europeans, it would eliminate the injury to the U.S. industry from those sales. The TPM promised to provide a satisfactory alternative for the domestic steel producers to the prosecution of numerous antidumping cases.[53]

---

[50] Wolff, *Ibid.*

[51] The Solomon Report estimated that the average antidumping complaint, from the date of filing until the final determination, took thirteen months to complete. Interagency Task Force, *Report to the President: A Comprehensive Program for the Steel Industry* (December 6, 1977).

[52] According to industry sources, President Carter personally appealed to industry leaders to accept the TPM and withdraw their cases, given the foreign policy concerns which the cases fostered. In addition, based on its conversations with Administration officials, the industry was concerned that if it did not accept the TPM, the Treasury Department rulings on pending antidumping actions would be adverse.

[53] Dumping cases typically do not produce results until well after injury has begun to occur to an industry. Moreover, while injury typically occurs across a broad range of product lines, each case must be focused on specific products from individual countries, (*e.g.*, wire rods from France, hot-rolled sheets from Belgium, etc.). The TPM offered the hope of a deterrent to (rather than a penalty for) dumping which would apply to all foreign countries across most product lines. Such a system would not only be more comprehensive, but, hopefully, would also forestall injury to the U.S. mills.

The TPM was fully in place by April 1978 and seemed to eliminate the worst foreign price undercutting for several months in late 1978 and early 1979. While the volume of European imports remained strong through the remainder of 1978, that fact was thought to reflect the filling of pre-TPM orders. In the first two quarters of 1979, import penetration fell to its lowest level in many years -- 12.5 and 13.6 percent, respectively.[54] U.S. firms' operating ratios reached 91 percent during the first half of the year, and operating profits reached their highest levels in years.[55]

This relief proved short-lived. Imports from European mills increased sharply during the latter portion of 1979, both in absolute tonnage and as a percent of U.S. consumption. Because trigger prices were based on Japanese production costs, less efficient, high cost European mills could sell above TPM levels (avoiding U.S. government antidumping scrutiny), but well below their own costs -- in effect, they could sell at prices which constituted dumping as defined by the U.S. trade laws. One analyst noted in 1980 that "Romanian steelmakers can sell their products on the West Coast for the same price as Japanese producers without violating the TPM. However, because Romanians are relatively inefficient steelmakers . . . when Romanian steel is sold on the West Coast for the same price as Japanese steel, it must of necessity be selling at less than its actual cost of production."[56] The General Accounting Office later observed that, as a result of this loophole, "European steel penetrated the West Coast,"[57] where it had not previously enjoyed a substantial presence, and increased its presence in other U.S. markets, depressing prices and eroding U.S. firms' market share.[58] Another wave of plant closings and layoffs followed.[59]   Finally in March 1980, U.S. Steel filed new antidumping complaints which covered about three-fourths of the volume of U.S. steel

---

[54] American Iron and Steel Institute.

[55] Imports from Europe were greatly reduced during this period — 3.0 percent of U.S. consumption in the first quarter of 1979, compared with 7.12 percent in the first quarter of 1978.

[56] John J. Range, "Trigger Price Mechanism," 5 *N.C. Journal of International Law and Commercial Regulation* 291 (Spring 1980).

[57] U.S. General Accounting Office, *New Strategy Required for Aiding Distressed Steel Industry*, January, 1981, pp. 6-8.

[58] In 1980 the U.S. International Trade Commission found that there was a reasonable indication that imports of steel from the European Community had materially injured the U.S. steel industry across a broad range of product lines. In 1980, eighteen U.S. producers accounting for 80 percent of U.S. production suffered a cumulative net operating loss of $703 million. U.S.I.T.C. Publication 1221, February 1982, p. I-36. U.S.I.T.C. Investigation 731-TA-18/24 (1980).

[59] U.S. Steel closed its Joliet-Waukegan (Illinois) Works, except for a rod mill at the Joliet plant; its New Haven (Connecticut) Works; its Torrance (California) Works; the 140" plate mill at Fairfield (Alabama) Works; the strip mill at Gary (Indiana) Works; the iron foundry at South (Chicago, Illinois) Works; and the rod mill at Pittsburg (California) Works. In addition, U.S. Steel's wire mill at Fairfield (Alabama) Works and Youngstown (Ohio) Works were also permanently shut down.

imports from the Community. The U.S. government suspended the TPM --
which had served as an alternative to such suits -- on the day of these filings.

The U.S. Steel filings roughly coincided with the Soviet invasion of
Afghanistan and the hostage crisis in Iran, when the Carter Administration
was seeking to enhance the solidarity of the western alliance, and the cases
were awkward in this context precisely because they appeared to warrant
imposition of duties. The U.S. International Trade Commission issued an
affirmative preliminary determination of injury, and as the antidumping
investigations proceeded and Commerce Department officials gained access
to European sales and production cost data, it became apparent that EC
dumping was significant and that "there was a real possibility of having to
impose substantial antidumping duties on most European steel imports
covered by the U.S. Steel suits."[60] EC Commissioner Davignon implied,
however, that if a compromise were not reached by September 1980, the EC
would be forced to reevaluate its entire trade relationship with the United
States.[61]

Concerned that enforcement of the trade laws by their terms might result
in a virtual embargo of European steel, and worried about the broader
political implications of a trade war with the European allies, the U.S.
government proposed an alternative solution -- a revised TPM.
Acknowledging the flaw in its original assumption that no injury could result
to the U.S. industry from imports at above trigger levels, the U.S. government
proposed to bolster the TPM by monitoring the degree of import penetration.
Whenever the imports of any particular product category "surged," the
Department of Commerce would identify the country from which the
increased imports were exported and examine the imports to determine if they
involved injurious dumping or subsidization.[62] If such unfair trade practices
were found, the Department promised to initiate a formal investigation of the
practice. U.S. Steel agreed to withdraw its antidumping cases in favor of this
strengthened TPM and the modified TPM began operation on October 21,
1980, shortly before the Carter Administration left office.

The Collapse of the Trigger Price Mechanism. Like its predecessors, the
revised TPM initially appeared to work effectively. In the first quarter of
1981, import pressure was noticeably less severe; by spring employment levels
had climbed from the trough period of 1980, and by April 1981, the industry

---

[60] Patrick and Sato, "Trade in Steel," pp. 220-221. In January 1980 jurisdiction to administer
the antidumping and countervailing duty laws was transferred from the Treasury to the
Commerce Department's International Trade Administration.

[61] *Ibid.*

[62] "Surges" were increases in imports that were disproportionate to changes in U.S. market
conditions, seasonal patterns, or traditional trade patterns. Commerce was directed to determine
whether the imports (a) were being dumped, whether on a cost or price basis; (b) were the result
of government subsidies; or (c) were the result of fair competition. The new TPM trigger prices
were about 12 percent higher than under the previous system.

was operating at 88.6 percent of capacity.[63] However, in that same month, imports from the EC more than doubled over the preceding month, and it was clear by June that some European mills were mounting a major export drive to the U.S. One firm, Usinor, publicly announced that it was selling in the U.S. below trigger price levels.[64] The Europeans justified these sales on the grounds that as a result of the appreciation of the dollar against European currencies, they could lower their dollar export prices to the United States without selling below cost.[65]

Given the fact that the TPM was essentially a monitoring regime designed to give "early warning" of surges of dumped and subsidized steel, the fact that the new U.S. Administration did not react decisively to the first open sales below TPM levels proved fatal. When it became apparent that the U.S. government was not prepared to take action against the first European mills who sought to test the system, the result was a flood of EC steel into the U.S. market; one U.S. observer commented that "by the end of the year there will be an avalanche of flat-rolled carbon steel sheet priced below trigger, and it's getting to be an auction out there."[66] By the end of 1981 quarterly import penetration levels had reached 23.7 percent, and the U.S. industry was undergoing another major contraction; between September and November 1981, U.S. steel producers closed more than 23 plants and laid off nearly 50,000 workers.[67] Steel analyst Peter Marcus commented that the "trigger price mechanism, with its legal loopholes (preclearance), price disparities and ineffective enforcement has developed into an economic tragedy of epic proportions."[68]

The Administration took no significant action until November 1981, when it self-initiated seven antidumping and countervailing duty investigations against European mills. In January 1982, the U.S. steel industry filed 132 antidumping and countervailing duty actions against seven EC and four non-EC countries, the largest filing of antidumping/countervailing cases in U.S. history. The TPM was suspended, never to be reinstated. The EC Commission's public reaction was one of anger; Commission Vice President

---

[63] American Metal Market (March 2, April 7, May 5, 15, 1981); AISI, Annual Statistical Report 1982.

[64] American Metal Market (June 1, 15, 1981). Thyssen and Hoogovens were reportedly selling steel on the West coast below trigger price levels, and deep undercutting of the trigger prices was reported in the Gulf region. American Metal Market (June 16, 1981).

[65] The European producers sought "preclearance" from the Commerce Department under the TPM, that is, a ruling by Commerce that, based on their costs, they could sell below TPM levels without dumping. The European mills argued that for purposes of this determination Commerce should ignore the subsidies which they were receiving.

[66] American Metal Market (November 5, 1981).

[67] Metal Bulletin (October 9, 1981); American Metal Market (October 12, 1981); Wall Street Journal (October 19, 1981).

[68] American Metal Market (September 16, 1981).

Davignon complained of "massive harassment" of European exporters, but "Commission officials spoke in private about the excesses which some EC companies had practiced in their sales to the USA."[69]

The U.S.-EC Arrangement, 1982. This time the U.S. government was better staffed to handle a large number of antidumping and countervailing duty investigations, and during early and mid-1982 the U.S. trade cases proceeded according to their statutory timetables, while the U.S. government and the Community pursued a negotiated solution to the dispute.[70] Informal discussions between Davignon and Commerce Secretary Baldrige over a possible VRA proved inconclusive.[71] On June 10, 1982, the Commerce Department announced its preliminary findings in the countervailing duty investigations, finding margins of subsidization which appalled the Europeans.[72] In late July, the Council of Ministers gave the Commission an "exclusive mandate" to negotiate a comprehensive steel arrangement with the United States.[73]

The 1982 cases were significant because, in contrast to prior proceedings, a large number of them proceeded sufficiently far to produce a thorough U.S. investigation of EC subsidy policies and dumping practices, resulting in published findings by the Commerce Department and the U.S. International Trade Commission. The margins found in these cases were substantial. The margin of subsidization on most imports from British Steel was 20.33 percent; on imports from France's Sacilor and Usinor, margins ranged from 11.30 to 21.42 percent, and the margins on many other producers were substantial, including Italsider (14.56 percent), and Cockerill Sambre (13.44 percent). Many of the heavily-subsidized firms were also found (in preliminary determinations) to be dumping by substantial margins, including Italy's Teksid (40.72 percent on CR sheet and strip), Sacilor (27.69 percent on CR sheet and strip), British Steel (18.84 percent on plate) and Cockerill-Sambre (10.84 percent on HR sheet). The West German mills were preliminarily found to

---

[69] *Metal Bulletin Monthly* (April 1983). Davignon himself was harshly critical of the EC producers for having provoked the U.S. action by their "reckless export tactics." *Metal Bulletin* (November 6, 1981). See also *Wirtschaftsdienst* (August 1981).

[70] The Commerce Department initiated an investigation with respect to 85 of the U.S. industry petitions involving the Community; the U.S.I.T.C. made affirmative injury determinations with respect to 36. 47 F.R. 5744 (1982); 47 F.R. 9087 (1982).

[71] The Community proposed an agreement that would limit ECSC carbon steel sales to 4.95 percent of the U.S. market, but which would exclude pipes and tubes from the VRA. The U.S., sought a 4.3 percent ceiling which would include pipes and tubes. *Commerce News* (June 11, 1982) in van der Ven and Grunert, "Transatlantic Steel Trade," p. 158.

[72] *Certain Steel Products from Belgium, et al.*, 47 F.R. 39304 (1982). British Steel faced preliminary margins of over 40 percent on some products; Cockerill-Sambre, 20-22 percent; Usinor and Sacilor, 20-30 percent, and Italsider, 18 percent.

[73] *Bull. EC* (July 7/8 1982), Point 1.1.2.

524

Table 7-2. 1982 Margins of EC Dumping and Subsidization in the U.S. Market

SUPPLIER	PRODUCT	DUMPING	SUBSIDIZATION
Belgium			
Cockerill-Sambre	Structurals	1.14%	13.23%
	Plate	5.17	13.44
	HR sheet, strip	10.88	13.44
Sidmar	Plate	-	2.77
	HR sheet, strip	-	2.77
Fabrique de Fer	Plate	-	2.17
Others	Structurals	1.14	13.23
	Plate	5.17	13.44
	HR sheet, strip	10.88	12.44
	HR sheet, strip	27.69	21.42
Italy			
Italsider	CR sheet, strip	2.07	14.56
	HR sheet, strip	9.72	14.56
Teksid	CR sheet, strip	40.72	14.56
Falck	CR sheet, strip	-	6.32
	CR sheet, strip	-	6.32
Others	CR sheet, strip	2.07	14.56
	HR sheet, strip	2.07	14.56
Britain			
British Steel	Structurals	10.61	20.33
	Plate	18.84	20.33
	HR bar	-	20.33
Brymbo	HR bar	-	1.88
Darlington-Simpson	Structurals	7.84	20.33
Others	Structurals	10.61	20.33
	Plate	-	20.33
	H.R. bar	-	20.33

SUPPLIER	PRODUCT	DUMPING	SUBSIDIZATION
France			
Sacilor	Structurals	9.06%	14.22%
	HR sheet, strip	23.16	21.42
	CR sheet, strip	27.69	19.49
Usinor	HR sheet, strip	2.39	17.98
	CR sheet, strip	1.33	11.30
	Structurals	-	11.30
Dilling	HR sheet, strip	-	4.04
	CR Sheet, strip	-	3.70
Others	Structurals	9.06	14.22
	CR sheet, strip	23.11	19.49
West Germany			
Thyssen	HR sheet, strip	19.17	...
	Plate	2.41	...
	CR sheet, strip	12.91	...
Rochling-Burbach	Structurals	10.90	1.31
Hoesch	Structurals	10.29	...
	CR sheet, strip	6.92	...
Dillinger	Plate	9.25	...
Klockner	Plate	3.60	...
Others	Structurals	10.90	1.31
	CR sheet, strip,	12.91	...
HR sheet, strip	19.17	-	

Note: All dumping margins based on U.S. Commerce Department preliminary determinations, subsidy margins based on final countervailing duty determinations. Dumping cases were terminated after U.S.-E.C. Arrangement was concluded before final margins were determined.

be dumping at substantial margins, ranging as high as 19.17 percent (Thyssen). The real implication of these findings was that if the U.S. trade laws were applied to the facts of the situation, a number of European firms would be excluded from the U.S. market entirely.[74]

In early August a tentative government-to-government agreement was reached, under which the U.S. would permit an ECSC share of 5.75 percent of the U.S. market, in return for which the U.S. industry would withdraw its cases. The U.S. industry rejected this arrangement on the grounds that the quota was too high and did not cover pipes and tubes. In early August, the Commerce Department published its preliminary determinations in the antidumping actions, finding margins as high as 41 percent. Later that month, final margins of subsidization were announced, which although lower than those in the preliminary determination, were substantial, and, if applied, would effectively exclude the large integrated producers of Belgium, France, Italy and Britain from the U.S. market. The imminent prospect of the imposition of duties provided substantial negotiating leverage for the U.S., and in late October a U.S.-EC Steel Arrangement was reached.[75]

Under the Arrangement, which ran from October 1, 1982 through the end of 1985, the Community agreed to limit its shipments to an average of 5.44 percent of U.S. consumption of specified "arrangement" products. The Arrangement provided for consultations in the event that diversion took place from covered to non-covered products ("consultation products"). The Commission enforced adherence to the Arrangement through the issuance of export licenses; special licenses could be issued in the event of short supply. The U.S. industry withdrew all of its cases, and undertook not to file any further trade actions during the duration of the Arrangement.[76]

The treatment of pipes and tubes was a sticking point which would aggravate U.S.-EC relations long after the conclusion of the Arrangement. Within the Community, the German and French producers were adamantly opposed to restrictions on pipe and tube exports to the U.S., while the U.S. industry opposed an agreement that did not cover those products. At the time the Arrangement was concluded, these differences were finessed by excluding them from the Arrangement, but addressing them in a separate exchange of side letters between Baldrige and Davignon providing a formula for regulating

---

[74] Mary F. Dominick, "Countervailing State Aids for Steel: A Case for International Consensus," in 21 *Common Market Law Review* 354, 372 (June 1984); van der Ven and Grunert, p. 158.

[75] Arrangement Concerning Trade in Certain Steel Products between the European Coal and Steel Community and the United States, *Official Journal* No. L. 307/12 (1982).

[76] For a synopsis of the terms of the Arrangement, see Frank Benyon and Jacques Bourgeois, "The European Community - United States Steel Arrangement," in 21 *Common Market Law Review* 283 (1984).

EC pipe and tube exports to the U.S. on the basis of EC shipments in the period 1979-81.[77]

Political leaders in both the EC and the US hailed these accords as eliminating a major trouble spot in relations between Europe and the United States. EC Commission officials presented the agreement as a victory for the Western European steel industry, and President Reagan indicated that the agreement provided reassuring evidence that America and its allies and trading partners could work together.[78] Industry spokesmen on both sides of the Atlantic, however, were more reserved, and subsequent events would show that the conclusion of the 1982 U.S.-EC accords by no means heralded the end of friction in steel between the U.S. and the Community.

The collapse of the TPM at the end of 1981 removed an impediment to Japanese exports to the U.S., and U.S. imports from Japan increased sharply in 1982 from 1981 levels, particularly in higher value added product lines like oil country tubular goods, line pipe and other tubular products. The U.S. steel industry brought several trade actions against Japan in 1982 and 1983 (including an antidumping action in pipes and tubes and a Section 301 action alleging that an EC-Japan agreement had diverted steel into the U.S. market).[79] By mid-1983, import pressure from Japan had abated.

The Influx From the Developing Countries. Pressure on the U.S. steel market from developing country suppliers had been increasing for a number of years, and U.S. producers had brought antidumping and countervailing duty actions resulting in affirmative findings against exporting countries in the early 1980s, most notably Brazil (plate and wire rod in 1982-83), Argentina (wire rod in 1982), South Korea (pipe, plate, HR sheet in 1982-83) and Taiwan (plate in 1979). However, in 1983, following the conclusion of the U.S.-EC arrangement, the U.S. experienced an "incredible surge"[80] of steel imports from the developing countries, as well as some "other industrialized" countries like Spain and South Africa. The influx was broad both in the range of products and the number of exporting countries involved. Penetration of the U.S. market by "other" suppliers (countries other than Canada, the EC and Japan) doubled, from 5.3 percent to 10.2 percent between 1982 and the first quarter of 1984.[81] U.S. steel producers responded to this influx with their own

---

[77] Baldrige to Davignon, October 21, 1982. The Pipe and Tube Arrangement provided that diversion from products subject to export licensing under the basic steel Arrangement to pipes and tubes would not occur insofar as EC pipe and tube did not exceed the 1979-81 average, which accounted for 5.9 percent of the U.S. market.

[78] van der Ven and Grunert, "Transatlantic Steel Trade."

[79] The Section 301 action was subsequently dismissed by the Office of the U.S. Trade Representative; the antidumping action eventually led to the imposition of duties.

[80] van der Ven and Grunert, "Transatlantic Steel Trade," p. 173.

[81] U.S. Department of Commerce; *Business Week* (October 3, 1983); *American Metal Market* (May 1, 1984).

price reductions in order to prevent further erosion of market share. This competition between U.S. and developing country mills was one reason cited for the depressed level of U.S. steel prices in 1982 and 1983, when the U.S. steel industry reported a cumulative net loss of approximately $5 billion.[82] The U.S. industry filed a succession of antidumping and countervailing duty petitions in 1983 and 1984.

Like the 1982 cases against the EC, many of the antidumping and countervailing duty actions filed by the U.S. industry against developing and "other industrialized" countries resulted, after investigation, in preliminary and in some cases final determinations of dumping and subsidization. These investigations were noteworthy not only because they resulted in the Commerce Department's finding of some of the highest margins of dumping and subsidization in the history of the U.S. trade laws (particularly against Brazil), but also because they revealed the breadth and scope of dumping and subsidization of steel exports to the U.S. market.[83] For example, between 1982 and 1986, affirmative findings of dumping and/or subsidization were made against Brazil in plate, wire rod, welded pipes and tubes, stainless steel bars, alloy tool steel, butt-weld pipe fittings, cold-rolled sheets, hot-rolled sheets, plate in coil, and oil country tubular goods.[84] During the same period, affirmative findings of dumping or subsidization were also made against Argentina, Australia, Austria, Canada, China, Finland, India, Israel, South Korea, Mexico, New Zealand, Peru, Poland, Romania, Saudi Arabia, South Africa, Spain, Sweden, Taiwan, Trinidad & Tobago, Turkey, Yugoslavia and Zimbabwe.[85] Some of these countries, such as Spain, South Korea and Argentina, were, like Brazil, the subject of affirmative dumping/subsidy findings in many different product areas. The cumulative evidentiary effect of these dozens of cases -- each of which involved a detailed investigation by the U.S. government -- was to demonstrate that in the early and mid-1980s, the U.S. was experiencing a wave of dumped and subsidized steel imports from virtually all points of the compass.

Origins of the Reagan Steel Program. In January 1984 Bethlehem Steel and the United Steelworkers of America jointly filed a petition under Section 201 of the Trade Act of 1974 (the "escape clause") seeking import relief on

---

[82] *American Metal Market* (January 13, 27, February 9, March 5, 19, April 22, 28, August 17, 1982; July 27, 1983). Peter Marcus observed that "price cutting remains more severe than at any time since the 1930s." *Business Week* (August 8, 1983).

[83] In 1984 Brazil's COSIPA was found to be dumping plate at a margin of 100.04 percent and hot-rolled sheet at a margin of 89.46 percent. *Hot-Rolled Carbon Steel Plate and Sheet from Brazil*, January 25, 1984 (49 F.R. 3102).

[84] U.S. Department of Commerce.

[85] U.S. Department of Commerce, *Summary of Steel Cases Since January 1981* (As of June 15, 1988).

Table 7-3. U.S. Department of Commerce Affirmative Antidumping and Countervailing Duty Findings Against Developing Country and "Other Industrialized" Steel Producers, 1982-88

Argentina

Wire Rod (CVD) [1]
Wire Rod (AD)
CR Sheet (CVD)
CR Sheet (AD) [3]
OCTG (CVD)
OCTG (AD) [3]
Barbed Wire (AD)

Australia

Galvanized
  Sheet (AD) [2]

Austria

HR Sheet (AD) [3]
HR Sheet (CVD) [3]
CR Sheet (CVD)

Brazil

Plate (CVD) [2]
Wire Rod (CVD) [2]
PC Strand (CVD) [3]
Welded Pipe &
  Tube (CVD) [2]
Stainless HR bar, CF Bar,
  Wire Rod (CVD) [1]
Alloy Tool Steel
  (CVD) [1]
Wire Rod (AD) [2]
HR Plate (AD) [2]
Butt-weld Pipe
  Fitting (AD)
HR Sheet (plate in
  coil) (AD) [2]
CR Sheet (AD) [3]
CR Sheet (CVD) [2]
HR Sheet (AD) [2]
HR Sheet (CVD) [2]
Plate in Coil (CVD) [2]
Large Diameter
  Pipe (AD) [2]
OCTG (AD) [2]
OCTG (VD) [2]

Canada

Sheet Piling (AD) [1]
Rebars (AD) [1]
Structurals & bars
  (AD) [1]
Rectangular Pipe &
  Tube (AD) [3]
OCTG (CVD)
OCTG (AD)

China

Wire Nails (AD) [1]
Small Diameter Pipe
  & Tube (AD) [3]

Finland

Plate (AD) [2]

India

Standard Pipe & Tube (AD)

Israel

OCTG (AD)
OCTG (CVD)

Korea

Welded Pipe (CVD) [2]
Wire Nails (AD) [2]
Plate (CVD) [2]
HR Sheet (CVD)
Galvanized Sheet (CVD) [2]
Circular Pipe & Tube
  (AD) [2]
Rectangular Pipe & Tube
  (AD) [2]
Plate (AD) [2]
CR Plate & Sheet (CVD) [2]

Malaysia

Wire Rod (CVD) [2]

Mexico

Bar (CVD) [1]
Rebar (CVD) [1]
Bar-Shaped Sizes
  (CVD) [1]
OCTG (CVD) [2]

New Zealand

Wire Rod (CVD)
Steel Wire (CVD)
Wire Nails (CVD)

Norway

Structurals (AD) [3]

Peru

Rebars (CVD)

Poland

Wire Rod (AD) [3]
Barbed Wire (AD) [2]

Saudi Arabia

Wire Rod (CVD)

Table 7-3. (continued)

Spain	Sweden	Turkey
PC Strand (CVD) [3]	Stainless Plate (AD)	Line Pipe (AD) [3]
Structurals (CVD) [2]	HR Sheet (CVD) [3]	Pipe & Tube
HR Plate (CVD) [2]	CR Sheet (CVD)	Pipe & Tube (CVD)
CR Sheet (CVD) [2]	Plate (CVD) [3]	
Galvanized Sheet	Stainless Hollow	
(CVD) [2]	Products (AD)	**Venezuela**
HR Bars (CVD) [2]	Stainless Hollow	
Cold Formed Bars	Products (CVD)	Wire Rod (AD) [3]
(CVD) [2]		
HR Stainless Bars		
(CVD) [3]	**Taiwan**	**Yugoslavia**
Cold Formed Stainless		
Bars (CVD)	Plate (AD)	Pipe & Tube, Line Pipe
Stainless Wire (CVD)	Circular Pipe &	(AD) [2]
Carbon Wire Rod (AD) [2]	Tube (AD)	Pipe & Tube, Line Pipe
Stainless CR Sheet	Line Pipe (AD) [3]	(CVD) [2]
(AD) [3]		
Stainless CR Strip		
(AD) [3]	**Trinidad & Tobago**	**Zimbabwe**
Structurals (AD) [2]		
Plate (AD) [2]	Wire Rod (AD)	Wire Rod (CVD)
HR Sheet (AD) [2]	Wire Rod (CVD) [1]	
CR Sheet (AD) [2]		
Galvanized Sheet (AD) [2]		
OCTG (AD) [2]		
OCTG (CVD) [2]		

Source: U.S. Department of Commerce
Notes: OCTG - Oil Country Tubular Goods;AD - Antidumping;
CVD - Countervailing Duty
[1] Suspended, terminated or revoked pursuant to agreement.
[2] Terminated pursuant to Reagan VRA program
[3] Negative injury determination

carbon and alloy steel products.[86] Concurrently, the U.S. industry filed a new round of antidumping and countervailing duty cases, principally against developing countries and industrialized nations outside of Japan and the

---

[86] The preceding year President Reagan had increased existing tariffs and imposed quantitative restrictions on imports of specialty steel products pursuant to a Section 201 action brought by the U.S. industry. Article XIX of the GATT permits signatories to "escape" their GATT obligations when imports cause serious injury to individual sectors in the domestic economy. Section 201, the U.S. statute which provides for "escape clause" relief, authorizes entities representative of an industry to petition the U.S. International Trade Commission for a determination that imports in increased quantities are (or threaten to be) a substantial cause of serious injury to a domestic industry. If the U.S.I.T.C. determination is affirmative, the Commission must recommend import restrictions or adjustment assistance to rectify the injury. The President has 60 days to determine what relief, if any, he will provide on the basis of the Commission's recommendations.

Community.[87] In July 1984, the U.S. International Trade Commission concluded that the U.S. industry had been injured by imports in five of the nine product categories under investigation, and recommended that the President establish quotas on imports of these products.[88] In September 1984, President Reagan announced that he would deny relief under Section 201, but that he would proceed to negotiate bilateral restraint arrangements (VRAs) with steel exporting countries, and would more vigorously enforce U.S. trade laws against unfairly traded steel.[89] Under this policy, the President indicated that it was his expectation that steel imports would be reduced to about 18.5 percent of U.S. consumption or 20.2 percent if semifinished steel was included. Within a matter of days the U.S. Congress passed legislation providing the President with statutory authority to enforce voluntary restraint arrangements, conditioned on a commitment by the U.S. steel industry to modernize its plant and provide retraining assistance for former workers.[90]

In late 1984 and early 1985, President Reagan negotiated VRAs with seven major U.S. suppliers, Japan, South Korea, Brazil, South Africa, Spain, Mexico and Australia, each establishing specific quantitative limits on U.S. imports; the pending U.S. antidumping and countervailing duty actions against VRA countries were withdrawn. On December 19, 1984, U.S. Steel filed antidumping and countervailing duty actions against nine non-VRA suppliers; eventually most of these countries also concluded VRAs with the U.S.[91] Exporting countries regarded the VRAs as preferable to antidumping and countervailing duty actions, since the agreements permitted the continuation of substantial steel exports to the U.S. market, whereas the cases in some instances raised the prospect of virtual exclusion from the U.S. market upon application of antidumping or countervailing duties.

The U.S.-EC Arrangement, 1984-88. The U.S.-EC Arrangements on carbon steel and pipes and tubes were characterized by continual controversy. In 1984, the U.S. called for consultations with the EC after the European mills

---

[87] The U.S. industry also backed legislation which would limit imports from all sources to 15 percent of the U.S. market.

[88] Report to the President, U.S.I.T.C. Investigation No. TA-201-51, U.S.I.T.C. Pub. No. 1553, July 1984. The Section 201 petition was timed to ensure that President Reagan would be required to decide on relief for steel prior to the 1984 Presidential election.

[89] Executive Communication 4046 (September 18, 1984).

[90] The President is required to certify on an annual basis to the House Ways and Means and Senate Finance Committees (a) that the major steel companies, taken as a whole, have committed substantially all of their net cash flow from steel operations to investments in modernization, and have taken sufficient action to maintain their international competitiveness, and (b) that each company has committed not less than 1 percent of net cash flow to the retraining of workers. *Steel Imports Stabilization Act,* 19 U.S.C. 2253 *et seq.*

[91] Venezuela, Norway, Austria, East Germany, Poland, Romania, Hungary, Czechoslovakia, Norway, Sweden. The President had set December 18 as the deadline for concluding the VRA negotiations; the filings were made the following day.

exceeded the 5.9 percent benchmark for pipe and tube shipments to the U.S., which by late 1984 were running at a level of 14 percent of U.S. consumption.[92] In November 1984, after negotiations on a "voluntary" EC quota proved inconclusive, the U.S. government announced a ban on further U.S. imports of EC pipes and tubes, on the grounds that the Community mills had already greatly exceeded their 5.9 percent limit.[93] In early 1985, the U.S. and EC reached a new accord pursuant to which the EC agreed to limit their pipe and tube shipments to 7.6 percent of the U.S. market.[94] Friction continued in this sector, however, because the EC sought, and the U.S. refused, short supply exemptions to permit EC mills to exceed the quantitative limits set down in the new agreement.[95]

A second source of friction was the growing U.S. concern over EC diversion of exports from "arrangement" products, which were subject to quantitative limits, to "consultation" products, such as semifinished steel, electrical sheets, blackplate, CR strip, rails, tin-free steel and alloy tool steels, which were not. In 1985, U.S. imports of some of these products from the EC were running at three times their 1982 levels.[96] The U.S. government called for consultations on six of these products in early 1985; although the 60-day consultation period ended without a resolution being reached, the U.S. refrained from unilateral action pending further negotiations.[97] In August, an agreement was reached under which the Community agreed to quantitative limits on 16 of 17 consultation products, but at levels permitting Community mills to export higher tonnages "than they had actually asked for in the negotiations."[98] A pleased EC Commission characterized the accord as "an equitable agreement taking into account the vital interests of European industry as well as the preoccupations of the U.S. government;" the U.S. industry complained that the U.S. government had been "completely

---

[92] *Metal Bulletin* (October 5, 1984). The overshipment occurred as the U.S. market for oil country tubular goods experienced a massive import influx. *Metal Bulletin* (August 3, 1984).

[93] 1984 shipments blocked by the ban were allowed to enter the U.S. in 1985, but would count against any quota agreed for 1985. *Metal Bulletin* (November 23, 1984).

[94] *Metal Bulletin* (March 5, 1985).

[95] *Metal Bulletin* (April 4, 19, 1985). Community suppliers sought to supply pipe to U.S. pipeline project. The Commerce Department rejected the request on the grounds that pipe was available from domestic suppliers. This particular dispute was resolved by a compromise allowing 100 thousand tons of EC pipe to enter the U.S. *BNA International Trade Reporter* (April 3, 1985); *Metal Bulletin* (June 7, 1985).

[96] *BNA International Trade Reporter* (June 12, 1985).

[97] *Metal Bulletin* (June 11, 1985). The U.S. government sought to establish quantitative limits on all 17 consultation products, including semifinished steel. The Community wanted restraints limited to six consultation products.

[98] The U.S. had entered the negotiations seeking a ceiling of 475 thousand tons; the EC had asked for a quota of 540 thousand tons. The U.S. ultimately agreed to limits which would permit the EC to ship about 690 thousand tons to the U.S. in 1985. *Metal Bulletin* (August 6, 1985).

outmaneuvered," and that the EC mills had been "rewarded" for violations of the U.S.-EC Arrangement.[99]

The U.S.-EC Arrangements were due to expire at the end of 1985. The U.S. government sought to negotiate a pact which embraced all steel products, including semifinished steel, pipes and tubes, and other consultation products; the EC opposed coverage of these products. A compromise, reached in November 1985, provided for extension of the U.S.-EC Arrangements (carbon steel and pipes and tubes) through September 1989. Coverage was extended to 11 former consultation products and ten other products; the quotas on former arrangement products were increased slightly, from an average of 5.46 percent to 5.57 percent. Semifinished products were excluded from strict controls.[100]   The Community industry was generally satisfied with the agreement, while the U.S. industry sharply attacked it, citing the nebulous treatment of semifinished steel and the fact that the EC mills were allowed to increase their share of the U.S. market.[101]

At the end of 1985 the U.S. government announced that it would establish a unilateral quota on imports of semifinished steel from the EC of 400 thousand short tons per year through 1989, with a discretionary quota of 200 thousand tons per year to meet contracts already in place, effective January 1, 1986.[102]   The Community called the action "unjustified" and imposed retaliatory restrictions on EC imports of U.S. coated paper, beef fat and fertilizers.[103]   After six months of complex negotiations, a compromise was reached under which the EC agreed to inclusion of semis in the coverage of the Arrangement, but at substantially higher quota levels than those announced by the U.S. government at the beginning of the year.[104]

The Reagan Steel Program, 1985-88. The Reagan steel program got off to an extremely shaky start. Trade data for the first six months of 1985 showed that imports had reached an all-time high, and accounted for 26.2 percent of U.S. consumption, compared with 24.2 percent a year earlier. The

---

[99] *Ibid.*; *BNA International Trade Reporter* (August 28, 1985).

[100] The U.S. government indicated that it expected overall semifinished imports from all sources, including the EC, to remain below 1.7 million short tons per year. Semis from the EC were subject to consultation if they exceeded 400 thousand tons per year.

[101] *Metal Bulletin* (November 8, 1985).

[102] The Community objected to the lack of consultations prior to the imposition of the quota. U.S. Trade Representative Clayton Yeutter responded that the semis issue had already been the subject of extensive talks, and that the quota was necessary to prevent diversion into semis from other arrangement product areas. The British were particularly upset by the U.S. limits because they planned to ship 300 thousand tons of slabs per year to a new steel plant in Tuscaloosa, Alabama, which was partly owned by British Steel. *Metal Bulletin* (January 3, 1986).

[103] *BNA International Trade Reporter* (March 12, 1986).

[104] The agreed tonnages were 620 thousand for 1987, 650 thousand for 1988, and 502.5 thousand for the first nine months of 1989.

apparent inadequacy of the policy measures taken was criticized by the U.S. industry and its Congressional supporters.[105]

A number of holes in the system quickly became apparent. Perhaps the most serious was the surges of imports into the U.S. from countries not yet subject to VRAs. As the negotiation of VRAs progressively limited shipments from traditional suppliers, new countries began increasing their steel shipments to the U.S., including such unlikely sources as Bulgaria, Saudi Arabia, New Zealand, Zimbabwe, China, Thailand, Peru and Singapore. This problem was partially mitigated over time by a series of antidumping and countervailing duty actions against the new suppliers, many of which resulted in affirmative findings of dumping and subsidization, and in some cases, the conclusion of VRAs with these countries.[106]

Another problem was the circumvention of VRA restrictions by supplying countries, usually by transshipment through third countries. In 1985 Brazil was reportedly transshipping steel to the U.S. through Panama, and had entered into an arrangement to produce pipe in Panama, made with flat-rolled Brazilian steel, for export to the U.S.[107] Customs reported entries of steel into the U.S. from countries which did not produce steel, such as Bhutan, Antigua and the Cayman Islands, a clear indicator of transshipment. In 1986, Commerce Department official Gilbert Kaplan expressed his concern in a letter to his counterparts in other governments over reports that steel mills were being constructed in countries not subject to VRAs in order to process steel from VRA countries for export to the U.S.[108]

A third problem was posed by several traditional major suppliers, notably Canada, Sweden, Argentina and Taiwan, which refused to enter into VRAs with the U.S. After major increases in imports from these countries occurred in 1986, the U.S. government called for consultations with them. A number of the non-VRA countries eventually worked out "gentlemen's agreements" with the U.S. on shipment levels, although refusing to accept formal quotas.[109] U.S. relations with Canada were complicated by concurrent negotiations to establish a U.S.-Canada Free Trade Area (FTA), an initiative which faced substantial opposition in both countries. U.S. imports of steel from Canada grew from traditional levels of about 3 percent of consumption to over 5 percent in early 1987, leading to charges that Canada was serving as a

---

[105] *BNA International Trade Reporter* (May 29, August 21, 1985).

[106] *BNA International Trade Reporter* (October 2, November 27, December 4, 1985; January 22, March 19, April 23, July 23, August 20, 1986).

[107] *BNA International Trade Reporter* (November 20, 1985).

[108] *BNA International Trade Reporter* (March 5, 1986).

[109] *BNA International Trade Reporter* (September 10, 1986). Taiwan, for example, was reported in 1986 to be limiting its exports to the U.S. to a fixed tonnage. *Metal Bulletin* (September 9, 1986).

transshipment point for steel from VRA countries. In response, the Canadian government implemented a system to monitor steel imports and exports.[110]

Despite the various problems encountered under the Reagan program, it was evident by mid-1986 that the system was beginning to work. U.S. import levels for June 1986 were 27 percent lower than for June of 1985, and the American Iron and Steel Institute concluded that "the figures show President Reagan's anti-import measures are working."[111] While import penetration levels remained above the 20.2 percent target set by the President, they have declined in each year of the program -- from 26.4 percent in 1984, 25.2 percent in 1985, 23 percent in 1986, to 21.3 percent in 1987.[112]

The main reason that the import penetration goal of the program was not met by 1987 was that imports from non-VRA countries (especially Canada) increased sharply. The VRA countries did not meet their import limits under the program in 1987. The VRA countries supplied 13.5 percent of the market for finished steel products, 20 percent less than the negotiated market share of 16.9 percent, and are shipping 14 percent less than their quota on semifinished steel.[113] The non-VRA countries increased their share of the U.S. market for finished and semifinished steel from 4.6 percent in 1984 to 6.8 percent in 1987.[114]

---

[110] *BNA International Trade Reporter* (April 1, 1987). The Canadian position with respect to the Reagan program was that Canada's traditional 3 percent share of the U.S. market had been won "by free and fair trade," and that Canada should not have this share reduced. The Canadians were concerned, however, that transshipments through Canada might provoke U.S. antidumping and countervailing duty actions against Canadian mills. Another fear was that European, Japanese and Korean steel transshipped through Canada would soon displace "real" Canadian steel exports to the U.S.

[111] *Metal Bulletin* (August 6, 1986).

[112] American Iron and Steel Industry, *1987 Annual Statistical Report*, table 1A. An assessment of the import restraints on the U.S. sheet and strip segment of the steel industry by the ITC indicated that the restraints themselves have had a "relatively small" positive impact. U.S. International Trade Commission, *Steel Sheet and Strip Industry*, pp. 11-130 to 11-135.

[113] David J. Cantor, "Steel Imports: Is the President's Program Working?," (Washington, D.C.: Congressional Research Service, March 17, 1988).

[114] U.S. International Trade Commission, *Monthly Report on Selected Steel Industry Data* (Washington, D.C.: U.S. International Trade Commission, March 1988), tables 5,7.

8

Policy Lessons for the 1990s

The lesson of international competition in steel is that national policies determine competitive outcomes. Governments make choices which affect both trade and investment. They can consciously create comparative advantage and, conversely, inadvertently, they can create comparative disadvantage.

Japan started the postwar period with virtually no industry, no raw materials, a shortage of capital, and a shortage of technically skilled engineers. Within fifteen years it had created a world class steel industry. Korea, Brazil, Italy, Taiwan, the United Kingdom, France and many other countries whose stories have been told in the foregoing pages set out to establish modern steel industries. To a significant extent, they succeeded, although in many cases the industries so created, while "modern," could only continue operating with massive government financial support. In many cases these countries' "success" was obtained at great cost to their national treasuries, their other industries and other countries' steel industries. The United States, by contrast, set out to create the world's most efficient market, and beyond any doubt, in this it has succeeded.

Government policies, both macroeconomic and sectoral, have altered the industrial landscape. There has been a substantial degree of consistency of purpose abroad, as governments have adopted long-term, concrete sectoral goals, and pursued them through direct subsidization, protection (a highly effective form of hidden subsidy), and the use of competition policy as an industrial policy tool. This is not to say that they have always been successful in meeting their objectives, or that significant errors in judgement were never made; many of the countries studied in this book have launched ambitious promotional efforts which have gone catastrophically awry. In others, such as Belgium, public intervention has consisted primarily of a succession of improvised measures to prevent the collapse of a sector deemed vital to the national economy. Nevertheless, other governments have been concerned with the sectoral composition of their economies and have acted to effect that composition when it has been deemed in their nation's best interest to do so. For better or worse, by such actions, they have changed the distribution of world steel-making facilities and changed the pattern of world trade.

After its own fashion, America's purpose never wavered. It set out to make the market the sole determinant of what was produced and what was consumed within the borders of the United States. U.S. economic philosophy required only inaction by the government, although events occasionally forced the government to intervene, however reluctantly. In those cases, invocation of the trade laws and political pressures caused trade measures to be implemented, but there was no longer-term objective other than to return to the normality of the free play of market forces as soon as the storm had passed. The U.S. was largely oblivious to the highly active role played by other governments.

A policy of inaction has its own consequences, however. According to the United States' *laissez faire* beliefs, if a problem of international competition arose, it could be dealt with on an *ad hoc* basis. If the problem did not fit neatly within the established categories provided by the trade laws, then perhaps there was no public interest to be served by government action and the problem should be left to the individual company to meet as best as it could.

This policy of noninterference, with relatively little appreciation of the effects of the policies of others, has been one of the central factors underlying the dramatic disinvestment in steel in the United States since the mid-1970s.[1] The effects of the overvalued dollar in the early 1980s compounded the severe adjustment difficulties of the U.S. steel industry caused by foreign industrial policies. The U.S. Government pursued a rigid policy of noninterference at the sectoral level, punctuated by occasional, partially effective trade restrictions.

THE LEGACY OF DIFFERING POLICY CHOICES

The adjustment problems faced by U.S. integrated steel producers over the past 15 years were part of a global structural crisis of overcapacity whose roots lay in the stagnation in western world steel consumption after 1974, coupled with the uneconomic expansion of steel producing capacity in many countries, begun prior to 1974 and continued for almost a decade afterwards. For the most part, the capacity expansion was state-supported or state-directed.

Some have argued that from an economic perspective it does not matter that government intervention was primarily responsible for the world's excess capacity. "A market-driven adjustment process . . . levels no such blame and makes no such distinction between national boundaries; it is the uncompetitive

---

[1] When the structural crisis began in 1975 the U.S. industry was already in the middle of adjusting to new conditions of competition in the world steel industry. In the decade prior to 1974 the U.S. industry made huge investments in installing BOF capacity and modern, large-scale hot-strip mills. To "round out" these investments required further investments in new blast furnaces and continuous casters. But because of stagnating consumption, world excess capacity and the resulting, generally poor operating rates, these investment plans were significantly slowed down or canceled altogether.

capacity that must be scrapped."[2] This type of reasoning accepts political intervention as the catalyst for the introduction of new capacity, but leaves it to the "market" to eliminate excess capacity. However the adjustment process, far from being "market-driven," is to a large extent "government-driven." It is true that the effects of government intervention found their expression in the market -- higher aggregate production levels, lower utilization rates, lower prices and decreased profitability. But the results cannot in any way be associated with what would have been a market outcome. Without government actions that forced new capacity, or sustained capacity that was uneconomic, the outcome of the adjustment process would have been much different.

In some cases the steelmaking capacity put in place as a result of government initiatives and assistance -- South Korea's Pohang Iron and Steel Company, Taiwan's China Steel -- was to approach world class standards. In other cases -- France's Fos-sur-Mer project, Britain's Ravenscraig works, or Brazil's Acominas project -- government-supported projects were a financial disaster. Regardless of the outcome, however, it was generally private companies that bore the brunt of the required adjustment.[3] While private companies with older facilities generally were at a disadvantage, newer facilities were also closed (*e.g.*, Kaiser's BOF capacity in Fontana, California and the USX Baytown, Texas plate mill), driven into insolvency (*e.g.*, Korf's Badische Stahlwerke in southern Germany) or burdened with huge losses (*e.g.*, Klöckner's Bremen hot strip mill, the most modern in Europe). Private sector steel firms in Italy, Britain, Canada and Germany have suffered severely as a result of government support for selected producers.

The crux of the problem is that governments desired an outcome that the market was unwilling to provide, namely, greater steelmaking capacity. In most cases governments had political, social or national security reasons for their actions, although in some, the motive was little more than a vague notion of national aggrandizement. The net result was a global capacity surplus which drove down prices, utilization rates and profits, and forced a severe adjustment process on other segments of the world steel industry through the mechanism of international trade.

Excess capacity has exacerbated an increasing conflict between private steel firms and state-supported steel firms over the past decade. By 1987, 44.1

---

[2] Jones, *World Steel Trade*, p. 62. Others have argued that, while government intervention did make a difference in permitting capacity and production "to expand without regard to the immediate economics of the investment decision," the shift of steel output to the third world would probably have occurred anyway. Barnett and Crandall, *Up From the Ashes*, pp. 12-13. However, with the notable exception of Korea and Taiwan, most steel operations in developing countries are inefficient, crisis-ridden and dependent upon government subsidies and trade protection for survival. The least efficient, highest cost steel producers are generally to be found in the developing world (*e.g.*, Nigeria). And even the industries in Korea and Taiwan owe their success to government support and assistance.

[3] The one major exception was the government-owned British Steel Corporation, which underwent major restructuring and huge layoffs in the early 1980s.

percent of raw steel production of the 47 major steelmakers in the western world was by state-owned firms (table 8-1). Outside of the four major national industries that are composed of predominately private firms (those of the United States, Japan, West Germany and Canada), 93 percent of raw steel production of the top steelmakers was by government-owned firms.

One way of assessing the result of government intervention in the world steel industry is to examine the effect of government-supported excess capacity on steel industry operating rates. Figure 8-1 presents the actual average western world capacity utilization rate for 1960 to 1986 and an adjusted capacity utilization rate for 1975 to 1986. The adjusted capacity utilization rate was based on capacity estimates for the 1975 to 1986 period assuming that government promoted capacity additions did not occur after 1974.[4] The effect of this counterfactual experiment is striking. The average actual operating rate for the western world steel industry from 1975 to 1986 was 69 percent.[5] When the effect of government-induced capacity expansion is adjusted for, the average estimated operating rate increases to 77 percent. For many steel producers, the difference between operating at 69 percent compared to 77 percent of capacity would have meant the difference between operating at a loss or operating at a profit.[6] For private companies, the difference has in some cases been that between survival and extinction.

In steel, public capital has been displacing private capital since the onset of the structural crisis. Given the depressed prices and poor operating results that characterized world steel production between 1975 and 1986, private capital markets have not been allocating investment funds to steel production. Government ministries, national parliaments and diets, however, have shown no such reluctance. As discussed in chapter 7, in the United States there has therefore been net disinvestment in the steel industry over the past 15 years, with the largest capacity reductions taking place since 1982. In Germany and Japan, where steel production also remains largely in private hands, the major producers are rapidly diversifying into non-steel businesses.[7]

U.S. private companies, especially integrated steel producers, have not been able to attract capital or generate sufficient internal cash flow to prevent

---

[4] As a practical matter after 1974 only net additions to capacity in the United States, Canada, Japan and West Germany are assumed to have proceeded without government intervention. All other capacity additions are assumed to depend on government support.

[5] The average operating rate for the period 1960 to 1974 was 80 percent.

[6] For example, the estimated breakeven operating rate for U.S. steel producers in the mid-1970s was approximately 73 to 75 percent.

[7] *Rheinische Merkur/Christ und Welt* (February 12, 1988); *Zaikai Tembo* (December 1985).

Table 8-1: Top Western World Steelmakers of 1987 (million tons raw steel)

		Output	Ownership	Country
1.	Nippon Steel	26.03	private	Japan
2.	Usinor-Sacilor	16.70	state	France
3.	Siderbras	14.11	state	Brazil
4.	BSC	13.61	state	United Kingdom
5.	Finsider	12.50	state	Italy
6.	Posco	11.34	state	Korea
7.	NKK	11.28	private	Japan
8.	Thyssen	10.90	private	Germany
9.	Bethlehem	10.47	private	United States
10.	LTV Steel	10.44	private	United States
11.	USS	10.39	private	United States
12.	Kawasaki	10.13	private	Japan
13.	Sumitomo Metal	10.12	private	Japan
14.	Sail	7.34	state	India
15.	Arbed	7.02	state	Luxembourg
16.	Iscor	6.49	state	South Africa
17.	Kobe Steel	5.88	private	Japan
18.	BHP	5.78	private	Australia
19.	Armco	5.38	private	United States
20.	Inland	5.01	private	United States
21.	Hoogovens	4.80	state	Netherlands
22.	National Steel	4.66	private	United States
23.	Stelco	4.48	private	Canada
24.	Cockerill Sambre	4.31	state	Belgium
25.	Sidermex	4.28	state	Mexico
26.	Voest Alpine	4.16	state	Austria
27.	Hoesch	3.93	private	Germany
28.	Krupp Stahl	3.80	private	Germany
29.	Ensidesa	3.68	state	Spain
30.	Dofasco	3.67	private	Canada
31.	China Steel	3.62	state	Taiwan
32.	Mannesmann	3.58	private	Germany
33.	Klockner	3.41	private	Germany
34.	Peine Salzgitter	3.39	state	Germany
35.	Nisshin Steel	3.36	private	Japan
36.	Sidor	3.30	state	Venezuela
37.	Tokyo Steel	3.16	private	Japan
38.	SSAB	2.96	state	Sweden
39.	Weirton	2.94	private	United States
40.	Rouge Steel	2.36	private	United States
41.	Algoma	2.35	private	Canada
42.	Saarstahl	2.33	private	Germany
43.	Tata Iron & Steel	2.30	private	India
44.	TDCI	2.30	state	Turkey
45.	Wheeling-Pittsburg	2.21	private	United States
46.	United Eng. Steels	2.10	private	United Kingdom
47.	Rautaruukki	2.05	state	Finland

Source: *Metal Bulletin* (February 15, 1988), p. 23 and authors' data.
Note: Top steelmakers include all those making 2 million tons or more of raw steel. State ownership is defined as an equity position exceeding 10 percent.

Figure 8-1: Western World Actual
Capacity Utilization and Adjusted
Utilization Rate 1960-1986

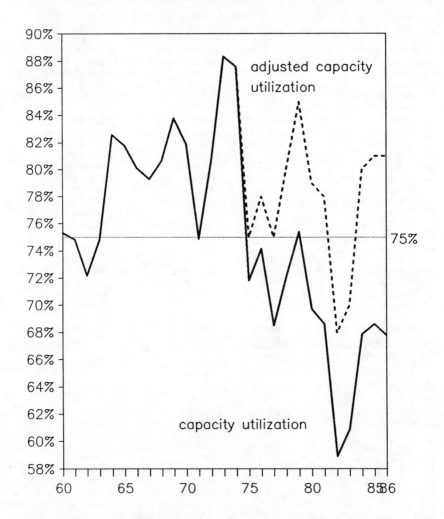

Source: Figure 2-4 and authors' estimates.

Note: Adjusted capacity utilization calculated by subtracting additions to
capacity after 1974 due to government intervention.

net disinvestment.[8] The only net expansion that has occurred has been in the semi-integrated, minimill sector, but the increase in minimill capacity has been only a fraction of the decline in the capacity of the integrated producers. Between 1977 and 1987 integrated producers shut down a cumulative total of 50 million metric tons of raw steel capacity, representing a 40 percent reduction in integrated producer capacity.[9] The net increase in minimill capacity was 5 million metric tons. While this is a 50 percent increase in minimill capacity, it represents only 10 percent of the capacity reduction by integrated producers.

Low prices and low expected returns have not justified construction of a new integrated steel plant in the United States for over two decades. Indeed some analysts have expressed the opinion that another integrated steelworks will *never* again be constructed in the United States, Europe or Japan, because of the huge costs and risk involved. There still exists a large volume of excess capacity in both Europe and Japan and future capacity reductions are planned or contemplated. In the United States, where capacity has been severely reduced, it is not at all clear that U.S. steel firms can earn sufficient profits to maintain and modernize existing capacity. If they cannot, the U.S. steel industry will face further contraction.[10] As figure 8-2 illustrates, the United States is the only major steel producing industrialized country that lacks self-sufficiency in steel.

---

[8] In the United States, the closest approximation to state intervention has been bankruptcy proceedings, which have played an important role recently. A significant number of firms in the United States have been restructured due to bankruptcy or the threat of bankruptcy (*e.g.,* McLouth Steel Products, Weirton Steel, Newport Steel, LTV, Wheeling-Pittsburg, Geneva Steel, California Steel, Gulf States Steel, etc.). These restructurings have in many cases significantly reduced production costs, for example, by allowing the renegotiation of supply and labor contracts.

[9] Almost half of the capacity that has been shut down has been open hearth capacity, which would have been retired in any event without a structural crisis in world steel. However, under the conditions of the last 15 years, this capacity has not been replaced with more modern steelmaking capability. (The capacity data is taken from Marcus and Kirsis, *Core Report BB*, chapter 2 and American Iron and Steel Industry.)

[10] Recent estimates of capital outlays required to just maintain existing capacity indicate expenditures of $25 per metric ton of capacity. For the U.S. steel industry this means that to maintain capacity at 1987 levels would require approximately $2.55 billion per year in capital outlays. According to AISI, the U.S. industry's capital expenditures from 1982 to 1986 averaged only $1.56 billion at a time when capacity was greater than it was in 1987. In fact, 1986 capital outlays reached a low of $863 million. The U.S. industry's capital spending was obviously significantly affected by the $11.7 billion in losses (net income) over this period. (Capital outlay estimate for sustaining capacity from Marcus and Kirsis, *Core Report BB*, exhibit BB-1-8; actual capital expenditures and net income data from AISI, *1986 Annual Statistical Report*, tables 1D and 2A.)

Figure 8—2: Self—Sufficiency in Steel

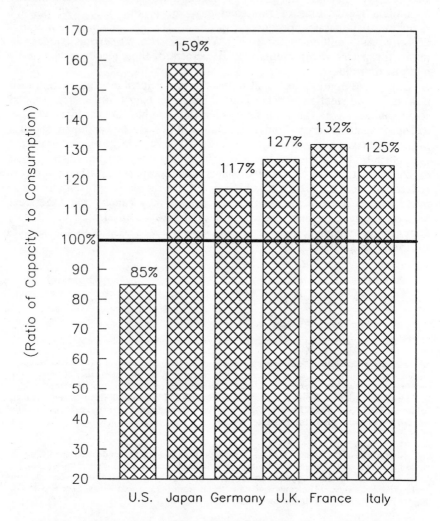

Source: Consumption data see table 2—4; capacity data see figure 2—4.

Note: Capacity data for all countries based on effective capacity estimates for U.S. of .92, Japan of .83 and EC countries of .86. See Marcus and Kirsis, World Steel Dynamics: Core Report BB (PaineWebber, Inc., January 1988), Exhibit BB—1—4. Consumption based on average for 1980 to 1986, capacity data based on 1987 for U.S., 1986 for all other countries.

LOOKING FORWARD

Over the long run, the market continues to signal American producers to exit the steel business. The rate of return on investment for producing steel continues to lag below the average manufacturing rate of return. The cost of building integrated facilities does not justify the expenditure. This circumstance has been shaped heavily by the policies of governments relative to each other. The future is still determined heavily by government policy -- the legacies of past policies and the continuing subsidization and protection of foreign industries.

Government-supported steel industries are currently some of the most aggressive competitors in international steel trade. The Korean and Taiwanese industries, East Asia's lowest-priced exporters, owe their existence and continued competitive strength to government support. In Europe, subsidies equivalent in value to tens of billions of dollars -- much of which has concededly been wasted -- have nevertheless enabled essentially bankrupt firms like SSAB and British Steel to modernize and expand their export presence, with the state absorbing their debt and capital costs. Brazil's expanding industry has repeatedly proven capable of surmounting its seemingly endless heavy losses and considerable operational and managerial failings through a volume of state subsidies which can only be characterized as stupendous, even for a country of Brazil's size and resources.

Given this world environment, what U.S. policies are appropriate?

Trade Policy. While the United States may not approve of the industrial promotional policies which are pervasive in the world steel industry, it is powerless to eliminate them, at least in the short run. Under such conditions it would be imprudent, if not foolhardy, to permit completely open access to the U.S. market, regardless of the circumstances or the consequences. To do so would, in effect, enable foreign industrial policy decisions to dictate the shape of the U.S. economy. The VRA program established by President Reagan -- along with the recovery in demand and the depreciation of the dollar -- while permitting a much higher level of import penetration than the EC or Japan would consider acceptable, has clearly helped the U.S. industry to return to profitability. The U.S. industry, under the Reagan program, has sharply reduced its costs and dramatically improved productivity and yield, while the falling dollar has taken away a significant factor depressing prices.

International Burden Sharing. Because the current VRA program, like prior U.S. trade policy measures on steel, is all too readily dismissed as being "protectionist," it is useful to put that program in global perspective. Without question, the current program has restricted import penetration of the U.S. market more effectively than any prior U.S. steel import program. However, the current VRA program has permitted an import penetration level far higher than most major steel producing countries would deem acceptable -- Japan has held import penetration to less than one quarter of U.S. levels, and the EC, to half the U.S. level. In many other countries, from Taiwan to South Africa, import penetration has been even more restricted.

Before a new level of import penetration is set, or the United States is returned to its former status of being the principal residual open market, the consequences of doing so should be examined. This analysis should take into account current and likely exchange rates and relative rates of growth, but should be guided fundamentally by the effects of others' policies on the composition of the United States economy. Factored into this calculation should be the implications for the national security and international responsibilities of the United States of continuing past policies not only of *laissez faire* but also of *les yeux fermé*.[11]

It will be necessary to negotiate increased openness abroad for purposes of burden-sharing and avoidance of diversion of steel trade flows to the U.S. market.

Longer Term International Negotiations. The United States steel program is, in international trade agreement terms, solely a comprehensive safeguard action. Safeguards are generally considered to be temporary and used for purposes of adjustment. But the disturbing question raised in this book is, adjustment to what? One of the basic dilemmas this book has focused on is the conflict and contradiction between private steel firms and state-owned and state-supported steel firms operating in the same world market. It is inappropriate to require continual adjustment to competitive outcomes which are not the result of a naturally superior competitive advantage of foreign industries in the aggregate. Rationalization of the American industry should not be deemed acceptable to accommodate foreign industrial policies which call for aggrandizement of steel production elsewhere.

It should be stipulated as a general rule that the United States should not desire to maintain permanent protection of any industry. And yet, there is no time certain when the justification for the current steel import restrictions will have lapsed. The principal problem is not one of temporary adjustment. Thus to avoid indefinite import restrictions, long-term changes in how world steel capacity is created and maintained must be brought about.

In the long run, any efforts to return international steel trade to the parameters of market-based competition must entail efforts to ameliorate trade distorting industrial policies in the steel sector. Obviously this will be extremely difficult given the social and political problems that led to government intervention in the first place. The objective of any international discussions should be the phasing out of existing policies that distort steel trade and the establishment of limitations on new distortions. The purpose should be to let the market decide which firms should expand and which

---

[11] The authors have consciously avoided prescriptions for domestic measures to strengthen the U.S. steel industry, which is really the subject for another book. Clearly, given the unlikelihood that others will abandon state intervention immediately, the need to continue some and review other appropriate measures will be unavoidable.

should contract based on their performance in the market and to take such decisions out of the hands of governments to the maximum extent possible. To the extent that this cannot be achieved, it will be necessary to retain some form of buffering measures between industries of created competitive advantage -- the state-supported industries -- and private industries.

Institutional Arrangements.   Trade liberalization is a very fine goal in its own right, but as repeatedly pointed out in this text, it must be understood what the results of premature liberalization can be in a sector characterized by pervasive government intervention.   To avoid costly errors, either in the direction of excessive illiberality or license, it will be necessary to have more knowledge of the factors determining the size of industries, their competitiveness following government intervention, and their causes of trade flows.   For enlightened policy measures to be formulated much more must be known about foreign industrial policies in the steel sector.   This book is one attempt at probing the subject, but far greater transparency will be needed to understand the nature and effects of government intervention in national steel industries.   Exchanges of information, the ability to notify other countries' practices, international surveillance and justification of measures will be a necessary forerunner of new substantive rules governing state intervention in steel.

There should be no illusions, however, as to the early demise of state intervention in steel.   It is too deeply entrenched.   The effects of past actions will be manifest far into the future, even were all intervention to cease in the near term.   Fundamentally, as in the current GATT subsidies code, the balance struck is between continued not wholly effective efforts to curb government intervention in promoting investment and trade, on the one hand, and a corresponding freedom of response by importing countries that would otherwise suffer irreparable harm to their industries because of such promotional policies.

With greater transparency and scrutiny, and with vigorous responsive measures, calculated to offset trade distortions caused by state intervention, there can be a negotiated reduction in the former in return for curbing the latter.   U.S. officials should not shrink from proclaiming the superiority of their vision of an efficient and growth-engendering structure for the world trading system.   Openness and market dictated results are to be sought, but generally, not just for the few countries where private industries will seek to preserve their existence in an environment where unacceptably high risks have been created by massive state intervention.

APPENDIX A

Steel Consumption Trends

The stagnation in world steel consumption after 1974, and the lack of adjustment to that situation by state-owned and controlled steel firms, were fundamental factors in the steel crisis of the last decade and a half. Given the importance of trends in steel consumption for the dynamics of international steel production and trade analyzed in this book, a more detailed discussion and analysis of some important issues pertaining to steel consumption is provided here.

ECONOMIC DEVELOPMENT AND DECLINING STEEL INTENSITY

The relationship between steel consumption and various macroeconomic variables (GNP, industrial production, gross domestic capital formation, etc.) has received considerable attention since the Second World War, especially in the context of economic development. For example, it has long been established that as industrialization and economic development proceeds, the intensity of steel usage declines.[1] The intensity of steel usage refers to the share of steel consumption in real GNP or industrial production.[2] Generally, advanced industrial countries such as the United States or the United Kingdom are used as illustrations of this phenomenon. But all countries going through the process of industrialization have experienced a declining intensity of steel usage.

---

[1] For example, see United Nations, Economic Commission for Europe, *Long-Term Trends and Problems of the European Steel Industry* (Geneva: United Nations, 1959) which concludes on page 124 that the "main point emerging from the foregoing analysis is that there is a tendency for the rate of growth of steel consumption to diminish as the absolute level increases."

[2] The level of "steel intensity" in various countries, the share of steel in real GNP, has also been related to per capita GNP, a proxy for the level of economic development. This relationship has also shown a declining level of steel intensity (steel/GNP) as higher levels of economic development (per capita GNP) are reached. International Iron and Steel Institute, *Steel Intensity and GNP Structure* (Brussels: IISI, 1974).

To quantify the declining intensity of steel usage, regression equations were estimated for the United States, Japan and South Korea.[3] The countries were chosen to provide a mix of countries at different stages of economic development that also had substantial steel industries. The estimated equations related steel intensity to a time factor to account for the trend in steel intensity as well as to gross fixed capital formation to control for the cylicality of steel consumption (most steel consumption reflects public and private capital investment). The regression equations and results follow.

1. United States: $\ln(CONS/IPI) = \beta + \beta_1 TIME + \beta_2 \ln RKF + e$
where
CONS: U.S. apparent consumption of steel in net tons.
(Source: American Iron and Steel Institute.)
IPI: U.S. industrial production index (1980=100).
(Source: International Monetary Fund, *International Financial Statistics*.)
RKF: U.S. real gross fixed capital formation (1980 U.S. dollars).
(Source: International Monetary Fund, *International Financial Statistics*.)

The equation was estimated using annual data for the years 1955 to 1986. The results of the estimation are provided below:

Independent Variable	Estimated Coefficient	Standard Error	t-statistic
TIME	-.0470	.0037	-12.575
RKF	.6426	.0936	6.862

$R^2 = .9645$
adjusted $R^2 = .9620$
F-Statistic (2,28) = 380.71
D.W. = 2.028
standard error = .0483
critical value of t is 2.763 (99.0%)

2. Japan: $\ln(CONS/IPI) = \beta + \beta_1 TIME + \beta_2 \ln RKF + e$
where
CONS: Japanese apparent consumption of steel in metric tons.
(Source: Organization for Economic Cooperation and Development.)
IPI: Japanese industrial production index (1980=100).
(Source: International Monetary Fund, *International Financial Statistics*.)
RKF: Japanese real gross fixed capital formation (1980 yen).
(Source: International Monetary Fund, *International Financial Statistics*).

---

[3] The equations were estimated with an ordinary least squares regression using the Cochrane-Orcutt iterative technique to control for first order serial correlation.

The equation was estimated using annual data for the years 1955 to 1986. The results of the estimation are provided below:

Independent Variable	Estimated Coefficient	Standard Error	t-statistic
TIME	-.0335	.0045	-7.48
RKF	.2358	.0455	5.184

R^2 = .7629
adjusted R^2 = .7459
F-Statistic (2,28) = 45.036
D.W. = 1.9416
standard error = .0746
critical value of t is 2.763 (99.0%)

3. Korea: $\ln(CONS/IPI) = \beta + \beta_1 TIME + \beta_2 \ln RKF + e$
where
CONS: Korean apparent consumption of steel in metric tons.
(Sources: Organization for Economic Cooperation and Development and International Iron and Steel Institute.)
IPI: Korean industrial production index (1980 = 100).
(Source: International Monetary Fund, *International Financial Statistics*.)
RKF: Korean real gross fixed capital formation (1980 won).
(Source: International Monetary Fund, *International Financial Statistics*.)

The equation was estimated using annual data for the years 1973 to 1986. The results of the estimation are provided below:

Independent Variable	Estimated Coefficient	Standard Error	t-statistic
TIME	-.0401	.0157	-2.555
RKF	.2882	.1422	2.027

R^2 = .5485
adjusted R^2 = .4581
F-Statistic (2,10) = 6.0732
D.W. = 2.2169
standard error = .0687
critical values of t are 1.812 (90.0%) and 2.228 (95.0%)

All of the regression results indicate a declining trend in the intensity of steel usage in the three countries.[4] Specifically, the growth in the consumption of steel has not keep pace with the growth in the economy as a whole (as measured by the industrial production index). The estimated trend coefficients indicate that industrial production must increase each year by approximately 4.6 percent in the United States, 3.3 percent in Japan and 4 percent in Korea to prevent a decline in steel consumption. The average annual growth rates for industrial production in each country for the years covered were 3.7 percent in the United States, 8.7 percent in Japan and 13.7 percent in Korea.

Table A-1. Distribution of U.S. Steel Shipments by Major Product Type (percent of total steel shipments)

	1920	1936	1967	1986
Rails	8.0%	3.6%	0.8%	0.6%
Plates	14.7%	7.4%	9.5%	5.1%
Sheet and Strip	10.7%	30.2%	38.8%	52.2%

Sources: American Iron and Steel Institute, *1986 Annual Statistical Report* (Washington, D.C.: AISI, 1987), table 9; Kenneth Warren, *World Steel: An Economic Geography* (New York: Crane, Russak & Company, Inc., 1975), table 16.

As discussed in chapter 2 the declining steel intensity associated with the process of economic development derives from changes in that process. These include the growth of the service sector (which uses relatively little steel), more sophisticated and less steel-intensive production processes, a relative decline in the level of infrastructure construction (ports, bridges, highways, etc., although at some point these must be replaced/repaired), and improvements in the efficiency of steel usage.

Another consequence of the process of economic development is the change in the structure of steel demand, generally entailing a shift from heavier to lighter steel products. The most pronounced shift is toward lighter, flat-rolled steel used in consumer durables.[5] Table A-1 illustrates this shift for the United States. In 1920 only 10.7 percent of steel production was

---

[4] The equation for Korea gave the poorest results in terms of the overall fit of the regression. This is probably accounted for by the earlier phase of industrialization that Korea is now in compared to the United States and Japan.

[5] Warren, *World Steel*, pp. 86-90.

comprised of sheet and strip products; by 1986 52.2 percent of the products of the U.S. steel industry were sheet and strip products. Table A-2 provides an international comparison of carbon steel shipments in 1986 for countries at various levels of economic development. The United States had the highest proportion of flat-rolled steel products at 51 percent, followed by Japan and Germany at 40 and 39 percent respectively. The other countries had even lower percentages of steel shipments of flat-rolled products, although Argentina's 38 percent was quite high given that country's level of economic development.

Table A-2. Distribution of Steel Shipments by Product Type, 1986 (percent of total carbon steel shipments)

1985 per capita GNP $(U.S.)		Sheet & Coil	Structurals & Bars	Wire & Rods	Plates
16,690	U.S.	50.9	21.9	7.1	3.9
11,300	Japan	39.9	30.9	5.6	10.4
10,890	Germany	39.1	12.4	9.2	12.4
4,290	Spain	20.6	47.8	7.6	4.6
2,130	Argentina	37.6	21.7	13.7	2.4
1,970	Portugal	11.9	57.5	22.5	0.0
1,640	Brazil	31.1	18.2	10.0	12.5

Sources: International Iron and Steel Institute, *Steel Statistical Yearbook 1987* (Brussels: IISI, 1987), table 6; *World Development Report 1987* (Washington, D.C.: World Bank, June 1987), table 1.

INDIRECT STEEL TRADE AND APPARENT STEEL CONSUMPTION

No statistical agency in any country keeps track of the actual consumption of steel. Rather the consumption data used throughout this book is referred to as apparent consumption. Apparent consumption is defined as domestic production or shipments less exports plus imports.

While the concept of apparent consumption does take into account exports and imports of steel mill products, indirect steel trade is ignored. Indirect steel trade refers to the steel content of other products that are traded but are

Figure A–1: U.S. Apparent Consumption of Steel Adjusted for Indirect Steel Trade, 1950–1987

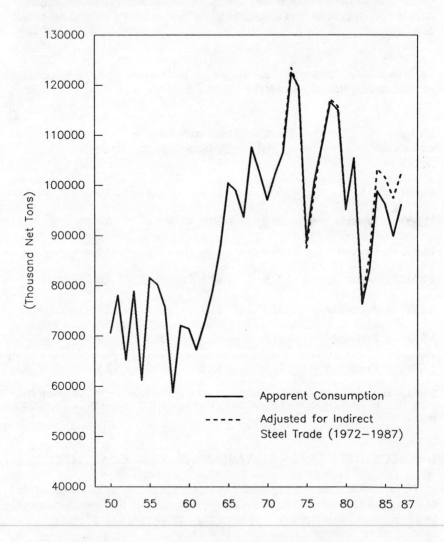

Source: American Iron and Steel Institute, <u>Annual Statistical Report</u> (various issues) and table A–3.

not included in the definition of steel mill products. Products made from steel, such as automobiles, various types of machinery, machine tools, ball and roller bearings and other products, obviously contain steel. If part of the steel production of country A is used to make automobiles which are then exported, that steel is not being consumed in country A, but rather in the country to which the automobiles were exported. However, under the traditional definition of apparent consumption, the steel in the automobiles that are exported are considered as part of the steel consumption of country A. Likewise, if country A imports a significant amount of machinery, it is consuming the steel content of that machinery, but that steel consumption is not included in the apparent consumption data of country A.

Historically, the failure of the apparent consumption measure to take into account indirect steel trade has not been a problem in providing an accurate gauge of consumption *trends* for the United States, primarily because of the relatively small level and variance of net indirect steel trade. However this was no longer the case in the 1980s with the huge increase in global trade imbalances in manufactured products. For other areas of the world the apparent consumption data has generally overstated consumption levels in Japan and the EC and understated consumption levels in the developing countries.[6]

The most detailed data on indirect steel trade available is for the United States and the EC. With respect to the United States, where the trade deficit in manufactured goods deteriorated by over $170 billion from 1980 to 1987, the net deficit in indirect steel trade grew significantly, from essential balance in 1980 to a deficit of almost 9 million net tons by 1987 (table A-3). While the EC also experienced a deterioration in net indirect steel trade, it was of a much smaller magnitude, declining from a surplus of 15.95 million metric tons in 1980 to a surplus of 13.46 million metric tons in 1986.[7]

The effect of U.S. indirect steel trade on the accuracy of the apparent consumption measure became significant by 1984 (figure A-1). For example, comparing U.S. steel consumption in 1980 with 1987 using the apparent consumption measure would indicate an increase of only 0.5 percent in U.S. steel consumption. However, when appropriate adjustments are made to the apparent consumption measure due to indirect steel trade, U.S. steel consumption in 1987 shows an increase of 7.4 percent compared to 1980.[8]

---

[6] The International Iron and Steel Institute publishes studies on indirect steel trade every three years or so. The last study was published in 1982. International Iron and Steel Institute, *World Indirect Steel Trade* (Brussels: IISI, 1982).

[7] Eurostat, *Iron and Steel Statistical Yearbook* (Brussels: Eurostat, 1987, 1983), table 5.11 (1987) and table 5.12 (1983).

[8] The U.S. regression equation discussed above was estimated again using the adjusted apparent consumption data. The secular decline in the measure of steel intensity changed to -4.5 percent instead of -4.6 percent. Obviously the adjusted data makes a significant difference in discussing trends in the 1980s, but does not change the overall direction or magnitude of the secular trend in steel intensity since the 1950s.

Table A-3: U.S. Indirect Steel Trade, 1972-1987
(million net tons)

	Exports	Imports	Net Exports
1972	6.9	8.4	-1.5
1973	8.1	9.2	-1.1
1974	8.9	8.3	0.6
1975	9.5	8.0	1.5
1976	10.0	8.3	1.7
1977	9.3	9.8	-0.5
1978	9.6	10.2	-0.6
1979	9.6	10.3	-0.7
1980	9.5	9.6	-0.1
1981	9.5	9.7	-0.2
1982	8.3	9.6	-1.3
1983	7.2	10.5	-3.3
1984	8.8	13.8	-5.0
1985	8.7	16.1	-7.4
1986	8.2	17.5	-9.3
1987	8.4	17.1	-8.7

Source: Peter F. Marcus and Karlis M. Kirsis, *World Steel Dynamics: Steel Strategist 14* (PaineWebber, Inc., December 10, 1987), p. 51 and Bethlehem Steel Corporation.

Glossary of Terms

Apparent consumption: Production minus exports plus imports of steel.

Bar: A finished steel product, commonly in flat, square, round or hexagonal shapes. Rolled from billets, bars are produced in two major types, merchant and special.

Billet: A piece of semifinished iron or steel that is nearly square and is longer than a bloom. Bars and pipe are made from billets.

Blast furnace: A large cylindrical structure in which iron ore is combined with coke and flux stone to produce molten iron.

Bloom: A semifinished product, large and mostly square in cross section. Blooms are shaped into girders, beams and other structural shapes.

Coke: A form of carbonized coal burned in blast furnaces to reduce iron ore or other iron-bearing materials to molten iron.

Coil: A finished steel product such as sheet or strip which has been wound or coiled after rolling.

Cold-rolling: The passing of sheet or strip that has been hot-rolled and pickled through cold rolls. Cold-rolling makes a product that is thinner, smoother and stronger than can be made by hot-rolling alone.

Continuous casting: A process for solidifying steel in the form of a continuous strand rather than individual ingots. Molten steel is poured into open-bottomed, water-cooled molds; as the molton steel passes through the mold the outer shell solidifies.

Crude steel: Steel in the first solid state after melting, suitable for further processing or for sale. Synonymous to raw steel.

Direct reduction: A family of processes for making iron from ore without exceeding the melting temperature. No blast furnace is needed.

Electric arc furnace: An electric furnace used to melt steel scrap or direct reduction iron.

Flat products: A term referring to a class of products, including sheet, strip and plate, that are made from slabs.

Hot-rolling: Rolling steel after it has been reheated.

Integrated steelmaker: A producer that converts iron ore into semifinished or finished steel products. Traditionally, this required coke ovens, blast furnaces, steelmaking furnaces and rolling mills. A growing number of integrated mills use the direct reduction process to produce sponge iron without coke ovens and blast furnaces.

Minimill: A small non-integrated or semi-integrated steel plant, generally based on electric furnace steelmaking. Most minimills produce rods, bars and small structural shapes.

Open-hearth process: A process for making steel from molten iron and scrap. The open-hearth process has been replaced by the basic oxygen process in most modern facilities.

Pellets: An enriched form of iron ore shaped like small balls.

Pig iron: High carbon iron made by the reduction of iron ore in the blast furnace.

Plate: A flat-rolled product rolled from slabs, of greater thickness than sheet or strip.

Reference price: A valuation for customs purposes of a product which may or may not correspond to the actual sales price of the product and which serves as the basis on which duty is levied.

Rolling mill: Equipment that reduces and transforms the shape of semifinished or intermediate steel products by passing the material through a gap between rolls that is smaller than the entering materials.

Semifinished products: Products such as slabs, billets and blooms which must be rolled or otherwise processed to create usable steel shapes.

Sheet: A flat-rolled product over 12 inches in width and of less thickness than plate.

Sintering: A process which combines ores too fine for efficient blast-furnace use with flux stone. The mixture is heated to form clumps, which allow better draft in the blast furnace.

Slab: A wide semifinished product made from an ingot or by continuous casting. Sheet, strip, plate and other flat rolled steel products are made from slabs.

Special steels: Steels containing alloys which provide special properties such as resistance to corrosion or to heavy loads.

Sponge iron: The product of the direct reduction process. Also known as direct reduction iron.

Strip: A flat-rolled product customarily narrower in width than sheet and often produced to more closely controlled thicknesses.

Bibliography

Adams, Walter, and Dirlam, Joel B. "Big Steel, Invention and Innovation."
Quarterly Journal of Economics 80 (May 1966): 167-189.

_____. "'Big Steel, Invention, and Innovation Reconsidered.'" *The
Quarterly Journal of Economics* 81 (August 1967): 475-480.

Adams, Walter, and Mueller, Hans. "The Steel Industry." In *The Structure
of American Industry* (6th ed.), ed. Walter Adams. New York: Macmillan
Publishing Co., Inc., 1982.

Albertson, L. and J. Zaragoza. "Estructura y Politica Siderurgica - de la
Acción Concertada a la Politica de Reconversión." *Informacíon
Commercial Española* (November 1982).

American Iron and Steel Institute. *Annual Statistical Report*. Washington,
D.C.: AISI, 1959-1986.

_____. *Steel at the Crossroads: The American Steel Industry in the 1980s.*
Washington, D.C.: AISI, January 1980.

Ault, D. "The Continued Deterioration of the Competitive Ability of the U.S.
Steel Industry: The Development of Continuous Casting." *Western
Economic Journal* 11 (March 1973): 89-97.

Barnett, Donald F. and Schorsch, Louis. *Steel: Upheaval in a Basic Industry.*
Cambridge, Mass.: Ballinger Publishing Company, 1983.

Bennett, James Paul. "Cyclical Determinants of Capital Expenditures: A
Regression Study of the United States Steel Industry." *Southern Economic
Journal,* Vol. 32, Issue 330 (1966).

Benyon, Frank and Bourgeois, Jacques. "The European Community - United
States Steel Arrangement." 21 *Common Market Law Review* 283 (1984).

Borrus, Michael. "The Politics of Competitive Erosion in the U.S. Steel
Industry." In *American Industry in International Competition,* ed. John
Zysman and Laura Tyson. Ithaca and London: Cornell University Press,
1983.

Bosworth, Barry P., and Rivlin, Alice M. *The Swedish Economy*. Washington, D.C.: The Brookings Institution, 1987.

Botsus, E. N. "Patterns of Trade." In *Europe in the 1980s*, ed. S. Fisher-Galati. Boulder and London: Westview Press, 1981.

Boylan, Jr., Myles G. *Economic Effects of Scale Increases in the Steel Industry: The Case of U.S. Blast Furnaces*. New York: Praeger, 1975.

Branson, William H. and Love, James P. "U.S. Manufacturing and the Real Exchange Rate." NBER Working Paper. Cambridge, Mass.: National Bureau of Economic Research, July 1987. (Revised).

Burgos, Juan Luis. "La Siderurgia Española Ante La CEE." In *Informacion Siderúrgica* (April 1985).

Campanna, Alberto. *Steel in Southern Italy*. Naples, 1979.

Capecelatro, E. *L'"Affaire" Accaio, Manipolazione di una Crisi*. Lerici, 1979.

Capron, Michael. "The State, the Regions and Industrial Redevelopment. The Challenge of the Belgian Steel Crisis." In *The Politics of Steel: Western Europe and the Steel Industry in the Crisis Years 1974-84*, ed. Yves Meny and Vincent Wright. Berlin and New York: Walter de Gruyther, 1987.

Carlsson, Bo. "Industrial Subsidies in Sweden: Macro-Economic Effects and an International Comparison." 32 *Journal of Industrial Economics* 1 (September 1983).

Central Intelligence Agency, National Foreign Assessment Center. *The Burgeoning LDC Steel Industry: More Problems for Major Steel Producers*. Washington, D.C.: CIA, 1979.

Cockerill, A., and Silberston, A. *The Steel Industry: International Comparisons of Industrial Structure and Performance*. University of Cambridge, Department of Applied Economics. Occasional Paper 42. Cambridge: Cambridge University Press, 1974.

Coetzee, J.B. "South Africa's Steel Industry and its Economic Potential-Consolidation." In *Symposium on South Africa's Steel Industry and its Economic Potential*. Johannesburg: March 20, 1970.

Colombo, V., Friderichs, M. and Mayoux, J. "Community Steel Policy: Analysis and Recommendations." ("Wise Men's Report") In EC

Commission, *Communication from the Commission to the Council*, COM (87) 640 final, November 26, 1987.

Commission of the European Communities. *Bulletin of Energy Prices: A Survey of Import and Consumer Prices for Oil, Coal, Gas and Electricity in the Community Up to January 1987*. Brussels: EC, 1987.

_____. Communication from the Commission to the Council, *Steel Policy*, COM (87) 388 final/2, September 11, 1987. Brussels: EC, 1987.

_____. Communication from the Commission to the Council, *External Commercial Policy in the Steel Sector*, COM (86) 585 final, November 13, 1986. Brussels: EC, 1986.

_____. *Report From the Commission to the Council on the Application of the Rules on Aids to the Steel Industry*, COM (86) 235 final, August 6, 1986. Brussels: EC, 1986.

_____. Communication from the Commission to the Council, *Concerning the Negotiation of Arrangements on Community Steel Imports for 1986*, COM (85) 535 final, October 14, 1985. Brussels: EC, 1985.

_____. *Fifth Report on the Application of the Rules for Aids to Steel Industry*, COM (84) 142 final, March 8, 1984. Brussels: EC, 1984.

_____. *Comments on the General Objectives Steel 1985*, COM (84) 89 final, February 16, 1984. Brussels: EC, 1984.

_____. *Steel: Short Term Measures*, COM (83) 691 final, November 14, 1983. Brussels: EC, 1983.

_____. *Fourth Report on the Application of the Rules for Aids to the Steel Industry*, COM (83) 178 Final, April 1983. Brussels: EC, 1983.

_____. *General Objectives Steel 1985*, COM (83) 239 final, April 22, 1983. Brussels: EC, 1983.

_____. *Summary of Arrangements for Iron and Steel Products*. Brussels: EC, April 5, 1983.

_____. *Initial Report on Application of Disciplinary Measures in the matter of Assistance to the Steel Industry*, COM (81) 71 Final, February 23, 1981. Brussels: EC, 1981.

Crandall, Robert W. "Investment and Productivity Growth in the Steel Industry: Some Implications for Industrial Policy." In *Ailing Steel: The*

Transoceanic Quarrel, ed. Walter H. Goldberg. New York: St. Martin's Press, 1986.

_____. *The U.S. Steel Industry in Recurrent Crisis: Policy Options in a Competitive World.* Washington, D.C.: The Brookings Institution, 1981.

_____ and Barnett, Donald F. *Up From The Ashes*. Washington, D.C.: The Brookings Institution, 1986.

Creutzberg, A. "The Demand for Money in Finland Revisited." Economic Planning Centre Report 9. Helsinki: 1983.

Dilley, David R. and McBride, David L. "Oxygen Steelmaking - Fact vs. Folklore." *Iron and Steel Engineer* 49 (October 1967): 131-152.

Dirlam, Joel B. and Mueller, Hans. "Import Restraints and Reindustrialization: The Case of the U.S. Steel Industry." *Journal of International Law*, Vol. 14, No. 3 (Summer 1982): 419-446.

Dod, D.P. "Bank Lending to Developing Countries." 67 *Federal Reserve Bulletin* 647 (September 1981).

Dominick, Mary Francis. "Countervailing State Aids: A Case for International Consensus." 21 *Common Market Law Review* 355 (June 1984).

Eichengreen, Barry. "International Competition in the Products of U.S. Basic Industries." NBER Working Paper No. 2190. Cambridge, Massachusetts: National Bureau of Economic Research, March 1987.

Eisenhammer, J. "Longwy and Bagnoli: A Comparative Study of Trade Union Response to the Steel Crisis in France and Italy." In *The Politics of Steel: Western Europe and the Steel Industry in the Crisis Years 1974-84*, ed. Yves Meny and Vincent Wright. Berlin and New York: Walter de Gruyther, 1987.

Eisenhammer, J. and Rhodes, M. "The Politics of Public Sector Steel in Italy: From the 'Economic Miracle' to the Crisis of the Eighties." In *The Politics of Steel: Western Europe and the Steel Industry in the Crisis Years 1974-84*, ed. Yves Meny and Vincent Wright. Berlin and New York: Walter de Gruyther, 1987.

Ericson, Bengt. *Huggsexan*. Stockholm: LT, 1979.

Esser, Josef and Väth, Werner. "Overcoming the Steel Crisis in the Federal Repubilc of Germany." In *The Politics of Steel: Western Europe and the*

Steel Industry in the Crisis Years 1974-84, ed. Yves Meny and Vincent Wright. Berlin and New York: Walter de Gruyther, 1987.

Eurostat, Statistical Office of the European Communities. *Iron and Steel Yearbook*. Luxembourg: EC, 1983-1987.

Franzmeyer, Fritz. "Industrielle Strukturprobleme und Sektorale Strukturpolitik." In *der Europaischen Gemeinschaft*. Berlin: Duncker and Humblot, 1979.

Freyssenet, Michel. *La Sidérurgie Française 1945-79. L'Histoire d'un Faillite. Les Solutions qui s'Affrontent.* Paris: Savelli, 1979. Cited in *The Politics of Steel: Western Europe and the Steel Industry in the Crisis Years 1974-84*, ed. Yves Meny and Vincent Wright. Berlin and New York: Walter de Gruyther, 1987.

Gandois, Jean. *Mission Acier; Mon Aventure Belge*. Paris: Ducolot, 1986.

Gerschenkron, Alexander. *Economic Backwardness in Historical Perspective.* Cambridge, Massachusetts: Harvard University Press, 1962.

Gold, Bela. "Transformation Tendencies in the World Steel Industry and Adaptive Strategies." In *Ailing Steel: The Transoceanic Quarrel*, ed. Walter H. Goldberg. New York: St. Martin's Press, 1986.

_____. "Protectionism and Steel: The Need to Replace Outworn Perspectives." *Journal of International Law*, Vol. 14, No. 3 (Summer 1982): 447-458.

_____. *Productivity, Technology, and Capital: Economic Analysis, Managerial Strategies, and Government Policies.* Lexington, Mass.: D. C. Heath and Company, 1979.

_____. "Factors Stimulating Technological Progress in Japanese Industries: The Case of Computerization in Steel." *Quarterly Review of Economics and Business*, Vol. 18, No. 4 (Winter 1978): 7-21.

_____. "Steel Technologies and Costs in the U.S. and Japan." *Iron and Steel Engineer* (April 1978): 32-37.

_____. "Evaluating Scale Economies: The Case of Japanese Blast Furnaces." *The Journal of Industrial Economics* 23 (1974/75).

_____ and Boylan, Myles G. "Capital Budgeting, Industrial Capacity, and Imports." *Quarterly Review of Economics and Business*, Vol. 15, No. 3 (Autumn 1975): 17-32.

Goldberg, Walter H., ed. *Ailing Steel: The Transoceanic Quarrel*. New York: St. Martin's Press, 1986.

Grossman, Gene M. "Imports As A Cause of Injury: The Case of the U.S. Steel Industry." Woodrow Wilson School of Public and International Affairs, Princeton University. Discussion Paper No. 78. Princeton: September 1984.

Grunwald, Oskar. "Steel and the State in Austria." 51 *Annals of Public and Cooperative Economy* 477 (December 1980).

Hagstrom, Tony. *1977 ars Specialstalutredning Del I.* Industri-Departmentet: 1977).

Harris, A. *U.S. Trade Problems in Steel*. New York: Praeger, 1983.

Hayward, Jack. "The Nemesis of Industrial Patriotism: The French Response to the Steel Crisis." In *The Politics of Steel: Western Europe and the Steel Industry in the Crisis Years 1974-84*, ed. Yves Meny and Vincent Wright. Berlin and New York: Walter de Gruyther, 1987.

Henning R. *Staten som Fortagare. En Studie au Statsforetag AB's Mal, Organisation och Effectivitet* (1974).

Heusdens and de Horn. "Crisis Policy in the European Steel Industry in the Light of the ECSC Treaty." 17 *Common Market Law Review* (February 1980).

Hexner, E. *The International Steel Cartel*. Westport, Ct.: Greenwood Press, 1943, 1976.

Himiltor, C. *Public Subsidies to Industry: The Case of Sweden and its Shipbuilding Industry*. World Bank Staff Working Paper No. 566. Washington, D.C.: World Bank, 1983.

Hiroshi, Iyori. "Antitrust and Industrial Policy in Japan: Competition and Cooperation." In *Law and Trade Issues of the Japanese Economy*, ed. Gary R. Saxonhouse and Kozo Yamamura. Seattle: University of Washington Press, 1986.

Hirschhorn, Joel S. "Restructuring of the United States Steel Industry Requires New Policies." In *Ailing Steel: The Transoceanic Quarrel*, ed. Walter H. Goldberg. New York: St. Martin's Press, 1986.

Hogan, William T. *World Steel in the 1980s: A Case of Survival*. Lexington, Mass.: Lexington Books, D.C. Heath & Company, 1983.

Hood, E. "Cyclical and Structural Problems in the Swedish Steel Industry." *Skkanndinaviska Enskilda Bankens Quarterly Review* (March-April 1978).

Hook, E. "Steel and the State in Sweden." 51 *Annals of Public and Cooperative Economy* 504 (December 1980).

Horders, F. "Konzentrationstendenzen in der Europaischen Wirtschaft." *Stahl und Eisen* (March 20, 1969).

Howell, Thomas R. "Steel and the State in Romania," in *Comparative Economic Studies*, Vol. XXIX, No. 2 (Summer 1987).

Hudec, Robert E. *The GATT Legal System and World Trade Diplomacy.* New York: Praeger, 1975.

Huettner, David A. "The Development of Continuous Casting in the U.S. Steel Industry: Comment." *Economic Inquiry* (June 1974): 265-277.

Imai, Ken'ichi. "Tekko." In *Industry and Business in Japan,* ed. Kazuo Sato. White Plains: M.E. Sharpe, Inc., 1980.

_____. "Iron and Steel." In *Industry and Business in Japan*, ed. Kazuo Sato. White Plains: M.E. Sharpe, Inc., 1980.

Instituto de Promoción Industrial de Valencia. *Repercusiones de la IV Planta Siderúrgica Integral de Sagunto.* Valencia: I.P.I., 1974.

International Iron and Steel Institute. *Steel Statistical Yearbook.* Brussels: IISI, 1981, 1987.

_____. *Steel Demand Forecasting.* Brussels: IISI, 1983.

_____. *World Indirect Steel Trade.* Brussels: IISI, 1982.

_____. *Steel Intensity and GNP Structure.* Brussels: IISI, 1974.

Johnson, Chalmers. *MITI and the Japanese Miracle.* Stanford: Stanford University Press, 1982.

Jones, Kent. *Politics vs Economics in World Steel Trade.* London: Allen & Unwin, 1986.

Kalzenstein, Peter J. *Corporatism and Change: Austria, Switzerland, and the Politics of Industry.* Ithaca: Cornell University Press, 1984.

Kaplan, Eugene. *Japan: The Government-Business Relationship*. Washington, D.C.: U.S. Department of Commerce, February 1972.

Karlson, Stephen H. "Adoption of Competing Inventions by United States Steel Producers." *The Review of Economics and Statistics* 68 (August 1986): 415-422.

Kawahito, Kiyoshi. *The Japanese Steel Industry With An Analysis of the U.S. Steel Import Problem*. New York: Praeger, 1972.

_____. "Sources of the Difference in Steel Making Yield Between Japan and the United States." Monograph Series No. 20. Murfreesboro, Tenn.: Middle Tennessee State University, 1979.

Kawasaki, Tsutomu. *The Japanese Steel Industry*. Tokyo: Tekko Shimbun Sha, 1985.

Keeling, Bernard. *World Steel - A New Assessment*. London: The Economist Intelligence Unit, Ltd., February 1988.

Kendrick, D., Meerhaus, A. and Alatorre, J. *The Planning of Investment Programs in the Steel Industry*. Baltimore: Johns Hopkins University Press, 1984.

Knight, P. T. *Economic Reform in Socialist Countries*. Washington, D.C.: World Bank, 1983.

Kohler, H.C. *Schriftenriehe der Wirtschaftsvereinigung Eisen und Stahlindustrie zur Wirtschafts Industriepolitik*. Dusseldorf: WES, 1977.

Kohler, H. C. "Vertragliche Formen der Zusammenarbeit in der Producktion und beim Verkauf Stahlerzeugnissen." *Stahl und Eisen* (April 17, 1969).

Koivisto, H. "The Importance of Real Rates of Interest." *Kansallis-Osake-Pankke Economic Review* (First Quarter 1977).

Liang, K. L. and Liang, C. H. "Incentive Policies for Import Substitution and Export Expansion in the Republic of China." International Commercial Bank of China *Economic Review* (November-December 1978).

Lim, Y. *Government Policy and Private Enterprise; Korean Experience in Industrialization*. Korea Research Monograph. Berkeley: Center for Korean Studies, 1981.

Lister, L. *Europe's Coal and Steel Community.* New York: Twentieth Century Fund, 1960.

Lodge, George C. and Vogel, Ezra, eds. *Ideology and National Competitiveness.* Boston: Harvard Business School Press, 1987.

Lynn, Leonard H. *How Japan Innovates; A Comparison with the U.S. in the Case of Basic Oxygen Steelmaking.* Boulder and London: Westview Press, 1982.

MacArthur, John H. and Scott, Bruce R. *Industrial Planning in France.* Boston: Harvard University Press, 1967.

MacPhee, Craig R. *Nontariff Barriers to International Trade in Steel.* Ann Arbor: University of Michigan Press, 1970.

Maddala, G. S. and Knight, Peter T. "International Diffusion of Technical Change - A Case Study of the Oxygen Steelmaking Process." *Economic Journal 77.* (September 1967): 531-558.

Magalhâes, F. *Historia da Siderurgia no Brasil.* São Paulo: Editora da Universidade de São Paulo, 1983.

Mancini, G. *Il Caso Gioia Tauro.* Reggio-Calabria: Casa del Libro Editrice, 1977.

Marcus, Peter F. and Kirsis, Karlis M. *World Steel Dynamics: Core Report BB; Global Steel Capacity Track.* New York: PaineWebber Incorporated, January 1988.

_____. *World Steel Dynamics: Steel Strategist 14.* New York: PaineWebber, Inc., 1987.

Marer, Paul. "U.S. Market Disruption Procedures Involving Romanian and Other CPE Products, with Policy Recommendations." In *New Horizons in East-West Economic and Business Relations,* ed. M.R. Jackson and J.D. Woodson. New York: Columbia University Press, 1984.

_____. *Polish-U.S. Industrial Cooperation in the 1980s.* Bloomington: Indiana University Press, 1981.

Masi, Anthony C. "Nuova Italsider - Taranto and the Steel Crisis: Problems, Innovations and Prospects." In *The Politics of Steel: Western Europe and the Steel Industry in the Crisis Years 1974-84,* ed. Yves Meny and Vincent Wright. Berlin and New York: Walter de Gruyther, 1987.

Maza, E. "Study Recommends Measures to Restore Steel Industry." *Proceso* (February 10, 1986).

McAdams, Alan K. "Big Steel, Invention, and Innovation Reconsidered." *The Quarterly Journal of Economics.* (August 1967): 457-474.

McGannon, Harold E., ed. *The Making, Shaping and Treating of Steel.* (9th Ed.) Pittsburgh, Pa.: United States Steel, 1971.

McKinsey & Co. *Un Programme de Redressment pour la Siderurgie Belgo-Luxembourgeoise.* Brussels: McKinsey & Co., 1978.

Meny, Yves and Wright, Vincent, eds. *The Politics of Steel: Western Europe and the Steel Industry in the Crisis Years 1974-84.* Berlin and New York: Walter de Gruyter, 1987.

Merrill Lynch, Inc. *Japanese Steel Industry: Comparison with its U.S. Counterpart.* New York: June 1977.

Messerlin, Patrick A. "The European Iron and Steel Industry and the World Crisis." In *The Politics of Steel: Western Europe and the Steel Industry in the Crisis Years 1974-84,* ed. Yves Meny and Vincent Wright. Berlin and New York: Walter de Gruyther, 1987.

Mueller, Hans and Kawahito, Kiyoshi. *Steel Industry Economics: A Comparative Analysis of Structure, Conduct and Performance.* New York: Japanese Steel Information Center, 1978.

_____. "Errors and Biases in the 1978 Putnam, Hayes and Bartlett Study on the Pricing of Imported Steel." Monograph Series No. 17. Murfreesboro, Tenn.: Middle Tennessee State University, January 1979.

Mughan, Anthony. "The Belgian Election of 1981; the Primacy of the Economic." 5 *West European Politics* (1982).

Nabseth, Lars. *Handel Stalindustrin infor 1980-talet.* Stockholm: 1977.

Nam, Chong Hyon. *Characteristics of the Iron and Steel Industry and its Supply and Demand Structure.* Berkeley: Center for Korean Studies, June 30, 1979.

National Academy of Sciences, National Academy of Engineering and National Research Council. *The Competitive Status of the U.S. Steel Industry.* Washington, D.C.: National Academy Press, 1985.

National Science Foundation. "Government Policies and the Adoption of Innovations in the Integrated Iron and Steel Industry." Report No. PB85-243673. Washington, D.C.: NSF, 1974.

Noguchi, Yukio. "The Government-Business Relationship in Japan: The Changing Role of Fiscal Resources." In *Policy and Trade Issues of the Japanese Economy*, ed. Kozo Yamamura. Seattle: University of Washington Press, 1982.

Old, Bruce S., Holloway, Frederic A. L. and Tenenbaum, Michael. *Brief Technology Assessment of the Domestic Steel Industry*. Bethlehem, Pa.: Lehigh University, January 1981.

Organization for Economic Cooperation and Development. *The Steel Market in 1986 and the Outlook for 1987*. Paris: OECD, 1987.

_____. *World Steel Trade Developments 1960-1983*. Paris: OECD, 1985.

Oster, Sharon. "The Diffusion of Innovation Among Steel Firms: The Basic Oxygen Furnace." *The Bell Journal of Economics* (Spring 1982): 45-56.

Patrick, Hugh, and Sato, Hideo. "The Political Economy of United States-Japan Trade in Steel" In *Policy and Trade Issues of the Japanese Economy*, ed. Kozo Yamamura. Seattle and London: University of Washington Press, 1982.

Putnam, Hayes and Bartlett, Inc. *The Economic Implications of Foreign Steel Pricing Practices in the U.S. Market*. Newton, Mass.: Putnam, Hayes and Bartlett, Inc., August 1978.

_____. *Economics of International Steel Trade: Policy Implications for the United States*. Newton, Mass.: Putnam, Hayes and Bartlett, 1977.

Radoi, A. "The Industrial Geography of Romania in the First and Second Five-Year Plans." *Natura* (September-October 1956).

Randall, L. *An Economic History of Argentina in the Twentieth Century*. New York: Columbia University Press, 1978.

Range, John Jay. "The Trigger Price Mechanism: Does It Prevent Dumping by Foreign Steelmakers?" 5 *N. C. Journal of International Law and Commercial Regulation* (Spring 1980): 279, 291.

Richardson, J.J. and Dudley, G. F. "Steel Policy in the U.K.: The Politics of Industrial Decline." In *The Politics of Steel: Western Europe and the Steel*

Industry in the Crisis Years 1974-84, ed. Yves Meny and Vincent Wright. Berlin and New York: Walter de Gruyther, 1987.

Roper, B. *Rationalisierungseffekte der Wahlzstahlkontore und der Rationalisierungsgruppen.* Berlin: Duncker and Humblot, 1974.

Rossegger, Gerhard. "Adjustment Through Piecemeal Innovation - the U.S. Experience." In *Ailing Steel: The Transoceanic Quarrel,* ed. Walter H. Goldberg. New York: St. Martin's Press, 1986.

Sato, Kazuo, ed. *Industry and Business in Japan.* White Plains: M.E. Sharpe, 1980.

Shepard, Geoffrey. "Japanese Exports and Europe's Problem Industries." In *Japan and Western Europe,* ed. Laukas Tsoukalis and Maureen White. New York: St. Martin's Press, 1982.

Singlet, Marc. *La Subsidisation de la Siderurgie Belge: Un Bilan Provisoire.* Brussels: Universite Libre de Bruxelles, 1986-87.

Sorci, Aldo. *L'Evoluzione del Settore Siderurgico in Italia.* In *L'Industria Siderurgica,* ed. L. Selleri and D. Velo. Milan: Giuffrè Editore, 1986.

Stegemann, Klaus. *Price Competition and Output Adjustment in the European Steel Market.* Kieler Studien 147. Tübingen: J.C.B. Mohr (Paul Siebeck), 1977.

Steinberg, D. *The Economic Development of Korea; Sui Genesis or Sui Generic?* A.I.D. Evaluation Special Study No. 6. Washington, D.C.: GPO, January 1982.

Stoffaes, Christian and Gadonniex, Pierre. "Steel and the State in France." In 4 *Annals of the Public Economy* 405 (1980).

Sumrall, James B. "Diffusion of the Basic Oxygen Furnace in the U.S. Steel Industry.." *Journal of Industrial Economics* 30 (June 1982): 421-437.

Torre, M. and Mercado, Y. *El Sector Sidérurgico Paraestatal.* Mexico City: Centro de Investigación y Doencia Económicas, 1983.

Trebat, T.J. *Brazil's State-Owned Enterprises.* Cambridge: Cambridge University Press, 1983.

Tsantis, Andreas and Pepper, Roy. *Romania: The Industrialization of an Agrarian Economy under Socialist Planning.* Washington, D.C.: World Bank, 1979.

United Kingdom. Chancellor of the Exchequer. *The Nationalized Industries*. London: HMSO, March 1978.

_____. House of Commons. *First Report of the Trade and Industry Committee*, H.C. 344, 208 iv (1983-84), "The British Steel Corporation's Prospects."

_____. House of Commons. *Fourth Report from the Industry and Trade Committee*, H.C. 336-II (1980-81), Minutes of Evidence.

_____. *Second Report of the Select Committee on Nationalized Industries*, H.C. 127 (1977-78), "British Steel Corporation," Vol. II.

_____. *Fifth Report from the Select Committee on Nationalized Industries*, H. 238 (1977-78), "Financial Forecasts of the British Steel Corporation."

_____. *First Report from the Select Committee on Nationalized Industries*, H.C. 62-11, Minutes of Evidence, April 7, 1976.

_____. Trade and Industry Committee, *The British Steel Corporation*, H.C. 444-i (1984-85), Mr. Crowther, M.P., Minutes of Evidence.

United Nations, Economic Commission for Europe. *Long-Term Trends and Problems of the European Steel Industry*. Geneva: United Nations, 1959.

U.S. Congress, Congressional Budget Office. "How Federal Policies Affect the Steel Industry." Washington, D.C.: February 1987.

_____. "The Effects of Import Quotas on the Steel Industry." Washington, D.C.: July 1984.

U.S. Congress, Office of Technology Assessment. *Technology and Steel Industry Competitiveness*. Washington, D.C.: June 1980.

U.S. Consulate General, Rio de Janeiro. "Brazil's Iron and Steel Industry 1983," Revista Bancaria Brasileira, March 1980.

U.S. Council on Wage and Price Stability. *Report to the President on Prices and Costs in the United States Steel Industry*. Washington, D.C.: U.S. Government Printing Office, October 1977.

U.S. Department of Commerce, Economic Affairs, Office of Business Analysis. *Studies in the Economics of Production: The U.S. Primary Iron and Steel Industry Since 1958*. Washington, D.C.: May 1985.

U.S. Department of Labor. "Industrial Policy Analysis for the U.S. Steel Industry: An Econometric Study of Policy Alternatives." Prepared by Economics Research Unit, University of Pennsylvania. Philadelphia: March 1982.

U.S. Federal Trade Commission, Bureau of Economics. *The United States Steel Industry and Its International Rivals: Trends and Factors Determining International Competitiveness.* Washington, D.C.: Government Printing OFfice, November 1977.

U.S. General Accounting Office. *Industrial Policy: Case Studies in the Japanese Experience.* Washington, D.C.: GAO, 1982.

_____. *New Strategy Required For Aiding Distressed Steel Industry. Report To The Congress By The Comptroller General of the United States.* EMD-81-29. Washington, D.C.: U.S. Government Printing Office, January 8, 1981.

U. S. International Trade Commission. *Monthly Report on Selected Steel Industry Data.* U.S.I.T.C. Pub. No. 2064, March 1988.

_____. *U.S. Global Competitiveness: Steel Sheet and Strip Industry.* U.S.I.T.C. Pub. No. 2050, January 1988.

_____. *Annual Survey Concerning Competitive Conditions in the Steel Industry and Industry Efforts to Adjust and Modernize.* U.S.I.T.C. Pub. No. 2019, September 1987.

_____. *The Effect of Developing Country Debt-Servicing Problems on U.S. Trade,* U.S.I.T.C. Pub. No. 1450, March 1987.

_____. *The Effects of Restraining U.S. Steel Imports on The Exports of Selected Steel-Consuming Industries.* U.S.I.T.C. Pub. No. 1788, December 1985.

_____. *Foreign Industrial Targeting and its Effects on U.S. Industries: Phase II: The European Community and Member States.* U.S.I.T.C. Pub. No. 1517, April 1984.

U.S. Library of Congress. Congressional Research Service. "Steel Imports: Is the President's Program Working?" Report by David J. Cantor. Washington, D.C.: March 17, 1988.

_____. "Steel Prices and Import Restraints." Report No. 88-204E, by David J. Cantor. Washington, D.C.: 1988.

_____. "Steel Markets in the United States: Where Have All the Buyers Gone?" Report No. 87-474 E, by David J. Cantor. Washington, D.C.: 1987.

_____. "The U.S. Steel Industry: Factors Influencing Gains in Industry Productivity." Report by David J. Cantor. Washington, D.C.: 1987.

_____. "Steel Manufacturing in the United States: Can A Smaller Industry Be Profitable?" Report No. 87-649 E, by David J. Cantor. Washington, D.C.: 1987.

U.S. National Advisory Council on International Monetary and Financial Policies. *Annual Report to Congress 1986.* Washington, D.C.: Government Printing Office, 1986.

U.S. Steel Advisory Committee. "State of the U.S. Steel Industry." Washington, D.C.: September 7, 1984.

U.S. Trade Representative. *Foreign Trade Barriers.* Washington, D.C.: Office of the U.S.T.R., 1987.

van der Ven, Hues and Grunert, Thomas. "The Politics of Transatlantic Steel Trade." In *The Politics of Steel: Western Europe and the Steel Industry in the Crisis Years 1974-84,* ed. Yves Meny and Vincent Wright. Berlin and New York: Walter de Gruyther, 1987.

Vaughan, William J., Russell, Clifford S. and Cochrane, Harold C. *Government Policies and the Adoption of Innovations in the Integrated Iron and Steel Industry.* Washington, D.C.: Resources for the Future, 1974.

Walstedt, Bertil. *State Manufacturing Enterprise in the Mixed Economy: The Turkish Case.* Baltimore and London: Johns Hopkins University Press, 1980.

Wang, Josephine. "A General Overview of Import Regulation (Taiwan)." *East Asian Executive Reports* (May 1986).

Warren, Kenneth. *World Steel: An Economic Geography.* New York: Crane, Russak & Company, Inc, 1975.

Winckler, Edwin A. "Statism and Familism on Taiwan." In *Ideology and National Competitiveness,* ed. George C. Lodge and Ezra Vogel. Boston: Harvard Business School Press, 1987.

Wirtschaftsvereinigung der Eisen and Stahlindustrie, *EG Stahlpolitik vor Neuer Berwährunsprobe*, Positionspapier der Deutschen Stahlindustrie Dusseldorf: WES, 1984.

_____. *Practical Experience with Governmental Assistance to the Steel Industry of the European Community.* Dusseldorf: WES, February 1982.

_____. *Fünfzehn Fragen and Fakten zur Europaischen Stahlpolitik.* Anlage IV. Dusseldorf: WES, December 1987.

Wolff, Alan Wm. "International Competitiveness of American Industry: The Role of U.S. Trade Policy." In *U.S. Competitiveness in the World Economy,* ed. Bruce R. Scott and George C. Lodge. Boston: Harvard Business School Press, 1985.

_____. "Evolution of the Executive-Legislative Relationship in the Trade Act of 1974." 19 *SAIS Review* 4 (1975).

World Bank. *China; Socialist Economic Development.* Vol. I. Washington, D.C.: World Bank, 1983.

Wormald, A. "Growth Promotion: The Creation of a Modern Steel Industry." In *The State as Entrepreneur,* ed. S. Holland. London: Weidenfeld and Nicolson, 1972.

Yamamura, Kozo. "Success That Soured: Administrative Guidance and Cartels in Japan." In *Policy and Trade Issues of the Japanese Economy,* ed. Kozo Yamamura. Seattle and London: University of Washington Press, 1982.

INDEX